THE **CFIN** SOLUT

Print + Online

CFIN⁵ delivers all the key terms and core concepts for the **Corporate Finance** course.

CFIN Online provides the complete narrative from the printed text with additional interactive media and the unique functionality of **StudyBits**—all available on nearly any device!

What is a StudyBit™? Created through a deep investigation of students' challenges and workflows, the StudyBit™ functionality of **CFIN Online** enables students of different generations and learning styles to study more effectively by allowing them to learn their way. Here's how they work:

COLLECT WHAT'S IMPORTANT
Create StudyBits as you highlight text, images or take notes!

WEAK

FAIR

STRONG

UNASSIGNED

RATE AND ORGANIZE STUDYBITS
Rate your understanding and use the color-coding to quickly organize your study time and personalize your flashcards and quizzes.

StudyBit™

TRACK/MONITOR PROGRESS
Use Concept Tracker to decide how you'll spend study time and study YOUR way!

85%

PERSONALIZE QUIZZES
Filter by your StudyBits to personalize quizzes or just take chapter quizzes off-the-shelf.

○ CORRECT
○ INCORRECT
○ INCORRECT
○ INCORRECT

CFIN5
Scott Besley and Eugene Brigham

Vice President, General Manager, 4LTR Press:
Neil Marquardt

Product Director, 4LTR Press: Steven E. Joos

Product Manager: Laura Redden

Content/Media Developer: Patricia Hempel

Product Assistant: Lauren Dame

Marketing Manager: Nathan Anderson

Marketing Coordinator: Eileen Corcoran

Content Project Manager: Jana Lewis

Manufacturing Planner: Ron Montgomery

Production Service: MPS Limited

Sr. Art Director: Bethany Casey

Internal Designer: Cmiller Design/Chris Miller

Cover Designer: Curio Press, LLC/Lisa Kuhn

Cover Image: Oleksiy Mark/Shutterstock.com

Title Page Images: Oleksiy Mark/Shutterstock.com

Intellectual Property Analyst: Brittani Morgan

Intellectual Property Project Manager:
Nick Barrows

Ad images:

    Computer and Tablet: © iStockphoto.com/
furtaev

    Smart Phone: © iStockphoto.com/dashadima

    Other Ad: iStockphoto.com/Rawpixel.com

Library of Congress Control Number: 2015959521

Student Edition ISBN: 978-1-305-66163-9

Student Edition with Online ISBN: 978-1-305-66165-3

Cengage Learning
20 Channel Center Street
Boston, MA 02210
USA

Cengage Learning is a leading provider of customized learning solutions with employees residing in nearly 40 different countries and sales in more than 125 countries around the world. Find your local representative at **www.cengage.com**

Cengage Learning products are represented in Canada by Nelson Education, Ltd.

To learn more about Cengage Learning Solutions, visit **www.cengage.com**

Purchase any of our products at your local college store or at our preferred online store **www.cengagebrain.com**

Printed in the United States of America
Print Number: 01   Print Year: 2015

BESLEY/BRIGHAM
CFIN⁵

BRIEF CONTENTS

Oleksiy Mark/Shutterstock.com

CONTENTS

PART 1
INTRODUCTION TO MANAGERIAL FINANCE

Pressmaster/Shutterstock.com

PART 2
ESSENTIAL CONCEPTS IN MANAGERIAL FINANCE

arka38/Shutterstock.com

PART 3

VALUATION— FINANCIAL ASSETS

PART 4

VALUATION—REAL ASSETS (CAPITAL BUDGETING)

Tashatuvango/Shutterstock.com

PART 5

COST OF CAPITAL AND CAPITAL STRUCTURE CONCEPTS

Sergey Nivens/Shutterstock.com

PART 6

WORKING CAPITAL MANAGEMENT

Jorg Greuel/Getty Images

PART 7
STRATEGIC PLANNING AND FINANCING DECISIONS

My Life Graphic/Shutterstock.com

APPENDIX A
Appendix: Using Spreadsheets to Solve Financial Problems 327

CFIN ONLINE

ACCESS TEXTBOOK CONTENT ONLINE—INCLUDING ON SMARTPHONES!

Includes Videos & Other Interactive Resources!

MANAGE MY COURSE ⌄   STUDENT

CFIN5

CHAPTER
1

An Overview of
Managerial Finance

CHAPTER
2

Income Statement

Financial
Statements

Analysis of Financial Statements

4LTR
PRESS

After you finish this chapter go to **PAGE 18** for **STUDY TOOLS**

LEARNING OUTCOMES

After studying this chapter, you will be able to…

LO1 Explain what finance entails and why everyone should have an understanding of basic financial concepts.

LO2 Identify different forms of business organization as well as the advantages and disadvantages of each.

LO3 Identify major goal that firms pursue and what a firm's primary goal should be.

LO4 Explain the roles ethics and good governance play in successful businesses.

LO5 Describe how foreign firms differ from U.S. firms and identify factors that affect financial decisions in multinational firms.

An Overview of Managerial Finance

1

In this chapter, we introduce finance by providing you with (1) a description of the discipline and (2) an indication of the goals companies should attain, as well as the conduct that is acceptable when pursuing these goals. As you will discover, a corporation acts in the best interests of its owners (stockholders) when decisions are made that increase the firm's value, which in turn increase the value of its stock.

1-1 What Is Finance?

In simple terms, finance is concerned with decisions about money. Financial decisions deal with how money is raised and used by businesses, governments, and individuals. To make sound financial decisions, you must understand three general, yet reasonable, concepts. Everything else equal, (1) more value is preferred to less; (2) the sooner cash is received, the more valuable it is; and (3) less risky assets are more valuable than (preferred to) riskier assets. These concepts are discussed in detail later in the book. At this point, we can state that firms that make decisions with these concepts in mind are able to provide better products to customers at lower prices, pay higher salaries to employees, and still provide greater returns to investors. In general, then, sound financial management contributes to the well-being of both individuals and the general population.

Although the emphasis in this book is on business finance, you will discover that the same concepts that firms apply when making sound business decisions can be used to make informed decisions relating to personal finances. For example, consider the decision you might have to make if you won a state lottery worth \$105 million. Which *would* you choose: a lump-sum payment of \$54 million today or a payment of \$3.5 million each year for the next 30 years? Which *should* you choose? In Chapter 4, we will show the time value of money techniques that firms use to make business decisions. These same techniques can be used to answer this and other questions that relate to personal finances.

1-1a General Areas of Finance

The study of finance consists of four interrelated areas:

1. *Financial markets and institutions*—Financial institutions, which include banks, insurance companies, savings and loans, and credit unions, are an integral part of the general financial services marketplace. The success of these organizations requires an understanding of factors that cause interest rates and other returns in the financial markets to rise and fall, regulations that affect such institutions, and various types of financial instruments, such as mortgages, automobile loans, and certificates of deposit, that financial institutions offer.

2. *Investments*—This area of finance focuses on the decisions made by businesses and individuals as they choose securities for their investment portfolios. The major functions in the investments area are (a) determining the values, risks, and returns associated with such financial assets as stocks and bonds and (b) determining the optimal mix of securities that should be held in a portfolio of investments, such as a retirement fund.

3. *Financial services*—Financial services refer to functions provided by organizations that deal with the management of money. Persons who work in these organizations, which include banks, insurance companies, brokerage firms, and similar companies, provide services that help individuals and companies

determine how to invest money to achieve such goals as home purchase, retirement, financial stability and sustainability, budgeting, and so forth.

4. ***Managerial (business) finance***—Managerial finance deals with decisions that all firms make concerning their cash flows, including both inflows and outflows. As a consequence, managerial finance is important in all types of businesses, whether they are public or private, and whether they deal with financial services or the manufacture of products. The duties encountered in managerial finance range from making decisions about plant expansions to choosing what types of securities should be issued to finance such expansions. Financial managers also have the responsibility for deciding the credit terms under which customers can buy, how much inventory the firm should carry, how much cash to keep on hand, whether to acquire other firms (merger analysis), and how much of each year's earnings should be paid out as dividends versus how much should be reinvested in the firm.

Although our concern in this book is primarily with managerial finance, because all areas of finance are interrelated, an individual who works in any one area should have a good understanding of the other areas as well. For example, a banker lending to a business must have a basic understanding of managerial finance to judge how well the borrowing company is operated. The same holds true for a securities analyst, who must understand how a firm's current financial position can affect its future prospects and thus its stock price. At the same time, corporate financial managers need to know what their bankers are thinking and how investors are likely to judge their corporations' performances when establishing their stock prices.

1-1b The Importance of Finance in Non-Finance Areas

Everyone is exposed to finance concepts almost every day. For example, when you borrow to buy a car or house, finance concepts are used to determine the monthly payments you are required to make. When you retire, finance concepts are used to determine the amount of the monthly payments you receive from your retirement funds. Further, if you want to start your own business, an understanding of finance concepts is essential for

survival. Thus, even if you do not intend to pursue a career in a finance-related profession, it is important that you have some basic understanding of finance concepts. Similarly, if you pursue a career in finance, it is important that you have an understanding of other areas in the business, including marketing, accounting, production, and so forth, to make well-informed financial decisions.

Let's consider how finance relates to some of the non-finance areas that students often study in a business college.

1. ***Management***—When we think of management, we often think of personnel decisions and employee relations, strategic planning, and the general operations of the firm. Strategic planning, which is one of the most important activities of management, cannot be accomplished without considering how such plans impact the overall financial well-being of the firm. Such personnel decisions as setting salaries, hiring new staff, and paying bonuses must be coordinated with financial decisions to ensure that needed funds are available. For these reasons, managers must have at least a general understanding of financial management concepts to make informed decisions in their areas.

2. ***Marketing***—If you have taken a basic marketing course, you learned that the *four Ps of marketing*—product, price, place, and promotion—determine the success of products that are manufactured and sold by companies. Clearly, the price that should be charged for a product and the amount of advertising a firm can afford for the product must be determined in conjunction with financial managers because the

firm will lose money if the price of the product is too low or too much is spent on advertising. Coordination of the finance function and the marketing function is critical to the success of a company, especially a small, newly formed firm because it is necessary to ensure that sufficient cash is generated to survive. For these reasons, people in marketing must understand how marketing decisions affect and are affected by such issues as funds availability, inventory levels, and excess plant capacity.

3. **Accounting**—In many firms (especially small ones), it is difficult to distinguish between the finance function and the accounting function. Because the two disciplines are closely related, often accountants are involved in finance decisions and financial managers are involved in accounting decisions. As our discussions will show, financial managers rely heavily on accounting information because making decisions about the future requires information that accountants provide about the past. As a consequence, accountants must understand how financial managers use accounting information in planning and decision making so that it can be provided in an accurate and timely fashion. Similarly, accountants must understand how accounting data are viewed (used) by investors, creditors, and others who are interested in the firm's operations.

4. **Information systems**—To make sound decisions, financial managers rely on accurate information that is available when needed. The process by which the delivery of such information is planned, developed, and implemented is costly, but so are the problems caused by a lack of good information. Without appropriate information, decisions relating to finance, management, marketing, and accounting could prove disastrous. Different types of information require different information systems, so information system specialists work with financial managers to determine what information is needed, how it should be stored, how it should be delivered, and how managing information affects the profitability of the firm.

5. **Economics**—Finance and economics are so similar that some universities offer courses related to these two subjects in the same functional area (department). Many tools used to make financial decisions evolved from theories or models developed by economists. Perhaps the most noticeable difference between finance and economics is that financial managers evaluate information and make decisions about cash flows associated with a particular firm or a group of firms, whereas economists analyze information and forecast changes in activities associated with entire industries and the economy as a whole. It is important that financial managers understand economics and that economists understand finance because economic activity and policy impact financial decisions, and vice versa.

Finance will be a part of your life no matter what career you choose. There will be a number of times during your life, both in business and in your personal finances, that you will make finance-related decisions. Therefore, it is vitally important that you have some understanding of general finance concepts. *There are financial implications in virtually all business decisions, and non-financial executives must know enough finance to incorporate these implications into their own specialized analyses.* For this reason, every student of business, regardless of his or her major, should be concerned with finance.

Finance in the Organizational Structure of the Firm. Although organizational structures vary from company to company, the chief financial officer (CFO), who often has the title of vice president of finance, generally reports to the president. The financial vice president's key subordinates are the treasurer and the controller. In most firms, the *treasurer* has direct responsibility for managing the firm's cash and marketable securities, planning how the firm is financed and when funds are raised, managing risk, and overseeing the corporate pension fund. The treasurer also supervises the credit manager, the inventory manager, and the director of capital budgeting, who analyzes decisions related to investments in fixed assets. The *controller* is responsible for the activities of the accounting and tax departments.

1-2 Alternative Forms of Business Organization

There are three major forms of business organization in the United States: (1) proprietorships, (2) partnerships, and (3) corporations. In terms of numbers, 70–75 percent of businesses are operated as proprietorships, 8–10 percent are partnerships, and the remaining 15–20 percent are corporations. Based on the dollar value of sales, however, approximately 83 percent of all business is conducted by corporations, while the remaining 17 percent is generated by proprietorships (3–4 percent) and partnerships (13–14 percent).[1] Because most business is conducted by corporations, we will focus on that form in this book. However, it is important to understand the differences among the three major forms of business, as well as the popular "hybrid" forms of business that have evolved from these major forms.

1-2a Proprietorship

A **proprietorship** is an unincorporated business owned by one individual. Starting a proprietorship is generally as easy as just beginning business operations.

The proprietorship has three important advantages:

1. It is easily and inexpensively formed. Not much "red tape" is involved when starting such a business; generally, only licenses required by the state and the municipality in which the business operates are needed.

2. It is subject to few government regulations. Large firms that potentially threaten competition are much more heavily regulated than small so-called mom-and-pop businesses, such as proprietorships.

3. It is taxed like an individual, not like a corporation; thus, earnings are taxed only once. The double taxation of dividends is discussed later in the chapter.

The proprietorship also has four important limitations:

1. The proprietor has unlimited personal liability for business debts because any debts of the business are considered obligations of the sole owner. With unlimited personal liability, the proprietor (owner) can potentially lose all of his or her personal assets, even those assets not invested in the business; thus, losses can far exceed the money that he or she has invested in the company. An explanation of this concept is given later in this chapter.

2. A proprietorship's life is limited to the time the individual who created it owns the business. When a new owner takes over the business, legally the firm becomes a new proprietorship (even if the name of the business does not change).

3. Transferring ownership is somewhat difficult. Disposing of the business is similar to selling a house in that the proprietor must seek out and negotiate with a potential buyer, which generally takes weeks or months to complete.

4. It is difficult for a proprietorship to obtain large sums of capital because the firm's financial strength generally is based only on the financial strength of the sole owner. A proprietorship's funds are derived from the owner's sources of credit, which include his or her credit cards, access to bank loans, loans from relatives and friends, and so forth. Unlike corporations, proprietorships cannot raise funds by issuing stocks and bonds to investors.

For these reasons, individual proprietorships are confined primarily to small business operations. In fact, only about 1 percent of all proprietorships have assets that are valued at $1 million or more; nearly 90 percent have assets valued at $100,000 or less. However, most businesses start out as proprietorships and then convert to corporations when their growth causes the disadvantages of being a proprietorship—namely, unlimited personal liability and the inability to raise large sums of money—to outweigh the advantages.

1-2b Partnership

A **partnership** is the same as a proprietorship, except that it has two or more owners. Partnerships can operate under different degrees of formality, ranging from informal, oral understandings to formal agreements filed with the secretary of the state in which the partnership does business. Most legal experts recommend that partnership agreements be put in writing.

The advantages of a partnership are the same as those of a proprietorship, except that most partnerships have more sources available for raising funds because there are more owners, with more relatives, more friends, and more opportunities to raise funds through credit. Even though they generally have greater capabilities than proprietorships to raise funds to support growth, partnerships still have difficulty in attracting substantial amounts of funds. This is not a major problem for a slow growing business. However, if a business's products really catch on and it needs to raise large amounts of funds to capitalize on its opportunities, the difficulty of attracting funds becomes a real drawback. For this reason, growth companies, such as Google Inc. and Amazon.com Inc., generally begin life as proprietorships or partnerships but at some point find it necessary to convert to corporations.

proprietorship An unincorporated business owned by one individual.

partnership An unincorporated business owned by two or more persons.

[1]The statistics provided in this section are based on business tax filings reported by the Internal Revenue Service (IRS), which can be found on the IRS website at http://www.irs.ustreas.gov/taxstats/.

Under partnership law, each partner is liable for the debts of the business. Therefore, if any partner is unable to meet his or her pro rata claim in the event the partnership goes bankrupt, the remaining partners must make good on the unsatisfied claims, drawing on their personal assets if necessary. Thus, the business-related activities of any of the firm's partners can bring ruin to the other partners, even though those partners are not direct parties to such activities.

1-2c Corporation

A corporation is a legal entity created by a state, which means that a corporation has the legal authority to act like a person when conducting business. It is separate and distinct from its owners and managers. This separateness gives the corporation four major advantages:

1. A corporation offers its owners *limited liability*. To illustrate the concept of limited liability, suppose you invested $10,000 to become a partner in a business formed as a partnership that subsequently went bankrupt, owing creditors $1 million. Because the owners are liable for the debts of a partnership, as a partner you would be assessed for a share of the company's debt; you could even be held liable for the entire $1 million if your partners could not pay their shares. This is the danger of *unlimited liability*. On the other hand, if you invested $10,000 in the stock of a corporation that then went bankrupt, your potential loss on the investment would be limited to your $10,000 investment.[2]

2. Ownership interests can be divided into shares of stock, which can be *transferred far more easily* than can proprietorship or partnership interests. Shares of stock can be bought and sold in minutes, whereas interests in proprietorships and partnerships generally cannot.

3. A corporation can continue after its original owners and managers no longer have a relationship with the business; thus it is said to have *unlimited life*. The life of a corporation is based on the longevity of its stock, not the longevity of those who own the stock (the owners).

4. The first three factors—limited liability, easy transferability of ownership interest, and unlimited life—make it much easier for corporations than for proprietorships or partnerships to raise money in the financial markets. In addition, corporations can issue stocks and bonds to raise funds, whereas proprietorships and partnerships cannot.

Even though the corporate form of business offers significant advantages over proprietorships and partnerships, it does have two major disadvantages:

1. Setting up a corporation, as well as periodic filings of required state and federal reports, is more complex and time-consuming than for a proprietorship or a partnership. When a corporation is created, (a) a corporate charter, which provides general information, including the name of the corporation, types of activities it will pursue, amount of stock that initially will be issued, and so forth, must be filed with the secretary of the state in which the firm incorporates; and (b) a set of rules, called bylaws, that specify how the corporation will be governed must be drawn up by the founder(s).

2. Because the earnings of the corporation are taxed at the corporate level and then any earnings paid out as dividends are again taxed as income to stockholders, corporate earnings are subject to *double taxation*.[3]

1-2d Hybrid Forms of Business: LLP, LLC, and S Corporation

Alternative business forms that include some of the advantages, and avoid some of the disadvantages, of the three major forms of business have evolved over time. These alternative forms of business combine some characteristics of proprietorships and partnerships with some characteristics of corporations. In this section, we provide brief descriptions of three popular *hybrid business forms* that exist today.

Limited Liability Partnership (LLP). In the earlier discussion of a partnership, we described the form of business that is referred to as a *general partnership*,

corporation A legal entity created by a state, separate and distinct from its owners and managers, having unlimited life, easy transferability of ownership, and limited liability.

corporate charter A document filed with the secretary of the state in which a business is incorporated that provides information about the company, including its name, address, directors, and amount of capital stock.

bylaws A set of rules drawn up by the founders of the corporation that indicates how the company is to be governed; includes procedures for electing directors, rights of stockholders, and how to change the bylaws when necessary.

[2]In the case of small corporations, the limited liability feature is often a fiction because bankers and credit managers frequently require personal guarantees from the stockholders of small, weak corporations.

[3]There was a push in Congress in 2003 to eliminate the double taxation of dividends by either treating dividends paid by corporations the same as interest—that is, making them a tax-deductible expense—or allowing dividends to be tax exempt to stockholders. Congress passed neither; instead, the tax on dividends received by investors was reduced from the ordinary tax rate to the capital gains rate.

Picsfive/Shutterstock.com

business. With this form of an LLP, only the general partners can participate in the management of the business; partners with limited liability are considered investors only. In other states, all partners in an LLP are fully liable for the general debts of the business, but an individual partner is not liable for the negligence, irresponsibility, or similar acts committed by any other partner (thus the limited liability). Some states require LLPs to file partnership agreements with the secretary of state, whereas other states do not.

Limited Liability Company (LLC). A **limited liability company (LLC)** is a relatively new business form that has become popular during the past couple of decades; it combines the features of a corporation and a partnership. An LLC offers the limited personal liability associated with a corporation, but the company can choose to be taxed as either a corporation or as a partnership. If an LLC is taxed like a partnership, income is said to pass through to the owners, so that it is taxed only once. The structure of the LLC is fairly flexible; owners generally can divide liability, management responsibilities, ownership shares, and control of the business any way they please. In addition, LLC owners, who are called members, can be individuals or other businesses. Unlike a partnership, an LLC can have a single owner. As with a corporation, legal paperwork, which is termed articles of organization, must be filed with the state in which the business is set up, and there are certain financial reporting requirements after the formation of an LLC. Because LLCs are created by state laws, which vary considerably from state to state, there can be substantial differences between how an LLC can be formed in one state versus another state. As this type of business organization becomes more widespread, state regulation likely will become more uniform.

S Corporation. A domestic corporation that has no more than 100 stockholders and only one type of stock outstanding can elect to file taxes as an **S corporation**. If a corporation elects the S corporation status, then its income is taxed the same as income earned by proprietorships and partnerships; that is, income passes through the company to the owners so that it is taxed only once. The major differences between an S corporation and an LLC are that an LLC can have more than 100 stockholders (members) and more than one type of stock (membership interest).

1-2e Which Form of Business Is Best?

Different forms of business serve different purposes. For the following reasons, however, the value of any

wherein each partner is personally liable for any of the debts of the business. It is possible to limit the liability faced by some of the partners by establishing a **limited liability partnership (LLP)**. The legal aspects of LLPs vary from state to state. Even so, an LLP generally is set up as one of two forms. In some states an LLP can be established that permits persons to invest in partnerships without exposure to the personal liability that general partners face. With this type of LLP, at least one partner is designated a *general partner* and the others are *limited partners*. The general partners remain fully personally liable for all business debts, whereas the limited partners are liable only for the amounts they have invested in the

limited liability partnership (LLP) A partnership wherein at least one partner is designated as a *general partner* with unlimited personal financial liability, and the other partners are *limited partners* whose liability is limited to amounts they invest in the firm.

limited liability company (LLC) Offers the limited personal liability associated with a corporation; however, the company's income is taxed like that of a partnership.

S corporation A corporation with no more than 100 stockholders that elects to be taxed in the same manner as proprietorships and partnerships, so that business income is only taxed once.

business, other than a very small concern, probably will be maximized if it is organized as a corporation:

1. Limited liability reduces the risks borne by investors. All else equal, *the lower the firm's risk, the higher its market value.*

2. *A firm's current value is related to its future growth opportunities,* and corporations can more easily attract funds to take advantage of growth opportunities than can unincorporated businesses (only corporations can issue stocks and bonds to raise funds).

3. Corporate ownership can be transferred more easily than ownership of either a proprietorship or a partnership. Therefore, all else equal, investors would be willing to pay more for a corporation than for a proprietorship or partnership, which means that the corporate form of organization can *enhance the value* of a business.

Most firms are managed with value maximization in mind, and this, in turn, has caused most large businesses to be organized as corporations.

1-3 What Goal(s) Should Businesses Pursue?

Depending on the form of business, one firm's major goals might differ somewhat from another firm's major goals. But, in general, every business owner wants the value of his or her investment in the firm to increase. The owner of a proprietorship has direct control over his or her investment in the company because it is the proprietor who owns and runs the business. As a result, a proprietor might choose to work three days per week and play golf or fish the rest of the week as long as the business remains successful and he or she is satisfied living this type of life. On the other hand, the owners (stockholders) of a large corporation have very little control over their investments because they generally do not run the business. Because they are not involved in the day-to-day decisions, these stockholders expect that the managers who run the business do so with the best interests of the owners in mind.

Investors purchase the stock of a corporation because they expect to earn an acceptable return on the money they invest. Because we know investors want to increase their wealth positions as much as possible, all else equal, it follows that managers should behave in a manner that is consistent with enhancing the firm's value. For this reason, throughout this book we operate on the assumption that management's primary goal is **stockholder wealth maximization**, which, as we will see, translates into maximizing the value of the firm as measured by the price of its common stock. Firms do, of course, have other objectives. In particular, managers who make the actual decisions are also interested in their own personal satisfaction, in their employees' welfare, and in the good of the community and of society at large. Still, *stock price maximization is the most important goal of most corporations.*

If a firm attempts to maximize its stock price, is this good or is this bad for society? In general, it is good. Aside from such illegal actions as attempting to form monopolies, violating safety codes, and failing to meet pollution control requirements, *the same actions that maximize stock prices also benefit society.* First, note that stock price maximization requires efficient, low-cost plants that produce high-quality goods and services that are sold at the lowest possible prices. Second, stock price maximization requires the development of products that consumers want and need, so the profit motive leads to new technology, to new products, and to new jobs. Finally, stock price maximization necessitates efficient and courteous service, adequate stocks of merchandise, and well located business establishments. These factors are necessary to maintain a customer base that generates sustainable profits. Therefore, most actions that help a firm increase the price of its stock also are beneficial to society at large. This is why profit-motivated, free-enterprise economies have been so much more successful than socialistic and communistic economic systems. Because managerial finance plays a crucial role in the operation of successful firms and because successful firms are necessary for a healthy, productive economy, it is easy to see why finance is important from a social standpoint.[4]

1-3a Managerial Actions to Maximize Shareholder Wealth

How do we measure value, and what types of actions can management take to maximize value? Although we will discuss valuation in

stockholder wealth maximization The appropriate goal for management decisions; considers the risk and timing associated with expected cash flows to maximize the price of the firm's common stock.

---

[4]People sometimes argue that firms, in their efforts to raise profits and stock prices, increase product prices and gouge the public. In a reasonably competitive economy, which exists in the United States, prices are constrained by competition and consumer resistance. If a firm raises its prices beyond reasonable levels, it will simply lose its market share. Of course, firms want to earn more, and they constantly try to cut costs or develop new products in an attempt to earn above-normal profits. Note, though, that if they are indeed successful and do earn above-normal profits, those very profits will attract competition that will eventually drive prices down so that normal profits are generated; again, the main long-term beneficiary is the consumer.

FIGURE 1.1   VALUE OF THE FIRM

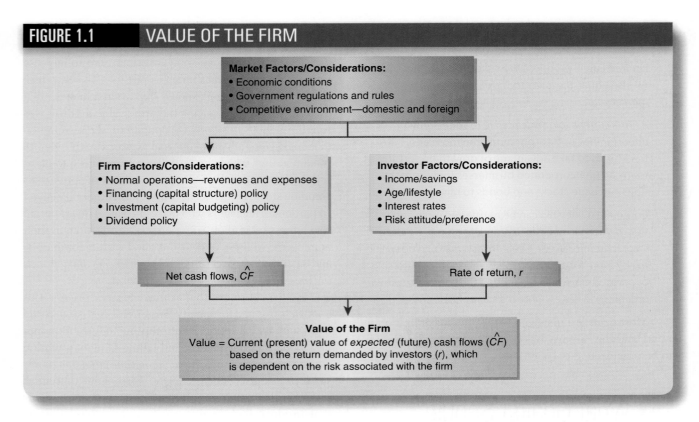

much greater detail later in the book, we introduce the concept of value here to give you an indication of how management can affect the price of a company's stock. First, the value of any investment, such as a stock, is based on the cash flows the asset is expected to generate during its life. Second, investors prefer to receive a particular cash flow sooner rather than later. And, third, investors generally are risk averse, which means they are willing to pay more for investments with more certain future cash flows than for investments with less certain, or riskier, cash flows, everything else equal. For these reasons, we know that managers can increase the value of a firm by making decisions that increase the firm's expected future cash flows, generate the expected cash flows sooner, increase the certainty of the expected cash flows, or produce any combination of these actions.

The financial manager makes decisions about the expected cash flows of the firm, which include decisions about how much and what types of debt and equity should be used to finance the firm (*capital structure decisions*); what types of assets should be purchased to help generate expected cash flows (*capital budgeting decisions*); and what to do with net cash flows generated by the firm—reinvest them in the firm or pay dividends (*dividend policy decisions*). Each of these topics will be addressed in detail later in the book. But, at this point, it should be clear that the decisions financial managers

make can significantly affect a firm's value because they affect the amount, timing, and riskiness of the cash flows the firm produces.

Although managerial actions affect the value of a firm's stock, external factors also influence stock prices. Included among these factors are legal constraints, the general level of economic activity, tax laws, and conditions in the financial markets. Based on both internal and external constraints, management makes a set of long-run strategic policy decisions that chart a future course for the firm. These policy decisions, along with the general level of economic activity and government regulations and rules (for instance, tax payments), influence the firm's expected cash flows, the timing of these cash flows, as well as their eventual transfer to stockholders in the form of dividends, and the degree of risk inherent in the expected cash flows.

Figure 1.1 diagrams the general relationships involved in the valuation process. As you can see, and as we will discuss in much greater detail throughout the book, a firm's value is ultimately a function of the cash flows it is expected to generate in the future and the rate of return at which investors are willing to provide funds to the firm for the purposes of financing operations and growth. Many factors, including conditions in the economy and financial markets, the competitive environment, and the general operations of the firm, affect the determination of the expected cash flows and the rates people demand when investing their funds. As we progress through the book, we will discuss these and other factors that affect a firm's value. For now, however, it is important to know that when we refer to value, we mean the worth of the expected future cash flows restated in current dollars—that is, the *present (current) value* of the future cash flows.

1-3b Should Earnings per Share (EPS) Be Maximized?

Will profit maximization also result in stock price maximization? In answering this question, we introduce the concept of *earnings per share* (EPS), which equals net income (NI) divided by the number of outstanding shares of common stock (Shares)—that is, EPS = NI/Shares. Many investors use EPS to gauge the value of a stock. A primary reason EPS receives so much attention is the belief that net income, and thus EPS, can be used as a barometer for measuring the firm's potential for generating future cash flows. Although current earnings and cash flows are generally highly correlated, as mentioned earlier, a firm's value is determined by the cash flows it is expected to generate in the future, as well as the risk associated with those expected cash flows. Thus, financial managers who attempt to maximize earnings might not maximize value because earnings maximization is a shortsighted goal. Most managers who focus solely on earnings do not consider the impact that maximizing earnings in the current period has on either future earnings (timing) or the firm's future risk position.

First, consider the *timing of the earnings*. Suppose Xerox has a project that will cause EPS to rise by $0.20 per year for five years, or $1 in total, whereas another project would have no effect on earnings for four years but would increase EPS by $1.25 in the fifth year. Which project is better? In other words, is $0.20 per year for five years better or worse than $1.25 in Year 5? The answer depends on which project contributes the most to the value of the firm, which in turn depends on the time value of money to investors. Thus, timing is an important reason to concentrate on wealth as measured by the price of the stock rather than on earnings alone.

Second, consider *risk*. Suppose one project is expected to increase EPS by $1, while another is expected to increase earnings by $1.20 per share. The first project is not very risky. If it is undertaken, EPS will almost certainly rise by approximately $1. However, the other project is quite risky. Although our best guess is that EPS will rise by $1.20, we must recognize the possibility that there might be no increase whatsoever or that the firm might even suffer a loss. Depending on how averse stockholders are to risk, the first project might be preferable to the second.

In many instances, firms have taken actions that increased earnings per share, yet the stock price decreased because investors believed that either the higher earnings would not be sustained in the future or the risk level of the firm would be increased substantially. Of course, the opposite effect has been observed as well. We see, then, that the firm's stock price, and thus its value, is dependent on (1) the cash flows the firm is expected to provide in the future, (2) when those cash flows are expected to occur, and (3) the risk associated with those cash flows. As we proceed through the book, you will discover that every significant corporate decision should be analyzed in terms of these factors and their effects on the firm's value and hence the price of its stock.

1-3c Managers' Roles as Agents of Stockholders

Because they generally are not involved in day-to-day operations, stockholders of large corporations "permit" (empower) the executives to make decisions about how the firms are run. Of course, the stockholders want the managers to make decisions that are consistent with the goal of wealth maximization. However, managers' interests can potentially conflict with stockholders' interests.

An *agency relationship* exists when one or more individuals, who are called the *principals*, hire another person, the *agent*, to perform a service and delegate decision-making authority to that agent. If a firm is a proprietorship, there is no agency relationship because the owner–manager operates the

value The present, or current, value of the cash flows that an asset is expected to generate in the future.

business in a fashion that will improve his or her own welfare, with welfare measured in the form of increased personal wealth, more leisure, or perquisites.[5] However, if the owner–manager incorporates and sells some of the firm's stock to outsiders, potential conflicts of interest immediately arise. For example, the owner–manager (agent) might now decide not to work as hard to maximize shareholder (principals') wealth because less of the firm's wealth will go to him or her, or he or she might decide to take a higher salary or enjoy more perquisites because part of those costs will fall on the outside stockholders. This potential conflict between two parties—the principals (outside shareholders) and the agents (managers)—is an **agency problem**.

The potential for agency problems is greatest in large corporations with widely dispersed ownership—for example, IBM and General Motors—because individual stockholders own extremely small proportions of the companies and managers have little, if any, of their own wealth tied up in these companies. For this reason, managers might be more concerned about pursuing their own agendas, such as increased job security, higher salaries, or more power, than about maximizing shareholder wealth.

Mechanisms used by large corporations to motivate managers to act in the shareholders' best interests include:

1. ***Managerial compensation (incentives)***—A common method used to motivate managers to operate in a manner consistent with stock price maximization is to tie managers' compensation to the company's performance. Such compensation packages should be developed so that managers are rewarded on the basis of the firm's performance over a long period of time, not on its performance in any particular year. For example, a company might implement a compensation plan where managers earn 100 percent of a specified reward when the company achieves a targeted growth rate. If the performance is above the target, higher rewards can be earned, whereas managers receive lower rewards when performance is below the target. Often the reward that managers receive is the stock of the company. If managers own stock in the company, they should be motivated to make decisions that will increase the firm's value and thus the value of the stock they own.

    All incentive compensation plans should be designed to accomplish two things: (1) Provide inducements to executives to act on those factors under their control in a manner that will contribute to stock price maximization. (2) Attract and retain top-level executives. Well-designed plans can accomplish both goals.

2. ***Shareholder intervention***—More than 25 percent of the individuals in the United States invest directly in stocks. Along with such institutional stockholders as pension funds and mutual funds, individual stockholders often "flex their muscles" to ensure that firms pursue goals that are in the best interests of shareholders rather than of the managers (where conflicts might arise). In addition, many institutional investors routinely monitor top corporations to ensure that managers pursue the goal of wealth maximization. When it is determined that action is needed to realign management decisions with the interests of investors, these institutional investors exercise their influence by suggesting possible remedies to management or by sponsoring proposals that must be voted on by stockholders at the annual meeting. Stockholder-sponsored proposals are not binding, but the results of the votes are noticed by corporate management.

    In situations where large blocks of the stock are owned by a relatively few large institutions that have enough clout to influence a firm's operations, these institutional owners often have enough voting power to overthrow management teams that do not act in the best interests of stockholders. Examples of major corporations whose managements have been ousted in past years include Coca-Cola, General Motors, and United Airlines.

3. ***Threat of takeover***—**Hostile takeovers**, instances in which management does not want the firm to be taken over, are most likely to occur when a firm's stock is undervalued relative to its potential, which often is caused by inefficient operations that result from poor management. In a hostile takeover, the managers of the acquired firm generally are fired, and those who stay on typically lose the power they had prior to the acquisition. Thus, to avoid takeover threats, managers have a strong incentive to take actions that maximize stock prices.

Because wealth maximization is a long-term goal rather than a short-term goal, management must be able to convey to stockholders that their best interests are being pursued. As you proceed through this book, you will discover that many factors affect the value of a stock,

agency problem A potential conflict of interest between outside shareholders (owners) and managers who make decisions about how to operate the firm.

hostile takeover The acquisition of a company over the opposition of its management.

[5]Perquisites (or "perks") are executive fringe benefits, such as luxurious offices, use of corporate planes and yachts, personal assistants, and general use of business assets for personal purposes.

which make it difficult to determine precisely when management is acting in the stockholders' best interests. However, a firm's management team will find it difficult to fool investors, both in general and for a long period, because stockholders can generally determine which major decisions increase value and which ones decrease value.

1-4 What Roles Do Ethics and Governance Play in Business Success?

In the previous section, we explained how the managers of a firm, who act as the agents of the owners, should make decisions that are in the best interests of the firm's investors. Would you consider it unethical for managers to act in their own best interests rather than the best interests of the owners? Would you invest in a firm that espoused unethical practices or had no direction about how the company's day-to-day operations should be handled? Probably not. In this section, we discuss business ethics and corporate governance, and the roles each of these concepts play in successful businesses.

phoelix/Shutterstock.com

1-4a Business Ethics

The word *ethics* can be defined as "moral behavior" or "standards of conduct." **Business ethics** can be thought of as a company's attitude and conduct toward its employees, customers, community, and stockholders. High standards of ethical behavior demand that a firm treat each party it deals with in a fair and honest manner. A firm's commitment to business ethics can be measured by the tendency of the firm and its employees to adhere to laws and regulations relating to such factors as product safety and quality, fair employment practices, fair marketing and selling practices, the use of confidential information for personal gain, community involvement, bribery, and illegal payments to foreign governments to obtain business.

Although most firms have policies that espouse ethical business conduct, in many instances large corporations have engaged in unethical behavior. Companies such as Arthur Andersen, Enron, and WorldCom MCI have fallen or have been changed significantly as the result of unethical, and sometimes illegal, practices. In some cases, employees (generally top management) have been sentenced to prison for illegal actions that resulted from unethical behavior. Not long ago, the number of high-profile instances in which unethical behavior provided substantial gains for executives at the expense of stockholders' positions increased to the point where public outcry resulted in legislation aimed at arresting the apparent tide of unethical behavior in the corporate world. A major reason for the legislation was that accounting scandals caused the public to be skeptical of accounting and financial information reported by large U.S. corporations. Simply put, the public no longer trusted what managers said. Investors felt that executives were pursuing interests that too often resulted in large gains for themselves and large losses for stockholders. As a result, Congress passed the Sarbanes-Oxley Act of 2002.

The 11 sections (*titles*) in the Sarbanes-Oxley Act of 2002 establish standards for accountability and responsibility in reporting financial information for publicly traded corporations. The act requires a publicly-traded corporation to (1) have a committee that consists of outside directors to oversee the firm's audits, (2) hire an external auditing firm that will render an unbiased (independent) opinion concerning the firm's financial statements, and (3) provide additional information about the procedures used to construct and report financial statements. In addition, the firm's chief executive officer (CEO) and CFO must certify financial reports that are submitted to the Securities and Exchange Commission. The act also stiffens the criminal penalties that can be imposed for producing fraudulent financial information and gives regulatory bodies greater authority to prosecute such actions.

Despite the decline in investor trust of financial reporting

> **business ethics** A company's attitude and conduct toward its stakeholders (employees, customers, stockholders, and community). Ethical behavior requires fair and honest treatment of all parties.

by corporations, the executives of most major firms in the United States believe their firms should, and do, try to maintain high ethical standards in all of their business dealings. Further, most executives believe that there is a positive correlation between ethics and long-run profitability because ethical behavior (1) prevents fines and legal expenses, (2) builds public trust, (3) attracts business from customers who appreciate and support ethical policies, (4) attracts and keeps employees of the highest caliber, and (5) supports the economic viability of the communities where these firms operate.

Today most large firms have in place strong codes of ethical behavior, and they conduct training programs designed to ensure that all employees understand what the correct behavior is in different business situations. It is imperative that executives and top management—the company's chairman, president, and vice presidents—be openly committed to ethical behavior and that they communicate this commitment through their own personal actions as well as through company policies, directives, and punishment/reward systems. Investors expect nothing less.

1-4b Corporate Governance

The term *corporate governance* has become a regular part of business vocabulary. As a result of the scandals uncovered at Arthur Andersen, Enron, WorldCom, and many other companies, stockholders, managers, and Congress have become quite concerned with how firms are operated. Corporate governance deals with the set of rules that a firm follows when conducting business. These rules provide the "road map" that managers follow to pursue the various goals of the firm, including maximizing its stock price. It is important for a firm to clearly specify its corporate governance structure so that individuals and entities that have an interest in the well-being of the business understand how their interests will be pursued. A good corporate governance structure should provide those who have a relationship with a firm with an understanding of how executives run the business and who is accountable for important decisions. As a result of the Sarbanes-Oxley Act of 2002 and increased stockholder pressure, most firms

corporate governance
Deals with the set of rules that a firm follows when conducting business; these rules identify who is accountable for major financial decisions.

stakeholders Those who are associated with a business, including managers, employees, customers, suppliers, creditors, stockholders, and other parties with an interest in the firm's well-being.

carefully write their corporate governance policies so that all stakeholders—managers, stockholders, creditors, customers, suppliers, and employees—better understand their rights and responsibilities.[6] In addition, from our previous discussions, it should be clear that maximizing shareholder wealth requires the fair treatment of all stakeholders.

Studies show firms that practice good corporate governance generate higher returns to stockholders than those that don't have good governance policies. Good corporate governance includes a board of directors with members who are independent of the company's management. An independent board generally serves as a checks-and-balances system that monitors important management decisions, including executive compensation. It has also been shown that firms that develop governance structures that make it easier to identify and correct accounting problems and potentially unethical or fraudulent practices perform better than firms that have poor governance policies (internal controls).[7]

1-5 Forms of Businesses in Other Countries

Large U.S. corporations can best be described as "open" companies because they are publicly traded organizations that, for the most part, are independent of each other and of the government. While most developed countries with free economies have business organizations that are similar to U.S. corporations, some differences exist relating to ownership structure and management of operations. Although a comprehensive discussion is beyond the scope of this book, this section provides some examples of differences between U.S. companies and non-U.S. companies.

Firms in most developed economies, such as corporations in the United States, offer equities with limited liability to stockholders that can be traded in domestic financial markets. However, such firms are not always called *corporations*. For instance, a comparable firm in England is called a *public limited company*, or PLC, while

---

[6]Broadly speaking, the term *stakeholders* should include the environment in which we live and do business. It should be apparent that a firm cannot survive—that is, remain sustainable—unless it treats both human stakeholders and environmental stakeholders fairly. A firm that destroys either the trust of its employees, customers, and shareholders, or the environment in which it operates, destroys itself.

[7]See, for example, Reshma Kapadia, "Stocks Reward Firms' Good Behavior," *The Wall Street Journal Online*, March 18, 2006, and David Reilly, "Checks on Internal Controls Pay Off," *The Wall Street Journal*, May 8, 2006, C3.

in Germany it is known as an *Aktiengesellschaft*, or AG. In Mexico, Spain, and Latin America, such a company is called a *Sociedad Anónima*, or SA. Some of these firms are publicly traded, whereas others are privately held.

Like corporations in the United States, most large companies in England and Canada are *open*, which means their stocks are widely dispersed among a large number of different investors, both individuals and institutions. On the other hand, in much of continental Europe, stock ownership is more concentrated; major investor groups include families, banks, and other corporations. In Germany and France, for instance, other domestic companies represent the primary group of shareholders, followed by families. Although banks in these countries do not hold large numbers of shares of stock, they can greatly influence companies because many shareholders assign banks their **proxy votes** for the directors of the companies. In addition, often the family unit has concentrated ownership and thus represents a major influence in many large companies in developed countries such as these. The ownership structures of these firms and many other large non-U.S. companies often are concentrated in the hands of a relatively few investors or investment groups. Such firms are considered *closed* because shares of stock often are not publicly traded, relatively few individuals or groups own the stock, and major stockholders generally are involved in the firms' daily operations.

The primary reason non-U.S. firms are likely to be more closed, and thus have more concentrated ownership, than U.S. firms results from the universal banking relationships that exist outside the United States. Financial institutions in other countries generally are less regulated than in the United States, which means foreign banks can provide businesses with a greater variety of services than U.S. banks can, including short-term loans, long-term financing, and even stock ownership. As a result, non-U.S. firms tend to have close relationships with individual banking organizations that also might take ownership positions in the companies. What this means is that banks in countries like Germany can meet the financing needs of family-owned businesses, even if they are very large. Therefore, such companies do not need to go public and thus relinquish control in order to finance additional growth. The opposite is true in the United States, where large firms do not have comparable "one-stop" financing outlets. Hence, their growth generally must be financed by bringing in outside owners, which results in more widely dispersed ownership.

In some parts of the world, firms belong to **industrial groups**, which are organizations composed of companies in different industries that have common ownership interests and, in some instances, shared management. Firms in an industrial group are linked by a major lender, typically a bank, which often also has a significant ownership interest, along with other firms in the group. The objective of an industrial group is to create an organization that ties together all the functions of production and sales from start to finish by including firms that provide the materials and services required to manufacture and sell the group's products. Thus, an industrial group encompasses firms involved in manufacturing, financing, marketing, and distribution of products: suppliers of raw materials, production organizations, retail stores, and creditors. A portion of the stocks of firms that are members of an industrial group might be traded publicly, but the lead company, which is typically a major creditor, controls the management of the entire group. Industrial groups are most prominent in Asian countries. In Japan, an industrial group is called a *keiretsu*, while it is called a *chaebol* in Korea. Well-known *keiretsus* include Mitsubishi, Toshiba, and Toyota, while Hyundai probably is the most recognizable *chaebol*. The success of industrial groups in Japan and Korea has inspired the formation of similar organizations in developing countries in Latin America and Africa as well as in other parts of Asia.

The differences in ownership concentration of non-U.S. firms might cause the behavior of managers, and thus the goals they pursue, to differ. For instance, often it is argued that the greater concentration of ownership of non-U.S. firms permits managers to focus more on long-term objectives, especially wealth maximization, than on short-term earnings, because these firms have easier access to credit in times of financial difficulty. In other words, creditors who also are owners generally have greater interest in supporting both short-term and long-term survival. On the other hand, it also has been argued that the ownership structures of non-U.S. firms create an environment where it is difficult to change managers, especially if they are significant stockholders. Such entrenchment could be detrimental to firms if management is inefficient. Whether the ownership structure of non-U.S. firms is an advantage or a disadvantage is debatable. What we do know is that the greater concentration of ownership in non-U.S. firms permits greater monitoring and control by individuals or groups than do the more dispersed ownership structures of U.S. firms.

proxy votes Voting power that is assigned to another party, such as another stockholder or institution.

industrial groups Organizations of companies in different industries with common ownership interests, which include firms necessary to manufacture and sell products; networks of manufacturers, suppliers, marketing organizations, distributors, retailers, and creditors.

1-5a Multinational Corporations

Large firms, both in the United States and in other countries, generally do not operate in a single country; rather, they conduct business throughout the world. Because large **multinational companies** are involved in all phases of the production process, from extraction of raw materials, through the manufacturing process, to distribution to consumers throughout the world, managers of such firms face a wide range of issues that are not present when a company operates in a single country.

U.S. and foreign companies "go international" for the following major reasons:

1. **To seek new markets**—After a company has saturated its home market, growth opportunities often are better in foreign markets. As a result, such homegrown firms as Coca-Cola and McDonald's have aggressively expanded into overseas markets, and foreign firms such as Sony and

multinational companies
Firms that operate in two or more countries.

Toshiba are major competitors in the U.S. consumer electronics market.

2. **To seek raw materials**—Many U.S. oil companies, such as ExxonMobil, have major subsidiaries around the world to ensure that they have continued access to the basic resources needed to sustain their primary lines of business.

3. **To seek new technology**—No single nation holds a commanding advantage in all technologies, so companies scour the globe for leading scientific and design ideas. For example, Xerox has introduced more than 80 different office copiers in the United States that were engineered and built by its Japanese joint venture, Fuji Xerox.

4. **To seek production efficiency**—Companies in countries where production costs are high tend to shift production to low-cost countries. The ability to shift production from country to country has important implications for labor costs in all countries. For example, when Xerox threatened to move its copier rebuilding work to Mexico, its union in Rochester, New York, agreed to work rule and productivity improvements that kept the operation in the United States.

5. **To avoid political and regulatory hurdles**—Many years ago, Japanese auto companies moved production to the United States to get around U.S. import quotas. Now, Honda, Nissan, and Toyota all assemble automobiles or trucks in the United States. Similarly, one of the factors that prompted U.S. pharmaceutical maker SmithKline and U.K. drug company Beecham to merge in 1989 was the desire to avoid licensing and regulatory delays in their largest markets. Now, GlaxoSmithKline, as the company is known, can identify itself as an inside player in both Europe and the United States.

The substantial growth that has occurred in multinational business during the past few decades has created an increasing degree of mutual influence and interdependence among business enterprises and nations, to which the United States is not immune. Political and social developments that influence the world economy also influence U.S. businesses and financial markets.

1-5b Multinational Versus Domestic Managerial Finance

In theory, the concepts and procedures discussed in the remaining chapters of this book are valid for both domestic and multinational operations. However, several problems associated with the international environment increase the complexity of the manager's task in a multinational corporation, and they often force the manager to change the way alternative courses of action are evaluated and compared. Six major factors distinguish managerial finance as practiced by firms operating entirely within a single country from management by firms that operate in several different countries:

1. *Different currency denominations*—Cash flows in various parts of a multinational corporate system often are denominated in different currencies. Hence, an analysis of exchange rates and the effects of fluctuating currency values must be included in all multinational financial analyses.

2. *Economic and legal ramifications*—Each country in which the firm operates has its own political and economic institutions, and institutional differences among countries can cause significant problems when a firm tries to coordinate and control the worldwide operations of its subsidiaries. For example, differences in tax laws among countries can cause after-tax consequences that differ substantially depending on where a transaction occurs. In addition, differences in legal systems of host nations complicate many matters, from the simple recording of a business transaction to the role played by the judiciary in resolving conflicts. Such differences can restrict multinational corporations' flexibility to deploy resources as they wish, and can even make procedures illegal in one part of the company that are required in another part. These differences also make it difficult for executives trained in one country to operate effectively in another.

3. *Language differences*—The ability to communicate is critical in all business transactions. Persons born and educated in the United States often are at a disadvantage because they generally are fluent only in English, whereas European and Asian businesspeople usually are fluent in several languages, including English. As a result, it is often easier for international companies to invade U.S. markets than it is for American firms to penetrate international markets.

4. *Cultural differences*—Even within geographic regions long considered fairly homogeneous, different countries have distinctive cultural heritages that shape values and influence the role of business in the society. Multinational corporations find that such matters as defining the appropriate goals of the firm, attitudes toward risk taking, dealing with employees, and the ability to curtail unprofitable operations can vary dramatically from one country to the next.

5. *Role of governments*—Most traditional models in finance assume the existence of a competitive marketplace in which the terms of trade are determined by the participants. The government, through its power to establish basic ground rules, is involved in this process, but its participation is minimal. Thus, the market provides both the primary barometer of success and the indicator of the actions that must be taken to remain competitive. This view of the process is reasonably correct for the United States and a few other major industrialized nations, but it does not accurately describe the situation in most of the world. Frequently, the terms under which companies compete, the actions that must be taken or avoided, and the terms of trade on various transactions are determined by direct negotiation between the host government and the multinational corporation rather than in the marketplace. This is essentially a political process, and it must be treated as such.

6. *Political risk*—The main characteristic that differentiates a nation from a multinational corporation is that the nation exercises sovereignty over the people and property in its territory. Hence, a nation is free to place constraints on the transfer of corporate resources and even to *expropriate*—that is, take for public use—the assets of a firm without compensation. This is *political risk*, and it tends to be a given rather than a variable that can be changed by negotiation. Political risk varies from country to country, and it must be addressed explicitly in any multinational financial analysis. Another aspect of political risk is terrorism against U.S. firms or executives abroad. For example, in the past, U.S. executives have been abducted and held for ransom in several South American and Middle Eastern countries.

These six factors complicate managerial finance within multinational firms, and they increase the risks these firms face. However, prospects for high profits often make it worthwhile for firms to accept these risks and to learn how to minimize or at least live with them.

exchange rates The prices at which the currency of one country can be converted into the currencies of other countries.

STUDY TOOLS

KEY MANAGERIAL FINANCE CONCEPTS

To conclude this chapter, we summarize some key concepts.

- Financial decisions deal with cash flows, both inflows and outflows.

- All else equal, investors prefer (1) more value rather than less value, (2) to receive cash sooner rather than later, and (3) less risk rather than more risk.

- The three principal forms of business organization in the United States are the (1) proprietorship, (2) partnership, and (3) corporation.

- The primary goal of the financial manager should be to maximize the value of the firm, which generally is measured by the firm's stock price.

- The managers of a firm are the decision-making agents of its owners (that is, the stockholders in a corporation). When managers do not make decisions that are in the best interests of the owners, agency problems exist. Agency problems can be mitigated by rewarding managers for making decisions that help maximize the firm's value.

- Firms that are ethical and have good governance policies generally perform better than firms that are less ethical or have poor governance policies.

- Firms "go international" for a variety of reasons, including to operate in new markets, to search for raw materials, to attain production efficiency, and to avoid domestic regulations.

- Foreign firms generally are less open—that is, have fewer owners (stockholders)—than U.S. firms.

PROBLEMS

1–1 What is finance? What types of decisions do people in finance make?

1–2 Why should persons who pursue careers in business have a basic understanding of finance even if their jobs are in areas other than finance, such as marketing or information systems?

1–3 What does it mean to maximize the value of a corporation?

1–4 In general terms, how is value measured? What three factors determine value? How does each factor affect value?

1–5 What is the difference between stock price maximization and profit maximization? Under what conditions might profit maximization not lead to stock price maximization?

1–6 What are some actions stockholders can take to ensure that management's interests and those of stockholders coincide? What are some other factors that might influence management's actions?

1–7 If you were the owner of a proprietorship, would you make decisions to maximize the value of your business or your personal satisfaction?

1–8 Suppose you are the president of a large corporation located in Seattle, Washington. How do you think the stockholders will react if you decide to increase the proportion of the company's assets that is financed with debt from 35 percent to 50 percent? In other words, what if the firm used much more debt to finance its assets.

1–9 What is corporate governance? How does corporate governance affect the returns generated for stockholders?

1–10 Why do U.S. corporations go international?

1–11 What are some factors that make financial decision making more complicated for firms that operate in foreign countries than for purely domestic firms?

1–12 Describe the four general areas included in the study of finance. Why is it important for a person who works in the financial markets to understand the responsibilities of a person who works in managerial finance?

1–13 Describe the major differences among the three primary forms of business organization (a proprietorship, a partnership, and a corporation).

1–14 Why do you think hybrid forms of business, such as limited liability partnerships (LLP) and limited liability companies (LLC), have evolved over time?

1–15 What does it mean to be ethical in business dealings? Should unethical business behavior be encouraged by business owners (stockholders) if such behavior increases the value of the stock they own in the short term?

1–16 Can a firm sustain its operations by maximizing stockholders' wealth at the expense of other stakeholders?

1–17 Compared to the ownership structure of U.S. firms, which are "open" companies, what are some advantages of the ownership structure of foreign firms, many of which are "closed" companies? Can you think of any disadvantages?

1–18 Should stockholder wealth maximization be thought of as a long-term goal or a short-term goal? Why?

1–19 Discuss the possibility of agency problems in a business that is a (a) proprietorship, (b) partnership with five partners, and (c) corporation with 100,000 stockholders.

1–20 Discuss the validity of the following statement: "When a firm's stock price falls, it is evidence that the firm's managers are not acting in the best interests of the shareholders."

part **2**

Income Statement

Financial Statements

Cash Flow

Equity

arka38/Shutterstock.com

After you finish this chapter go to **PAGE 39** for **STUDY TOOLS**

LEARNING OUTCOMES

After studying this chapter, you will be able to...

LO1 Describe the basic financial information that is produced by corporations and explain how the firm's stakeholders use such information.

LO2 Describe the financial statements that corporations publish and the information that each statement provides.

LO3 Describe how ratio analysis should be conducted and why the results of such an analysis are important to both managers and investors.

LO4 Discuss potential problems (caveats) associated with financial statement analysis.

Analysis of Financial Statements

2

Financial statement analysis involves evaluation of a firm's financial position to identify its current strengths and weaknesses and to suggest actions that the firm might pursue to take advantage of those strengths and correct any weaknesses to accomplish its goal of wealth maximization. In this chapter, we discuss how to evaluate a firm's current financial position using its financial statements. In later chapters, we examine actions that a firm can take to improve its financial position in the future, thereby increasing the price of its stock.

2-1 Financial Reports

Of the various reports that corporations provide to their stockholders, the **annual report** probably is the most important. This report provides two types of information:

1. **Discussion of operations**—describes the firm's operating results during the past year and discusses new developments that will affect future operations.

2. **Basic financial statements**—include (a) the balance sheet, (b) the income statement, (c) the statement of cash flows, and (d) the statement of retained earnings. Taken together, these statements give an accounting picture of the firm's operations and its financial position. Detailed data are provided for the two most recent years, along with historical summaries of key operating statistics for the past five to 10 years.[1]

The quantitative and verbal information contained in the annual report are equally important. The financial statements indicate what actually happened to the firm's financial position and to its earnings and dividends over the past few years, whereas the verbal statements attempt to explain both why things turned out the way they did and how management expects the firm to perform in the future. To illustrate how annual reports can prove helpful, we will use data taken from a fictitious company called Unilate Textiles. Unilate is a manufacturer and distributor of a wide variety of textiles and clothing items that was formed in 1990 in North Carolina. The company has grown steadily and has earned a reputation for selling quality products. In the most recent annual report, management reported that earnings were lower than forecasted due to losses associated with a poor cotton crop and from increased costs caused by a three-month employee strike and a retooling of the factory. Management then went on to paint a more optimistic picture for the future, stating that full operations had been resumed, several unprofitable businesses had been eliminated, and profits were expected to rise during the next year. Of course, an increase in profitability might not occur, and analysts should compare management's past statements with subsequent results to determine whether this optimism is justified. In any event, *investors use the information*

---

[1] Firms also provide quarterly reports, but they are much less comprehensive than the annual reports. In addition, larger publicly-traded firms file even more detailed statements that give breakdowns for each major division or subsidiary with the Securities and Exchange Commission (SEC). These reports, called *10-K reports*, are made available to stockholders upon request to a company's corporate secretary. Many companies also post these reports on their websites. Finally, many larger firms also publish *statistical supplements* that give financial statement data and key ratios going back 10 to 20 years.

> **annual report** A report issued by a corporation to its stockholders that contains basic financial statements, as well as the opinions of management about the past year's operations and the firm's future prospects.

contained in an annual report to form expectations about future earnings and dividends. Clearly, then, investors are quite interested in a company's annual report.

Because this book is intended to provide an introduction to managerial finance, Unilate's financial statements are constructed so that they are simple and straightforward. At this time, the company uses only debt and common stock to finance its assets—that is, Unilate does not have outstanding preferred stock or other financing instruments. Moreover, the company has only the basic assets that are required to conduct business, including cash and marketable securities, accounts receivable, inventory, and ordinary fixed assets. In other words, Unilate does not have items that require complex accounting applications.

FIGURE 2.1 SIMPLE BALANCE SHEET FORMAT

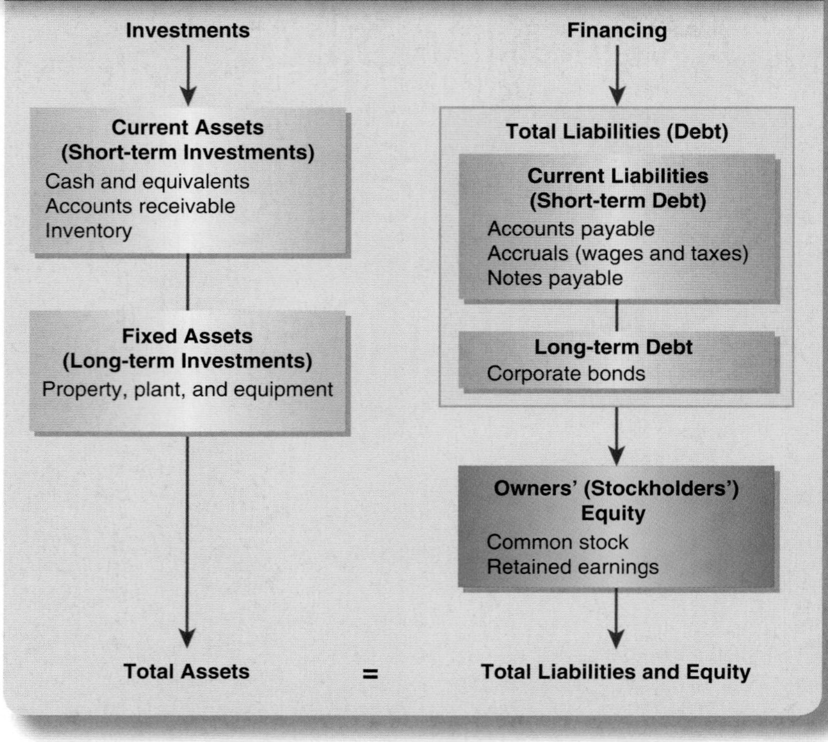

2-2 Financial Statements

Before we evaluate Unilate's financial position to form an opinion about its future prospects, let's take a look at the financial statements the company publishes.

2-2a The Balance Sheet

The **balance sheet** represents a picture taken *at a specific point in time (date)* that shows a firm's assets and how those assets are financed (debt or equity). Figure 2.1 shows the general set up for a simple balance sheet. Table 2.1 shows Unilate's balance sheets on December 31 for the years 2015 and 2016. December 31 is the end of the fiscal year, which is when Unilate "takes a snapshot" of its existing assets, liabilities, and owners' equity to construct the balance sheet. In this section, we concentrate on the more recent balance sheet—that is, December 31, 2016.

Assets, which represent the firm's investments, are classified as either short term (current) or long term (see Figure 2.1). Current assets generally include items that the firm expects to liquidate and thus convert into cash within one year, whereas long-term, or fixed, assets

balance sheet A statement that shows the firm's financial position—assets and liabilities and equity—at a specific point in time.

include investments that help generate cash flows over longer periods. As Table 2.1 shows, at the end of 2016, Unilate's current assets, which include cash and equivalents, accounts receivable (amounts due from customers), and inventory, totaled $465 million; its long-term assets, which include the building and equipment used to manufacture the textile products it sells, had a net value on the balance sheet equal to $380 million. Thus, its total assets were $845 million.

To finance its assets, a firm uses debt, equity (stock), or both forms of financing. Debt represents the loans the firm has outstanding, and it generally is divided into two categories—short-term debt and long-term debt (see Figure 2.1). Short-term debt, which is labeled "Current liabilities," represents debt that is due to be paid off within one year, and includes accounts payable (amounts owed to suppliers), accruals (amounts owed to employees and state and federal governments), and notes payable (amounts owed to banks). Table 2.1 shows that Unilate's short-term debt totaled $130 million in 2016. Long-term debt includes the bonds and similar debt instruments the firm has issued in previous years that are paid off over periods longer than one year. At the end of 2016, Unilate had outstanding bonds equal to $300 million. In combination, the total amount of debt Unilate used to finance its assets was $430 million. Thus, according to Table 2.1, about 51 percent

Table 2.1

Unilate Textiles: December 31 Balance Sheets ($ millions, except per-share data)

	2016		2015	
	Amount	**Percentage of Total Assets**	**Amount**	**Percentage of Total Assets**
Assets				
Cash and equivalents	$ 15.0	1.8%	$ 40.0	5.3%
Accounts receivables	180.0	21.3	160.0	21.3
Inventory	270.0	32.0	200.0	26.7
Total current assets	$465.0	55.0%	$400.0	53.3%
Net plant and equipment[a]	380.0	45.0	350.0	46.7
Total assets	$845.0	100.0%	$750.0	100.0%
Liabilities and Equity				
Accounts payable	$ 30.0	3.6%	$ 15.0	2.0%
Accruals	60.0	7.1	55.0	7.3
Notes payable	40.0	4.7	35.0	4.7
Total current liabilities	$130.0	15.4%	$105.0	14.0%
Long-term bonds	300.0	35.5	255.0	34.0
Total liabilities (debt)	$430.0	50.9%	$360.0	48.0%
Common stock (25 million shares)	130.0	15.4	130.0	17.3
Retained earnings	285.0	33.7	260.0	34.7
Total common equity	$415.0	49.1%	390.0	52.0
Total liabilities and equity	$845.0	100.0%	$750.0	100.0%
Book value per share = (Common equity)/Shares	$16.60		$15.60	
Market value per share (stock price)	$23.00		$25.00	
Additional Information:				
Net working capital = Current assets − Current liabilities	$335.0		$295.0	
Net worth = Total assets − Total liabilities	415.0		390.0	
[a]Breakdown of net plant and equipment account:				
Gross plant and equipment	$680.0		$600.0	
Less: Accumulated depreciation	(300.0)		(250.0)	
Net plant and equipment	$380.0		$350.0	

of the firm's assets were financed using debt, most of which (70 percent of total liabilities) was in the form of long-term bonds.

Equity represents stockholders' ownership, which, unlike debt, does not have to be paid off. Total equity is the amount that would be paid to stockholders if the firm's assets could be sold at the values reported on the balance sheet and its debt could be paid off in the amounts reported on the balance sheet. Thus, the firm's **stockholders' equity**, or **net worth**, equals total assets minus total liabilities. Table 2.1 shows that Unilate's net worth was $415 million at the end of 2016, which, based on the amounts shown on the balance sheet, implies that stockholders would receive $415 million if Unilate were to liquidate its assets and pay off all of its outstanding debt. However, because the firm probably would not be able to sell all of the

stockholders' equity (net worth) The funds provided by common stockholders—common stock, paid-in capital, and retained earnings.

assets at the values shown on the balance sheet, common stockholders actually would receive some amount different (higher or lower) from that shown in the equity section if the firm were actually liquidated. Thus, the risk of asset value fluctuations (both positive and negative) is borne by the stockholders.

Note that in Table 2.1, the assets are listed in order of their liquidity, or the length of time it typically takes to convert them to cash. The claims (liabilities and equity) are listed in the order in which they must be paid. For example, accounts payable generally must be paid within 30 to 45 days, accruals are payable within 60 to 90 days, and so on, down to the stockholders' equity accounts, which represent ownership that never needs to be repaid.

Often assets, liabilities, and equity are reported both in dollars and as a percentage of total assets, as shown in Table 2.1. This type of balance sheet is termed a common size balance sheet because it can be easily compared with statements of larger or smaller firms or with those of the same firm over time.

Some additional points about the balance sheet are worth noting.

1. **Cash and equivalents versus other assets**—Although the assets are all stated in terms of dollars, only the "Cash and equivalents" account represents actual money that can be spent. The other noncash assets should produce cash over time, but they do not represent cash in hand. The amount of cash they would bring in if sold today could be either higher or lower than the values that are reported on the balance sheet.

2. **Accounting alternatives**—Not every firm uses the same method to determine the account balances shown on the balance sheet. For instance, Unilate uses the FIFO (first-in, first-out) method to determine the inventory value shown on its balance sheet. It could have used the LIFO (last-in, first-out) method instead. During a period of rising prices, when compared to LIFO, FIFO will produce a higher balance sheet inventory value but a lower cost of goods sold, and thus a higher net income (less expensive goods are "used" first).

In some cases, a company might use one accounting method to construct financial statements provided to stockholders and another accounting method for tax purposes, internal reports, and so forth. For example, a company generally uses the most accelerated method permissible to calculate depreciation for tax purposes because accelerated methods lower taxable income in the early years of the asset's life, which means lower taxes are paid. The same company might use straight-line depreciation for constructing financial statements reported to stockholders because this method results in a higher net income. There is nothing illegal or unethical about this practice, but when evaluating firms, users of financial statements must be aware that more than one accounting alternative is available for constructing financial statements.

3. **Breakdown of the common equity account**—The equity section of Unilate's balance sheet contains two accounts: common stock and retained earnings. The amount shown in the retained earnings account represents the total amount of income that was saved and reinvested in assets—that is, the amount that was not paid out as dividends—since the firm started business. According to Table 2.1, Unilate has kept $285 million of all the income generated since 1990. This amount could have been paid to stockholders as dividends over the years, but Unilate instead decided to use these funds to finance growth in assets.

The common stock account shows the amount that stockholders paid to the company when it issued stock to raise funds. Unilate issued 25 million shares of stock at $5.20 per share to raise $130 million when it started business in 1990. No stock has been issued since. Thus, Unilate's stockholders provided the company with $130 million of funds to invest in its assets. Because Unilate's common stock does not have a par value, the entire amount of the issue is reported in the "Common stock" account.

The common equity section might include three accounts: common stock at par, paid-in capital, and retained earnings. For example, if Unilate's common stock had a par value equal to $2 per share, then the funds raised through the stock issue would have to be reported in two accounts: "Common stock at par" and "Paid-in capital." The amount reported in the "Common stock at par" account would equal the total value of the stock issue stated in terms of its par value, and it would be computed as follows:

common size balance sheet Dollar amounts on the balance sheet are stated as a percent of total assets.

retained earnings The portion of the firm's earnings that have been reinvested in the firm rather than paid out as dividends.

$$
\begin{aligned}
\text{Common stock at par} &= \text{Total shares issued} \times \text{Per share par value} \\
&= \quad 25,000,000 \quad \times \quad \$2 \\
&= \quad \$50,000,000
\end{aligned}
$$

The amount that was paid above the par value is reported in the "Paid-in capital" account. In this case, because the total value of the stock Unilate issued in 1990 was $130 million, the remaining $80 million (=$130 million − $50 million) would be reported in the "Paid-in capital" account.

The breakdown of the common equity accounts shows whether the company actually earned the funds reported in its equity accounts or generated the funds mainly from selling (issuing) stock. This information is important to both creditors and stockholders. For instance, a potential creditor would be interested in the amount of money that the owners (stockholders) put up, and stockholders would want to know the form of stockholders' funds.

4. *Book values versus market values*—The values, or accounting numbers, that are reported on the balance sheet are called *book values*, and they are generated using generally accepted accounting principles (GAAP). In many cases, the book values of the assets are not the same as the prices (values) for which they can actually be sold in the marketplace. For example, when Unilate built its original distribution center in 1995, the value of the building was $90 million, which represented its market value at that time. Today, the book value of the building is $30 million because $60 million has been depreciated over the years. However, the appraised (market) value of the building is $58 million.

The book values of assets often are not equal to their market values, especially for long-term assets. On the other hand, because most debt represents a contractual obligation to pay a certain amount at a specific time, the book values of a firm's debt generally are either equal to or very close to the market values of the firm's liabilities. The equity section of the balance sheet, which represents the book value of the firm's equity, must equal the book value of assets minus the book value of liabilities (see Figure 2.1).

5. *The time dimension*—The balance sheet can be thought of as a snapshot of the firm's financial position *at a particular point in time*. The balance sheet changes every day as inventories are increased or decreased, as fixed assets are added or retired, as liabilities are incurred or paid off, and so on. Companies whose businesses are seasonal experience especially large changes in their balance sheets during the year. As a result, firms' balance sheets will change over the year, depending on the date on which the statements are constructed.

2-2b The Income Statement

The income statement, which is also referred to as the *profit and loss statement*, presents the results of business operations *during a specified period of time* such as a quarter or a year. It summarizes the revenues generated and the expenses incurred by the firm during the accounting period. Table 2.2 gives the 2015 and 2016 income statements for Unilate Textiles. Net sales are shown at the top of the statement, followed by various costs, including income taxes, which are subtracted to determine the net income (earnings) available to common stockholders. A report on earnings and dividends per share appears at the bottom of the statement. In business, earnings per share (EPS) is called "the bottom line" because EPS is often considered the most important item on the income statement. Unilate earned $2.16 per share in 2016, down from $2.36 in 2015, but it still raised the per-share dividend from $1.08 to $1.16.

Should Firms with Identical Assets/Operations Report the Same Net Income? The obvious answer is yes. However, although two firms have identical operating structures—that is, facilities, employees, and production methods—they might be financed differently. For example, one firm might be financed with a substantial amount of debt, whereas the other firm is financed only with stock. Interest payments to debt holders are tax deductible; dividend payments to stockholders are not. The firm that is financed with debt will have greater tax-deductible expenses as a result of the interest expense and thus will report a lower net income than the firm that is financed with equity only. For this reason, when comparing the operations of two firms, analysts often examine the *net operating income (NOI)*, also known as the *earnings before interest and taxes (EBIT)*, because this figure represents the result of normal operations before considering the effects of the firm's financing choices (financial structure). Unilate's EBIT was $130 million in 2016. A firm that has the same operating structure (and follows the same accounting procedures) as Unilate should have reported EBIT equal to $130 million as well, even if it does not use the same amount of debt as Unilate does to finance its assets.

Does Net Income Determine Value? Investors often focus on the net income when

book values Amounts reported in financial statements—accounting numbers.

market values Values of items—such as assets, liabilities, and equities—in the marketplace outside the firm.

income statement A statement summarizing the firm's revenues and expenses over an accounting period, generally a quarter or a year.

Table 2.2

Unilate Textiles: Income Statements for Years Ending December 31 ($ millions, except per share data)[a]

	2016		2015	
	Amount	Percentage of Total Sales	Amount	Percentage of Total Sales
Net sales	$1,500.0	100.0%	$1,435.0	100.0%
Variable operating costs (82% of sales)	(1,230.0)	(82.0)	(1,176.7)	(82.0)
Gross profit	$ 270.0	18.0%	$ 258.3	18.0%
Fixed operating costs except depreciation	(90.0)	(6.0)	(85.0)	(5.9)
Earnings before interest, taxes, depreciation, and amortization (EBITDA)	$ 180.0	12.0%	173.3	12.1%
Depreciation	(50.0)	(3.3)	(40.0)	(2.8)
Net operating income (NOI) = Earnings before interest and taxes (EBIT)	$ 130.0	8.8%	133.3	9.3%
Interest	(40.0)	(2.7)	(35.0)	(2.4)
Earnings before taxes (EBT)	$ 90.0	6.0%	98.3	6.9%
Taxes (40%)	(36.0)	(2.4)	(39.3)	(2.7)
Net income	$ 54.0	3.6%	$ 59.0	4.1%
Preferred dividends	0.0		0.0	
Earnings available to common stockholders (EAC)	$ 54.0		$ 59.0	
Common dividends	(29.0)		(27.0)	
Addition to retained earnings	$ 25.0		$ 32.0	
Per share data (25,000,000 shares):				
Earnings per share = (EAC)/Shares	$ 2.16		$ 2.36	
Dividends per share = (Common dividends)/Shares	$ 1.16		$ 1.08	

[a]The parentheses indicate a negative value.

determining how well a firm has performed during a particular time period. However, *if investors are concerned with whether management is pursuing the goal of maximizing the firm's stock price, net income might not be the appropriate measure to examine.*

Recall from your accounting courses that, for most corporations, the income statement is generated using both the accrual method of accounting and the matching principle. That is, revenues are recognized when they are earned, not when the cash is received, and expenses are recognized when they are incurred, not when the cash is paid. As a result, not all of the amounts shown on the income statement represent cash flows. However, as we mentioned in Chapter 1, the value of an investment, such as the firm's stock price, is determined by the cash flows it generates. Therefore, although the firm's net income is important, cash flows are even more important because cash is needed

to continue normal business operations, including the payment of financial obligations, the purchase of assets, and the payment of dividends. As a result, in finance we focus on *cash flows* rather than net income.

One item on Unilate's income statement that we know is a noncash item is *depreciation*. The cash payment for a fixed asset, such as a building, occurs when the asset is originally purchased. However, because the asset is used to generate revenues and its life extends for more than one year, depreciation is the method that is used to match the expense associated with the decrease in the value of an asset to the years in which revenues are generated by its use. For example, Table 2.2 shows that Unilate's net income for 2016 was $54 million and the depreciation expense for the year was $50 million. Because depreciation was not an expense that required a cash payment during the year, Unilate's net cash flow must be at least $50 million higher than the $54 million that is reported as net income. If the only noncash item on its income statement is depreciation, then the net cash flow that Unilate generated in 2016 was $104 million.

When a firm sells all of its products for cash and pays cash for all of the expenses reported on its income statement except depreciation and amortization, its net cash flow can be computed using Equation 2.1:

2.1

Net cash flow = Net income + Depreciation and amortization

$$= \$54 \text{ million} + \$50 \text{ million}$$
$$= \$104 \text{ million}$$

Managers and analysts often use this equation to estimate the net cash flow generated by a firm, even when some customers have not paid for their purchases or the firm has not paid all of the bills for supplies, employees' salaries, and the like. In such cases, Equation 2.1 often is used to get a rough estimate of the firm's net cash flow. To get a better estimate of net cash flow, as well as to examine in detail which of the firm's actions provided cash and which actions used cash, a statement of cash flows should be constructed. We discuss the statement of cash flows in the next section.

For our purposes, it is useful to divide cash flows into two categories: (1) operating cash flows and (2) other cash flows. Operating cash flows arise from normal operations, and they represent, in essence, the difference between cash collections and cash expenses, including taxes paid, that are associated with the manufacture and sale of inventory. Other cash flows arise from borrowing, from the purchase or sale of fixed assets, from the sale or repurchase of common stock, and from paying dividends. Our focus here is on operating cash flows.

We know that operating cash flows can differ from accounting profits (or operating income) when a firm sells on credit, some operating expenses are not cash costs, or both situations occur. For example, we know that depreciation and amortization expenses represent costs that do not use cash in the current period. For this reason, analysts often compute a firm's *earnings before interest, taxes, depreciation, and amortization (EBITDA)* when evaluating its operations. Because both depreciation, which recognizes the decline in the values of tangible assets (buildings, equipment, and so forth), and amortization, which recognizes the decline in the values of intangible assets (patents, trademarks, and so forth) are noncash expenses, EBITDA provides an indication of the cash

flows that are generated by normal operations. Unilate's EBITDA was $180 million in 2016. This is higher than the reported EBIT of $130 million because the depreciation expense was $50 million. Unilate has no amortization expense.

2-2c Statement of Cash Flows

The statement of cash flows is designed to show how the firm's operations have affected its cash position by examining the firm's investment decisions (uses of cash) and financing decisions (sources of cash) during a particular accounting period. The information contained in the statement of cash flows can help answer questions such as the following: Is the firm generating the cash needed to purchase additional fixed assets for growth? Does it have excess cash flows that can be used to repay debt or to invest in new products? Because this information is useful for both financial managers and investors, the statement of cash flows is an important part of the annual report.

Constructing a statement of cash flows is relatively easy. First, to some extent, the income statement shows the cash flow effects of a firm's operations. For example, Unilate reported its 2016 net income as $54 million, which we know includes a $50 million depreciation expense that is a noncash operating cost. As reported earlier, if the $50 million depreciation expense is added back to the $54 million net income, we can estimate that the cash flow generated from normal operations is $104 million. For most firms, however, some of the reported revenues have not been collected, and some of the reported expenses have not been paid at the time the income statement is constructed. To adjust the estimate of cash flows obtained from the income statement and account for cash flow effects not reflected in the income statement, we need to examine the changes in the balance sheet accounts during the period in question. To accomplish this, we look at the changes in the balance sheet accounts from the beginning of the year to the end of the year to identify which items provided cash (*sources*) and which items used

operating cash flows Those cash flows that arise from normal operations; the difference between cash collections and cash expenses associated with the manufacture and sale of inventory.

accounting profits A firm's net income as reported on its income statement.

statement of cash flows A statement that reports the effects of a firm's operating, investing, and financing activities on cash flows over an accounting period.

cash (uses) during the year. To determine whether a change in a balance sheet account was a source of cash or a use of cash, we follow these simple rules:

Sources of Cash	Uses of Cash
Increase in a Liability or Equity Account	**Decrease in a Liability or Equity Account**
Borrowing funds or issuing stock provides cash.	Paying off a loan or buying back stock uses cash.
Decrease in an Asset Account	**Increase in an Asset Account**
Selling inventory or collecting receivables provides cash.	Buying fixed assets or buying more inventory uses cash.

Using these rules, we can identify which changes in Unilate's balance sheet accounts provided cash during 2016 and which changes used cash. Table 2.3 shows the results of this exercise. Note that the changes in the balance sheet accounts "used" a net $100 million in cash; the accounts' changes provided $70 million, but used $170 million. Earlier we estimated that, ignoring the balance sheet effects, a $104 million cash flow was generated from income. However, because $29 million was paid in common stock dividends, the net effect of the activities shown on the income statement was $75 million ($104 million − $29 million).

When we combine this effect with the cash flow effects from the balance sheet (shown in Table 2.3), the overall net effect was a $25 million decrease in the cash account—that is, −$25 million = $75 million − $100 million.

Using the information provided in Tables 2.2 and 2.3, we constructed the Statement of Cash Flows shown in Table 2.4.[2] Each cash flow effect shown in Table 2.4 is classified as resulting from (1) operations, (2) long-term investments, or (3) financing activities. Operating cash flows are those associated with the production and sale of goods and services. The estimate of cash flows obtained from the income statement is the primary operating cash flow, but changes in accounts payable, accounts receivable, inventories, and accruals are also classified as operating cash flows because these accounts are directly affected by the firm's day-to-day operations. Investment cash flows arise from the purchase or sale of plant, property, or equipment. Financing cash inflows result when the firm issues debt or common stock; financing cash outflows occur when the firm pays dividends, repays debt (loans), or repurchases stock. The cash inflows and outflows from these three activities are summed to determine their effect on the firm's liquidity position, which is measured by the change in the cash and equivalents account from one year to the next.

[2]The cash flow statement is presented in either of two formats. The method used here is called the *indirect method*. Cash flows from operations are calculated by starting with net income, adding back expenses not paid out of cash, and subtracting revenues that do not provide cash. With the *direct method*, operating cash flows are found by summing all revenues that provide cash and then subtracting all expenses that are paid in cash. Both formats produce the same result, and both are accepted by the Financial Accounting Standards Board.

Table 2.3

Unilate Textiles: Cash Sources and Uses from Balance Sheet Accounts, 2016 ($ million)

	Account Balances as of:		Change	
	12/31/16	**12/31/15**	**Sources**	**Uses**
Balance Sheet Effects (Adjustments)				
Cash and marketable securities[a]	$ 15.0	$ 40.0	—	
Accounts receivable	180.0	160.0		$ 20.0
Inventory	270.0	200.0		70.0
Gross plant and equipment	680.0	600.0		80.0
Accounts payable	30.0	15.0	$15.0	
Accruals	60.0	55.0	5.0	
Notes payable	40.0	35.0	5.0	
Long-term bonds	300.0	255.0	45.0	
Common stock (25 million shares)	130.0	130.0		
Total balance sheet effects			$70.0	$170.0

[a]Because we are trying to account for the change in the Cash and Marketable Securities account, the change is identified as neither a source nor a use in this table.

Table 2.4

Unilate Textiles: Statement of Cash Flows for the Period Ending December 31, 2016 ($ millions)

	Cash Flows	Net Amounts
Cash Flows from Operating Activities		
Net income	$ 54.0	
Additions (adjustments) to net income		
Depreciation[a]	50.0	
Increase in accounts payable	15.0	
Increase in accruals	5.0	
Subtractions (adjustments) from net income		
Increase in accounts receivable	(20.0)	
Increase in inventory	(70.0)	
Net cash flow from operations		$ 34.0
Cash Flows from Long-Term Investing Activities		
Acquisition of fixed assets[b]		$ (80.0)
Cash Flows from Financing Activities		
Increase in notes payable	$ 5.0	
Increase in bonds	45.0	
Dividend payment	(29.0)	
Net cash flow from financing		$ 21.0
Net change in cash		$ (25.0)
Cash at the beginning of the year		40.0
Cash at the end of the year		$ 15.0

[a]Depreciation is a noncash expense that was deducted when calculating net income. It must be added back to show the correct cash flow from operations.

[b]See footnote a in Table 2.1.

The top part of Table 2.4 shows cash flows generated by and used in operations. For Unilate, normal operations provided net cash flows of $34 million. This amount is determined by adjusting the firm's net income to account for noncash items. In 2016, Unilate's day-to-day operations provided $104 million of funds ($54 million net income plus $50 million depreciation), but the increase in inventories and investment in receivables during the year accounted for a combined use of funds equal to $90 million, whereas increases in accounts payable and accruals only provided $20 million in additional operating (short-term) funds. The second section in Table 2.4 shows the company's long-term investing activities. Unilate purchased fixed assets totaling $80 million, which was its only investment activity during the year. Unilate's financing activities, shown in the bottom section of Table 2.4, included borrowing from banks (notes payable), selling new bonds, and paying dividends to its common stockholders. The company raised $50 million by borrowing, but it paid $29 million in dividends, so its net inflow of funds from financing activities was $21 million.

When we total all of these sources of cash and uses of cash, we see that Unilate had a $25 million cash shortfall (deficit) during the year—that is, Unilate's cash outflows were $25 million greater than its cash inflows. It met this shortfall by drawing down its cash and equivalents from $40 million to $15 million, as shown in the firm's balance sheet (Table 2.1).

Unilate's statement of cash flows should raise some concerns for its financial manager and outside analysts. The company spent $80 million on new fixed assets and it paid out another $29 million in dividends. These cash outlays were covered by the $34 million in cash that was generated from operations, by borrowing heavily, by selling off marketable securities (cash equivalents), and by drawing down the company's bank account. Obviously, this situation cannot continue indefinitely. We will consider some of the actions that the financial manager might recommend later in this chapter.

2-2d Statement of Retained Earnings

Changes in the common equity accounts between balance sheet dates are reported in the

Table 2.5

Unilate Textiles: Statement of Retained Earnings for the Period Ending December 31, 2016 ($ millions)

Balance of retained earnings, December 31, 2015	$260.0
Add: 2015 net income	54.0
Less: 2015 dividends paid to stockholders	(29.0)
Balance of retained earnings, December 31, 2016	$285.0

statement of retained earnings. Unilate's statement is shown in Table 2.5. Of the $54 million that it earned, Unilate decided to keep $25 million for reinvestment in the business. Thus, the balance sheet item called "Retained earnings" increased from $260 million at the end of 2015 to $285 million at the end of 2016.

It is important to understand that the retained earnings account represents a *claim against assets,* not assets per se. Firms retain earnings primarily to expand their businesses, which means funds are invested in plant and equipment, in inventories, and so forth, but *not* necessarily in a bank account (cash). As a result, *the amount of retained earnings as reported on the balance sheet does not represent cash and is not "available" for the payment of dividends or anything else.*[3]

2-3 Financial Statement (Ratio) Analysis

statement of retained earnings A statement reporting the change in the firm's retained earnings as a result of the income generated and retained during the year. The balance sheet figure for retained earnings is the sum of the earnings retained for each year that the firm has been in business.

liquid asset An asset that can be easily converted into cash without significant loss of the amount originally invested.

As we discovered in previous sections, financial statements provide information about a firm's position at a specific point in time, as well as its operations over some past period. Nevertheless, the real value of financial statements lies in the fact that they can be used to help predict the firm's financial position in the future and to determine expected earnings and dividends. From an investor's standpoint, *predicting the future is the purpose of financial statement analysis;* from management's standpoint, *financial statement analysis is useful both as a way to anticipate future conditions and, more importantly, as a starting point for planning actions that will influence the firm's future course of events.*

The first step in a financial analysis typically includes an evaluation of the firm's ratios, which are designed to show relationships between financial statement accounts *within* firms and *between* firms. Translating accounting numbers into relative values, or *ratios,* allows us to compare the financial position of one firm with the financial position of another firm, even if their sizes are significantly different.

Table 2.6 shows the solutions for various ratios for Unilate Textiles in 2016. In this section, we discuss the five categories of ratios shown in this table and evaluate Unilate's financial results in relation to the industry averages. Note that all dollar amounts used in the ratio calculations given in the table are in millions, except where per-share values are used. Also note that there are literally hundreds of ratios that are used by management, creditors, and stockholders to evaluate firms; we show only a few of the most-often used ratios in Table 2.6.

2-3a Liquidity Ratios

A **liquid asset** is one that can be easily converted to cash without significant loss of its original value. Converting assets—especially current assets such as inventory and receivables—to cash is the primary means by which a firm obtains the funds needed to pay its current bills. Therefore, a firm's *liquidity position* deals with the question of how well the company is able to meet its current obligations, which include amounts owed to suppliers (accounts payable), amounts owed to employees (wages payable), and so forth. Short-term, or *current*, assets are more easily converted to cash (more liquid) than are long-term assets. In general, then, one firm is considered more liquid than another firm if it has a greater proportion of its total assets in the form of current assets.

[3]A positive number in the retained earnings account indicates only that in the past, according to generally accepted accounting principles, the firm has earned income, but its dividends have been less than its reported income. Even though a company reports record earnings and shows an increase in the retained earnings account, it still might be short of cash. The same situation holds for individuals. You might own a new BMW (no loan), lots of clothes, and an expensive sound system and therefore have a high net worth. If you had only $0.23 in your pocket plus $5.00 in your checking account, you would still be short of cash.

Table 2.6

Unilate Textiles: Summary of Financial Ratios, 2016 ($ million, except per-share dollars)

Ratio		Formula for Calculation	Calculation		Ratio Value	Industry Average	Comment
Liquidity							
Current	$=$	$\dfrac{\text{Current assets}}{\text{Current liabilities}}$	$\dfrac{\$465.0}{\$130.0}$	$=$	3.6×	4.1×	Low
Quick	$=$	$\dfrac{\text{Current assets } - \text{ Inventory}}{\text{Current liabilities}}$	$\dfrac{\$195.0}{\$130.0}$	$=$	1.5×	2.1×	Low
Asset Management							
Inventory turnover	$=$	$\dfrac{\text{Cost of goods sold}}{\text{Inventory}}$	$\dfrac{\$1,230.0}{\$270.0}$	$=$	4.6×	7.4×	Low
Days sales outstanding (DSO)	$=$	$\dfrac{\text{Accounts receivable}}{[(\text{Annual sales})/360]}$	$\dfrac{\$180.0}{\$4.17}$	$=$	43.2 days	32.1 days	Poor
Fixed assets turnover	$=$	$\dfrac{\text{Sales}}{\text{Net fixed assets}}$	$\dfrac{\$1,500.0}{\$380.0}$	$=$	3.9×	4.0×	OK
Total assets turnover	$=$	$\dfrac{\text{Sales}}{\text{Total assets}}$	$\dfrac{\$1,500.0}{\$845.0}$	$=$	1.8×	2.1×	Low
Debt Management							
Debt ratio	$=$	$\dfrac{\text{Total liabilities}}{\text{Total assets}}$	$\dfrac{\$430.0}{\$845.0}$	$=$	50.9%	42.0%	Poor
Times interest earned (TIE)	$=$	$\dfrac{\text{EBIT}}{\text{Interest charges}}$	$\dfrac{\$130.0}{\$40.0}$	$=$	3.3×	6.5×	Low
Fixed charge coverage[a]	$=$	$\dfrac{\text{EBIT } + \text{ Lease payments}}{\text{Interest charges} + \text{Lease payments} + \left[\dfrac{\text{Sinking fund payments}}{(1 - \text{Tax rate})}\right]}$	$\dfrac{\$140.0}{\$63.33}$	$=$	2.2×	5.8×	Low
Profitability							
Net profit margin	$=$	$\dfrac{\text{Net income}}{\text{Sales}}$	$\dfrac{\$54.0}{\$1,500.0}$	$=$	3.6%	4.9%	Poor
Return on assets (ROA)	$=$	$\dfrac{\text{Net income}}{\text{Total assets}}$	$\dfrac{\$54.0}{\$845.0}$	$=$	6.4%	10.3%	Poor
Return on equity (ROE)	$=$	$\dfrac{\text{Net income}}{\text{Common equity}}$	$\dfrac{\$54.0}{\$415.0}$	$=$	13.0%	17.7%	Poor
Market Value							
Price/Earnings (P/E)	$=$	$\dfrac{\text{Market price per share}}{\text{Earnings per share}}$	$\dfrac{\$23.00}{\$2.16}$	$=$	10.6×	15.0×	Low
Market/Book (M/B)	$=$	$\dfrac{\text{Market price per share}}{\text{Book value per share}}$	$\dfrac{\$23.00}{\$16.60}$	$=$	1.4×	2.5×	Low

[a]The values given in the numerator and the denominator reflect the lease payments and sinking fund payments that Unilate must make each year.

According to its balance sheet, Unilate has debts totaling $130 million that must be paid off within the coming year—that is, its current liabilities equal $130 million. Will it have trouble satisfying those obligations? A full liquidity analysis requires the use of cash budgets (described in Chapter 15). Nevertheless, by relating the amount of cash and other current assets to the firm's current obligations, ratio analysis provides a quick, easy-to-use measure of liquidity. Two commonly used liquidity ratios are discussed next.

$$\text{Current ratio} = \frac{\text{Current assets}}{\text{Current liabilities}}$$

Current assets normally include cash and equivalents, accounts receivable, and inventories, and current liabilities consist of accounts payable, short-term notes payable, long-term debt that matures in the current period (current maturities of long-term debt), accrued taxes, and other accrued expenses (principally wages). Because the current ratio provides the best single indicator of the extent to which the claims of short-term creditors are covered by assets that are expected to be converted to cash fairly quickly (i.e., current assets), it is the most commonly used measure of short-term solvency. When a company experiences financial difficulty, it pays its bills (e.g., accounts payable) more slowly, borrows more from its bank, and so forth. If current liabilities are rising more rapidly than current assets, the current ratio will fall, which could spell trouble.

$$\text{Quick ratio} = \frac{\text{Current assets} - \text{Inventories}}{\text{Current liabilities}}$$

Inventories typically are the least liquid of a firm's current assets, so they are the assets on which losses are most likely to occur in the event of an "emergency" liquidation. Therefore, having a measure of the firm's ability to pay off short-term obligations without relying on the sale of inventories is important.

Evaluation. Unilate's liquidity ratios are below the industry averages, which suggests that Unilate's liquidity position currently is weaker than average. Even so, with a current ratio of 3.6×, Unilate could liquidate current assets at only 28 percent of

book value and still pay off its current creditors in full.[4] Unfortunately, the value of the quick ratio suggests that Unilate's level of inventories is high relative to the rest of the industry. Even so, if the accounts receivable can be collected, the company can pay off its current liabilities even without having to liquidate its inventory. To get a better idea of why Unilate is in this position, we must examine its asset management ratios.

2-3b Asset Management Ratios

Firms invest in assets to generate revenues both in the current period and in future periods. To purchase their assets, Unilate and other companies must borrow or obtain funds from other sources. If firms have too many assets, their interest expenses will be too high; hence, their profits will be depressed. On the other hand, because production is affected by the capacity of assets, if assets are too low, profitable sales might be lost due to the firm's inability to manufacture enough products.

Asset management ratios measure how effectively the firm is managing its assets. These ratios are designed to answer the following question: Does the total amount of each type of asset as reported on the balance sheet seem reasonable, too high, or too low in view of current and projected sales levels? A few asset management ratios are discussed in this section.

$$\text{Inventory turnover} = \frac{\text{Cost of goods sold}}{\text{Inventory}}$$

provides an indication of how well the firm is managing its inventory.[5] On average, each item of Unilate's inventory is sold and restocked, or turned over, 4.6 times per year (every 78 days), which is considerably lower than the industry average of 7.4 times (every 49 days).[6] This ratio suggests that Unilate is holding excess stocks of inventory, some of which might be damaged or obsolete goods (for example, styles and patterns of textiles from previous years) that are not actually worth their stated value.

liquidity ratios Ratios that show the relationship of a firm's cash and other current assets to its current liabilities; they provide an indication of the firm's ability to meet its current obligations.

asset management ratios A set of ratios that measure how effectively a firm is managing its assets.

[4]Unilate's current ratio is 3.577, and 1/3.577 = 0.2796, which is 28 percent when rounded to two decimal places. Note that 0.2796 ($465.0) = $130, which is the amount of current liabilities.

[5]*Turnover* is a term that originated many years ago with the old Yankee peddler, who would load up his wagon with goods, then go off on his route to peddle his wares. The merchandise was his working capital because it was what he actually sold, or turned over, to produce his profits. His turnover was the number of trips that he took each year. Annual sales divided by inventory equaled turnover, or trips per year. If the peddler made 10 trips per year, stocked 100 pans, and made a gross profit of $5 per pan, his annual gross profit would be 100 × $5 × 10 = $5,000. If the peddler went faster and made 20 trips per year, his gross profit would double, other things held constant.

[6]Some compilers of financial ratio statistics, such as Dun & Bradstreet, use the ratio of sales to inventories carried at cost to depict inventory turnover. If this form of the inventory turnover ratio is used, the true turnover will be overstated, because sales are given at market prices, whereas inventories are carried at cost.

You should use care when calculating and using the inventory turnover ratio, because purchases of inventory (and thus the cost of goods sold) occur over the entire year, whereas the inventory figure applies to one point in time (perhaps December 31). For this reason, it is better to use an average inventory measure.[7] If the firm's business is highly seasonal, or if a strong upward or downward sales trend has occurred during the year, it is essential to make such an adjustment. To maintain comparability with industry averages, however, we did not use the average inventory figure in our computations.

$$\text{Days sales outstanding (DSO)} = \frac{\text{Accounts receivable}}{[\text{Annual sales/360}]}$$

also called the *average collection period (ACP)*, is used to evaluate the firm's ability to collect its credit sales in a timely manner.[8] The DSO represents the average length of time that the firm must wait after making a credit sale before receiving cash—that is, its average collection period. Unilate has about 43 days of sales outstanding, which is much higher than both the 32-day industry average and the company's sales terms, which call for payment within 30 days.

$$\text{Fixed assets turnover} = \frac{\text{Sales}}{\text{Net fixed assets}}$$

measures how effectively the firm uses its plant and equipment to help generate sales. Unilate's ratio of 3.9× is almost equal to the industry average, indicating that the firm is using its fixed assets about

danleap/iStockphoto.com

as efficiently as the other members of its industry. Unilate seems to have neither too many nor too few fixed assets in relation to similar firms.

$$\text{Total assets turnover} = \frac{\text{Sales}}{\text{Total assets}}$$

measures the turnover of all of the firm's assets. Unilate's ratio is somewhat lower than the industry average, indicating that the company is not generating a sufficient volume of business given its total investment in assets. To become more efficient, Unilate should increase its sales, dispose of some assets, or pursue a combination of these steps.

Evaluation. Our examination of Unilate's asset management ratios shows that its fixed assets turnover ratio is very close to the industry average, but its total assets turnover is below average. The fixed assets turnover ratio excludes current assets, whereas the total assets turnover ratio includes them. Therefore, comparison of these ratios confirms our conclusion from the analysis of the liquidity ratios: Unilate seems to have a liquidity problem. The fact that the company's inventory turnover ratio and average collection period are worse than the industry averages suggests, at least in part, that the firm might have problems with inventory and receivables management. Slow sales and tardy collections of credit sales suggest that Unilate might rely more heavily on external funds, such as loans, than the industry does to pay current obligations. Examining Unilate's debt management ratios will help us determine whether this assessment actually is the case.

2-3c Debt Management Ratios

The extent to which a firm uses debt financing has three important implications:

1. By raising funds through debt, the firm avoids diluting stockholder ownership.

2. Creditors look to the equity, or owner-supplied funds, to provide a margin of safety. If the stockholders have provided only a small proportion of the total financing, the risks of the enterprise are borne mainly by its creditors.

[7]Preferably, the average inventory value should be calculated by dividing the sum of the monthly figures during the year by 12. If monthly data are not available, you could add the beginning-of-year and end-of-year figures and divide by 2; this calculation will adjust for growth but not for seasonal effects. Using this approach, Unilate's average inventory for 2016 would be $235 = ($200 + $270)/2, and its inventory turnover would be 5.2 = $1,230/$235, which still is well below the industry average.

[8]To compute DSO using this equation, we must assume that all of the firm's sales are on credit. We usually compute DSO in this manner because information on credit sales is rarely available. Because not all firms have the same percentage of credit sales, the days sales outstanding could be misleading. Also, note that by convention, much of the financial community uses 360 rather than 365 as the number of days in the year for purposes such as this. The DSO is discussed further in Chapters 14 and 15.

3. If the firm earns more on investments financed with borrowed funds than it pays in interest, the return on the owners' capital is magnified, or *leveraged*.

Financial leverage, or borrowing, affects the expected rate of return realized by stockholders for two reasons. First, the interest on debt is tax deductible, whereas dividends are not, so paying interest lowers the firm's tax bill, everything else being equal. Second, if the firm has healthy operations, it typically invests the funds it borrows at a rate of return that is greater than the interest rate on its debt. In combination with the tax advantage that debt offers compared to stock, the higher investment rate of return produces a magnified positive return to the stockholders. Under these conditions, leverage works to the advantage of the firm and its stockholders. Unfortunately, however, financial leverage is a double-edged sword. When the firm experiences poor business conditions, typically sales are lower and costs are higher than expected, but the cost of borrowing, which generally is contractually fixed, still must be paid. Therefore, the required interest payments might impose a very significant burden on a firm that has liquidity problems. In fact, if the interest payments are high enough, a firm with a positive operating income could end up with a negative return to stockholders. Under these conditions, leverage works to the detriment of the firm and its stockholders.

In general, then, we can conclude that firms with relatively high debt ratios have higher expected returns when business is normal or good, but are exposed to risk of loss when business is poor. Conversely, firms with low debt ratios are less risky, but they also forgo the opportunity to leverage up their returns on equity. The prospects of high returns are desirable, but the average investor is averse to risk. Therefore, decisions about the use of debt require firms to balance the desire for higher expected returns against the increased risk that results from using more debt. Determining the optimal amount of debt for a given firm is a complicated process, and we will defer discussion of this topic until Chapter 12. Here, we will simply look at two procedures that analysts use to examine the firm's debt in a financial statement analysis: (1) examining balance sheet ratios to determine the extent to which borrowed funds have been used to finance assets and (2) evaluating income statement ratios to determine how well operating profits can cover fixed charges such as

interest. These two sets of ratios are complementary, so analysts use both types. A few **debt management ratios** are discussed next.

$$\text{Debt ratio} = \frac{\text{Total liabilities}}{\text{Total assets}}$$

measures the percentage of the firm's assets financed by borrowing (loans). Total liabilities (debt) includes both current liabilities and long-term debt. Thus, $(1 - \text{Debt ratio})$ represents the proportion of the firm's funds that is provided by stockholders. Creditors prefer low debt ratios, because the lower the ratio, the greater the cushion against creditors' losses in the event of liquidation of the firm. The owners, on the other hand, can benefit from leverage because it magnifies earnings, thereby increasing the return to stockholders. However, too much debt often leads to financial difficulty, which eventually could cause bankruptcy.

$$\frac{\text{Times interest}}{\text{earned (TIE)}} = \frac{\text{EBIT}}{\text{Interest charges}}$$

measures the extent to which a firm's operating earnings—before interest and taxes (EBIT), also called *net operating income (NOI)*—can decline before these earnings are no longer sufficient to cover annual interest costs. Failure to meet this obligation can bring legal action by the firm's creditors, possibly resulting in bankruptcy. Note that EBIT, rather than net income, is used in the numerator because interest is paid with pre-tax dollars.

Fixed charge coverage ratio =

$$\frac{\text{EBIT + Lease payments}}{\left(\begin{matrix}\text{Interest}\\\text{charges}\end{matrix}\right) + \left(\begin{matrix}\text{Lease}\\\text{payments}\end{matrix}\right) + \left(\frac{\text{Sinking fund payments}}{1 - \text{Tax rate}}\right)}$$

is similar to the TIE ratio, but it is more inclusive because it recognizes that many firms lease rather than buy long-term assets and they also must make sinking fund (required) payments.[9] Leasing is widespread in certain industries, making this ratio preferable to the TIE ratio for many purposes. Because sinking fund payments are paid with after-tax dollars, whereas interest and lease payments are paid with pre-tax dollars, to be consistent, we must convert the sinking fund payments to pre-tax dollars, which is accomplished by

---

financial leverage The use of debt financing.

debt management ratios Ratios that provide an indication of how much debt the firm has and whether the firm can take on more debt.

---

[9]Generally, a *long-term lease* is defined as one that extends for more than one year. Thus, rent incurred under a six-month lease would not be included in the fixed charge coverage ratio, but rental payments under a one-year or longer lease would be defined as a fixed charge and would be included. A *sinking fund* is a required annual payment designed to reduce the balance owed on a bond or the amount of preferred stock a firm has outstanding.

dividing the after-tax payment by (1 − Tax rate). In the numerator of the fixed charge coverage ratio, the lease payments are added to EBIT because we want to determine the firm's ability to cover its fixed financing charges from the income generated before any fixed financing charges are considered (deducted). Because the EBIT figure represents the firm's operating income net of (after subtracting) lease payments, the lease payments must be added back.

Evaluation. Our examination of Unilate's debt management ratios indicates that the company has a debt ratio that is higher than the industry average (51 percent versus 42 percent), and it has coverage ratios that are substantially lower than the industry averages ($\text{TIE}_{\text{Unilate}} = 3.3\times$; $\text{TIE}_{\text{Industry}} = 6.5\times$). This finding suggests that Unilate is in a somewhat dangerous position with respect to leverage (debt). In fact, the firm might have great difficulty borrowing additional funds until its debt position improves. In the worst case, if the company cannot pay its current obligations, it might be forced into bankruptcy. To see how Unilate's debt position has affected its profits, we next examine its profitability ratios.

2-3d Profitability Ratios

Profitability is the net result of a number of policies and decisions. The ratios examined thus far provide some information about the way the firm is operating, but the profitability ratios discussed in this section show the combined effects of liquidity management, asset management, and debt management on operating results.

$$\text{Net profit margin} = \frac{\text{Net profit}}{\text{Sales}}$$

measures the profit (earnings) per dollar of sales; that is, the percentage of each $1 of sales that remains after all expenses, including taxes, are paid.

$$\frac{\text{Return on total}}{\text{assets (ROA)}} = \frac{\text{Net income}}{\text{Total assets}}$$

provides an indication of the return that the firm generates on its investment in assets; that is, the average percentage return that is generated on funds provided by all shareholders (both creditors and stockholders).

$$\text{Return on equity (ROE)} = \frac{\text{Net income}}{\text{Common equity}}$$

or the *rate of return on stockholders' investment*, measures the percentage return that the firm generates on the funds provided only by common stockholders (the owners of the firm).

Evaluation. Unilate's net profit margin of 3.6 percent is lower than the industry average of 4.9 percent, indicating that its sales might be too low, its costs might be too high, or both conditions exist. Recall that, according to its debt ratio, Unilate has a greater proportion of debt than the industry average, and its TIE ratio shows that the company is not covering its interest payments as well as other firms in the industry are covering their interest payments. This partly explains why Unilate's profit margin is low. To see this fact, we can compute the ratio of EBIT (operating income) to sales, which is called the *operating profit margin*. Unilate's operating profit margin of 8.7 percent (=$130.0/$1,500.0) is exactly the same as the industry average, so the cause of its low net profit margin is the relatively high interest attributable to the firm's higher-than-average use of debt. Unilate's high use of debt has also depressed its ROA and ROE, both of which are much lower than the industry's measures.

Our examination of Unilate's profitability ratios shows that the company's operating results have suffered due to its poor liquidity position, its poor asset management, and its above-average debt. In the final group of ratios, we examine Unilate's market value ratios to see how investors feel about the company's current financial position.

2-3e Market Value Ratios

The market value ratios relate the firm's stock price to its earnings and book value per share. These ratios give management an indication of what *investors* think of the company's future prospects based on its past performance. If the firm's liquidity ratios, asset management ratios, debt management ratios, and profitability ratios are all good, then its market value ratios will be high and its stock price will probably be as high as can be expected. Of course, the opposite also is true.

$$\frac{\text{Price/Earnings}}{\text{(P/E) ratio}} = \frac{\text{Market price per share}}{\text{Earnings per share}}$$

shows how much investors are willing to pay for the firm's stock for each dollar of reported profits. Because Unilate's stock sells for $23.00 and its EPS is $2.16, its P/E ratio is 10.6.

If other things hold constant, P/E ratios are higher for firms with high growth prospects and lower for riskier firms. Because Unilate's P/E ratio is lower than that of other textile manufacturers, it

profitability ratios A group of ratios showing the effect of liquidity, asset management, and debt management on operating results.

market value ratios A set of ratios that relate the firm's stock price to its earnings and book value per share.

suggests that the company is regarded as being somewhat riskier than most of its competitors, as having poorer growth prospects, or both. From our analysis of its debt management ratios, we know that Unilate has higher-than-average risk associated with leverage. However, we do not know whether its growth prospects are poor.

$$\frac{\text{Market/Book}}{\text{(M/B) ratio}} = \frac{\text{Market price per share}}{\text{Book value per share}}$$

gives another indication of how investors regard the company. The stocks of companies with relatively high rates of return on equity generally sell at higher multiples of book value than do those with low returns.

Evaluation. Unilate's P/E and M/B ratios (10.6× and 1.4×, respectively) are much lower than the industry averages (15.0× and 2.5×, respectively). Investors are willing to pay less for Unilate's book value than for that of an average textile manufacturer. This finding should not be surprising because, as we discovered previously, Unilate has generated below-average returns with respect to both total assets and common equity. In general, our examination of Unilate's market value ratios indicates that investors are not excited about the future prospects of the company's common stock as an investment. Perhaps they believe that Unilate is headed toward serious financial difficulties, perhaps even bankruptcy, unless the firm takes actions to correct its liquidity and asset management problems and to improve its leverage position. One approach used to determine the direction in which a firm is headed is to evaluate the trends of the ratios over the past few years and thereby answer the following question: Is the firm's financial position improving or deteriorating?

2-3f Comparative Ratios (Benchmarking) and Trend Analysis

Our analysis of Unilate's ratios indicates that the firm's current financial position is poor compared to the industry norm. The type of analysis we completed in the previous sections is called comparative ratio analysis—that is, the ratios calculated for Unilate were compared with those of other firms in the same industry at the same point in time.[10] Comparative ratio analysis indicates how well the firm is currently performing, but it does not

comparative ratio analysis An analysis based on a comparison of a firm's ratios with those of other firms in the same industry at the same point in time.

trend analysis An evaluation of changes (trends) in a firm's financial position over a period of time, perhaps years.

tell us whether the company is in a better or a worse financial position now than it was in previous years.

To forecast the direction in which the firm is headed, we must analyze trends in ratios. By examining the paths taken in the past, trend analysis provides information about whether the firm's financial position is more likely to improve or to deteriorate in the future. A simple approach to trend analysis is to construct graphs containing both the firm's ratios and the industry averages for the past five years. Using this approach, we can examine both the direction of the movement in, and the relationships between, the firm's ratios and the industry averages. If we were to graphically compare Unilate's ratios from 2016 with those from 2009–2015, we would discover that Unilate's financial position has deteriorated, not strengthened, over this period. This is not a good trend.

2-3g Summary of Ratio Analysis: The DuPont Analysis

Management and analysts often evaluate ratios using the DuPont approach, named after the company whose managers developed the evaluation technique. The idea is to attain greater detail by dissecting a single ratio into two or more related ratios. For example, using the basic DuPont approach we can compute the return on assets (ROA) by multiplying the net profit margin by total assets turnover as shown in Equation 2.2:

2.2

$$\text{ROA} = \text{Net profit margin} \times \text{Total assets turnover}$$
$$= \frac{\text{Net income}}{\text{Sales}} \times \frac{\text{Sales}}{\text{Total assets}}$$
$$= \frac{\text{Net income}}{\text{Total assets}}$$

In 2016, Unilate made a profit of 3.6 percent, or 3.6 cents, on each dollar of sales, and assets were turned over 1.8 times during the year, which indicates that every \$1 that was invested in assets generated \$1.80 in sales. The company earned a return of 6.4 percent on

[10]Comparative ratios for a large number of industries are available from several sources, including Dun & Bradstreet (D&B), Robert Morris Associates, the U.S. Department of Commerce, and trade associations. There are often definitional differences in the ratios presented by different sources; so before using any source, verify the exact definitions of the ratios to ensure consistency with your work.

its assets. Applying the DuPont equation, ROA can be restated as follows:

$$ROA = \frac{\$54}{\$1{,}500} \times \frac{\$1{,}500}{\$845} = 0.036 \times 1.775$$

$$= 0.0639 = 6.4\%$$

If the company were financed only with common equity—that is, if it had no debt—the ROA and the ROE would be the same, because total assets would equal the amount of common equity such that (Net income)/(Total assets) = (Net income)/(Owners' equity). However, nearly 51 percent of Unilate's capital consists of debt. Because ROA shows the average return that is earned by both debt holders and stockholders (that is, all investors), ROE, which shows the return to common stockholders only, must be greater than the ROA of 6.4 percent. To translate the ROA into the ROE, we must multiply ROA by the *equity multiplier*, which is the number of times by which the total assets exceed the amount of common equity. (It is also the inverse of the proportion of total assets that is financed with equity.) Using this approach, we can write ROE as shown in Equation 2.3:

2.3

$$ROE = ROA \times \text{Equity multiplier}$$

$$= \frac{\text{Net income}}{\text{Total assets}} \times \frac{\text{Total assets}}{\text{Common equity}}$$

$$= 6.4\% \times \frac{\$845.0}{\$415.0}$$

$$= 6.4\% \times 2.036 = 13.0\%$$

We can combine Equations 2.2 and 2.3 to form the *extended DuPont equation*, which is written as shown in Equation 2.4:

2.4

$$ROE = \left[\left(\begin{matrix}\text{Profit} \\ \text{margin}\end{matrix}\right)\right] \times \left(\begin{matrix}\text{Total assets} \\ \text{turnover}\end{matrix}\right) \times \left(\begin{matrix}\text{Equity} \\ \text{multiplier}\end{matrix}\right)$$

$$= \left[\frac{\text{Net income}}{\text{Sales}} \times \frac{\text{Sales}}{\text{Total assets}}\right] \times \frac{\text{Total assets}}{\text{Common equity}}$$

$$= 3.6\% \times 1.775 \times 2.036 = 13.0\%$$

Our previous evaluations showed that Unilate's ROE is lower than that for the industry because Unilate's profit margin and total assets turnover (efficiency) are lower than the industry's. Unilate's management can use the DuPont analysis to evaluate ways to improve the firm's performance. Focusing on the net profit margin, Unilate's marketing personnel can study the effects of raising prices (or lowering them to increase volume); of selling new products or moving into markets with higher margins; and so forth. The company's cost accountants can study various expense items and, working with engineers, purchasing agents, and other operating personnel, seek ways of holding down costs. To improve the turnover of assets, Unilate's financial analysts, working with both production and marketing personnel, can investigate ways of minimizing its investment in various types of assets. At the same time, its treasury staff can analyze the effects of alternative financing strategies, seeking to hold down interest expense and the risk of debt while still using leverage to increase the rate of return on equity.

2-4 Uses and Limitations of Ratio Analysis

Although ratio analysis can provide useful information concerning a company's operations and financial condition, it does have inherent problems and limitations that necessitate care and judgment. Some potential problems follow.

1. Many large firms operate a number of divisions in very different industries. In such cases, it is difficult to develop a meaningful set of industry averages for comparative purposes. Consequently, general ratio analysis tends to be more useful for small, narrowly focused firms than for large, multidivisional ones.

2. Most firms want to be better than average, so merely attaining average performance is not necessarily good. As a target for high-level performance, it is best to focus on the industry leaders' ratios. Thus, the industry average is not a magic number that all firms should strive to maintain. If a firm's ratios are far removed from the average for its peers or the industry, however, an analyst should question why this deviation has occurred.

3. Inflation might distort firms' balance sheets. Because many recorded values are historical, they could be substantially different from the "true" values in the marketplace. For example, everything else the same, if we are comparing an old firm that acquired its fixed assets many years ago at low prices with a new company that acquired its fixed assets recently, we probably would find that the old firm has a higher

fixed assets turnover ratio because the book values of its assets are lower. Furthermore, because inflation affects both depreciation charges and inventory costs, it also affects profits. For these reasons, a ratio analysis for one firm over time, or a comparative analysis of firms of different ages, must be carefully interpreted.

4. Seasonal factors can distort a ratio analysis. For example, the inventory turnover ratio for a textile firm will be radically different if the balance sheet figure used for inventory is the one just before the fall fashion season rather than the one just after the close of the season. You can minimize this problem by using monthly averages for inventory (and receivables) when calculating ratios such as turnover.

5. Firms can employ **window-dressing techniques** to make their financial statements look stronger. To illustrate, consider a Chicago builder that borrowed on a five-year basis on December 30, 2015, held the proceeds of the loan as cash for a few days, and then paid off the loan ahead of time on January 3, 2016. This activity

window-dressing techniques
Techniques employed by firms to make their financial statements look better than they actually are.

improved the company's current and quick ratios, and it made the firm's year-end 2015 balance sheet look good. The improvement was strictly window dressing, however; one week later, the balance sheet was back at the old level.

6. Different accounting practices can distort comparisons. As noted earlier, inventory valuation and depreciation methods can affect financial statements. The fact that different methods can be used to measure the same event makes comparisons among firms difficult.

7. It is difficult to generalize about whether a particular ratio is "good" or "bad." For example, a high current ratio might indicate a strong liquidity position, which is good, or excessive cash, which is bad (because excess cash in the bank is a nonearning asset). Similarly, a high fixed asset turnover ratio might denote either a firm that uses its assets efficiently or one that is undercapitalized and cannot afford to buy enough assets to produce sufficient amounts of its product in order to satisfy customers' demands.

8. A firm might have some ratios that look good and others that look bad, making it difficult to tell whether the company is, on balance, strong or weak. Statistical procedures

can be used to analyze the net effects of a set of ratios and thereby clarify the situation. No matter what method is used to interpret ratios, however, you should perform a complete analysis of the firm's financial statements before reaching conclusions. Do not form opinions about a firm's financial position based on only a few ratios.

Ratio analysis is useful, but analysts should be aware of these problems and make adjustments as necessary. When conducted in a mechanical, unthinking manner, this type of analysis is dangerous. Used intelligently and with good judgment, however, it can provide useful insights into a firm's operations. Probably *the most important and most difficult input to successful financial statement (ratio) analysis is the judgment used when interpreting the results to reach an overall conclusion about the firm's future financial position.*

2-4a Accounting in an International Setting

Traditionally, the manner in which firms have recorded and reported their financial activities has varied substantially from one country to the next. As more firms have gone "global," however, there has been increasing pressure for countries to adopt a standardized reporting system that allows companies, investors, and regulators to compare financial statements produced by companies around the world. The push to develop international accounting standards is not new; it actually started in the mid-1970s. But it wasn't until the early 2000s that the movement toward general acceptance of such an accounting system made substantial progress. In 2001, the International Accounting Standards Board (IASB) was created to develop and approve a set of common international accounting rules that are referred to as the International Financial Reporting Standards (IFRS).[11] Proponents of IFRS argue that using one set of accounting standards will improve global financial reporting and the ability to monitor firms, no matter their country of origin.

Today more than 120 countries either require or recommend that firms operating within their borders follow IFRS. Even with its acceptance worldwide, it is interesting that publicly traded companies in the United States are not required to use IFRS. In 2007, the Securities and Exchange Commission (SEC), which oversees the financial reporting of publicly traded companies in the United States, allowed publicly traded foreign companies to use IFRS rather than the Generally Accepted Accounting Principles (GAAP), which is used in the United States, when submitting their financial statements if IFRS was the accounting system used in their home country. And, in 2010, the SEC announced its support for IFRS. But at the time we write this book in 2016, the SEC has not required U.S. firms to use IFRS when filing their financial statements. Even so, it appears there is a good chance that all firms that are publicly traded in the United States will be required to adopt IFRS in the near future. And, as a result of the movement to require firms throughout the world, especially multinational firms, to adhere to IFRS, it is clear that financial statements produced by American companies in the future will have a different form than what we described in this chapter.

---

[11]More information about International Financial Reporting Standard (IFRS) can be found on the IFRS website, which is located at http://www.irfs.org.

STUDY TOOLS

LOCATED AT BACK OF THE TEXTBOOK

- ☐ Problems are found at the end of this chapter.
- ☐ A tear-out Chapter Review card is located at the back of the textbook.

LOCATED AT WWW.CENGAGEBRAIN.COM

- ☐ Review Key Term flashcards and create your own cards.
- ☐ Track your knowledge and understanding of key concepts in corporate finance.
- ☐ Complete practice and graded quizzes to prepare for tests.
- ☐ Complete interactive content within CFIN5 Online.
- ☐ View the chapter highlight boxes for CFIN5 Online.

KEY FINANCIAL STATEMENT ANALYSIS CONCEPTS

To conclude this chapter, we summarize some financial statement analysis concepts that were discussed.

- The information provided in financial reports is used by the firm's managers, its creditors and stockholders, potential creditors and stockholders, and other stakeholders and interested parties.

- If a financial analyst could use only one of the financial statements mentioned in this chapter, he or she probably would choose the statement of cash flows because it provides information about how a firm generated funds during the year and how those funds were used.

- Although ratio analysis provides information about a firm's current financial position, *the primary purpose of such an analysis is to provide an indication of the direction the firm's operations are headed in the future.*

- When evaluating the financial position of a firm, an analyst must be aware that different accounting techniques exist to measure the same event; that the firm might use techniques to "dress up" its financial statement; that the effects of inflation can distort values from different time periods; and so forth. The most important ingredient in financial statement analysis is the judgment the analyst uses when interpreting the results.

PROBLEMS

2–1 What kind of financial information is a publicly traded company required to provide to its stockholders? Which financial statement do you think provides the best information for investors?

2–2 Differentiate (compare) among the information that is provided in each of the following financial statements: (1) balance sheet, (2) income statement, and (3) statement of cash flows.

2–3 Discuss some of the limitations associated with performing ratio (financial statement) analysis. What is the most important ingredient (input) in completing ratio analysis? Explain why.

2–4 Robust Robots (RR) recently issued 100,000 shares of common stock at $7 per share. The stock has a par value equal to $3 per share. What amount of the $700,000 that RR raised should be reported in the "common stock at par" account, and what amount should be reported in the "Paid-in capital" account?

2–5 Crooked Golf's most recent income statement shows that net income was $90,000, depreciation was $25,000, and taxes were $60,000. What was Crooked Golf's net cash flow?

2–6 HighTech Wireless just published its current income statement, which shows net income equal to $240,000. The statement also shows that operating expenses were $500,000 before including depreciation, depreciation was $100,000, and the tax rate was 40 percent. If HighTech has no debt, what were its sales revenues? What was its net cash flow?

2–7 Credit Card of America (CCA) has a current ratio of 3.5 and a quick ratio of 3.0. If its total current assets equal $73,500, what are CCA's (a) current liabilities and (b) inventory?

2–8 At the end of the year, Wrinkle Free Laundry (WFL) had $150,000 in total assets. (a) If WFL's total assets turnover was 2.0, what were its sales revenues? (b) If WFL's return on assets was 6 percent, what were its net income *and* net profit margin?

2–9 The balance sheet for Panoramic Open Pictures (POP) shows $300,000 in total assets and $200,000 in total liabilities. POP's return on assets (ROA) is 5 percent. Compute POP's (a) net income for the year and (b) its return on equity (ROE). POP has no preferred stock.

2–10 Legacy Cleaning has a debt ratio equal to 40 percent, total assets equal to $750,000, return on assets (ROA) at 6 percent, and total assets turnover of 3.0. (a) If it has no preferred stock, what amount of common equity does Legacy have? (b) What is Legacy's net profit margin?

2–11 At the end of the year, Water Works International (WWI) had $10,000 in total assets. Its total assets turnover was 2.5, and its return on assets (ROA) was 4 percent. What were WWI's (a) sales revenues and (b) net profit margin?

2–12 Last year, Delightful Desserts had a quick ratio of 1.8, a current ratio of 5.0, an inventory turnover of 7, total current assets of $340,000, and cash and equivalents of $43,000. If the cost of goods sold equaled 80 percent of sales, what were Bailey's annual sales and DSO?

2–13 Wiley's Wilderness pays 6 percent interest on its outstanding debt, which equals $200,000. The company's sales are $540,000, its tax rate is 40 percent, and its net profit margin is 4 percent. (a) What is Wiley's TIE? (b) If Wiley's wants to maintain a TIE equal to 6.0, what must its sales equal?

2–14 The most recent balance sheet of Infinity Information Systems (IIS) shows that the company has $35 million of common equity and 7 million shares of common stock outstanding. The company's common stock has a market value equal to $8 per share. IIS's net income was $14 million. What are IIS's (a) P/E ratio and (b) M/B ratio?

2–15 Smitty's Finger-Licking BBQ has a total assets turnover equal to 2.0, a return on equity (ROE) equal to 15 percent, and a debt ratio equal to 60 percent. If Smitty's is financed with debt and common stock, what are its (a) return on assets (ROA) and (b) net profit margin?

2–16 Duncan Boutique's total assets are $440,000, its return on assets (ROA) is 8 percent, and its debt ratio is 20 percent. What are Duncan's (a) net income and (b) return on equity (ROE)?

2–17 Horatio's Hot Dogs' current assets equal $260,000. The company's return on assets (ROA) is 4 percent, its net income is $140,000, its long-term debt equals $1,755,000, and 35 percent of its assets are financed with common equity. Horatio's has no preferred stock. Compute the company's current ratio.

2–18 Fido's Dog Spa's financial statements show that its total assets equal $100,000, its return on assets (ROA) is 3 percent, and its return on equity (ROE) is 5 percent. (a) Compute the company's net income. (b) What portion of total assets is financed with debt? Fido's has no preferred stock.

2–19 Sixty (60) percent of Extreme Well Drilling's assets are financed with common equity, which is the only type of equity financing the company has. Extreme's current ratio is 5.0, its total assets turnover is 4.0, current assets equal $150,000, and its sales equal $1,800,000. What amount of Extreme's total liabilities is long term, and what amount is short term (current liabilities)?

2–20 North/South Airlines generated the following information from its financial statements: (1) P/E ratio equals 15.0, (2) common stock market price per share is $30, (3) fixed assets turnover equals 8.0, (4) current ratio equals 5.0, (5) current liabilities equal $300,000, (6) net profit margin equals 4 percent, and (7) 60,000 shares of common stock are outstanding. What are North/South's (a) return on assets (ROA) and (b) total assets turnover?

After you finish this chapter go to **PAGE 58** for **STUDY TOOLS**

LEARNING OUTCOMES

After studying this chapter, you will be able to…

LO1 Describe the role that financial markets play in improving the standard of living in an economy.

LO2 Describe how various financial markets are differentiated.

LO3 Discuss the role that an investment banking house plays in the financial markets.

LO4 Describe the role that financial intermediaries play in the financial markets, and explain why there are so many different types of intermediaries.

LO5 Describe how financial markets and financial intermediaries in the United States differ from those in other parts of the world.

The Financial Environment:
Markets, Institutions, and Investment Banking

Businesses, individuals, and governments often need to raise funds to finance operations or to invest in assets. For example, suppose Tampa Electric Company (TECO) forecasts an increase in the demand for electricity in Florida, and the company decides to build a new power plant. Because TECO almost certainly will not have the hundreds of millions of dollars necessary to pay for the plant, the company will have to raise these funds by borrowing or by issuing new stock. This chapter examines the financial markets where such funds are raised, securities are traded, and the prices for stocks and bonds are established.[1]

3-1 What Are Financial Markets?

Although some individuals and firms need funds, others have funds to invest because their incomes are greater than their current living expenses. People who need money are brought together with those who have surplus funds in the *financial markets*. Note that *markets* is plural; a great many different financial markets exist, each of which includes many institutions and individuals, in a developed economy such as that of the United States. Unlike *physical asset markets*, which deal with products such as wheat, autos, real estate, and machinery, *financial asset markets* deal with stocks, bonds, mortgages, and other *claims on real assets* with respect to the distribution of the future cash flows generated by such assets.

In a general sense, the term *financial market* refers to a conceptual mechanism rather than a physical location or a specific type of organization or structure. We usually define the **financial markets** as a system that includes individuals and institutions, instruments, and procedures that bring together borrowers and savers, no matter the location.

3-1a Importance of Financial Markets

The primary role of financial markets is to facilitate the flow of funds *from* individuals and businesses that have surplus funds *to* individuals, businesses, and governments that have needs for funds in excess of their incomes. The more efficient the flow of funds process is, the more productive the economy is, in terms of both manufacturing and financing.

3-1b Flow of Funds

The financial markets allow us to consume amounts different from our current incomes by providing *mechanisms* that help us transfer

> **financial markets** A system consisting of individuals and institutions, instruments, and procedures that bring together borrowers and savers.

[1]Throughout much of this chapter, we primarily refer to corporations as the users, or issuers, of such financial assets as debt and equity. In reality, governments, government agencies, and individuals also issue debt. For example, an individual "issues" a mortgage when he or she finances the purchase of a house. Because corporations issue a variety of debt instruments and can also issue equity, we will identify them as the issuers more often than governments or individuals in the examples.

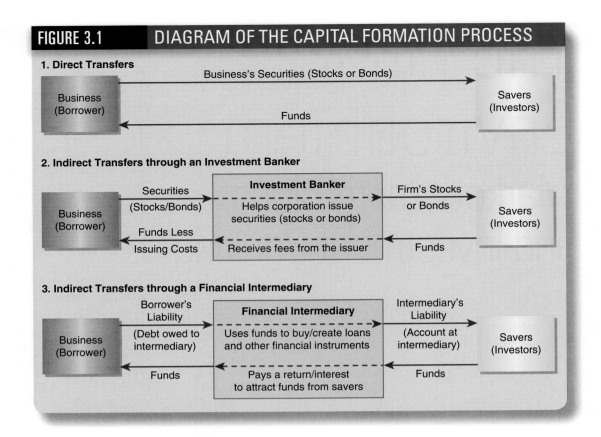

FIGURE 3.1   DIAGRAM OF THE CAPITAL FORMATION PROCESS

1. Direct Transfers

Business's Securities (Stocks or Bonds)

Business (Borrower) → Savers (Investors)

Funds

2. Indirect Transfers through an Investment Banker

Investment Banker

Business (Borrower)

Securities (Stocks/Bonds)

Helps corporation issue securities (stocks or bonds)

Firm's Stocks or Bonds

Savers (Investors)

Funds Less Issuing Costs

Receives fees from the issuer

Funds

3. Indirect Transfers through a Financial Intermediary

Financial Intermediary

Business (Borrower)

Borrower's Liability

(Debt owed to intermediary)

Uses funds to buy/create loans and other financial instruments

Intermediary's Liability

(Account at intermediary)

Savers (Investors)

Funds

Pays a return/interest to attract funds from savers

Funds

---

income through time.[2] When we borrow, for example, we sacrifice future income to supplement (increase) current income; when we save, or invest, we sacrifice current income in exchange for greater expected income (spending) in the future. The ability to transfer income to different time periods allows us to pass through three financial phases during our lives that would not be possible without financial markets.

1. As young adults, we generally consume more than our incomes to buy such items as houses and cars. To do so, we borrow based on our ability to generate future income that will be used to pay off the debt.

2. As older working adults in the prime of our careers, we generally earn more than we consume, so we save some of our income. Such savings are often designated for use during retirement.

3. As retired adults, we use funds accumulated in earlier years to at least partially replace income that is lost when we retire from our careers.

In the absence of financial markets, consumption would be restricted to income earned each year plus any amounts put aside (perhaps in a coffee can) in previous years. As a result, because it would be difficult to transfer income to periods prior to when it is earned, our standard of living would be much lower than exists with financial markets.

Funds are transferred (flow) from those with surpluses (savers) to those with needs (borrowers) by the three different processes diagrammed in Figure 3.1.

1. A *direct transfer* of money and securities, as shown in the top section, occurs when a business sells its stocks or bonds directly to savers (investors) without going through any type of intermediary or financial institution. The business delivers its securities to savers, who in turn provide the firm with some of the money it needs.

2. As shown in the middle section, a transfer can also go through an *investment banking house,* which serves as a middleman that facilitates the issuance of securities by firms that need to raise funds. The firm's securities and the savers' money merely "pass through" the

---

[2]Throughout this chapter, we often refer to the parties involved in financial market transactions as borrowers or lenders, which implies that only loans are traded in the financial markets. In reality, stocks, options, and many other financial assets also are traded in the financial markets. In our general discussions, we will use the term borrowers to refer to parties such as individuals and government units that raise needed funds through various types of loans, as well as corporations that use both loans and stock issues to raise needed funds. We will use the term lenders to refer to those parties who provide funds by investing in such instruments as stocks (equity) and bonds (debt).

investment banking house. The investment banking process is described later in this chapter.

3. Transfers can also be made through a *financial intermediary,* such as a bank or a mutual fund. In this case, the intermediary obtains funds from savers and then uses the money to lend out or to purchase another company's securities. The existence of intermediaries greatly increases the efficiency of the financial markets. More information concerning the roles and descriptions of financial intermediaries is provided later in this chapter.

Direct transfers of funds from savers to borrowers are possible and do occur on occasion. Generally, however, corporations and government entities use investment bankers to help them raise needed capital in the financial markets, whereas individuals use financial intermediaries to help them borrow (raise) needed funds. Individuals also use financial intermediaries to help them save to meet such future financial goals as retirement.

3-1c Market Efficiency

If the financial markets did not provide efficient funds transfers, the economy simply could not function as it does now. Because Tampa Electric Company would have difficulty raising needed capital, Miami's citizens would pay more for electricity. Likewise, you would not be able to buy the house you want when you want it or earn a decent rate on funds you save. Clearly, the level of employment and productivity, and hence our standard of living, would be much lower. Therefore, it is essential that our financial markets function efficiently—not only quickly, but also at a low cost. When we speak of *market efficiency*, we generally mean either economic efficiency or informational efficiency.

Economic Efficiency. The financial markets are said to have achieved economic efficiency if funds are allocated to their optimal use at the best costs (interest rates). In economically efficient markets, businesses and individuals invest their funds in assets that yield the highest returns, and the costs of searching for such opportunities are lower than those observed in less efficient markets.

Informational Efficiency. The prices of investments bought and sold in the financial markets are based on available information. If these prices reflect existing information and adjust very quickly when new information becomes available, then the financial markets have achieved informational efficiency. When the financial markets have a large number of participants in search of the most profitable investments, informational efficiency generally exists. Informational efficiency typically is classified into one of the following three categories:

1. **Weak-form efficiency**—states that all information contained in *past price movements* is fully reflected in current market prices. Therefore, information about past trends (including recent ones) in investment prices is of no use in selecting "winning" investments; the fact that an investment has risen for the past three days, for example, gives us no clues as to what it will do today or tomorrow.

2. **Semistrong-form efficiency**—states that current market prices reflect all *publicly available information,* whether it is historical or newly released (perhaps a few minutes earlier). In this case, it does no good to scrutinize such published data as a company's financial statements to seek *abnormal returns,* because market prices will adjust to any good news or bad news contained in such reports as soon as they are made public. An abnormal return is defined as a return that is greater than is justified by the risk associated with the investment. For example, if you and all of your friends invest in similar-risk securities, you should all earn about the same return. However, if you earn a 20 percent return and your friends earn a 12 percent return on investments with the same risk, the additional 8 percent is considered an abnormal return.

3. **Strong-form efficiency**—states that current market prices reflect *all pertinent information,* whether it is publicly available or privately held. If this form of efficiency holds, even company insiders would find it impossible to earn abnormal returns in the financial markets.

The informational efficiency of the financial markets has received a great deal of attention. The results of most market efficiency studies suggest that the financial markets are highly efficient in the weak form and reasonably efficient in the semistrong form, but strong-form efficiency does not appear to hold.

Generally, when financial markets are informationally efficient, they are also economically efficient. This situation arises because investors can expect prices to reflect appropriate information that permits them to make intelligent choices about which investments will likely provide the best returns.

economic efficiency Funds are allocated to their optimal use at the lowest costs in the financial markets.

informational efficiency The degree to which prices of investments reflect existing information and how quickly they adjust when new information enters the markets.

abnormal return Return that exceeds what is justified by the risk associated with the investment.

3-2 Types of Financial Markets

Many financial markets, with a variety of investments and participants, exist today. We generally differentiate among financial markets based on the types of investments, maturities of investments, types of borrowers and lenders, locations of the markets, and types of transactions. There are too many different financial markets to discuss here. Instead, we only describe a few of the more common classifications.

1. **Money markets versus capital markets**—Some borrowers need funds for short periods; others need funds for extended periods. Similarly, some investors prefer to invest for short periods, but others prefer to invest for longer periods. The markets for short-term financial instruments are termed the *money markets*, and the markets for long-term financial instruments are called the *capital markets*. More specifically, the money markets include debt instruments that have maturities equal to one year or less when originally issued, and the capital markets include instruments with original maturities greater than one year. By definition, then, money markets include only debt instruments, because stocks (equities) have no specific maturities, whereas capital markets include both equity instruments and such long-term debt instruments as mortgages, corporate bonds, and government bonds.

The money markets and capital markets provide us with financial instruments with different maturities that permit us to better match our cash inflows with cash outflows. The primary function of the money markets is to provide liquidity to businesses, governments, and individuals so that they can meet their short-term needs for cash, because, in most cases, the receipt of cash inflows does not coincide exactly with the payment of cash outflows. The primary function of the capital markets is to provide us with the opportunity to transfer cash surpluses or deficits to future years. For example, individuals transfer income through time so that they can afford to buy houses with mortgages that are paid off as income is generated in future years.

2. **Debt markets versus equity markets**—Simply stated, the debt markets are where loans are traded, and the equity markets are where stocks are traded. A debt instrument is a contract that specifies how and when a borrower must repay a lender. In contrast, equity represents "ownership" in a corporation that entitles the stockholder to share in future cash distributions generated by the firm.

   Debt markets generally are described (labeled) according to the characteristics of the debt that is traded. In many cases, the segmentation of the debt markets is based on the maturity of the instrument (money or capital market instruments), the type of debt (consumer, government, or corporate), and the participant (borrowers and investors). Characteristics of stock markets are discussed later in the chapter.

3. **Primary markets versus secondary markets**—The *primary markets* are where "new" securities are traded, and the *secondary markets* are where "used" securities are traded. Primary markets are the markets in which corporations raise new funds. The corporation selling a newly created stock receives the proceeds from the sale (less issuing costs) in a primary market transaction. Secondary markets are markets in which existing, previously issued securities are traded among investors. The corporation whose securities are traded in the secondary market is not involved in the transaction and, therefore, does not receive any funds from the transaction; rather, funds are transferred from one investor to another investor.

4. **Derivatives markets**—Options, futures, and swaps are some of the securities traded in the derivatives markets. These securities are called *derivatives* because their values are determined, or derived, directly from other assets. For example, a *call option* allows the option buyer (owner) to purchase a certain number of shares of stock (or some other security) from the option seller at a specific price—say, $50—for a particular period of time—say, 60 days. Because the option contract fixes the purchase price of the stock, the value of the call option changes as the *market value* of the stock on which the option is written changes. For example, if the per-share price of the "underlying" stock increases to $60 (decreases to $45), the value of the option increases (decreases) because the person who owns the option can "exercise" his or her right to purchase the stock for the contracted

money markets The segments of the financial markets where the instruments that are traded have original maturities equal to one year or less.

capital markets The segments of the financial markets where the instruments that are traded have maturities greater than one year.

debt markets Financial markets where loans are traded.

equity markets Financial markets where corporate stocks are traded.

primary markets Markets in which various organizations raise funds by issuing new securities.

secondary markets Markets where financial assets that have previously been issued by various organizations are traded among investors.

derivatives markets Financial markets where options and futures are traded.

$50 per share from the option seller regardless of the existing market price of the stock.

Although many investors use derivatives to speculate about the movements of prices in the financial markets, these instruments are typically employed to help manage risk. Individuals, corporations, and governments use derivatives to *hedge* risk by contracting to set (fix) future prices, which offsets exposures to uncertain price changes in the future.

3-2a Stock Markets

During the past couple of decades, individuals have expressed greater interest in stocks than ever before. A major reason for this increased interest is the fact that the stock markets generated record-breaking returns during the 1990s. Although there exists a great deal of uncertainty in the movements of stock prices, the potential to earn huge returns intrigues investors, and interest in the markets continues to grow. For this reason, we describe some of the characteristics of stock markets in this section.

3-2b Types of General Stock Market Activities

We generally classify basic stock market activities into three distinct categories:

1. ***Trading in the outstanding, previously issued stock of established, publicly owned companies: the secondary market***—If the owner of 100 shares of IBM sells his or her stock to another investor, the trade is said to have occurred in the *secondary market*. The company (e.g., IBM) receives no new money when sales occur in this market.

2. ***Additional (new) shares sold by established, publicly owned companies: the primary market***—If IBM decides to sell (or issue) new shares of stock to raise funds for expansion, this transaction is said to occur in the *primary market*. In this case, the company receives

the funds that are raised when its securities are sold (issued), less any issuing costs.

3. ***New public offerings of stock by privately held firms: the initial public offering (IPO) market; the primary market***—When a privately held corporation raises funds by issuing stock to the public for the first time, the company is said to be *going public*, and the market for stocks in companies that have recently gone public is called the initial public offering (IPO) market.

On a given day, nearly all stock transactions occur in the secondary markets. Nevertheless, primary market transactions are important to corporations that need to raise funds for capital projects.

Traditionally, we have categorized stock markets in the United States into two basic types: (1) physical stock exchanges, which include the New York Stock Exchange (NYSE) and regional exchanges, such as the Chicago Stock Exchange, and (2) the less formal over-the-counter (OTC) market, which consists of a network of dealers around the country and includes the well-known NASDAQ market. As a result of heated competition, stock markets have changed substantially in recent years through mergers and by introducing new, more efficient trading systems. As a result, it is now difficult to differentiate between the two categories of stock markets. Even so, we generally still refer to stock markets as having the general characteristics of either a physical stock exchange or the OTC/NASDAQ market.

3-2c Physical Stock Exchanges[3]

The physical stock exchanges are tangible physical entities. They include national exchanges, such as the New York Stock Exchange (NYSE), and regional exchanges, such as the Chicago Stock Exchange (CHX).[4] The prices of stocks listed on the physical stock exchanges are determined by auction processes whereby investors (through their brokers) bid for stocks.

Until the late 1990s, most physical stock exchanges were not-for-profit organizations that were owned by their members, who were said to hold "seats" on the exchanges (although everyone stood up). These seats, which were bought and sold, gave the holder the right to trade on the exchange.[5] Organizations such as these, which are owned and operated by their members, are said to

---

[3]The statistics and other information provided in this section are based on information that is reported by various stock exchanges. Additional statistics and information can be found on the websites of the exchanges: http://www.nyse.com and http://www.chx.com.

[4]The NYSE, which is more than 200 years old, is the largest physical stock exchange in the world in terms of the total value of stocks traded. In the past, regional stock exchanges existed in Philadelphia, Chicago, San Francisco, and Boston. As the result of competition, most regional exchanges have been acquired by either the NYSE or the NASDAQ market in recent years.

[5]NYSE stocks were not traded continuously until 1871. Prior to that time, stocks were traded sequentially according to their position on a stock roll, or roster, sheet. Members were assigned chairs, or "seats," in which to sit while the roll call of stocks proceeded. The number of "seats" changed as the number of members changed, until the number was fixed at 1,366 in 1868. The demutualization of the NYSE marked the end of the NYSE's traditional seat membership (ownership). Now trading licenses are awarded to successful bidders through the SEATS (Stock Exchange Auction Trading System) auction.

initial public offering (IPO) market Market consisting of stocks of privately held companies that have recently gone public for the first time.

physical stock exchanges Formal organizations with physical locations that facilitate trading in designated ("listed") securities. The major U.S. stock exchange is the New York Stock Exchange (NYSE).

lev radin/Shutterstock.com

specialists, are considered the most important participants in NYSE transactions because their role is to ensure that the auction trading process is completed in a fair and efficient manner. To accomplish this task, the DMM raises or lowers prices of the stocks that he or she is assigned to oversee in an effort to keep supply and demand in balance. The DMM must stand ready to make a market when either buyers or sellers are needed; that is, he or she might have to buy (sell) stock when not enough buyers (sellers) exist.

have *mutual ownership* structures. Although most stock exchanges were set up as mutual ownership structures when they were started many decades ago, the recent trend has been to convert stock exchanges from not-for-profit mutual ownership organizations to for-profit organizations that are owned by outside stockholders and are publicly traded. The process of converting an exchange from a mutual ownership organization to a stock ownership organization is called *demutualization*. Some exchanges that have "demutualized" are the Chicago Stock Exchange and the NYSE. Many foreign stock exchanges have also demutualized, including the Australian Securities Exchange, the Hong Kong Stock Exchange, the Stock Exchange of Singapore, and the Toronto Stock Exchange, to name a few. To date, more than 80 percent of the world's developed stock markets have demutualized.

Exchange Membership (Licenses). Exchange members are charged with different trading responsibilities, depending on which type of license (trading permit) they own. For example, trading licenses on the NYSE are classified into one of three general categories.

1. **Trading floor brokers** act as agents for investors who want to buy or sell securities. They trade stocks and bonds for clients, not for themselves, and they are employed by brokerage firms, such as Bank of America/Merrill Lynch.

2. **Designated market makers (DMMs),** which previously were called

3. **Supplemental liquidity providers (SLPs)** deal with high-volume trades to ensure that the best price quotes are received. SLPs enhance liquidity in large block trades by maintaining continuous up-to-date prices for the securities they are assigned.

Listing Requirements. For a stock to be traded on an exchange, it must be *listed*. Each exchange has established listing requirements, which indicate the quantitative and qualitative characteristics that a firm must possess to be listed. Table 3.1 provides examples of the listing requirements for some U.S. exchanges. The primary purpose of these requirements is to ensure that investors have some interest in the listed company so that the firm's stock will be actively traded on the exchange.

A listed firm pays a relatively small annual fee to the exchange to receive such benefits as the marketability offered by continuous trading activity and the publicity and prestige associated with being an exchange-listed firm. Many people believe that listing has a beneficial effect on the sales of the firm's products and that it is advantageous in terms of lowering the return investors demand when they buy the firm's common stock. Investors respond favorably to a listed firm's increased information and liquidity, and they have confidence that its quoted price is not being manipulated.

3-2d The Over-the-Counter (OTC) Market and NASDAQ

If a security is not traded on an organized exchange, it has been customary to say that it is traded in the over-the-counter (OTC) market, which is a trading system that consists of a network of brokers and dealers around

Table 3.1

Listing Requirements for Stock Exchanges and the NASDAQ

	NYSE	Regional Exchanges	NASDAQ
Round-lot (100 shares) shareholders	400	800	300
Number of public shares (millions)	1.1	0.5	1.1
Assets ($ millions)	$75	$4	$50
Pre-tax income ($ millions)	$2.00	$0.75	$1.00

Sources: Information for the listing requirements was taken from the websites of the New York Stock Exchange (https://nyse.nyx.com/), the Chicago Stock Exchange (http://www.chx.com/index.asp), and NASDAQ (http://www.nasdaq.com/).

the country. Traditionally, the OTC market has been defined as including all of the facilities needed to conduct securities transactions not conducted on the physical exchanges. These facilities consist of (1) the *dealers* who hold inventories of OTC securities and who are said to "make a market" in these securities, (2) the *brokers* who act as *agents* in bringing the dealers together with investors, and (3) the *electronic networks* that provide a communications link between dealers and brokers. Unlike physical exchanges, the OTC market generally does not operate as an auction market. The dealers who make a market in a particular stock continuously quote a price at which they are willing to buy the stock (the *bid price*) and a price at which they will sell shares (the *asked price*). Each dealer's prices, which are adjusted as supply and demand conditions change, can be read off computer screens across the country. The spread between the bid and asked prices (called the *dealer's spread*) represents the dealer's markup, or profit.

NASDAQ. Brokers and dealers who participate in the OTC market are members of a self-regulating body known as the *National Association of Securities Dealers* (NASD), which licenses brokers and oversees trading practices. The computerized trading network used by NASD is known as the NASD Automated Quotation system, or NASDAQ. Today, the NASDAQ is considered a sophisticated market of its own, separate from the OTC market. In fact, unlike the general OTC market, the NASDAQ includes *market makers* who continuously monitor trading activities in various stocks to ensure that such stocks are available to traders who want to buy or sell them. The role of the NASDAQ market maker is similar to that of the designated market makers on the NYSE. Another feature of the NASDAQ

that is similar to the NYSE is that companies must meet minimum financial requirements to be *listed*, or included, on the NASDAQ (see Table 3.1); the OTC market has no such requirements.

In terms of *numbers of issues,* most stocks are traded over the counter. Even though the OTC market includes some very large companies that qualify to be listed on the physical exchanges, most of the stocks traded over the counter involve small companies that do not meet the requirements to be listed on a physical exchange.[6] But, because the stocks of larger companies generally are listed on the physical exchanges, approximately two-thirds of the total *dollar volume of stock trading* takes place on these exchanges.

3-2e Electronic Communications Networks (ECN)

Today many trades are executed electronically using trading systems known as electronic communications networks (ECN). ECNs, which are registered with the **Securities and Exchange Commission (SEC)**, are electronic systems that quickly transfer information about securities transactions to facilitate the execution of orders at the best available prices. ECNs automatically match the buy and sell orders by price for a large number of investors. Investors use ECNs through accounts they have at brokerage firms that offer online trading services and subscribe to ECNs. When an order (buy or sell) is placed electronically, the process is seamless in the sense that investors have no indication that an ECN is used to execute their transactions. ECNs provide an alternative trading medium, which has increased competition with the stock exchanges. In fact, as a result of the increased competition and to improve its

Securities and Exchange Commission (SEC) The U.S. government agency that regulates the issuance and trading of stocks and bonds.

[6]It is not required that a qualified firm be listed on an exchange. Listing is the choice of the firm.

competitive position, in 2006 the NYSE merged with the Archipelago Exchange (ArcaEX), an ECN started in 1997, to form the NYSE Group.

3-2f Competition Among Stock Markets

Competition among the major stock markets has become increasingly fierce in recent years. In the United States, the major stock markets, especially the NYSE and NASDAQ, continuously explore ways to improve their competitive positions. Two factors have changed the competitive arena of the stock markets. First, whereas many years ago stocks could be listed and traded on only one stock exchange, today many popular stocks are *dual listed*. A stock with a dual listing is eligible (registered) to be traded in more than one stock market. Dual listing increases liquidity because a stock has more exposure through a greater number of outlets than if it were listed on only one market. Various stock markets compete to list stocks that are actively traded because increased trading activity translates into increased profits.

Second, in 2005, the Securities and Exchange Commission adopted Regulation NMS (National Market Structure), which mandates that the *trade-through rule* be used when securities are traded. The trade-through rule states that a stock trade should be executed at the best price that is available in all of the stock markets. In other words, a trade order continues to pass through the markets until the best price is reached.

As a result of the increased competition among the stock markets, both the NYSE and NASDAQ have taken actions to improve their competitive positions. For example, we mentioned earlier that in 2006 the NYSE merged with ArcaEX to form the NYSE Group. The "new and improved" NYSE Group effectively consists of two distinct stock (securities) exchanges. The physical stock exchange called the NYSE still exists, and the products and services that it offers are similar to those offered prior to the merger. In addition, the NYSE Group offers a fully electronic exchange through NYSE Arca. In 2007, the NYSE Group merged with Euronext, which includes leading stock markets throughout Europe, to form NYSE Euronext. And in 2008, NYSE Euronext acquired the American Stock Exchange (AMEX), the second largest national stock market in the United States at the time, to broaden its offerings of financial instruments. Clearly, NYSE Euronext has positioned itself as a leader in global financial markets.

Soon after the announcement of the NYSE-ArcaEx merger in 2005, NASDAQ acquired Instinet, an electronic exchange that improved the technology and efficiency of NADAQ trading and helped it compete better with the NYSE. In addition, since 2005, NASDAQ has acquired regional stock exchanges (Philadelphia Stock Exchange and the Boston Stock Exchange) and the OMX, which operates stock exchanges in northern Europe.

A recent example of the "stock market wars" took place at the beginning of 2011, when NASDAQ made an $11 billion bid to take over the NYSE. In May of 2011, however, the U.S. Justice Department denied the hostile takeover attempt because it felt that investors (competition) would be hurt by the consolidation of the two markets. And, in 2012, an attempt to merge the NYSE and a German stock market company named Deutsche Börse was also blocked by regulators because it was felt the megamarket that would be created would stifle competition. However, in 2013, regulators did permit IntercontinentalExchange (ICE) to purchase NYSE Euronext to form the world's largest network of exchanges, including exchanges for stocks, debt, and derivatives.

Increased competition among global stock markets assuredly will result in alliances among various exchanges and markets in the future. Clearly, the playing field on which the exchanges compete will be much different in the future.

3-2g Regulation of Securities Markets

Sales of new securities, such as stocks and bonds, as well as operations in the secondary markets, are regulated by the SEC and, to a lesser extent, by each of the 50 states. For the most part, the SEC regulations are intended to ensure that investors receive fair disclosure of financial and nonfinancial information from publicly traded companies and to discourage fraudulent and misleading behavior by firms' investors, owners, and employees who might contemplate manipulating stock prices.

The primary elements of SEC regulations include (1) jurisdiction over most interstate offerings of new securities to the general investing public, (2) regulation of national securities exchanges, (3) power to prohibit manipulation of securities prices (deliberate manipulation of securities prices is illegal), and (4) control over stock trades by corporate *insiders*, which include the officers, directors, and major stockholders of a company.[7]

dual listing When stocks are listed for trading in more than one stock market.

---

[7]Insiders must file monthly reports of changes in their holdings of the corporation's stock, and any *short-term* profits from trading in the stock must be handed over to the corporation.

3-3 The Investment Banking Process

When a business needs to raise funds in the financial markets, it generally enlists the services of an **investment banker** (see the middle panel in Figure 3.1). Such organizations perform three tasks: (1) They help corporations design securities with the features that are most attractive to investors, given existing market conditions; (2) they generally buy these securities from the corporations; and (3) they resell the securities to investors (savers). Although the securities are sold twice, this process is actually one primary market transaction, with the investment banker acting as a middleman (agent) as funds are transferred from investors to businesses. The major investment banking houses often are divisions of large financial service corporations that engage in a wide range of activities (e.g., Bank of America/Merrill Lynch).

Daniilantiq/Shutterstock.com

In this section we describe the general procedures that are followed when stocks and bonds are issued in the financial markets with the aid of investment bankers.

3-3a Raising Capital: Stage I Decisions

A corporation that needs to raise funds makes some preliminary decisions on its own, including the following:[8]

1. *Dollars to be raised*—How much new capital is needed?

2. *Type of securities used*—Should stock, bonds, or a combination of these instruments be used?

3. *Competitive bid versus negotiated deal*—Should the company simply offer a block of its securities for sale to the investment banker that submits the highest bid of all interested investment bankers, or should it sit down and negotiate a deal with a single investment banker? These two procedures are called *competitive bids* and *negotiated deals (purchases)*, respectively. Only a handful of the largest firms, whose securities are already well known to the investment banking community, are in a position to use the competitive bid process.

4. *Selection of an investment banker*—If the issue is to be negotiated, which investment banker should the firm use? Older corporations that have "been to market" before will already have established relationships with investment bankers. A firm that is going public for the first time will have to choose an investment banker, and different investment banking houses are better suited for different companies. Some investment bankers deal mainly with large companies such as IBM, whereas others specialize in more speculative issues such as initial public offerings (IPOs).

3-3b Raising Capital: Stage II Decisions

Stage II decisions, which are made jointly by the firm and its selected investment banker, include the following:

1. *Reevaluating the initial decisions*—The firm and its investment banker will reevaluate the initial decisions about the size of the issue and the type of securities to use to determine whether revisions are needed, given current market conditions.

2. *Best-efforts or underwritten issue*—The firm and its investment banker must

> **investment banker** An organization that underwrites and distributes new issues of securities; it helps businesses and other entities obtain needed financing.

[8]For the most part, the procedures described in this section also apply to government entities. Governments issue only debt, however; they do not issue stock.

decide whether the investment banker will work on a best-efforts basis or underwrite the issue. In an **underwritten arrangement**, the investment banker generally assures the company that the entire issue will be sold, so *the investment banker bears significant risks* in such an offering. With this type of arrangement, the investment banking firm typically buys the securities from the issuing firm and then sells the securities in the primary markets, hoping to make a profit. In a **best-efforts arrangement**, the issue is handled on a contingency basis so that the investment banker receives a commission based on the amount of the issue that is sold. The investment banker essentially promises to exert its best efforts when selling the securities, which means *the issuing firm takes the chance* that the entire issue will not be sold and that all needed funds will not be raised.

3. *Issuance (flotation) costs*—The investment banker's fee must be negotiated, and the firm must estimate the other expenses that it will incur in connection with the issue, including lawyers' fees, accountants' costs, printing and engraving costs, and so forth. The investment banker will buy the issue from the company at a discount below the price at which the securities are to be offered to the public. The difference between the issuing price and the net proceeds received by the issuing firm, which is the *underwriter's spread,* covers the investment banker's costs and provides for a profit. Generally, the issuing costs, called **flotation costs**, associated with public issues are higher for stocks than for bonds, and they are also higher for small issues than for large issues (because certain fixed costs exist).

To show how flotation costs affect decisions firms make when issuing securities to raise new funds, suppose a firm needs $325,000 to support its growth. The firm plans to raise the needed funds by issuing new common stock, which will require it to pay its investment banker 4 percent of the issue's total value. In addition, the firm must pay $35,000 to cover other expenses related to the issue (e.g., legal fees, printing costs, and so forth). If the firm needs

exactly $325,000 for its growth, then it must issue more than $325,000 in common stock to ensure that $325,000 is left over after covering all issuing costs. How much common stock does the firm need to issue? We can answer this question by recognizing that the amount of funds the firm will net from the stock issue is computed as follows:

$$\text{Net proceeds} = \text{Amount of issue} - \text{Flotation costs}$$
$$= \text{Amount of issue} \times (1 - F) - OC$$

where F represents the flotation costs stated in decimal form, and OC represents other flotation costs stated in dollars.

If we plug into the preceding equation the information we know for our example, we have

$$\$325{,}000 = \text{Amount of issue} \times (1 - 0.04) - \$35{,}000$$
$$\text{Amount of issue} = \frac{\$360{,}000}{0.96} = \$375{,}000$$

If the firm issues $375,000 in common stock, the flotation costs will be $50,000 = $375,000(0.04) + $35,000; thus $325,000 will be left over after all flotation costs are paid.

Equation 3.1 generalizes the relationship we discussed here. This equation can be used to determine the amount a firm must issue to net a specific dollar amount after paying flotation costs.

3.1
$$\text{Amount of issue} = \frac{NP + OC}{(1 - F)}$$

Here NP represents the net proceeds from the issue, which is the amount that the firm receives (needs) after paying flotation costs, F is the flotation costs stated in decimal form, and OC is the other flotation costs stated in dollars.

4. *Setting the offering price*—If the company is already publicly owned, the *offering price* will be based on the existing market price of the stock or the yield on the firm's existing bonds. An investment banker has an easier job of selling the issue if it carries a relatively low price, but the issuer of the securities naturally wants as high a price as possible. Therefore, an inherent conflict of interest on price exists between the investment banker and the issuer. If the issuer is financially sophisticated and its stock is actively traded, however, the investment banker will be forced to price the issue close to the market price.

underwritten arrangement Agreement for the sale of securities in which the investment bank guarantees the sale by purchasing the securities from the issuer, thus agreeing to bear any risks involved in selling the securities in the financial markets.

best-efforts arrangement Agreement for the sale of securities in which the investment bank handling the transaction gives no guarantee that the securities will be sold.

flotation costs The costs associated with issuing new stocks or bonds.

The stock of a company that is going public for the first time (an IPO) will not have an established price. Consequently, the investment banker must estimate the equilibrium price at which the stock will sell after it is issued. If the offering price is set below the true equilibrium price, the stock price will rise sharply after issue, and the company and its original (founding) stockholders will have "given away" too many shares to raise the required capital. If the offering price is set above the true equilibrium price, either the issue will fail, or, if the investment bankers succeed in selling the stock, their clients will be unhappy when the price subsequently falls to its equilibrium level. For these reasons, it is important that the equilibrium price be estimated as accurately as possible.

3-3c Raising Capital: Selling Procedures

Once the company and its investment banker have decided how much money to raise, the types of securities to issue, and the basis for pricing the issue, they will prepare and file a registration statement and prospectus with the SEC. The **registration statement** provides financial, legal, and technical information about the company, whereas the **prospectus** summarizes the information in the registration statement and is provided to prospective investors for use in selling the securities. When the SEC approves the registration statement and the prospectus, it merely validates that the required information has been furnished; it does not judge the quality or value of the issue.

The final price of the stock (or the interest rate on a bond issue) generally is set at the close of business on the day before the securities are offered to the public. Typically, investment bankers sell the stock within a day or two after the offering begins. On occasion, however, they are unable to quickly move the issue at a good price, so they hold it for a longer period.

Underwriting Syndicate. Because investment bankers are exposed to large potential losses, an investment banker typically does not handle the purchase and distribution of an issue alone unless it is fairly small. Often an investment banker will form an **underwriting syndicate** whereby the issue is distributed to a number of investment firms around the country in an effort to minimize the amount of risk that is carried by each firm. The investment banking house that sets up the deal is called the *lead*, or *managing, underwriter.*

In addition to the underwriting syndicate, larger offerings might require the services of still more investment bankers as part of a *selling group.* The selling group, which handles the distribution of securities to individual investors, includes all members of the underwriting syndicate plus additional dealers who take relatively small *participations* (shares of the total issue) from the syndicate members. Members of the selling group act as selling agents and receive commissions for their efforts. The number of investment banking houses in a selling group depends partly on the size of the issue.

Shelf Registrations. The selling procedures described here apply to many securities sales. However, a large, well-known public company (called a *seasoned* company) that frequently issues securities will often file a master registration statement with the SEC and then update it with a short-form statement just prior to each individual offering. In such a case, the company could decide at 10 a.m. to sell registered securities and have the sale completed before noon. This procedure is known as **shelf registration** because, in effect, the company puts its new securities "on the shelf" and then sells them to investors when it thinks the market is right.

Maintenance of the Secondary Market. In the case of a large, established firm, the investment banking firm's job is finished once it has issued the stock and the net proceeds have been turned over to the company. But, if a company is going public for the first time, the investment banker has an obligation to maintain a market for the shares after the issue has been completed. Such stocks typically are traded in the OTC market, and the lead underwriter generally agrees to "make a market" in the stock and keep it reasonably liquid. The issuing company wants a good market to exist for its stock, as do its stockholders. Therefore, if the investment banking house wants to do business with the company in the future, to keep its own brokerage customers happy, and to have future referral business, it will hold an inventory of the shares and help maintain an active secondary market in the stock.

registration statement A statement of facts filed with the SEC about a company that plans to issue securities.

prospectus A document describing a new security issue and the issuing company.

underwriting syndicate A group of investment banking firms formed to spread the risk associated with the purchase and distribution of a new issue of securities.

shelf registration Registration of securities with the SEC for sale at a later date. The securities are held "on the shelf" until the sale.

3-4 Financial Intermediaries and Their Roles in Financial Markets

Financial intermediaries include such financial services organizations as commercial banks, savings and loan associations, pension funds, and insurance companies. In simple terms, **financial intermediaries** facilitate the transfer of funds from those who have funds (savers) to those who need funds (borrowers) by *manufacturing* a variety of financial products. When intermediaries accept funds (generally called *deposits*) from savers, they issue *securities* with such names as savings accounts, money market funds, and pension plans, that represent claims, or liabilities, against the institutions. The funds received by intermediaries are, in turn, lent to businesses and individuals via debt instruments created by these institutions, which include automobile loans, mortgages, commercial loans, and similar types of debt. The process by which financial intermediaries transform funds provided by savers into funds used by borrowers is called *financial intermediation*. The lower panel of Figure 3.1 illustrates the financial intermediation process. The arrows at the top portion of the boxes (pointing to the right) indicate the changes in the balance sheets of savers, borrowers, and intermediaries that result from the intermediation process. The arrows at the bottom portion of each box (pointing to the left) show the flow of funds from savers to borrowers through intermediaries.

Without financial intermediaries, savers would have to provide funds directly to borrowers, which would be a difficult task for those who do not possess such expertise; such loans as mortgages and automobile financing would be much more costly, so the financial markets would be much less efficient economically. Clearly, the presence of intermediaries improves economic well-being. In fact, financial intermediaries were created to reduce the inefficiencies that would otherwise exist if users of funds could get loans only by borrowing directly from individual savers.

Improving economic well-being is only one of the benefits associated with intermediaries. Following are other benefits:

1. ***Reduced costs***—Without intermediaries, the net cost of borrowing would be greater, and the net return earned by savers would be less, because individuals with funds to lend would have to seek out appropriate borrowers themselves, and vice versa. Intermediaries are more cost-efficient than individuals because they (a) create combinations of financial products that better match the funds provided by savers with the needs of borrowers and (b) spread the costs associated with these activities over large numbers of transactions, thus achieving economies of scale.

2. ***Diversification (risk)***—The loan portfolios of intermediaries generally are well diversified, because they provide funds to a large number and variety of borrowers by offering many different types of loans. Thus, intermediaries spread their risks by "not putting all their financial eggs in one basket."

3. ***Funds divisibility/pooling***—Intermediaries pool funds provided by individuals to offer loans or other financial products with different denominations and different maturities. For example, an intermediary can offer a large loan to a single borrower by combining the funds provided by many small savers, and vice versa.

4. ***Financial flexibility***—Because intermediaries offer a variety of financial products—that is, different types of loans and savings instruments—savers and borrowers have greater choices, or financial flexibility, than can be achieved with direct placements with respect to denominations, maturities, and other characteristics.

5. ***Related services***—A system of specialized intermediaries offers more than just a network of mechanisms to transfer funds from savers to borrowers. Many intermediaries provide other financial services, such as check clearing services, insurance, retirement funds, and trust services.

3-4a Types of Financial Intermediaries

In the United States, a large set of specialized, highly efficient financial intermediaries has evolved. Although each type of intermediary originated to satisfy a particular need in the financial markets, recent competition and government policy have created such a rapidly changing arena that different institutions currently offer financial products and perform services that previously were reserved for others. This trend has caused the lines among the various types of intermediaries to become blurred. Still, some degree of institutional identity persists, and these distinctions are discussed in this section.

financial intermediaries
Organizations that create various loans and investments from funds provided by depositors.

Commercial Banks. *Commercial banks*, commonly referred to simply as *banks*, are the traditional "department stores of finance"—that is, they offer a wide range of products and services to a variety of customers. Originally, banks were established to serve the needs of commerce, or business—hence the name "commercial banks." Today, commercial banks, which represent one of the largest types of financial intermediaries, still represent the primary source of business loans. Historically, banks were the institutions that handled checking accounts and provided mechanisms for clearing checks. Also, they traditionally provided the medium through which the supply of money was expanded or contracted. Today, however, several other institutions provide checking and check clearing services and significantly influence the money supply. At the same time, banking companies offer a greater range of services than before.

Credit Unions. A *credit union* is a depository institution that is owned by its depositors, who often are members of a common organization or association, such as an occupation, a religious group, or a community. Credit unions operate as not-for-profit businesses and are managed by member depositors elected by other members.

The purpose of the original credit unions, which were established in Europe more than 160 years ago, was to create savings pools that could be used to provide credit to neighboring farmers who suffered temporary losses of income due to crop failures or other catastrophes. The common bonds possessed by the members generated a help-thy-neighbor attitude within the savings pools. Today, credit unions differ significantly from their earliest forms; they are much larger and hence less personal. Nevertheless, the spirit of credit unions remains unchanged—to serve depositor members. Members' savings are still loaned to other members, but the loans are primarily for automobile purchases, home improvements, and the like. Because credit unions are not-for-profit organizations, loans from these intermediaries often are the cheapest source of funds for individual borrowers.

Thrift Institutions. *Thrift institutions*, also known as *savings and loan associations* or *S&Ls*, cater to savers, especially individuals who have relatively small savings or need long-term loans to purchase houses. Thrifts were originally established because the services offered by commercial banks were designed for businesses rather than individuals, who have substantially different financial needs. S&Ls were first set up so that depositors could pool their savings to create loans that helped other depositors build houses in a particular geographic area. Each savings association was eventually liquidated when the building goals were achieved and all of the loans were repaid. Today, S&Ls not only take the funds of many small savers and then lend this money primarily to home buyers, but also to other types of borrowers.

Mutual Funds. *Mutual funds* are *investment companies* that use funds provided by savers to buy various types of financial assets, including stocks and bonds. These organizations pool investors' funds, reducing risks through diversification. They also achieve economies of scale, which lower the costs of analyzing securities, managing portfolios, and buying and selling securities.

Literally hundreds of different types of mutual funds exist, offering a variety of instruments to meet the objectives of many different types of savers. Investors can find mutual funds to meet almost any financial goal. For example, investors who prefer to receive current income can invest in *income funds*, which are comprised of financial instruments that generate fairly constant annual incomes. Investors who are willing to accept higher risks in hopes of obtaining higher returns can invest in *growth funds*, which include investments that generate little or no income each year but exhibit high growth potential that can result in significant increases in the values of the investments (that is, capital gains) in the future.

Whole-Life Insurance Companies.[9] Broadly speaking, the purpose of life insurance is to provide a beneficiary, such as a spouse or other family members, with protection against financial distress or insecurity that might result from the premature death of a breadwinner or other principal wage earner. In a general sense, life insurance can be labeled either term insurance or whole-life insurance. *Term life insurance* is a relatively short-term contract that provides financial protection for a temporary period— perhaps for one year or for five years at a time—and it must be renewed each period to continue such protection. On the other hand, *whole-life insurance* is a long-term contract that provides lifetime protection.

The cost of term insurance, called the *premium*, generally increases with each renewal, because the risk of premature death increases as the insured ages. In contrast, the premiums associated with whole-life insurance policies are fixed payments computed as an average of the premiums required over the expected life of the insured person. As a consequence, the premiums in the early years exceed what is needed to provide the appropriate coverage, whereas the premiums in the later years

---

[9]Insurance is intended to reduce the consequences of risk by transferring some of the economic consequences to others—namely insurance companies—that are better able to absorb such risk. Insurance companies achieve risk reduction by *pooling*, or diversifying, the risks of individuals, companies, and governments.

are less than what is needed. The excess amounts in the early years are invested to make up for the deficits in later years. These invested amounts provide savings features that create cash values for the whole-life insurance policies. In contrast, term life insurance policies do not provide such savings features because the premiums are fixed for only a short time period (generally five years or less); for this reason, the premiums are based on the existing risks only and change at renewal when risks change. Thus, whole-life polices offer both insurance coverage and a savings feature, whereas term life policies do not.[10]

Pension Funds. *Pensions* are retirement plans funded by corporations or government agencies for their workers. Pension plans are administered primarily by the trust departments of commercial banks or by life insurance companies. Probably the most famous pension plan is Social Security, which is a government-sponsored plan established in 1935 that is funded by tax revenues collected by the federal government. Most state and municipal governments and large corporations also offer pension plans to their employees. Many of these plans have been established to accept both employer and employee contributions, which often are shielded from taxes until the assets are withdrawn from the plan. These contributions are invested by pension fund managers, primarily in long-term investments (stocks and bonds) that will provide retirement income at some later date.

3-5 International Financial Markets[11]

Financial markets have become much more global during the past few decades. As the economies of developing countries have grown, greater numbers of investors have provided funds to these financial markets. In 1970, U.S. stocks accounted for nearly two-thirds of the value of worldwide stock markets. Today, U.S. stock markets represent 35–40 percent of the total value worldwide. But the markets in the United States are still much larger

than individual stock markets in any country. During the past decade, the areas of greatest worldwide growth lay in the emerging markets of China, India, and Brazil. In addition, although fairly small in size, the financial markets of countries that were previously part of the Soviet Union—for example, Russia, Serbia, and Ukraine—have experienced substantial growth in recent years.

Even with the expansion of stock markets internationally, exchanges in the United States continue to account for the greatest numbers of trades, with respect to both volume and value. U.S. trading activity accounts for nearly 50 percent of worldwide trading activity each year.

The international market for bonds has experienced growth similar to that of the international stock markets. Even so, the bond markets in the United States and in the countries that comprise Euroland continue to dominate the international bond markets, with approximately 60 percent of the total value (United States, 38 percent; Eurozone, 22 percent).[12]

The financial markets truly are global in nature, as can be seen by how recent economic events in the United States have affected economies around the world, and vice versa, especially in Europe and Asia.

While the globalization of financial markets continues and international markets offer investors greater frontiers of opportunity, investing overseas can be challenging due to restrictions imposed or barriers erected by foreign countries. In many cases, individual investors find it difficult or unattractive to invest directly in foreign stocks. Many countries prohibit or severely limit the ability of foreigners to invest in their financial markets, or make it extremely difficult for such investors to access reliable information concerning the companies that are traded in their stock markets.

3-5a Financial Organizations in Other Parts of the World

Two notable factors distinguish financial institutions in the United States from those in other countries. These differences can be traced to the regulatory climate that has existed historically in the United States. Generally speaking, U.S. financial institutions have been much more heavily regulated and faced greater limitations than have their foreign

[10]Premiums charged by other insurance companies, such as health insurance, property and casualty insurance, and the like, are based only on the risks faced and are changed over time as the risks change. In other words, they reflect the cost of the peril (risk) that is insured at the time at which the premium is paid. There is no savings function, because individuals pay only for the insurance services offered by such companies. Such insurance companies do not perform the same intermediary function as whole-life insurance companies.

[11]Information about worldwide stock markets was compiled from "Market Capitalization of Listed Companies," *The World Bank*, http://data.worldbank.org/indicator/cm.mkt.lcap.cd. Information about worldwide bond markets can be found on the Bank for International Settlements website in the publication *BIS Quarterly Review*, June 2015, which is available at http://www.bis.org/publ/quarterly.htm.

[12]A group of 11 countries—Austria, Belgium, Finland, France, Germany, Ireland, Italy, Luxembourg, the Netherlands, Portugal, and Spain—originally was called *Euroland*. The *Eurozone* currently consists of the 11 countries from the original Euroland plus Cyprus, Estonia, Greece, Latvia, Malta, Slovakia, and Slovenia. Euroland members created a common currency (the *euro*) and a common debt instrument that is denominated in the euro and traded in a unified financial market called the *Euromarket*. The emergence of Euroland was intended to reduce or eliminate the effects of country boundaries with respect to member countries' economic and trading policies.

counterparts with regard to expansion (branching), the services that could be offered, and relationships with nonfinancial businesses. Such regulations have imposed an organizational structure and competitive environment that have curbed the ability of individual financial intermediaries in the United States to grow, especially in international markets.

First, prior to the deregulation that began in the 1980s, laws existed that restricted the ability of financial intermediaries to operate nationwide through branches. As a result, the U.S. banking system traditionally has been characterized by a large number of independent financial institutions of various sizes, rather than the few very large institutions that might exist if branching was not restricted. Consider, for example, that there are approximately 13,500 individual banks, credit unions, and thrift institutions in the United States (in 2015), whereas Japan has fewer than 150 licensed banks; there are about 20 Australian-owned banks (four of which are considered large commercial banks), and Canada has only 70 chartered banks (seven of which operate both nationally and internationally). Even India, which has a population about four times larger than that of the United States, has fewer than 300 individual banks. In India and other countries, however, each financial intermediary generally has many branches. For instance, the State Bank of India alone has more than 10,000 offices (branches). The financial institutions of nearly every other country in the world have been allowed to branch with few, if any, limitations, and as a result, their banking systems include far fewer individual, or unit, institutions than exist in the United States.

Second, most foreign financial institutions are allowed to engage in nonbanking (nonfinancial) business activities, whereas the nonbanking activities of U.S. intermediaries have been severely restricted until recently. Developed countries such as the United Kingdom, France, Germany, and Switzerland, to name a few, permit financial firms and commercial businesses to interact without restriction; banking firms can own commercial firms, and vice versa. Other countries, including Canada, Japan, and Spain, allow the mixing of financial institutions and commercial firms with some restrictions.

In the past, regulations that restricted the nonbanking activities of U.S. financial institutions put these organizations at a competitive disadvantage internationally. However, Congress has shown that it is willing to remove existing competitive restraints to allow U.S. institutions to better compete in the global financial arena. To be more like their international counterparts, U.S. financial intermediaries must have the ability to engage in more aspects of multilayer financial deals, which means that these organizations must be able to offer such services as investment banking, commercial lending, insurance, and other necessary financial services. Being able to operate as a company's lender, owner, investment banker, and insurer permits foreign financial organizations to be a "one-stop shop" for financial services and products. Because a single financial institution can offer such financial products as a package, it is possible to reduce the aggregate costs associated with financial services.

It should not be surprising that foreign banks dominate international banking activities. In recent years, however, the presence of U.S. banks in international banking has grown rapidly. At the same time, even though they face greater restrictions than in their home country, many foreign banks have found it attractive to expand to the United States. The presence of foreign banking operations in the United States has expanded greatly during the past couple of decades, especially in California, where large Japanese banks

3-5b Recent Legislation of Financial Markets

During 2007–2008, financial markets worldwide experienced substantial declines, some to the point of near collapse. For example, the U.S. stock markets lost more than 50 percent of their total value from November 2007 through February 2009. Much of the blame for this financial crisis was directed toward the actions of financial institutions, especially with regard to some of their lending practices. As a result, governments around the world imposed new regulations to rein in the powers of financial institutions and to provide accountability to world financial systems. Recent major legislative actions include:

Dodd-Frank Wall Street Reform and Consumer Protection Act. Passed in the summer of 2010, this legislation represents the most significant revision of financial regulations in the United States since the 1930s. The purpose of the Act was to restore confidence in the financial markets by requiring accountability and limiting the actions of all participants. Major provisions include:

▶ Created new organizations to: (1) Help (a) provide consumers clear and accurate information related to credit so that better-informed decisions can be made and (b) protect consumers from unreasonable credit fees. (2) Monitor rules associated with the capital, liquidity, and risk of institutions to help prevent future failures of mega financial organizations.

▶ Restricts the ability of the U.S. government to use taxpayers' funds to bail out large financial institutions.

▶ Requires greater transparency for trading exotic securities, such as derivatives and hedge funds. Nearly all complex, risky securities transactions must now be monitored.

▶ Permits stockholders to have a say on corporate governance, including executive compensation, through nonbinding votes.

▶ Strengthens the supervision of banks, S&Ls, and bank holding companies.

Basel III Accord (2010). Representatives from 27 countries agreed to increase their banks' capital (owners' equity) requirements in an effort to reduce the risk that mega bank failures will cause future financial crises.

Emergency Economic Stabilization Act of 2008. (1) Permitted the U.S. government to purchase up to $700 billion in troubled mortgages in an attempt to improve liquidity in the financial markets (called the Troubled Asset Relief Program, or TARP). (2) Extended certain tax incentives to encourage capital spending. (3) Extended some protections for homeowners whose houses were valued lower than their mortgages. (4) Limited salaries of executives whose companies received TARP funds.

STUDY TOOLS

LOCATED AT BACK OF THE TEXTBOOK

☐ Problems are found at the end of this chapter.

☐ A tear-out Chapter Review card is located at the back of the textbook.

LOCATED AT WWW.CENGAGEBRAIN.COM

☐ Review Key Term flashcards and create your own cards.

☐ Track your knowledge and understanding of key concepts in corporate finance.

☐ Complete practice and graded quizzes to prepare for tests.

☐ Complete interactive content within CFIN5 Online.

☐ View the chapter highlight boxes for CFIN5 Online.

KEY FINANCIAL ENVIRONMENT CONCEPTS

To conclude this chapter, we summarize some essential concepts that were discussed.

- Financial markets represent the system, or mechanisms, by which borrowers and lenders are brought together.

- Financial markets permit companies and individuals to move income from one time period to another—income is moved from future periods to the current period through borrowing, whereas income is moved from the present period to future periods through investing.

- Corporations generally use the services of investment banking houses when raising funds through issues of stocks and bonds. Investment bankers provide advice and help firms issue securities to raise needed funds.

- Financial intermediaries, which include banks, credit unions, pension funds, and so forth, are an important component of the financial markets. Such intermediaries generally take deposits and create loans (perhaps through investments) that are needed by individuals and businesses. If financial intermediaries did not exist, our standard of living would be much lower because the financial markets would not be able to bring together borrowers and lenders as efficiently as they currently do.

- Even though foreign financial markets have increased their prominence during the past couple of decades, U.S. financial markets continue to dominate financial markets throughout the world.

- On a relative basis, in most developed countries, there are many fewer individual banks, which are larger, than the number of banks in the United States. In addition, foreign banks often are permitted to engage in nonbanking business activities that U.S. banks are prohibited from doing.

PROBLEMS

3–1 How do financial markets that run freely and efficiently affect the standard of living in a country?

3–2 What does it mean for a financial market to be considered (a) informationally efficient and (b) economically efficient?

3–3 Do you think investors can earn abnormal returns in financial markets that are at least semistrong-form efficient?

3–4 When the SEC approves a stock issue, it does not provide an opinion about the value of the stock. Do you think the SEC should give an opinion to investors on the appropriate value of the stock being issued? Explain.

3–5 What economic functions do financial intermediaries perform?

3–6 Do you think that the financial services industry will be more reregulated or deregulated in the future? Explain.

3–7 How do you think intermediaries' characteristics will change in the future?

3–8 How do financial institutions in the United States differ from financial institutions in other parts of the world? Why?

3–9 Express Courier (EC) needs $141 million to support future growth. If it issues common stock to raise the needed funds, EC will have to pay its investment banker 6 percent of the issue's total value. If EC can issue common stock at a market price of $80 per share, how many shares must be issued so that the company has $141 million *after flotation costs* to fund the planned growth?

3–10 Jewel Regal Cars (JRC) must raise $240 million to support operations. To do so, JRC plans to issue new bonds. Investment bankers have informed JRC that the flotation costs will be 4 percent of the total amount issued. If the market value of each bond is $1,000, how many bonds must JRC sell to *net* $240 million *after flotation costs*? Assume that fractions of bonds cannot be issued.

3–11 Bearskin Rugs needs $115 million to build a new distribution center. If it issues common stock to raise the funds, the issuance costs will be 8 percent of the total amount issued. If Bearskin can issue stock at $40 per share, how many shares of common stock must be issued so that it has $115 million *after flotation costs* to use to fund the construction of its distribution center?

3–12 Persian Rugs needs $600 million to support growth next year. If it issues new common stock to raise the funds, the flotation (issuance) costs will be 4 percent. If Persian can issue stock at $125 per share, how many shares of common stock must be issued so that it has $600 million *after flotation costs* to use for its planned growth?

3–13 Gerald Morris Corporation (GM) plans to issue bonds to raise $95 million. GM's investment banker will charge flotation costs equal to 5 percent of the total amount issued. The market value of each bond at issue time will be $1,000. How many bonds must GM sell to *net* $95 million *after flotation costs*? Assume that fractions of bonds cannot be issued. Show how much of the total amount issued will consist of flotation costs and how much GM will receive *after flotation costs* are paid.

3–14 Grand Energy Corporation (GE) plans to issue bonds to raise $345 million. GE's investment banker will charge flotation costs equal to 8 percent of the total amount issued. The market value of each bond at issue time will be $1,000. How many bonds must GE sell to net $345 million *after flotation costs*? Assume that fractions of bonds cannot be issued. Show how much of the total amount issued will consist of flotation costs and how much GE will receive *after flotation costs* are paid.

3–15 Boat Emporium (BE) must raise $225 million. To do so, BE expects to issue new common stock. BE's Investment banker will charge issuing costs equal to 10 percent of the total amount issued. If the stock can be issued for $160 per share, how many shares must BE sell to *net* $225 million *after flotation costs*. Show how much of the issue will consist of flotation costs and how much BE will receive after the flotation costs are paid.

3–16 Jasmine Flowers must raise $345 million for its future expansion. To do so, Jasmine expects to issue new common stock. Investment bankers have informed the company that the flotation costs will be 6.5 percent of the total amount issued and that the company will incur another $576,000 in costs associated with the issue. Jasmine can issue its stock for $55 per share. Determine how many shares Jasmine must sell to *net* $345 million *after flotation costs*.

3–17 Wilderness World (WW) needs to raise $84 million in debt. To issue the debt, WW must pay its underwriter a fee equal to 3 percent of the total issue. The company estimates that other expenses associated with the issue will total $487,000. If the face value of each bond is $1,000, how many bonds must be issued to net the needed $84 million? Assume that the firm cannot issue a fraction of a bond.

3–18 Bushwhacker Mowing needs $360 million to support growth. If it issues new common stock to raise the funds, the flotation costs charged by the investment banker will be 4 percent. Additional costs associated with the issue will total $288,000. If Bushwhacker can issue stock at $60 per share, how many shares of common stock must be issued so that it has $360 million *after flotation costs*? Show how much of the issue will consist of flotation costs and how much Bushwhacker will receive *after flotation costs* are paid.

3–19 Mom's Motel Corporation (MM) plans to issue bonds to raise $175 million that it needs to support future operations. MM's investment banker will charge 2.5 percent of the total amount issued to help MM raise the funds. In addition, MM will incur other costs associated with the issue that equal $500,000. The market value of each bond at issue time will be $1,000. How many bonds must MM sell to *net* $175 million *after flotation costs*? Assume that fractions of bonds cannot be issued. Show how much of the issue will consist of flotation costs and how much MM will receive *after flotation costs* are paid.

3–20 United Uninsured Underwriters (U^3) needs to raise $192 million. If it issues new common stock to raise the funds, the flotation costs will be 8 percent. The new issue will also require U^3 to pay $280,000 in fees to its lawyers, printing costs, and other costs associated with the issue. U^3 can issue stock at $25 per share. How many shares of common stock must be issued so that it has $192 million *after flotation costs*? Show how much of the total dollar amount will be flotation costs and how much U^3 will receive after the flotation costs are paid.

CFIN ONLINE

STUDY YOUR WAY WITH STUDYBITS!

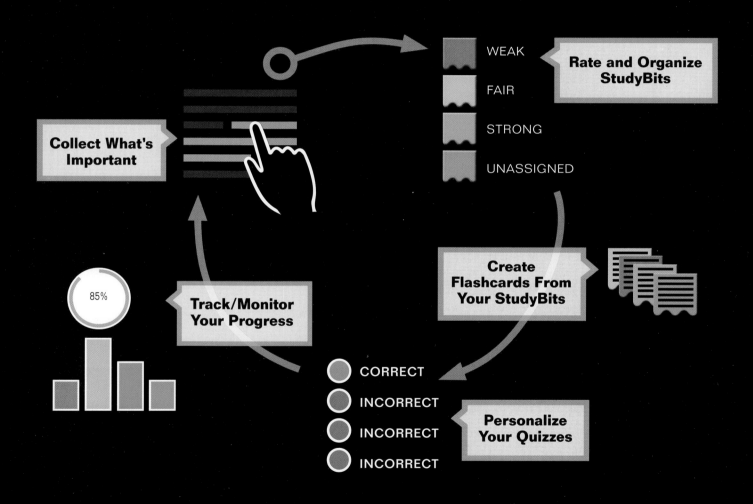

WEAK

FAIR

STRONG

UNASSIGNED

Rate and Organize StudyBits

Collect What's Important

Create Flashcards From Your StudyBits

Track/Monitor Your Progress

85%

CORRECT

INCORRECT

INCORRECT

INCORRECT

Personalize Your Quizzes

4LTR PRESS

Access CFIN ONLINE at www.cengagebrain.com

After you finish this chapter go to **PAGE 79** for **STUDY TOOLS**

LEARNING OUTCOMES

After studying this chapter, you will be able to...

LO1 Identify various types of cash flow patterns (streams) seen in business.

LO2 Compute the future value of different cash flow streams. Explain the results.

LO3 Compute the present value of different cash flow streams. Explain the results.

LO4 Compute (a) the return (interest rate) on an investment (loan) and (b) how long it takes to reach a financial goal.

LO5 Explain the difference between the annual percentage rate (APR) and the effective annual rate (EAR). Explain when it is appropriate to use each.

LO6 Describe an amortized loan. Compute (a) amortized loan payments and (b) the amount that must be paid on an amortized loan at a specific date during the life of the loan.

Time Value of Money

4

A basic financial principle states that, all else equal, the sooner cash is received, the more valuable it is. The logic is simple—*the sooner a dollar is received, the more quickly it can be "put to work" (invested) to increase its value*. So does this mean that receiving $700 today is better than receiving $935 in three years? Not necessarily because the $935 payoff in three years is much greater than the $700 payoff today. To determine which payoff is more valuable, the dollar payoffs of each option must be compared at the same point in time. For example, we can restate (revalue) the future payoff of $935 in terms of current (today's) dollars and then compare the result to the $700 payoff today. The concept used to revalue payments from different time periods, such as the ones described here, is termed the **time value of money (TVM)**.

To make sound financial decisions, you must understand fundamental TVM concepts that are presented in this chapter. To begin, *an important TVM "rule" states that dollar amounts from different time periods should never be compared; rather, amounts should be compared only when they are stated in dollars at the same point in time, such as December 31 of a particular year*. The reasoning behind this "rule" is simple: Dollars from different time periods have opportunities to earn different amounts (numbers of periods) of interest. For example, the $935 payoff in three years is not directly comparable to the $700 payoff today, because these two values contain different amounts of interest. The $700 payoff today contains no future interest, whereas the $935 payoff in three years

includes interest that will be accumulated at some rate over the next three years. We restate, or translate, dollars to the same time period by computing either the future value of current dollars or the present value of future dollars. To "move" a value from one period to another, we use TVM techniques to adjust the interest, or *return*, that the amount has the opportunity to earn over the period of time for which it can be invested. For example, we can illustrate the solution to the question posed earlier using a *cash flow timeline*, which is depicted as follows:

Year (n):	0 r = return = 10%	1	2	3

Cash flow: Option A: $PV_A = \$700$ —— Translate the current $700 into an FV amount by *adding* interest. —→ $? = FV_{A3}$

or

Option B: $PV_B = ?$ ←—— Translate the future $935 into a PV amount by *taking out* interest. —— $\$935 = FV_{B3}$

Following are the definitions of the variables shown in the cash flow timeline:

PV = *Present value*, or beginning amount, that can be invested. PV also represents the current value of some future amount. In our example, the PV of Option A is $700 because this is the amount that will be paid today. At this point, we do not know the PV of Option B.

FV_n = *Future value*, which is the value to which an amount invested today will grow at the end of n periods (years, in this case), after accounting for interest that can be earned during the investment period. In our example, the FV of Option B in Year 3 is $935. At this point, we do not know the FV of Option A in Year 3.

(continued)

time value of money (TVM) The principles and computations used to revalue cash payoffs from different times so they are stated in dollars of the same time period.

A cash flow timeline, such as the one shown here, is an essential TVM tool that is used much like a road map to help visualize the financial situation that is being analyzed. On the timeline, we place the time above the line so that Time 0 is today, Time 1 is one period from today—perhaps one year, one month, or some other time period—and so forth. The cash flows are placed below the tick marks that correspond to the period in which they are either paid or received, and the interest rate, or *return*, is shown directly above the timeline. According to the cash flow timeline we show here, to answer the question we posed earlier, we must either compute the FV in Year 3 of the $700 current payment from Option A and compare it to the $935 payment of Option B to be received in Year 3, or compute the PV of the $935 payment in Year 3 from Option B and compare it to the $700 PV (current value) of Option A. We show these computations in the sections that follow.

opportunity cost rate The rate of return on the best available alternative investment of equal risk.

lump-sum amount A single payment (received or made) that occurs either today or at some date in the future.

annuity A series of payments of an equal amount at fixed, equal intervals for a specified number of periods.

ordinary annuity An annuity with payments that occur at the end of each period.

annuity due An annuity with payments that occur at the beginning of each period.

uneven cash flows Multiple payments of different amounts over a period of time.

future value (FV) The amount to which a cash flow or series of cash flows will grow over a given period of time when compounded at a given interest rate.

compounding The process of determining the value to which an amount or a series of cash flows will grow in the future when compound interest is applied.

4-1 Cash Flow Patterns

The three cash flow patterns that we normally see in business include:

▶ *Lump-sum amount*—A single, or one-time, payment (received or made) that occurs either today or at some date in the future. The cash flows given in the earlier examples and shown in the cash flow timeline are lump-sum amounts.

▶ *Annuity*—Multiple payments of the same amount over equal time periods. For example, an investment of $400 in each of the next three years represents an annuity. If the payment is made at the end of the period, the annuity is referred to as an ordinary annuity because this is the way most payments are made between businesses. On the other hand, if the payment is made at the beginning of the period, the annuity is referred to as an annuity due, because in such situations a business has paid for, and is due to receive, certain products or services.

▶ *Uneven cash flows*—Multiple payments of different amounts over a period of time. For example, investments of $400 this year, $300 next year, and $250 the following year represent an uneven cash flow stream.

4-2 Future Value (FV)

To compute the future value of an amount invested today (a current amount), we "push forward" the current amount by *adding interest* for each period the money can earn interest in the future. This process is called compounding because, as you will soon discover, when interest that is earned in prior years is left to grow along with the amount that was originally invested, the interest that is earned in each future year increases; that is, interest *compounds*. Following is a cash flow timeline that shows how we "push forward" the current $700 payment from Option A in our example by adding annual interest (at a 10 percent rate) to determine its value at the end of Year 3.

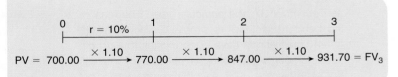

This example shows that if you invest $700 today at a 10 percent annual return (interest), your money will grow to $770 in one year, to $847 in two years, and to $931.70 in three years. Using this information, we can now answer the question that was posed earlier: Assuming that all future payments are guaranteed, you should prefer to receive the $935 payment from Option B in three years rather than the $700 payment from Option A today. The logic is simple: If you take the $700 payment today from Option A and invest it at a 10 percent annual return, it will grow to only $931.70 in three years, which is $3.30 less than the $935 you would receive with Option B at the same point in time—that is, at the end of three years.

4-2a FV of a Lump-Sum Amount—FV_n

The computations given on the cash flow timeline show that we can determine the future value of a $700 investment that is made today by multiplying the value of the investment at the beginning of each of the three years by $(1 + r) = (1.10)$. As a result, in our example, we would get the same ending balance of $931.70 if we multiplied the initial $700 investment by $(1.10) \times (1.10) \times (1.10) = (1.10)^3$. That is,

$$FV_3 = \$700(1.10)^3 = \$700(1.33100) = \$931.70$$

When this concept is generalized, the future value of an amount invested today can be computed by applying Equation 4.1.

4.1

$$FV_n = PV(1 + r)^n$$

Equation 4.1 shows that the future value (FV) of an amount invested today (PV) is based on the multiple by which the initial investment will increase in the future, $(1 + r)^n$. As you can see, the value of this multiple depends on both the interest rate (r) and the length of time (n) interest is earned—that is, $(1 + r)^n$; it is greater when r (interest rate) is higher, when n (investment time period) is greater, or when both conditions exist.

Equation 4.1 shows one approach that can be used to solve a TVM problem—the equation solution. Such problems can also be solved using a financial calculator or a spreadsheet. Each approach gives the same answer to a particular problem, because each performs the same computation. In this chapter, we primarily show the equation solutions and the financial calculator solutions to the problems that are presented.

FV of a Lump-Sum Amount—Equation Solution. The equation solution to our current situation was shown in the previous section with the application of Equation 4.1; that is, $FV = 700(1.10)^3 = 700(1.33100) = 931.70$.[1]

FV of a Lump-Sum Amount—Financial Calculator Solution. Equation 4.1 and most other TVM equations have been programmed directly into *financial calculators*. These calculators have five keys that correspond to the five most commonly used TVM variables. On a Texas Instruments BAII PLUS financial calculator, which is the calculator we use throughout this book, N = number of periods interest is paid, I/Y = interest rate paid each period, PV = present (today's) value of some amount, FV = future value of an amount, and PMT = amount of an annuity payment (if the problem includes such a cash flow pattern).

Following is an illustration of the financial calculator solution for the current example:

Inputs:	3	10	−700	0	?
	N	I/Y	PV	PMT	FV
Output:					= 931.70

Throughout the book, we show the values that must be entered into the calculator above the illustrations of the TVM keys and show the result of the computation below the keys. Note that financial calculators require all cash flows to be designated as either inflows or outflows, because the computations are based on the fact that we generally pay money, which is a *cash outflow* (a negative cash flow), to receive a benefit, which is a *cash inflow* (a positive cash flow). When entering the cash flows into the calculator, you must designate a cash outflow with a negative sign. In our illustration, because the initial $700 is invested today—that is, an investment is purchased—PV is entered as −700. If you forget the negative sign and enter 700, then the calculator assumes you receive $700 in the current period and that you must pay it back with interest in the future, so the FV solution would appear as −931.70, a cash outflow.

FV of a Lump-Sum Amount—Spreadsheet Solution. You probably will use a financial calculator to solve the TVM problems assigned in class. Because most businesses use spreadsheets to solve such problems, however, you should have some familiarity with the TVM functions that are programmed into spreadsheets. As a result, we briefly discuss how to set up a spreadsheet to solve the current TVM problem. To solve the problems that we discuss in the remainder of this chapter, similar

---

[1] To reduce clutter, we do not show the dollar signs in the solutions in the remainder of this chapter.

setups are used; you simply use the appropriate spreadsheet TVM function. (Appendix A, which is titled Using Spreadsheets to Solve Financial Problems, provides a detailed discussion about how to use spreadsheet TVM functions to solve the problems mentioned in this chapter.)

To access the TVM functions that are programmed into Microsoft Excel 2013, you must click on the Insert Function option, which is designated f_x and can be found in the Formulas menu on the toolbar at the top of the spreadsheet.[2] Each preprogrammed function is standardized so that numbers must be entered in a specific order to solve the problem correctly. Figure 4.1 shows the setup and the results of using the FV function to compute the future value in three years of $700 invested today at 10 percent. Because a spreadsheet and a financial calculator have similar functions to solve TVM problems, the labels given in Row 1 through Row 4 of Column A in Figure 4.1 correspond to the TVM keys on a financial calculator. Note that the $700 that is invested today is entered into the spreadsheet as a negative value, just as it is when using a financial calculator to solve the problem. Values should be entered in the spreadsheet in the same way as they are entered in the financial calculator, with the exception of

the interest rate. The interest rate is entered as a percentage (10 in our example) in the financial calculator, whereas it is entered as a decimal (0.10 in our example) in the spreadsheet.

4-2b FV of an Ordinary Annuity—FVA_n

Suppose Alice decides to deposit $400 each year for three years in a savings account that pays 5 percent interest per year. If Alice makes the first deposit one year from today, how much will be in the account when she makes the final deposit? Because the first deposit is at the end of the year (one year from today), this series of deposits represents an *ordinary annuity*. One way to determine the future value of this annuity, which we designate FVA_n, is to compute the future value of *each* individual payment using Equation 4.1 and then sum the results. Using this approach, we find that $FVA_3 = \$1,261$.

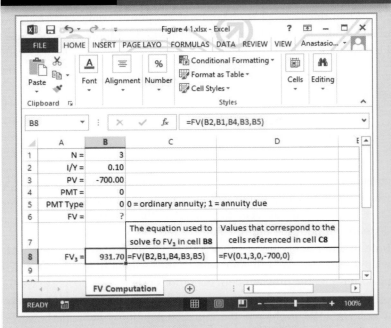

FIGURE 4.1 USING EXCEL'S FV FUNCTION TO COMPUTE THE FUTURE VALUE OF A LUMP-SUM AMOUNT, FV

Note: According to the equation shown in cell **C8**, the input values must be entered in a specific order: I/Y, N, PMT, PV, and PMT type (not used for this problem). It is a good idea to set up a table that contains the data needed to solve the problem, and then refer to the cell where each number is located when you apply the FV equation. If you follow this technique, you can change any number in the table you set up and the result of the change will immediately show in the cell where the equation is located. For example, if the current problem is changed so that $500 rather than $700 is deposited in a bank account, you would change the value in cell **B3** to -500, and the result of 665.50 would appear in cell **B8**.

[2]The Insert Function selection can also be found on the Home menu under the summation sign (Σ).

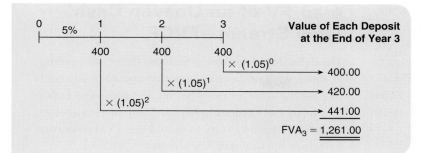

Value of Each Deposit at the End of Year 3

$$FVA_3 = 1,261.00$$

FVA$_n$—Financial Calculator Solution. To solve for FVA$_n$ using a financial calculator, we use the PMT (annuity) key. In our example, we input PMT $= -400$ because Alice will deposit $400 each year in the bank account; this deposit is considered a cash outflow. Thus, the inputs and the result are as follows:

Inputs:	3	5	0	−400	?
	N	I/Y	PV	PMT	FV
Output:					= 1,261.00

FVA$_n$—Equation Solution. The timeline solution shows that we can compute the future value of this $400 ordinary annuity as follows:

$$\begin{aligned} FVA_3 &= 400(1.05)^2 + 400(1.05)^1 + 400(1.05)^0 \\ &= 400[(1.05)^2 + (1.05)^1 + (1.05)^0] \\ &= 400(1.1025 + 1.0500 + 1.0000) \\ &= 400(3.1525) = 1,261.00 \end{aligned}$$

Because an annuity represents a *series of equal payments*, we can generalize this computation to obtain Equation 4.2 to solve for the FVA of any ordinary annuity.

4-2c FV of an Annuity Due—FVA(DUE)$_n$

Now suppose Alice's twin brother, Alvin, thinks that his sister's savings plan is a good idea, so he decides to copy her by also depositing $400 each year for three years in a savings account that pays 5 percent interest per year. However, Alvin plans to make his first deposit today rather than one year from today, which means that his series of deposits represents an *annuity due*. Using Equation 4.1 to solve for the future value of the individual payments for this annuity, which we designate FVA(DUE)$_n$, we find

4.2

$$\begin{aligned} FVA_n &= PMT[(1 + r)^{n-1} + (1 + r)^{n-2} + \cdots + (1 + r)^0] \\ &= PMT\sum_{t=0}^{n-1}(1 + r)^t \\ &= PMT\left[\frac{(1 + r)^n - 1}{r}\right] \end{aligned}$$

Here the symbol Σ indicates summation, which means that $\sum_{t=0}^{n-1}(1 + r)^t = (1 + r)^0 + (1 + r)^1 + \cdots + (1 + r)^{n-1}$ in Equation 4.2. The same interpretation applies to equations that include Σ in the remainder of the book.

Entering the information from our example into Equation 4.2, we have the following solution:[3]

$$FVA_3 = 400\left[\frac{(1.05)^3 - 1}{0.05}\right] = 400(3.152500)$$
$$= 1,261.00$$

[3]The version of Equation 4.2 given on the third line is derived from the equation given on the first line by applying the algebra of geometric progressions.

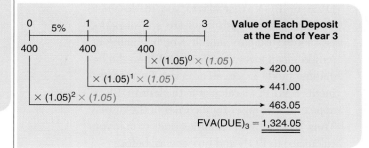

Value of Each Deposit at the End of Year 3

$$FVA(DUE)_3 = 1,324.05$$

FVA(DUE)$_n$—Equation Solution. As you can see from the cash flow timeline, the future value of Alvin's deposits—FVA(DUE)$_3$ = $1,324.05—is greater than the future value of Alice's deposits—FVA$_3$ = $1,261.00. Even though both annuities have the same total amount (cash flows) deposited over the three-year period, each year Alvin makes his deposit at the beginning of the year (annuity due), whereas Alice makes her deposit at the end of the year (ordinary annuity). As a result, each of Alvin's deposits earns one additional year's worth of interest compared to Alice's deposits, which amounts to $63.05 additional interest (= $1,324.05 − $1,261.00).

As the cash flow timeline shows, Equation 4.2, which we used to solve for FVA, must be adjusted to solve for $FVA(DUE)_n$. Specifically, because the payments are made at the beginning of the year, we must give each annuity payment one additional year of interest, $(1 + r)$, compared to an ordinary annuity. Thus, Equation 4.2 can be restated to form Equation 4.3, which is used to solve $FVA(DUE)_n$.

4.3

$$FVA(DUE)_n = PMT\sum_{t=0}^{n-1}(1 + r)^t \, (1 + r)$$

$$= PMT\left\{\left[\frac{(1 + r)^n - 1}{r}\right] \times (1 + r)\right\}$$

The adjustment that is made to Equation 4.2 to generate Equation 4.3 is shown in italics and highlighted in red. Using Equation 4.3, we find

$$FAV(DUE)_3 = 400\left\{\left[\frac{(1.05)^3 - 1}{0.05}\right] \times (1.05)\right\}$$

$$= 400(3.310125) = 1,324.05$$

$FVA(DUE)_n$—Financial Calculator Solution. Financial calculators have a switch, or key, generally marked DUE or BGN, that allows you to designate whether annuity cash flows are end-of-period payments (ordinary annuity) or beginning-of-period payments (annuity due). When the beginning mode is activated on the Texas Instruments BAII PLUS calculator, the letters "BGN" appear in the upper right corner of the display. Thus, to deal with annuities due, switch your calculator to BGN and proceed as before:[4]

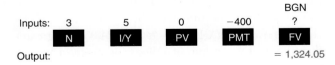

Inputs:	3	5	0	−400	BGN ?
	N	I/Y	PV	PMT	FV
Output:					= 1,324.05

payment (PMT) This term designates constant cash flows—that is, the amount of an annuity payment.

cash flow (CF) This term designates cash flows in general, including uneven cash flows.

terminal value The future value of a cash flow stream.

Because most problems specify end-of-period cash flows—that is, ordinary annuities— *you should always switch your calculator back to the END mode after you work an annuity due problem.*

4-2d FV of an Uneven Cash Flow Stream—FVCF$_n$

The definition of an annuity includes the words *constant*, or *equal, amount*, because annuities consist of payments that are the same for every period. Because some important financial decisions involve uneven, or *nonconstant*, cash flows, it is necessary to extend our TVM discussion to include *uneven cash flow streams*.

Throughout the book, we use the term **payment (PMT)** to identify situations where the cash flows are constant such that the cash flow pattern represents an annuity, and we use the term **cash flow (CF)** to denote a cash flow series in general, which *includes both uneven cash flows and annuities*. When all cash flows in a series are nonconstant, $CF_1 \neq CF_2 \neq \ldots \neq CF_n$, which represents an uneven cash flow stream; when all cash flows in a series are equal, $CF_1 = CF_2 = \ldots = CF_n = PMT$, which represents an annuity.

The future value of an uneven cash flow stream, sometimes called the **terminal value**, is found by compounding each payment to the end of the stream and then summing the future values. For example, suppose that rather than depositing $400 each year in her bank account, Alice managed to deposit $400 at the end of the first year, $300 at the end of the second year, and $250 at the end of the third year. If the account earns 5 percent interest each year, the future value of this uneven cash flow stream is

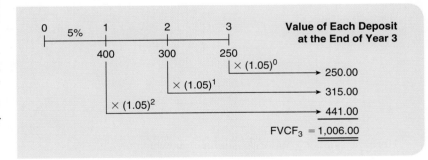

$FVCF_n$—Equation Solution. You can find the *future value of any cash flow stream by summing the future values of the individual cash flows* as shown in the cash flow timeline. Stated in equation form, the future value of *any* cash flow stream can be computed using Equation 4.4.

[4]See the operating instructions for the financial calculator you are using to determine how to switch to the "begin" mode.

4.4

$$FVCF_n = CF_1(1 + r)^{n-1} + \cdots + CF_n(1 + r)^0$$

$$= \sum_{t=1}^{n} CF_t(1 + r)^{n-t}$$

Equation 4.2 and Equation 4.3 can *only* be used to compute the future values of cash flow streams that represent annuities—that is, when the cash flows are the same each period—whereas Equation 4.4 can be used to find the future value for *any* cash flow stream (annuity or uneven). Because the cash flows shown in the previous cash flow timeline are not equal, Equation 4.4 cannot be simplified further for our example. Thus, to compute the future value of an uneven cash flow stream, you must compute the future value of each cash payment and then sum the results. In our example, the computation is

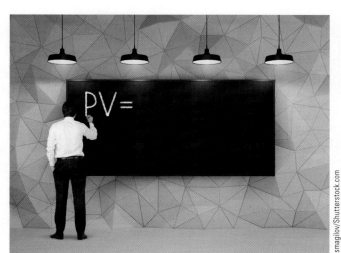

$$FV_3 = 400(1.05)^2 + 300(1.05)^1 + 250(1.05)^0$$
$$= 400(1.1025) + 300(1.0500) + 250(1.0000)$$
$$= 1,006.00$$

This process can be quite tedious if the uneven cash flow stream covers many years. Fortunately, financial calculators have *cash flow registers* that can be used to make such computations more manageable. We will discuss use of the cash flow register on the financial calculator to compute the future value of an uneven cash flow stream at the end of the next section.

4-3 Present Value (PV)

To compute the **present value** of a future amount, we "bring back" the future amount by *taking interest out* for each future period that the money has the

opportunity to earn interest; that is, we "de-interest" the future amount. This process, which is called **discounting**, is essentially the opposite of determining the future value of a current amount. The following timeline shows how we discount $935 to be received in three years if investors have the opportunity to invest at a 10 percent return.

0		1		2		3
	10%					

$$\frac{1}{(1.10)} \times \quad \frac{1}{(1.10)} \times \quad \frac{1}{(1.10)} \times$$

PV = 702.48 ← 772.73 ← 850.00 ← 935.00 = FV_3

This example shows that if you want to receive $935 in three years and you can earn a 10 percent annual return, you must invest $702.48 today. Thus, if you were offered the choice of a payment of $700 today (Option A) or a payment of $935 in three years (Option B) and you have the opportunity to earn a 10 percent return (the situation we described at the beginning of the chapter), everything else equal, you should choose the payment of $935 in three years because it has a current (present) value that is greater than $700. Another interpretation is to view the present value as either the current cost or the selling price of the future amount. In our example, the cost to produce $935 in three years if investors can earn a 10 percent return is $702.48; thus, anyone who owns the right to receive $935 in three years should be able to sell it today for $702.48, which is $2.48 greater than the option to receive $700 today.

4-3a PV of a Lump-Sum Amount—PV

The timeline solution shows that we compute the present value of the $935 payment in three years by taking away three years worth of interest from the $935, which can be accomplished by *dividing* the value of the investment at the end of each of the three years by $(1 + r) = (1.10)$. As a result, in our

present value (PV) The value today—that is, the current value—of a future cash flow or series of cash flows.

discounting The process of determining the present value of a cash flow or a series of cash flows to be received (paid) in the future; the reverse of compounding.

example, we would get the same present value of $702.48 if we divided the $935 to be received in three years by $(1.10)^3$, which discounts the $935 by the 10 percent interest that it will earn over the next three years. That is,

$$PV = \frac{935}{(1.10)^3} = 935\left[\frac{1}{(1.10)^3}\right]$$

$$= 935(0.751315) = 702.48$$

PV of a Lump-Sum Amount—Equation Solution. When we generalize the process shown in the previous computation and in the cash flow timeline, the present value of a future lump-sum payment can be computed by applying Equation 4.5:

4.5

$$PV = \frac{FV_n}{(1 + r)^n} = FV_n\left[\frac{1}{(1 + r)^n}\right]$$

According to Equation 4.5, to compute the present value (PV) of a future amount (FV), we must discount the future amount by the interest that it could earn from the present period until some future period. This discount factor, $1/(1 + r)^n$, depends on both the interest rate (r) and the length of time (n) interest is earned. The PV is lower when r (interest) is higher, when n (time) is greater, or when both conditions exist.

Applying Equation 4.5, we find the solution to our current problem is

$$PV = 935\left[\frac{1}{(1.10)^3}\right] = 935(0.751315) = 702.48$$

PV of a Lump-Sum Amount—Financial Calculator Solution. When solving this problem using a financial calculator, input the known information into the appropriate TVM locations and solve as follows:

Inputs:	3	10	?	0	935
	N	I/Y	PV	PMT	FV

Output: = −702.48

4-3b PV of an Ordinary Annuity—PVA$_n$

Suppose that Alice, whom we introduced earlier, has decided that she wants to pay herself—that is, take out of savings—$400 each year for the next three years rather than deposit these amounts in her savings account. If she can invest a lump-sum amount in a savings account that pays 5 percent per year, how much money does she need to deposit today to accomplish her goal? Alice would make the first $400 withdrawal from the savings account at the end of this year, which means that the series of cash flows represents an ordinary annuity. Using Equation 4.5, we can compute the present value of each of Alice's annual withdrawals and sum the results to determine the present value of this ordinary annuity, which we designate PVA$_n$.

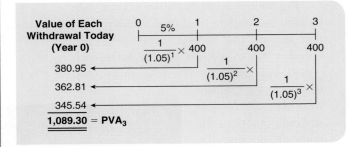

This result indicates that if Alice deposits $1,089.30 today in a savings account that pays 5 percent interest per year, she will be able to pay herself (withdraw) $400 at the end of each of the next three years.

PVA$_n$—Equation Solution. According to the timeline solution, we can compute the present value of this $400 ordinary annuity as follows:

$$PVA_3 = 400\left[\frac{1}{(1.05)^1}\right] + 400\left[\frac{1}{(1.05)^2}\right] + 400\left[\frac{1}{(1.05)^3}\right]$$

$$= 400\left[\frac{1}{(1.05)^1} + \frac{1}{(1.05)^2} + \frac{1}{(1.05)^3}\right]$$

$$= 400(0.952381 + 0.907029 + 0.863838)$$

$$= 400(2.723248) = 1,089.30$$

When this concept is generalized, the present value of an ordinary annuity can be computed by applying Equation 4.6:

4.6

$$PVA_n = PMT\left[\sum_{t=1}^{n}\frac{1}{(1 + r)^t}\right]$$

$$= PMT\left[\frac{1 - \frac{1}{(1 + r)^n}}{r}\right]$$

Entering the information from our example into Equation 4.6, we find that

$$PVA_3 = 400\left[\frac{1 - \frac{1}{(1.05)^3}}{0.05}\right] = 400(2.72325) = 1,089.30$$

PVA$_n$—Financial Calculator Solution. To solve for PVA$_3$ in our example using a financial calculator, the inputs and the result are

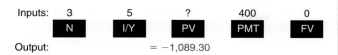

Inputs: 3 [N] 5 [I/Y] ? [PV] 400 [PMT] 0 [FV]

Output: = −1,089.30

4-3c PV of an Annuity Due— PVA(DUE)$_n$

Suppose that Alice's twin brother, Alvin, again wants to copy his sister. However, Alvin plans to make the first $400 withdrawal from his savings account today rather than one year from today. The series of deposits now represents an *annuity due*. Using Equation 4.5, we can compute the PVs of the individual payments and sum the results to find the PV of the annuity due, which we designate PVA(DUE)$_n$.

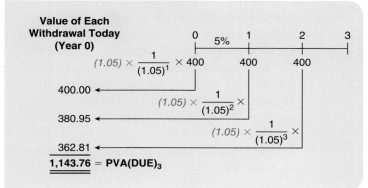

Value of Each Withdrawal Today (Year 0)

0   5%   1   2   3

$(1.05) \times \frac{1}{(1.05)^1} \times 400$ 400   400

400.00 ←

$(1.05) \times \frac{1}{(1.05)^2} \times$

380.95 ←

$(1.05) \times \frac{1}{(1.05)^3} \times$

362.81 ←

1,143.76 = PVA(DUE)$_3$

Note that the PV of Alvin's annuity ($1,143.76) is greater than the PV of Alice's annuity ($1,089.30). You should have expected this result because Alvin will need to deposit more money today if he wants to pay himself each of the $400 withdrawals one year earlier than Alice pays herself. In other words, Alvin's money earns less interest because it is invested for a shorter time than Alice's money, which means he must start with a greater amount to withdraw the same total amount as his sister over the three years.

PVA(DUE)$_n$—Equation Solution. Because an annuity due payment is made at the beginning of the year, to compute PVA(DUE)$_n$, we adjust Equation 4.6 to reflect the fact that each annuity payment is discounted one less year (one less year of interest can be earned) compared to an ordinary annuity. Thus, the equation is now stated as Equation 4.7:

4.7

$$PVA(DUE)_n = PMT\left\{\sum_{t=1}^{n}\left[\frac{1}{(1+r)^t}\right](1+r)\right\}$$

$$= PMT\left\{\left[\frac{1 - \frac{1}{(1+r)^n}}{r}\right] \times (1+r)\right\}$$

The adjustment that is made to Equation 4.6 to generate Equation 4.7 is shown in italics and highlighted in red. Applying Equation 4.7 to our example, we find

$$PVA(DUE)_3 = 400\left\{\left[\frac{1 - \frac{1}{(1.05)^3}}{0.05}\right] \times (1.05)\right\}$$

$$400(2.859410) = 1,143.76$$

PVA(DUE)$_n$—Financial Calculator Solution. As described earlier, to deal with annuities due, you must switch your calculator to the BGN mode. The inputs and the result for the current situation are

Inputs: 3 [N] 5 [I/Y] ? [PV] 400 [PMT] BGN 0 [FV]

Output: = −1,143.76

4-3d Perpetuities

Although most annuities call for payments to be made over some limited period of time, some annuities go on indefinitely, or perpetually. These *perpetual annuities* are called **perpetuities**. The present value of a perpetuity is found by applying Equation 4.8, which is simply Equation 4.6 when n = ∞:

4.8

$$PVP = PMT\left[\frac{1}{r}\right] = \frac{PMT}{r}$$

Suppose an investment promises to pay $100 per year in perpetuity. What is this investment worth if the opportunity cost rate is 5 percent? The answer is $2,000:

$$PVP = \frac{100}{0.05} = 2,000$$

Suppose the interest rate increases to 10 percent.

perpetuities Streams of equal payments that are expected to continue forever.

What would happen to the investment's value? The value would drop to $1,000:

$$PVP = \frac{100}{0.10} = 1,000$$

We see that the value of a perpetuity changes dramatically when interest rates change. This example demonstrates an important financial concept: Everything else equal, when the *interest rate changes, the value of an investment changes in an opposite direction*—a higher (lower) interest rate means that a lower (higher) amount needs to be invested today to accumulate a specific amount in the future.

4-3e PV of an Uneven Cash flow Stream—PVCF$_n$

We mentioned earlier that an uneven, or nonconstant, cash flow stream consists of payments that are not all equal; thus, we cannot use the annuity equations to determine their present values. Let's return to the previous example where Alice deposits $400, $300, and $250 at the end of each of the next three years. The present value of this uneven cash flow stream is

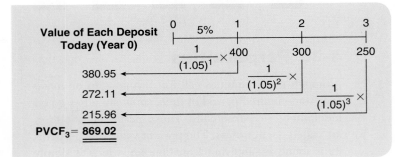

PVCF$_n$—Equation Solution. You can find the *present value of any cash flow stream by summing the present values of the individual cash flows* as shown in the previous cash flow timeline. Stated in equation form (Equation 4.9), the present value of any cash flow stream is:

4.9

$$PVCF_n = CF_1\left[\frac{1}{(1 + r)^1}\right] + \cdots + CF_n\left[\frac{1}{(1 + r)^n}\right]$$

$$= \sum_{t=1}^{n} CF_t\left[\frac{1}{(1 + r)^t}\right]$$

Because the cash flows shown in the previous cash flow timeline are not equal, Equation 4.9 cannot be simplified further for our situation. Thus, to compute the

present value of an uneven cash flow stream, you must compute the present value of each cash payment and then sum the results as shown in the cash flow timeline.

PVCF$_n$—Financial Calculator Solution. Financial calculators have "cash flow registers" that can be used to make the computation of PVCF$_n$ more manageable. When using a financial calculator, you first input the individual cash flows in chronological order into the cash flow register. Cash flows usually are designated CF$_0$, CF$_1$, CF$_2$, and so on. Next, you enter the interest rate. At this point, you have entered all the known values of Equation 4.9, so you only need to press the NPV key to find the present value of the cash flow stream. The calculator has been programmed to find the PV of each cash flow, including CF$_0$, and then to sum these values to find the PV of the entire stream, which is called the NPV, or net present value. To input the cash flows for this problem, enter 0 (because CF$_0$ = 0), 400, 300, and 250 in that order into the calculator's cash flow register, enter I = 5, and then press NPV to get the answer, -869.02. Because we discuss the application of this function in much greater detail in Chapter 9, we will wait until then to describe in more detail the process of solving for NPV using a financial calculator.

After computing the present value of an uneven cash flow stream, we can use either Equation 4.1 or a financial calculator to determine its future value. For the current situation, FVCF$_3$ = $869.02(1.05)^3$ = $1,006. This is the same result we found earlier using Equation 4.4.[5]

4-3f Comparison of FV with PV—Understanding the Numbers

It is important that you get the correct solutions when solving TVM problems; more important, however, is that you interpret the solutions correctly when making business decisions. The secret to understanding FV and PV values is to realize that an FV amount contains interest, whereas a PV amount does not. For example, earlier we showed that a $700 investment will grow to $931.70 in three years if the opportunity cost rate is 10 percent; that is, the $700 investment will accumulate $231.70 of interest over the three-year period. Let's examine what this

[5]Some financial calculators are programmed to compute both the net present value, NPV, and the net future value, NFV. The NFV is the future value of the cash flows from Period 0 through Period n; that is, NFV = NPV(1 + r)^n.

means when making business decisions by considering the following question:

If the opportunity cost rate is 10 percent, which amount is it better (preferred) to receive, a $700 payment today or a guaranteed (certain) payment of $931.70 in three years?

To answer this question, remember that the reason we perform TVM computations is to restate dollars from one time period to another time period; that is, "move values through time." Also remember that we move dollars through time by adjusting the amount of interest that those dollars have the opportunity to earn, because today's dollars do not contain the same amount of interest as future dollars. Different dollar amounts can be compared only when they have comparable amounts of interest; that is, they are stated in values from the same time period. For example, when we computed the FV in three years of the $700 payment today, we "pushed forward" the $700 by adjusting the interest that this money has the opportunity to earn during the next three years. The $700 is a current (present value) amount that includes no future interest, whereas the $931.70 is a future value amount that includes the interest that can be accumulated during the next three years at a 10 percent interest rate. As a result, the $700 payment today and the $931.70 guaranteed payment in three years should be considered equally desirable, because the $700 can be invested at 10 percent and its value will grow to $931.70 at the end of three years.

To illustrate the reason the two payoffs mentioned here are equally desirable, let's suppose you won a contest that gives you a choice between either a $700 payment today or a *guaranteed* payment of $931.70 in three years. If only one opportunity cost rate exists for all investors, 10 percent, which prize should you choose? Based on our discussion, you should answer this question by shrugging your shoulders and saying, "I don't care which prize I get, because they both are equally desirable." For example, suppose that you choose the $700 prize, and then you realize that you actually prefer the payment of $931.70 in three years. Did you make a mistake? No, because you can invest the $700 at 10 percent today, and in three years, the investment's value will be $931.70.

Now, let's assume that you won the contest just mentioned and you are a student with no money in the bank who has to pay rent today. Coincidentally your rent payment equals $700. If you were in this situation, which prize *should* you select (prefer)? If you are like most people, your first impulse probably would be to choose the $700 check, because your rent must be paid today. But the particular circumstances a person faces have no impact on the values of money at different points in time. In other words, just because your rent is due today does

Stephen Stickler/he Image Bank/Getty Images

not change the fact that the two prizes are identical when we evaluate them using the TVM methods described in this chapter. To show that this is correct, let's now suppose that you won the contest described here, but the prize you get is determined by drawing from a hat that contains two pieces of paper—one paper is a check for $700 that can be cashed today and the other paper states that the owner can collect $931.70 in three years. Because your rent is due today, you probably are hoping that you draw the $700 check. Consider what happens if you draw the piece of paper that states the owner will be paid $931.70, but not until three years from today. How are you going to pay your rent? Remember that the piece of paper you drew from the hat has value today, which is equal to the PV of the $931.70 that will be paid in three years. Because the PV of $931.70 to be received in three years is $700 = $931.70/(1.10)^3, you should be able to immediately sell your prize for $700 to someone who prefers to receive a payment of $931.70 in three years. With the $700 in hand, you can pay your rent today.[6]

This illustration shows that to make a rational business decision based on monetary payments from different time periods, the payments must first be adjusted so that they are stated on a comparable basis, which means that the payments must be stated in dollars at the same point

[6]For the sale to occur quickly and for you to receive $700, we assume no commissions, taxes, or other costs are associated with the sale of the prize and that there are many people who would want to buy such a prize; that is, there are many people who want to invest $700 today at 10 percent so that they will have $931.70 to spend in three years.

in time. Following is an expanded cash flow timeline that illustrates how a $700 investment that earns 10 percent interest each year grows to $931.70 in three years:

Note that the values given under the tick marks for each year differ only because they contain different amounts of interest, which is shown in the boxes below the values. In other words, on a time value of money basis, if your opportunity rate is 10 percent, you should be indifferent if you had to choose whether to take $700 today, $770 in one year, $847 in two years, or $931.70 in three years. These values differ only by the amount of interest they contain, which is interest that can be earned by everyone who invests for the specified period of time. In fact, if we take out all of the interest in each of the future amounts, the current (present) value of each is $700.

Let's apply the logic presented here to the ordinary annuity we discussed earlier in the chapter, where we showed that if, beginning in one year, Alice deposits $400 per year in a savings account that pays 5 percent interest annually, her account will have a balance of $1,261 at the end of three years. We also discovered that Alice would need to deposit $1,089.30 today in a savings account that pays 5 percent interest annually if she wants to pay herself $400 per year for the next three years, assuming that she withdraws the first $400 from the account at the end of this year.

Suppose you win a raffle that allows you to choose from one of three prizes: (1) $1,089.30 that will be paid to you today; (2) $1,261 that will be paid to you in three years; or (3) three payments of $400 at the end of each of the next three years. The payoff for each prize is guaranteed. If your opportunity cost rate is 5 percent, which prize *should* you choose? Based on the discussion presented earlier in this section, you should conclude that each prize is equally desirable. It is easy to see that they are identical when we compute the PV of each prize because PV(Prize 1) = PV(Prize 2) = PV(Prize 3) = $1,089.30. As a result, to select a prize, you should take three identical pieces of blank paper, write the number 1 on one piece of paper, the number 2 on another piece of paper, and the number 3 on a third piece of paper; put the three pieces of paper in a hat; and, with your eyes closed, draw one piece of paper out of the hat. Whichever prize you choose (receive) can be transformed into either of the other prizes. For example, let's assume that you choose the prize that pays you $1,089.30 today. If you don't need the money, you can invest the $1,089.30 at 5 percent and it will grow to $1,261 in three years. That is, $FV_3 = \$1,089.30(1.05)^3 = \$1,261.00$. Conversely, if you choose the prize that pays you $1,261 in three years, you can sell the prize today for its present value of $1,089.30. And, if you want the annuity payment, you can invest $1,089.30 at 5 percent annual interest and pay yourself $400 at the end of each of the next three years. Table 4.1 shows that this statement is indeed correct.

These simple examples show that when we apply TVM techniques, we simply restate dollars (values) from

Table 4.1

Creating a $400 Annuity Payment

Year	Balance at the Beginning of the Year	Annual Interest Earned @ 5%[a]	Balance at the End of the Year	Withdrawal at the End of the Year
1	$1,089.30	$54.47	$1,143.77	$400.00
2	743.77	37.19	780.96	400.00
3	380.96	19.05	400.01[b]	400.00

[a]Annual interest is computed by multiplying the balance at the beginning of the year by 0.05. For example, the interest earned in the first year is $54.47 = $1,089.30 × 0.05.
[b]There is a $0.01 difference due to rounding.

one time period in terms of their *equivalent* values at some other point in time. To determine the *future value* of a current amount, we *add interest* that can be earned over the investment period; to determine the *present value* of a future amount, we *take out interest* that can be earned over the investment period.

4-4 Solving for Interest Rates (r) or Time (n)

The equations that we presented in the previous sections include variables labeled PV, FV, r, n, and PMT. If we know the values of all these variables except one, we can solve for the value of the unknown variable. To this point, we have solved for present values and future values. In many situations, however, we need to solve for either r or n. In this section, we give a couple of situations where we might want to solve for these variables. We show the financial calculator solutions only, because the algebraic (equation) solutions are more complicated.

4-4a Solving for r

Suppose you can buy a security at a price of $78.35 that will pay you $100 after five years. What annual rate of return will you earn if you purchase the security? Here you know PV, FV, and n, but you do not know r, the interest rate that you will earn on your investment. The timeline setup is:

Using your financial calculator, enter the known values into the appropriate locations—that is, N = 5, PV = −78.35, PMT = 0, and FV = 100—and then solve for the unknown value.

Inputs: 5   ?   −78.35   0   100.00
         [N]   [I/Y]   [PV]   [PMT]   [FV]
Output: = 5.00

4-4b Solving for n

Suppose you know that a security will provide a return of 10 percent per year, it will cost $68.30 to purchase, and you want to keep the investment until it grows to a value of $100. How long will it take the investment to grow to $100? In this case, we know PV, FV, and r, but we do not know n, the number of periods. The timeline setup is:

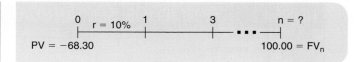

Using your financial calculator, enter I/Y = 10, PV = −68.30, PMT = 0, and FV = 100; then solve for n = 4.

Inputs: ?   10   −68.30   0   100.00
        [N]   [I/Y]   [PV]   [PMT]   [FV]
Output: = 4.0

The same steps can be applied to solve for r and n for annuities. We will discuss how to determine r for an uneven cash flow stream later in the book.

4-5 Annual Percentage Rate (APR) and Effective Annual Rate (EAR)

In all of our examples to this point, we assumed that interest was compounded once per year or annually. This is called **annual compounding**. Suppose, however, that you earn interest more often than once per year—say, twice per year (**semiannual compounding**), four times per year (quarterly compounding), or every day (daily compounding). In this section, we compare the rate of return that is earned when interest is paid once per year (annually) with the rate that is earned when interest is paid more than once per year.

4-5a Semiannual and Other Compounding Periods

To illustrate semiannual compounding, let's return to the example we introduced at the beginning of the chapter: Assume that $700 is invested at an annual interest rate of 10 percent for a period of three years. Earlier we showed what happens when interest is *compounded annually*: The interest that is earned will grow the investment to $931.70 at the end of three years.

How would the future value change if interest is paid twice each year, that is, semi-annually? Look at the timeline in Figure 4.2.

> **annual compounding** The process of determining the future (or present) value of a cash flow or series of cash flows when interest is paid once per year.
>
> **semiannual compounding** The process of determining the future (or present) value of a cash flow or series of cash flows when interest is paid twice per year.

FIGURE 4.2   TIMELINE: SEMIANNUAL COMPOUNDING

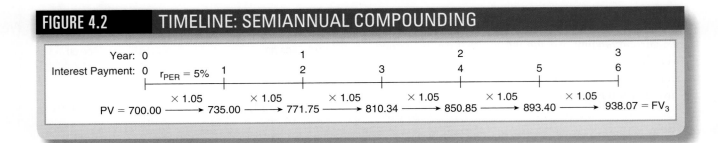

To find the future value, we apply Equation 4.1, generally after making the two adjustments that are shown on the cash flow timeline: (1) convert the annual interest rate to a rate per period (*periodic rate*) and (2) convert the investment period from the number of years to the number of interest payments (compounding periods) during the life of the investment. These two conversions are shown in Equations 4.10 and 4.11:

4.10

$$\text{Periodic rate} = r_{PER} = \frac{\left(\begin{array}{c}\text{Stated annual}\\\text{interest rate}\end{array}\right)}{\left(\begin{array}{c}\text{Number of interest}\\\text{payments per year}\end{array}\right)}$$

$$= \frac{r_{SIMPLE}}{m}$$

4.11

$$\text{Number of interest periods} = n_{PER} = \left(\begin{array}{c}\text{Number}\\\text{of years}\end{array}\right) \times \left(\begin{array}{c}\text{Number of interest}\\\text{payments per year}\end{array}\right)$$

$$= n_{YRS} \times m$$

Here m is the number of interest payments per year, r_{SIMPLE} is the simple (noncompounded) annual interest rate, r_{PER} is the rate of interest that is paid *each* compounding period, n_{YRS} is the number of years interest is earned, and n_{PER} is the total number of interest payments during the n_{YRS} years (periods). Note that $r_{PER} = r_{SIMPLE}$ and $n_{PER} = n_{YRS}$ only when interest is compounded annually; when interest is compounded more than once per year, $r_{PER} < r_{SIMPLE}$ and $n_{PER} > n_{YRS}$.

In our current example, if interest is paid semiannually for three years, there are $n_{PER} = 2 \times 3 = 6$ interest payments during the life of the investment, and interest is paid at a rate equal to $r_{PER} = r_{SIMPLE}/m = 10\%/2 =$

5% every six months. If we make these adjustments and apply Equation 4.1, we find:

$$FV_3 = \$700 \left(1 + \frac{0.10}{2}\right)^{3 \times 2} = \$700(1.05)^6$$

$$= \$700(1.340096) = \$938.07$$

The financial calculator solution is

Inputs:	6	5	−700	0	?
	N	I/Y	PV	PMT	FV
Output:					= 938.07

As you can see, the value in three years of $700 invested today at a 10 percent interest rate is higher when interest is compounded semiannually ($938.07) than when interest is compounded annually ($931.70). We discuss the reason for this difference next.

4-5b Comparison of Different Interest Rates

In the previous section we showed that the dollar interest earned on an investment is greater when interest is computed (*compounded*) more than once per year. In simple terms, this means that the *effective* return earned on an investment is higher than the stated, or simple, return (r_{SIMPLE}) when interest is paid more than once per year. For example, in previous sections we discovered that $700 invested for three years at 10 percent will grow to $931.70 when interest is compounded annually, whereas the same $700 will grow to $938.07 when interest is compounded semiannually. Because the total interest earned is greater when interest is compounded semiannually, the effective annual return that is earned with semiannual compounding is greater than with annual compounding.

Because different compounding periods are used for different types of investments, we must state returns on a comparable basis to make correct financial decisions. This requires us to distinguish between the *simple* (or *quoted*) *interest rate* and the *effective annual rate (EAR)* that an investment earns.

▶ In our example, the **simple, or quoted, interest rate**, which we designate r_{SIMPLE}, is 10 percent. Often interest is quoted as a simple annual rate along with an indication of the number of times interest will be paid during the year. In our current example, the quoted rate is *10 percent, compounded semiannually*. The simple rate is also called the **annual percentage rate**, or **APR**, and it is generally one of the rates that is reported to you by lenders when you borrow money. The APR is a noncompounded interest rate because it does not consider the effect of compounding when interest is paid more than once per year.

▶ To compare loans (or investments) when interest is paid at different times during the year, we must compare the loans' (investments') effective annual interest rates, not their APRs. The **effective (equivalent) annual rate**, which we designate (r_{EAR}), is defined as the rate that would produce the same future value when annual interest compounding exists. To find r_{EAR}, we convert the APR to its equivalent annual rate of return based on the number of interest payments each year—that is, we adjust APR to include the effects of compounded interest.

▶ If interest is computed once each year—that is, compounded annually—$r_{EAR} = r_{SIMPLE} =$ APR. But, *if compounding occurs more than once per year, the effective annual rate is greater than the simple, or quoted, interest rate*; that is, $r_{EAR} > r_{SIMPLE}$.

In our example, r_{EAR} is the rate that will grow a $700 investment today to $938.07 at the end of three years if interest is paid once per year rather than twice per year. Thus, we have the following situation:

Year: 0	r_{EAR} = ?	1	2	3
−700				938.07

Using a financial calculator, enter N = 3, PV = −700, PMT = 0, and FV = 938.07; then solve for I/Y = 10.25 = r_{EAR}.

We can compute the effective annual rate, given the simple rate, r_{SIMPLE}, and the number of compounding periods per year, m, by solving Equation 4.12:

4.12

$$\text{Effective annual rate (EAR)} = r_{EAR} = \left(1 + \frac{r_{SIMPLE}}{m}\right)^m - 1.0$$
$$= (1 + r_{PER})^m - 1.0$$

Using Equation 4.12 to find the r_{EAR} if the simple rate is 10 percent and interest is paid semiannually, we have:

$$r_{EAR} = \left(1 + \frac{0.10}{2}\right)^2 - 1.0$$
$$= (1.05)^2 - 1.0 = 1.1025 - 1.0$$
$$= 0.1025 = 10.25\%$$

To compute r_{EAR} for this situation using a financial calculator, enter N = 2 = number of interest payments each year, I/Y = 5 = interest rate for each interest payment, PV = −1 (assume $1 is invested today), and PMT = 0; then solve for FV = 1.1025. The result indicates to what amount an investment of $1 will grow in one year. We compute the return that would be earned during the year by subtracting 1.0 and converting the result to a percentage; that is, r_{EAR} = 1.1025 − 1.000 = 0.1025 = 10.25%.

Now let's determine to what amount an investment of $700 will grow if it earns 10.25 percent interest that is *compounded annually* for three years:

$$FV_3 = \$700(1.1025)^3$$
$$= \$700(1.340096)$$
$$= \$938.07$$

Using a financial calculator, enter N = 3, I/Y = 10.25, PV = −700, and PMT = 0; then solve for FV = 938.07.

Note that when $700 is invested for

hywards/Shutterstock.com

simple (quoted) interest rate (r_{SIMPLE}) The annual, non-compounded rate, quoted by borrowers and lenders; it is used to determine the rate earned per compounding period (periodic rate, r_{PER}).

annual percentage rate (APR) Another name for the simple interest rate, r_{SIMPLE}; does not consider the effect of interest compounding.

effective (equivalent) annual rate (r_{EAR}) The annual rate of interest actually being earned, as opposed to the quoted rate; considers the compounding of interest.

three years at 10.25 percent compounded annually, the future value is the same as when $700 is invested for three years at 10 percent compounded semiannually. As a result, we can conclude that the investment that pays 10 percent compounded semiannually earns the same rate of return as the investment that pays 10.25 percent compounded annually. This means that both investments have an *effective*, or actual, rate of return that equals 10.25 percent—that is, $r_{EAR} = 10.25\%$. Also, note that the answer to the question that was posed at the beginning of the chapter is different if interest is compounded more than once per year. We discovered earlier that you should choose a payment of $935 in three years rather than a payment of $700 today if your opportunity cost is 10 percent compounded annually, because the $700 would grow to only $931.70 if it were invested for three years. However, the current example shows that when interest is compounded semiannually, this same $700 would grow to $938.07 in three years, which is greater than the $935 payment that Option B promises. Thus, when interest is compounded semiannually, Option A, which pays $700 today, is preferable to Option B.

4-6 Amortized Loans

One of the most important applications of compound interest involves loans that are paid off in installments over time. Included in this category are automobile loans, home mortgages, student loans, and some business debt. If a loan is to be repaid in equal periodic amounts (monthly, quarterly, or annually), it is said to be an **amortized loan**.[7]

To illustrate, suppose that you borrow $15,000 for a business that you own, and the loan is to be repaid in three equal payments at the end of each of the next three years. The lender will charge 8 percent interest on the amount of the loan balance that is outstanding at the beginning of each year. Our first task is to determine the amount that you must repay each year; that is, the annual loan payment. To find this amount,

amortized loan A loan that requires equal payments over its life; the payments include both interest and repayment of the debt.

amortization schedule A schedule showing precisely how a loan will be repaid. It gives the payment required on each payment date and a breakdown of the payment, showing how much is interest and how much is repayment of principal.

recognize that the $15,000 represents the present value of an ordinary annuity of PMT dollars per year for three years, discounted at 8 percent.

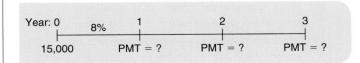

Using a financial calculator, the solution is

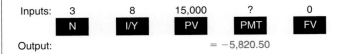

The payments represent an ordinary annuity because each payment is made at the end of the year.

Each payment on an amortized loan consists partly of interest and partly of repayment of the amount borrowed (called the *principal*). This breakdown is given in the **amortization schedule** shown in Table 4.2. Note that the interest component is largest in the first year when the greatest amount is owed (outstanding) on the loan, and it declines as the outstanding balance of the loan decreases. For tax purposes, a business borrower reports the interest component shown in Column 3 as a deductible cost each year, whereas the lender reports this amount as taxable income. The same logic that is presented in Table 4.2 can be used to create amortization schedules for home mortgages, automobile loans, and other amortized loans.[8]

Column 5 in Table 4.2 shows the outstanding balance that is due for our illustrative loan at the end of each year. If you do not have an amortization schedule, you can still determine the outstanding balance of the loan by computing the present value of the *remaining* loan payments. For example, after the first loan payment of $5,820.50 is made at the end of Year 1, the loan agreement calls for two more payments equal to $5,820.50 each. Remember that a portion of each $5,820.50 payment includes a payment for interest on the amount of the loan that has not been repaid; the

---

[7]The word *amortized* comes from the Latin *mors*, meaning death, so an amortized loan is one that is "killed off" over time.

[8]Financial calculators and spreadsheets are programmed to calculate amortization tables—you simply enter the data and apply the appropriate built-in function. If you have a financial calculator, it is worthwhile to read the appropriate section of the manual and learn how to use its amortization feature. Similarly, it is worth your time to learn how to set up an amortization table using a spreadsheet.

Table 4.2

Loan Amortization Schedule; $15,000 Loan at 8 Percent Interest Rate

Year	Beginning of Year Balance (1)	Payment (2)	Interest @ 8%[a] (3) = (1) × 0.08	Repayment of Principal[b] (4) = (2) − (3)	Remaining Loan Balance[c] (5) = (1) − (4)
1	$15,000.00	$5,820.50	$1,200.00	$4,620.50	$10,379.50
2	10,379.50	5,820.50	830.36	4,990.14	5,389.36
3	5,389.36	5,820.50	431.15	5,389.35	0.01

[a]Interest is calculated by multiplying the loan balance in Column 1 by the interest rate (0.08). For example, the interest in Year 2 is $10,379.50 × 0.08 = $830.36.

[b]Repayment of principal (shown in Column 4) is equal to the payment of $5,820.50 in Column 2 minus the interest charge for each year in Column 3. For example, the repayment of principal in Year 2 is $5,820.50 − $830.36 = $4,990.14.

[c]The $0.01 remaining balance at the end of Year 3 results from a rounding difference.

© Cengage Learning 2013

remainder of the $5,820.50 represents repayment of the loan. Thus, to determine the total amount of these payments that represents repayment of the loan only, you must take out the portion of each payment that represents interest. We can "de-interest" the future payments by computing the present value of the two remaining payments. Using a financial calculator, enter N = 2, I/Y = 8, PMT = −5,820.50, and FV = 0; then solve for PV = 10,379.49 = PVA$_1$, which is the remaining balance at the end of Year 1 that is shown in Column 5 in Table 4.2 (there is a rounding difference in the table).

STUDY TOOLS

LOCATED AT BACK OF THE TEXTBOOK

- ☐ Problems are found at the end of this chapter.
- ☐ A tear-out Chapter Review card is located at the back of the textbook.

LOCATED AT WWW.CENGAGEBRAIN.COM

- ☐ Review Key Term flashcards and create your own cards.
- ☐ Track your knowledge and understanding of key concepts in corporate finance.
- ☐ Complete practice and graded quizzes to prepare for tests.
- ☐ Complete interactive content within CFIN5 Online.
- ☐ View the chapter highlight boxes for CFIN5 Online.

KEY TIME VALUE OF MONEY CONCEPTS

To conclude this chapter, we summarize some TVM concepts (rules) that were discussed.

- Before making financial decisions, dollars from different time periods must be stated in the same "time value"—that is, all dollars must be valued at the same time period before they can be compared.

- Everything else equal, an amount that is invested at a higher rate or for a longer time period will grow to a greater future amount (future value), because a greater amount of interest is earned.

- The further in the future an amount is received (paid) or the higher the interest rate, the lower the present value of the future amount; less money must be invested today to accumulate the future amount because more interest is earned during the investment period. Based on this TVM rule, we know that, everything else equal, the current value of an investment is lower the higher the interest rate it earns in the future. This is an important financial concept that we will discuss throughout the book.

- Everything else equal, the greater the number of compounding periods per year, the greater the effective rate of return that is earned on an investment. In other words, the total dollar amount of interest that is earned on an investment is greater when interest is compounded more often during the year.

PROBLEMS

4–1 If Samantha invests $700 today in an account that pays 4 percent interest compounded annually, how much will she have in her account four years from today?

4–2 Fifteen (15) years ago, your parents purchased an investment for $2,500. If the investment earned 6 percent interest each year, how much is it worth today?

4–3 Fiona plans to invest $500 later today. She wants to know to what amount her investment will grow in 20 years if she earns 12 percent interest compounded (a) annually, (b) quarterly, and (c) monthly.

4–4 Staci invested $950 five years ago. Her investment paid 7.2 percent interest compounded monthly. Staci's twin sister Shelli invested $900 at the same time. But Shelli's investment earned 8 percent interest compounded quarterly. How much is each investment worth today?

4–5 What is the present value of $1,500 due in 14 years at a (a) 5 percent interest rate and (b) 10 percent rate. Explain why the present value is lower when the interest rate is higher.

4–6 Matt is considering the purchase of an investment that will pay him $12,500 in 12 years. If Matt wants to earn a return equal to 7 percent per year (annual compounding), what is the maximum amount he should be willing to pay for the investment today?

4–7 What is the present value (PV) of an investment that will pay $2,500 in five years if the opportunity cost rate is 9 percent compounded (a) annually, (b) quarterly, and (c) monthly? Explain why the PV is lowest when interest is compounded monthly.

4–8 If Quincy can invest at an opportunity cost rate equal to 12 percent compounded monthly, what lump-sum amount should he invest today so that he has $22,000 to buy a new car in three years?

4–9 Suppose you invest $385 at the end of each of the next eight years. (a) If your opportunity cost rate is 7 percent compounded annually, how much will your investment be worth after the last $385 payment is made? (b) What will be the ending amount if the payments are made at the beginning of each year?

4–10 At the end of each of the past 14 years, Vanessa deposited $450 in an account that earned 8 percent compounded annually. (a) How much is in the account today? (b) How much would be in the account if the deposits were made at the beginning each year rather than at the end of each year?

4–11 Suppose your opportunity cost rate is 11 percent compounded annually. (a) How much must you deposit in an account today if you want to pay yourself $230 at the end of each of the next 15 years? (b) How much must you deposit if you want to pay yourself $230 at the beginning of each of the next 15 years?

4-12 Compute the amount Amanda must deposit in an account today so that she can pay herself $450 per month for the next nine years if her opportunity cost rate is 8.4 percent compounded monthly. How much must Amanda deposit today if she wants to pay herself at the beginning of each month?

4-13 Kym plans to deposit $100 in an account at the end of each month for the next five years so that she can take a trip. (a) If Kym's opportunity cost rate is 6 percent compounded monthly, how much will she have in the account in five years? (b) How much will be in the account if the deposits are made at the beginning of each month?

4-14 Rebecca would like to set up an account to supplement her parents' retirement income for the next 15 years. (a) If the account earns 7.2 percent compounded monthly, how much will Rebecca have to deposit today so that her parents are paid $150 at the end of each month? (b) How much would she have to deposit if her parents wanted to receive the $150 payment at the beginning of each month?

4-15 If the opportunity cost rate is 7.5 percent, what is the present value of an investment that pays $500 at the end of this year, $400 at the end of the next year, and $300 at the end of the following year? What is the present value if the payments are made at the beginning of each year?

4-16 Suppose Jennifer deposits $500 in an account at the end of this year, $400 at the end of the next year, and $300 at the end of the following year. If her opportunity cost rate is 7.5 percent, how much will be in the account immediately after the third deposit is made? How much will be in the account at the end of three years if the deposits are made at the beginning of each year?

4-17 Compute the present value (PV) of an annuity that pays $320 forever if the opportunity cost rate is (a) 4 percent, (b) 8 percent, and (c) 10 percent. Why does the PV decrease as the opportunity cost increases?

4-18 Ten years ago, Bruce invested $1,250. Today, the investment is worth $3,550. If interest is compounded annually, what annual rate of return did Bruce earn on his investment?

4-19 Tina owes $12,000 on her automobile loan, which has an interest rate equal to 4.8 percent compounded monthly. If Tina pays $526 at the end of each month, how long will it take her to repay the loan?

4-20 Mario wants to take a trip that costs $4,750, but currently he only has $2,260 saved. If Mario invests this money at 7 percent compounded annually, how long will it take for his investment to grow to $4,750?

4-21 CanAm Financial offers investments that pay 12 percent interest compounded monthly, whereas UniMex Financial offers investments that pay 12.25 percent interest compounded semiannually. Which investment offers the better effective annual return?

4-22 Yolanda's bank advertises a savings investment that pays 6 percent compounded monthly. What is the investment's (a) annual percentage rate (APR) and (b) effective annual rate (r_{EAR})?

4-23 William recently graduated from NFA University. While at NFA, William took out a $50,000 student loan. His loan requires him to make monthly payments for a 10-year period. (a) If the simple annual interest is 4.2 percent, what are William's monthly payments? (b) To the nearest dollar, how much will William owe on his student loan after he makes payments for three years?

4-24 When Sarah Jean purchased her house 12 years ago, she took out a 30-year mortgage for $220,000. The mortgage has a fixed interest rate of 6 percent compounded monthly. (a) Compute Sarah Jean's monthly mortgage payments. (b) If Sarah Jean wants to pay off her mortgage today, for how much should she write a check? She made her most recent mortgage payment earlier today.

4-25 Nona purchased a new car earlier today for $32,000. She financed the entire amount using a five-year loan with a 3 percent interest rate (compounded monthly). (a) Compute the monthly payments for the loan. (b) How much will Nona owe on the loan after she makes payments for two years (i.e., after 24 payments)?

part **3**

After you finish this chapter go to **PAGE 98** for **STUDY TOOLS**

LEARNING OUTCOMES

After studying this chapter, you will be able to…

LO1 Describe the cost of money and factors that affect the cost of money (interest rates).

LO2 Describe how interest rates are determined.

LO3 Describe a yield curve and discuss how a yield curve might be used to forecast future interest rates.

LO4 Discuss how government actions and general business activity affect interest rates.

LO5 Describe how changes in interest rates (returns) affect the values of stocks and bonds.

The Cost of Money (Interest Rates)

In a free economy such as that of the United States, the excess funds of lenders are allocated to borrowers in the financial markets through a pricing system that is based on the supply of and the demand for funds. This system is represented by interest rates, or the *cost of money*, which permits those borrowers who are willing to pay the rates that prevail in the financial markets to use funds provided by others. In this chapter, we describe basic concepts associated with interest rates, including factors that affect rates and methods for forecasting them.

dollar return as a percentage of the dollar amount that was originally invested. Thus, the yield on an investment is computed as shown in Equation 5.1:

5.1

$$\text{Yield} = \frac{\text{Dollar return}}{\text{Beginning value}} = \frac{\text{Dollar income} + \text{Capital gains}}{\text{Beginning value}}$$

$$= \frac{\text{Dollar income} + (\text{Ending value} - \text{Beginning value})}{\text{Beginning value}}$$

Here, "Beginning value" represents the market value of the investment at the beginning of the period for which the yield is computed, and "Ending value" represents its market value at the end of the period.

If the financial asset is debt, the income from the investment consists of the *interest* paid by the borrower. If the financial asset is equity, the income from the investment is the *dividend* paid by a corporation. Although the "Dollar income" must be either zero or positive, "Capital gains" can be negative if the value of the investment decreases during the period it is held.

To illustrate the concept of yield, consider the return that you would earn if you purchased a corporate bond on January 2, 2016, for $980 and sold it one year later for $990.25. If the bond paid $100 interest on December 31, 2016, the bond's one-year yield, or *percentage return*, would be

$$\begin{aligned}\text{Yield} \atop \text{(\% return)} &= \frac{\$100.00 + (\$990.25 - \$980.00)}{\$980.00} \\ &= \frac{\$110.25}{\$980.00} = 0.1125 = 11.25\%\end{aligned}$$

5-1 The Cost of Money

In this section, we explain what the cost of money is and discuss general factors that affect interest rates (the cost of money). The discussion is meant to provide only a simple overview of the cost of money.

5-1a Realized Returns (Yields)

Investors determine rates of return through their buying and selling actions in the financial markets. Regardless of the type of investment, the dollar return an investor earns is divided into two categories: (1) income paid by the *issuer* of the financial asset (perhaps a stock or a bond) and (2) the change in the market value of the asset (capital gains) over some time period. To determine an investment's yield, we state its

In this example, investors who purchased the bond at the beginning of 2016, and held it for one year would have earned a one-year holding-period return equal to 11.25 percent. If we assume that this is the same return that investors expected to earn when they purchased the bond at the beginning of the year, then this yield represents the average rate of return that investors required to provide their funds to the company that issued the bond. In other words, the *cost of money* for such a corporation was essentially 11.25 percent in 2016. In the remainder of this chapter, we discuss factors that determine the cost of money and examine what causes the cost of money to change.

5-1b Factors That Affect the Cost of Money

Four fundamental factors affect the cost of money: (1) *production opportunities*, (2) *time preferences for consumption*, (3) *risk*, and (4) *inflation*. To see how these factors operate, imagine an isolated island community where the people survive by eating fish. They have a stock of fishing gear that permits them to live reasonably well, but they would like to have more fish. Now suppose Mr. Crusoe has a bright idea for a new type of fishnet that would enable him to increase his daily catch substantially. It would take him one year to perfect his design, build his net, and learn how to use it efficiently. Mr. Crusoe probably would starve before he could put his new net into operation. Recognizing this problem, he might suggest to Ms. Robinson, Mr. Friday, and several others that if they would give him one fish each day for one year, he would return two fish per day during all of the following year. If Ms. Robinson accepted the offer, then the fish that she gave to Mr. Crusoe would constitute *savings* that she is willing to *invest* in the fishnet, and the extra fish the net produced in the future would constitute a *return on the investment*. Obviously, the more productive Mr. Crusoe thought the new fishnet would be—that is, the higher the **production opportunity**—the higher his expected return on the investment would be, and the more he could afford to offer potential investors to attract their savings. In this example, we assume that Mr. Crusoe thinks he will be able to pay, and thus has offered to give back two fish for every one fish he receives, which is a 100 percent rate of return. He might have tried to attract savings for less—say, 1.5 fish next year for every one fish he receives this year.

The attractiveness of Mr. Crusoe's offer to a potential saver would depend in large part on the saver's **time preference for consumption**. For example, Ms. Robinson might be thinking of retirement, and she might be willing to trade fish today for fish in the future on a one-for-one basis, whereas Mr. Friday might be unwilling to "lend" a fish today for anything less than three fish next year because he has a wife and several young children to feed with his current fish. Mr. Friday is said to have a *high time preference for consumption*, whereas Ms. Robinson has a *low time preference for consumption*. Note also that if the entire population is living at the subsistence level, everything else the same, time preferences for current consumption would necessarily be high, aggregate savings would be low, interest rates would be high, and capital formation would be difficult.

The **risk** inherent in the fishnet project, and thus in Mr. Crusoe's ability to repay the loan, also affects the return required by investors: The higher the perceived risk, the higher the required rate of return. For example, if Mr. Crusoe has a history of not always following through with his ideas, those who are interested in Mr. Crusoe's new fishnet would consider the investment to be fairly risky, and thus they might provide Mr. Crusoe with one fish per day this year only if he promises to return four fish per day next year. In addition, a more complex society includes many businesses like Mr. Crusoe's, many goods other than fish, and many savers like Ms. Robinson and Mr. Friday. Furthermore, most people use money as a medium of exchange rather than bartering with fish. When a society uses money, its value in the future, which is affected by inflation, comes into play. That is, the higher the expected rate of **inflation**, the greater the return required to compensate investors for the loss in purchasing power caused by the inflation.

This simple illustration shows that the interest rate paid to savers depends in a basic way on (1) *the rate of return that producers expect to earn on their invested capital*, (2) *savers' time preferences for current consumption versus future consumption*, (3) *the riskiness of the loan*, and (4) *the expected future rate of inflation*. The returns that borrowers expect to earn by investing borrowed funds set an upper limit on how much they can pay for such funds. In turn, consumers' time preferences for consumption establish how much consumption they are willing to defer, and hence how much they will save at different levels of interest offered by borrowers. Higher risk and higher inflation also lead to higher interest rates.

production opportunity The return available within an economy from investment in a productive (cash-generating) asset.

time preference for consumption The preference of a consumer for current consumption as opposed to saving for future consumption.

risk In a financial market context, the chance that a financial asset will not earn the return promised.

inflation The tendency of prices to increase over time.

5-1c Interest Rate Levels

Funds are allocated among borrowers by interest rates. Firms with the most profitable investment opportunities are willing and able to pay the most for capital, so they tend to attract it away from less-efficient firms or from firms whose products are not in demand. Of course, our economy is not completely free in the sense of being influenced only by market forces. As a result, the federal government supports agencies that help designated individuals or groups obtain credit on favorable terms. Among those eligible for this kind of assistance are small businesses, certain minorities, and firms willing to build facilities in areas characterized by high unemployment. Even with these government interventions, most capital in the U.S. economy is allocated through the price system (i.e., interest rates).

Figure 5.1 shows how supply and demand interact to determine interest rates in two capital markets. Markets A and B represent two of the many capital markets in existence. The going interest rate, which we designate as r for this discussion, initially is 6 percent for the low-risk securities in Market A. That is, borrowers whose credit is strong enough to qualify for this market can obtain funds at a cost of 6 percent, and investors who want to put their money to work without much risk can obtain a 6 percent return. Riskier borrowers must borrow higher-cost funds in Market B. Investors who are willing to take on more risk invest in Market B expecting to earn a 9 percent return, but they also realize that they might actually receive much less (or much more).

If the demand for funds declines, as it typically does during business recessions, the demand curves will shift to the left, as shown in Curve D_{A2} in Market A. The market-clearing, or *equilibrium*, interest rate in this example then falls to 5 percent. Similarly, you should be able to visualize what would happen if the supply of funds tightens: The supply curve, S_{A1}, would shift to the left, which would raise interest rates and lower the level of borrowing in the economy.

Financial markets are interdependent. For example, if Markets A and B were in equilibrium before the demand shifted to D_{A2} in Market A, it means

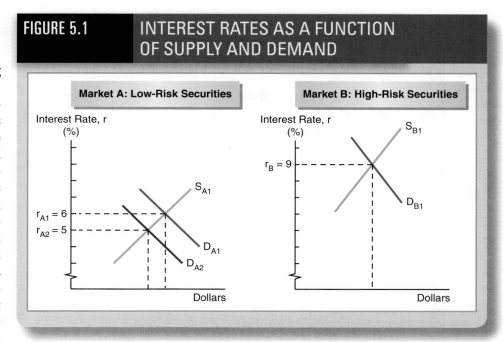

FIGURE 5.1   INTEREST RATES AS A FUNCTION OF SUPPLY AND DEMAND

that investors were willing to accept the higher risk in Market B in exchange for a *risk premium* of 3% = 9% − 6%. After the shift to D_{A2}, the risk premium would initially increase to 4% = 9% − 5%. In all likelihood, this larger premium would induce some of the lenders in Market A to shift to Market B, which in turn would cause the supply curve in Market A to shift to the left (or up) as funds flow out and the supply curve in Market B to shift to the right as funds from Market A are invested. The transfer of capital between markets would raise the interest rate in Market A and lower it in Market B, thereby bringing the risk premium closer to the original level, 3 percent. We know, for example, that when rates on Treasury securities increase, the rates on corporate bonds and mortgages generally follow suit.

As discussed in Chapter 3, many financial markets are found in the United States and throughout the world. There are markets for short-term debt, long-term debt, home loans, student loans, business loans, government loans, and so forth. Prices are established for each type of funds, and these prices change over time as shifts occur in supply and demand conditions. Figure 5.2 illustrates how long- and short-term interest rates paid by business borrowers have varied since 1990. Notice that short-term interest rates are especially prone to rise during booms and then fall during recessions. (The tall blue-shaded areas of the chart indicate recessions.) When the economy is expanding, firms need capital, and this demand for capital pushes rates higher. Inflationary pressures are strongest during business booms, which also exert upward pressure on rates. Conditions are reversed during recessions, such as the ones during 2001

FIGURE 5.2   LONG- AND SHORT-TERM INTEREST RATES, 1990–2015

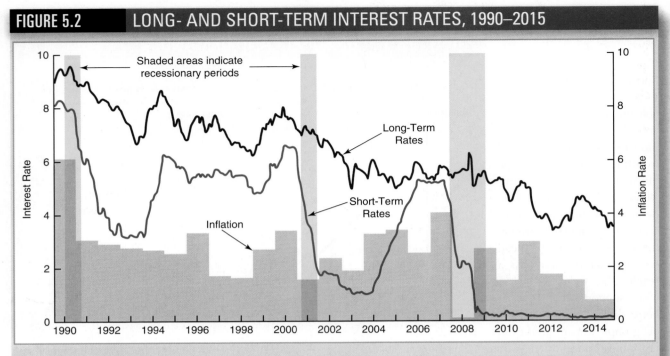

Notes:

1. Short-term interest rates are measured by three-month loans to very large, strong corporations, and long-term rates are measured by AAA corporate bonds.
2. Tick marks on the *X*-axis represent the middle of the year—that is, July 1.

Sources: Interest rates are found at the Federal Reserve website at www.federalreserve.gov/; information about recessions can be found at the National Bureau of Economic Research website at www.nber.org/cycles.html/, and CPI data are found at the website of the U.S. Department of Labor, Bureau of Labor, at www.bls.gov.

and 2007–2009. In these periods, a slowdown in business reduces the demand for credit, the rate of inflation falls, and thus interest rates generally decline.

These tendencies do not hold exactly. For example, the price of oil fell dramatically in 1985 and 1986, reducing inflationary pressures on other prices and easing fears of serious long-term inflation. In earlier years, these fears had pushed interest rates to record high levels (e.g., greater than 15 percent in 1982). From 1984 to 1987, the economy was fairly strong, but dwindling fears about inflation more than offset the normal tendency of interest rates to rise during good economic times, and the net result was lower interest rates.[1]

5-2 Determinants of Market Interest Rates

In general, the quoted (or nominal) interest rate, r, on *any* security traded in the financial markets is composed of a risk-free rate of interest plus a premium that reflects the riskiness of the security. This relationship can be expressed as shown in Equation 5.2:

5.2

$$\text{Rate of return} = r = \left(\begin{array}{c}\text{Risk-free} \\ \text{rate}\end{array}\right) + \left(\begin{array}{c}\text{Risk} \\ \text{premium}\end{array}\right)$$

This relationship is illustrated in Figure 5.3, which shows that investors require greater returns to invest in securities with greater risks. Although we discuss risk and return in detail in Chapter 8, the discussion in this section will give you an indication as to the general factors that affect interest rates on such debt securities as bonds.

The interest on *debt* can be expressed as shown in Equation 5.3:

5.3

$$r = r_{RF} + \qquad\qquad RP$$
$$= r_{RF} + [DRP + LP + MRP]$$

[1]Short-term rates respond to current economic conditions, whereas long-term rates primarily reflect long-run expectations for inflation. As a result, short-term rates are sometimes higher than and sometimes lower than long-term rates. The relationship between long-term and short-term rates is called *term structure of interest rates*. This topic is discussed later in the chapter.

FIGURE 5.3

RATE OF RETURN (INTEREST RATE)

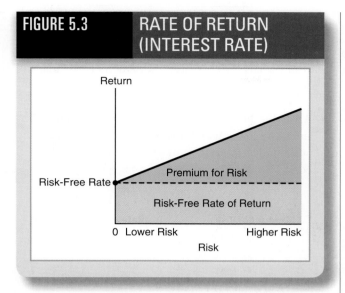

The variables in Equation 5.3 are defined as follows:

- **r** = the quoted, or *nominal*, rate of interest on a given security.[2] There are many different securities with different levels of risk; hence, there are many different quoted interest rates.

- r_{RF} = the quoted risk-free rate of return. Theoretically, this rate is the return associated with an investment that has a guaranteed outcome in the future—that is, it has no risk.

- **RP** = risk premium, which is the return that exceeds the risk-free rate of return, r_{RF}, and thus represents payment for the risk associated with an investment. RP = r − r_{RF} = DRP + LP + MRP.

- **DRP** = default risk premium, which reflects the chance that the borrower—that is, the issuer of the security—will not pay the debt's interest or principal on time.

- **LP** = liquidity, or marketability, premium, which reflects the fact that some investments are more easily converted into cash on short notice at a reasonable price than are other securities.

- **MRP** = maturity risk premium, which accounts for the fact that longer-term bonds experience greater price reactions to interest rate changes than do short-term bonds.

[2] The term *nominal* as it is used here means the *stated* rate as opposed to the *real* rate, which is adjusted to remove the effects of inflation. If you bought a 10-year Treasury bond in May 2015, the quoted, or nominal, rate was about 2.1 percent, but because inflation was expected to average 1.1 percent over the next 10 years, the real rate was 1.0% = 2.1% − 1.1%.

[3] Clearly, relationships exist among the components that we include in Equation 5.3, which means that they are not strictly additive. To simplify our discussion, however, we assume that these components are additive (independent).

We discuss the components whose sum makes up the quoted, or *nominal*, rate on a given security in the following sections.[3]

5-2a The Nominal, or Quoted, Risk-Free Rate of Interest, r_{RF}

The **nominal**, or **quoted, risk-free rate**, r_{RF}, is the interest rate on a security that has absolutely no risk at all—that is, one that has a guaranteed outcome in the future, regardless of the market conditions. No such security exists in the real world; hence, there is no observable truly risk-free rate. However, there is one security that is free of most risks: a U.S. Treasury bill (T-bill), which is a short-term security issued by the U.S. government.

The nominal risk-free rate, r_{RF}, is comprised of two components: the *"real" risk-free rate*, which we designate r°, and an adjustment for the average inflation that is expected during the life of the investment, which we designate IP, or the *inflation premium*. As a result, r_{RF} = r° + IP in Equation 5.3.

The **real risk-free rate of interest**, **r***, is defined as the interest rate that would exist on a risk-free security *if inflation is expected to be zero* during the investment period. It can be thought of as the rate of interest that would exist on short-term U.S. Treasury securities in an *inflation-free world*. The real risk-free rate changes over time depending on economic conditions, especially (1) the rate of return corporations and other borrowers are willing to pay to borrow funds and (2) people's time preferences for current versus future consumption. It is difficult to measure the real risk-free rate precisely, but most experts think that r° fluctuates in the range of 2 to 4 percent in the United States.

No matter what investments they make, all *investors are affected by inflation*. For this reason, the minimum rate earned on any security, *no matter its risk*, must include compensation for the loss of purchasing power (due to inflation) that is expected during the life of the investment. Thus, r_{RF} must include a component for the average inflation, or purchasing power loss, that investors expect in the future.

5-2b Inflation Premium (IP)

Inflation has a major effect on interest rates because it erodes the purchasing power of the dollar and thus lowers the real rate of

nominal (quoted) risk-free rate, r_{RF} The rate of interest on a security that is free of all risk; r_{RF} is proxied by the T-bill rate and includes an inflation premium.

real risk-free rate of interest, r* The rate of interest that would exist on default-free U.S. Treasury securities if no inflation were expected.

return on investments. To illustrate, suppose you invested $1,000 in a certificate of deposit that matures in one year and pays 4.5 percent interest. At the end of the year you will receive $1,045: your original $1,000 plus $45 of interest. Now suppose the inflation rate during the year is 10 percent and that it affects all items equally. If pizza cost $1.00 per slice at the beginning of the year, it would cost $1.10 at the end of the year. Therefore, your $1,000 could buy $1,000/$1.00 = 1,000 slices of pizza at the beginning of the year but only $1,045/$1.10 = 950 slices at year's end. *In real terms,* therefore, you would be worse off at the end of the year: You would receive $45 in interest, but that amount would not be sufficient to offset the effect of inflation. In this case, you would be better off buying 1,000 slices of frozen pizza (or some other storable asset such as land, timber, apartment buildings, wheat, or gold) than investing in the certificate of deposit.

Investors are well aware of the effect of inflation. When they lend money, therefore, they build in an **inflation premium (IP)** equal to the *average inflation rate expected over the life of the security.* Thus, if the real risk-free rate of interest, r°, is 3 percent, and if inflation is expected to be 2 percent during the next year (and hence IP = 2%), then the quoted rate of interest on one-year T-bills would be $r_{RF} = 3\% + 2\% = 5\%$.[4]

It is important to note that the rate of inflation built into interest rates is the *rate of inflation expected in the future,* not the rate experienced in the past. Note also that the inflation rate reflected in the quoted interest rate of an investment is the *average inflation expected over the life of the investment.* Consequently, the inflation rate that is built into a one-year bond is the expected inflation rate for the next year, but the inflation rate built into a 10-year bond is the average rate of inflation expected over the next 10 years.

inflation premium (IP) A premium investors add to the real risk-free rate of return to account for inflation that is expected to exist during the life of an investment.

default risk premium (DRP) The difference between the interest rate on a U.S. Treasury bond and a corporate bond of equal maturity and marketability; compensation for the risk that a corporation will not meet its debt obligations.

5-2c Default Risk Premium (DRP)

The risk that a borrower will *default* on a loan—that is, not pay the interest or the principal according to the loan contract—also affects the market interest rate on a security: The greater the default risk, the higher the interest rate that lenders charge (demand). Treasury securities have no default risk because everyone believes that the U.S. government will pay its debt on time. For corporate bonds, the better the bond's overall credit rating (AAA is the best), the lower its default risk and consequently the lower its interest rate.[5] Following are some representative interest rates on 10-year bonds that existed in May 2015:[6]

Type of Debt	Amount of Risk	Rate, r	DRP = r − r_{RF}
U.S. Treasury, $r_{Treasury}$	No default risk, r_{RF}	2.1%	—
AAA corporate bond	Default risk greater than T-bonds	4.1	2.0%
BBB corporate bond	Default risk greater than AAA corporate bonds	4.9	2.8
CCC corporate bond	Default risk much greater than BBB corporate bonds	8.8	6.7

Assuming that these bonds have identical provisions, the only reason their rates differ is because their default risks differ. As a result, the difference between the quoted interest rate on a T-bond and that on a corporate bond with similar maturity, liquidity, and other features is the **default risk premium (DRP)**. Thus, if the bonds listed here were otherwise similar, the default risk premium would be DRP = $r_{Corporate\ bond}$ − r_{T-bond}. Default risk premiums vary somewhat over time. Because investors were uncertain about the future of the economy in May 2015, the figures shown in the table are somewhat higher than normal, especially for corporate bonds with high default risks.

5-2d Liquidity Premium (LP)

Liquidity generally is defined as the ability to convert an asset into cash on short notice and reasonably capture the amount initially invested. The more easily an asset

[4]In reality, we should recognize that the purchasing power of the real risk-free rate is also affected by inflation. As a result, it is more appropriate to compute the nominal risk-free rate as $r_{RF} = (1 + r^*)(1 + IP) − 1$, which means that the appropriate rate in our example is $r_{RF} = (1.03)(1.02) − 1 = 0.0506 = 5.06\%$. The additional 0.06 percent represents the increase in the nominal rate associated with the real risk-free rate, r^*, that is needed to ensure investors' wealth actually increases by 3 percent.

[5]Bond ratings, and bonds' riskiness in general, are discussed in more detail in Chapter 6. For this example, note that bonds rated AAA are judged to have less default risk than are bonds rated BBB, and BBB bonds are less risky than CCC bonds.

[6]Sources: http://www.federalreserve.gov/releases/h15/data.htm, http://finance.yahoo.com /bonds/composite_bond_rates, and http://www.bloomberg.com.

can be converted into cash at a price that substantially recovers the initial amount invested, the more liquid it is considered. Clearly, assets have varying degrees of liquidity, depending on the characteristics of the markets in which they are traded. For instance, such financial assets as government securities trade in very active and efficient secondary markets, whereas the markets for real estate are much more restrictive. In addition, it generally is easier to convert an asset into cash at a "good" price the closer the asset's life is to its maturity date. Thus, financial assets generally are more liquid than real assets, and short-term financial assets generally are more liquid than long-term financial assets.

Because liquidity is important, investors evaluate liquidity and include a **liquidity premium (LP)** when the market rate on a security is established. Although it is difficult to accurately measure liquidity premiums, a differential of at least two, and perhaps four or five, percentage points exists between the least liquid and the most liquid financial assets of similar default risk and maturity.

5-2e Maturity Risk Premium (MRP)

The prices of long-term bonds decline (increase) sharply whenever interest rates rise (decline). Because interest rates can and do occasionally rise, *all* long-term bonds—even Treasury bonds—have an element of risk called *interest rate risk*. As a general rule, the bonds of any organization have more interest rate risk the longer the maturity of the bonds.[7] Therefore, the required interest rate must include a **maturity risk premium (MRP)**, which is higher the longer the time to maturity. Such a premium, like the other types of premiums, is extremely difficult to measure. Nevertheless, two things seem clear: (1) The MRP appears to vary over time, rising when interest rates are more volatile and uncertain, then falling when interest rates are more stable; and (2) the MRP on T-bonds with

20–30 years to maturity normally is in the range of one or two percentage points.[8]

To illustrate the effect of time to maturity on the prices of bonds, consider two investments that are identical except for their maturity dates. Both investments promise to pay $1,000 at maturity, but Investment A matures in two years, whereas Investment B matures in 10 years. To simplify this example, let's assume that there currently is no MRP so that the return on both investments is the same. When interest rates are 10 percent and 12 percent, the values of the two bonds are shown here:

Investment	Maturity	Value @ 10%	Value @ 12%	$ Change in Value	% Change in Value
A	2 years	$826.45	$797.19	−$29.26	−3.5%
B	10 years	385.54	321.97	−63.57	−16.5

Note that both the dollar change and the percentage change are greater for the investment with the longer term to maturity—that is, Investment B. This simple example, which illustrates the general concept of maturity risk, shows why investors normally demand higher MRPs for investments with longer terms to maturity.

Although long-term bonds are heavily exposed to interest rate risk, short-term investments are more vulnerable to *reinvestment rate risk*. When short-term investments mature and the proceeds are reinvested, or *rolled over*, a decline in interest rates would necessitate reinvestment at a lower rate, and hence would lead to a decline in interest income. Thus, although investing short-term preserves one's principal, the interest income provided by short-term investments varies from year to year, depending on reinvestment rates. The implications of interest rate risk and reinvestment rate risk are discussed in greater detail in Chapter 6.

5-3 The Term Structure of Interest Rates

A study of Figure 5.2 reveals that at certain times, such as in 2002–2004 and 2008–2010, short-term interest rates are lower than long-term rates. At other times, such as in 2007, short-term rates are

[7]For example, if you had bought a 30-year Treasury bond for $1,000 in 1972, when the long-term interest rate was 7 percent, and held it until 1981, when the long-term T-bond rate was 14.5 percent, the value of the bond would have declined to $514. That decrease would represent a loss of almost half the money, and it demonstrates that long-term bonds—even U.S. Treasury bonds—are not riskless. If you had purchased short-term T-bills in 1972 and subsequently reinvested the principal each time the bills matured, however, you would still have $1,000. This point will be discussed in Chapter 6.

[8]The total MRP from long-term government securities has averaged 1.5–2.0 percent over the last 65–70 years. Thus, the MRP per additional year of maturity has averaged 0.05–0.07 percent. See *Ibbotson SBBI Classic Yearbook: Market Results for Stocks, Bonds, Bills, and Inflation* (Chicago: Morningstar, 2015).

liquidity premium (LP) A premium added to the rate on a security if the security cannot be converted to cash on short notice at a price that is close to the original cost.

maturity risk premium (MRP) A premium that reflects interest rate risk; bonds with longer maturities have greater interest rate risk.

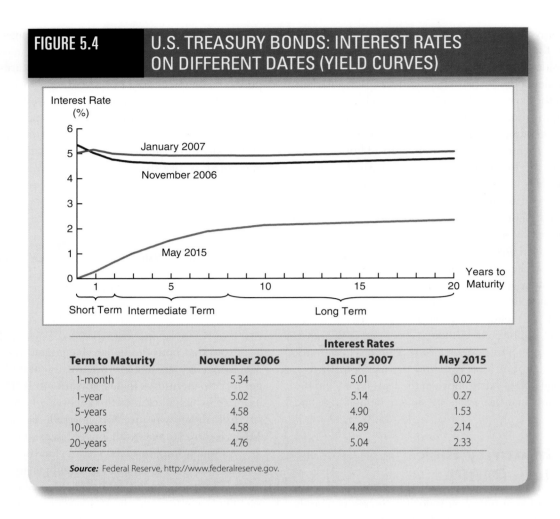

FIGURE 5.4 U.S. TREASURY BONDS: INTEREST RATES ON DIFFERENT DATES (YIELD CURVES)

| | Interest Rates | | |
Term to Maturity	November 2006	January 2007	May 2015
1-month	5.34	5.01	0.02
1-year	5.02	5.14	0.27
5-years	4.58	4.90	1.53
10-years	4.58	4.89	2.14
20-years	4.76	5.04	2.33

Source: Federal Reserve, http://www.federalreserve.gov.

higher than long-term rates. The relationship between long- and short-term rates, which is known as the **term structure of interest rates**, is important to corporate treasurers, who must decide whether to borrow by issuing long- or short-term debt, and to investors, who must decide whether to buy long- or short-term bonds. For these reasons, it is important to understand (1) how long- and short-term rates are related, and (2) what causes shifts in their relative positions.

The relationship between long- and short-term bonds varies and generally is dependent on the supply-and-demand relationship that exists for these bonds at a particular point in time. For example, the tabular section of Figure 5.4 includes interest rates for different maturities on three different dates. The set of data for a given date, when plotted on a graph such as that in Figure 5.4,

term structure of interest rates The relationship between yields and maturities of securities.

yield curve A graph showing the relationship between yields and maturities of securities on a particular date.

normal yield curve An upward-sloping yield curve.

is called the **yield curve** for that date. The yield curve provides a snapshot of the relationship between short- and long-term rates on a particular date. The yield curve changes both in position and in slope over time. For example, in November 2006 the yield curve was *downward sloping* (although not substantially); but, in May 2015 all rates were substantially lower, and long-term rates were higher than short-term rates, so the yield curve at that time was *upward sloping*.[9] In January 2007, rates were similar to those in November 2006, but short- and long-term rates did not differ much, so the yield curve was fairly *flat*, or *horizontal*.

Historically, long-term rates have generally been higher than short-term rates, so the yield curve normally has been upward sloping. For this reason, people often refer to an upward-sloping yield curve as a **normal yield curve**. On the other hand, because a downward-sloping yield curve is pretty rare, we normally refer to this

[9]The yield curve exhibited a fairly dramatic downward slope in March 1980, when short-term rates hovered around 16 percent and long-term rates were approximately 12 percent. During this recessionary period, interest rates remained at historically high levels for several months.

type of curve as an *inverted*, or *abnormal*, *yield curve*. Thus, in Figure 5.4, the yield curve for November 2006 was inverted, but the yield curve for August 2013 was a normal shape (even though all rates were low). In the next section, we discuss three explanations for the shape of the yield curve and explain why an upward-sloping yield curve is considered normal.

5-3a Why Do Yield Curves Differ?

It is clear from Figure 5.4 that the shape of the yield curve at one point in time can be significantly different from the yield curve at another point in time. For example, the yield curve was downward sloping in 2006 whereas it was upward sloping in 2015. Remember that interest rates consist of (1) a risk-free return, r_{RF}, which includes the real risk-free return (r^*) and an adjustment for expected inflation (IP) and (2) a risk premium that rewards investors for various risks, including default risk (DRP), liquidity risk (LP), and maturity risk (MRP). Although the real risk-free rate of return, r^*, does change at times, it generally is relatively stable from period to period. As a result, when interest rates shift to substantially different levels, it generally is because investors have changed either their expectations concerning future inflation or their attitudes concerning risk. Because changes in investors' risk attitudes generally evolve over time (years), *inflation expectations represent the most important factor in the determination of current interest rates,* and thus the shape of the yield curve.

To illustrate how inflation impacts the shape of the yield curve, let's examine interest rates on U.S. Treasury securities. First, the rate of return on these securities can be written as in Equation 5.4:

5.4

$$r_{Treasury} = r_{RF} + MRP = (r^* + IP) + MRP$$

This equation is the same as Equation 5.3, except that neither the default risk premium (DRP) nor the liquidity premium (LP) is included because we generally consider Treasury securities to be liquid (marketable), default-free investments. As a result, DRP = 0 and LP = 0. The maturity risk premium (MRP) is included in the equation because Treasury securities vary in maturity from as short as a few days to as long as 30 years. All else equal, *investors generally prefer to*

hold short-term securities, because such securities are less sensitive to changes in interest rates and provide greater investment flexibility than longer-term securities. As a result, investors will generally accept lower yields on short-term securities, which leads to relatively low short-term rates. *Borrowers,* on the other hand, *generally prefer long-term debt* because short-term debt exposes them to the risk of having to refinance the debt under adverse conditions (e.g., higher interest rates). Accordingly, borrowers want to lock into long-term funds, which means they are willing to pay higher rates, other things held constant, for long-term funds than for short-term funds, which also leads to relatively low short-term rates. Taken together, these two sets of preferences imply that under normal conditions, a positive maturity risk premium (MRP) exists, and the MRP increases with years to maturity, causing the yield curve to be upward sloping. In economics, the general theory that supports this conclusion is referred to as the **liquidity preference theory**, which simply states that long-term bonds normally yield more than short-term bonds, all else equal, primarily because MRP > 0 and MRP increases with time to maturity.

During the past decade, we have observed three basic shapes for the yield curve associated with Treasury securities. Each of the three shapes is shown in Figure 5.4: a normal, or upward-sloping, yield curve; an inverted, or downward-sloping, yield curve; and a flat yield curve. For this reason, although MRP > 0, which supports the *liquidity preference theory,* it appears that this theory does not fully explain the shape of the yield curve. Remember that the nominal risk-free rate of return, r_{RF}, consists of two components: the real risk-free rate of return, r^*, which is considered to be relatively constant from one year to the next, and an adjustment for the inflation expectations of investors, IP—that is, $r_{RF} = r^* + IP$. Expectations about future inflation do vary over time. However, the inflation premium, IP, that is included in interest rates is somewhat predictable because it is the average of the inflation rates that are expected to occur during the life of the investment (a Treasury security in this case). In fact, the yield curve is often used as an aid when forecasting future interest rates because both investors and borrowers base their current decisions on expectations regarding which way interest rates will move in the future. For example, because interest rates were at extremely low levels in 2015, most people

inverted (abnormal) yield curve
A downward-sloping yield curve.

liquidity preference theory
The theory that, all else being equal, lenders prefer to make short-term loans rather than long-term loans; hence, they will lend short-term funds at lower rates than they lend long-term funds.

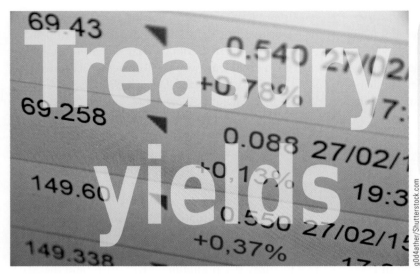

Year	Increasing Inflation	Decreasing Inflation
1	1.0%	5.0%
2	1.8	4.2
3	2.0	4.0
4	2.4	3.4
5	2.8	3.2
After Year 5	3.0	2.4

believed rates most certainly would have to increase in the future. The attitude was that rates could not possibly drop any lower. As a result, homeowners with higher-interest mortgages refinanced their houses to take advantage of, and thus "lock in," lower rates, whereas investors primarily purchased short-term securities in hopes that rates would increase in the future, at which time they would be able to lock in the higher rates. Clearly, the expectations of the participants in the financial markets—that is, investors and borrowers—greatly impact interest rates. The **expectations theory** states that the shape of the yield curve depends on *expectations* concerning future inflation rates. More specifically, the yield curve should be upward sloping when investors expect inflation, and thus interest rates, to increase, and vice versa. We illustrate how expectations can be used to help *forecast* interest rates in the next section.

Let's consider the impact of inflation expectations on the determination of interest rates when inflation is expected to (1) increase in the future and (2) decrease in the future. For both situations, assume the real risk-free rate, r°, is 2 percent and that investors demand a 0.1 percent maturity risk premium for each year remaining until maturity for any debt with a term to maturity greater than one year, with a maximum value of 1 percent. Thus, if a Treasury bill matures in one year, MRP = 0; but, if a Treasury bond matures in five years, MRP = 0.5%, and bonds that mature in 10 years or longer will have MRP = 1.0%. Also, suppose that inflation expectations are as follows for the two situations:

expectations theory The theory that the shape of the yield curve depends on investors' expectations about future inflation rates.

Note that these two situations are not related; that is, we are not assuming that these two patterns of expected inflation can exist at the same time; rather, they are mutually exclusive.

Using this information, we can compute the interest rates for Treasury securities with any term to maturity. To illustrate, consider a bond that matures in five years. For the case in which inflation is expected to *increase*, the interest rate, or yield, on this bond should be 4.5% = 2% + 2% + 0.5% because r° = 2%, IP = 2.0% = (1.0% + 1.8% + 2.0% + 2.4% + 2. 8%)/5, and MRP = 0.5% = 0.1% × 5 years. Note that IP is the average of the inflation rates that investors expect each year during the bond's five-year life. Had we evaluated a 10-year bond, IP would have been the average of the inflation rates that investors expect each year during the next 10 years (IP = 2.5%) and MRP would have been 1 percent (MRP = 0.1% × 10); thus r = 2% + 2.5% + 1% = 5.5%.

Figure 5.5 shows the yield curves for both inflationary situations. The yields are given in the tables in the figure. As the graphs show, when inflation is expected to increase, the yield curve is upward sloping, and vice versa. In either case, economists often use the yield curve to form expectations about the future of the economy. For example, when inflation is high and expected to decline, as Panel B of Figure 5.5 indicates, the yield curve generally is downward sloping. In many cases a downward-sloping yield curve suggests that the economy will weaken in the future: Consumers delay purchases because they expect prices to decline in the future, borrowers wait to borrow funds because they believe rates will be lower in the future, and investors provide more long-term funds to the financial markets in an effort to capture (lock in) higher current long-term rates. All of these actions lead to long-term rates that are lower than short-term rates in the current period.

FIGURE 5.5 ILLUSTRATIVE YIELD CURVES FOR TREASURY SECURITIES

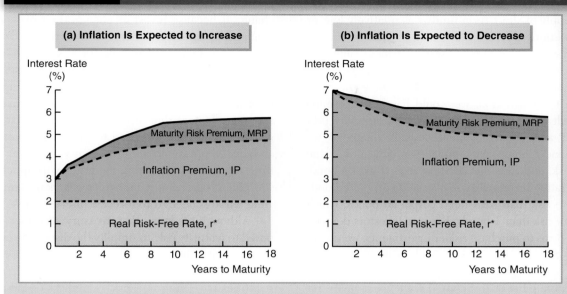

Inflation Is Expected to Increase					Inflation Is Expected to Decrease				
Maturity	**r***	**IP**	**MRP**	**Yield**	**Maturity**	**r***	**IP**	**MRP**	**Yield**
1 year	2.0%	1.0%	0.0%	3.0%	1 year	2.0%	5.0%	0.0%	7.0%
5 years	2.0	2.0	0.5	4.5	5 years	2.0	4.0	0.5	6.5
10 years	2.0	2.5	1.0	5.5	10 years	2.0	3.2	1.0	6.2
20 years	2.0	2.8	1.0	5.8	20 years	2.0	2.8	1.0	5.8

Note: The inflation premium is the average of the expected inflation rates during the life of the security. Therefore, in the case where inflation is expected to *increase*, IP_{10} is computed as follows:

$$IP_{10} = \frac{1.0\% + 1.8\% + 2.0\% + 2.4\% + 2.8\% + 3.0\% + 3.0\% + 3.0\% + 3.0\% + 3.0\%}{10} = \frac{25\%}{10} = 2.5\%$$

There are times when the yield curve exhibits either humps or dips for bonds in a particular range of terms to maturity because the supply/demand condition in one range of maturities is significantly different from those in other maturity ranges. When such a situation exists, interest rates for bonds in the affected maturity range are either substantially higher or substantially lower than rates in the maturity ranges on either side. In such cases, the resulting yield curve is not smooth or uniform; rather, there is a hump in the yield curve if rates are higher, and a dip if rates are lower. The reason these humps and dips occur is because there are instances when investors and borrowers prefer bonds with specific maturity ranges. For example, a person borrowing to buy a long-term asset like a house, or an electric utility borrowing to build a power plant, would want a long-term loan. However, a retail firm borrowing in September to build its inventories for Christmas would prefer a short-term loan. Similar differences exist among savers. For example, a person saving to take a vacation next summer would want to lend (save) in the short-term market, but someone saving for retirement 20 years hence would probably buy long-term securities.

According to the **market segmentation theory** that has been developed by economists, the slope of the yield curve depends on supply/demand conditions in the long- and short-term markets. Thus, the yield curve could at any given time be flat, upward sloping, or downward sloping, and could have humps or dips. Interest rates would be high in a particular segment compared to other segments when there was a low supply of funds in that segment relative to demand, and vice versa. The slight hump in the January 2007 yield curve shown in Figure 5.4 for bonds with a maturity of one year suggests that the demand for one year loans was high relative to the supply; that is, in relative terms, borrowers

market segmentation theory The theory that every borrower and every lender has a preferred maturity, and that the slope of the yield curve depends on the supply of and the demand for funds in the long-term market relative to the short-term market.

demanded more one-year loans than longer-term loans, fewer investors bought bonds that matured in one year, so the supply of short-term funds was relatively low, or both conditions existed.

In this section, we use Treasury securities to illustrate concepts relating to the shape of the yield curve. The same concepts apply to corporate bonds. To include corporate bonds in the illustration, we would have to determine the default risk premium, DRP, and the liquidity premium, LP, associated with such bonds. In Chapter 6, we discuss bond ratings, which provide an indication of the default risk, and thus the DRP, associated with a bond. In bond-rating terminology, BBB-rated corporate bonds have more risk than AAA-rated corporate bonds, which have more risk than T-bonds. Because investors demand higher returns to purchase riskier investments, we expect that $r_{BBB} > r_{AAA} > r_{Treasury}$. As a result, if we were to add yield curves for AAA-rated corporate bonds and BBB-rated corporate bonds to Figure 5.4, the yield curves for the AAA-rated bonds would be positioned above the yield curves for T-bonds, and the yield curve for the BBB-rated bonds would be positioned above the yield curves for both the AAA-rated bonds and the T-bonds.

5-3b Does the Yield Curve Indicate Future Interest Rates?

It was mentioned earlier that the *expectations theory* states that the shape of the yield curve depends on expectations concerning future inflation rates. It was also mentioned that the primary reason interest rates change is because investors change their expectations concerning future inflation rates. If this is true, can we use the yield curve to help forecast future interest rates? In this section, we examine Treasury securities to illustrate how interest rates might be forecast using information provided by a yield curve. Because there are many factors that affect interest rates in the real world, models that are used to forecast interest rates are very complex and not always very accurate. Therefore, the discussion in this section is very much oversimplified; significantly more analysis than examining a yield curve is needed to forecast interest rates.

Although we know that Treasury securities are exposed to maturity risk, to simplify the discussion here, we assume that MRP = 0 in the determination of interest rates for these securities. If MRP = 0, then all Treasury securities have the same risk, regardless of their terms to maturity, and neither investors nor borrowers should have a preference for securities with particular maturities because all securities are interchangeable. In other words, a person who wants to invest for a five-year period should not care whether the funds are invested in a Treasury bond that matures in five years or a Treasury bond that matures in one year that can be turned over in each of the next five years. The Treasury securities should be perfect substitutes for each other so that the investor earns the same return if the money is invested in one five-year Treasury bond or in five one-year Treasury bonds that mature one after the other. The bonds are considered interchangeable because the yield on the five-year T-bond should be the average of the yields on the five one-year T-bonds.

To illustrate, suppose that on January 2, 2017, the real risk-free rate of interest was $r° = 3\%$ and expected inflation rates for the next three years are as shown here:[10]

Year	Expected Annual (One-Year) Inflation Rate	Expected Average Inflation Rate from January 2, 2017 to December 31 of Indicated Year		
2017	2.0%	$IP_1 =$		$(2\%)/1 = 2.0\%$
2018	4.0	$IP_2 =$		$(2\% + 4\%)/2 = 3.0\%$
2019	6.0	$IP_3 =$	$(2\% + 4\% + 6\%)/3 = 4.0\%$	

[10]In this example, we compute simple *arithmetic* average. Technically, we should be using *geometric* average, but the differences are not material in this example.

Roman Gorielov/Shutterstock.com

Given these expectations, the following table shows the interest rate pattern that should exist:

Bond Type	Real Risk-Free Rate (r^*)		Inflation Premium (IP_t) = Average Expected Inflation Rate		Nominal Rate for Each Type of Bond (r_{RF})
1-year bond	3.0%	+	2.0%	=	5.0%
2-year bond	3.0%	+	3.0%	=	6.0%
3-year bond	3.0%	+	4.0%	=	7.0%

If the yields on these hypothetical bonds were plotted, the yield curve would be upward sloping, similar to the May 2015 yield curve in Figure 5.4. Had the pattern of expected inflation rates been reversed, with inflation expected to fall from 6 percent to 2 percent during the three-year period, the pattern of interest rates would have produced an inverted yield curve like the November 2006 yield curve shown in Figure 5.4, except the downward slope would have been much more pronounced.

Because the yield on any bond is the average of the annual, or one-year, interest rates that are expected during its life, we know the relationship shown in Equation 5.5 exists:

5.5

$$\text{Yield (\%) on an n-year bond} = \frac{R_1 + R_2 + \cdots + R_n}{n}$$

Here, R_1 is the interest rate expected only during the first year of the bond's remaining life (Year 1), R_2 is the interest rate expected only during the second year of its remaining life (Year 2), and so forth.

We should be able to reverse the averaging process shown in Equation 5.5 to forecast the interest rate expected in each year (R_1, R_2, and so forth) by examining the yields that currently exist on bonds with various maturities. For example, suppose that currently the yield on a one-year T-bill is 5 percent and the yield on a two-year T-bond is 6 percent. Plugging in the known information, we have

$$6\% = \frac{5\% + R_2}{2}$$

Solving for R_2, we have

$$5\% + R_2 = 6\%(2) = 12\%,$$
$$\text{so} \quad R_2 = 12\% - 5\% = 7\%$$

Therefore, if today were January 2, 2017, according to this example, investors would expect the interest rate to be 5 percent in 2017 and 7 percent in 2018. If this were true, then the average yield over the next two years would be 6% = (5% + 7%)/2. You can see that the yield curve is upward sloping whenever interest rates are expected to increase in future years because the *average yield* increases as higher interest rates are included in the computation.

This information can also be used to determine the expected inflation rate. In the current example, the interest rate consists of the real risk-free rate, r^*, which is constant, and an adjustment for inflation. Therefore, to determine the expected inflation rate each year, we simply subtract r^* from the nominal interest rate that is expected to occur during the year. Remember that we assumed the real risk-free rate, r^*, is 3 percent per year. As a result, in the current example, investors expect inflation to be 2% = 5% − 3% in 2017 and 4% = 7% − 3% in 2018. These results are the same as the expected inflation rates that were reported earlier.

5-4 Other Factors That Influence Interest Rate Levels

Factors other than those discussed earlier also influence both the general level of interest rates and the shape of the yield curve. The four most important factors are discussed here.

5-4a Federal Reserve Policy

You probably learned two important points in your economics courses: (1) The money supply has a major effect on both the level of economic activity and the rate of inflation; and (2) in the United States, the Federal Reserve (the Fed) controls the money supply. If the Fed wants to slow (control) growth in the economy, it slows growth in the money supply. Such an action initially causes interest rates to increase and inflation to stabilize. The opposite effect occurs when the Fed loosens the money supply.

The most important tool used by the Fed to manage the supply of money is **open market operations**,

open market operations Operations in which the Federal Reserve buys or sells Treasury securities to expand or contract the U.S. money supply.

which involve buying or selling U.S. Treasury securities to change bank reserves. When the Fed wants to increase the money supply, it *purchases* government securities from *primary dealers* who have established trading relationships with the Federal Reserve. The Fed pays for the securities by sending funds to the banks where the primary dealers have accounts. This action increases the deposit balances of the dealers, which in turn increases the overall reserves of the banking system. Banks have additional funds to lend, so the money supply increases, which causes interest rates to decline. To increase rates, the Fed would decrease the money supply by *selling* government securities. The Fed carries out "normal" open market operations on a continuous basis to maintain economic activity within defined limits, and it shifts its open market strategies toward heavier-than-normal buying or selling when more substantial adjustments are required.

Frank L. Junior/Shutterstock.com

5-4b Federal Deficits

If the federal government spends more than it takes in from tax revenues, it runs a *deficit*. Deficit spending must be covered either by borrowing or by printing money. If the government borrows, the added demand for funds pushes up interest rates. If it prints money, the expectation is that future inflation will increase, which also drives up interest rates. Thus, other things held constant, the larger the federal deficit, the higher the level of interest rates. Whether long- or short-term rates are affected to a greater extent depends on how the deficit is financed. Consequently, we cannot generalize about how deficits will influence the slope of the yield curve.

5-4c International Business (Foreign Trade Balance)

Businesses and individuals in the United States buy from and sell to people and firms in other countries. If Americans import more than they export (buy more than they sell), the United States is said to be running a *foreign trade deficit*. When trade deficits occur, they must be financed, and the main source of financing is debt.[11] Therefore, the larger the trade deficit, the more the United States must borrow. As the country increases its borrowing, interest rates are driven up. In addition, foreigners are willing to hold U.S. debt only if the interest rate on this debt is competitive with interest rates in other countries. Therefore, if the Federal Reserve attempts to lower interest rates in the United States, causing U.S. rates to fall below rates abroad, foreigners will sell U.S. bonds. This activity will depress bond prices and cause U.S. interest rates to increase. As a result, the existence of a deficit trade balance hinders the Fed's ability to combat a recession by lowering interest rates.

5-4d Business Activity

We can return to Figure 5.2 to see how business conditions influence interest rates.

1. During periods of inflation, the general tendency is toward higher interest rates.

2. During recessions, both the demand for money and the rate of inflation tend to fall. At the same time, the Federal Reserve tends to increase the money supply in an effort to stimulate the economy. As a result, interest rates typically decline during recessions.

3. When the U.S. economy shows signs of expanding too quickly, the Fed normally takes actions to increase interest rates to discourage too much expansion and to control future growth so that it does not result in high inflation.

---

[11]The deficit could also be financed by selling assets, including gold, corporate stocks, entire companies, or real estate. The United States has financed its massive trade deficits by all of these approaches, but the primary method has been by borrowing.

4. During recessions, short-term rates decline more sharply than do long-term rates. This situation occurs for two reasons. First, the Fed operates mainly in the short-term sector, so its intervention has the strongest effect here. Second, long-term rates reflect the average expected inflation rate over the next 20 to 30 years. This expectation generally does not change much, even when the current rate of inflation is low because of a recession.

5-5 Interest Rate Levels and Stock Prices

Interest rates have two effects on corporate profits. First, because interest is a cost, the higher the rate of interest, the lower a firm's profits, other things held constant. Second, interest rates affect the level of economic activity, and economic activity affects corporate profits. Interest rates obviously affect stock prices because of their effects on profits. Perhaps even more important, they influence stock prices because of competition in the marketplace between stocks and bonds. If interest rates rise sharply, investors can obtain higher returns in the bond market, which induces them to sell stocks and transfer funds from the stock market to the bond market. A massive sale of stocks in response to rising interest rates obviously would depress stock prices. Of course, the reverse would occur if interest rates decline. Indeed, the 11 percent increase in the Dow Jones Industrial Index in October 2002 was the result of a sharp drop in long-term interest rates during the prior few months. On the other hand, at least to some extent, the poor performance exhibited by the market in 2000, when the prices of common stocks declined, resulted from increases in interest rates.

5-5a The Cost of Money as a Determinant of Value

In this chapter, we have discussed some of the factors that determine the cost of money. For the most part, these same factors also affect other rates of return, including rates earned on stocks and other investments. In Chapter 1, we mentioned that the value of an asset is a function of the cash flows it is expected to generate in the future and the *rate of return* at which investors are willing to provide funds to purchase the investment. We know that many factors, including conditions in the economy and financial markets, affect the determination of the expected cash flows and the rate people demand when investing their funds; thus, the process of determining value can be fairly complex. In Chapter 4, however, you should have discovered that the value of an asset can be stated in simple mathematical terms as the present value of the future cash flows that the asset is expected to generate during its life. Thus, to compute the value of an asset, you must solve Equation 5.6:

5.6

$$\text{Value of an asset} = \frac{\hat{CF}_1}{(1+r)^1} + \frac{\hat{CF}_2}{(1+r)^2} + \cdots + \frac{\hat{CF}_n}{(1+r)^n}$$
$$= \sum_{t=1}^{n} \frac{\hat{CF}_t}{(1+r)^t}$$

In this equation, $\hat{CF}_t$ is the cash flow that the asset is expected to generate in Period t, and r represents the cost of funds. As a result, you can see that mathematically, as r increases, the denominator in Equation 5.6 increases, which decreases the present value. In general, then, when the cost of money increases, the value of an asset decreases. Let's consider the logic of this statement with a simple example. Suppose that you are offered an investment that will pay you a constant $100 per year forever (a perpetuity). If you want to earn a 10 percent return on this investment, you should be willing to pay $1,000 = $100/0.10 to purchase it. But would the amount you are willing to pay for the investment be different if interest rates on similar investments increase to 12 percent before you have a chance to purchase the perpetuity? Because the $100 annual payment that you will receive from the investment does not change, you must change the amount that you are willing to pay for the perpetuity if you want to earn the higher 12 percent return. To earn the higher return, you must lower the price you are willing to pay for the investment to $833.33 = $100/0.12. In other words, if you purchase the investment for $833.33, you will earn 12 percent because $100 is 12 percent of $833.33.

As you can see, the cost of money—that is, the interest rate (return)—affects the prices of investments. In general, *when rates in the financial markets increase, the prices (values) of financial assets decrease.* In the next couple of chapters, we discuss the valuation of stocks and bonds to give you a better understanding of this fundamental valuation concept.

STUDY TOOLS

LOCATED AT BACK OF THE TEXTBOOK

☐ Problems are found at the end of this chapter.

☐ A tear-out Chapter Review card is located at the back of the textbook.

LOCATED AT WWW.CENGAGEBRAIN.COM

☐ Review Key Term flashcards and create your own cards.

☐ Track your knowledge and understanding of key concepts in corporate finance.

☐ Complete practice and graded quizzes to prepare for tests.

☐ Complete interactive content within CFIN5 Online.

☐ View the chapter highlight boxes for CFIN5 Online.

KEY COST OF MONEY (INTEREST RATE) CONCEPTS

To conclude this chapter, we summarize some cost-of-money concepts that were discussed.

- The yield, or return, that is earned on an investment is comprised of two components: (1) income paid by the *issuer* of the financial asset and (2) the change in the market value of the financial asset over some time period.

- The cost of money (interest rates) is based on (1) the rate of return that borrowers expect to earn on their investments, (2) savers' preferences to spend income in the current period rather than delay consumption until some future period, (3) the risks associated with investments/loans, and (4) expected inflation.

- In general, the rate of return on an investment, or the interest rate on a loan, includes a minimum payment for delaying consumption until some future date, which is termed the risk-free rate of return, r_{RF}, and

payment for the risk associated with the investment/loan, which is termed a risk premium, RP. Risks can include the risk that the borrower will default on the loan, the risk associated with the liquidity of the investment, and so forth.

- In most instances, long-term interest rates are greater than short-term interest rates; that is, the yield curve is upward sloping. However, there are rare instances when the yield curve is inverted, or downward sloping, which occurs when long-term interest rates are lower than short-term interest rates. An inverted yield curve is likely to appear when the economy is in a recession.

- Everything else equal, when interest rates (returns) increase, the prices (values) of investments decrease. In other words, when investors want to receive higher returns, they lower the amount they are willing to pay for investments.

PROBLEMS

5–1 Yesterday Travis sold 1,000 shares of stock that he owned for $29 per share. Travis purchased the stock one year ago for $28 per share. During the year, Travis received a quarterly dividend equal to $0.10 per share. What return (yield) did Travis earn during the time he owned the stock?

5–2 One year ago, Richard purchased 40 shares of common stock for $10 per share. During the year, he received one dividend payment in the amount of $0.50 per share. If the stock currently is worth $9 per share, what yield did Richard earn on his investment for the year?

5–3 One year ago, Regina purchased $1,050 worth of Elite Electrician's common stock for $42 per share. During the year, Regina received two dividend payments, each equal to $0.05 per share. The current market value of the stock is $44 per share. What yield did Regina earn on her investment during the year?

5–4 Wilma just sold all the shares of International Inns stock that she owned for $156 per share. She purchased the stock one year ago for $150 per share. If Wilma did not receive any dividend payments during the year, what yield did she earn on her investment?

5–5 Yesterday Sandi sold 1,000 shares of stock that she owned for $45 per share. When she purchased the stock two years ago, Sandi paid $50 per share. Every three months during the time that she held the stock, Sandi received a quarterly dividend equal to $0.50 per share. A total of eight dividends were received. (a) What return (yield) did Sandi earn during the two years she held the stock? (b) If the price of the stock was $45 per share one year ago, what return did Sandi earn in *each* year she held the stock?

5–6 Earlier today, Stuart sold 200 shares of stock he owned. He purchased the stock three years ago for $28 per share. Following is a table that shows the market value of the stock at the end of each year and the amount of the dividend that Stuart received during the year:

Year	Market Value (per share)	Dividend (per share)
1	$26	$0.60
2	28	0.60
3	32	0.60

(a) What total return (yield) did Stuart earn during the three-year period he held the stock? (b) What return did Stuart earn for *each* year he held the stock?

5–7 Suppose the yield on a two-year Treasury bond is 5 percent and the yield on a one-year Treasury bond is 4 percent. If the maturity risk premium (MRP) on these bonds is zero (0), what is the expected one-year interest rate during the second year (Year 2)?

5–8 The interest rate on one-year Treasury bonds is 1.0 percent, the rate on two-year T-bonds is 0.9 percent, and the rate on three-year T-bonds is 0.8 percent. Using the expectations theory, compute the expected *one-year* interest rates in (a) the second year (Year 2 only) and (b) the third year (Year 3 only).

5–9 The interest rate on one-year Treasury bonds is 0.4 percent, the rate on two-year T-bonds is 0.8 percent, and the rate on three-year T-bonds is 1.1 percent. Using the expectations theory, compute the expected *one-year* interest rates in (a) the second year (Year 2 only) and (b) the third year (Year 3 only).

5–10 The interest rate on five-year Treasury bonds is 3.1 percent, the rate on six-year T-bonds is 2.9 percent, and the rate on seven-year T-bonds is 2.6 percent. Using the expectations theory, compute the expected *one-year* interest rates in (a) Year 6 only and (b) Year 7 only.

5–11 The interest rate on two-year Treasury bonds is 1.2 percent, the rate on three-year T-bonds is 1.4 percent, and the rate on four-year T-bonds is 1.9 percent. Using the expectations theory, compute the expected *one-year* interest rates in (a) the third year (Year 3 only) and (b) the fourth year (Year 4 only).

5–12 The rate of inflation for the next 12 months (Year 1) is expected to be 1.4 percent; it is expected to be 1.8 percent the following year (Year 2); and it is expected to be 2.0 percent every year after Year 2. Assume the real risk-free rate, r^*, is 3 percent for all maturities. What should be the yield to maturity on risk-free bonds that mature in (a) one year, (b) five years, and (c) 10 years.

5–13 Economists expect the inflation rate to be 1.5 percent for the coming year and the following year, and then after Year 2 inflation will settle at a constant rate greater than 1.5 percent. The yield is the same on one-year bonds and two-year bonds; the yield on three-year bonds is 0.5 percent greater than on one-year and two-year bonds. The real risk-free rate is 2 percent for all bonds. If the bonds are risk-free, what rate of inflation is expected in Year 3 and beyond?

5–14 Today is January 2, 2017, and investors expect the *annual* risk-free interest rates in 2017 through 2019 to be:

Year	One-Year Rate (r_{RF})
2017	2.2%
2018	1.8
2019	2.9

What is the yield to maturity for Treasury bonds that mature at the *end* of (a) 2018 (a two-year bond) and (b) 2019 (a three-year bond)? Assume the bonds have no risks.

5–15 Suppose today is January 2, 2017, and investors expect the *annual* inflation rates in 2017 through 2019 to be:

Year	One-Year Inflation Rate
2017	2.1%
2018	1.5
2019	0.9

To yield a real risk-free rate, r*, equal to 2 percent, what would the average nominal rate be on a (a) one-year bond, (b) two-year bond, and (c) three-year bond? Assume the bonds are risk-free.

5–16 Suppose today is January 2, 2017, and investors expect the *annual* risk-free interest rates in 2021 and 2022 to be:

Year	One-Year Rate (r_{RF})
2021	4.5%
2022	2.3

Currently a four-year Treasury bond that matures on December 31, 2020 has an interest rate equal to 2.5 percent. What is the yield to maturity for Treasury bonds that mature at the end of (a) 2021 (a five-year bond) and (b) 2022 (a six-year bond)? Assume the bonds have no risks.

5–17 *The Wall Street Journal* reports that the yield on a nine-month Treasury bond is 2.3 percent, the yield on a three-year Treasury bond is 2.9 percent, and the yield on a 10-year Treasury bond is 4.3 percent. Although no liquidity premium is associated with Treasury securities, there is a maturity risk premium (MRP) for Treasuries with maturities equal to one year or greater. What is the MRP?

5–18 Currently, a six-month Treasury bill is yielding 3.2 percent. Company F's three-year bond has a yield equal to 5.0 percent, and its seven-year bond has a yield equal to 5.8 percent. Although none of the bonds has a liquidity premium, any bond with a maturity equal to one year or longer has a maturity risk premium (MRP). Except for their terms to maturity, the characteristics of the bonds are the same. Compute the (a) *annual* MRP and (b) default risk premium (DRP) associated with the bonds.

5–19 Suppose economists expect that the nominal risk-free rate of return, r_{RF}, which is also the rate on a one-year Treasury note, will be 3.2 percent long into the future. You are evaluating two corporate bonds that are identical except for their terms to maturity. The bonds have the same default risk, and neither bond has a liquidity premium. Bond T matures in five years and has a yield equal to 5.3 percent, whereas Bond Q matures in eight years and has a yield equal to 5.9 percent. Compute (a) the annual maturity risk premium (MRP) and (b) the bonds' default risk premium (DRP).

5–20 Economists expect that the nominal risk-free rate of return, r_{RF}, on one-year Treasury bonds will be 2.4 percent long into the future. General Machinery's (GM) one-year bond has a yield equal to 4.8 percent. The yield on the GM bond includes a liquidity premium equal to 0.3 percent. Suppose the maturity risk premium (MRP) for all bonds with maturities *greater* than one year is 0.15 percent per year. Based on this information, what should be the yield on GM's five-year bonds?

CFIN ONLINE

PREPARE FOR TESTS ON THE STUDYBOARD!

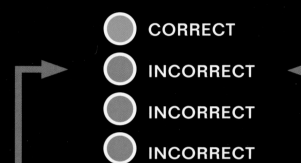

CORRECT

INCORRECT

INCORRECT

INCORRECT

Personalize Quizzes from Your StudyBits

Take Practice Quizzes by Chapter

CHAPTER QUIZZES

Chapter 1

Chapter 2

Chapter 3

Chapter 4

4LTR
PRESS

Access CFIN ONLINE at www.cengagebrain.com

After you finish this chapter go to **PAGE 119** for **STUDY TOOLS**

LEARNING OUTCOMES

After studying this chapter, you will be able to...

LO1 Describe the basic characteristics of debt and some of the different types of debt.

LO2 Discuss bond ratings and the information that they provide to investors.

LO3 Explain how bond prices are determined.

LO4 Explain how bond yields (market rates) are determined.

LO5 Describe the relationship between bond prices and interest rates (yields), and explain why it is important for investors to understand this relationship.

Bonds (Debt)— Characteristics and Valuation

In this chapter, we discuss debt. First, we describe the general characteristics and features of debt. Then, we show how bonds are valued and discuss factors that affect the values of bonds. It is important to understand the valuation concepts presented in this and the next few chapters because they represent the general foundations of finance.

6-1 Characteristics and Types of Debt

In this section, we describe some of the characteristics of debt. Far too many types of debt with different features exist to cover everything here; thus, we only include the most common types of debt and the features associated with those debt instruments.

6-1a Debt Characteristics[1]

Simply stated, **debt** is a loan to a firm, a government, or an individual. Many types of debt instruments exist: home mortgages, commercial paper, bonds, and unsecured notes, among others. Often, we identify debt by describing three of its features: the principal amount that must be repaid, the interest payments, and the time to maturity. For instance, a $1,000, 10-year, 8 percent bond consists of

debt with a $1,000 principal due in 10 years that pays interest equal to 8 percent of the principal amount, or $80, per year. In this section, we explain the meanings of these terms and describe some of the general features associated with debt.

Principal Value, Face Value, Maturity Value, and Par Value. The *principal value* of debt represents the amount owed to the lender, which must be repaid at some point during the life of the debt. For much of the debt issued by corporations, the principal amount is repaid at the maturity date. Consequently, we also refer to the principal value as the *maturity value*. In addition, the principal value generally is written on the face, or outside cover, of the debt contract, so it is sometimes called the *face value*. When the market value of debt is the same as its face value, it is said to be selling at *par;* thus, the principal amount is also referred to as the *par value*. For most debt, therefore, the terms *par value, face value, maturity value,* and *principal value* are used interchangeably to designate the borrowed amount that must be repaid by the borrower.

Interest Payments. In most cases, owners of (investors in) debt instruments receive periodic payments of interest, which are computed as a percentage of the principal amount. But some debt does not pay interest; to generate a positive return for investors, such financial assets must sell for less than their par, or maturity, values. Securities that sell for less than their par values when issued are called **discounted securities**.

Maturity Date. The maturity date represents the date on which the principal amount of a debt is due. As long as

---

[1]In this chapter, we primarily discuss bonds (debt) from the perspective of a corporation. Most of the characteristics we describe for corporate debt also apply to government debt.

debt A loan to a firm, government, or individual.

discounted securities Securities selling for less than par value.

interest has been paid when due, once the total principal amount is repaid, the debt obligation has been satisfied. Some debt instruments, called *installment loans*, require the principal amounts to be repaid in several payments during the lives of the loans. In such cases, the maturity date is the date the last installment payment is due.

Priority to Assets and Earnings. Corporate debt holders have priority over stockholders with regard to distribution of earnings and liquidation of assets; that is, they must be paid before any stockholders can be paid.

Control of the Firm (Voting Rights). Corporate debt holders do not have voting rights, so they cannot attain control of the firm. Nevertheless, debt holders can affect the management and operations of a firm by placing restrictions on the use of the funds as part of the loan agreement.

6-1b Types of Debt

Many types of debt instruments exist, some of which we describe in this section. Whereas most long-term debt instruments pay interest, most short-term debt instruments do not; rather, they are sold as discounted securities when issued, so that the difference between their purchase prices and maturity values represent the dollar returns earned by investors.

6-1c Short-Term Debt

Short-term debt refers to debt instruments with original maturities of one year or less. Some of the more common short-term debt instruments are described here.

Treasury Bills. Treasury bills (T-bills) are discounted securities issued by the U.S. government to finance its operations and programs. When the U.S. Treasury issues T-bills, the prices are determined by an auction process: interested investors and investing organizations submit competitive bids to purchase T-bill issues.[2] T-bills are issued electronically with face values ranging from $1,000 to

$5 million, and with maturities that range from a few days to 52 weeks at the time of issue.

Repurchase Agreements (Repos). A repurchase agreement (also called a *repo*) is an arrangement whereby a firm that needs funds sells some of its financial assets to another firm that has excess funds to invest, with a promise to *repurchase* the securities at a higher price at a later date. The price at which the securities will be repurchased is agreed to at the time the *repo* is arranged. Although some repos last for days or even weeks, most repos last only a few hours, which means they are essentially overnight agreements.

Federal Funds. Often referred to simply as *fed funds*, federal funds represent loans from one bank to another bank. Banks generally use the fed funds market to adjust their reserves: Banks that need additional funds to meet the reserve requirements of the Federal Reserve borrow from banks with excess reserves. The interest rate associated with such debt is known as the *federal funds rate*. Federal funds have very short maturities, often overnight.

Banker's Acceptances. A banker's acceptance might be best described as a postdated check. More accurately, a banker's acceptance is a *time draft*, which is an instrument issued by a bank that obligates it to pay a specified amount to the holder of the draft at some future date. Generally used in international trade, a banker's acceptance arrangement is established between a bank and a firm, essentially to guarantee that a payment the firm submits to its international trading partner can be collected from the bank at some future date, perhaps in 30 days. The time between when a banker's acceptance is created and cash payment is made is sufficient to verify the completion of the international transaction. A banker's acceptance is generally sold at a discount by the original owner before its maturity to raise immediate cash.

Commercial Paper. Commercial paper is a type of *promissory note*, or "legal IOU," issued by large, financially sound firms. Like a T-bill, commercial paper does not pay interest, so it is issued at a discount. The maturity on commercial paper varies from one to nine months, with an average of about five months.[3] Generally, commercial paper is issued in denominations of $100,000

Treasury bills (T-bills) Discounted debt instruments issued by the U.S. government.

repurchase agreement An arrangement where one firm sells some of its financial assets to another firm with a promise to *repurchase* the securities at a later date.

federal funds Overnight loans from one bank to another bank.

banker's acceptance An instrument issued by a bank that obligates the bank to pay a specified amount at some future date.

commercial paper A discounted instrument that is a type of promissory note, or "legal" IOU, issued by large, financially sound firms.

[2]The U.S. Treasury also sells T-bills on a noncompetitive basis to investors or investment organizations offering to buy a certain dollar amount. In such cases, the purchase price is based on the average of the competitive bids received by the Treasury.

[3]The maximum maturity without SEC registration is 270 days. In addition, commercial paper can be sold only to sophisticated investors; otherwise, SEC registration would be required even for maturities of less than 270 days.

or more, so few individuals can afford to directly invest in the commercial paper market. Instead, commercial paper is sold primarily to other businesses, including insurance companies, pension funds, money market mutual funds, and banks.

Certificates of Deposit (CDs). A certificate of deposit represents a time deposit at a bank or other financial intermediary. Traditional CDs, which generally earn periodic interest, must be kept at the issuing institution for a specified time period. To liquidate a traditional CD prior to maturity, the owner must return it to the issuing institution, which normally applies an interest penalty (lower interest) to the amount paid out. *Negotiable CDs,* however, can be traded to other investors prior to maturity because they can be redeemed by whoever owns them at maturity. Often called *jumbo CDs,* these investments typically are issued in denominations of $1 million and greater, and they have maturities that range from a few months to a few years.

Eurodollar Deposits. A Eurodollar deposit is a deposit in a bank outside the United States that is not converted into the currency of the foreign country; instead, it is denominated in U.S. dollars. Such deposits are not exposed to *exchange rate risk*, which is the risk associated with converting dollars into foreign currencies. Eurodollar deposits earn rates offered by foreign banks and are not subject to the same regulations imposed on deposits in U.S. banks. Consequently, the rate that can be earned on Eurodollars is sometimes considerably greater than the rate that can be earned in the United States.

Money Market Mutual Funds. Money market mutual funds consist of investment dollars that are pooled to purchase large amounts of short-term financial (money market) assets, such as those described here. The mutual funds are professionally managed by firms, called *investment companies*, that specialize in investing money that is provided by many individual investors. These funds offer individual investors the ability to indirectly invest in such short-term securities as T-bills, commercial paper, and Eurodollars, which they otherwise would not be able to purchase because such investments either are sold in denominations that are too large or are not available to individual investors.

[4]Most term loans are *amortized*, which means that they are paid off in equal installments over the life of the loan. Amortization protects the lender against the possibility that the borrower will not make adequate provisions for the loan's retirement during the life of the loan. (Chapter 4 reviews the concept of amortization.) In addition, if the interest and principal payments required under a term loan agreement are not met on schedule, the borrowing firm is said to have *defaulted*, and it can then be forced into bankruptcy.

6-1d Long-Term Debt

Long-term debt refers to debt instruments with maturities greater than one year. Owners of such debt generally receive periodic payments of interest. This section describes common types of long-term debt.

Term Loans. A term loan is a contract under which a borrower agrees to make a series of interest and principal payments to the lender on specific dates. Term loans usually are negotiated directly between the borrowing firm and a financial institution, such as a bank, an insurance company, or a pension fund. For this reason, they are often referred to as *private debt*. Although term loans' maturities vary from two years to 30 years, most maturities are in the three- to 15-year range.[4]

Term loans have three major advantages over public debt offerings such as corporate bonds: *speed, flexibility*, and *low issuance costs*. Because they are negotiated directly between the lender and the borrower, formal documentation is minimized. The key provisions of a term loan can be worked out much more quickly than can those for a public issue, and it is not necessary for the loan to go through the Securities and Exchange Commission (SEC) registration process because it is not sold to the public. In addition, unlike typical corporate bonds that have many different bondholders, a company often can sit down with the lender in a term loan arrangement and work out mutually agreeable modifications to the contract if necessary. The interest rate on a term loan can be either fixed for the life of the loan or it can be variable.

Bonds. A bond is a long-term contract under which a borrower (issuer) agrees to make payments of interest and principal on specific dates to the bondholder (investor). The interest payments are determined by the coupon rate, which represents the total interest paid each year, stated as a percentage of the bond's face value. Typically, interest is paid semiannually, although bonds that pay interest annually,

---

certificate of deposit An interest-earning time deposit at a bank or other financial intermediary.

Eurodollar deposit A deposit in a foreign bank that is denominated in U.S. dollars.

money market mutual funds Pools of funds managed by investment companies that are primarily invested in short-term financial assets.

term loan A loan, generally obtained from a bank or insurance company, on which the borrower agrees to make a series of payments consisting of interest and principal.

bond A long-term debt instrument.

coupon rate Interest paid on a bond or other debt instrument stated as a percentage of its face (maturity) value.

Hiroshi Watanabe/Photodisc/Getty Images

funds for projects that will generate revenues that contribute to payment of interest and the repayment of the debt, such as a roadway that generates revenues through tolls. *General obligation bonds* are backed by the government's ability to tax its citizens; special taxes or tax increases are used to generate the funds needed to service such bonds. Generally, the income that an investor earns from munis is exempt from federal taxes.

2. As the name implies, **corporate bonds** are issued by businesses called *corporations*. A corporate bond issue generally is advertised, offered to the public, and sold to many different investors. The interest rate typically remains fixed, although the popularity of floating-rate bonds has grown during the past couple of decades. Several types of corporate bonds exist, the more important of which are discussed in the remainder of this section.

3. With a **mortgage bond**, the corporation pledges certain tangible (real) assets as security, or *collateral*, for the bond. In addition to original, or *first,* mortgages, firms can issue *second-mortgage bonds* secured by the same assets. In the event of liquidation, the holders of these second mortgage bonds (called *junior mortgages)* would have a claim against the property, but only after the first-mortgage (called *senior-mortgage*) bondholders have been paid off in full.

4. A **debenture** is an unsecured bond; as such, it provides no lien, or *claim*, against specific property as security for the obligation. Therefore, debenture holders are general creditors whose claims are protected by property not otherwise pledged as collateral. A **subordinated debenture** is an unsecured bond that ranks below, or is inferior to, other debt with respect to claims on cash distributions made by the firm. In the event of bankruptcy, for instance, *subordinated debt* has claims on assets only after senior debt has been paid off. Debentures are often issued by companies, such as large mail-order houses, that are in industries in which it would not be practical to provide security through a mortgage on fixed assets.

quarterly, and monthly also exist, and the principal amount is generally paid in a lump-sum amount at the end of the bond's life (maturity date).

Some of the more common bonds issued by both governments and corporations are listed below.

1. **Government bonds** are issued by the U.S. government, state governments, and local or municipal governments. U.S. government bonds are issued by the U.S. Treasury and are called either *Treasury notes* or *Treasury bonds*. Both types of debt pay interest semiannually. The primary difference between Treasury notes and Treasury bonds is that the original maturities on T-notes can be from more than one year to 10 years, whereas the original maturities on T-bonds exceed 10 years.

Municipal bonds, or *munis,* are similar to Treasury bonds, except they are issued by state and local governments. The two principal types of munis are revenue bonds and general obligation bonds. *Revenue bonds* are used to raise

government bonds Debt issued by a federal, state, or local government.

municipal bonds Bonds issued by a state or local government.

corporate bonds Long-term debt instruments issued by corporations.

mortgage bond A bond backed by tangible (real) assets. First-mortgage bonds are senior in priority to second-mortgage bonds.

debenture A long-term bond that is not secured by a mortgage on specific property.

subordinated debenture A bond which, in the event of liquidation, has a claim on assets only after the senior debt has been paid off.

5. Several other types of corporate bonds are used sufficiently often to merit mention.

   ▶ **Income bonds** pay interest only when the firm generates sufficient income to cover the interest payments. As a consequence, when income is insufficient, missing interest payments on these securities cannot bankrupt a company. From an investor's standpoint, these bonds are riskier than bonds that require fixed interest payments.

   ▶ **Putable bonds** are bonds that can be turned in to the firm prior to maturity in exchange for cash at the bondholder's option if the firm takes some specified action—for example, if the firm is acquired by a weaker company or its outstanding debt increases substantially.

   ▶ **Indexed**, or **purchasing power, bonds** pay interest based on an inflation index, such as the consumer price index (CPI). The interest paid rises automatically when the inflation rate rises, thereby protecting bondholders against inflation.

   ▶ **Floating-rate bonds** are similar to *indexed bonds* except the coupon rates on these bonds float with market interest rates rather than with the inflation rate. Thus, when interest rates rise, the coupon rates increase, and vice versa. In many cases, limits are imposed on how high and low the rates on such debt can go (referred to as caps and collars, respectively).

6. *Original issue discount bonds (OIDs),* commonly referred to as **zero coupon bonds**, were created during the 1980s. These securities were offered at substantial discounts below their par values because they paid little or no coupon interest. OIDs have since lost their attraction for many individual investors, primarily because the interest income that must be reported each year for tax purposes includes any cash interest actually received, which is $0 for zero coupon bonds, plus the annual *prorated* capital appreciation (price increase) that would be received if the bond were held to maturity. Thus, capital appreciation is taxed before it is actually received. For this reason, most OID bonds currently are held by institutional investors, such as pension funds and mutual funds, rather than by individual investors.

7. Another innovation from the 1980s is the **junk bond**, a high-risk, high-yield bond often issued to finance a management buyout (MBO), a merger, or a troubled company. In junk bond deals, firms generally have significant amounts of debt, so bondholders must bear as much risk as stockholders normally would. The high yields on these bonds reflect this fact.

6-1e Bond Contract Features

A firm's managers are concerned with both the effective cost of debt and any restrictions in debt contracts that might limit the firm's future actions. This section discusses the features that generally are included in bond contracts, which can affect the firm's cost of debt and its future financial flexibility.

Bond Indenture. An **indenture** is a document that spells out the legalities of the bond issue, including any features or legal restrictions associated with the bond and the rights of the bondholders (lenders) and the corporation (bond issuer). A *trustee*, usually a bank, is assigned to represent the bondholders and to guarantee that the terms of the indenture are carried out. The indenture, which could be several hundred pages long, includes *restrictive covenants* that cover such points as the conditions under which the issuer can pay off the bonds prior to maturity, the levels at which various financial measures (such as the ability to pay interest) must be maintained if the company is to sell additional bonds, and restrictions on the payment of dividends to stockholders when earnings do not meet certain specifications. The Securities and Exchange Commission approves indentures for publicly traded bonds and verifies that all previous indenture provisions have been met before allowing a company to sell new securities to the public.

Call Provision. Most corporate bonds contain a **call provision**, which gives the issuing firm the right to "call in" the bonds for redemption

> **income bond** A bond that pays interest to the holder only if the interest is earned by the firm.
>
> **putable bond** A bond that can be redeemed at the bondholder's option when certain circumstances exist.
>
> **indexed (purchasing-power) bond** A bond that has interest payments based on an inflation index to protect the holder from loss of purchasing power.
>
> **floating-rate bond** A bond whose interest rate fluctuates with shifts in the general level of interest rates.
>
> **zero coupon bond** A bond that pays no annual interest but sells at a discount below par, thus providing compensation to investors in the form of capital appreciation.
>
> **junk bond** A high-risk, high-yield bond; used to finance mergers, leveraged buyouts, and troubled companies.
>
> **indenture** A formal agreement (contract) between the issuer of a bond and the bondholders.
>
> **call provision** A provision in a bond contract that gives the issuer the right to redeem the bonds under specified terms prior to the normal maturity date.

prior to maturity. A call provision generally states that the company must pay the bondholders an amount greater than the bond's par value when it is called. This additional amount, which is termed a *call premium,* typically equals one year's interest if the bond is called during the first year in which a call is permitted; the premium declines at a constant rate each year thereafter. Bonds usually are not callable until several years (generally five to 10) after they are issued; bonds with such *deferred calls* are said to have *call protection.* Call provisions allow firms to refinance debt, much as individuals might refinance mortgages on their houses: when interest rates decline, firms can *recall* (refund) high-cost debt that is outstanding and replace it with new, lower-cost debt.

Sinking Fund. A sinking fund is a provision that facilitates the orderly retirement of a bond issue. Typically, the sinking fund provision requires the firm to retire a portion of the bond issue each year. On rare occasions, the firm might be required to deposit money with a trustee, which invests the funds and then uses the accumulated sum to retire the bonds when they mature. Often the firm has the right to handle the sinking fund in two ways: by randomly calling for redemption (at par value) a certain percentage of the bonds each year or by purchasing the required amount of bonds in the open market. The firm will choose the lower-cost method. A sinking fund call does not require the company to pay a call premium, but only a small percentage of the issue is normally redeemable in any one year.

Convertible Feature. A conversion feature permits the bondholder (investor) to exchange, or *convert,* the bond into shares of the company's common stock at a fixed price. Investors have greater flexibility with a *convertible bond* than with a straight (regular) bond because they can choose whether to hold the company's

bond or convert the bond into its stock. Once the conversion is made, investors cannot convert back to bonds.

An important provision of a convertible bond is the *conversion ratio,* which is defined as the number of shares of stock that the bondholder receives upon conversion. Related to the conversion ratio is the *conversion price,* which is the price that is effectively paid for the common stock obtained by converting a bond into stock. For example, a $1,000 convertible bond with a conversion ratio of 20 can be converted into 20 shares of common stock, so the conversion price is $50 = $1,000/20. If the market value of the stock rises above $50 per share, it would be beneficial for the bondholder to convert his or her bonds into stock (ignoring any costs associated with conversion).

6-1f Foreign Debt Instruments

Any debt sold outside the country of the borrower is called *international debt.* Two important types of international debt exist:

1. **Foreign debt** is debt sold by a foreign borrower, but it is denominated in the currency of the country in which the issue is sold. For instance, Bell Canada might need U.S. dollars to finance the operations of its subsidiaries in the United States. If it decides to raise the needed capital in the U.S. bond market, the bond will be underwritten by a syndicate of U.S. investment banking firms, denominated in U.S. dollars, and sold to U.S. investors in accordance with SEC and applicable state regulations. Except for the foreign origin of the borrower

sinking fund A required annual payment designed to amortize a bond issue.

conversion feature Permits bondholders to exchange their investments for a fixed number of shares of common stock.

foreign debt Debt sold by a foreign borrower but denominated in the currency of the country where it is sold.

donfiore/Shutterstock.com

Table 6.1

Moody's and Standard & Poor's (S&P) Bond Ratings

Investment Risk	High Quality Low		Investment Grade Medium		Junk Bonds			
					Substandard High		Speculative Extremely High	
Moody's	Aaa	Aa	A	Baa	Ba	B	Caa	C
S&P	AAA	AA	A	BBB	BB	B	CCC	D

Note: Both Moody's and S&P use modifiers for bonds rated below triple-A. S&P uses a plus and minus system; that is, A+ designates the strongest A-rated bonds, and A− indicates the weakest. Moody's uses a 1, 2, or 3 designation, with 1 denoting the strongest and 3 the weakest; thus, within the double-A category, Aa1 is the best, Aa2 is average, and Aa3 is the weakest.

(Canada), this bond is indistinguishable from bonds issued by equivalent U.S. corporations. Foreign bonds often are labeled according to the country in which they are issued. For example, if foreign bonds are issued in the United States, they are called *Yankee bonds;* if they are issued in Japan, they are called *Samurai bonds;* and if they are issued in the United Kingdom, they are called *Bulldog bonds.*

2. The term **Eurodebt** is used to designate any debt sold in a country other than the one in whose currency it is denominated. An example of a *Eurobond* is a bond issued by Ford Motor Company in Germany that remains denominated in U.S. dollars. The institutional arrangements by which Eurobonds are marketed are different from those for most other bond issues, with the most important distinction being a far lower level of required disclosure than normally applies to bonds issued in domestic markets, particularly in the United States. Governments tend to be less strict when regulating securities denominated in foreign currencies than they are with home-currency securities because the bonds' purchasers generally are sophisticated investors. The lower disclosure requirements result in lower total transaction costs for Eurobonds. In addition, Eurobonds generally are issued in bearer form rather than as registered bonds, so the names and nationalities of investors are not recorded. Individuals who desire anonymity, whether for privacy reasons or for tax avoidance, find Eurobonds to their liking. Similarly, most governments do not withhold taxes on interest payments associated with Eurobonds. Other types of *Eurodebt* include *Eurocredits, Euro-commercial paper (Euro-CP),* and *Euronotes.*

[5]In the discussion to follow, a reference to the S&P code is intended to imply the Moody's code as well. Thus, "triple-B bonds" means both BBB and Baa bonds; "double-B bonds" means both BB and Ba bonds; and so on.

Eurocredits are bank loans that are denominated in the currency of a country other than that where the lending bank is located. Many of these loans are very large, so the lending bank often forms a loan syndicate to help raise the needed funds and to spread out some of the risk associated with the loan. Euro-CP is similar to commercial paper issued in the United States, except that there is not as much concern about the credit quality of Euro-CP issuers as there is about U.S. commercial paper issuers. Euronotes, which represent medium-term debt, typically have maturities ranging from one to 10 years. The general features of Euronotes closely resemble those of longer-term debt instruments like bonds. The principal amount is repaid at maturity, and interest often is paid semiannually.

Interest rates on short-term Eurodebt typically are tied to a standard rate known by the acronym **LIBOR**, which stands for *London Interbank Offered Rate.* LIBOR is the rate of interest offered by the largest and strongest London banks on deposits of other large banks of the highest credit standing.

6-2 Bond Ratings

Bonds are often assigned quality ratings that reflect their probabilities of going into default. The two major rating agencies are Moody's Investors Service (Moody's) and Standard & Poor's Corporation (S&P). Table 6.1 shows these agencies' rating designations and gives an indication of the investment risk that is associated with the particular ratings.[5]

Eurodebt Debt sold in a country other than the one in whose currency the debt is denominated.

LIBOR The London Interbank Offered Rate; the interest rate offered by the best London banks on deposits of other large, very creditworthy banks.

FIGURE 6.1   YIELDS ON SELECTED LONG-TERM BONDS, 1990–2015

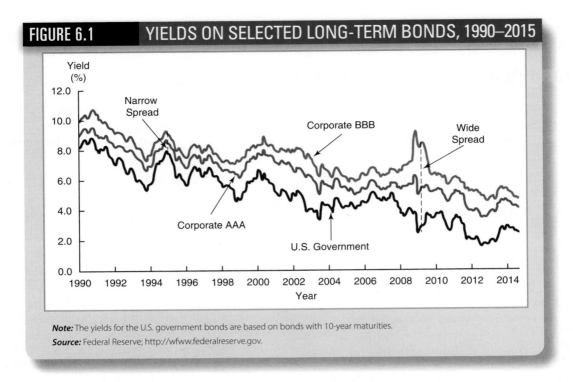

Note: The yields for the U.S. government bonds are based on bonds with 10-year maturities.

Source: Federal Reserve; http://wfww.federalreserve.gov.

6-2a Bond Rating Criteria

Bond ratings are based on both qualitative and quantitative factors. Factors considered by the bond rating agencies include the financial strength of the company as measured by various ratios, collateral provisions, the seniority of the debt, restrictive covenants, such provisions as a sinking fund or a deferred call, litigation possibilities, regulation, and so on. Representatives of the rating agencies have consistently stated that no precise formula is used to set a firm's rating; all the factors listed, plus others, are taken into account, but not in a mathematically precise manner.

6-2b Importance of Bond Ratings

Bond ratings are important to both issuers and investors for several reasons. First, because a bond's rating serves as an indicator of its default risk, the rating has a direct, measurable influence on the bond's interest rate and the firm's cost of using such debt. As we discussed in Chapter 5, the greater a bond's default risk, the greater the *default risk premium (DRP)* associated with the bond. Second, most bonds are purchased by institutional investors rather than individuals, and many institutions are restricted to *investment-grade*, or high-quality, securities. If a firm's bonds fall below a BBB rating, it will therefore have a difficult time selling new bonds because many potential purchasers will not be

allowed to buy them. As a result of their higher risk and more restricted market, lower-grade bonds offer higher returns than high-grade bonds. Figure 6.1 illustrates this point. In each of the years shown on the graph, U.S. government bonds (least amount of risk) have the lowest yields, AAA-rated corporate bonds have the next lowest, and BBB-rated corporate bonds (riskiest) have the highest yields. The figure also shows that the gaps between yields on the three types of bonds vary over time, indicating that the cost differentials, or *risk premiums*, fluctuate as well.

6-2c Changes in Ratings

Changes in a firm's bond rating affect both its ability to borrow long-term capital and the cost of such funds. Rating agencies review outstanding bonds on a periodic basis, occasionally upgrading or downgrading a bond as a result of its issuer's changed financial circumstances. For example, firms that were financially distressed by the poor economic conditions that existed from 2007 through 2011 saw their bond ratings downgraded. Not even the U.S. government is immune to ratings changes; its debt was downgraded from AAA to AA+ at the end of July 2011 due to concerns about its financial stability. Firms that had their credit ratings downgraded discovered that their costs of raising funds in the financial markets increased because their bankruptcy risks were perceived by investors to be higher than they were prior to the downgrades.

Valuation of Bonds

Suppose that on January 2, 2016, Genesco Manufacturing borrowed $25 million by selling 25,000 individual bonds for $1,000 each. Genesco received the $25 million, and it promised to pay the holders of each bond interest equal to $100 per year and to repay the $25 million at the end of 15 years.[6] The lenders (investors), who wanted to earn a 10 percent return on their investment, were willing to provide Genesco $25 million, so the value of the bond issue was $25 million. But how did investors decide that the issue was worth $25 million?

As we will see, a bond's market price is determined by the cash flows that it generates: both the interest that is paid over its life, which depends on the coupon interest rate, and the principal amount that must be repaid at maturity ($1,000 per bond in our example). *At the time a bond is issued, the coupon rate generally is set at a level that will cause the market price of the bond to equal its par value.* With a lower coupon rate, investors would not be willing to pay $1,000 for the bond. With a higher coupon rate, investors would clamor for the bond and bid its price up over $1,000. As a result, a new bond's coupon rate of interest normally is set to equal the market yield on similar-risk bonds that exist at the time the new bond is issued. *After it is issued, however, the value of the outstanding bond can vary widely from its par value.* Annual interest payments that bondholders receive are fixed (constant). Consequently, when economic conditions change, a bond that sold at par when it was issued will sell for more or less than par after its issue, depending on the relationship between the prevailing market rates and the bond's coupon rate.

6-3a The Basic Bond Valuation Model

The value of any financial asset is based on the cash flows that investors expect the asset to generate during its life. In the case of a bond, the cash flows consist of interest payments during the life of the bond plus a return of the principal amount borrowed (the par value) when the bond matures. In a cash flow timeline format, here is the situation:

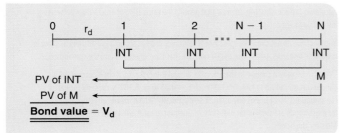

Here,

r_d = the average rate of return investors require to invest in the bond (the letter *d* stands for "debt"). For the Genesco Manufacturing bond issue, r_d = 10%.[7]

N = the number of years before the bond matures. For the Genesco bonds, N = 15. Note that N declines each year the bond is outstanding, so a bond that had a maturity of 15 years when it was issued (original maturity = 15) will have N = 14 one year after issue, N = 13 two years after issue, and so on.

M = maturity value, which is the principal amount that must be paid off at maturity; M = $1,000 per bond in our example.

INT = dollars of interest paid each year = $C \times M$; where C is the coupon rate of interest stated as a decimal and M is the bond's maturity value. In our example, each bond requires an annual interest payment equal to $100, which means that the coupon rate is 10 percent because $100 = 0.10($1,000). In financial calculator terminology, INT = PMT = 100.

We can now redraw the cash flow timeline for Genesco's bond to show the numerical values for all variables except the bond's current value:

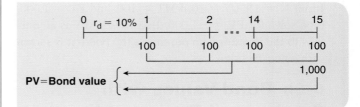

As the timeline shows, the value of a bond is determined by computing the present value of the interest payments, which represent an ordinary annuity, and the present value of the maturity value, which represents a lump-sum payment. Combining the equations from Chapter 4 that we used to compute the present value of an ordinary annuity (PVA) and the present value of a lump-sum amount (PV) forms Equation 6.1, which can be used to determine the value of a bond.

---

[6]Actually, Genesco would receive some amount less than $25 million because of costs associated with issuing the bond, such as legal fees, investment banking fees, and so forth. For our discussion here, we choose to ignore issuing costs to simplify the explanations. Chapter 3 describes the topics of issuing costs and the investment banking process.

[7]The appropriate interest rate on debt securities was discussed in Chapter 5. The bond's riskiness, liquidity, and years to maturity, as well as supply and demand conditions in the capital markets, influence the interest rates on bonds.

6.1

$$\underset{\text{value}}{\text{Bond}} = V_d = INT\left(\frac{1 - \frac{1}{(1 + r_d)^N}}{r_d}\right) + M\left[\frac{1}{(1 + r_d)^N}\right]$$

Inserting the values relevant to Genesco's bond into Equation 6.1, we find:[8]

$$V_d = \$100\left(\frac{1 - \frac{1}{(1.10)^{15}}}{0.10}\right) + \$1,000\left(\frac{1}{(1.10)^{15}}\right)$$
$$= \$100(7.60608) \quad + \$1,000(0.23939)$$
$$= \$760.61 + \$239.39 = \$1,000$$

The value of the bond can be computed using any of the three approaches discussed in Chapter 4: (1) equation (numerical) solution, which requires us to use Equation 6.1 as shown here; (2) financial calculator solution, which requires use of all five of the calculator's time-value-of-money (TVM) keys; or (3) spreadsheet solution, which is essentially the same as using a financial calculator. In this chapter, we primarily use the financial calculator to compute the value of a bond.[9] For Genesco's bond, the setup on the financial calculator is:

Inputs:	15	10	?	100	1,000
	N	I/Y	PV	PMT	FV
Output:			= −1,000.00		

Input N = 15, I/Y = 10, PMT = 100, and FV = 1,000; then solve for PV = −1,000. Because the PV is an outflow to the investor who purchases the bond, it is shown with a negative sign.

6-3b Bond Values with Semiannual Compounding

Although some bonds pay interest annually, *most* pay interest semiannually. To evaluate semiannual payment bonds, we must modify the bond valuation equation just as we did in Chapter 4 when we discussed interest compounding that occurs more than once per year. In this case, we use Equation 6.2, which is simply a modified version of Equation 6.1 to value a bond with semiannual interest payments:

6.2

$$V_d = \left(\frac{INT}{2}\right)\left[\frac{1 - \frac{1}{(1 + r_d/2)^{2 \times N}}}{(r_d/2)}\right] + \frac{M}{(1 + r_d/2)^{2 \times N}}$$

To illustrate, assume that Genesco's bonds pay $50 interest every six months rather than $100 at the end of each year. Each interest payment is now only half as large as before, but there are twice as many payments. Suppose the going (simple) rate of interest drops to 8 percent one year after the bond is issued such that there are 14 years remaining until maturity. In this scenario, the value of the bond is found as follows:[10]

Inputs:	28	4	?	50	1,000
	N	I/Y	PV	PMT	FV
Output:			= −1,166.63		

Input N = 28 = 14 × 2, I/Y = 4 = 8/2, INT = PMT = 50 = 100/2, and M = FV = 1,000; compute PV = −1,166.63.

6-4 Finding Bond Yields (Market Rates): Yield to Maturity and Yield to Call

Suppose that you were offered a 10-year, 8 percent coupon, $1,000 par value bond at a price of $875. Interest from this bond is paid semiannually. What rate of interest, or *yield*, would you earn if you bought this bond? In this section, we show you how to compute the yield, or return, you would earn if you purchase a bond with these characteristics.

6-4a Yield to Maturity (YTM)

If you buy a bond and hold it until it matures, the average rate of return you will earn per year is called the

[8]The bond prices quoted by brokers are calculated as described. If you bought a bond between interest payment dates, however, you would have to pay the basic price plus accrued interest. Thus, if you purchased a Genesco bond six months after it was issued and market rates had not changed, your broker would send you an invoice stating that you must pay $1,000 as the basic price of the bond plus $50 interest, representing one-half the annual interest of $100. The seller of the bond would receive $1,050. If you bought the bond the day before its interest payment date, you would pay $1,000 + (364/365)($100) = $1,099.73. Of course, you would receive an interest payment of $100 at the end of the next day. Throughout the chapter, we assume that the bond is being evaluated immediately after an interest payment date. Some financial calculators include a built-in calendar that permits the calculation of exact values between interest payment dates.

[9]Although we do not show the spreadsheet solutions, you can set up a spreadsheet as show in the online resources; that is, use the PV function that is programmed into the spreadsheet.

[10]We also assume a change in the effective annual interest rate, from 8 percent with annual compounding to EAR = $(1.04)^2 − 1 = 0.0816 = 8.16\%$ with semiannual compounding. Most bonds pay interest semiannually, which means effective annual rates for most bonds are somewhat higher than the quoted rates, which, in effect, represent the APRs for the bonds.

bond's **yield to maturity (YTM)**. To find a bond's yield to maturity, we solve Equation 6.1 or Equation 6.2 for r_d. For the current situation, we know that investors who buy the bond today and hold it to maturity will receive $40 = (0.08 \times \$1,000)/2$ interest every six months for the next 10 years and a $1,000 principal payment when the bond matures in 10 years. Because investors have determined that this bond is currently worth $875, based on Equation 6.2, we know the following relationship exists:

$$V_d = \frac{\$40}{\left(1 + \frac{r_d}{2}\right)^1} + \frac{\$40}{\left(1 + \frac{r_d}{2}\right)^2} + \cdots + \frac{\$40 + \$1,000}{\left(1 + \frac{r_d}{2}\right)^{20}}$$

$$= \frac{\$40}{\left(1 + \frac{YTM}{2}\right)^1} + \frac{\$40}{\left(1 + \frac{YTM}{2}\right)^2} + \cdots + \frac{\$40 + \$1,000}{\left(1 + \frac{YTM}{2}\right)^{20}}$$

$$= \$875$$

Using a financial calculator, input $N = 2 \times 10 = 20$, PV = −875 (this is a cash outflow when you buy the bond), INT = PMT = 80/2 = 40, and M = FV = 1,000, and then compute I/Y = 5.0, which represents the yield *per interest payment period* (six months in our example).

Inputs:	20	?	−875	40	1,000
	N	**I/Y**	**PV**	**PMT**	**FV**
Output:		= 5.0			

In this case, the yield is 5 percent per six months; thus the annual yield to maturity for this bond is $r_d = 10.0\% = 5.0\% \times 2$. Note that the YTM is stated as an annual return, and it is not a compounded return; rather, it is an APR as described in Chapter 4.

For this bond, the going rate of return, or yield, is 10 percent (YTM = 10.0% = 5.0% × 2). Thus, an investor who purchases this bond today for $875 and holds it until it matures in 10 years will receive an *average* of 10 percent return each year.

Notice that YTM = 10% > coupon = 8%. When the bond was issued, which might have been five years ago, the yield for similar bonds was 8 percent. We know that this is the case because a firm sets the coupon rate on a bond immediately before it is issued so that the bond's issuing price equals its face (par) value. However, as market conditions change, the bond's yield to maturity changes, which causes its market price to change. In our example, market

interest rates have increased since the time the bond was issued, so the price (value) of the bond has decreased below its face value. In reality, the calculated YTM and thus the price of a bond will change frequently before it matures because market conditions change frequently. We will discuss the relationship between YTM changes and price changes in greater detail later in the chapter.

6-4b Yield to Call (YTC)

Bonds that contain call provisions (*callable bonds*) often are called by the firm prior to maturity. In cases where a bond issue is called, investors do not have the opportunity to earn the yield to maturity because the bond issue is retired before its maturity date arrives. Thus, for callable bonds, we generally compute the **yield to call (YTC)** in addition to the YTM. The computation for the YTC is the same as that for the YTM, except that we substitute the *call price* of the bond for the maturity (par) value and the number of years until the bond can be first called for the years to maturity. To calculate the YTC for a bond with annual interest payments, then, we modify Equation 6.1, and solve the following equation for r_d:

$$V_d = \frac{INT}{(1 + r_d)^1} + \frac{INT}{(1 + r_d)^2} + \cdots + \frac{INT + Call\ price}{(1 + r_d)^{N_c}}$$

$$= \frac{INT}{(1 + YTC)^1} + \frac{INT}{(1 + YTC)^2} + \cdots + \frac{INT + Call\ price}{(1 + YTC)^{N_c}}$$

Here N_c is the number of years until the company can first call the bond; "Call price" is the price that the company must pay to call

yield to maturity (YTM) The average rate of return earned on a bond if it is held to maturity.

yield to call (YTC) The average rate of return earned on a bond if it is held until the first call date, when it is called.

the bond on the first call date; and r_d now represents the YTC. To solve for the YTC, we proceed just as we did to solve for the YTM of a bond.

Suppose the bond we are currently examining has a call provision that kicks in four years from today—that is, the bond is callable six years before it matures. If it calls the bond on the first date possible, the firm will have to pay a call price equal to $1,080. Using a financial calculator, you would find the YTC equals 13.7 percent:

Inputs:	8	?	−875	40	1,080
	N	I/Y	PV	PMT	FV

Output: = 6.87

Input N = 2 × 4 = 8, PV = −875 (this is a cash outflow if you buy the bond), INT = PMT = 40 = 80/2, and Call price = FV = 1,080, and then compute I/Y = 6.87, which is the six-month yield. As a result, YTC = 6.87% × 2 =13.7%. Thus, investors who purchase the bond today expect to earn an average annual return equal to 13.7 percent if the bond is called in four years, which could occur.

6-5 Interest Rates and Bond Values

Because they are contractually fixed, the interest payment, maturity value, and maturity date of a bond do not change during the bond's life. Conversely, the market value of a bond fluctuates continuously during its life as a result of changing market conditions. To see why the values of bonds change, let's again examine Genesco's bonds to see what happens when market interest rates change.

First, let's assume that you purchased one of the Genesco bonds we described earlier on the day it was issued. Remember that the bond matures in 15 years and has a 10 percent coupon rate of interest (annual payments), and the market interest rate at the time of issue was 10 percent. As we showed earlier, the price of the bond on the day of issue is $1,000. Suppose that *immediately after you purchased* the bond, interest rates on similar bonds increased from 10 percent to 12 percent. How would the value of your bond be affected?

Because the cash flows associated with the bond—that is, interest payments and principal repayment—remain constant, the value of the bond will decrease

when interest rates increase. In present value terms, the decrease in value makes sense. If you want to mimic the Genesco bond—that is, pay yourself $100 each year for 15 years and then pay yourself $1,000 at the end of the fifteenth year—and your opportunity cost is 10 percent, you must deposit $1,000 in a savings account. However, if you found a savings account that pays 12 percent interest annually, you could deposit some amount less than $1,000 and pay yourself the same $100 each year and receive $1,000 in 15 years because your deposit would earn greater interest. The same logic applies when we consider how an interest rate change affects the value of Genesco's bond.

If market rates *increase* from 10 percent to 12 percent immediately after you purchase Genesco's bond, the value of the bond would decrease to $863.78 (assuming annual interest payments):

Inputs:	15	12	?	100	1,000
	N	I/Y	PV	PMT	FV

Output: = − 863.78

Input N = 15, I/Y = 12, INT = PMT = 100, and M = FV = 1,000; then compute PV = −863.78.

What would be the price of Genesco's bond if interest rates had *decreased* from 10 percent to 8 percent immediately after it was issued? The value of the bond would increase to $1,171.19:

Inputs:	15	8	?	100	1,000
	N	I/Y	PV	PMT	FV

Output: = −1,171.19

Input N = 15, I/Y = 8, INT = PMT = 100, and M = FV = 1,000; then compute PV = −1,171.19.

The fact that r_d has declined to 8 percent means that if you had $1,000 to invest, you could buy *new* bonds such as Genesco's, except that these new bonds would pay $80 of interest each year rather than the $100 interest paid by Genesco. Naturally, you would prefer $100 to $80, so you would be willing to pay more than $1,000 for Genesco's bonds to get its higher interest payments. Because all investors would recognize these facts, the Genesco Manufacturing bonds would be bid up in price to $1,171.19. At that price, the Genesco bonds would provide the same rate of return to potential investors as the new bonds: 8 percent.

Following is a table that summarizes the relationship between the value of Genesco's bond and its yield to maturity.

Relationship of Market Rate, r_d, with Coupon Rate C = 10%	Bond Value, V_d (N = 15, PMT = 100, FV =1,000, and I/Y = r_d)	Relationship of Market Price, V_d, and Maturity Value, M = $1,000
$r_d = 10\% = C$	$1,000.00	V_d = M; bond sells at par
$r_d = 12\% > C$	863.78	V_d < M; bond sells at a discount
$r_d = 8\% < C$	1,171.19	V_d > M; bond sells at a premium

These same relationships exist for all bonds. When the market yield (r_d = YTM) and the coupon rate of interest are equal, the bond sells for its par value; when the market yield is greater than the coupon rate of interest, the bond sells for less than its par value, or at a *discount*. When the market yield is less than the coupon rate of interest, the bond sells for greater than its par value, or at a *premium*.

6-5a Changes in Bond Values over Time

Let's again assume that immediately after Genesco issued its bond interest rates in the economy fell from 10 to 8 percent. In the previous section, we showed that the price of the bond would increase from $1,000 to $1,171.19. Assuming that interest rates remain constant at 8 percent for the next 15 years, what will happen to the value of Genesco's bond as time passes and the maturity date approaches? It will decrease gradually from $1,171.19 at present to $1,000 at maturity, when Genesco will redeem each bond for $1,000. We can illustrate this point by calculating the value of the bond one year from now, when it has 14 years remaining to maturity:

Inputs:	14	8	?	100	1,000
	N	I/Y	PV	PMT	FV

Output: = −1,164.88

As you can see, the value of the bond will decrease from $1,171.19 to $1,164.88, or by $6.31. If you were to calculate the bond's value at other future dates using r_d = 8%, its price must decline as the maturity date approaches—when N = 13, V_d = $1,158.08, when N = 12, V_d = $1,150.72, and so on. At maturity, the value of the bond must equal its par value of $1,000 (as long as the firm does not go bankrupt).

Suppose that Sherman purchased a Genesco bond *just after* the market rate dropped to 8 percent, so he paid $1,171.19 for the bond. If he sold the bond one year later for $1,164.88, Sherman would realize a capital *loss* of $6.31, or a total dollar return of $93.69 = $100.00 − $6.31. The percentage rate of return that Sherman would earn on the bond consists of an *interest yield* (called the **current yield**) plus a **capital gains yield**. These yields are calculated using Equation 6.3:

6.3

$$\text{Bond yield} = \text{Current yield} + \text{Capital gains yield}$$
$$= \frac{\text{INT}}{V_{d,\text{Begin}}} + \frac{V_{d,\text{End}} - V_{d,\text{Begin}}}{V_{d,\text{Begin}}}$$

Here, $V_{d,\text{Begin}}$ represents the value of the bond at the beginning of the year (period) and $V_{d,\text{End}}$ is the value of the bond at the end of the year (period).

The yields Sherman would earn by holding Genesco's bond for one year are computed as follows:

Current yield =	$100.00/$1,171.19 =	0.0854 =	8.54%
Capital gains yield =	−$6.31/$1,171.19 =	−0.0054 =	−0.54%
Total rate of return (yield) =	$93.69/$1,171.19 =	0.0800 =	8.00%

Had interest rates risen from 10 to 12 percent rather than fallen immediately after issue, the value of the bond would have immediately decreased to $863.78. In this case, because the bond's value must equal the principal, or par, amount at maturity (as long as bankruptcy does not occur), its value will gradually increase from the current price of $863.78 to its maturity value of $1,000. The value of the bond would increase to $867.44 at N = 14, to $871.53 at N = 13, to $876.11 at N = 12, and so forth. The total expected

current (interest) yield The interest payment divided by the market price of the bond.

capital gains yield The percentage change in the market price of a bond over some period of time.

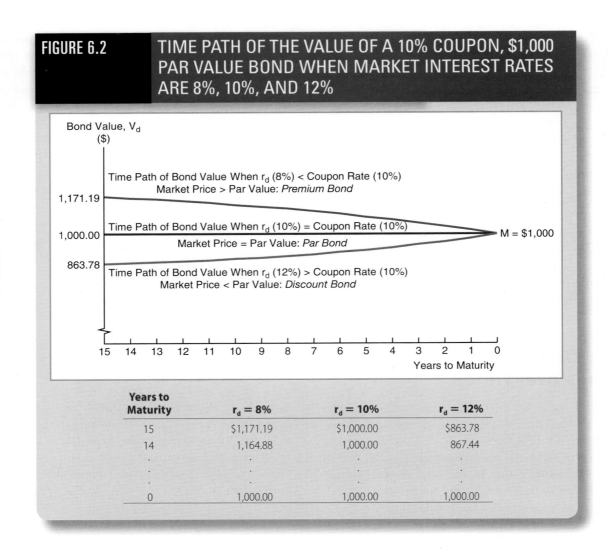

FIGURE 6.2

TIME PATH OF THE VALUE OF A 10% COUPON, $1,000 PAR VALUE BOND WHEN MARKET INTEREST RATES ARE 8%, 10%, AND 12%

Bond Value, V$_d$ ($)

Time Path of Bond Value When r$_d$ (8%) < Coupon Rate (10%)
Market Price > Par Value: *Premium Bond*

1,171.19

Time Path of Bond Value When r$_d$ (10%) = Coupon Rate (10%)
Market Price = Par Value: *Par Bond*

1,000.00

M = $1,000

863.78

Time Path of Bond Value When r$_d$ (12%) > Coupon Rate (10%)
Market Price < Par Value: *Discount Bond*

15 14 13 12 11 10 9 8 7 6 5 4 3 2 1 0

Years to Maturity

Years to Maturity	r$_d$ = 8%	r$_d$ = 10%	r$_d$ = 12%
15	$1,171.19	$1,000.00	$863.78
14	1,164.88	1,000.00	867.44
.	.	.	.
.	.	.	.
0	1,000.00	1,000.00	1,000.00

future yield on the bond would again consist of a current yield and a capital gains yield. However, now the capital gains yield would be positive, and the total yield on the bond would be 12 percent (assuming market rates remain constant).

Figure 6.2 graphs the value of Genesco's bond over time, assuming that interest rates in the economy (1) remain constant at 10 percent, (2) fall to 8 percent immediately after issue and then remain constant at that level for the next 15 years, or (3) rise to 12 percent immediately after issue and remain constant at that level. Of course, if interest rates do not remain constant, the price of the bond will fluctuate. However, regardless of what interest rates do in the future, *the bond's price will approach its face value ($1,000) as it nears its maturity date* (barring bankruptcy, in which case the bond's value might drop to zero).

interest rate price risk The risk of changes in bond prices to which investors are exposed as the result of changing interest rates.

6-5b Interest Rate Risk on a Bond

As we saw in Chapter 5, interest rates change over time. Furthermore, changes in interest rates affect bondholders in two ways. First, as shown earlier, an increase in interest rates leads to a decline in the values of outstanding bonds. (At r$_d$ = 10%, the value of Genesco's 15-year bond was $1,000; at r$_d$ = 12%, V$_d$ = $863.78.) Thus, because interest rates can rise, bondholders face the risk of suffering losses in the market values of their bond portfolios. This risk is called **interest rate price risk**. Second, many bondholders buy bonds to build funds for some future use. These bondholders reinvest each interest payment when it is received (generally every six months) and the principal repayment when it is received at maturity (or when the bond is called). If interest rates decline—say, from 10 percent to 8 percent—the bondholders will earn a lower rate of return on *reinvested cash flows*, which will reduce the

FIGURE 6.3

VALUE OF LONG-TERM AND SHORT-TERM 10% ANNUAL COUPON RATE BONDS AT DIFFERENT MARKET INTEREST RATES (r_d)

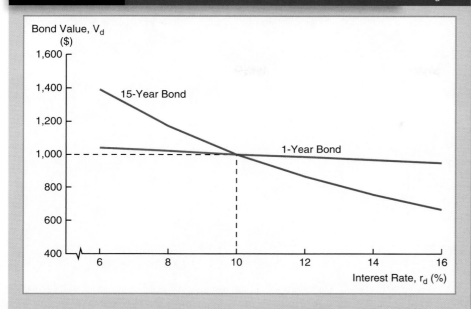

Bond Value, V_d ($)

Current Market Interest Rate, r_d	Value of	
	1-Year Bond	15-Year Bond
6%	$1,037.74	$1,388.49
8	1,018.52	1,171.19
10	1,000.00	1,000.00
12	982.14	863.78
14	964.91	754.31
16	948.28	665.47

An investor's exposure to interest rate price risk is greater on bonds with long maturities than on those that will mature in the near future. We can demonstrate this fact by considering how the value of a one-year bond with a 10 percent coupon fluctuates with changes in r_d and then comparing these changes with the effects on a 15-year bond, as calculated previously. Figure 6.3 shows the values for a one-year bond and a 15-year bond at several different market interest rates, r_d. The values for the bonds were computed assuming that the coupon interest payments for the bonds occur annually. Notice how much more sensitive the price of the long-term bond is to changes in interest rates. At a 10 percent interest rate, both the long- and short-term bonds are valued at $1,000. When rates rise to 12 percent, the value of the long-term bond decreases to $863.78, or by 13.6 percent, but the value of the short-term bond falls to only $982.14, which is a 1.8 percent decline.

future values of their portfolios relative to the values they would have accumulated if interest rates had not fallen. This risk is called **interest rate reinvestment risk**.

We can see, then, that any given change in interest rates has two separate effects on bondholders: (1) It changes the current market values of their portfolios (price risk), and (2) it changes the rates of return at which the cash flows from their portfolios can be reinvested (reinvestment risk). These two risks tend to offset one another. For example, an increase in interest rates will lower the current value of a bond portfolio. However, the future value of the portfolio will increase because the cash flows produced by the portfolio can be reinvested at the higher rates of return.

For bonds with similar coupons, this differential sensitivity to changes in interest rates always holds. *The longer the maturity of the bond, the more significantly its price changes in response to a given change in interest rates.* Thus, if two bonds have exactly the same risk of default, the bond with the longer maturity typically is exposed to more price risk from a change in interest rates.[11]

The logical explanation for this difference in interest rate price risk is simple. Suppose that you bought a 15-year bond that yielded 10 percent, or $100 per year. Now suppose that interest rates on comparable-risk bonds increased to 12 percent. You would be stuck with only $100 of interest for the next 15 years. On the other hand, had you bought a one-year bond, you would have received

[11]If a 10-year bond were plotted in Figure 6.3, its curve would lie between the curves for the 15-year and one-year bonds. The curve of a one-month bond would be almost horizontal, indicating that its price would change very little in response to an interest rate change. A perpetuity would have a very steep slope.

interest rate reinvestment risk The risk that income from a bond portfolio will vary because cash flows must be reinvested at current market rates.

Nikada/iStockphoto.com

a low return for only one year. At the end of the year, you would get your $1,000 back, and you could then reinvest it and receive 12 percent, or $120 per year, for the next 14 years. As you can see, interest rate price risk reflects the length of time one is committed to a given investment. As we described in Chapter 5, the longer a bond's term to maturity, the higher its maturity risk premium (MRP), which accounts for its higher interest rate risk.

Although a one-year bond has less interest rate price risk than a 15-year bond, the one-year bond exposes the buyer to more interest rate reinvestment risk. Suppose that you bought a one-year bond that yielded 10 percent, and then interest rates on comparable-risk bonds fell to 8 percent so that newly issued bonds now pay $80 interest. After one year, when you get your $1,000 back, you would have to invest your funds at only 8 percent. As a result, you would lose $100 – $80 = $20 in annual interest. Had you bought the 15-year bond, you would have continued to receive $100 in annual interest payments even if rates fell. If you reinvested those coupon payments, you would have to accept a lower reinvestment rate of return, but you would still be much better off than if you had been holding the one-year bond.

6-5c Bond Prices in Recent Years

From Chapter 5, we know that interest rates fluctuate. We have also just seen that the prices of outstanding bonds rise and fall inversely with changes in interest rates. When interest rates fall, many firms refinance by issuing new, lower-cost debt and using the proceeds to repay higher-cost debt. In 2003, interest rates dropped to levels that had not been seen in more than 45 years. Not surprisingly, firms that had issued higher-cost debt in earlier years refinanced much of their debt at that time. In 2015, rates were still at extremely low levels, which enticed many firms to refinance their bonds once again.[12]

Suppose that you bought a five-year bond that a corporation issued on January 3, 2011, when the average interest rate on AAA-rated bonds was 4.8 percent. Because the bond would have a coupon rate equal to 4.8 percent, you would have received $24 every

[12]In some cases, corporate bonds could not be refinanced at the lower rates due to restrictions that existed in the debt contracts or because firms (issuers) were not financially sound.

six months ($48 per year) until the bond matured on December 31, 2015. The following table shows the market price of the bond on the first trading day of January until it matured in 2015:

value by $36.79 and resulted in a 3.68 percent capital gain. Also, note that by the maturity date of the bond, interest rates had dropped to 3.4 percent, which means the rate at which you could reinvest the $1,000

Date	Years to Maturity	Market Rate of Return (%)	Market Price	Current Yield (%)	Capital Gain Yield (%)	Total Yield(%)
January 3, 2011	5	4.8%	$1,000.00			
January 2, 2012	4	3.8	1,036.79	4.80%	3.68%	8.48%
January 2, 2013	3	3.8	1,028.10	4.63	−0.84	3.79
January 2, 2014	2	4.4	1,007.58	4.67	−2.00	2.67
January 2, 2015	1	3.4	1,013.65	4.76	0.60	5.37
December 31, 2015	0		1,000.00	4.74	−1.35	3.39

Note that because market rates were lower than the bond's coupon rate, the bond was selling for a premium each year. The total yield shown in the far right column indicates the yield you would have earned if you bought the bond on the first trading day of January in a particular year and then sold it the following January. For example, if you bought the bond January 3, 2011, and sold it on January 2, 2012, you would have earned an 8.48 percent return in 2011. The return for this one-year period is higher than the bond's coupon rate because market rates decreased in 2011 from 4.8 percent to 3.8 percent in 2012, which increased the bond's

maturity value that you received on December 31, 2015 was 3.4 percent. In other words, AAA-rated corporate bonds issued on December 31, 2015 had a coupon rate of interest equal to 3.4 percent; thus any new bonds you bought on that date paid $34 interest per year (compared to $48 in 2011).

Although market rates might differ when you read this book, this illustration shows that (1) bond prices change as market rates change (in an opposite direction) and (2) the value of a bond approaches its par value as the maturity date gets closer (assuming the firm is financially healthy).

STUDY TOOLS

LOCATED AT BACK OF THE TEXTBOOK

- ☐ Problems are found at the end of this chapter.
- ☐ A tear-out Chapter Review card is located at the back of the textbook.

LOCATED AT WWW.CENGAGEBRAIN.COM

- ☐ Review Key Term flashcards and create your own cards.
- ☐ Track your knowledge and understanding of key concepts in corporate finance.
- ☐ Complete practice and graded quizzes to prepare for tests.
- ☐ Complete interactive content within CFIN5 Online.
- ☐ View the chapter highlight boxes for CFIN5 Online.

KEY BOND VALUATION AND CHARACTERISTICS CONCEPTS

To conclude this chapter, we summarize some bond valuation concepts (rules) that were discussed.

- Other things held constant, the higher the coupon rate, the higher the market price of a bond.

- When interest rates change, the values of bonds change in an opposite direction; that is, when rates increase, bond prices decrease, and vice versa.

- Whenever the going rate of interest, r_d, equals the coupon rate, a bond will sell at its par value; whenever r_d is greater than the coupon rate, a bond's price will fall below its par value (a discount bond); whenever r_d is less than the coupon

rate, a bond's price will rise above its par value (a premium bond).

- The going rate of interest, r_d, which represents the return that investors earn when buying and holding a bond to its maturity, is comprised of a return that is associated with (1) the annual interest payment, which is called the current yield, and (2) the annual change in the market value of the bond, which is called the capital gains yield.

- The market value of a bond will always approach its par value as its maturity date approaches, provided that the firm does not go bankrupt.

PROBLEMS

6–1 Swift Bicycles plans to issue convertible bonds to finance its future growth. Each convertible bond has a face value equal to $1,000 and can be converted into 25 shares of common stock. What is the minimum stock price that would make it beneficial for bondholders to convert their bonds?

6–2 Many years ago, Winding Road Maps issued a convertible bond with a conversion ratio equal to 40. The bond's face value is $1,000. (a) For how many shares of stock can a bondholder convert each bond? (b) At what stock price should bondholders convert?

6–3 Suppose you own a convertible bond that has a conversion ratio equal to 50. Each convertible bond has a face value equal to $1,000. The current market value of the company's common stock is $19, and the bond is selling for $980. If you want to liquidate your position today because you need money to pay your rent, should you sell the bond or should you convert the bond into common stock and then sell the stock? Explain your answer.

6–4 Lightning Electric's outstanding bond has a $1,000 maturity value and a 4.5 percent coupon rate of interest (paid *semiannually*). The bond, which was issued five years ago, matures in 10 years. If investors require a return equal to 6 percent to invest in similar bonds, what is the current market value of Lightning's bond?

6–5 Eleven years ago, Elite Elements issued a 15-year bond with a $1,000 face value and a 5 percent coupon rate of interest (paid *semiannually*). If investors require a return equal to 7 percent to invest in similar bonds, what is the current market value of Elite's bond?

6–6 Fine Fishing Lures (FFL) has an outstanding bond with a $1,000 face value and a 9 percent coupon rate of interest (paid *semiannually*). The bond, which was issued 22 years ago, matures in eight years. If investors require a return equal to 4 percent to invest in similar bonds, what is the market value of FFL's bond?

6–7 Tracer Manufacturers issued a 10-year bond six years ago. The bond's maturity value is $1,000, and its coupon interest rate is 6 percent. Interest is paid *semiannually*. The bond matures in four years. If investors require a return equal to 5 percent to invest in similar bonds, what is the current market value of Tracer's bond?

6–8 Buner Corp.'s outstanding bond, which has a coupon rate equal to 8 percent and a $1,000 face value, matures in six years. If investors require a rate of return equal to 12 percent on similar bonds and interest is paid *semiannually*, what should be the market price of Buner's bond?

6–9 The Desreumaux Company has two bonds outstanding. Both bonds pay $100 *annual* interest plus $1,000 at maturity. Bond L matures in 15 years, whereas Bond S matures in one year. One interest payment remains on Bond S. What will be the values of these bonds when the going rate of interest is (a) 5 percent and (b) 7 percent?

6–10 Filkins Farm Equipment's five-year zero coupon bond is currently selling for $621. The bond's maturity value is $1,000. What is the bond's yield to maturity (YTM)?

6–11 Severn Company's bond has four years remaining to maturity. Interest is paid *semiannually*, the bonds have a $1,000 par value, and the coupon interest rate is 9 percent. Compute the yield to maturity for the bonds if the current market price is (a) $851 and (b) $1,105.

6–12 Décor Interiors has an outstanding bond that was issued 20 years ago. The bond has a $1,000 maturity value and a 5.5 percent coupon rate of interest. Interest is paid *semiannually*. The bond, which matures in five years, is currently selling for $1,022. What is the bond's yield to maturity?

6–13 Four years ago Messy House Painting issued a 20-year bond with a $1,000 maturity value and a 4 percent coupon rate of interest. Interest is paid *semiannually*. The bond is currently selling for $714. (a) What is the bond's yield to maturity? (b) If the bond can be called in three years for a redemption price of $1,016, what is the bond's yield to call?

6–14 Three years ago, Jack's Automotive Jacks issued a 20-year callable bond with a $1,000 maturity value and an 8.5 percent coupon rate of interest. Interest is paid *semiannually*. The bond is currently selling for $1,046. (a) What is the bond's yield to maturity? (b) If the bond can be called in four years for a redemption price of $1,089, what is the bond's yield to call?

6–15 Quiver Archery's bond currently is selling for $1,006; its value one year ago was $996. The bond has a $1,000 maturity value and a coupon rate equal to 7 percent, and it matures in eight years. Interest is paid *annually*. Compute (a) the current yield and capital gains yield Quiver's bondholders earned during the year and (b) the bond's yield to maturity today.

6–16 Gabby's Garage issued a bond with a 10-year maturity, a $1,000 par value, a 10 percent coupon rate, and *semiannual* interest payments. Two years after the bond was issued, the going rate of interest on similar-risk bonds fell to 6 percent. Suppose the market rate stays at this level for the remainder of the bond's life. Compute the (a) current yield and (b) capital gains yield that the bond will generate in the third year (Year 3) of its life.

6–17 Dynamic Systems has an outstanding bond that has a $1,000 par value and a 7 percent coupon rate. Interest is paid *semiannually*. The bond has 11 years remaining until it matures. Today the going interest rate is 10 percent, and it is expected to remain at this level for many years in the future. Compute the (a) current yield and (b) capital gains yield that the bond will generate this year.

6–18 One year ago, Henderson Honey issued a 10-year bond for $1,000. The bond's coupon rate of interest is 4 percent, and interest is paid *annually*. If the current value of the bond is $929, what are (a) the current yield and capital gains yield Henderson's bondholders earned during the year and (b) the bond's yield to maturity today.

6–19 Eight years ago, Over-the-Top Trampolines issued a 15-year bond with a $1,000 par value and a 6 percent coupon rate (interest is paid *annually*). Today the going rate of interest on similar bonds is 6 percent. (a) What is the bond's current value? If the market rate stays at 6 percent for the remainder of the bond's life, what (b) current yield and (c) capital gains yield will bondholders receive during the next two years (i.e., Years 9 and 10)?

6–20 Many years ago, Topnotch Knives issued a zero coupon bond with a $1,000 face value. The bond matures in three years. If the current market rate on similar bonds is 11 percent, (a) what is the bond's current value? Suppose the market rate stays at 11 percent for the next three years. What (b) current yield and (c) capital gains yield will bondholders receive each year during the remainder of the bond's life?

After you finish this chapter go to **PAGE 136** for **STUDY TOOLS**

LEARNING OUTCOMES

After studying this chapter, you will be able to…

LO1 Explain what equity is, and identify some of the features and characteristics of (a) preferred stock and (b) common stock.

LO2 Describe how stock prices (values) are determined when (a) dividends grow at a constant rate and (b) dividend growth is nonconstant.

LO3 Describe some approaches (techniques) other than strict application of time value of money models that investors use to value stocks.

LO4 Identify factors that affect stock prices.

Stocks (Equity)— Characteristics and Valuation

7

Each corporation issues at least one type of stock, or equity, called *common stock*. Some corporations issue more than one type of common stock, and some issue *preferred stock* in addition to common stock. As the names imply, most equity takes the form of common stock, and preferred shareholders have preference over common shareholders when a firm distributes funds to stockholders. In this chapter, we discuss the general characteristics of both preferred stock and common stock and then give an indication as to how equity is valued.

7-1 Types of Equity

In this section, we describe some of the characteristics of equity. Far too many types of stock with different features exist to cover everything here; thus, we include only the most common features associated with preferred stock and common stock.

7-1a Preferred Stock

Preferred stock is often referred to as a *hybrid* security because it is similar to bonds (debt) in some respects, but similar to common stock in other respects. For example, like debt, preferred stock traditionally pays a constant income (called a dividend) to investors each year. At the same time, like common stock, preferred stock is safer to use than debt because a firm cannot be forced into bankruptcy if it is misses preferred dividend payments. Like bondholders, preferred stockholders have a higher priority claim to distributions made by the firm than common

stockholders. And, like debt, if the firm is highly successful, the common stockholders do not share that success with preferred stockholders because their dividend payment is fixed. We see, then, that preferred stock shares some characteristics with debt and some characteristics with common stock; that is, the characteristics of preferred stock fall between debt and common stock.

Preferred stock is issued in situations where neither debt nor common stock is entirely appropriate. For instance, a corporation might find preferred stock to be an ideal instrument when it needs to raise funds and already has a considerable amount of debt. In this situation, its creditors might be reluctant to lend more funds, and, at the same time, its common stockholders might not want their ownership shares diluted.

Some of the features that are associated with preferred stock are described next.

Par Value. Most preferred stock has a par value or its equivalent under some other name, such as *liquidation value* or *liquidation preference*. The par value is important for two reasons: (1) it establishes the amount due to the preferred stockholders in the event the firm is liquidated and (2) the preferred dividend generally is stated as a percentage of the par value.

Cumulative Dividends. Most preferred stock provides for **cumulative dividends**, a feature that requires any preferred dividends not paid in previous periods to be paid before common stock dividends can be distributed. The cumulative feature acts as a protective device. If the preferred stock dividends were not cumulative, a firm could avoid paying preferred and common stock dividends for, say, 10 years, plowing back

> **cumulative dividends** A protective feature on preferred stock that requires preferred dividends previously not paid to be disbursed before any common stock dividends can be paid.

all of its earnings into the company, and then pay a huge common stock dividend but only the stipulated annual dividend to the preferred stockholders. Obviously, such an action would effectively void the preferential position that the preferred stockholders are supposed to enjoy. The cumulative feature helps prevent such abuses.[1]

Maturity. Preferred stock generally has no specific maturity date. However, as we describe later in this section, firms can essentially incorporate a maturity proviso by including a call provision with the preferred stock issue.

Priority to Assets and Earnings. Preferred stockholders have priority over common stockholders, *but not debt holders*, with regard to earnings and assets. Thus, dividends must be paid on preferred stock before they can be paid on common stock, and, in the event of bankruptcy, the claims of the preferred shareholders must be satisfied before the common stockholders receive anything. To reinforce these features, most preferred stocks have coverage requirements similar to those placed on bonds. These restrictions limit the amount of preferred stock that a company can use, and they require a minimum level of retained earnings before the firm can pay any dividends to common stockholders.

Control of the Firm (Voting Rights). Nearly all preferred stock is *nonvoting stock*, which means that preferred stockholders neither elect the members of the board of directors nor vote on corporate issues. However, preferred stockholders often are given the right to vote for directors if the company does not pay the preferred dividend for a specified period, such as two years.

Convertibility. Most preferred stock that has been issued in recent years is convertible into common stock. The conversion feature works the same as for a bond (discussed in Chapter 6). The preferred stockholder has the option to convert each share of preferred stock into a certain number of shares of common stock (at the *conversion price*).

Other Provisions. Other provisions occasionally found in preferred stocks include the following:

1. **Call provision**—A call provision gives the issuing corporation the right to call in the preferred stock for redemption. As in the case of bonds, call provisions generally state that the company must pay an amount greater than the par value of the preferred stock, with the additional amount being dubbed a **call premium**.

2. **Sinking fund**—Most newly issued preferred stocks have sinking funds that call for the repurchase and retirement of a given percentage of the preferred stock each year. By including a call provision with a sinking fund, a firm essentially adds a

maturity option to a preferred stock issue, because it is likely that the issue will be called and retired by the firm at some future date.

3. **Participating**—A rare type of preferred stock is one that participates with the common stock in sharing the firm's earnings. Participating preferred stocks generally work as follows. (a) The stated preferred dividend is paid—for example, $5 per share. (b) The common stock is then entitled to a dividend in an amount up to the preferred dividend. (c) If the common dividend is raised, say, to $5.50, the preferred dividend must likewise be raised to $5.50.

7-1b Common Stock

We usually refer to common stockholders as the owners of the firm, because investors in common stock have certain rights and privileges generally associated with property ownership. Common stockholders are entitled to any earnings that remain after interest payments are made to bondholders and dividends are paid to preferred stockholders. Because debt and preferred stock are generally *fixed-payment* securities, common stockholders do not have to share earnings that exceed the amounts that the firm is required to pay to these shareholders. As a result, common stockholders benefit when the firm performs well. On the other hand, the payments due to bondholders and preferred stockholders do not change when the company performs poorly. In this case, payment of mandatory fixed financial obligations might reduce the common stockholders' (owners') equity. Thus, it is the common stockholders who bear most of the risk associated with a firm's operations.

The most common characteristics and rights associated with common stock are discussed next.

Par Value. In many cases, common stock does not have a par value. However, corporations that are chartered in certain states are required to assign par values to their common stocks. Legally, the par value of a common stock represents a stockholder's minimum financial obligation in the event the corporation is liquidated and its debts are repaid. For example, if a stock has a par value equal to $10, then the investor is obligated to contribute $10 per share to repay the firm's debt upon liquidation. If a newly issued stock is purchased for more than $10 per share, the investor's obligation is satisfied; but if the stock is purchased for less than $10—say, for $6—then the stockholder is required to make up the difference—$4 in this case—if the firm goes bankrupt and additional funds are needed

call premium The amount in excess of par value that a company must pay when it calls a security.

---

[1] Most cumulative plans do not provide for compounding; in other words, the unpaid preferred dividends themselves earn no return. In addition, many preferred issues have a limited cumulative feature; for example, unpaid preferred dividends might accumulate for only three years.

to repay creditors. In nearly every instance, new common stock is sold for more than its par value, so investors generally are not concerned with a stock's par value. As you will discover later in this chapter, the par value and market value of a common stock are not related—that is, *par value does not determine market value, and vice versa.*

Dividends. The firm has no obligation, contractual or implied, to pay common stock dividends. Some firms pay relatively constant dividends year after year; other companies do not pay dividends for many years after they go public. The return that investors receive when they own a company's common stock is based on both the change in the stock's market value (capital gain) and the dividend paid by the company. Stocks that produce returns that are based primarily on dividends are traditionally called **income stocks** because dividend payments represent income to investors. Stocks of companies that retain most, if not all, of their earnings each year to help fund growth opportunities are called **growth stocks** because the returns on such stocks are often generated primarily by capital gains, which are associated with the companies' growth rates.

Maturity. Like preferred stock, common stock has no specified maturity; that is, it is perpetual. At times, however, companies repurchase shares of their common stock in the financial markets. Stock repurchases might be undertaken when (1) the firm has excess cash but no good investment opportunities; (2) the price of the firm's stock is undervalued; or (3) management wants to gain more ownership control of the firm by repurchasing stock from *other* investors, thereby increasing the percentage owned by management.

Priority to Assets and Earnings. Common stockholders can be paid dividends only after interest on debt and preferred dividends are paid. In the event the company is liquidated, common stockholders are last to receive any of the proceeds from the liquidation. Thus, as investors, the *common stockholders are last in line to receive any cash distributions from the corporation.*

Control of the Firm (Voting Rights). The common stockholders have the right to elect the firm's directors, who in turn appoint the officers who manage the business. Stockholders also vote on shareholders' proposals, mergers, and changes in the firm's charter. In a small firm, the major stockholder typically assumes the positions of president and chairperson of the board of directors. In a large, publicly owned firm, the managers typically own some stock, but their personal holdings are insufficient to provide voting control. Thus, if stockholders decide that the management team of a large, publicly owned company is not effective, they can join together to vote to remove the executives.

Numerous state and federal laws stipulate how stockholder control is to be exercised. Corporations must hold elections of directors at their annual meetings. Each share of stock normally has one vote, so the owner of 1,000 shares has 1,000 votes. Stockholders of large corporations, such as General Motors, can appear at the annual meeting and vote in person, but in most cases they transfer their right to vote to a second party by means of an instrument known as a **proxy**. The management of large firms solicits, and thus usually gets, stockholders' proxies. If earnings are poor and stockholders are dissatisfied, however, an outside group might solicit the proxies in an effort to overthrow management and take control of the business. This kind of battle is known as a *proxy fight.*

Managers who do not have majority control (more than 50 percent of their firms' stock) are very much concerned about proxy fights and takeovers from other companies, and many attempt to get stockholder approval for changes in their corporate charters that would make takeovers more difficult. For example, in the past, companies have persuaded their stockholders to agree to the following provisions: (1) to elect only one-third of the directors each year (rather than electing all directors each year); (2) to require 75 percent of the stockholders (rather than 50 percent) to approve a merger; and (3) to approve a "poison pill" provision that would allow the stockholders of a firm that is taken over by another firm to buy shares in the second firm at a substantially reduced price. The third provision makes the acquisition unattractive and therefore wards off hostile takeover attempts. Managements seeking such changes generally cite a fear that the firm will be picked up at a bargain price, but it often appears that managers' concerns about their own positions might be an even more important consideration.

income stocks Stocks of firms that traditionally pay large, relatively constant dividends each year.

growth stocks Stocks that generally pay little or no dividends so as to retain earnings to help fund growth opportunities.

proxy A document giving one person the authority to act for another; typically it gives them the power to vote shares of common stock.

Preemptive Right. A preemptive right requires a firm to offer existing stockholders shares of a new stock issue in proportion to their current ownership holdings before such shares can be offered to other investors. The purpose of the preemptive right is twofold. First, it protects the power of control of current stockholders. If not for this safeguard, the management team of a corporation could prevent the stockholders from removing the managers from office by issuing a large number of additional shares and purchasing these shares themselves. Second, and more importantly, a preemptive right protects stockholders against the dilution of value that would occur if new shares were sold at relatively low prices. Although most common stock issues do not have preemptive rights (because most states do not require such rights to be included in corporate charters), we mention it here to provide information about the benefits the preemptive right offers stockholders.

Types of Common Stock. Although most firms have only one type of common stock, in some instances classified stock is used to meet the special needs of a company. Generally, when special classifications of stock are used, one type is designated Class A, another Class B, and so on. For example, a company that is going public might designate Class A stock for sale to the public. Investors who purchase this class of stock will receive any dividends that are paid by the firm, but they will not have voting rights until perhaps five years after the stock's issuance. The company's Class B stock, which might be called founders' shares, will be retained by the organizers of the firm. The holders of this class of stock will have full voting rights for five years, but will not receive dividends until the company establishes its earning power by building up retained earnings to a designated level. In this case, the use of classified stock enables the public to take a position in a company without sacrificing income, while the founders retain control during the crucial early stages of the firm's development. At the same time, outside investors are protected against excessive withdrawals of funds by the original owners.

Note that "Class A," "Class B," and so on have no standard meanings. One firm could designate its Class B shares as founders' shares and its Class A shares as those sold to the public, whereas another firm might reverse these designations. Still other firms could use stock classifications for entirely different purposes.[2]

7-1c Equity Instruments in International Markets

For the most part, the financial securities of companies in other countries are similar to those in the United States. Some differences do exist, however, as discussed in this section.

American Depository Receipts. In the United States, most foreign stock is traded through American depository receipts (ADRs). ADRs are not foreign stocks; rather, they are certificates that represent ownership in stocks of foreign companies held in trust by a bank that created the ADRs and is located in the country where the stocks are traded. ADRs provide U.S. investors with the ability to invest in foreign companies with less complexity and difficulty than might otherwise be possible.

In many cases, investors can purchase foreign securities directly, but such investments might be complicated by legal issues, the ability to take funds such as dividends out of the country, and translation of value and information into domestic terms. ADRs enable investors to participate in the international financial markets without having to bear risks greater than the risks associated with the corporations in which the investments are made. Each ADR certificate represents a certain number of shares of stock of a foreign company, and it entitles the owner to receive any dividends paid by the company in U.S. dollars. ADRs are traded in the stock markets in the United States, which often are more liquid than foreign markets. All financial information, including value, is denominated in dollars and stated in English, thereby eliminating potential problems with exchange rates and language translations.

Foreign Equity (Stock). The primary difference between stocks of foreign companies and stocks of U.S. companies is that U.S. regulations provide greater protection of stockholders' rights than do the regulations of most other countries. In the international markets,

[2]When General Motors (GM) acquired Hughes Aircraft for $5 billion in 1985, it paid for the purchase in part with a new Class H common stock (designated as GMH). The GMH stock had limited voting rights, and its dividends were tied to Hughes's performance as a GM subsidiary. The company created the new stock for the following reasons: (1) GM wanted to limit voting privileges on the new classified stock because of management's concern about a possible takeover and (2) Hughes's employees wanted to be rewarded more directly based on Hughes's own performance than would have been possible with regular GM stock. At the time, GM's deal posed a problem for the New York Stock Exchange, which had a rule against listing any company's common stock if the firm had any nonvoting common stock outstanding. GM made it clear that it was willing to delist if the NYSE did not change its rules. The NYSE concluded that such arrangements as GM had made were logical and were likely to be made by other companies in the future, so it changed its rules to accommodate GM.

---

preemptive right A provision that gives existing common stockholders the right to purchase new issues of common stock on a pro rata basis before any shares can be offered to other investors.

classified stock Common stock that is given a special designation, such as Class A, Class B, and so forth, to meet special needs of the company.

founders' shares Stock, owned by the firm's founders, that has sole voting rights but generally pays out only restricted dividends (if any) for a specified number of years.

American depository receipts (ADRs) "Certificates" created by organizations such as banks; represent ownership in stocks of foreign companies that are held in trust by banks located in the countries where the stocks are traded.

equity generally is referred to as either *Euro stock* or *Yankee stock*. With the exception of stock traded in the United States, any stock that is traded in a country other than the issuing company's home country is called **Euro stock**. Thus, if the stock of a Japanese company is sold in Germany, it would be considered a Euro stock. On the other hand, **Yankee stock** is issued by foreign companies and traded in the United States. For example, if a Japanese company sells its stock in the United States, it is termed a Yankee stock in the international markets.

7-2 Stock Valuation—The Dividend Discount Model (DDM)

A stock's value is found in the same manner as the values of other assets; by determining the present value of the expected future cash flow stream. The expected future cash flows that an investor receives as the result of purchasing a stock consist of dividends, which include regular dividends, *special* dividends (not regularly scheduled), or *liquidating* dividends (paid when a firm liquidates its assets and after its debts are paid).

Before we present the general stock valuation model, let's define some terms and notations that we use in the remainder of the chapter.

$\hat{D}_t$ = pronounced "D hat t"; the dividend stockholders expect to receive at the end of Year t. We designate expected value by placing a hat (^) above the variable. D_0 is the most recently paid dividend, which already has been paid; $\hat{D}_1$ is the next dividend that is expected to be paid at the end of this year; $\hat{D}_2$ is the dividend expected at the end of Year 2; and so forth. Because D_0 has already been paid, its value is known, and thus we do not place a hat over the D.

$P_0 = V_s$ = the *actual* market price (value) of the stock today.

$\hat{P}_t$ = the *expected* price of the stock at the end of each Year t. $\hat{P}_0$ is the intrinsic, or theoretical, value of the stock today as seen by a particular investor; $\hat{P}_1$ is the price *expected* at the end of Year 1; and so on. Note that $\hat{P}_0$ is the intrinsic value of the stock today based on a particular investor's estimate of the stock's expected dividend stream and the riskiness of that stream. Whereas P_0 is fixed and is identical for all investors because it represents the actual price at which the stock currently can be purchased in the stock market, $\hat{P}_0$ can differ among investors depending on what they feel the firm (stock) actually is worth. An investor would buy the stock only if his or her estimate of $\hat{P}_0$ is equal to or greater than the current selling price, P_0; that is, the stock is a good investment if $\hat{P}_0 \geq P_0$.

g = the expected growth rate in dividends as predicted by an average investor. If we assume that dividends are expected to grow at a constant rate, then g is also equal to the expected rate of growth in the stock's price (*capital gains*).

r_s = the minimum acceptable, or required, rate of return on the stock that investors demand, considering both its riskiness and the returns available on other investments. The determinants of r_s are discussed in detail in Chapter 8.

$\dfrac{\hat{D}_1}{P_0}$ = the expected dividend yield on the stock during the coming year.

$\dfrac{\hat{P}_1 - P_0}{P_0}$ = the expected capital gains yield on the stock during the coming year; it is the expected change in the stock's value stated as a percentage.

$\hat{r}_s$ = the expected rate of return, which is the return that an investor who buys the stock *expects* to receive. The value of $\hat{r}_s$ could be above or below the required rate of return, r_s, but an investor should buy the stock only if $\hat{r}_s$ is equal to or greater than r_s; that is, a stock is considered a good investment if $\hat{r}_s \geq r_s$.

7-2a Expected Dividends as the Basis for Stock Values

In our discussion of bonds, we found that the value of a bond is the present value of the interest payments over the life of the bond plus the present value of the bond's maturity (par) value. Stock prices are likewise computed as the present value of a stream of cash flows, and the basic stock valuation equation resembles the bond valuation equation shown in Chapter 6 (Equation 6.1).

To determine the cash flows that corporations provide to their stockholders, think of yourself as an investor who buys a stock with the intention of holding it

Euro stock Stock traded in countries other than the home country of the company, not including the United States.

Yankee stock Stock issued by foreign companies and traded in the United States.

market price (value), P_0 The price at which a stock currently sells in the market.

intrinsic (theoretical) value, $\hat{P}_0$ The value of an asset that, in the mind of a particular investor, is justified by the facts; $\hat{P}_0$ can be different from the asset's current market price, its book value, or both.

growth rate, g The expected rate of change in dividends per share.

required rate of return, r_s The minimum rate of return that stockholders consider acceptable on a common stock.

dividend yield The next expected dividend divided by the current price of a share of stock, $\hat{D}_1/P_0$.

capital gains yield The change in price (capital gain) during a given year divided by the price at the beginning of the year; $(\hat{P}_1 - P_0)/P_0$.

expected rate of return, $\hat{r}_s$ The rate of return that an individual stockholder expects to receive on a common stock. It is equal to the expected dividend yield plus the expected capital gains yield, $\hat{r}_s = \hat{D}_1/P_0 + (\hat{P}_1 - P_0)/P_0$.

(in your family) forever. In this case, all that you (and your heirs) will receive from your investment in the stock is a stream of dividends. Thus, the value of the stock today is calculated as the present value of an infinite stream of dividends (we assume the firm remains in business forever), which is depicted on a cash flow timeline as follows:

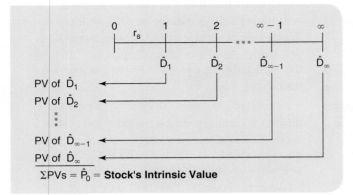

This cash flow timeline shows that the general equation to compute the value of a stock can be stated as Equation 7.1:

7.1

$$\text{Stock value} = V_s = \hat{P}_0 = \frac{\hat{D}_1}{(1 + r_s)^1} + \cdots + \frac{\hat{D}_\infty}{(1 + r_s)^\infty}$$

$$= \sum_{t=1}^{\infty} \frac{\hat{D}_t}{(1 + r_s)^t}$$

According to Equation 7.1, the value of a stock is determined by computing the present value of the dividends that the corporation is expected to pay stockholders during its life, which we generally assume is infinite for a going concern. From an investor's viewpoint, however, a stock's expected cash flows consist of two elements: (1) the dividends expected in each year the stock is held and (2) the price that is received when the stock is sold at the end of the holding period. So how do you determine the value of $\hat{P}_0$ when you plan to hold the stock for a specific (finite) period and then sell it, which is the typical scenario followed by investors? Unless the company is likely to be liquidated, and therefore disappear, *the value of the stock is still determined by Equation 7.1*. To see why, recognize that for any individual investor, the expected cash flows consist of expected dividends plus the expected price of the stock when it is sold. However, the sale price that the current investor receives

depends on the dividends that the *future investor expects* to be paid by the company from that point forward. As a consequence, for all present and future investors, expected cash flows include *all* of the expected future dividends. Put another way, unless the corporation is liquidated or sold to another concern, *the cash flows that it provides stockholders will consist only of a stream of dividends*. Therefore, the value of a share of stock must equal the present value of the dividend stream that the company is expected to pay throughout its life.

The general validity of Equation 7.1 can be confirmed by considering the following scenario: Suppose you buy a stock and expect to hold it for one year. You will receive dividends during the year plus the value of the stock when you sell it at the end of the year. The value of the stock at the end of the year—that is, $\hat{P}_1$—equals the present value of the dividends during Year 2 plus the stock price at the end of that year, which in turn is determined as the present value of another set of future dividends and an even more distant stock price. This process can be continued forever, with the ultimate result being Equation 7.1.

Equation 7.1 is a generalized stock valuation model in the sense that over time the value of $\hat{D}_t$ can follow any pattern: $\hat{D}_t$ can be rising, falling, or constant, or it can even fluctuate randomly, and Equation 7.1 will still hold. Often, however, the projected stream of dividends follows a systematic pattern, in which case we can develop a simplified (easier to apply) version of the stock valuation model expressed in Equation 7.1. In the following sections, we show how to apply Equation 7.1 when the firm grows at a constant rate as well as when the firm's growth rate is not constant.

7-2b Valuing Stocks with Constant, or Normal, Growth (g)

Even though expected growth rates vary from company to company, for many firms it is not uncommon for investors

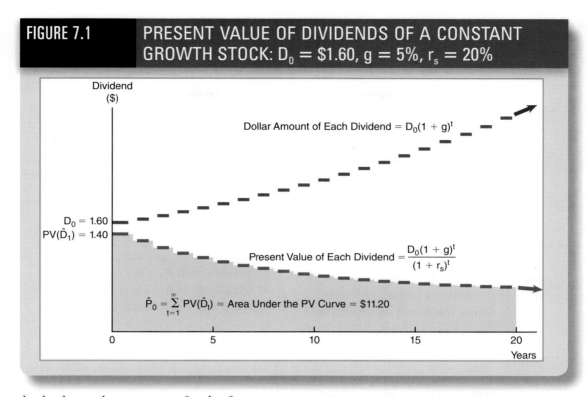

FIGURE 7.1   PRESENT VALUE OF DIVIDENDS OF A CONSTANT GROWTH STOCK: $D_0 = \$1.60$, $g = 5\%$, $r_s = 20\%$

Dividend ($)

Dollar Amount of Each Dividend $= D_0(1 + g)^t$

$D_0 = 1.60$
$PV(\hat{D}_1) = 1.40$

Present Value of Each Dividend $= \dfrac{D_0(1 + g)^t}{(1 + r_s)^t}$

$\hat{P}_0 = \displaystyle\sum_{t=1}^{\infty} PV(\hat{D}_t) =$ Area Under the PV Curve $= \$11.20$

0   5   10   15   20

Years

to expect dividend growth to continue for the foreseeable future at about the same rate as that of the *nominal gross national product* (real GNP plus inflation). On this basis, we might expect the dividend of an average, or "normal," company to grow at a rate of 3–5 percent per year. Thus, if the last dividend paid by such a normal, or constant, growth company was D_0, the firm's dividend in any future Year t can be forecast as $\hat{D}_t = D_0(1 + g)^t$, where g is the constant expected rate of growth each year. For example, if a firm just paid a dividend of $1.60—that is, $D_0 = \$1.60$—and investors expect a 5 percent growth rate, the estimated dividend one year hence would be $\hat{D}_1 = \$1.60(1.05) = \$1.68$; $\hat{D}_2$ would be $\$1.60(1.05)^2 = \$1.764$; and so on. When g is constant such that $g = g_1 = g_2 = \cdots = g_\infty$, we can use this method for estimating dividends for any period in the future, which allows us to rewrite Equation 7.1 as Equation 7.2:[3]

7.2

$$\hat{P}_0 = \frac{D_0(1 + g)^1}{(1 + r_s)^1} + \frac{D_0(1 + g)^2}{(1 + r_s)^2} + \cdots + \frac{D_0(1 + g)^\infty}{(1 + r_s)^\infty}$$

$$= \frac{D_0(1 + g)}{r_s - g} = \frac{\hat{D}_1}{r_s - g}$$

$$= \text{value of a constant growth stock}$$

[3]The second line in Equation 7.2 is derived by applying the algebra of geometric progressions.

[4]The constant growth model as set forth in the last term of Equation 7.2 is often called the *Gordon model*, after Myron J. Gordon, who did much to develop and popularize it.

The form of the equation given in the second line of Equation 7.2, which is often referred to as the **constant growth model**, is merely a simplification of Equation 7.1 under the condition that dividends grow at a constant rate, g.[4] Note that for the simplified form of Equation 7.2 (shown in the second line) to yield meaningful results, r_s must be greater than g. In situations where $r_s < g$, the results are meaningless because the denominator in the simplified form of Equation 7.2 is negative—that is, $(r_s - g) < 0$—which gives a negative value for $\hat{P}_0$. $\hat{P}_0 < 0$ doesn't make sense in the world of finance.

Inserting values from our illustrative stock, we find that when investors require a 20 percent return, the value of the stock should be $11.20:

$$\hat{P}_0 = \frac{\$1.60(1.05)}{0.20 - 0.05} = \frac{\$1.68}{0.15} = \$11.20$$

Figure 7.1 illustrates the concept underlying the valuation process for this constant growth stock. Dividends are growing at the rate g = 5%. Because $r_s > g$, however, the present value of each future dividend is declining. For example, the dividend in Year 1 is $\hat{D}_1 = D_0(1 + g)^1 = \$1.60(1.05) = \$1.68$. The present value of this dividend, discounted at 20 percent, is $PV(\hat{D}_1) = \$1.68/(1.20)^1 = \$1.40$. The dividend expected in Year 2 grows to $\hat{D}_2 = \$1.68(1.05) = \$1.764$, but the present value of this dividend falls to $PV(\hat{D}_2) = \$1.225$.

constant growth model Also called the Gordon model, it is used to find the value of a stock that is expected to experience constant growth.

Continuing, $\hat{D}_3 = \$1.8522$ and $PV(\hat{D}_3) = 1.0719$, and so on. As you can see, the expected future dividends are growing, but the present value of each successive dividend is declining because the dividend growth rate, 5 percent, is less than the rate used for discounting the dividends to the present, 20 percent.

If we summed the present values of each future dividend, this summation would equal the value of the stock, $\hat{P}_0$. When g is constant, this summation is equal to $\hat{D}_1/(r_s-g)$, as shown in Equation 7.2. Therefore, if we extended the lower step function curve in Figure 7.1 to infinity and added up the present values of all future dividends, the summation would be identical to the value given by solving Equation 7.2; that is, $11.20.

Growth in dividends occurs primarily as a result of growth in *earnings per share (EPS)*. Earnings growth, in turn, results from a number of factors, including the amount of earnings that is *reinvested*, or plowed back into the firm. If the firm's earnings are not all paid out as dividends—that is, if the firm retains some fraction of its earnings—the dollars of investment behind each share will increase over time, which should lead to growth in future earnings and dividends. On the other hand, when all earnings are paid out as dividends, the firm retains nothing for reinvestment; thus, everything else equal, the growth rate equals zero.

Special Case of Constant Growth: g = 0. Equation 7.2 is sufficiently general to encompass the case where g = 0; that is, there is no growth, so constant growth is equal to 0 percent. When g = 0, which is simply a special case of constant growth, the simplified form of Equation 7.2 becomes:

$$\hat{P}_0 = \frac{D_0(1 + g)}{r_s - g} = \frac{D}{r_s}$$

We eliminated the subscript and the hat for D, because all future dividends will be the same as the most recently paid dividend, which means that $D_0 = \hat{D}_1 = \hat{D}_2 = \cdots = \hat{D}_\infty = D$. This stream of dividends represents a perpetuity, and the equation given here is the same as the equation given in Chapter 4 to compute the present value of a perpetuity. This equation can be used to determine the value of preferred stock, because the constant preferred dividend represents a perpetuity.

Expected Rate of Return on a Constant Growth Stock. We can solve Equation 7.2 for r_s, again using the

[5]The r_s value of Equation 7.2 is a *required* rate of return. When we transform this equation to obtain Equation 7.3, we are finding an *expected* rate of return. Obviously, the transformation requires that $r_s = \hat{r}_s$. This equality holds if the stock market is in equilibrium, a condition discussed in Chapter 8.

hat to denote that we are dealing with an expected rate of return (Equation 7.3):[5]

7.3

Expected rate of return	=	Expected dividend yield	+	Expected growth rate, or capital gains yield

$$\hat{r}_s = \frac{\hat{D}_1}{P_0} + g$$

For example, imagine that you buy a stock for a price $P_0 = \$11.20$, and that you expect the stock to pay a dividend $\hat{D}_1 = \$1.68$ at the end of the year and to grow at a constant rate of g = 5% in the future. In this case, your expected rate of return will be 20 percent:

$$\hat{r}_s = \frac{\$1.68}{\$11.20} + 0.05 = 0.15 + 0.05$$
$$= 0.20 = 20.0\%$$

In this form, we see that $\hat{r}_s$ is the *expected total return* and that it consists of an *expected dividend yield*, $\hat{D}_1/P_0 = 15\%$, plus an *expected growth rate or capital gains yield*, g = 5%.

Suppose we had conducted this analysis on January 2, 2017. In other words, $P_0 = \$11.20$ is the January 2, 2017, stock price and $\hat{D}_1 = \$1.68$ is the dividend expected at the end of 2017 (December 31). What would be the expected stock price at the end of 2017 (or the beginning of 2018)? We would again apply Equation 7.2, but this time we would use the expected 2018 dividend, $\hat{D}_2 = \hat{D}_1(1+g) = \hat{D}_{2018} = \hat{D}_{2017}(1+g) = \$1.68\ (1.05) = \$1.764$, and solve for $\hat{P}_1$.

$$\hat{P}_1 = \hat{P}_{1/2/18} = \frac{\hat{D}_{12/31/18}}{r_s - g} = \frac{\$1.764}{0.20 - 0.05} = \$11.76$$

Notice that $\hat{P}_1 = \$11.76$ is 5 percent greater than $\hat{P}_0$, the \$11.20 price on January 2, 2017; that is, $\hat{P}_{1/2/18} = \$11.20(1.05) = \$11.76$. In this case, we would expect to make a capital gain of \$0.56 = \$11.76 − \$11.20 during the year, which represents a capital gains yield of 5 percent:

$$\text{Capital gains yield} = \frac{\$\text{Capital gain}}{\text{Beginning price}} = \frac{\hat{P}_1 - P_0}{P_0}$$
$$= \frac{\$11.76 - \$11.20}{\$11.20}$$
$$= \frac{\$0.56}{\$11.20} = 0.05 = 5.0\%$$

Here P_0 represents the actual stock price at the beginning of the period, and $\hat{P}_1$ represents the expected price of the stock at the end of one period (one year in this case).

We could extend this analysis further, if desired. In each future year the expected capital gains yield would equal g = 5%, the expected dividend growth rate. Continuing, we could estimate the dividend yield in 2018 as follows:

$$\text{Dividend yield}_{2018} = \frac{\hat{D}_1}{P_0} = \frac{\hat{D}_{12/31/18}}{P_{1/2/18}} = \frac{\$1.764}{\$11.76}$$

$$= 0.15 = 15.0\%$$

We could also calculate the dividend yield for 2019, which would again be 15 percent. Thus, for a constant growth stock, the following conditions must hold:

1. The dividend is expected to grow forever at a constant rate, g. The stock price is expected to grow at this same rate, g. As a result, the expected capital gains yield is also constant, and it is equal to g.

2. The expected dividend yield is a constant, such that $\hat{D}_1/P_0, = \hat{D}_2/P_1, = \cdots = \hat{D}_\infty/P_{\infty-1}$.

3. The expected total rate of return, $\hat{r}_s$, is equal to the expected dividend yield plus the expected growth rate: $\hat{r}_s = \hat{D}_1/P_0 + g$.

We should clarify the meaning of the term *expected* here. It means expected in a probabilistic sense: the statistically expected outcome. Thus, if we say the growth rate is expected to remain constant at 5 percent, we mean that the best prediction for the growth rate in any future year is 5 percent. We do not literally expect the growth rate to be exactly equal to 5 percent in each future year. In this sense, the constant growth assumption is a reasonable one for many large, mature companies.

7-2c Valuing Stocks with Nonconstant Growth

Firms typically go through *life cycles*. During the early parts of their lives, their growth rates greatly exceed that of the economy as a whole. Later, their growth matches the economy's growth. In the final stage of its life, a firm's growth lags behind that of the economy.[6] Automobile manufacturers in the 1920s, computer software firms such as Microsoft in the 1990s, and the Wi-Fi (which

[6]The concept of a life cycle could be broadened to include a *product cycle*, which would include small start-up companies and large companies such as IBM that periodically introduce new products that boost sales and earnings. We should also mention *business cycles*, which alternately depress and boost sales and profits. The growth rate just after a major new product has been introduced, or just after a firm emerges from the depths of a recession, is likely to be much higher than the expected long-run average growth rate, which is the proper value to use for evaluating the project.

stands for *wireless fidelity*) industry in the 2000s are examples of firms in the early part of their cycles. On the other hand, firms, such as those in the tobacco industry or coal industry, are currently in the waning stages of their life cycles. That is, their growth is not keeping pace with the general economic growth. (In some cases, their growth actually is negative.) Firms with growth rates that are not essentially the same each year are called nonconstant growth firms.

Because it is applicable only when *all* the future dividends grow at a constant rate, g, Equation 7.2 cannot be used to estimate the value of a nonconstant growth stock. But we can easily estimate the value of a nonconstant growth stock if we assume that, at some point during its life, the firm stops growing at a nonconstant rate and begins to grow at a constant rate. With this assumption, we can follow these three steps to determine the current value of a nonconstant growth stock:

▶ **Step 1**—Start computing the dividends that are expected to be paid during the nonconstant growth period; continue computing dividends until you compute the last dividend that is affected by nonconstant growth. Using the investors' required rate of return, r_s, compute the present values of all the nonconstant growth dividends, and sum these present values.

▶ **Step 2**—Compute the first dividend that is affected by the constant, or normal, growth rate, and use this dividend to compute the value of the stock at the *end of the nonconstant growth period*. Because at this point all future dividends will grow at a constant rate, which we designate g_{norm}, we can use the modified version of Equation 7.2 shown in Equation 7.4 to compute the value of the stock at the end of the nonconstant growth period, $\hat{P}_t$:

7.4

$$\hat{P}_t = \frac{\left(\begin{array}{c}\text{First constant}\\\text{growth dividend}\end{array}\right)}{r_s - g_{norm}} = \frac{\hat{D}_t(1 + g_{norm})}{r_s - g_{norm}} = \frac{\hat{D}_{t+1}}{r_s - g_{norm}}$$

$\hat{D}_t$ is the last nonconstant growth dividend the firm is expected to pay, and $\hat{D}_{t+1}$ represents the first dividend that grows at the constant rate, g_{norm}. As a result, $\hat{P}_t$, which is the expected value of the stock in Year t, represents the value of all the dividends that are expected to be paid in Year t + 1 and beyond. That is, $\hat{P}_t$ represents the value

nonconstant growth The part of the life cycle of a firm in which its growth is either much faster or much slower than that of the economy as a whole.

of all the future constant growth dividends at the end of Year t because $\hat{D}_{t+1}, \hat{D}_{t+2}, \ldots \hat{D}_\infty$ are all dividends that grow at the same rate, g_{norm}.

After computing $\hat{P}_t$, find its present value: PV of $\hat{P}_t = \hat{P}_t/(1 + r_s)^t$.

▶ **Step 3**—To determine the current intrinsic value of the stock, add the present value of the nonconstant growth dividends computed in Step 1 to the present value of the future stock price computed in Step 2. In other words, $\hat{P}_0 = $ (PV of nonconstant growth dividends) + (PV of $\hat{P}_t$).

Year	Growth Rate, g_t	Dividend, $\hat{D}_t = \hat{D}_{t-1}(1 + g_t)$	(PV of $\hat{D}_t$) = $\hat{D}_t/(1 + r_s)^t$
1	20.0%	\$1.2000 = \$1.00(1.20)	\$1.0435 = \$1.2000/(1.15)^1
2	20.0	1.4400 = 1.20(1.20)	1.0888 = 1.4400/(1.15)^2
3	20.0	1.7280 = 1.44(1.20)	1.1362 = 1.7280/(1.15)^3

$$\sum(\text{PV of } \hat{D}_t) = \$3.2685$$

To illustrate the valuation of a nonconstant growth stock using these steps, let's suppose that the dividends paid by a firm are expected to grow at a 20 percent rate for the next three years, and then the growth rate is expected to fall to 5 percent and remain at that level for the remainder of the firm's life. Clearly, the growth rate for this firm is not constant, because different growth rates are expected during the remainder of the firm's life (i.e., $g_1 = g_2 = g_3 = 20\%$, but $g_4 = g_5 = \cdots = g_\infty = 5\%$). In this example, even though the growth rate is not the same for all future years, the stock becomes a constant growth stock at the end of the period of supernormal growth, which is at the end of Year 3 because, after that point in time, the firm grows at a constant rate forever, $g_{norm} = 5\%$.

To determine the current value of the stock for our example, let's assume that investors require a 15 percent return to invest in the company's stock. If the last (most recent) dividend paid by the company was \$1.00, we can follow the steps outlined previously to find the current value of the stock.

▶ **Step 1**—Compute the values of the nonconstant growth dividends, and then compute the sum of the present values of these dividends. The computations and the results of this step are shown in the following table:

▶ **Step 2**—Using Equation 7.4, compute the value of the stock at the end of the nonconstant growth period. In our example, because nonconstant growth ends after the Year 3 dividend, $\hat{D}_3$, is paid, we have

$$\hat{P}_3 = \frac{\hat{D}_3(1 + g_{norm})}{r_s - g_{norm}} = \frac{\hat{D}_4}{r_s - g_{norm}}$$

$$= \frac{\$1.7280(1.05)}{0.15 - 0.05} = \frac{\$1.8144}{0.10} = \$18.1440$$

This result indicates that in Year 3 the value of the constant growth dividends $\hat{D}_4, \hat{D}_5, \ldots, D_\infty$ is \$18.14. In other words, the stock should be selling for \$18.14 at the end of Year 3, after the last nonconstant growth dividend, $\hat{D}_3$, is paid.

Compute the present value of $\hat{P}_3$: (PV of $\hat{P}_3$) = \$18.1440/(1.15)^3 = \$11.9300.

▶ **Step 3**—To determine the current intrinsic value of the stock, sum the result of Step 1 and the result of Step 2. Thus, $\hat{P}_0 = \$3.2685 + \$11.9300 = \$15.1985 \approx \$15.20$. Figure 7.2 shows the cash flow timeline with the actual

FIGURE 7.2   DETERMINING THE VALUE OF A NONCONSTANT GROWTH STOCK

Note: $\hat{P}_3 = \dfrac{\hat{D}_4}{r_s - g_{norm}} = \dfrac{\$1.8144}{0.15 - 0.05} = \$18.1440$

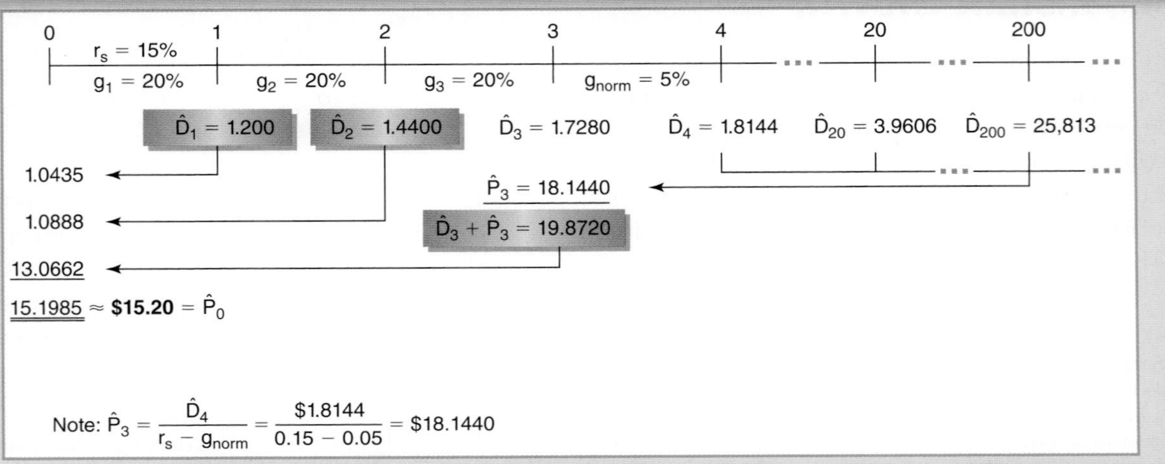

cash flows and the results we found for our example. Note that at the end of the last year of nonconstant growth two cash flows are included: (1) the last nonconstant dividend, which is $\hat{D}_3$ in our example, and (2) the value of the stock after nonconstant growth ends, $\hat{P}_3$, which represents the value of the constant growth dividends that will be paid during the remainder of the firm's life, Year 4 through Year ∞ in our example.

If you think about the steps we followed to determine the value of the stock in our example, we can summarize the process of computing the intrinsic value of a nonconstant growth stock in simple terms: When valuing a nonconstant growth stock, assume that you buy the stock and hold it only for the nonconstant growth period, and then you sell the stock to another investor immediately after the last nonconstant growth dividend is paid. With this scenario, you would receive all of the nonconstant growth dividends ($\hat{D}_1$, $\hat{D}_2$, and D_3 in our example), and then you would sell all of the constant growth dividends to another investor (in our example, $\hat{P}_3$ represents all the future constant dividends valued at the end of the nonconstant growth period, Year 3). In this case, the value of the stock today is the present value of all of the future nonconstant growth dividends you receive from owning the stock plus the present value of the future price for which you can sell the stock when nonconstant growth ends.

To give a different perspective of the valuation process presented in Steps 1–3, let's assume that the same situation exists for the stock that we are currently evaluating, except investors expect the company to pay dividends for the next 50 years and then go bankrupt (at which point its stock is worthless) rather than continue to pay dividends forever. Table 7.1 shows the dividend that would be paid each year, as well as the present value of all of the dividends that would

Table 7.1

Present Value of the Dividends Received from a Stock Investment During a 50-Year Period

Year	Growth Rate, g_t	Dividend $\hat{D}_t = \hat{D}_{t-1}(1 + g_t)$	PV of Dividend $= \hat{D}_t/(1.15)^t$	Year	Growth Rate, g_t	Dividend $\hat{D}_t = \hat{D}_{t-1}(1 + g_t)$	PV of Dividend $= \hat{D}_t/(1.25)^t$
1	20	1.2000	1.0435	26	5	5.3076	0.1402
2	20	1.4400	1.0888	27	5	5.5730	0.1280
3	20	1.7280	1.1362	28	5	5.8516	0.1169
4	5	1.8144	1.0374	29	5	6.1442	0.1067
5	5	1.9051	0.9472	30	5	6.4514	0.0974
6	5	2.0004	0.8648	31	5	6.7740	0.0890
7	5	2.1004	0.7896	32	5	7.1127	0.0812
8	5	2.2054	0.7210	33	5	7.4683	0.0742
9	5	2.3157	0.6583	34	5	7.8417	0.0677
10	5	2.4315	0.6010	35	5	8.2338	0.0618
11	5	2.5530	0.5488	36	5	8.6455	0.0565
12	5	2.6807	0.5010	37	5	9.0778	0.0515
13	5	2.8147	0.4575	38	5	9.5317	0.0471
14	5	2.9555	0.4177	39	5	10.0083	0.0430
15	5	3.1032	0.3814	40	5	10.5087	0.0392
16	5	3.2584	0.3482	41	5	11.0341	0.0358
17	5	3.4213	0.3179	42	5	11.5858	0.0327
18	5	3.5924	0.2903	43	5	12.1651	0.0299
19	5	3.7720	0.2650	44	5	12.7734	0.0273
20	5	3.9606	0.2420	45	5	13.4120	0.0249
21	5	4.1586	0.2210	46	5	14.0826	0.0227
22	5	4.3666	0.2017	47	5	14.7868	0.0208
23	5	4.5849	0.1842	48	5	15.5261	0.0189
24	5	4.8141	0.1682	49	5	16.3024	0.0173
25	5	5.0549	0.1536	50	5	17.1175	0.0158

$$\sum \text{PV of Dividends} = \underline{\$15.0326}$$

Information: Last dividend payment, $D_0 = \$1.00$
Dividend growth rates: $g_{super} = g_1 = g_2 = g_3 = 20\%$; $g_{norm} = g_4 = \cdots = g_{50} = 5\%$
Required rate of return, $r_s = 15\%$

be paid during the 50-year period. Notice that the present value of the dividends equals $15.0326, which is about $0.17 less than the result we computed earlier (shown in Figure 7.2). Because the only difference between the result shown in Table 7.1 and the result shown in Figure 7.2 is that Table 7.1 excludes the dividends that would be received beyond Year 50, $0.17 represents the present value of the dividends from Year 51 to Year ∞. This is a small value.

Clearly, it is very easy to compute the dividends and their present values for 50 years (or even 1,000 years), using a spreadsheet if we know the annual growth rates. However, it is easier to compute the dividends during the nonconstant growth period, use Equation 7.4 to compute the value of the stock at the point when nonconstant growth ends, and then add the present values of these future cash flows to determine $\hat{P}_0$ (as illustrated in Figure 7.2).

7-3 Other Stock Valuation Methods

Investors often use more than one method to determine (estimate) the value of a stock. In this section, we describe two other valuation methods that are popular with investors. It is important to keep in mind that to apply any model literally, certain assumptions must be met. There are few, if any, instances where all the assumptions associated with a model are met in the real world. Therefore, models such as those described in this chapter should be used as guidance when determining the value of a stock; that is, the results should not be taken to mean that a stock should be selling for precisely the same price that a model predicts.

7-3a Valuation Using P/E Ratios

Many analysts consider the P/E ratio, or *earnings multiplier*, to be a good indicator of the value of a stock in relative terms. The P/E ratio mentioned here is the same as that described in Chapter 2; it is computed by dividing the current market price per share, P_0, by the firm's earnings per share, EPS_0. The higher (lower) the P/E ratio, the more (less) investors are willing to pay for each dollar earned by the firm.

In a sense, the P/E ratio gives an indication of a stock's "payback period." For example, if a firm's P/E ratio is 12, then, assuming that the firm distributes all of its earnings as dividends, it would take 12 years for an investor to recover his or her initial investment. If we view P/E ratios as measures of payback, all else equal, lower earnings multipliers are better. In fact, it has been suggested that firms with low P/E ratios relative to other firms in their industries can earn above-average risk-adjusted returns, and vice versa. The rationale is that if a company's P/E ratio is too low relative to that of similar firms, its earnings have not been fully captured in the existing stock value; thus the price will be bid up as soon as investors recognize the stock is undervalued. Similarly, if the firm's P/E ratio is too high relative to that of similar firms, the market has overvalued its current earnings, and its stock price must decrease.

Generally, investors examine whether a stock's P/E ratio is higher or lower than "normal" to decide whether the price is too high or too low. If we can determine what value is appropriate for the P/E ratio, we can then multiply that value by the firm's EPS to estimate the appropriate stock price. Determining the appropriate P/E requires judgment, so analysts do not always agree as to what the preferred P/E ratio for a firm should be.

7-3b Evaluating Stocks Using the Economic Value Added Approach

Economic value added (EVA) is an approach, developed by Stern Stewart Management Services, that is based on the concept that the earnings generated by a company must be sufficient to compensate investors who provide its funds. EVA measures by how much a firm's economic value is increased based on the decisions it makes. The change in a firm's economic value, or its EVA, is determined by decreasing its after-tax operating income by the costs associated with both the debt and the equity issued by the firm. Equation 7.5 gives the basic EVA equation:

P/E ratio The current market price of a stock divided by the earnings per share; P_0/EPS_0.

economic value added (EVA) An analytical method that seeks to evaluate the earnings generated by a firm to determine whether they are sufficient to compensate the suppliers of funds—both the bondholders and the stockholders.

7.5

$$\text{Economic value added} = EVA = EBIT(1 - T) - \left[\left(\begin{array}{c} \text{Average cost} \\ \text{of funds} \end{array} \right) \times \left(\begin{array}{c} \text{Invested} \\ \text{capital} \end{array} \right) \right]$$

The bull and bear statues at the Frankfurt Stock Exchange in Germany. Bull markets occur when the economy is on the upswing, and bear markets describe an economy in a recession or long-term decline.

In this equation, EBIT represents the earnings before interest and taxes as reported on the firm's income statement, T is the firm's marginal tax rate, "Invested capital" is the amount of funds provided by investors (both debt and equity), and "Average cost of funds" is the average interest rate, or percentage return, that the firm pays for its debt and equity (invested capital). We discuss the cost of funds in detail in Chapter 11. For the purposes of our discussion here, we simply define the percentage cost of funds as the *average* rate of return that must be paid to investors—both bondholders and stockholders—who provide funds to the firm. As a result, when EVA is greater than zero, the firm's value should increase because its operating earnings exceed the amount that must be paid to investors who have provided the funds that the firm uses to finance its assets.

To illustrate the use of the EVA approach, suppose the following information has been gathered from the financial statements of a company:

Operating income, EBIT	$15.0 million
Total invested capital = Long-term debt + Equity	$60.0 million
Marginal tax rate	40%
Number of outstanding shares of common stock	2.5 million
Average cost of funds	7.0%

If we apply Equation 7.5, we find the company's EVA as follows:

$$EVA = [\$15.0 \text{ million} \times (1 - 0.4)] - (0.07 \times \$60.0 \text{ million})$$
$$= \$9.0 \text{ million} - \$4.2 \text{ million} = \$4.8 \text{ million}$$

According to this computation, the EVA approach suggests that investors demanded $4.2 million in compensation for providing funds to the firm. Because the firm generated $9 million in net operating profits after taxes to cover the compensation associated with financing, we can conclude that it was able to use its funds to earn higher returns than those demanded by investors. Thus, the firm should be attractive to investors. The company's stock should be especially attractive to common stockholders, because they have the right to any amounts earned in excess of their required rate of return.

We can use the EVA concept to determine the maximum dividend per share that can be paid to stockholders before we would expect the firm's current value to be threatened. The computation is simple: Divide the computed EVA by the number of outstanding shares. For our illustrative firm, the maximum dividend suggested by EVA is $1.92 = ($4.8 million) ÷ (2.5 million shares).

The EVA approach has gained attention as a valuation technique because it is based on the fundamental principle of wealth maximization, which should be the goal of every firm. Prospective EVA users should be aware that to obtain a precise estimate of the economic performance of a firm, it might be necessary to make several adjustments to the accounting numbers contained in the firm's financial statements. For instance, Stern Stewart indicates that it has identified more than 160 possible adjustments to accounting values contained in financial statements that can be made to provide a better estimate of the true economic value of a firm's performance. Knowing how to apply such adjustments often takes considerable expertise.

7-4 Changes in Stock Prices

Stock prices are not constant: They sometimes change significantly, as well as very quickly. For example, on October 19, 1987, the Dow Jones Industrial Average (DJIA) dropped 508 points, and the average stock lost about 23 percent of its value in just one day. Some stocks lost more than half of their values on that day. More recently, the DJIA decreased by nearly 1,880 points the week of October 6, 2008, through October 10, 2008; the average stock lost nearly 25 percent of its value during the week. On the following Monday, October 13, 2008, however, the DJIA rebounded, increasing by almost 940 points and the value of the average stock increased by more than 11 percent. To see how such changes can occur, assume you own the stock of a company that just paid a $2.50 dividend ($D_0 = \$2.50$). The company's growth has been constant for many years, so it is expected that the company will continue to grow at the same rate, 6 percent, in the future ($g = 6\%$). Currently, investors require a return equal to 15 percent for such investments. Therefore, the expected value of the company's stock should be:

$$\hat{P}_0 = \frac{\$2.50(1.06)}{0.15 - 0.06} = \frac{\$2.65}{0.09} = \$29.44$$

Now consider what would happen to the stock price if the value of any of the variables used to compute the current price changes. For instance, how would the price be affected if investors demand a higher rate of return—say, 18 percent? If we change the value for r_s to 18 percent in the previous equation, we find that the expected value of the stock becomes:

$$\hat{P}_0 = \frac{\$2.50(1.06)}{0.18 - 0.06} = \frac{\$2.65}{0.12} = \$22.08$$

The new price is lower (-25%) because investors demand a higher return for receiving the same future cash flows.

How will the price change if the future cash flows differ from the expected cash flows, but the required return is 15 percent? Consider the effect if the company's growth rate is 4 percent rather than 6 percent:

$$\hat{P}_0 = \frac{\$2.50(1.04)}{0.15 - 0.04} = \frac{\$2.60}{0.11} = \$23.64$$

Again, the new price is lower (-19.7%) than the original price of $29.44. In this case, however, the price is lower because the cash flows that the stock is expected to provide in the future are smaller than previously expected.

From this simple example, you should have concluded that changes in stock prices occur for two reasons: (1) investors change the rates of return they require to invest in stocks and (2) expectations about the cash flows associated with stocks change. From the preceding example, we can generalize how such changes affect stock prices: *Stock prices move opposite changes in rates of return, but they move in the same direction as changes in cash flows expected from the stock in the future.* Therefore, if investors demand higher (lower) returns to invest in stocks, then prices should fall (increase). If investors expect their investments to generate lower (higher) future cash flows, then prices should also fall (increase).

Of course, we generally do not know (cannot compute) the "true" (intrinsic) price of a stock, because it is unlikely that (1) the company's future growth pattern is exactly as analysts forecast and (2) all the assumptions of the model that is used to estimate the equilibrium value are met. However, the various valuation techniques we discussed in this chapter give some indication of a stock's *equilibrium*, or intrinsic, value.

Evidence suggests that stocks—especially those of large NYSE companies—adjust rapidly to disequilibrium situations. Consequently, equilibrium ordinarily exists for any given stock, and, in general, required returns (r) and expected returns (r̂) are equal. Stock prices certainly change, sometimes violently and rapidly, but these changes simply reflect different conditions and expectations. We discuss stock market equilibrium in greater detail in Chapter 8.

STUDY TOOLS

LOCATED AT BACK OF THE TEXTBOOK

- [ ] Problems are found at the end of this chapter.
- [ ] A tear-out Chapter Review card is located at the back of the textbook.

LOCATED AT WWW.CENGAGEBRAIN.COM

- [ ] Review Key Term flashcards and create your own cards.
- [ ] Track your knowledge and understanding of key concepts in corporate finance.
- [ ] Complete practice and graded quizzes to prepare for tests.
- [ ] Complete interactive content within CFIN5 Online.
- [ ] View the chapter highlight boxes for CFIN5 Online.

KEY STOCK VALUATION CONCEPTS

To conclude this chapter, we summarize some stock valuation concepts that were discussed.

- The current value of a stock is based on the stream of dividends investors expect the firm to pay during its life (generally considered to be infinite).

  a. The current value of a stock is computed as the present value of the dividends the stock is expected to generate during the remainder of its life. If a company's dividends grow at a constant rate, its stock can be valued using a simple equation: $\hat{P}_0 = [D_0(1 + g)]/(r_s - g)$.

  b. When a person sells stock that he or she owns, the investor who purchases the stock pays for the dividends that the stock is expected to generate in the future (during the remainder of the firm's life).

- Everything else equal, if the dividends that are expected to be paid in the future increase, the value of a stock also increases.

- Everything else equal, when investors demand higher rates of return—that is, when market rates increase—stock prices decrease. In other words, to earn higher rates of return, investors lower the prices they are willing to pay for their investments (stocks in this case).

- Investors often use P/E ratios to estimate the intrinsic values of stocks. The value of a stock can be estimated by multiplying a "normal" P/E ratio by the firm's earnings per share (EPS).

- The economic value added (EVA) approach can be used to determine whether the actions taken by a firm are sufficient to generate the funds that are needed to pay investors (stockholders and bondholders) who provide funds to the firm. If the firm generates more operating profits than are needed to pay its taxes and cover its costs of funds, then its economic value increases.

PROBLEMS

7–1 One year ago, James Sirlank bought Dell Computer common stock for $20 per share. Today the stock is selling for $19 per share. During the year, James received four dividend payments, each in the amount of $0.20 per share. (a) What rate of return did James earn during the year? (b) What were the (1) dividend yield and (2) the capital gains yield associated with the stock for the year?

7–2 Last year, Julie Johnson bought one share of common stock for $950. During the year, Julie received a $47.50 dividend. Earlier today, she sold the stock for $988. (a) What rate of return did Julie earn on her investment? (b) What were the (1) dividend yield and (2) the capital gains yield associated with holding the stock?

7–3 Express Surgery Center's (ESC) preferred stock, which has a par value equal to $110 per share, pays an annual dividend equal to 9 percent of the par value. If investors require a 15 percent return to purchase ESC's preferred stock, what is the stock's market value?

7–4 The Ape Copy Company's preferred stock pays an annual dividend equal to $16.50. If investors demand a return equal to 11 percent to purchase Ape's preferred stock, what is its market value?

7–5 Out-of-Sight Telecommunications (OST) has preferred stock outstanding with a par value of $40 per share that pays an annual dividend equal to 5 percent. (a) If investors who purchase similar investments require a 10 percent return, what is the market value of OST's preferred stock? (b) What would be the market value of the stock if investors require an 8 percent return?

7–6 Your broker offers to sell you shares of Wingler & Company common stock, which paid a dividend of $2 *yesterday*. You expect the dividend to grow at a rate of 5 percent per year into perpetuity. If the appropriate rate of return for the stock is 12 percent, what is the market value of Wingler's stock?

7–7 Alpine Ski Resort has grown at a constant rate, which equals 4 percent, for as long as it has been in business. This growth rate is expected to continue long into the future. A couple of days ago, Alpine paid common stockholders a dividend equal to $3 per share. If investors require a 10 percent rate of return to purchase Alpine's common stock, what is the market value of its common stock?

7-8 Since it started business 10 years ago, Alphafem Company has paid a constant $1.20 per share dividend to its common stockholders. Next year and every year thereafter, the company plans to increase the dividend at a constant rate equal to 2.5 percent per year. If investors require a 15 percent rate of return to purchase Alphafem's common stock, what is the market value of its common stock?

7-9 Suppose your company is expected to grow at a constant rate of 6 percent long into the future. In addition, its dividend yield is expected to be 8 percent. If your company expects to pay a dividend equal to $1.06 per share at the *end of the year*, what is the value of your firm's stock?

7-10 Ocala Company's stock is currently selling for $19.50 per share. *At the end of the year*, the company plans to pay a dividend equal to $2.34 per share. For the remainder of the company's life, dividends are expected to grow at a constant rate, and investors are expected to require a 16 percent return to invest in Ocala's stock. What should be the value of Ocala's stock five years from now?

7-11 Since it has been in business, FoolsGold Jewelry has never paid a dividend. The company will not pay a dividend at the end of this year. However, two years from today—at the end of Year 2—FoolsGold expects to pay a dividend equal to $0.50 per share, which it plans to increase by 6 percent each year thereafter for the remainder of the company's life. If investors require a 14 percent rate of return to purchase its common stock, what should be the market value of FoolsGold's stock today?

7-12 Minimight Company has never paid a dividend, and there are no plans to pay dividends during the next three years. But, in four years—that is, at the end of Year 4—the company expects to start paying a dividend equal to $3 per share. This same dividend will be paid for the remainder of Minimight's existence. If investors require a 10 percent rate of return to purchase the company's common stock, what should be the market value of Minimight's stock today?

7-13 Since it has been in business, FreeFin has paid a $1 per share annual dividend. The company plans to pay a $1 dividend for the next two years. Beginning in three years, however, FreeFin plans to increase the dividend by 8 percent each year for the remainder of the company's life. If investors require a 17 percent rate of return to purchase FreeFin's common stock, what should be the market value of its stock today?

7-14 Forral Company has never paid a dividend. But, the company plans to start paying dividends in two years—that is, at the end of Year 2. The first dividend is expected to equal $2 per share. The second dividend and every dividend thereafter are expected to grow at a 5 percent rate. If investors require a 15 percent rate of return to purchase Forral's common stock, what should be the market value of its stock today?

7-15 Xtinct Artifacts has not paid a dividend during the past 10 years. However, at the end of this year, the company plans to pay a $1.50 dividend and a $2 dividend the following year (Year 2). Starting in three years, the dividend will begin to grow by 5 percent each year for as long as the firm is in business. If investors require an 11 percent rate of return to purchase Xtinct's common stock, what should be the market value of its stock today?

7-16 Sparkle Jewelers expects to pay dividends (per share) of $0.60, $0.90, $2.40, and $3.50 during the next four years. Beginning in the fifth year, the dividend is expected to grow at a rate of 4 percent indefinitely. If investors require a 20 percent return to purchase Sparkle's stock, what is the current value of the company's stock?

7-17 Georgetown Motorcars' (GM) common stock normally sells for 19 times its earnings; that is, its P/E ratio equals 19. If GM's earnings per share are $3.70, what should be its stock price under normal circumstances?

7-18 For the past 15 years, the P/E ratio of North/South Travel has been between 28 and 30. If North/South's earnings per share equal $4, in what price range would you estimate its stock should be selling?

7-19 RJS generated $65,000 *net* income this year. The firm's financial statements also show that its interest expense was $40,000, its marginal tax rate was 35 percent, and its invested capital was $800,000. If its average cost of funds is 12 percent, what was RJS's economic value added (EVA) this year?

7-20 Backhaus Beer Brewers (BBB) just announced that the current fiscal year's *net* income was $1.2 million. BBB's marginal tax rate is 40 percent, its interest expense for the year was $1.5 million, it has $8 million of invested capital, and its average cost of funds was 10 percent. What is BBB's economic value added (EVA) for the current year?

After you finish this chapter go to **PAGE 158** for **STUDY TOOLS**

LEARNING OUTCOMES

After studying this chapter, you will be able to...

LO1 Explain what it means to take risk when investing.

LO2 Compute the risk and return of an investment, and explain how the risk and return of an investment are related.

LO3 Identify relevant and irrelevant risk, and explain how irrelevant risk can be reduced.

LO4 Describe how to determine the appropriate reward—that is, rate of return—that investors should earn for purchasing an investment.

LO5 Describe actions that investors take when the return they require to purchase an investment is different from the return they expect the investment to produce.

LO6 Identify different types of risk, and classify each as relevant or irrelevant with respect to determining an investment's required rate of return.

Risk and Rates of Return

8

E arlier in the book, we showed that the return (interest rate) on debt is equal to the nominal risk-free rate, r_{RF}, plus several premiums that reflect the riskiness of the debt instrument in question (Chapter 5). In this chapter, we define the term *risk* more precisely in terms of how it relates to investments in general, we examine procedures used to measure risk, and we discuss the relationship between risk and return.

8-1 Defining and Measuring Risk

Although most people view risk as a chance of loss, in reality *risk occurs any time we cannot be certain about the future outcome of a particular activity or event*. Consequently, risk results from the fact that an action such as investing can produce *more than one outcome in the future*. When multiple outcomes are possible, some of the possible outcomes are considered "good" and some of the possible outcomes are considered "bad." Thus, when we think of investment risk, along with the chance of receiving less than expected, we should consider the chance of receiving more than expected. If we consider investment risk from this perspective, then we can define **risk** as the chance of receiving an actual return that differs from the one that is expected. This definition simply means that there is *variability in the returns* or outcomes from the investment. Therefore, investment risk can be measured by the variability of all the investment's returns, both "good" and "bad." *The greater the variability of the possible outcomes, the riskier the investment.*

8-1a Probability Distributions

When deciding whether to purchase an investment, most people think about the range of possible payoffs that the investment is expected to return in the future. In most cases, analysts formalize this process by trying to identify all of the possible payoffs and then determining the chance, or probability, that each payoff will occur. A listing of all of the possible outcomes associated with an investment along with their probabilities is called a **probability distribution**.

To illustrate probability distributions, let's consider two fictitious companies—Martin Products, Inc. and U.S. Electric. Martin Products manufactures equipment that is used in the data transmission industry, which is quite cyclical; that is, the firm's profits generally rise and fall with business cycles. On the other hand, U.S. Electric supplies electricity, which is considered an essential service, and thus its profits are fairly stable and predictable.

Suppose that analysts have created the following probability distributions for Martin Products and U.S. Electric:

State of the Economy	Probability of This State Occurring	Rate of Return on the Stock if the Economic State Occurs	
		Martin Products	U.S. Electric
Boom	0.2	110%	20%
Normal	0.5	22	16
Recession	0.3	−60	10
	1.0		

This probability distribution indicates that there is a 20 percent chance of a booming economy in the future, in which case both

risk The chance that an outcome other than the expected one will occur.

probability distribution A listing of all possible outcomes or events, with a probability (chance of occurrence) assigned to each outcome.

companies will have high returns, there is a 50 percent probability that the two companies will operate in a normal economy and offer moderate returns, and there is a 30 percent chance of a recession, which will mean low returns will be generated by the companies.[1] Although the general pattern of returns is the same for both companies, notice that there is a fairly high probability that the value of Martin's stock will vary substantially, possibly resulting in a loss of 60 percent or a gain of 110 percent; conversely, there is no chance of a loss for U.S. Electric, and its maximum gain is 20 percent.[2] Thus, according to the probability distributions, Martin's rate of return could vary far more dramatically than that of U.S. Electric. Based on our definition of risk, then, Martin Products seems to be a riskier investment than U.S. Electric.

8-2 Expected Rate of Return

The probability distribution given in the previous section shows that the most likely outcome is for the economy to be normal, in which case Martin Products will return 22 percent and U.S. Electric will return 16 percent. Because other outcomes are also possible, however, we need to summarize all of the information contained in the probability distributions into a single measure that can be used to make decisions. That measure is called the expected value, or **expected rate of return**, and it is measured by computing the *weighted average* of the outcomes using the probabilities as the weights. The expected rate of return, $\hat{r}$, can be calculated using Equation 8.1:

8.1

Expected rate of return $= \hat{r} = Pr_1r_1 + \cdots + Pr_nr_n$

$$= \sum_{i=1}^{n} Pr_i r_i$$

expected rate of return $\hat{r}$
The rate of return expected to be realized from an investment, which is the mean value of the probability distribution of possible results.

standard deviation, σ A measure of the tightness, or variability, of a set of outcomes.

Here r_i is the *i*th possible outcome, Pr_i is the probability that the *i*th outcome will occur, and n is the number of possible outcomes. Applying Equation 8.1, the expected returns for Martin Products and U.S. Electric are

$$\hat{r}_{Martin} = 0.2(110\%) + 0.5(22\%) + 0.3(-60\%)$$
$$= 15.0\%$$
$$\hat{r}_{US} = 0.2(20\%) + 0.5(16\%) + 0.3(10\%)$$
$$= 15.0\%$$

Notice that neither expected rate of return equals any of the possible payoffs given in the probability distributions. Simply stated, the expected rate of return represents the *average payoff* that investors will receive in the future if the probability distributions do not change over a long period of time. For example, if the probability distribution for Martin Products is correct, then 20 percent of the time the economy will be booming and investors will earn a 110 percent rate of return, 50 percent of the time the economy will be normal and investors will earn 22 percent, and 30 percent of the time the economy will be in a recession and investors will earn −60 percent. On average, then, Martin Products' investors should earn 15 percent over some period of time, say, 10 years.

8-2a Measuring Total (Stand-Alone) Risk: The Standard Deviation (σ)

Because we have defined risk as the variability of returns, we can measure it by examining the tightness of the probability distribution associated with the possible outcomes. In general, the width of a probability distribution indicates the amount of *scatter*, or variability, of the possible outcomes. The measure we use most often to evaluate variability is the **standard deviation**, the symbol for which is σ, the Greek letter *sigma*. *The smaller the value of the standard deviation*, the tighter the probability distribution, and, accordingly, *the lower the total risk associated with the investment*. The standard deviation of returns can be calculated using Equation 8.2:

8.2

Standard deviation $= \sigma = \sqrt{(r_1 - \hat{r})^2 Pr_1 + \cdots + (r_n - \hat{r})^2 Pr_n}$

$$= \sqrt{\sum_{i=1}^{n} (r_i - \hat{r})^2 Pr_i}$$

[1]The probability distributions given in the table are called *discrete*, because the number of outcomes is limited, or finite. In reality of course, the state of the economy could actually range from a deep depression to a fantastic boom, with an unlimited number of possible states in between. The probability distribution for such a situation is called *continuous* because the number of possible outcomes is infinite within a particular range.

[2]It is, of course, completely unrealistic to think that any stock has no chance of a loss. Only in hypothetical examples could this situation occur.

Table 8.1

Calculating Martin Products' Standard Deviation

Payoff r_i (1)	Expected Return $\hat{r}$ (2)		Deviation $r_i - \hat{r}$ (1) − (2) = (3)	$(r_i - \hat{r})^2$ (3) × (3) = (4)	Probability (5)	$(r_i - \hat{r})^2 \, Pr_i$ (4) × (5) = (6)
110%	− 15%	=	95	9,025	0.2	9,025 × 0.2 = 1,805.0
22	− 15	=	7	49	0.5	49 × 0.5 = 24.5
−60	− 15	=	−75	5,625	0.3	5,625 × 0.3 = 1,687.5
					Variance = σ^2 =	3,517.0

$$\text{Standard deviation} = \sigma = \sqrt{\sigma^2} = \sqrt{3{,}517} = 59.3\%$$

Equation 8.2 shows that the standard deviation is a weighted average deviation from the expected value, which gives an idea as to how far above or below the expected value the actual value is likely to be. Note that the standard deviation is the square root of the variance—that is, Standard deviation = $\sigma = \sqrt{\sigma^2} = \sqrt{\text{Variance}}$.

Table 8.1 shows the steps you should follow to compute σ_{Martin} = 59.3%. Using these same procedures, we find U.S. Electric's standard deviation to be 3.6 percent. The larger standard deviation for Martin Products indicates a greater variation of returns for this firm, and hence a greater chance that the actual, or realized, return will differ significantly from the expected return. Consequently, according to this measure of risk, Martin Products is considered a riskier investment than U.S. Electric.

To this point, the example we have used to compute the expected return and standard deviation has been based on data that take the form of a known probability distribution, which includes estimates of all future outcomes and the chances that these outcomes will occur in a particular situation. In many cases, however, the only information we have available consists of data over some *past period*. For example, suppose we have observed the following returns associated with a common stock during the past six years ($\ddot{r}$ = historical returns):

Year	$\ddot{r}_t$	Year	$\ddot{r}_t$
2014	16%	2011	20%
2013	13	2010	17
2012	−5	2009	23

We can use this information to *estimate* the risk associated with the stock by estimating the standard deviation of returns. The estimated standard deviation can be computed using a series of past, or *observed*, returns to solve Equation 8.3:

8.3

$$\text{Estimated } \sigma = s = \sqrt{\frac{\sum_{t=1}^{n}(\ddot{r}_t - \bar{r})^2}{n-1}}$$

Here $\ddot{r}_t$ represents the past realized rate of return in Period t, and $\bar{r}$ (pronounced "r bar") is the arithmetic average of the annual returns earned during the last n years. We compute $\bar{r}$ using Equation 8.4:

8.4

$$\bar{r} = \frac{\ddot{r}_1 + \ddot{r}_2 + \cdots + \ddot{r}_n}{n} = \frac{\sum_{t=1}^{n}\ddot{r}_t}{n}$$

Continuing with our current example, we compute the arithmetic average and *estimate* the value for σ as follows:[3]

[3]You should recognize from statistics courses that a sample of six observations is not sufficient to make a good estimate. We use six observations here only to simplify the illustration.

$$\bar{r} = \frac{16\% + 13\% + (-5\%) + 20\% + 17\% + 23\%}{6} = \frac{84\%}{6} = 14.0\%$$

Estimated $\sigma = s$

$$= \sqrt{\frac{(16\% - 14\%)^2 + (13\% - 14\%)^2 + (-5\% - 14\%)^2 + (20\% - 14\%)^2 + (17\% - 14\%)^2 + (23\% - 14\%)^2}{6 - 1}}$$

$$= \sqrt{\frac{492}{5}} = \sqrt{98.4} = 9.9\%$$

The historical standard deviation is often used as an estimate of the future standard deviation because $s \approx \sigma$. On the other hand, the historical return generally is not used as an estimate of the expected return because the past *level* of returns generally will not be repeated in the future; that is, $\bar{r} \neq \hat{r}$, especially for young, high-growth firms.

8-2b Coefficient of Variation (Risk/Return Ratio)

Another useful measure for evaluating risky investments is the **coefficient of variation (CV)**, which is the standard deviation divided by the expected return (Equation 8.5):

8.5

$$\text{Coefficient of variation} = CV = \frac{\text{Risk}}{\text{Return}} = \frac{\sigma}{\hat{r}}$$

The coefficient of variation shows the risk per unit of return. It provides a more meaningful basis for comparison when the expected returns and the risk associated with two investments differ. Because both U.S. Electric and Martin Products have the same expected return, it is not necessary to compute the coefficient of variation to compare the two investments. In this case, most people would prefer to invest in U.S. Electric because it offers the same expected return as Martin Products but with lower risk.

The coefficient of variation is more useful when we consider investments that have different expected rates of return *and* different levels of risk. For example, Biobotics Corporation is a biological research and development firm that, according to

coefficient of variation (CV) A standardized measure of the risk per unit of return. It is calculated by dividing the standard deviation by the expected return.

stock analysts, offers investors an expected rate of return equal to 35 percent with a standard deviation of 7.5 percent. Biobotics offers a higher expected return than U.S. Electric, but it is also riskier. If we calculate the coefficient of variation for Biobotics, we find that it is $0.21 = 7.5\%/35\%$, which is slightly less than U.S. Electric's coefficient of variation of $0.24 = 3.6\%/15\%$. Thus, Biobotics actually has less risk per unit of return than U.S. Electric, even though its standard deviation is much higher. In this case, the additional return offered by Biobotics is more than sufficient to compensate investors for taking on the additional risk.

Because the coefficient of variation captures the effects of both risk and return, it is a better measure than the standard deviation for evaluating total (stand-alone) risk in situations where investments differ with respect to both their amounts of total risk and their expected returns.

8-2c Risk Aversion and Required Returns

Suppose you have worked hard and saved $1 million, which you now plan to invest. You can buy a 10 percent U.S. Treasury note, and at the end of one year you will have a sure $1.1 million, which consists of your original investment plus $100,000 in interest. Alternatively, you can buy stock in R&D Enterprises. If R&D's research

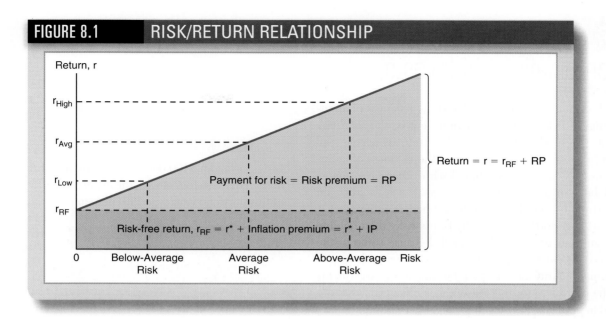

FIGURE 8.1   RISK/RETURN RELATIONSHIP

Return, r

r_{High}

r_{Avg}

r_{Low}

r_{RF}

Return = r = r_{RF} + RP

Payment for risk = Risk premium = RP

Risk-free return, r_{RF} = r* + Inflation premium = r* + IP

0   Below-Average   Average   Above-Average   Risk
Risk   Risk   Risk

programs are successful, the value of your stock will increase to $2.2 million. Conversely, if the firm's programs fail, the value of your stock will go to zero, and you will be penniless. You regard R&D's chances of success or failure as being 50–50, so the expected value of the stock investment is $1,100,000 = 0.5($0) + 0.5($2,200,000). Subtracting the $1 million cost of the stock leaves an expected profit of $100,000, or an expected (but risky) 10 percent rate of return; that is, $\hat{r}$ = $100,000/$1,000,000 = 0.10 = 10.0%.

In this case, you have a choice between a sure $100,000 profit (representing a 10 percent rate of return) on the Treasury note and a risky expected $100,000 profit (also representing a 10 percent expected rate of return) on the R&D Enterprises stock. Which one would you choose? Because most investors are risk averse, they would choose the less risky investment—that is, the U.S. Treasury note—in this situation.

What does it mean to be risk averse? Simply stated, a risk-averse person requires positive rewards to take on risks, and higher risks require higher rewards. When this concept is applied to investments, other things held constant, the higher a security's risk, the higher the return investors demand, and thus the less they are willing to pay for the investment. To see how **risk aversion** affects security prices, we can analyze the stocks of U.S. Electric and Martin Products. Suppose each stock sells for $100 per share and each has an expected rate of return of 15 percent. To simplify our discussion, let's assume both firms pay a perpetual dividend equal to $15 per share. In this case, rational risk-averse investors would prefer U.S. Electric because there is less variability in its payoffs (less risk). People with money to invest would bid for U.S. Electric

stock rather than Martin Products stock, and Martin's stockholders would start selling their stock and using the money to buy U.S. Electric stock. Buying pressure would drive up the price of U.S. Electric's stock, and selling pressure would simultaneously cause Martin's price to decline. These price changes, in turn, would alter the expected rates of return on the two securities. Suppose, for example, that the price of U.S. Electric stock was bid up from $100 to $125, whereas the price of Martin's stock declined from $100 to $75. This development would cause U.S. Electric's expected return to fall to 12 percent, whereas Martin's expected return would rise to 20 percent. The difference in returns, 8% = 20% − 12%, is a **risk premium** that represents the compensation investors require for assuming the *additional* risk of buying Martin's stock.

This example demonstrates a very important principle: In a market dominated by risk-averse investors, *riskier securities must have higher expected returns*, as estimated by the average investor, than less risky securities. If this situation does not hold, investors will buy and sell investments, and prices will continue to change until the higher-risk investments have higher expected returns than the lower-risk investments. Figure 8.1 illustrates this relationship.

We will consider the question of how much higher the returns on risky securities should be later in the chapter, after we examine how diversification affects the way risk should be measured.

risk aversion Risk-averse investors require higher rates of return to invest in higher-risk securities.

risk premium (RP) The portion of the expected return that can be attributed to the additional risk of an investment. It is the difference between the expected rate of return on a given risky asset and the expected rate of return on a less risky asset.

8-3 Portfolio Risk—Holding Combinations of Investments

To this point, we have considered the riskiness of an investment that is held in isolation; that is, the *total* risk of an investment if it is held by itself, which we call *stand-alone* risk. Now we analyze the riskiness of an investment when it is combined with other investments and held in a portfolio.[4] As we shall see, holding an investment—whether it is a stock, bond, or other asset—as part of a portfolio generally is less risky than holding the same investment all by itself, because some of the total, or stand-alone, risk that is associated with the individual security can be spread to the other investments in the portfolio. For this reason, most financial assets are held in portfolios. From an average investor's standpoint, then, the fact that the price of a particular stock goes up or down is not very important. What is important is the return on his or her portfolio and the overall risk of the portfolio. As a result, *the risk and return characteristics of an investment should not be evaluated in isolation; instead, the risk and return of an individual security should be analyzed in terms of how the security affects the risk and return of the portfolio in which it is held.*

Portfolio Returns. The expected return on a portfolio, $\hat{r}_p$, is simply the weighted average of the expected returns on the individual stocks that are held in the portfolio, with each stock's weight being the proportion of the total funds invested in that stock (Equation 8.6):

8.6

$$\text{Portfolio return} = \hat{r}_p = w_1\hat{r}_1 + w_2\hat{r}_2 + \cdots + w_N\hat{r}_N$$
$$= \sum_{j=1}^{N} w_j\hat{r}_j$$

Here $\hat{r}_j$ represents the expected return on Stock j, w_j is the weight that represents the proportion of the total funds that is invested in Stock j, and the portfolio includes N stocks (investments). Note two points: (1) w_j is equal to the value of the investment in Stock j divided by the total value of the portfolio and (2) the w_js must sum to 1.0.

To illustrate, suppose securities analysts estimate the following expected returns on four large companies:

Company	Expected Return, $\hat{r}$
Citigroup	6%
General Electric	14
Johnson & Johnson	8
Microsoft	16

If we formed a $100,000 portfolio by investing $25,000 in each of these four stocks, the expected portfolio return of this portfolio would be 11.0 percent:

$$\hat{r}_p = w_{Citi}\hat{r}_{Citi} + w_{GE}\hat{r}_{GE} + w_{JNJ}\hat{r}_{JNJ} + w_{Micro}\hat{r}_{Micro}$$
$$= 0.25(6\%) + 0.25(14\%) + 0.25(8\%) + 0.25(16\%)$$
$$= 11.0\%$$

Of course, after the fact and one year later, the actual realized rate of return, $\ddot{r}$, on each stock will almost certainly differ from its expected value, so $\ddot{r}_p$ will be somewhat different from $\hat{r}_p = 11\%$. For example, Microsoft's stock might double in price and provide a return of +100 percent, whereas Citigroup's stock price might fall sharply and provide a return of −75 percent. Note, however, that those two events would offset each other somewhat, so the portfolio's realized return might still be close to its expected return, even though the individual stocks' actual returns turned out to differ significantly from their expected returns.

Portfolio Risk. Although the expected return of a portfolio is a weighted average of the expected returns of the individual stocks in the portfolio, the risk of a portfolio (σ_p) generally *cannot* be computed as a weighted average of the standard deviations of the individual securities in the portfolio. Instead, the portfolio's risk usually is *smaller* than the weighted average of the individual stocks' standard deviations. In fact, it is theoretically possible to combine two stocks that by themselves are quite risky, as measured by their individual standard deviations, and form a completely riskless portfolio—that is, the portfolio has $\sigma_p = 0$.

To illustrate the effect of combining securities, suppose that you have $5,000 invested in the stock of Martin Products (introduced earlier) and you are considering investing an equal amount in the stock of American Business Collections (ABC), a company that collects delinquent accounts receivable for manufacturing firms. The

expected return on a portfolio, $\hat{r}_p$ The weighted average of the expected returns on stocks held in a portfolio.

realized rate of return, $\ddot{r}$ The return that is actually earned. The actual return ($\ddot{r}$) usually differs from the expected return ($\hat{r}$).

[4]A *portfolio* is a collection of investment securities or assets. If you owned some General Motors stock, some ExxonMobil stock, and some IBM stock, you would be holding a three-stock portfolio. For the reasons set forth in this section, the majority of all stocks are held as parts of portfolios.

Table 8.2

Probability Distributions for Martin Products, American Business Collections (ABC), and a Portfolio Consisting of Both Stocks ($\rho = -1.0$)

State of the Economy	Probability of This State Occurring	Individual Stock Returns		Return on a Portfolio That Consists of 50% Martin and 50% ABC	
		Martin Products	ABC		
Boom	0.2	110.0%	−80.0%	15.0% =	110%(0.5) + (−80%)(0.5)
Normal	0.5	22.0	8.0	15.0% =	22%(0.5) + 8%(0.5)
Recession	0.3	−60.0	90.0	15.0% = (−60%)(0.5) +	90%(0.5)
Expected return, r̂		15.0%	15.0%	15.0%	
Standard deviation, σ		59.3%	59.3%	0.0%	

probability distributions for these two stocks and a portfolio that consists of 50 percent Martin and 50 percent ABC are shown in Table 8.2. The information provided in the table shows that $\hat{r} = 15\%$ for both stocks as well as for the portfolio. Note that both stocks have a fair amount of stand-alone risk, because $\sigma_{\text{Martin}} = \sigma_{\text{ABC}} = 59.3\%$. However, the risk associated with a portfolio that includes equal amounts invested in each stock is zero; that is, $\sigma_P = 0.0\%$.

The stocks of Martin Products and ABC can be combined to form a riskless portfolio because their returns tend to move in opposite directions; when Martin's returns are low, American's returns are high, and vice versa. In statistical terms, we state that the relationship between the returns of these two stocks is negative. This relationship exists because ABC's stock price rises during recessions when its collection business is booming, whereas the prices of other stocks, such as Martin's, tend to decline when the economy slumps. Therefore, holding ABC in a portfolio with a "normal" stock like Martin Products tends to stabilize returns on the portfolio, and thus lowers the effect of ABC's stand-alone risk on a person's investment funds. The concept of reducing the stand-alone risk of an individual investment by combining it with other investments to form a portfolio is called **diversification**.

The relationship between two variables, such as the return on Martin's stock and the return on ABC's stock, is called *correlation*, and it is determined by computing the **correlation coefficient**, ρ, which measures both the direction and the strength of the relationship between two variables,[5] If we compute the correlation coefficient for the returns on Martin's stock and ABC's stock, we would find that $\rho = -1.0$, which means that they are perfectly negatively related. Variables that are perfectly negatively correlated exhibit the same relative movement, but in opposite directions.

The opposite of perfect negative correlation ($\rho = -1.0$) is perfect positive correlation ($\rho = +1.0$). Returns on two perfectly positively correlated stocks exhibit the same relative movement in the same direction. A portfolio consisting of two such stocks would be exactly as risky as the individual stocks, because the stocks would seem like identical twins with respect to the variability of their returns. In this case, there is no diversification effect—that is, *risk is not reduced if the portfolio contains perfectly positively correlated stocks*.

From our discussion, we know that (1) two stocks that are perfectly negatively correlated can be combined to form a portfolio that has no risk which means $\sigma_P = 0$; and (2) when two perfectly positively correlated stocks with the same risk are combined, the portfolio risk is equal to the risk associated with the individual stocks which means $\sigma_P = \sigma_{\text{Stock1}} = \sigma_{\text{Stock2}}$. In reality, however, the correlation coefficient (ρ) for the returns on two

[5]The *correlation coefficient*, ρ, can range from $+1.0$ (denoting that the two variables move in the same direction with exactly the same degree of synchronization every time movement occurs) to -1.0 (denoting that the variables always move with the same degree of synchronization, but in opposite directions). A correlation coefficient of zero suggests that the two variables are not related to each other—that is, changes in one variable occur *independently* of changes in the other variable.

diversification Reduction of stand-alone risk of an individual investment by combining it with other investments in a portfolio.

correlation coefficient, ρ A measure of the degree of relationship between two variables.

Table 8.3

Probability Distributions for Martin Products, Anderson Mechanical, and a Portfolio Consisting of Both Stocks ($\rho = +0.21$)

State of the Economy	Probability of This State Occurring	Individual Stock Returns		Return on a Portfolio That Consists of 50% Martin and 50% Anderson
		Martin Products	Anderson Mechanical	
Boom	0.2	110.0%	104.0%	107.0% = 110%(0.5) + 104%(0.5)
Normal	0.5	22.0	−41.0	−9.5% = 22%(0.5) + (−41%)(0.5)
Recession	0.3	−60.0	49.0	−5.5% = (−60%)(0.5) + 49%(0.5)
Expected return, r̂		15.0%	15.0%	15.0%
Standard deviation, σ		59.3%	59.2%	46.0%

$$\hat{r}_p = 107\%(0.2) + (-9.5\%)(0.5) + (-5.5\%)(0.3) = 15.0\%$$

$$\sigma_p = \sqrt{0.2(107.0\% - 15.0\%)^2 + 0.5(-9.5\% - 15.0\%)^2 + 0.3(-5.5\% - 15.0\%)^2} = \sqrt{2,119} = 46.0\%$$

randomly selected stocks generally lies in the range from +0.3 to +0.6. However, as we will show, even though it cannot be completely eliminated, risk is reduced when positively related stocks are combined to form portfolios as long as $\rho \neq +1.0$.

Suppose you are considering investing equal amounts in the stock of Martin Products and in the stock of Anderson Mechanical, a company that manufactures water meters, calibrators, and other measuring devices. The probability distribution of returns that is given in Table 8.3 shows that the expected return on Anderson's stock is 15 percent and it has about the same risk as Martin's stock ($\sigma_{Martin} = 59.3\%$ and $\sigma_{Anderson} = 59.2\%$). The correlation coefficient for the returns on these two stocks is +0.21, which means that there exists a less than perfectly positive relationship between the stocks' returns. As Table 8.3 shows, however, when a portfolio is formed by investing equal amounts in both stocks, the portfolio's return is 15 percent, but its standard deviation is 46 percent, which is less than the standard deviation of either stock individually ($\sigma_{Martin} \approx \sigma_{Anderson} \approx 59\%$). This example shows that the stocks have less risk when held in a portfolio than when either is held all by itself.

We can conclude from our discussion that risk can be completely eliminated in one extreme case ($\rho = -1.0$), whereas diversification does no good in the other extreme case ($\rho = +1.0$). In between these extremes, combining two stocks into a portfolio reduces, but does not eliminate, the riskiness inherent in the individual stocks. The weaker (lower) the positive correlation *or* the stronger (higher) the negative correlation two stocks exhibit, the more risk can be reduced when they are combined in a portfolio—that is, the greater the diversification effect.

8-3a Firm-Specific Risk Versus Market Risk

From our discussion of portfolio risk, you should have concluded that an individual stock (or other investment) generally is less risky when it is held in a portfolio that includes other investments than when it is held by itself. In other words, some of the risk that is associated with an individual stock can be eliminated by combining it with other investments to form a diversified portfolio. But we know that most stocks are positively correlated, because most companies, and thus their stocks, tend to do well when the economy is strong and to do poorly when it is weak.[6] So, how do investors eliminate some of a stock's risk by combining a bunch of positively correlated investments?

[6]It is not too difficult to find a few stocks that happened to rise because of a particular set of circumstances in the past while most other stocks were declining. It is much more difficult to find stocks that could logically be *expected* to go up in the future when other stocks are falling. American Business Collections, the collection agency discussed earlier, is one of those rare exceptions.

FIGURE 8.2

EFFECTS OF PORTFOLIO SIZE ON PORTFOLIO RISK FOR AVERAGE STOCKS

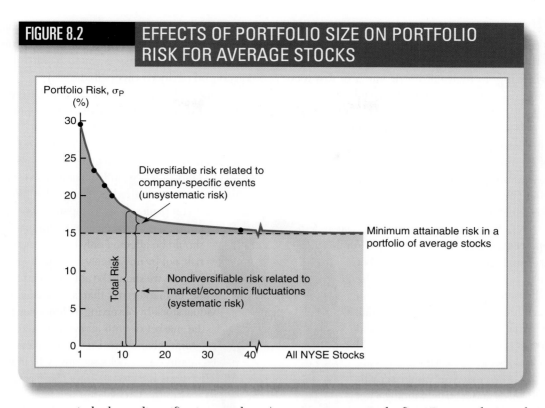

To see more precisely how diversification works, consider Figure 8.2. This figure shows how portfolio risk is affected by forming ever larger portfolios of randomly selected stocks listed on the New York Stock Exchange (NYSE). Standard deviations are plotted for an average one-stock portfolio, for a two-stock portfolio, and so on, up to a portfolio consisting of all common stocks listed on the NYSE. As the graph illustrates, the riskiness of a portfolio consisting of average NYSE stocks generally tends to decline and to approach some minimum limit as the size of the portfolio increases. The figure shows that almost half of the riskiness inherent in an average individual stock can be eliminated if the stock is held as part of a reasonably well-diversified portfolio—namely, a portfolio containing 40 or more stocks. Some risk always remains, so it is virtually impossible to diversify away the effects of broad stock market (economic) movements that affect all stocks.

The portion of the risk of a stock that can be eliminated by diversification generally is called *diversifiable risk, firm-specific risk,* or *unsystematic risk,* whereas the part that cannot be eliminated is called *nondiversifiable risk, market risk,* or *systematic risk.* Although the name given to the risk is not especially important, the fact that a large portion of the riskiness of any individual stock can be eliminated through portfolio diversification is vitally important.

Firm-specific, or diversifiable, risk is caused by such things as lawsuits, loss of key personnel, strikes, the winning and losing of major contracts, and other events that are unique to a particular firm. Because the actual outcomes of these events are generally unpredictable (fairly random), their effects on a portfolio can be eliminated by diversification; that is, unexpected bad events in one firm will be offset by unexpected good events in another. Market, or nondiversifiable, risk, on the other hand, stems from factors that *systematically* affect all firms, such as war, inflation, recessions, and high interest rates. Because all companies, and thus their stocks, are somehow affected by economic, or market, events, such *systematic risk* cannot be eliminated by portfolio diversification.

We know that investors demand a premium for bearing risk. That is, the riskier a security, the higher the expected return required to induce investors to buy (or to hold) it, which is the relationship that is given in Figure 8.1. However, if investors really are primarily concerned with *portfolio risk* rather than the risk of the individual securities in the portfolio, how should we measure the riskiness of an individual stock? The answer is this: *The relevant riskiness of an individual stock is its contribution to the riskiness of a well-diversified portfolio.* In other words, the riskiness of General Electric's stock to a doctor who has a

firm-specific (diversifiable) risk That part of a security's risk associated with random outcomes generated by events or behaviors, specific to the firm. It *can* be eliminated by proper diversification.

market (nondiversifiable) risk The part of a security's risk associated with economic, or market, factors that systematically affect all firms to some extent. It *cannot* be eliminated by diversification.

portfolio of 40 stocks, or to a trust officer managing a 150-stock portfolio, is the contribution that the GE stock makes to the entire portfolio's riskiness. A stock might be quite risky if held by itself, but if much of this total (stand-alone) risk can be eliminated through diversification, then its **relevant risk**—that is, its *contribution to the portfolio's risk*—is much smaller than its total risk.

A simple example will help clarify this point. Suppose you are offered the chance to flip a coin once. If a head comes up, you win $20,000; if the coin comes up tails, you lose $16,000. This proposition is a good bet: The expected return is $2,000 = 0.5($20,000) + 0.5(−$16,000). It is a highly risky proposition, however, because you have a 50 percent chance of losing $16,000. For this reason, you might refuse to make the bet. Alternatively, suppose you were offered the chance to flip a coin 100 times. You would win $200 for each head but lose $160 for each tail. It is possible that you would flip all heads and win $20,000. It is also possible that you would flip all tails and lose $16,000. The chances are very high, however, that you would actually flip about 50 heads and 50 tails, winning a net of about $2,000. Although each individual flip is a risky bet, collectively this scenario is a low-risk proposition because most of the stand-alone risk that is associated with each flip has been diversified away. This concept underlies the practice of holding portfolios of stocks rather than just one stock.

8-3b The Concept of Beta[7]

Are all stocks equally risky in the sense that adding them to a well-diversified portfolio would have the same effect on the portfolio's riskiness? The answer is no. Because not all companies are affected in the same way by such economic factors as levels of interest rates and consumer prices, different stocks will affect the portfolio differently, which means that different securities have different degrees of relevant (systematic) risk. How can we measure the relevant risk of an individual stock? As we have seen, all risk except that related to broad market (economic) movements can, and presumably will, be diversified away. After all, why accept risk that we can easily eliminate? The risk that remains after diversifying is called *market risk,* because it

relevant risk The portion of a security's risk that cannot be diversified away; the security's market risk. It reflects the security's contribution to the risk of a portfolio.

beta coefficient, β A measure of the extent to which the returns on a given stock move with the stock market.

is the risk that remains in a portfolio that consists of all investments available in both the financial markets and the markets for real assets. Such a portfolio might be considered perfectly diversified.

Suppose that you are able to purchase every investment that exists in the financial markets. Because you would have an extremely well-diversified portfolio, the overall return that you earn on your portfolio of investments should be affected by movements in general economic factors that affect all companies (e.g., inflation and interest rates) rather than movements caused by factors that affect only specific companies (e.g., company labor problems or poor marketing campaigns). Thus, such a portfolio should be affected only by systematic, or market, risk, not by unsystematic, or firm-specific, risk. As a result, we should be able to measure the systematic, or market, risk that is associated with an individual stock by observing its tendency to move with the market or with an average stock that has the same characteristics as the market. The measure of a stock's sensitivity to market fluctuations is called its **beta coefficient**, designated with the Greek letter β.

An *average-risk stock* is defined as one that tends to move up and down in step with the general market as measured by some index, such as the Dow Jones Industrial Average (DJIA) or the Standard & Poor's 500 Index (S&P 500). Because such a stock mirrors the market, *by definition* its beta (β) is 1.0. This value indicates that, in general, if the market moves up by 10 percent, the average stock price will also increase by 10 percent; if the market falls by 10 percent, the average stock price will decline by 10 percent. If β = 0.5, the stock's systematic risk is only half as volatile as the market, which means that a change in return associated with risk will be only half as much as the average stock. If β = 2.0, the stock's relevant risk is twice as volatile as the market portfolio, so it is considered twice as risky as an average stock.

Because the beta coefficient measures a stock's volatility relative to an average stock (or the market), which has β = 1.0, we can calculate a stock's beta by comparing its returns to the market's returns over some time period. This comparison can be examined by plotting a line like the one shown in Figure 8.3. The slope of the line shows how the stock's returns move in response to movements in the general market; thus, the slope represents the stock's beta coefficient.[8] Betas for literally

[7]Although we refer to the beta coefficient (β) as a measure of a stock's systematic risk in this section, the concept of beta applies to any investment, including bonds.

[8]A stock's beta coefficient generally is computed by performing simple regression analysis, where the dependent variable is the return on the stock and the independent variable is the return on the market.

FIGURE 8.3

VOLATILITY OF A STOCK'S RETURNS RELATIVE TO VOLATILITY OF THE MARKET'S RETURNS, β

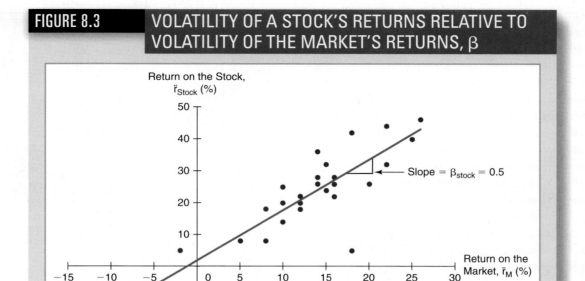

thousands of companies are calculated and published by Bank of America Merrill Lynch, Value Line, Inc., and numerous other organizations. For example, the May 30, 2015, issue of the *S&P Capital IQ* report indicates that E*TRADE (β = 2.15), an online investment service, and Avalon Rare Metals (β = 3.72), a company that mines rare metals and minerals, have betas greater than 1.0; Northern Trust (β = 1.05), a wealth management and banking company, and Northrop Grumman Corporation (β = 1.00), a provider of military equipment and services, have betas approximately equal to 1.0, which is the average for all stocks; and Campbell Soup (β = 0.32), General Mills (β = 0.18), and PepsiCo (β = 0.43) have betas less than 1.0.[9]

If we add a higher-than-average-beta stock (β_{Stock} > 1.0) to an average-beta portfolio ($\beta_{Portfolio}$ = 1.0), then the beta and consequently the riskiness, of the portfolio will increase. Conversely, if we add a lower-than-average-beta stock (β_{Stock} < 1.0) to an average-risk portfolio, the portfolio's beta and risk will decline. *Thus, because a stock's beta measures its contribution to the riskiness of a well-diversified portfolio, theoretically beta is the correct measure of the stock's riskiness.*

[9]In theory, betas can be negative. For example, if a stock's returns tend to rise when those of other stocks decline, and vice versa, then the regression line in a graph such as Figure 8.3 will have a downward slope, and the beta will be negative. Note, however, that few stocks have negative betas. American Business Collections, the fictitious collection agency introduced earlier, probably would have a negative beta.

We can summarize our discussion to this point as follows:

1. A stock's risk consists of two components: *market risk* and *firm-specific risk.*

2. *Firm-specific risk* can be eliminated through diversification. Most investors do diversify, either by holding large portfolios or by purchasing shares in mutual funds, which consist of large portfolios of investments. We are left, then, with *market, or economic, risk,* which is caused by general economic movements that are reflected in the stock market. *Market risk is the only risk that is relevant to a rational, diversified investor because it cannot be eliminated (or reduced).*

3. Investors must be compensated for bearing risk. That is, the greater the riskiness of an investment, the higher its required return. Such *compensation is required only for risk that cannot be eliminated by diversification.* If risk premiums existed on investments with high diversifiable risk, well-diversified investors would start buying these securities and bidding up their prices, and their final (equilibrium) expected returns would eventually reflect only nondiversifiable market (systematic) risk.

An example might help clarify this point. Suppose half of Stock A's risk is market risk (it occurs because Stock A moves in tandem with the market), and the other half of Stock A's risk is diversifiable. You hold only Stock A, so you are exposed to all of its risk—that is, its stand-alone (total) risk. As compensation for bearing so much risk, *you want* a risk premium that is 8 percent higher than the 5 percent Treasury bond rate; that is, you demand a return of 13 percent (= 5% + 8%) on this investment. But suppose other investors, including your professor, are well diversified: They also hold Stock A, but they have eliminated its diversifiable risk and thus are exposed to only half as much risk as you are. Consequently, their risk premium will be only half as large as yours, and they will *require* a return of only 9 percent (=5% + 4%) to invest in the stock.

If the stock actually yielded more than 9 percent in the market, other investors, including your professor, would buy it. If it yielded the 13 percent you demand, you would be willing to buy the stock, but well diversified investors would compete with you for its acquisition. They would bid its price up and its yield down, which would keep you from getting the stock at the return you need (want) to compensate you for taking on its *total risk*. In the end, you would have to accept a 9 percent return or else keep your money in the bank. Thus, risk premiums in a market populated with *rational* investors—that is, those who diversify—will reflect only market risk.

4. The systematic (nondiversifiable) risk of a stock is measured by its *beta coefficient*, which is an index of the stock's relative volatility compared with that of the entire market because a portfolio that includes all available investments—that is, a market portfolio—is perfectly diversified and thus exhibits systematic risk *only*. The benchmark is the market beta, which is 1.0. Firms with greater systematic risk volatilities than the market have betas that are greater than 1.0 (i.e., $\beta > 1.0$), and firms with smaller systematic risk volatilities than the market have betas that are less than 1.0 (i.e., $\beta < 1.0$).

5. *Because a stock's beta coefficient determines how the stock affects the riskiness of a diversified portfolio, beta (β) is a better measure of a stock's relevant risk than is standard deviation (σ), which measures total, or standalone, risk.*

capital asset pricing model (CAPM) A model used to determine the required return on an asset, which is based on the proposition that an asset's return should be equal to the risk-free return plus a risk premium that reflects the asset's nondiversifiable (relevant) risk.

8-3c Portfolio Beta Coefficients

A portfolio consisting of low-beta securities will itself have a low beta, because the beta of any set of securities is a weighted average of the individual securities' betas, as shown in Equation 8.7:

8.7

$$\text{Portfolio beta} = \beta_p = w_1\beta_1 + \cdots + w_N\beta_N$$
$$= \sum_{j=1}^{N} w_j\beta_j$$

Here β_p, the beta of the portfolio, reflects how volatile the portfolio is in relation to the market; w_j is the fraction of the portfolio invested in the *j*th stock; and β_j is the beta coefficient of the *j*th stock. For example, if an investor holds a $105,000 portfolio consisting of $35,000 invested in each of three stocks, and each of the stocks has a beta of 0.7, then the portfolio's beta will be $\beta_{P1} = 0.7$:

$$\beta_{P1} = (1/3)(0.7) + (1/3)(0.7) + (1/3)(0.7) = 0.7$$

Such a portfolio will be less risky than the market, which means it should experience narrower price swings and demonstrate smaller rate-of-return fluctuations than the market. When graphed in a fashion similar to Figure 8.3, the slope of its regression line would be 0.7, which is less than that of a portfolio of average stocks.

Now suppose one of the existing stocks is sold and replaced by a stock with $\beta_j = 2.5$. This action will increase the riskiness of the portfolio from $\beta_{P1} = 0.7$ to $\beta_{P2} = 1.3$:

$$\beta_{P2} = (1/3)(0.7) + (1/3)(0.7) + (1/3)(2.5) = 1.3$$

Had the beta coefficient of the replacement stock been 0.4 rather than 2.5, the portfolio beta would have declined from 0.7 to 0.6. Adding a low-beta stock, therefore, would reduce the riskiness of the portfolio.

(8-4) The Relationship between Risk and Rates of Return: The CAPM[10]

Now that we know beta is the appropriate measure of a stock's relevant risk, we must specify the relationship between relevant risk and return. To determine an investment's *required rate of return*, we use a theoretical model called the **capital asset pricing model (CAPM)**. The CAPM shows how the relevant risk of an investment, as measured by its beta coefficient, is used to determine the investment's appropriate required rate of return.

[10]This concept is discussed in more detail in investment textbooks. Some of the assumptions of the CAPM theory are unrealistic. As a consequence, the theory does not hold exactly.

First, note from Figure 8.1 that the risk premium for any investment is the return that is generated in excess of the risk-free rate of return. Thus, for Stock j the required risk premium, RP_j, is the required rate of return on Stock j minus the risk-free rate, r_{RF}—that is, $RP_j = r_j - r_{RF}$. Using this same logic, we can state the market risk premium as $RP_M = r_M - r_{RF}$. This risk premium represents the additional return above the risk-free rate that is required to compensate investors for taking on the *average amount of risk* that is associated with the market portfolio, or average-risk stock, that has $\beta = 1.0$. Because the market portfolio contains only systematic, or market, risk, RP_M represents the return that investors require to be compensated for taking an average amount of relevant, or systematic, risk. It follows then that if the systematic (relevant) risk of a stock is twice as risky (volatile) as the market, or average systematic risk, the stock's *risk premium* should be twice as high as the market's risk premium, and vice versa. Furthermore, because we can measure a stock's relevant risk by computing its beta coefficient, β_j, we should be able to determine its appropriate risk premium by multiplying the market risk premium by the stock's beta, as shown in Equation 8.8:

8.8

Risk premium for Stock j $= RP_j = RP_M \times \beta_j$
$$= (r_M - r_{RF})\beta_j$$

For example, if $\beta_j = 0.5$ and $RP_M = 6\%$, then $RP_j = 3.0\% = 6\% \times 0.5$.

As Figure 8.1 shows, the required return for any investment can be expressed in general terms as shown in Equation 8.9:

8.9

$$\begin{array}{c} \text{Required} \\ \text{return} \end{array} = \begin{array}{c} \text{Risk-free} \\ \text{return} \end{array} + \begin{array}{c} \text{Premium} \\ \text{for risk} \end{array}$$
$$r_j = r_{RF} + RP_j$$

If we substitute the definition of RP_j given in Equation 8.8 into Equation 8.9, we have Equation 8.10, which is the equilibrium pricing equation for the CAPM:

[11]Students sometimes confuse beta with the slope of the SML. This is a mistake. The slope of any line is equal to the "rise" divided by the "run," or $(Y_1 - Y_0)/(X_1 - X_0)$. Consider Figure 8.4 *on the next page*. If we let $Y = r$ and $X = \beta$, and we go from the origin to $\beta = 1.0$, we see that the slope is $(r_M - r_{RF})/(\beta_M - \beta_{RF}) = (11\% - 5\%)/(1 - 0) = 6\%$. Thus the slope of the SML is equal to $(r_M - r_{RF})$, the market risk premium. In Figure 8.4, $r_j = 5\% + (6\%)\beta_j$, so a doubling of beta (for example, from 1.0 to 2.0) would produce a six-percentage point increase in r_j.

8.10

$$r_j = r_{RF} + (RP_M)\beta_j$$
$$= r_{RF} + (r_M - r_{RF})\beta_j$$

To illustrate the application of the CAPM, suppose that the market's required rate of return is 11 percent, the risk-free rate of return is 5 percent, and Stock L has a beta coefficient equal to 0.5. Applying Equation 8.10, the stock's required rate of return would be

$$r_L = 5\% + (11\% - 5\%)(0.5) = 5\% + 6\%(0.5)$$
$$= 8\%$$

If Stock H had $\beta_H = 2.0$, then its required rate of return would be 17 percent:

$$r_H = 5\% + (6\%)2.0 = 17\%$$

In addition, an average stock, with $\beta = 1.0$, would have a required return of 11 percent, the same as the market return:

$$r_A = 5\% + (6\%)1.0 = 11\% = r_M$$

Equation 8.10 is often expressed in graph form. The line that represents the required rate of return is called the **security market line (SML)**. Figure 8.4 shows the SML when $r_{RF} = 5\%$ and $r_M = 11\%$. Note the following points:

1. *Required rates of return* are shown on the vertical axis, and risk as measured by beta is shown on the horizontal axis.

2. Riskless securities have $\beta_j = 0$; therefore, $r_{RF} = 5\%$ appears as the vertical axis intercept in Figure 8.4.

3. The slope of the SML reflects the degree of *risk aversion* in the economy; that is, the slope is RP_M. The greater the average investor's aversion to risk, (a) the steeper the slope of the line, (b) the greater the risk premium for any stock, and (c) the higher the required rate of return on stocks.[11]

4. The values we worked out for stocks with $\beta_L = 0.5$, $\beta_A = 1.0$, and $\beta_H = 2.0$ agree with the values shown on the graph for r_{Low}, r_{Avg}, and r_{High}.

security market line (SML) The line that shows the relationship between risk as measured by beta and the required rate of return for individual securities.

FIGURE 8.4   **THE SECURITY MARKET LINE (SML)**

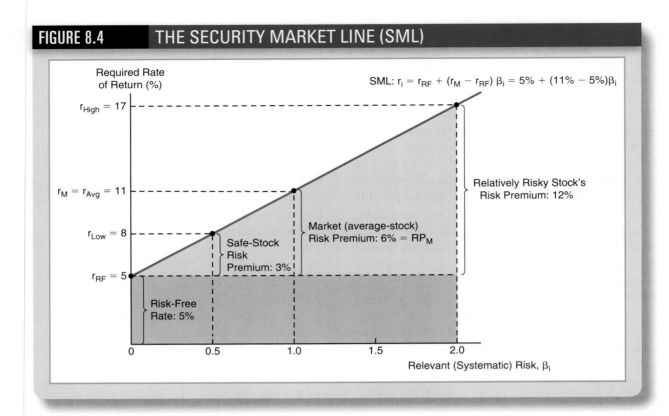

Both the SML and a company's position on it change over time because of changes in interest rates, investors' risk aversion, and individual companies' betas. Such changes are discussed in the following sections.

8-4a The Impact of Inflation

As we learned in Chapter 5, the risk-free rate of return, r_{RF}, is the price of money to a riskless borrower. We also learned in Chapter 5 that r_{RF} as measured by the rate on U.S. Treasury securities is called the *nominal*, or *quoted*, rate, and it consists of two elements: (1) a *real inflation-free rate of return*, r^*, and (2) *an inflation premium, IP*, equal to the anticipated rate of inflation.[12] Thus, $r_{RF} = r^* + IP$.

If the expected rate of inflation rose by 2 percent, r_{RF} would also increase by 2 percent. In this case, the SML shown in Figure 8.4 would shift upward so that it is parallel to the existing line, which indicates that the 2 percent increase in expected inflation causes r_{RF} to increase by 2 percent.[13] Because the inflation premium is built into the required rates of return of both riskless and risky assets,

market risk premium (RP_M) The additional return over the risk-free rate needed to compensate investors for assuming an average amount of risk.

the increase in expected inflation would cause an *equal increase in the rates of return on all risky assets.* Suppose r_{RF} increases from 5 percent to 7 percent. Because inflation affects r_{RF}, the market risk premium will not change; thus, $RP_M = 6\%$. Therefore, the effect on the returns on a stock with $\beta = 1.0$ and a stock with $\beta = 2.0$ would be

Investment	RP_M	$r_{RF} + (RP_M)\beta = r$	
Stock A, $\beta_A = 1.0$	6%	$r_{A1} = 5\% + (6\%)1.0 = 11\%$	$\Delta = 2\%$
	6%	$r_{A2} = 7\% + (6\%)1.0 = 13\%$	
Stock H, $\beta_H = 2.0$	6%	$r_{H1} = 5\% + (6\%)2.0 = 17\%$	$\Delta = 2\%$
	6%	$r_{H2} = 7\% + (6\%)2.0 = 19\%$	

Thus, all securities' returns increase by 2 percentage points.

8-4b Changes in Risk Aversion

The **market risk premium (RP_M)** depends on the degree of aversion that investors on average have to risk,

[12]Long-term Treasury bonds also contain a maturity risk premium (MRP). Here we consider short-term T-bills; thus, MRP = 0.

[13]Note that r_{RF} in a CAPM analysis can be proxied by either a long-term rate (the T-bond rate) or a short-term rate (the T-bill rate). We use the T-bill rate here.

which is reflected in the slope of the security market line (SML). The steeper the slope of the line, the greater the average investor's risk aversion, and thus the greater the return investors require as compensation for risk. *As risk aversion increases, so does the risk premium,* and, therefore, so does the slope of the SML.[14]

If the average investor were to become more risk averse, the SML shown in Figure 8.4 would pivot upward so that its slope was steeper but its intersection with the y-axis remained at r_{RF} = 5% in our example. The intersection does not change because neither component of r_{RF}—the real risk-free rate of return, r^*, or the inflation premium, IP—is affected by changes in investors' risk attitudes. Consider what would happen if investors become more risk averse so that the market risk premium increased from 6 percent to 8 percent, and r_M increased from r_{M1} = 11% to r_{M2} = 13%. The returns on other risky assets would also rise. However, because each stock's risk premium is a multiple of both the market risk premium, RP_M, and the beta coefficient for the individual stock, β_j, the effect of this shift in risk aversion would be *more pronounced on riskier securities* than less risky investments. As a result, for our example, the change in the risk premium for Stock j can be stated as $\Delta RP_j = \Delta RP_M(\beta_j) = (13\% - 11\%)\beta_j = (2\%)\beta_j$. The effects of this change on the stock with β = 1.0 and the stock with β = 2.0 in Figure 8.4 would be

Investment	RP_M	$r_{RF} + (RP_M)\beta = r$	
Stock A, β_A = 1.0	6%	r_{A1} = 5% + (6%)1.0 = 11%	Δ = 2%
	8%	r_{A2} = 5% + (8%)1.0 = 13%	
Stock H, β_H = 2.0	6%	r_{H1} = 5% + (6%)2.0 = 17%	Δ = 4%
	8%	r_{H2} = 5% + (8%)2.0 = 21%	

As you can see, the securities' returns increased by $\Delta RP_M(\beta_j)$. Because Stock H's beta coefficient is two times Stock A's beta coefficient, the effect of the risk premium change was twice as much for Stock H. Thus, *when the average investor's aversion to risk changes, investments with higher beta coefficients experience greater changes*

[14]If investors were *indifferent* to risk, and if r_{RF} was 5 percent, then all risky assets would also provide an expected return of 5 percent. If there were no risk aversion, there would be no risk premium, so the SML would be horizontal.

in their required rates of return than investments with lower betas.

8-4c Changes in a Stock's Beta Coefficient

As we will see later in this book, a firm can affect its beta risk by changing the composition of its assets and by modifying its use of debt financing. External factors, such as increased competition within a firm's industry or the expiration of basic patents, can also alter a company's beta. When such changes occur, the required rate of return, r, changes as well. Suppose some action occurred that caused Stock L's beta to increase from 0.5 to 0.8. Stock L's required rate of return would increase from r_{L1} = 8% to

$$r_{L2} = 5\% + (11\% - 5\%)0.8 = 9.8\%$$

Any change that affects the required rate of return on a security, such as a change in its beta coefficient or in expected inflation, will affect the price of the security.

8-4d A Word of Caution

A word of caution about betas and the CAPM is in order here. First, the model originally was developed under very restrictive assumptions, including: (1) all investors have the same information, which leads to the same expectations about future stock prices; (2) everyone can borrow and lend at the risk-free rate of return; (3) stocks (or any other security) can be purchased in any denomination or fraction of shares; and (4) taxes and transaction costs (commissions) do not exist.

Second, the entire theory is based on *expected* conditions, yet we have available only *past* data. The betas we calculate show how volatile a stock has been in the past, but future conditions could certainly change. The stock's *future volatility*, which is the item of real concern to investors, might therefore differ quite dramatically from its past volatility. For this reason, many investors and analysts use the CAPM and the concept of β to provide "ballpark" figures for further analysis. The concept that investors should be rewarded only for taking relevant risk makes sense. Moreover, the CAPM provides an easy way to get a "rough" estimate of the relevant risk and the appropriate required rate of return of an investment (or a portfolio of investments).

8-5 Stock Market Equilibrium

Suppose the risk-free return is 5 percent, the market *risk premium* is 6 percent, and Stock Q has a beta of 1.5 ($\beta_Q = 1.5$). In this case, an average investor will require a return on Stock Q of $r_Q = 5\% + 6\%(1.5) = 14\%$. The average investor will want to buy Stock Q if the *expected rate of return*, $\hat{r}_Q$, exceeds 14 percent, will want to sell it if $\hat{r}_Q < 14\%$, and will be indifferent (and therefore will hold but not buy or sell Stock Q) if $\hat{r}_Q = 14\%$. Now suppose the investor's portfolio contains Stock Q, and he or she analyzes the stock's prospects and concludes that its earnings, dividends, and price can be expected to grow at a constant rate of 4 percent per year forever. The last dividend paid was $D_0 = \$3$, so the next expected dividend is $\hat{D}_1 = \$3.00(1.04) = \$3.12$. Our *average* (marginal) investor observes that the present price of the stock, P_0, is \$34.67. Should he or she purchase more of Stock Q, sell the present holdings, or maintain the present position?

Recall from Chapter 7 that we can calculate Stock Q's *expected rate of return* using Equation 7.3:

$$\hat{r}_Q = \frac{\hat{D}_1}{P_0} + g = \frac{\$3.12}{\$34.67} + 0.04$$

$$= 0.09 + 0.04 = 0.13 = 13\%$$

Because the expected rate of return, $\hat{r}_Q = 13\%$, is less than the required return, $r_Q = 14\%$, this marginal investor would want to sell the stock, as would other stockholders. Because few people would want to buy at the \$34.67 price, the present owners would be unable to find buyers unless they cut the price of the stock. The price would therefore decline, and this decline would continue until the stock's price reached \$31.20. At that point, the market for this security would be in equilibrium because the expected rate of

equilibrium The condition under which the expected return on a security is just equal to its required return, $\hat{r} = r$, and the price is stable.

return, 14 percent, would be equal to the required rate of return:

$$\hat{r}_Q = \frac{\$3.12}{\$31.20} + 0.04 = 0.10 + 0.04$$

$$= 0.14 = 14\% = r_Q$$

Had the stock initially sold for less than \$31.20—say, \$28.36—events would have been reversed. Investors would have wanted to buy the stock because its expected rate of return ($\hat{r} = 15\%$) would have exceeded its required rate of return, and buy orders would have driven the stock's price up to \$31.20.

To summarize, two conditions must hold in equilibrium:

1. The expected rate of return, $\hat{r}_j$, as seen by the marginal (average) investor must equal the required rate of return, r_j; that is, $\hat{r}_j = r_j$.

2. The actual market price of the stock, P_0, must equal its intrinsic value, $\hat{P}_0$, as estimated by the marginal investor; that is, $P_0 = \hat{P}_0$.

Of course, some individual investors might believe that $\hat{r}_j > r_j$ and $P_0 < \hat{P}_0$; hence they would invest most of their funds in the stock. Other investors might ascribe to the opposite view and sell all of their shares. Nevertheless, it is the marginal investor who establishes the actual market price. For this investor, $\hat{r}_j = r_j$ and $P_0 = \hat{P}_0$. If these conditions do not hold, trading will occur until they do hold.

8-6 Different Types of Risk

In Chapter 5, we introduced the concept of risk in our discussion of interest rates. However, we did not discuss risk evaluation in detail; rather, we described some of the factors that determine the total risk associated with debt, such as default risk (DRP), liquidity risk (LP), and maturity risk (MRP). In reality, these risks also affect other types of investments, including equity. Equity does not represent a legal contract that requires the firm to pay defined amounts of dividends at particular times or to "act" in specific ways. There is, however, an expectation that positive returns will be generated through future distributions of cash because dividends will be paid, capital gains will be generated through growth, or both events will occur. Investors also expect the firm to behave "appropriately." If these expectations are not met, investors generally consider the firm to be in "default" of their expectations. In such cases, as long as no laws have been broken, stockholders generally do not have legal recourse, as would be the case for a default on debt. As a result, investors penalize the firm by selling their stock, which causes the value of the firm's stock to decline.

In this chapter, we build on the general concept that was introduced in Chapter 5 by showing how the risk premium associated with any investment should be determined (at least in theory). The basis of our discussion is Equation 5.2, which we develop further in this chapter as follows:

$$r_j = \text{Risk-free rate} + \text{Risk premium}$$
$$= r_{RF} + (r_M - r_{RF})\beta_j = \text{CAPM}$$

According to the CAPM, investors should not expect to be rewarded for all of the risk associated with an individual investment—that is, its total, or stand-alone, risk—because some risk can be eliminated through diversification. The *relevant risk*, and thus the risk for which investors should be compensated, is that portion of the total risk that cannot be diversified away. Thus, in this chapter we showed the following:

Systematic risk is represented by an investment's beta coefficient, β, in Equation 8.10.

The specific types and sources of risk to which a firm or an investor is exposed are numerous, and vary considerably depending on the situation. A detailed discussion of all the different types of risks and the techniques used to evaluate risks is beyond the scope of this book. However, you should recognize that risk is an important factor in the determination of the required rate of return (r), which, according to the following equation, is one of the two variables we need to determine the value of an asset:

$$\text{Value} = \frac{\hat{CF}_1}{(1 + r)^1} + \cdots + \frac{\hat{CF}_n}{(1 + r)^n} = \sum_{t=1}^{n} \frac{\hat{CF}_t}{(1 + r)^t}$$

According to this equation, the value of an asset, which could be a stock, bond, or any other investment, is based on the cash flows that the asset is expected to generate during its life, $\hat{CF}_t$, and the rate of return, r, that investors require to "put up" their money to purchase the investment. In this chapter, we provide you with an indication as to how r should be determined, and we show that investors demand higher rates of return to compensate them for taking greater amounts of "relevant" risk.

Because it is an important concept and has a direct effect on value, we continue to discuss risk in the remainder of the book. Table 8.4 shows the risks that are discussed in this book and indicates whether each risk is considered a component of systematic (nondiversifiable) risk or of unsystematic (diversifiable) risk. Note that (1) this table oversimplifies risk analysis, because some risks are not easily classified as either systematic or unsystematic; and (2) some of the risks included in the table will be discussed later in the book. Even so, this table should show you the relationships among the different risks discussed in the book.

Total risk = σ = Market (systematic) risk + Firm-specific (unsystematic) risk

= Nondiversifiable risk + Diversifiable risk

Relevant risk = Nondiversifiable (systematic) risk

Table 8.4

Different Types (Sources) of Risk

General Type of Risk	Name of Risk	Brief Description
I. Systematic risks (nondiversifiable risk; market risk; relevant risk)	Interest rate risk	When interest rates change, (1) the values of investments change (in opposite directions) and (2) the rate at which funds can be reinvested also changes (in the same direction).
	Inflation risk	The primary reason interest rates change is because investors change their expectations about future inflation.
	Maturity risk	Long-term investments experience greater price reactions to interest rate changes than do short-term investments.
	Liquidity risk	Reflects the fact that some investments are more easily converted into cash on a short notice at a "reasonable price" than are other securities.
	Exchange rate risk	Multinational firms deal with different currencies; the rate at which the currency of one country can be *exchanged* into the *currency* of another country—that is, the exchange rate—changes as market conditions change.
	Political risk	Any action by a government that reduces the value of an investment.
II. Unsystematic risks (diversifiable risk; firm-specific risk)	Business risk	Risk that would be inherent in the firm's operations if it used no debt—factors such as labor conditions, product safety, quality of management, competitive conditions, and so forth, affect firm-specific risk.
	Financial risk	Risk associated with how the firm is financed; that is, its credit risk.
	Default risk	Part of financial risk, the chance that the firm will not be able to service its existing debt.
III. Combined risks (some systematic risk and some unsystematic risk)	Total risk (Stand-alone risk)	The combination of systematic risk and unsystematic risk; also referred to as stand-alone risk, because this is the risk an investor takes if he or she purchases only one investment, which is tantamount to "putting all your eggs into one basket."
	Corporate risk	The riskiness of the firm without considering the effect of stockholder diversification; based on the combination of assets held by the firm (inventory, accounts receivable, plant and equipment, and so forth). Some diversification exists because the firm's assets represent a portfolio of investments in real assets.

STUDY TOOLS

LOCATED AT BACK OF THE TEXTBOOK

- ☐ Problems are found at the end of this chapter.
- ☐ A tear-out Chapter Review card is located at the back of the textbook.

LOCATED AT WWW.CENGAGEBRAIN.COM

- ☐ Review Key Term flashcards and create your own cards.
- ☐ Track your knowledge and understanding of key concepts in corporate finance.
- ☐ Complete practice and graded quizzes to prepare for tests.
- ☐ Complete interactive content within CFIN5 Online.
- ☐ View the chapter highlight boxes for CFIN5 Online.

KEY RISK AND RETURN CONCEPTS

To conclude this chapter, we summarize some risk/return concepts that were discussed.

- In finance, we define risk as the chance that you will not receive the return that you expect, regardless of whether the actual outcome is better than expected or worse than expected.

- Riskier investments must have higher expected returns than less risky investments; otherwise, people will not purchase investments with higher risks.

- The total risk of any investment can be divided into two components: diversifiable risk and nondiversifiable risk. Diversifiable risk is not important to informed investors, because they will eliminate its

effects through diversification. Thus, the relevant risk is nondiversifiable risk, because it cannot be eliminated, even in a perfectly diversified portfolio.

- The effects of nondiversifiable risk, which is also labeled systematic risk or market risk, can be determined by computing the beta coefficient (β) of an investment. The beta coefficient measures the volatility of an investment relative to the volatility of the market, which, in theory, is perfectly diversified and thus is affected only by systematic risk.

- According to the capital asset pricing model (CAPM), an investment's required rate of return can be computed as $r_i = r_{RF} + (r_{RF} - r_M)\beta_i = r_{RF} + (RP_M)\beta_i$.

PROBLEMS

8-1 What are the (a) expected return, (b) standard deviation, and (c) coefficient of variation for an investment with the following probability distribution?

Probability	Payoff
0.2	19.0%
0.7	9.0
0.1	4.0

8-2 Calculate the (a) expected return, (b) standard deviation, and (c) coefficient of variation for an investment with the following probability distribution:

Probability	Payoff
0.45	32.0%
0.35	−4.0
0.20	−20.0

8-3 Compute the (a) expected return, (b) standard deviation, and (c) coefficient of variation for investments with the following probability distributions:

Probability	r_A	r_B
0.3	30.0%	5.0%
0.2	10.0	15.0
0.5	−2.0	25.0

8-4 Suppose you are an average risk-averse investor who can purchase *only one* of the following stocks. Which should you purchase? Explain your reasoning.

Investment	Expected Return, $\hat{r}$	Standard Deviation, σ
Stock M	6.0%	4.0%
Stock N	18.0	12.0
Stock O	12.0	7.0

8-5 Which of the following investments has the greater *relative* risk?

Investment	Expected Return, $\hat{r}$	Standard Deviation, σ
F	16.0%	7.0%
G	27.0	13.0

8-6 Rebecca invested $9,000 in a stock that has an expected return equal to 18 percent and $21,000 in a stock with an 8 percent expected return. What is the portfolio's expected return?

8-7 What is the expected return of the following portfolio of investments, $\hat{r}_p$:

Investment	$\hat{r}$	Amount Invested
DEF	4%	$30,000
JKL	24	25,000
TUV	14	45,000

8-8 Currently, the risk-free return is 3 percent, and the expected market rate of return is 9 percent. What is the expected return of the following three-stock portfolio?

Amount Invested	Beta
$350,000	1.0
250,000	0.2
400,000	2.5

8-9 Compute the (a) expected return and (b) standard deviation of the following investments:

Probability	r_{ABC}	r_{RST}
0.1	22.0%	−2.0%
0.6	12.0	12.0
0.3	2.0	30.0

(c) Suppose you form a portfolio that consists of 60 percent Investment ABC and 40 percent Investment RST. Compute the expected return and standard deviation of the portfolio. (d) Compare the portfolio's standard deviation with the individual investments' standard deviations.

8-10 Of the $60,000 invested in a two-stock portfolio, 40 percent is invested in Stock S and 60 percent is invested in Stock X. If Stock S has a beta coefficient equal to 1.5 and the beta of the portfolio is 2.1, what is the beta coefficient of Stock X?

8-11 Pete's investment portfolio contains five stocks that have a total value equal to $40,000. The beta coefficient of this portfolio is 1.2. Pete wants to invest an additional $10,000 in a stock that has beta equal to 2.2. After he adds this stock, what will be the portfolio's new beta?

8-12 Willis currently has $120,000 invested in a four-stock portfolio with a beta coefficient equal to 0.8. Willis plans to sell one of the stocks in his portfolio for $48,000, which will increase the portfolio's beta to 1.0. What is the beta coefficient of the stock Willis plans to sell?

8-13 Sharon's portfolio, which is valued at $200,000, contains six stocks and has a beta coefficient equal to 1.5. Later today, Sharon is going to sell one of the stocks in her portfolio for $40,000. After the sale, the portfolio's beta will be 1.3. What is the beta coefficient of the stock that Sharon plans to sell?

8-14 The current risk-free rate of return, r_{RF}, is 3 percent and the market *risk premium*, RP_M, is 6 percent. If the beta coefficient associated with a firm's stock is 1.5, what should be the stock's required rate of return?

8-15 Suppose the risk-free rate of return, r_{RF}, is 4 percent, and the market return, r_M, is expected to be 12 percent. What is the required rate of return for a stock with a beta coefficient, β, equal to 2.5?

8-16 ZR Corporation's stock has a beta coefficient equal to 0.8 and a required rate of return equal to 11 percent. If the expected return on the market is 12.5 percent, what is the risk-free rate of return, r_{RF}?

8-17 Stock V has a beta coefficient of 2.0, and Stock W has a beta of 0.5. The expected rate of return on an average stock is 11 percent, and the risk-free rate of return is 5 percent. By how much does the required return on the riskier stock exceed the required return on the less risky stock?

8-18 Recently, Kellie determined that the required rate of return for Stock Q is 11 percent. In her analysis, she determined that the risk-free rate of return, r_{RF}, is 4 percent and that the required return on the market portfolio, r_M, is 9 percent. Today, however, Kellie received new information that indicates the market risk premium, RP_M, is actually 1 percent higher than she estimated in her original analysis. Based on this new information, what should be the required rate of return for Stock Q?

8-19 Suppose the risk-free rate of return is 3.5 percent and the market *risk premium* is 7 percent. Stock U, which has a beta coefficient equal to 0.9, is currently selling for $28 per share. The company is expected to grow at a 4 percent rate forever, and the most recent dividend paid to stockholders was $1.75 per share. Is Stock U correctly priced? Explain.

8-20 High Energy (HE) Company recently paid a $2 per share dividend, which is expected to grow at a constant rate forever. HE's stock, which has a beta coefficient equal to 1.1, is selling for $37.50 per share. Currently, the risk-free rate of return is 4 percent, and the return on an average stock is 10 percent. If HE's stock is selling at its equilibrium price, what is its growth rate?

part 4

After you finish this chapter go to **PAGE 178** for **STUDY TOOLS**

LEARNING OUTCOMES

After studying this chapter, you will be able to...

LO1 Describe the importance of capital budgeting decisions and the general process that is followed when making decisions about investing in fixed (capital) assets.

LO2 Describe how the net present value (NPV) technique and the internal rate of return (IRR) technique are used to make investment (capital budgeting) decisions.

LO3 Compare the NPV technique with the IRR technique, and discuss why the two techniques might not always lead to the same investment decisions.

LO4 Describe how conflicts that might arise when using the NPV and IRR techniques can be resolved by using the modified internal rate of return (MIRR) technique.

LO5 Describe other capital budgeting techniques used by businesses to make investment decisions and which techniques are used most often in practice.

Capital Budgeting Techniques

In the previous three chapters, we showed how financial assets are valued and how required rates of return are determined. Now we apply these concepts to investment decisions involving the fixed assets of a firm, or *capital budgeting*. Here the term *capital* refers to fixed (long-term) assets used in production, whereas a *budget* is a plan that details projected cash inflows and cash outflows during some future period. Thus, the capital budget is an outline of planned expenditures on fixed (real) assets, and **capital budgeting** is the process of analyzing projects and deciding (1) which are acceptable investments and (2) which should actually be purchased.

Our treatment of capital budgeting is divided into two chapters. First, in this chapter we give an overview and explain the basic evaluation techniques used in capital budgeting analysis. In Chapter 10, we show how the cash flows associated with capital budgeting projects are estimated and how risk is considered in capital budgeting decisions.

9-1 Importance of Capital Budgeting

A number of factors combine to make capital budgeting decisions among the most important ones that financial managers must make. First, the impact of capital budgeting is long term; thus, the firm loses some decision-making flexibility when capital projects are purchased. For example, when a firm invests in an asset with a 10-year economic life, its operations are affected for 10 years—that is, the firm is "locked in" by the capital budgeting decision. Further, because asset expansion is fundamentally related to expected future sales, a decision to buy a fixed asset that is expected to last 10 years involves an implicit 10-year sales forecast. An error in the forecast of asset requirements can have serious consequences. If the firm invests too much in fixed assets, it will incur unnecessarily heavy expenses. But if it does not spend enough on fixed assets, it might find that inefficient production and inadequate capacity lead to lost sales that are difficult, if not impossible, to recover.

Timing is also important in capital budgeting. Capital assets must be ready to come on line when they are needed; otherwise, opportunities might be lost. For example, consider what happened to Decopot, a decorative tile manufacturer with no formal capital budgeting process. Decopot attempted to operate at full capacity as often as possible. This was not a bad idea, because demand for Decopot's products and services was relatively stable. A few years ago, however, Decopot began to experience intermittent spurts of additional demand for its products. Decopot could not satisfy the additional demand because it did not have the capacity to produce any more products, and customers had to be turned away. The spurts in demand continued, so senior management decided to add capacity to increase production so the additional orders could be filled in the future. It took nine months to get the additional production capacity ready. Finally, Decopot was ready to meet the increased demand the next time it arrived. Unfortunately, the "next time" never came because competitors had expanded their operations six months earlier, which allowed them to fill customers' orders when Decopot could not. Many of Decopot's original customers are now its competitors' customers. If Decopot had properly forecasted demand and planned its capacity requirements, it would have been able to maintain or perhaps even increase its market share; instead, its market share decreased.

> **capital budgeting** The process of planning and evaluating expenditures on assets whose cash flows are expected to extend beyond one year.

Effective capital budgeting can improve both the timing of asset acquisitions and the quality of assets purchased. A firm that forecasts its needs for capital assets in advance will have an opportunity to purchase and install the assets before they are needed. Unfortunately, like Decopot, many firms do not order capital goods until they approach full capacity or are forced to replace worn-out equipment. If many firms order capital goods at the same time, backlogs result, prices increase, and firms are forced to wait for the delivery of machinery; in general, the quality of the capital goods deteriorates. If a firm foresees its needs and purchases capital assets early, it can avoid these problems.

Finally, capital budgeting is important because the acquisition of fixed assets typically involves substantial expenditures, and before a firm can spend a large amount of money, it must have the funds available. Large amounts of money are not available automatically. Therefore, a firm contemplating a major capital expenditure program must arrange its financing well in advance to ensure that the required funds are available.

9-1a Generating Ideas for Capital Projects

The same general concepts that we developed for valuing financial assets are involved in capital budgeting. However, whereas a set of stocks and bonds already exists in the financial markets and investors select from this set, capital budgeting projects are created by the firm. For example, a sales representative might report that customers frequently ask for a particular product that the company does not currently produce. The sales manager then discusses the idea with the marketing research group to determine the size of the market for the proposed product. If it appears likely that a significant market does exist, cost accountants and engineers will be asked to estimate production costs. If those estimates show the product can be produced and sold at a sufficient profit, the project will be undertaken.

A firm's growth, and even its ability to remain competitive and to survive, depends on a constant flow of ideas for new products, ways to make existing products better, and ways to produce output at lower costs. Accordingly,

replacement decisions
Decisions whether to purchase capital assets to take the place of existing assets to maintain or improve existing operations.

expansion decisions Decisions whether to purchase capital projects and add them to existing assets to increase existing operations.

independent projects Projects whose cash flows are not affected by decisions made about other projects.

mutually exclusive projects A set of projects in which the acceptance of one project means the others cannot be accepted.

a well-managed firm will go to great lengths to develop good capital budgeting proposals. Some firms even provide incentives to employees to encourage suggestions that lead to beneficial investment proposals. If a firm has capable and imaginative executives and employees and its incentive system works properly, many ideas for capital investment will be advanced.

9-1b Project Classifications

Capital budgeting decisions generally are termed either *replacement decisions* or *expansion decisions*. Replacement decisions involve determining whether new assets (projects) should be purchased to take the place of existing assets that might be worn out, damaged, or obsolete. Usually the replacement projects are necessary to maintain or improve profitable operations using the *existing* production levels. On the other hand, an expansion decision is made when a firm determines whether it should add assets either to produce more of its existing products or to offer entirely new products.

In general, relatively simple calculations, and only a few supporting documents, are required for replacement decisions, especially maintenance-type investments in profitable plants. Analysis that is more detailed is required for cost-reduction replacements, for expansion of existing product lines, and especially for investments in new products or areas. In addition, within each category, projects are broken down by their dollar costs: Larger investments require both analysis that is more detailed and approval at a higher level within the firm.

Some capital budgeting decisions involve *independent projects*, while others involve *mutually exclusive* projects. Independent projects are projects whose cash flows are not affected by one another, so the acceptance of one project does not affect the acceptance of the other project(s). *All independent projects can be purchased if they all are acceptable.* For example, if South-Western Cengage Learning, which publishes this book, decides to purchase the ABC television network, it still could publish new textbooks. Conversely, if a capital budgeting decision involves mutually exclusive projects, then when one project is taken on, the others must be rejected. In other words, *only one mutually exclusive project can be purchased, even if they all are acceptable.* For example, suppose Global Sports and Entertainment Ltd. has a parcel of land on which it wants to build either a children's amusement park or a domed baseball stadium. Because the land is not large enough for both alternatives, if Global chooses to build the amusement park, it cannot build the stadium, and vice versa.

9-1c The Post-Audit

An important aspect of the capital budgeting process is the **post-audit**, which involves (1) comparing actual results with those predicted by the project's sponsors and (2) explaining why any differences occurred.

The post-audit has two main purposes:

To Improve Forecasts. When decision makers are forced to compare their projections to actual outcomes, there is a tendency for estimates to improve, conscious or unconscious biases to be observed and eliminated, and new forecasting methods to be sought as the need for them becomes apparent. People simply tend to do everything better, including forecasting, if they know that their actions are being monitored.

To Improve Operations. Businesses are run by people, and people can perform at higher or lower levels of efficiency. When a divisional team has made a forecast about an investment, its members are, in a sense, putting their reputations on the line. If costs are above predicted levels, sales are below expectations, and so on, executives in production, marketing, and other areas will strive to improve operations and to bring results in line with forecasts.

The post-audit is not a simple process; a number of factors can cause complications. First, we must recognize that each element of the cash flow forecast is subject to uncertainty, so a percentage of all projects undertaken by any reasonably venturesome firm will necessarily go awry. This fact must be considered when appraising the performances of the operating executives who submit capital expenditure requests. Second, projects sometimes fail to meet expectations for reasons beyond the control of the operating executives and for reasons that no one could realistically be expected to anticipate. Third, it is often difficult to separate the operating results of one investment from those of a larger system. Although some projects stand alone and permit ready identification of costs and revenues, the actual cost savings that result from a new computer system, for example, might be hard to measure. Fourth, it is often hard to hand out blame or praise, because the executives who were actually responsible for a given decision might have moved on by the time the results of a long-term investment are known.

Because of these difficulties, some firms tend to downplay the importance of the post-audit. However, observations of both businesses and governmental units suggest that the best run and most successful organizations are the ones that put the greatest emphasis on post-audits. Accordingly, we regard the post-audit as being an extremely important element in a good capital budgeting system.

9-2 Evaluating Capital Budgeting Projects

To make capital budgeting decisions, we must value the assets, or projects, that are being evaluated. Not surprisingly, then, capital budgeting involves the same steps used in general asset valuation that were described in the last few chapters:

1. Estimate the cash flows expected to be generated by the asset during its life. (We discuss this topic in Chapter 10.) This is similar to estimating the future dividends that a stock will generate.

2. Evaluate the riskiness of the projected cash flows to determine the appropriate rate of return to use for computing the present value of the estimated cash flows. (We discuss this topic further in Chapters 10 and 11.)

3. Compute the present value of the expected cash flows—that is, compute the investment's value. This is equivalent to finding the present value of the dividends a stock is expected to pay during its life. For a real asset, such as a machine, we can solve the following equation:

$$\text{PV of CF} = \frac{\hat{CF}_1}{(1 + r)^1} + \frac{\hat{CF}_2}{(1 + r)^2} + \cdots + \frac{\hat{CF}_n}{(1 + r)^n}$$

$$= \sum_{t=1}^{n} \frac{\hat{CF}_t}{(1 + r)^t}$$

4. Compare the present value of the future expected cash flows with the initial investment, or cost, required to acquire the asset. Alternatively, the expected rate of return on the project can be calculated and compared with the rate of return that is considered appropriate (required) for the project. *If a firm identifies (or creates) an investment opportunity with a present value (the value of the investment to the firm) that is greater than its cost, the value of the firm will increase if the investment is purchased.* Thus, there is a direct link between capital budgeting and stock values: The more effective the firm's capital budgeting procedures, the higher the price of its stock.

Because some investment projects will be good and others will not, procedures must be established for evaluating the worth of such projects to the firm. Our topic in the remainder of this chapter is the evaluation of the acceptability of capital projects.

> **post-audit** A comparison of the actual and expected results for a given capital project.

9-2a Net Present Value (NPV)

Following the steps outlined in the previous section, to determine the acceptability of a capital budgeting project, we must determine its value and then compare this value to the project's purchase price. Remember from our previous discussions that the value of an asset can be determined by computing the present value of the cash flows it is expected to generate during its life. If we subtract the purchase price of the asset from the present value of its expected future cash flows, the result is the net dollar value, or the net benefit that accrues to the firm if the asset is purchased. This net benefit is called the asset's **net present value (NPV)**. We use Equation 9.1 to compute NPV:

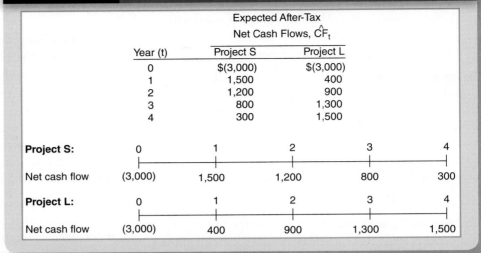

FIGURE 9.1   NET CASH FLOWS FOR PROJECT S AND PROJECT L

Expected After-Tax Net Cash Flows, $\hat{CF}_t$

Year (t)	Project S	Project L
0	$(3,000)	$(3,000)
1	1,500	400
2	1,200	900
3	800	1,300
4	300	1,500

Project S:

	0	1	2	3	4
Net cash flow	(3,000)	1,500	1,200	800	300

Project L:

	0	1	2	3	4
Net cash flow	(3,000)	400	900	1,300	1,500

> **NPV Decision Rule:** A project is acceptable if NPV > $0.

9.1

$$NPV = \hat{CF}_0 + \frac{\hat{CF}_1}{(1 + r)^1} + \frac{\hat{CF}_2}{(1 + r)^2} + \cdots + \frac{\hat{CF}_n}{(1 + r)^n}$$

$$= \sum_{t=0}^{n} \frac{\hat{CF}_t}{(1 + r)^t}$$

Here $\hat{CF}_t$ is the expected net cash flow in Period t, and r is the rate of return required by the firm to invest in this project.[1] Cash outflows (expenditures on the project, such as the cost of buying equipment or building factories) are treated as negative cash flows. $\hat{CF}_0$ generally is a negative cash flow because it represents the initial investment in the project, which normally is a cash outflow when the project is purchased (Period 0).[2]

The NPV shows by how much a firm's value, and thus stockholders' wealth, will increase if a capital budgeting project is purchased. *If the net benefit computed on a present value basis—that is, NPV—is positive, then the asset (project) is considered an acceptable investment.* In other words, to determine whether a project is acceptable using the NPV technique, we apply the following decision rule:

To illustrate the application of the NPV method and the other capital budgeting techniques discussed in this chapter, we use the cash flow data shown in Figure 9.1 for Project S and Project L. Throughout this chapter we assume that these projects are equally risky and that their expected cash flows are known with certainty. In the next chapter, we discuss how these cash flows are determined and how risk should be considered in capital budgeting analyses. The expected cash flows, $\hat{CF}_t$, shown in Figure 9.1 are the "bottom-line," after-tax cash flows, which we assume occur at the end of the designated year. For Project S and Project L, only $\hat{CF}_0$ is negative, but for many large projects, such as the Alaska Pipeline or an electric generating plant, outflows occur for several years before operations begin and cash flows turn positive. Incidentally, the S stands for "short" and the L for "long": Project S is a short-term project in the sense that its cash inflows tend to come in sooner than those of Project L. We use these two illustrative projects to simplify our presentations.

net present value (NPV) The present value of an asset's future cash flows minus its purchase price (initial investment).

[1]The rate of return required by the firm generally is termed the firm's *cost of capital*, because it is the average rate the firm must pay for the funds used to purchase capital projects. The concept of cost of capital is discussed in Chapter 11.

[2]We describe how the cash flows that are associated with a capital budgeting project are determined in Chapter 10.

At a 10 percent required rate of return, Project S's net present value, NPV$_S$, is $161.33:

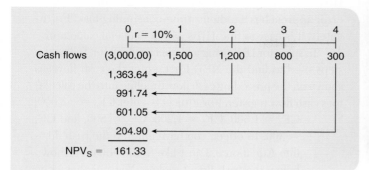

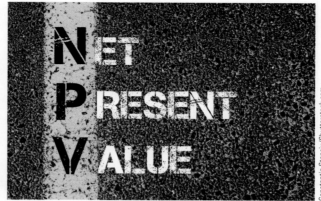

As this cash flow timeline shows, to find the NPV, we compute the present value of each cash flow, including $\hat{CF}_0$, and sum the results. Using Equation 9.1, the numerical solution for NPV$_S$ is:

$$NPV_s = (3,000) + \frac{1,500}{(1.10)^1} + \frac{1,200}{(1.10)^2} + \frac{800}{(1.10)^3} + \frac{300}{(1.10)^4}$$

$$= (3,000) + 1,363.64 + 991.74 + 601.05 + 204.90$$

$$= 161.33$$

It is not difficult to calculate the NPV using Equation 9.1 and a regular calculator, as we did here. Nevertheless, the most efficient way to find the NPV is by using a financial calculator. Although all financial calculators are not set up identically, they all have a section of memory called the *cash flow register* that is used for computing the present value of uneven cash flows such as those in Project S (as opposed to equal annuity cash flows). As we saw in Chapter 4, a solution process for Equation 9.1 is literally programmed into financial calculators. Simply input the cash flows in the order in which they occur (being sure to observe the signs), along with the value of I/Y = r. For Project S, enter CF$_0$ = −3,000, CF$_1$ = 1,500, CF$_2$ = 1,200, CF$_3$ = 800, CF$_4$ = 300, and I/Y = r = 10%. At this point, you have entered in your calculator the cash flows and the interest rate displayed on the timeline shown in Figure 9.1 for Project S, and you have provided the calculator with the values that are needed to solve Equation 9.1 for the project. There is one unknown, NPV. Now you simply ask the calculator to solve the equation for you; the answer, 161.33, will appear on the screen.[3]

Using this same process for Project L, we find NPV$_L$ = $108.67. On this basis, both projects should be purchased if they are *independent*, but Project S should be the one chosen if they are *mutually exclusive*, because NPV$_S$ = $161.33 > NPV$_L$ = $108.67.

The rationale for the NPV method is straightforward. An NPV of zero signifies that the project's cash flows are just sufficient to repay the invested capital and to provide the required rate of return (r) on that capital. If a project has a positive NPV, then it generates a return that is greater than is needed to pay for funds provided by investors, and this excess return accrues solely to the firm's stockholders. Therefore, if a firm takes on a project with a positive NPV, the position of the stockholders is improved because the firm's value increases. In our example, shareholders' wealth will increase by $161.33 if the firm takes on Project S, but by only $108.67 if it takes on Project L. Viewed in this manner, it is easy to see why Project S is preferred to Project L, and it is also easy to see the logic of the NPV approach. If the two projects are independent, both should be purchased, because shareholders' wealth would increase by $270.00 = $161.33 + $108.67.[4]

9-2b Internal Rate of Return (IRR)

In Chapter 6, we presented procedures for finding the yield to maturity (YTM), or rate of return, on a bond. Recall that if you invest in a bond and hold it to maturity, the average return you can expect to earn on the money you invest is the YTM. Exactly the same concept is employed in capital budgeting to determine the **internal rate of return (IRR)**, which is the rate of return the firm expects to earn if a project is purchased and held for its useful life (maturity). In essence, a project's IRR is its yield to maturity. The IRR

internal rate of return (IRR) The discount rate that forces the PV of a project's expected cash flows to equal its initial cost; IRR is the same as the YTM on a bond.

---

[3] Refer to the manual that came with your calculator to determine how the CF function is used.

[4] This description of the process is somewhat oversimplified. Both analysts and investors anticipate that firms will identify and accept positive NPV projects, and current stock prices reflect these expectations. Thus, stock prices react to announcements of new capital projects only to the extent that such projects were not already expected. In this sense, we can think of a firm's value as consisting of two parts: (1) the value of its existing assets and (2) the value of its growth opportunities, or projects with positive NPVs.

is defined as the discount rate that equates the present value of a project's expected future cash flows to the initial amount invested. *As long as the project's IRR, which is the average return it is expected to generate each year of its life, is greater than the rate of return required by the firm for such an investment, the project is acceptable.* In other words, to determine whether a project is acceptable using the IRR technique, we apply the following decision rule:

IRR Decision Rule: A project is acceptable if IRR > r

where r is the firm's required rate of return.

We can use Equation 9.2 to solve for a project's IRR:

9.2

$$NPV = \hat{CF}_0 + \frac{\hat{CF}_1}{(1 + IRR)^1} + \cdots + \frac{\hat{CF}_n}{(1 + IRR)^n} = 0$$

or

$$\hat{CF}_0 = \frac{\hat{CF}_1}{(1 + IRR)^1} + \cdots + \frac{\hat{CF}_n}{(1 + IRR)^n}$$

For Project S, the cash flow timeline for the IRR computation is as follows:

Using Equation 9.2, here is the setup for computing IRR_S:

$$(3,000) + \frac{1,500}{(1 + IRR)^1} + \frac{1,200}{(1 + IRR)^2} + \frac{800}{(1 + IRR)^3} + \frac{300}{(1 + IRR)^4} = 0$$

Although it is fairly easy to find the NPV without a financial calculator, the same is *not* true of the IRR. Without a financial calculator, you must solve Equation 9.2 by trial and error; that is, you

must try different discount rates until you find the one that forces NPV to equal zero. This discount rate is the IRR. For a project with a fairly long life, the trial-and-error approach is a tedious, time-consuming task. Fortunately, it is easy to find IRRs with a financial calculator.

To solve for IRR using a financial calculator, follow the steps used to find the NPV. First, enter the cash flows as shown on the preceding cash flow timeline into the calculator's cash flow register. For Project S, enter $CF_0 = -3,000$, $CF_1 = 1,500$, $CF_2 = 1,200$, $CF_3 = 800$, and $CF_4 = 300$. In effect, you have entered the cash flows into Equation 9.2, just like in the equation shown below the cash flow timeline. You now have one unknown, IRR, or the discount rate that forces NPV to equal zero. The calculator has been programmed to solve for the IRR, and you activate this program by pressing the key labeled "IRR." Following are the IRRs for Project S and Project L, found using a financial calculator:

$$IRR_S = 13.1\%$$
$$IRR_L = 11.4\%$$

A project is acceptable if its IRR is greater than the firm's **required rate of return**, *or* **hurdle rate**. For example, if the hurdle rate required by the firm is 10 percent, then both Project S and Project L are acceptable. If they are mutually exclusive, then Project S is more acceptable than Project L because $IRR_S > IRR_L$. On the other hand, if the firm's required rate of return is 12 percent, only Project S is acceptable; and, if r = 15%, neither project is acceptable.

Notice from Equation 9.2 that *you do not need to know the firm's required rate of return (r) to solve for IRR.* However, you need the required rate of return to make a decision as to whether a project is acceptable once its IRR has been computed. Also, note that (1) the IRR is the rate of return that will be earned by *anyone* who purchases the project and (2) the IRR is dependent on the project's cash flow characteristics (that is, the amounts and the timing of the cash flows), not the firm's required rate of return. As a result, *the IRR of a particular project is the same for all firms, regardless of their particular required rates of return.* A project might be acceptable to some firms (Project S would be acceptable to firms with required rates of return less than 13.1 percent), but not acceptable to other firms (Project S is not acceptable to firms with required rates of return greater than 13.1 percent).

Why is a project acceptable if its IRR is greater than its required rate of return? Because the IRR on a project is the rate of return that the project is expected to generate,

FIGURE 9.2   NPV PROFILES FOR PROJECT S AND PROJECT L

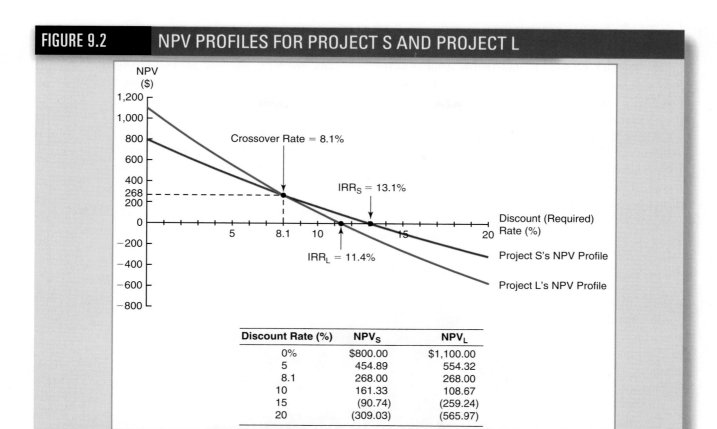

Discount Rate (%)	NPV$_S$	NPV$_L$
0%	$800.00	$1,100.00
5	454.89	554.32
8.1	268.00	268.00
10	161.33	108.67
15	(90.74)	(259.24)
20	(309.03)	(565.97)

and if this return exceeds the cost of the funds used to finance the project, a surplus remains after paying for the funds. This surplus accrues to the firm's stockholders. Therefore, *taking on a project whose IRR exceeds the firm's required rate of return (cost of funds) increases shareholders' wealth*. On the other hand, if the IRR is less than the cost of funds, then taking on the project imposes a cost on current stockholders that decreases wealth. For example, consider what would happen if you borrowed funds at a 10 percent interest rate to invest in the stock market. The 10 percent interest is your *cost of funds*, which is the rate that you must earn on your investments to break even. You would lose money if you earned less than 10 percent, and you would gain money (wealth) if you earned more than 10 percent. This break-even characteristic makes the IRR useful in evaluating capital projects.

9-3 Comparison of the NPV and IRR Methods

We found that the NPV for Project S is $161.33, which means that the firm's value will increase by $161.33 if the project is purchased. The IRR for Project S is 13.1 percent, which means that the firm will earn a 13.1 percent

rate of return on its investment if Project S is purchased. We generally measure wealth in dollars, so the NPV method should be used to accomplish the goal of maximizing shareholders' wealth. In reality, using the IRR method could lead to investment decisions that increase wealth, but do not maximize it. We choose to discuss the IRR method and compare it to the NPV method because many corporate executives are familiar with the meaning of IRR, it is entrenched in the corporate world, and it does have some virtues. For these reasons, it is important to understand the IRR method and be prepared to explain why a project with *a lower IRR might sometimes be preferable to one with a higher IRR* (discussed later in the chapter).

9-3a NPVs and Required Rates of Return—NPV Profiles

A graph that shows a project's NPV at various discount rates (required rates of return) is termed the project's **net present value (NPV) profile**. Figure 9.2 shows the NPV profiles for Project L and Project S. To construct the profiles, we calculate the projects' NPVs at various discount rates— say, 0, 5, 10, and

> **net present value (NPV) profile**
> A graph that shows the NPVs for a project at various discount rates (required rates of return).

15 percent—and then plot these values. The points plotted on our graph for each project are shown at the bottom of Figure 9.2.[5] Because the IRR is defined as the discount rate at which a project's NPV equals zero, the point where its *NPV profile crosses the X-axis indicates a project's internal rate of return.*

Figure 9.2 shows that the NPV profiles for Project L and Project S decline as the discount rate (required rate of return) increases. Notice, however, that Project L has the higher NPV at low discount rates, whereas Project S has the higher NPV at high discount rates. According to the graph, $NPV_S = NPV_L = \$268$ when the discount rate equals 8.1 percent. We call this point the *crossover rate* because, below this rate, $NPV_S < NPV_L$, and above this rate, $NPV_S > NPV_L$; however, the NPVs are equal and thus the two NPV profile lines intersect at 8.1 percent.[6]

Figure 9.2 also indicates that Project L's NPV is more sensitive to changes in the discount rate than is Project S's NPV. That is, Project L's NPV profile has the steeper slope, indicating that a given change in r has a larger effect on NPV_L than on NPV_S. Project L is more sensitive to changes in r because the cash flows from Project L are received later in its life than those from Project S. As a general rule, the impact of a change in the discount rate is much greater on distant cash flows than on near-term cash flows. To illustrate, consider the present value of $100 to be received in one year versus $100 to be received in 10 years. The present values of each $100, discounted at 10 percent and at 15 percent, are as follows:

Future Value	Year Received	PV @ 10%	PV @ 15%	Percent Difference
$100	1	$90.91	$86.96	−4.3%
100	10	38.55	24.72	−35.9

[5]Note that the NPV profiles are curved; they are *not* straight lines. Also, the NPVs approach the cost of the project as the discount rate increases without limit. The reason is that, at an infinitely high discount rate, the PV of the future cash flows would be zero, so NPV at $r = \infty$ is $\hat{CF}_0$, which in our example is −$3,000.

[6]The crossover rate is easy to calculate. Simply go back to Figure 9.1, where we first show the two projects' cash flows. Now calculate the difference in the cash flows for Project S and Project L in each year. The differences are computed as $\hat{CF}_S - \hat{CF}_L$. Thus, the cash flow differences for Projects S and L are $CF_0 = \$0$, $CF_1 = +\$1,100$, $CF_2 = +\$300$, $CF_3 = -\$500$, and $CF_4 = -\$1,200$, respectively. To compute the crossover rate using a financial calculator, enter these numbers in the order given here into the cash flow register, and then ask the calculator to compute the IRR. You should find IRR = 8.11%.

We can conclude from this discussion that if a project has most of its cash flows coming in the early years, its NPV will not be lowered as much if the required rate of return increases as the NPV of a project whose cash flows come later in its life. Accordingly, Project L, which has its largest cash flows in the later years, is hurt badly when the required rate of return is high, whereas Project S, which has relatively rapid cash flows, is affected less by high discount rates.

9-3b Independent Projects

Note that the IRR formula, Equation 9.2, is simply the NPV formula, Equation 9.1, solved for the particular discount rate that forces the NPV to equal zero. Thus, the same basic equation is used for both methods. Mathematically, the NPV and IRR methods will *always* lead to the same accept/reject decisions for all projects that are evaluated. In other words, *if a project's NPV is positive, its IRR will exceed r; if NPV is negative, r will exceed the IRR.* To see why this is so, look back at Figure 9.2, focus on Project L's profile, and note that

▶ The IRR criterion for acceptance is that the required rate of return must be less than (or to the left of) the IRR_L (11.4 percent). In other words, if $r < IRR_L = 11.4\%$, Project L is acceptable; otherwise, it is not.

▶ Whenever the required rate of return is less than the IRR_L (11.4 percent), Project L's NPV is greater than zero, which means that the project is acceptable; that is, when $r < 11.4\%$, $NPV_L > 0$.

Thus, at any required rate of return less than 11.4 percent, Project L will be acceptable using both the NPV and the IRR criteria; both methods reject the project if the required rate of return is greater than 11.4 percent. Project S—and all other projects under consideration—can be analyzed similarly, and *in every case, if a project is acceptable using the IRR method, then the NPV method also will show that it is acceptable.* If the firm wants to maximize wealth, *all independent* projects that are evaluated as acceptable should be purchased (regardless of how acceptable they are).

9-3c Mutually Exclusive Projects

If Project S and Project L are *mutually exclusive* rather than independent, then only one project can be *purchased*. If you use IRR to make the decision as to which project is better, you would choose Project S because $IRR_S = 13.1\% > IRR_L = 11.4\%$. If you use NPV to make the decision, you might reach a different conclusion, depending on the firm's required rate of return. Note from Figure 9.2 that if the required rate of return is less than the crossover rate of 8.1 percent, $NPV_L > NPV_S$, but $NPV_L < NPV_S$ if the required rate of return is greater than 8.1 percent. As a result, using the NPV technique, Project L is preferred if the firm's required rate of return is less than 8.1 percent, but Project S is preferred if the firm's required rate of return is greater than 8.1 percent.

As long as the firm's required rate of return is greater than 8.1 percent, using either NPV or IRR will result in the same decision—that is, Project S should be purchased—because $NPV_S > NPV_L$ and $IRR_S > IRR_L$. But, if the firm's required rate of return is less than 8.1 percent, a person who uses NPV will reach a different conclusion as to which mutually exclusive project should be purchased: he or she will choose Project L because $NPV_L > NPV_S$. For example, the table in Figure 9.2 shows that $NPV_L = \$554 > \$455 = NPV_S$ when r = 5 percent. In this situation—that is, the required rate of return is less than 8.1 percent—*a conflict exists* because NPV says to choose Project L over Project S, whereas IRR says just the opposite. Which answer is correct? Logic suggests that the NPV method is better because it selects the project that adds more value to shareholder wealth.

Two basic conditions can cause NPV profiles to cross, and thus lead to conflicts between NPV and IRR: (1) when *project size (or scale) differences* exist, meaning that the cost of one project is much larger than that of the other; and (2) when *timing differences* exist, meaning that the timings of cash flows from the two projects differ so that most of the cash flows from one project come in the early years and most of the cash flows from the other project come in the later years, as occurs with Projects L and S.[7]

When either size or timing differences occur, the firm will have different amounts of funds to invest in the various years, depending on which of the two mutually exclusive projects it chooses. For example, if one project costs more than the other project, then the firm will have more money at t = 0 to invest elsewhere if it selects the lower-cost project. Similarly, for projects of equal size, the one with the larger early cash inflows provides more funds for reinvestment in the early years. Given this situation, the rate of return at which differential cash flows can be invested is an important consideration.

The critical issue in resolving conflicts between mutually exclusive projects is this: How useful is it to generate cash flows earlier rather than later? The value of early cash flows depends on the rate at which we can reinvest these cash flows. *The NPV method implicitly assumes that the rate at which cash flows can be reinvested is the firm's required rate of return, r, whereas the IRR method implies that the firm has the opportunity to reinvest at the project's IRR.* These assumptions are inherent in the mathematics of the discounting process.

Which is the better assumption: that cash flows can be reinvested at the firm's required rate of return or that they can be reinvested at the project's IRR? To reinvest at the IRR associated with a capital project, the firm must be able to reinvest the project's cash flows in another project with an identical IRR. Such projects generally do not continue to exist, or it is not feasible to reinvest in such projects because competition in the investment markets drives their prices up and their IRRs down. On the other hand, at the very least, a firm could repurchase the bonds and the stock it has issued to raise capital budgeting funds and thus repay some of its investors, which would be the same as investing at its required rate of return. Thus, we conclude that the *more realistic* reinvestment rate assumption *is the required rate of return, which is implicit in the NPV method.* This, in turn, leads us to prefer the NPV method, at least for firms willing and able to obtain new funds at a cost reasonably close to their current cost of funds.

Remember that when projects are independent, the NPV and IRR methods provide the same accept/reject decision. As a result, when evaluating independent projects, it doesn't matter whether the NPV technique or the IRR technique is used to make the investment decision, because the firm only wants to know whether the projects are acceptable (value increasing) or unacceptable (value decreasing). In this case, it is not necessary to determine which project is most acceptable, because all acceptable projects should be purchased. However, when evaluating mutually exclusive projects, especially those that differ in scale or timing, the NPV method should be used to determine which project should be purchased. In this case, because only one project can be purchased, the firm must determine which project is most acceptable; that is, which project adds the greatest value to the firm.

---

[7]Of course, it is possible for mutually exclusive projects to differ with respect to both scale and timing. Also, if mutually exclusive projects have different lives (as opposed to different cash flow patterns over a common life), this introduces further complications, and for meaningful comparisons, some mutually exclusive projects must be evaluated over a common life.

reinvestment rate assumption The assumption that cash flows from a project can be reinvested (1) at the firm's required rate of return, if using the NPV method or (2) at the internal rate of return, if using the IRR method.

9-3d Cash Flow Patterns and Multiple IRRs

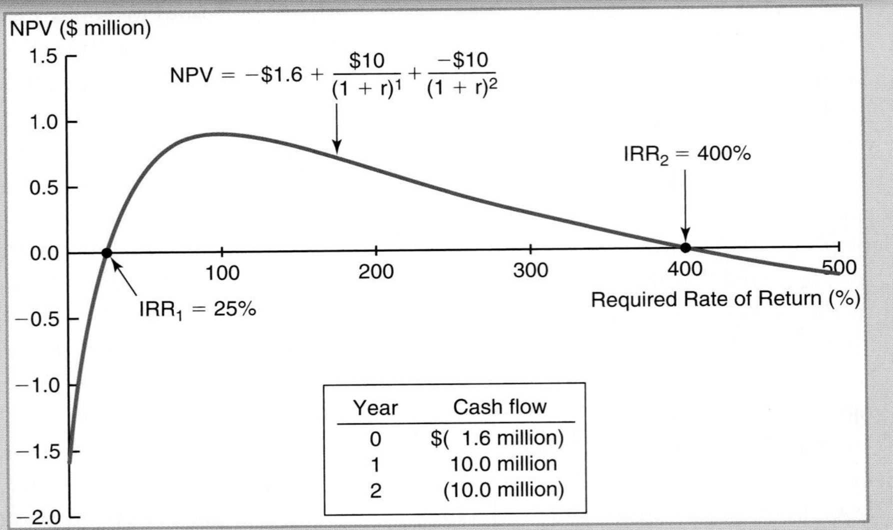

A project has a *conventional* cash flow pattern if it has cash outflows (costs) in one or more consecutive periods at the beginning of its life, followed by a series of cash inflows. If, however, a project has a large cash outflow at the beginning of its life, and then has another cash outflow either at some time during its life or at the end of it, then it has an *unconventional* cash flow pattern. Projects with unconventional cash flow patterns present unique difficulties when the IRR method is used, including the possibility of multiple IRRs.[8] Following are examples of conventional and unconventional cash flow patterns:

FIGURE 9.3   NPV PROFILE FOR PROJECT M

NPV ($ million)

$$NPV = -\$1.6 + \frac{\$10}{(1+r)^1} + \frac{-\$10}{(1+r)^2}$$

$IRR_2 = 400\%$

Required Rate of Return (%)

$IRR_1 = 25\%$

Year	Cash flow
0	$(1.6 million)
1	10.0 million
2	(10.0 million)

Conventional cash
    flow patterns: (1) − + + + + + (2) − − − + + +
Unconventional cash
    flow patterns: (1) − + + − + + + (2) − − + + + − −

There exists an IRR solution for each time the *direction* of the cash flows associated with a project is interrupted, that is, each time outflows change to inflows. For example, each of the conventional cash-flow patterns shown here has only one change in the signs (direction) of the cash flows from negative (outflow) to positive (inflow); thus, there is only one IRR solution. On the other hand, each of the unconventional cash flow patterns shown here has two interruptions, and thus two IRR solutions.

Figure 9.3 illustrates the multiple-IRR problem with a strip-mining project that costs $1.6 million. The mine will produce a cash inflow of $10 million at the end of Year 1, but $10 million must be spent at the end of Year 2 to restore the land to its original

condition. Two IRRs exist for this project: 25 percent and 400 percent. The NPV profile for the mine shows that the project would have a positive NPV, and thus be acceptable, if the firm's required rate of return is between 25 percent and 400 percent.

9-4 Modified Internal Rate of Return

Despite a strong academic preference for NPV, surveys indicate that many business executives prefer IRR. It seems that many managers find it intuitively more appealing to analyze investments in terms of percentage rates of return (IRR) rather than dollars (NPV). However, remember from our earlier discussion that the IRR method assumes the cash flows from the project are reinvested at a rate of return equal to the IRR, which we generally view as unrealistic. Given this fact, can we devise a rate of return measure that is better than the regular IRR? The answer is yes: We can modify the IRR and make it a better indicator of relative profitability, hence better for use in capital budgeting. This "modified" return is called the modified IRR, or MIRR, and it is defined as follows:

[8]Multiple IRRs result from the manner in which Equation 9.2 must be solved to arrive at a project's IRR. The mathematical rationale and the solution to multiple IRRs will not be discussed here. Instead, we want you to be aware that multiple IRRs can exist because this possibility complicates capital budgeting evaluation using the IRR method.

multiple IRRs The situation in which a project has two or more IRRs.

modified IRR (MIRR) The discount rate at which the present value of a project's cash outflows is equal to the present value of its terminal value, where the terminal value is found as the sum of the future values of the cash inflows compounded at the firm's required rate of return and the present value of the cash outflows is found using the same required rate of return.

9.3

$$\text{PV of cash outflows} = \frac{TV}{(1 + MIRR)^n}$$

$$\sum_{t=0}^{n} \frac{COF_t}{(1 + r)^t} = \frac{\sum_{t=1}^{n} CIF_t(1 + r)^{n-t}}{(1 + MIRR)^n}$$

Here COF refers to the cash outflows (all negative numbers), and CIF refers to the cash inflows (all positive numbers) associated with a project. The term on the left side of the equals sign is simply the present value (PV) of the investment outlays (cash *outflows*) when discounted at the firm's required rate of return, r, and the numerator of the term on the right side of the equals sign is the future value of the cash *inflows*, assuming that these inflows are reinvested at the firm's required rate of return. The future value of the cash inflows is also called the *terminal value*, or TV. The discount rate that forces the PV of the TV to equal the PV of the costs is defined as the MIRR.[9]

We can illustrate the calculation of MIRR with Project S:

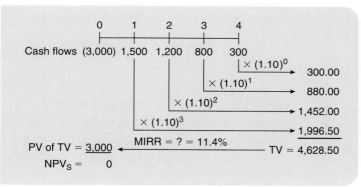

Using the cash flows as set out on the cash flow timeline, first find the terminal value by compounding each cash inflow at the 10 percent required rate of return. Then, enter into your calculator PV = −3,000, which is the present value of the project's cash outflows,

FV = 4,628.50, which is the future value of the project's cash inflows, and N = 4; compute I/Y = 11.4% = MIRR$_S$. Using the same process, we find MIRR$_L$ = 11.0%.

To determine whether a project is acceptable using the MIRR technique, we apply the following decision rule:

MIRR Decision Rule: A project is acceptable if MIRR > r.

The modified IRR has a significant advantage over the traditional IRR measure. MIRR assumes that cash flows are reinvested at the required rate of return, whereas the traditional IRR measure assumes that cash flows are reinvested at the project's own IRR. Because reinvestment at the required rate of return generally is more correct, the MIRR is a better indicator of a project's true profitability. MIRR also solves the multiple-IRR problem. To illustrate, using a required rate of return equal to 10 percent, the strip mine project described earlier has an MIRR equal to 5.6 percent, so it should be rejected. This is consistent with the decision based on the NPV method, because at r = 10%, NPV = −$0.77 million.

Is MIRR as good as NPV for choosing between mutually exclusive projects? If two projects are of equal size and have the same life, then NPV and MIRR will always lead to the same project selection decision. Thus, for any projects like Projects S and L, if NPV$_S$ > NPV$_L$, then MIRR$_S$ > MIRR$_L$, and the kinds of conflicts we encountered between NPV and the traditional IRR will not occur. Furthermore, if the projects are of equal size, but have different lives, the MIRR will always lead to the same decision as the NPV if the MIRRs for both projects are calculated using the terminal year of the project with the longer life. (Just fill in zeros for the shorter project's missing cash flows.) However, if the projects differ in size, conflicts can still occur. For example, if we were choosing between a large project and a small, mutually exclusive one, we might find NPV$_{Large}$ > NPV$_{Small}$ and MIRR$_{Large}$ < MIRR$_{Small}$.

Our conclusion is that the MIRR is superior to the regular (traditional) IRR as an indicator of a project's "true" rate of return, or expected long-term rate of return, but the NPV method is still better for choosing among mutually exclusive projects that differ in size because it provides a better indicator of the extent to which each project will increase the value of the firm; thus, NPV is still the recommended approach.

[9]There are several alternative definitions for the MIRR. The differences relate primarily to whether negative cash flows that occur after positive cash flows begin should be compounded and treated as part of the TV, or discounted and treated as a cost. Our definition (which treats all negative cash flows as investments and thus discounts them) generally is the most appropriate procedure. For a complete discussion, see William R. McDaniel, Daniel E. McCarty, and Kenneth A. Jessell, "Discounted Cash Flow with Explicit Reinvestment Rates: Tutorial and Extension," *The Financial Review*, August 1988, 369–385.

FIGURE 9.4

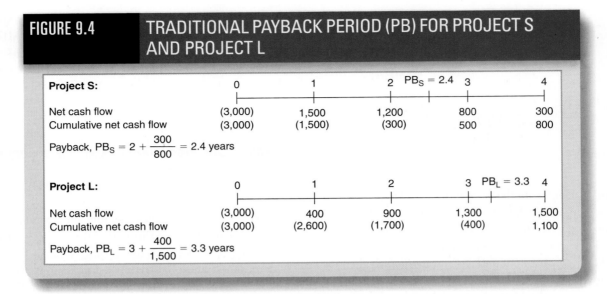

9-5 Use of Capital Budgeting Techniques in Practice

In this section, we describe two additional techniques that firms use when making capital budgeting decisions. And, then we discuss the information that is provided by all of the capital budgeting techniques covered in this chapter and indicate which techniques are most often used in practice.

and, as far as we know, the oldest *formal* method used to evaluate capital budgeting projects. To compute a project's payback period, simply add up the expected cash flows for each year until the cumulative value equals the amount that is initially invested. The total amount of time, including the fraction of a year if appropriate, that it takes to recapture the original amount invested is the payback period. Figure 9.4 shows the process for computing the payback periods for both Project S and Project L.

The exact payback period can be found using Equation 9.4:

9.4

$$\text{Payback period} = \left(\begin{array}{c} \text{The year just } prior \\ \text{to the year of full recovery} \\ \text{of initial investment} \end{array} \right) + \left(\dfrac{\begin{array}{c} \text{Amount of initial investment that is} \\ unrecovered \text{ at the start of the recovery year} \end{array}}{\begin{array}{c} \text{Total cash flow generated} \\ \text{during the recovery year} \end{array}} \right)$$

9-5a Payback Period: Traditional (Nondiscounted) and Discounted

Many managers like to know how long it will take a project to repay its initial investment (cost) from the cash flows it is expected to generate in the future. Thus, many firms compute a project's **traditional payback period (PB)**, which is defined as the expected number of years required to recover the original investment (the cost of the asset). Payback is the simplest

traditional payback period (PB)
The length of time it takes to recover the original cost of an investment from its unadjusted (raw) expected cash flows.

As Figure 9.4 shows, the payback period for Project S is between two years and three years. Using Equation 9.4, the exact payback period for Project S is computed as follows:

$$\text{PB}_\text{S} = 2 + \frac{300}{800} = 2.4 \text{ years}$$

Applying the same procedure to Project L, we find $\text{PB}_\text{L} = 3.3$ years.

Using payback to make capital budgeting decisions is based on the concept that it is better to recover the cost of (investment in) a project sooner rather than later. Therefore, Project S is considered better than

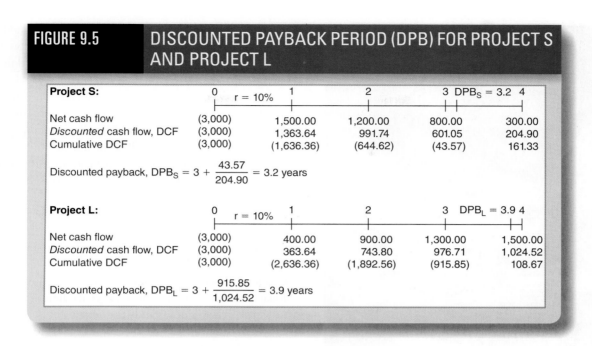

Project L because it has a shorter payback period. *As a general rule, a project is considered acceptable if its payback period is less than the maximum cost-recovery time established by the firm.* In other words, when we use the traditional payback period method, we apply the following decision rule:

PB Decision Rule: A project is acceptable if PB < n*

where $n°$ is the recovery period that the firm has determined is appropriate. For example, if the firm requires projects to have a payback of three years or less, Project S will be acceptable but Project L will not.

The payback method is simple, which explains why it traditionally has been one of the most popular capital budgeting techniques. However, because the traditional payback period computation ignores the time value of money, relying solely on this method can lead to incorrect decisions, at least if our goal is to maximize value. If a project has a payback of three years, we know how quickly the initial investment will be covered by the expected cash flows, but this information does not provide any indication of whether the return on the project is sufficient to cover the cost of the funds invested. In addition, when payback is used, the cash flows beyond the payback period are ignored. For example, even if Project L had a fifth year of cash flows equal to $50,000, its payback would remain 3.3 years, which is less desirable than the payback of 2.4 years for Project S. However, with the

additional $50,000 cash flow, Project L most likely would be preferred.

To correct for the fact that the traditional payback method does not consider the time value of money, we can compute the discounted payback period (DPB), which is the length of time it takes for the project's *discounted* cash flows to recapture the cost of the investment. Applying the general payback concept, we can easily compute how long it takes to Project S's the initial outlay of $3,000 using the *discounted* (present value of the) cash flows given in the cash flow timeline shown in Figure 9.5. The sum of the present values of the cash flows for the first three years is $2,956.43 = $1,363.64 + $991.74 + $601.05, so all of the $3,000 cost is not recovered until 3.2 years = 3 years + [($3,000 − $2,956.43)/$204.90] years. Therefore, on a *present value basis*, it takes 3.2 years for Project S to recover, or pay back, its original cost. DPB = 3.9 years for Project L; so Project S is more acceptable. Figure 9.5 shows the DPB computations for Projects S and L.

Unlike the traditional payback computation, the discounted payback period computation considers the time value of money. If you look at the cash flow timeline that shows the NPV computation for Project S, you can see that the reason it has a positive NPV is because the initial investment of $3,000 is recovered on a present value basis prior to the end of the project's useful life. Thus, using the discounted payback method, a project should be accepted when its DPB is less than its useful life.

discounted payback period (DPB) The length of time it takes for a project's discounted cash flows to repay the cost of the investment.

DPB Decision Rule: A project is acceptable if DPB < Project's useful life.

As Figure 9.5 shows, when a project's discounted payback is less than its useful life, the present value of the future cash flows that the project is expected to generate exceeds the initial cost of the asset—that is, NPV > 0. Note that the final value given in the row labeled "Cumulative DCF" is simply the project's NPV, because it is the result of summing the present values of all of the cash flows, including the initial cost, that are associated with the project.

9-5b Conclusions on the Capital Budgeting Decision Methods

Earlier in this chapter, we compared the NPV and IRR methods to highlight their relative strengths and

weaknesses for evaluating capital projects, and in the process we probably created the impression that "sophisticated" firms should use only one method in the decision process—NPV. However, virtually all capital budgeting decisions are analyzed by computer, so it is easy to calculate and list all the decision measures we discussed: traditional payback (PB), discounted payback (DPB), NPV, IRR, and MIRR. In making the accept/reject decision, most large, sophisticated firms, such as IBM, General Electric, and General Motors, calculate and consider multiple measures because each provides decision makers with a somewhat different piece of relevant information.

Traditional payback and discounted payback provide information about both the risk and the *liquidity* of a project. A long payback means that (1) the investment dollars will be locked up for many years, hence the project is relatively illiquid; and (2) the project's cash flows must be forecast far out into the future, hence the project is probably quite risky.[10] A good analogy for this is the bond valuation process. An investor should never compare the yields to maturity on two bonds without considering their terms to maturity, because a bond's riskiness is influenced by its maturity.

NPV is important because it gives a direct measure of the dollar benefit (on a present value basis) to the firm's shareholders, so we regard NPV as the best single measure of *profitability*. IRR also measures profitability, but here it is expressed as a percentage rate of return, which many decision makers, especially nonfinancial managers, seem to prefer. Further, IRR contains information concerning a project's "safety margin," which is not inherent in NPV. To illustrate, consider the following two projects: Project T costs $10,000 at t = 0 and is expected to return $16,500 at the end of one year, while Project B costs $100,000 and has an expected payoff of $115,500 after one year. At a 10 percent required rate of return, both projects have an NPV of $5,000, so by the NPV rule we should be indifferent between the two. However, Project T actually provides a much larger margin for error. Even if its realized cash inflow turns out to be almost 40 percent below the $16,500 forecast, the firm will still recover its $10,000 investment. On the other hand, if Project B's inflow falls by only 14 percent from the forecasted $115,500, the firm will not recover its investment. Further, if no inflows are generated at all, the firm will lose only $10,000 with Project T but will lose $100,000 if it takes on Project B.

The NPV contains no information about either the safety margin inherent in a project's cash flow forecasts

---

[10]We generally define *liquidity* as the ability to convert an asset into cash quickly while maintaining the original investment. Thus, in most cases, short-term assets are considered more liquid than long-term assets. We discuss liquidity in greater detail later in the book.

or the amount of capital at risk, but the IRR does provide "safety margin" information: Project T's IRR is a whopping 65 percent, whereas Project B's IRR is only 15.5 percent. As a result, the realized return could fall substantially for Project T, and it would still make money. Note, however, that the IRR method has a reinvestment assumption that probably is unrealistic, and that it is possible for projects to have multiple IRRs. Both of these problems can be corrected using the MIRR calculation.

In summary, the different methods provide different types of information. Because it is easy to calculate them, all should be considered in the decision process. For any specific decision, more weight might be given to one method than another method, but it would be foolish to ignore the information provided by any of the methods.

In addition, you should have discovered from our discussion that *all capital budgeting methods that consider the time value of money provide the same accept/reject decisions*; that is, they all give the same answer to the question as to whether a project is a good investment or a bad investment. But when projects are mutually exclusive, depending on which capital budgeting technique is used, there could be ranking conflicts that might lead to different investment (purchase) decisions.

At this point, we should note that multinational corporations use essentially the same capital budgeting techniques described in this chapter. However, foreign governments, international regulatory environments, and financial and product markets in other countries pose certain challenges to U.S. firms that must make capital budgeting decisions for their foreign operations. We will wait to discuss some of these challenges/differences until the next chapter.

9-5c Capital Budgeting Methods Used in Practice

Many surveys have been conducted over the years to determine which techniques firms rely on when making capital budgeting decisions. The results consistently show that firms rely on each of the methods discussed in this chapter to some extent to help them make final decisions about the acceptability of capital budgeting projects. As technology has advanced, firms have shifted to using the more sophisticated techniques, such as NPV and IRR. The following table shows to what extent this shift has occurred since the 1970s. The results given in the table were compiled from surveys conducted during each decade.[11] The

numbers represent the average percentage of respondents who indicated that their firms use the particular capital budgeting technique "always" or "almost always." In most cases, those who were surveyed were not asked to indicate the primary and secondary methods that were used.

Period	Traditional Payback Period	NPV	IRR
1970s	85%	65%	80%
1980s	78	75	88
1990s	60	80	79
2000s	53	85	77

As the data show, the use of the traditional payback period and IRR methods has declined, whereas the use of the NPV method has increased. Prior to the 1970s, many firms relied heavily on the payback period to make capital budgeting decisions. As technology and understanding of the discounting techniques improved, both NPV and IRR became more popular. It appears that, for the most part, financial managers recognize that these techniques provide correct decisions with respect to value maximization.

For the most part, studies have shown that companies (1) use more sophisticated capital budgeting techniques today than in previous times and (2) do not rely on a single evaluation method to make decisions about investing in capital projects. Clearly, firms still use payback period in their capital budgeting analyses. However, even firms that previously relied on the traditional payback period seem to have switched to the discounted payback period. Thus, indications are that firms do use the methods we profess in finance courses.

[11]Studies that were examined include Lawrence J. Gitman and John R. Forrester, Jr., "A Survey of Capital Budgeting Techniques Used by Major U.S. Firms," *Financial Management*, Fall 1977, 66–71; David J. Oblak and Roy J. Helm, Jr., "Survey and Analysis of Capital Budgeting Methods Used by Multinationals," *Financial Management*, Winter 1980, 37–41; Marjorie T. Stanley and Stanley B. Block, "A Survey of Multinational Capital Budgeting," *Financial Review*, March 1984, 36–51; Glenn H. Petry and James Sprow, "The Theory of Finance in the 1990s," *The Quarterly Review of Economics and Finance*, Winter 1993, 359–381; Erika Gilbert and Alan Reichert, "The Practice of Financial Management among Large United States Corporations," *Financial Practice and Education*, Spring/Summer 1995, 16–23; Patricia Chadwell-Hatfield, Bernard Goitein, Philip Horvath, and Allen Webster, "Financial Criteria, Capital Budgeting Techniques, and Risk Analysis of Manufacturing Firms," *Journal of Applied Business Research*, Winter 1996/1997, 95–104; John R. Graham and Campbell R. Harvey, "The Theory and Practice of Corporate Finance: Evidence from the Field," *Journal of Financial Economics*, Vol. 60, No. 2–3, May/June 2001, 197–243; Patricia A. Ryan and Glenn P. Ryan "Capital Budgeting Practices of the Fortune 1000: How Have Things Changed?" *Journal of Business and Management*, Fall 2002, 335–364; John Graham and Campbell Harvey, "How Do CFOs Make Capital Budgeting and Capital Structure Decisions," *Journal of Applied Corporate Finance*, Vol. 15, No. 1, Spring 2002, 8–23.

STUDY TOOLS

LOCATED AT BACK OF THE TEXTBOOK

- ☐ Problems are found at the end of this chapter.
- ☐ A tear-out Chapter Review card is located at the back of the textbook.

LOCATED AT WWW.CENGAGEBRAIN.COM

- ☐ Review Key Term flashcards and create your own cards.
- ☐ Track your knowledge and understanding of key concepts in corporate finance.
- ☐ Complete practice and graded quizzes to prepare for tests.
- ☐ Complete interactive content within CFIN5 Online.
- ☐ View the chapter highlight boxes for CFIN5 Online.

KEY CAPITAL BUDGETING CONCEPTS

To conclude this chapter, we summarize some of the capital budgeting concepts (rules) that were discussed.

- Capital budgeting decisions are important because they involve long-term assets; thus, the firm loses some financial flexibility when such assets are purchased.

- The process of valuing a capital budgeting project (investment) to determine whether it should be purchased is the same process that is used to value financial assets, such as stocks and bonds: (1) Compute the present value of the cash flows the asset is expected to generate during its useful life, and (2) compare the present value of the asset to its purchase price (cost). If the present value of the project's cash flows is greater than its cost, the asset should be purchased.

- When making capital budgeting decisions, we generally compute an asset's net present value (NPV). NPV equals the present value of the cash flows the asset is expected to generate during its useful life minus the cost of the asset. Thus, the NPV indicates by how much the firm's current value will change if the capital budgeting project is purchased. A project should be purchased if its NPV is positive.

- A project's internal rate of return (IRR) represents the average rate of return that a company will earn if

the project is purchased and held until the end of its useful life. The IRR is the same for all companies that purchase a particular project. A project should be purchased if its IRR is greater than the firm's required rate of return.

- A ranking conflict might occur when evaluating two mutually exclusive projects using the NPV technique and the IRR technique; that is, the NPV technique might favor one project whereas the IRR technique might favor the other project. This conflict, which results from the reinvestment assumptions associated with each of these capital budgeting techniques, generally can be resolved by using the modified internal rate of return (MIRR) technique rather than the traditional IRR technique.

- All capital budgeting techniques that consider the time value of money will provide the same accept–reject decisions; that is, for a particular project, if $NPV > 0$, then we know that $IRR > r$, $MIRR > r$, and $DPB <$ Project's useful life, all of which indicate that the project is acceptable. However, ranking conflicts could exist, depending on which techniques are used, when mutually exclusive projects are evaluated. Such conflicts are not a concern when independent projects are evaluated, because all acceptable independent projects should be purchased regardless of their rankings.

9–1 Wandering RV is evaluating a capital budgeting project that is expected to generate $36,950 per year during its six-year life. If its required rate of return is 10 percent, what is the value of the project to Wandering RV?

9–2 Zebra Fashions is evaluating a capital budgeting project that should generate $104,400 per year for four years. (a) If its required rate of return is 16 percent, what is the value of the project to Zebra? (b) If Leopard Fashions evaluates the same project with its required rate of return of 12 percent, what will it determine the value of the project to be?

9–3 Conventional Corporation is evaluating a capital budgeting project that will generate $600,000 per year for the next 10 years. The project costs $3.6 million, and Conventional's required rate of return is 11 percent. Should the project be purchased?

9–4 The CFO of HairBrain Stylists is evaluating a project that costs $42,000. The project will generate $11,000 each of the next five years. If HairBrain's required rate of return is 9 percent, should the project be purchased?

9–5 What is the internal rate of return (IRR) of a project that costs $20,070 if it is expected to generate $8,500 per year for three years?

9–6 What is the internal rate of return (IRR) of a project that costs $74,000 if it is expected to generate $16,500 per year for six years?

9–7 Piping Hot Food Services (PHFS) is evaluating a capital budgeting project that costs $75,000. The project is expected to generate after-tax cash flows equal to $26,000 per year for four years. PHFS's required rate of return is 14 percent. Compute the project's (a) net present value (NPV) and (b) internal rate of return (IRR). (c) Should the project be purchased?

9–8 Kansas Furniture Corporation (KFC) is evaluating a capital budgeting project that costs $34,000 and is expected to generate after-tax cash flows equal to $14,150 per year for three years. KFC's required rate of return is 12 percent. Compute the project's (a) net present value (NPV) and (b) internal rate of return (IRR). (c) Should the project be purchased?

9–9 Construct an NPV profile for a capital budgeting project that costs $64,000 and is expected to generate $18,200 per year for five years. Using the NPV profile, determine the project's internal rate of return (IRR) and its net present value (NPV) at required rates of return equal to 10 percent, 13 percent, and 15 percent.

9–10 Using a required rate of return equal to 12 percent, compute the modified internal rate of return (MIRR) for a project that costs $82,000 and is expected to generate $35,000, $70,000, and −$10,450, respectively, during the next three years. Should the project be purchased?

9–11 What is the internal rate of return (IRR) for a project that costs $5,500 and is expected to generate $1,800 per year for the next four years? If the firm's required rate of return is 8 percent, what is the project's modified internal rate of return (MIRR)? Should the firm purchase the project?

9–12 Rascal Clothing is evaluating a new weaving machine that costs $90,000. It is expected that the machine will generate after-tax cash flows equal to $54,000 per year for two years. Rascal's required rate of return is 9 percent. Compute the project's (a) internal rate of return (IRR) and (b) modified internal rate of return (MIRR). (c) Should the project be purchased?

9–13 Compute both the traditional payback period (PB) and the discounted payback period (DPB) for a project that costs $270,000 if it is expected to generate $75,000 per year for five years. The firm's required rate of return is 11 percent. Should the project be purchased?

9–14 Compute the traditional payback period (PB) for a project that costs $64,000 if it is expected to generate $16,000 per year for six years? If the firm's required rate of return is 12 percent, what is the project's discounted payback period (DPB)? Should the project be purchased?

9–15 Komfy Karz is evaluating a project that costs $365,000 and is expected to generate $260,000 and $175,000, respectively, during the next two years. If Komfy's required rate of return is 13 percent, what is the project's (a) net present value, (b) internal rate of return (IRR), and (c) modified internal rate of return (MIRR)?

9–16 Compute the (a) net present value, (b) internal rate of return (IRR), and (c) discounted payback period (DPB) for each of the following projects. The firm's required rate of return is 14 percent.

Year	Project Alpha	Project Beta
0	$(270,000)	$(300,000)
1	120,000	0
2	120,000	(80,000)
3	120,000	555,000

Which project(s) should be purchased if they are independent? Which project(s) should be purchased it they are mutually exclusive?

9–17 Compute the (a) net present value, (b) internal rate of return (IRR), (c) modified internal rate of return (MIRR), and (d) discounted payback period (DPB) for each of the following projects. The firm's required rate of return is 13 percent.

Year	Project AB	Project LM	Project UV
0	$(90,000)	$(100,000)	$ (96,500)
1	39,000	0	(55,000)
2	39,000	0	100,000
3	39,000	147,500	100,000

Which project(s) should be purchased if they are independent? Which project(s) should be purchased it they are mutually exclusive?

9–18 Following are the estimated after-tax cash flows for two *mutually exclusive* projects:

Year	Project S	Project T
0	($16,000)	($15,000)
1	14,000	2,000
2	6,000	18,600

The company's required rate of return is 16 percent. What is the internal rate of return (IRR) of the project(s) the company should purchase?

9–19 Following is information about two *independent* projects that a company is evaluating:

Capital Budgeting Technique	Project X	Project Y
Net present value	$5,000	$4,950
Internal rate of return	15.5%	17.0%
Discounted payback period	5.1 years	4.6 years

(a) Which project(s) should be chosen? Explain why.
(b) What can be concluded about the company's required rate of return, r?

9–20 The CFO of Horatio's Hotels gave three college interns three different *independent* projects to evaluate. Following are the results of their analyses:

Intern's Name	Project's Life	NPV	IRR	Discounted Payback	Decision
Albert	7 years	$5,300	12.0%	6.8 years	Accept
Josie	6	(1,800)	8.0	5.8	Reject
Kenny	10	4,500	10.0	9.6	Accept

The CFO agrees with the final accept/reject decision that each intern made. But she spotted an error in the numbers reported by one of the interns. (a) Which intern's report has the error? (b) Does the information given here provide an indication of the firm's required rate of return? Explain your answers.

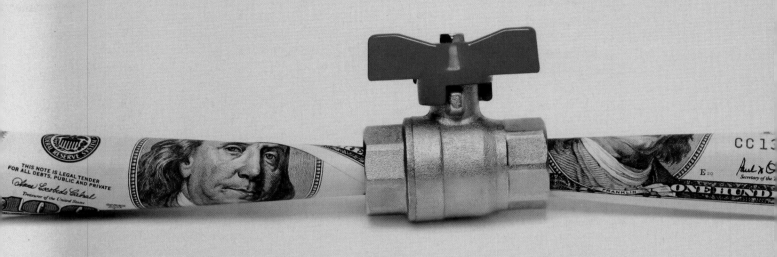

LEARNING OUTCOMES

After studying this chapter, you will be able to…

LO1 Describe the relevant cash flows that must be forecast to make informed capital budgeting decisions.

LO2 Identify the relevant cash flows and perform a capital budgeting analysis for (a) an expansion project and (b) a replacement project.

LO3 Describe how the riskiness of a capital budgeting project is evaluated and how the results are incorporated in capital budgeting decisions.

LO4 Describe how capital budgeting decisions differ for firms that have foreign operations and for firms that only have domestic operations.

Project Cash Flows and Risk

10

The basic principles of capital budgeting and the methods used to evaluate capital budgeting projects were covered in Chapter 9. In this chapter, we examine some additional issues, including cash flow estimation and incorporating risk into capital budgeting decisions. In addition, we present some of the challenges multinational firms face when making capital budgeting decisions.

10-1 Cash Flow Estimation

The most important, and also the most difficult, step in the analysis of a capital project is estimating its cash flows. The relevant cash flows include the investment outlays needed to purchase the project and the net cash flows (both inflows and outflows) the project is expected to generate after it is purchased. Many variables are involved in cash flow estimation, and many individuals and departments participate in the process. For example, the forecasts of unit sales and sales prices normally are made by the marketing group based on its knowledge of advertising effects, the state of the economy, competitors' reactions, and trends in consumers' tastes. Similarly, the capital outlays associated with a new product generally are determined by the engineering and product-development staffs, while operating costs are estimated by cost accountants, production experts, personnel specialists, purchasing agents, and so forth. As difficult as plant and equipment costs are to estimate, sales revenues and operating costs over the life of the project generally are even more uncertain.

The financial staff's role in the forecasting process includes (1) coordinating the efforts of the other departments, such as engineering and marketing; (2) ensuring that everyone involved with the forecast uses a consistent set of economic assumptions; and (3) making sure that no biases are inherent in the forecasts. This last point is extremely important because division managers often become emotionally involved with pet projects or develop empire-building complexes (egos), both of which can lead to cash flow forecasting biases that make bad projects look good on paper.

Although substantial difficulties can be encountered when forecasting cash flows for capital budgeting projects, it is all but impossible to overstate the importance of these forecasts. If cash flows fail to meet the forecasted levels, the company might lose hundreds of millions of dollars. Companies recognize that if cash flow estimates are not reasonably accurate, any analytical technique, no matter how sophisticated, can lead to poor decisions and hence to operating losses and lower stock prices. In this chapter, we give you a sense of some of the inputs that are involved in forecasting the cash flows associated with a capital project and in minimizing forecasting errors.

10-1a Relevant Cash Flows

One important element in cash flow estimation is the determination of **relevant cash flows**, which are defined as the specific set of cash flows that should be considered in the capital budgeting decision. This process can be rather difficult, but two important rules should be followed:

▶ Capital budgeting decisions must be based on *cash flows after taxes*, not accounting income.

relevant cash flows The specific cash flows that should be considered in a capital budgeting decision.

Table 10.1

Unilate's Accounting Profits Versus Net Cash Flows ($ thousands)

	Accounting Profits	Cash Flows
I. 2018 Situation		
Sales	$50,000	$50,000
Costs except depreciation	(25,000)	(25,000)
Depreciation	(15,000)	
Net operating income or cash flow	$10,000	$25,000
Taxes based on operating income (30%)	(3,000)	(3,000)
Net income or net cash flow	$ 7,000	$22,000
Net cash flow = Net income + Depreciation = $7,000 + $15,000 = $22,000		
II. 2023 Situation		
Sales	$50,000	$50,000
Costs except depreciation	(25,000)	(25,000)
Depreciation	(5,000)	
Net operating income or cash flow	$20,000	$25,000
Taxes based on operating income (30%)	(6,000)	(6,000)
Net income or net cash flow	$14,000	$19,000
Net cash flow = Net income + Depreciation = $14,000 + $5,000 = $19,000		

▶ Only *incremental cash flows*—that is, cash flows that change if the project is purchased—are relevant to the accept/reject decision.

Cash Flow Versus Accounting Income. In capital budgeting analysis, *after-tax cash flows, not accounting profits,* are used, because cash, not profits, pays the bills, and cash can be invested in capital projects. Cash flows and accounting profits can be very different. To illustrate, consider Table 10.1, which shows how accounting profits and cash flows are related. We assume that Unilate Textiles, the textile manufacturer introduced in Chapter 2, is planning to start a new division at the end of 2017; that sales and all costs, except depreciation, represent actual cash flows and are projected to be constant over time; and that the division will use accelerated depreciation, which will cause its reported depreciation charges to decline with the passage of time.[1]

The top section of Table 10.1 shows the situation in the first year of operations, 2018. Accounting profits are $7 million, but the division's net cash flow—money that is available to Unilate—is $22 million. The $7 million profit is the *return on the funds* originally invested,

while the $15 million of depreciation is a *return of part of the funds* originally invested, so the $22 million cash flow consists of both a return *on* and a return *of* part of the invested capital.

The bottom part of the table shows the situation projected for 2023. Here, reported profits have doubled because of the decline in depreciation, but net cash flow is down sharply because taxes, which require cash payments (outflows), have doubled. The amount of money received by the firm is represented by the cash flow figure, not the net income figure. Although accounting profits are important for some purposes, only cash flows are relevant for the purposes of determining the value of a project. Cash flows can be reinvested to create value; profits cannot. Therefore, in capital budgeting, we are interested in net cash flows,

[1]Depreciation procedures are discussed in detail in accounting courses, but we provide a summary and review in Appendix 10A at the end of this chapter. The tables provided in Appendix 10A are used to calculate depreciation charges used in the chapter examples. In some instances, we simplify the depreciation assumptions to reduce the arithmetic. Because Congress changes depreciation procedures fairly frequently, it is always necessary to consult the latest tax regulations before developing actual capital budgeting cash flows.

not in accounting profits per se.[2] In most cases, we can estimate an asset's operating cash flows as

$$\text{Operating cash flow} = \text{Net income} + \text{Depreciation}$$
$$= \text{Return } on \text{ capital} + \text{Return } of \text{ capital}$$

10-1b Incremental (Marginal) Cash Flows

In evaluating a capital project, we are concerned only with those cash flows that result directly from the decision to accept the project. These cash flows, called incremental (marginal) cash flows, represent the changes in the firm's total cash flows that occur as a direct result of purchasing the project. Thus, to determine whether a specific cash flow is considered relevant, we must determine whether it is affected by the purchase of the project. Cash flows that change if the project is purchased are *incremental cash flows* that must be included in the capital budgeting evaluation; they are relevant cash flows. Cash flows that are not affected by the purchase of the project are *not* relevant to the capital budgeting decision, thus they should not be included in the evaluation. Unfortunately, identifying the relevant cash flows for a project is not always as simple as it seems. Some special problems in determining incremental cash flows are discussed next.

Sunk Costs. A sunk cost is an outlay that the firm has already committed or that has already occurred, and hence is not affected by the accept/reject decision under consideration. As a result, sunk costs should not be included in the analysis. To illustrate, in 2015 Unilate Textiles considered building a distribution center in New England in an effort to increase sales in that area of the country. To help with its evaluation, Unilate hired a consulting firm to perform a site analysis and to provide a feasibility study for the project; the study's cost was $100,000, and this amount was expensed for tax purposes in 2015. This expense is *not* a relevant cost that should be included in the capital budgeting evaluation of the prospective distribution center because Unilate

cannot recover this money, regardless of whether the new distribution center is built. Therefore, the $100,000 is a sunk cost because it will not change no matter what decision Unilate makes.

Opportunity Costs. The second potential problem relates to opportunity costs, which are defined as the cash flows that could be generated from assets the firm *already owns* if they are not used for the project in question. To illustrate, Unilate already owns a piece of land that is suitable for the proposed New England distribution center. When evaluating the prospective center, should the cost of the land be disregarded because no additional cash outlay would be required? The answer is no, because there is an opportunity cost inherent in the use of the property. In this case, the land could be sold to yield $750,000 after taxes. Use of the site for the distribution center would require forgoing this inflow, so the $750,000 must be charged as an opportunity cost against the project. Note that the proper land cost in this example is the $750,000 market-determined current value (after taxes), irrespective of whether Unilate originally paid $50,000 or $1 million for the property. (What Unilate paid would, of course, have an effect on taxes, and hence on the after-tax opportunity cost.) The $750,000 opportunity cost must be included as part of the distribution center's overall investment cost.

Externalities: Effects on Other Parts of the Firm. The third potential problem involves the effects of a project on existing cash flows in other parts of the firm or on the environment in which the firm operates. Economists call these effects externalities. For example, Unilate currently has customers in New England who would use the new distribution center, if it is built, because its location would be more convenient than the North Carolina distribution center they have been using. The sales, and hence the cash flows, generated by these customers would not be new to Unilate; rather, they would represent a transfer of existing sales from one distribution center to another. Thus, the net revenues produced by these customers should not be treated as new (incremental) cash flows in the capital budgeting decision. Although they often are difficult to quantify, *externalities* such as these must be identified because they

---

[2]Actually, operating cash flow should be adjusted to reflect all noncash charges, not just depreciation. However, for most projects, depreciation is by far the largest noncash charge. Also, note that Table 10.1 ignores interest charges, which would be present if the firm used debt. Most firms do use debt, and hence finance part of their capital budgets with debt. Therefore, the question has been raised as to whether interest charges should be reflected in capital budgeting cash flow analysis. The consensus is that interest charges should not be dealt with explicitly in capital budgeting; rather, the effects of debt financing are reflected in the cost of funds, or required rate of return, which is used to discount the cash flows. If interest is subtracted and cash flows are then discounted, we would be double-counting the cost of debt.

incremental (marginal) cash flow The change in a firm's net cash flow attributable to an investment project.

sunk cost A cash outlay that has already been incurred and that cannot be recovered regardless of whether the project is accepted or rejected.

opportunity cost The return on the best alternative use of an asset; the highest return that will not be earned if funds are invested in a particular project.

externalities The effect accepting a project will have on the cash flows in other parts (areas) of the firm.

might *not* represent new revenues or relevant cash flows, in which case they should *not* be included in the analysis of the new capital budgeting project.

Shipping and Installation Costs. When a firm acquires fixed assets, it often incurs substantial costs for shipping and installing the assets. These charges are added to the invoice price of the assets when the total cost of the project is determined. In addition, for depreciation purposes, the *depreciable basis* of an asset, which is the total amount that can be depreciated during the asset's life, includes the purchase price and any additional expenditures required to make the asset operational, including shipping and installation. Therefore, the full cost of the asset, including shipping and installation costs, is used to determine annual depreciation expenses.

Keep in mind that *depreciation is a noncash expense, so there is not a cash outflow associated with the recognition of depreciation expense each year.* Nevertheless, because depreciation is a tax-deductible expense, *it affects the taxable income of a firm, and thus the amount of taxes paid by the firm, which is a cash flow.*

Inflation. Inflation is a fact of life, and it should be recognized in capital budgeting decisions. If expected inflation is not built into the determination of expected cash flows, then the calculated net present value and internal rate of return will be incorrect: both will be artificially low. It is easy to avoid inflation bias; simply build inflationary expectations into the cash flows used in the capital budgeting analysis. Expected inflation should be reflected in the revenue and cost figures, and thus in the annual net cash flow forecasts. The required rate of return should not be adjusted for inflation expectations, because investors include such expectations when establishing the rate at which they are willing to allow the firm to use their funds. (We discussed this concept in Chapter 5.)

10-1c Identifying Incremental Cash Flows

Generally, when we identify the incremental cash flows associated with a capital project, we separate them according to when they occur during the life of the project. In most cases, we classify a project's incremental cash flows into one of these three categories:

▶ Cash flows that occur *only at the start* of the project's life (Period 0) are part of the *initial investment outlay.*

▶ Cash flows that *continue throughout* the project's life (Periods 1 through n) are part of the *supplemental operating cash flows.*

▶ Cash flows that occur *only at the end* of the project's life (Period n) and that are associated with the disposal, or termination, of the project are part of the *terminal cash flow.*

We discuss these three incremental cash flow classifications and identify some of the relevant cash flows next. Keep in mind, however, that when identifying the relevant cash flows for capital budgeting, the primary question is which cash flows will be affected by purchasing the project. *If a cash flow does not change, it is not relevant to the capital budgeting analysis.*

Initial Investment Outlay. The **initial investment outlay**, which we designate CF_0, refers to the incremental cash flows that *occur only at the start of a project's life.* CF_0 includes such cash flows as the purchase price of the new project and shipping and installation costs. If the capital budgeting decision is a *replacement decision,* then the initial investment must also take into account the cash flows associated with the disposal of the old, or replaced, asset. This amount includes any cash received or paid to scrap the old asset and any tax effects associated with its disposal.

In many cases, the addition or replacement of a capital asset also affects the firm's short-term assets and liabilities, which are known as its *working capital accounts.* For example, additional inventories might be required to support a new operation, and increased inventory purchases will increase accounts payable. The difference between current assets and current liabilities is called *net working capital.* Thus, the difference between the required change in current assets and the spontaneous change in current liabilities is the change in net working capital. If this change is positive, as it generally is for expansion projects, then additional financing, over and above the cost of the project, is needed to fund the increase.[3] *The change in net working capital that results from the acceptance of a project is an incremental cash flow that must be considered in the capital budgeting analysis.* Because the change in net working capital requirements occurs at the start of the project's life, this cash flow impact is an incremental cash flow that is included as a part of the initial investment outlay.

---

[3]We should note that there are instances in which the change in net working capital associated with a capital project actually results in a decrease in the firm's current funding requirements, which frees up cash flows for investment. Usually this occurs if the project being considered is much more efficient than the existing asset(s).

Supplemental Operating Cash Flows. Supplemental operating cash flows are the changes in day-to-day operating cash flows that result from the purchase of a capital project. These changes occur throughout the life of the project; thus, they continue to affect the firm's cash flows until the firm disposes of the asset.

In most cases, the *supplemental operating cash flows* for each year can be computed directly by using Equation 10.1:

10.1

Supplemental
operating $\hat{CF}_t$ = ΔCash revenues$_t$ − ΔCash expenses$_t$ − ΔTaxes$_t$
$$= \Delta NOI_t \times (1 - T) + \Delta Depr_t$$
$$= (\Delta NOI_t + \Delta Depr_t) \times (1 - T) + T\Delta Depr_t$$

The symbols in Equation 10.1 are defined as follows:

Δ = the Greek letter *delta*, which indicates the change in something.
ΔNOI_t = NOI$_{t,\,accept}$ − NOI$_{t,\,reject}$ = the change in net operating income in Period t that results from accepting the capital project; the subscript *accept* indicates the firm's operations that would exist if the project is accepted and the subscript *reject* indicates the level of operations that would exist if the project is rejected (the existing situation without the project).
$\Delta Depr_t$ = Depr$_{t,\,accept}$ − Depr$_{t,\,reject}$ = the change in depreciation expense in Period t that results from accepting the project.
T = marginal tax rate.

We have emphasized that depreciation is a *noncash* expense. So why is the change in depreciation expense included in the computation of supplemental operating cash flow shown in Equation 10.1? The change in depreciation expense must be computed because when depreciation changes, taxable income changes, and so does the amount of income taxes paid; the amount of taxes paid is a cash flow.

Terminal Cash Flow. The terminal cash flow occurs at the end of the life of the project. It is associated with (1) the final disposal of the project, including any tax

effects, and (2) the return of the firm's operations to where they were before the project was purchased. Consequently, the terminal cash flow includes (1) the salvage, or disposal, value, which can be either positive (selling the asset) or negative (paying for removal) and (2) the tax impact associated with the disposal of the project. Also, (3) because we assume the firm will return to the operating level that existed prior to the acceptance of the project, any changes in net working capital that occurred at the beginning of the project's life will be *reversed* at the end of its life. For example, as an expansion project approaches the end of its useful life, inventories will be sold off and not replaced. In this case, the firm will receive an end-of-project cash inflow equal to the net working capital requirement that was incurred when the project was begun.

10-2 Capital Budgeting Project Evaluation

To this point, we have discussed several important aspects of cash flow analysis. Now we illustrate cash flow estimation for (1) an expansion project and (2) a replacement project.

10-2a Expansion Projects

Remember from Chapter 9 that an expansion project is one that calls for the firm to invest in new assets to *increase* sales. We illustrate expansion project analysis with a project that is being considered by Household Energy Products (HEP), a Dallas-based technology company. HEP's research and development department has created a computerized home appliance-control device that will increase a home's energy efficiency by simultaneously controlling all household appliances and electronic devices. At this point, HEP wants to decide whether it should proceed with full-scale production of the appliance-control device.

supplemental operating cash flows The changes in day-to-day cash flows that result from the purchase of a capital project and continue until the firm disposes of the asset.

terminal cash flow The *net* cash flow that occurs at the end of the life of a project, including the cash flows associated with (1) the final disposal of the project and (2) returning the firm's operations to where they were before the project was accepted.

expansion project A project that is intended to increase sales.

HEP's marketing department plans to target sales of the appliance computer to the owners of larger homes, because the computer is cost-effective only in homes with 4,000 or more square feet of living space. The marketing vice president believes that annual sales will be 15,000 units if each unit is priced at $2,000; thus, annual sales are estimated at $30 million. The engineering department has determined the firm would need no additional manufacturing or storage space; it would just need the equipment to manufacture the devices. The necessary equipment would be purchased and installed late in 2017. The invoice cost is $9.5 million, which does not include the $500,000 that would have to be paid for shipping and installation. The equipment would fall into the Modified Accelerated Cost Recovery System (MACRS) 5-year class for the purposes of depreciation. (See Appendix 10A at the end of this chapter for depreciation rates and an explanation of MACRS.)

The project will require an initial increase in net working capital equal to $4 million, primarily because the raw materials required to produce the devices will significantly increase the amount of inventory HEP currently holds. The investment necessary to increase net working capital will be made on December 31, 2017, when the decision to manufacture the appliance-control device is made. The project's estimated economic life is four years. At the end of that time, the equipment is expected to have a market value of $2 million and a

book value of $1.7 million. The production department has estimated that variable manufacturing costs will total 60 percent of sales and fixed overhead costs, excluding depreciation, will be $5 million per year. Depreciation expenses will vary from year to year in accordance with the MACRS rates. HEP's marginal tax rate is 40 percent; its cost of funds, or required rate of return, is 15 percent; and, for capital budgeting purposes, the company's policy is to assume that operating cash flows occur at the end of each year. If it is determined to be an acceptable investment, manufacture of the new product will begin on January 2, 2018, and the first *supplemental operating cash flows* will occur on December 31, 2018. Table 10.2 shows the computations for the three categories of cash flows associated with the appliance-control device: initial investment outlay, supplemental operating cash flows, and terminal cash flow.

Analysis of the Cash Flows. The first step in the analysis is to summarize the initial investment outlay required for the project; this is done in the 2017 column of Table 10.2. For HEP's appliance-control device project, the initial cash flows consist of the purchase price of the needed equipment, the cost of shipping and installation, and the required investment in net working capital (NWC). Notice that these cash flows do not carry over in the years 2018 through 2021; they occur only at the start of the project. Thus, the *initial investment* outlay is a cash outflow equal to $14 million.

Having estimated the investment requirements, we must now estimate the cash flows that will occur once production begins and will continue throughout the project's life. These are set forth in the 2018 through 2021 columns of Table 10.2. The supplemental operating cash flow estimates are based on information provided by HEP's various departments. The depreciation amounts were obtained by multiplying the depreciable basis, $10 million ($9.5 million purchase price plus $0.5 million shipping and installation), by the MACRS recovery allowance rates as set forth in the footnote to Table 10.2. As you can see from the computations given in footnote a in the table, the supplemental operating cash flow differs each year only because the depreciation expense, and thus the impact depreciation has on taxes, differs each year.

The final cash flow component we need to compute is the terminal cash flow. For this computation, remember that the $4 million investment in net working capital that is made in 2017 will be recovered in 2021. In addition, we need an estimate of the net cash flows from the disposal of the equipment in 2021. Table 10.3 shows the calculation of the net salvage value

Table 10.2

HEP Expansion Project Net Cash Flows, 2017–2021 ($ thousands)

	2017	2018	2019	2020	2021
I. Initial Investment Outlay					
Cost of new asset	$(9,500)				
Shipping and installation	(500)				
Increase in net working capital	(4,000)				
Initial investment	$(14,000)				
II. Supplemental Operating Cash Flow[a]					
Sales revenues		$30,000	$30,000	$30,000	$30,000
Variable costs (60% of sales)		(18,000)	(18,000)	(18,000)	(18,000)
Fixed costs		(5,000)	(5,000)	(5,000)	(5,000)
Depreciation on new equipment[b]		(2,000)	(3,200)	(1,900)	(1,200)
Earnings before taxes (EBT)		5,000	3,800	5,100	5,800
Taxes (40%)		(2,000)	(1,520)	(2,040)	(2,320)
Net income		3,000	2,280	3,060	3,480
Add back depreciation		2,000	3,200	1,900	1,200
Supplemental operating cash flows		$ 5,000	$ 5,480	$ 4,960	$ 4,680
III. Terminal Cash Flow					
Return of net working capital					$ 4,000
Net salvage value (see Table 10.3)					1,880
Terminal cash flow					$ 5,880
IV. Incremental Cash Flows					
Total net cash flow per period	$(14,000)	$5,000	$5,480	$4,960	$10,560

[a]Using Equation 10.1, the supplemental operating cash flows can also be computed as follows:

Year	Supplemental Operating Cash Flow Computation
2018	$5,000 = ($30,000 − $18,000 − $5,000)(1 − 0.4) + $2,000(0.4)
2019	$5,480 = ($30,000 − $18,000 − $5,000)(1 − 0.4) + $3,200(0.4)
2020	$4,960 = ($30,000 − $18,000 − $5,000)(1 − 0.4) + $1,900(0.4)
2021	$4,680 = ($30,000 − $18,000 − $5,000)(1 − 0.4) + $1,200(0.4)

[b]Depreciation for the new equipment was calculated using MACRS (see Appendix 10A at the end of this chapter):

Year	2018	2019	2020	2021
Depreciated	20%	32%	19%	12%

These percentages are multiplied by the depreciable basis of $10,000 = $9,500 + $500 to get the depreciation expense each year.

for the equipment. It is expected that the equipment will be sold for more than its book value, which means the company will have to pay taxes on the capital gain because, in essence, the equipment was depreciated too quickly, which allowed HEP to reduce its tax liability by too much in the years 2018–2021. The book value is calculated as the depreciable basis (purchase price plus shipping and installation) minus the accumulated depreciation. The net cash flow from salvage is merely the sum of the salvage value and the tax impact resulting from the sale of the equipment, $1.88 million in this case. Thus, the *terminal cash flow* totals $5.88 million: the $1.88 million net cash flow from salvage plus the $4 million cash flow from the return of the investment in net working capital.

Notice that the *total* net cash flow for 2021 is the sum of the supplemental operating cash flow for the year and the terminal cash flow. Thus, in the final year of a project's useful (economic) life, the firm incurs two types of cash flows: (1) the last supplemental operating cash

Table 10.3

HEP Expansion Project Net Salvage Value, 2021 ($ thousands)

I. Book Value of HEP's Project, 2021

Cost of new asset, 2017	$ 9,500
Shipping and installation	500
Depreciable basis of asset	$10,000
Depreciation, 2018–2021	
$= (0.20 + 0.32 + 0.19 + 0.12) \times \$10,000$	(8,300)
Book value, 2021	$ 1,700

II. Tax Effect of the Sale of HEP's Project, 2021

Selling price of asset, 2021	$ 2,000	
Book value of asset, 2021	(1,700)	
Gain (loss) on sale of asset	$ 300	
Taxes (40%)	$ 120	$= \$300 \times 0.4$

III. Net Salvage Value, TCF, 2021

Cash flow from sale of project	$ 2,000
Tax effect of sale	(120)
Net cash flow from salvage	$ 1,880

flow attributed to the project's normal operation in the final year of its life and (2) the terminal cash flow associated with the disposal of the project. For the appliance-control device project HEP is considering, the supplemental operating cash flow in 2021 is $4.68 million and the terminal cash flow is $5.88 million, so the total expected net cash flow in 2021 is $10.56 million.

Making the Decision. A summary of the data and the computation of the project's NPV are provided with the cash flow timeline that follows. The amounts are in thousands of dollars, just like in Table 10.2.

The project appears to be acceptable using the NPV and IRR methods, and it also would be acceptable if HEP required a maximum payback period of three years. Note, however, that the analysis thus far has been based on the assumption that the project has the same degree of risk as the company's average project. If the project were judged to be riskier than an average project, it would be necessary to increase the required rate of return used to compute the NPV. Later in this chapter, we will extend the evaluation of this project to include an analysis of its risk.

10-2b Replacement Analysis

All companies make *replacement decisions* to determine when older, worn assets should be replaced with newer assets to continue normal operations. The analysis relating to replacements is the same as that for expansion projects: Identify the relevant cash flows, and then find the net present value of the project. However, identifying the *incremental* cash flows associated with a replacement

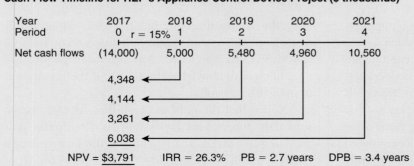

Cash Flow Timeline for HEP's Appliance-Control Device Project ($ thousands)

Year	2017	2018	2019	2020	2021
Period	0	r = 15% 1	2	3	4
Net cash flows	(14,000)	5,000	5,480	4,960	10,560
	4,348				
	4,144				
	3,261				
	6,038				

NPV = $3,791   IRR = 26.3%   PB = 2.7 years   DPB = 3.4 years

project is more complicated than for an expansion project because the cash flows from both the new asset *and* the old asset must be considered. The relevant cash flows are determined by the net differences between the *new* cash flows and the *old* cash flows because the cash flows from the new project replace the cash flows from the old (replaced) project. We illustrate **replacement analysis** with another HEP example.

HEP has a lathe for trimming molded plastics that was purchased 10 years ago at a cost of $7,900. The machine had an expected life of 15 years at the time it was purchased, and management originally estimated, and still believes, that the salvage value will be $400 at the end of its 15-year life (in five more years). The machine has been depreciated on a straight-line basis; therefore, its annual cash depreciation charge is $500 = ($7,900 − $400)/15, and its present book value is $2,900 = $7,900 − 10($500).

HEP is considering the purchase of a new special-purpose machine to replace the lathe. The new machine, which can be purchased for $12,000 (this price includes shipping and installation), will reduce labor and raw materials usage sufficiently to cut annual cash operating costs from $8,000 to $4,500.

It is estimated that the new machine will have a useful life of five years, after which it can be sold for $2,000. If the new machine is purchased, the old lathe will be sold to another company for $1,600, which is below its $2,900 book value, rather than exchanged for the new machine.

Net working capital requirements will increase by $1,400 if the old lathe is replaced with the new machine; this increase will occur at the time of replacement. Under an IRS ruling, the new machine falls into the 3-year MACRS class, and because the risk associated with the new machine is considered average for HEP, the project's required rate of return is 15 percent. Should the replacement be made?

Table 10.4 shows the worksheet format HEP uses to analyze replacement projects. Determining the relevant cash flows for a replacement decision is more involved than for an expansion decision because we need to consider the fact that the cash flows associated with the replaced asset will not continue after the new asset is purchased; that is, *the cash flows associated with the new asset will take the place of the cash flows associated with the old asset.* Because we want to evaluate how the acceptance of a capital budgeting project *changes* cash flows, we must compute the increase or decrease (change) in cash flows that results from the replacement of the old asset with the new asset.

Analysis of Cash Flows. The initial investment outlay of $11,280 includes the cash flows associated with the cost of the new asset and the change in net working capital. However, when a replacement asset is purchased, the asset being replaced generally can be sold to another firm or to a scrap dealer. If the firm disposes of the old asset at a value different from its book value (its purchase price less accumulated depreciation), there is a tax effect. In our example, the *old* asset has a current book value equal to $2,900, but it can be sold for only $1,600. So HEP will incur a capital loss equal to −$1,300 = $1,600 − $2,900 if it replaces the lathe with the new machine. This loss will result in a *tax savings* equal to $520 = Capital loss × T = $1,300 × 0.4, which accounts for the fact that HEP did not adequately depreciate the old asset to reflect its market value. Consequently, the disposal of the old asset will generate a positive cash flow equal to $2,120 which equals to the $1,600 selling price plus the $520 tax savings. As a result, disposal of the lathe effectively reduces the amount of cash required to purchase the new machine, and thus reduces the initial investment outlay. Any cash flows associated with disposing of the old asset must be included in the computation of the initial investment because they affect the net amount of cash required to purchase the asset.[4]

Next, we need to compute the annual supplemental operating cash flows. Section II of Table 10.4 shows these computations. The procedure is the same as before: determine how operating cash flows will change if the new machine is purchased to replace the lathe. Remember, the lathe is expected to decrease cash operating costs from $8,000 to $4,500, and thus increase cash operating profits by $3,500;

---

[4]If you think about it, the computation of the initial investment outlay for replacement decisions is similar to determining the amount you would need to purchase a new automobile to replace your old one. If the purchase price of the new car is $30,000 and the dealer is willing to give you $5,000 for your old car as a trade-in, then the amount you need is only $25,000. However, if you need to pay someone to take your old car out of the garage because that is where you are going to keep the new car at night, the total amount you need to purchase the new car is, in fact, greater than $30,000.

replacement analysis An analysis involving the decision as to whether to replace an existing asset with a new asset.

Table 10.4

HEP Replacement Project Net Cash Flows, 2017–2022

	2017	2018	2019	2020	2021	2022
I. Initial Investment Outlay						
Cost of new asset	$(12,000)					
Change in net working capital	(1,400)					
Net cash flow from sale of old asset[a]	2,120					
Initial investment	$(11,280)					
II. Supplemental Operating Cash Flows						
Δ Operating costs = $8,000 − $4,500		$3,500	$3,500	$3,500	$3,500	$3,500
Δ Depreciation[b]		(3,460)	(4,900)	(1,300)	(340)	500
Δ Operating income before taxes (EBT)		40	(1,400)	2,200	3,160	4,000
Δ Taxes (40%)		(16)	560	(880)	(1,264)	(1,600)
Δ Net operating income		24	(840)	1,320	1,896	2,400
Add back Δ depreciation		3,460	4,900	1,300	340	(500)
Supplemental operating cash flows		$3,484	$4,060	$2,620	$2,236	$1,900
III. Terminal Cash Flow						
Return of net working capital						$1,400
Net salvage value of *new* asset[c]						1,200
Net salvage value of *old* asset[d]						(400)
Terminal cash flow						$2,200
IV. Incremental Cash Flows						
Total net cash flow per period	$(11,280)	$3,484	$4,060	$2,620	$2,236	$4,100

[a]The net cash flow from the sale of the old (replaced) asset is computed as follows:

Selling price (market value)	$1,600
Subtract book value	(2,900)
Gain (loss) on sale of asset	(1,300)
Tax impact of sale of asset (40%) = (1,300) × 0.4 =	$(520) = a tax refund

Net cash flow from the sale of asset = $1,600 + $520 = $2,120

[b]The change in depreciation expense is computed by comparing the depreciation of the new asset with the depreciation that would have existed if the old asset was not replaced. The old asset has been depreciated on a straight-line basis, with five years of $500 annual depreciation remaining. The new asset will be depreciated using the rates for the 3-year MACRS class (see Appendix 10A at the end of this chapter). The change in annual depreciation would be

Year	New Asset Depreciation		Old Asset Depreciation		Change in Depreciation
2018	$12,000 × 0.33 = $ 3,960	−	$ 500	=	$3,460
2019	12,000 × 0.45 = 5,400	−	500	=	4,900
2020	12,000 × 0.15 = 1,800	−	500	=	1,300
2021	12,000 × 0.07 = 840	−	500	=	340
2022	= 0	−	500	=	(500)
Accumulated depreciation	= $12,000				

[c]The book value of the new asset in 2022 will be zero because the entire $12,000 has been written off. The net salvage value of the new asset in 2022 is computed as follows:

Selling price (market value)	$2,000
Subtract book value	(0)
Gain (loss) on sale of asset	2,000
Tax impact of sale of asset (40%)	$(800) = 2,000 × 0.4

Net salvage value of the new asset in 2022 = $2,000 − $800 = $1,200

[d]If the old lathe is not replaced, HEP could sell it for $400 in 2022. If HEP purchases the new machine, it will not receive this cash flow in 2022. Because the old lathe would have a book value of $400 in 2022, there would be no tax effect from the sale.

that is, less cash will have to be spent to operate the new machine. Had the replacement resulted in an increase in sales in addition to the reduction in costs, this amount would also be reported. Also, note that the $3,500 cost savings is constant over the years 2018–2022. Had the annual savings been expected to change over time, this fact would have to be built into the analysis.

The change in depreciation expense must be computed to determine the impact such a change will have on the taxes paid by the firm because taxes require cash payments. If the new machine is purchased, the $500 depreciation expense of the lathe (old asset) no longer will be relevant for tax purposes; instead, the depreciation expense for the new machine will be used. For example, in 2018, the depreciation expense for the new machine will be $3,960 because, according to the 3-year MACRS classification, 33 percent of the cost of the new asset can be depreciated in the year it is purchased. Because HEP will dispose of the existing lathe if it buys the new machine, in 2018 it will replace the $500 depreciation expense associated with the lathe with the $3,960 depreciation expense associated with the new machine; thus the depreciation expense will increase by $3,460 = $3,960 – $500. The computations for the remaining years are the same. Note that in 2022 the change in depreciation is negative. This occurs because the new machine will be fully depreciated at the end of 2021, so there is nothing left to write off in 2022; thus, if the lathe is replaced, its depreciation of $500 will be replaced by the new machine's depreciation of $0 in 2022, which is a change of –$500.

The terminal cash flow includes $1,400 for the return of net working capital, because we assume the firm's normal net working capital level, which is the level that existed before buying the new machine, is restored at the end of the new machine's life. Any additional accounts receivables created by the purchase of the new machine will be collected, and any additional inventories required by the new machine will be drawn down and not replaced. The net salvage value of the *new* machine is $1,200; it is expected that the new machine can be sold in 2022 for $2,000, but $800 in taxes will have to be paid on the sale because the new machine will be fully depreciated at the time of the sale. We must also recognize that if the new machine is purchased to replace the old lathe, the firm no longer will have the *opportunity* to sell the *old* machine for its estimated salvage value in 2022, which is $400. In other words, if the new machine

is purchased, the firm will dispose of the old machine in 2017 rather than in 2022. Although we recognize the financial effects of disposing of the old machine in the initial investment outlay in 2017, we must now recognize the fact that the firm will no longer be able to sell the old machine in 2022 for its estimated $400 salvage value. Because it is estimated that the old machine could be sold at its book value in 2022, there would be no tax effect (i.e., the gain on the sale would be $0), and the net salvage value of the old machine would be $400. This amount appears as a negative cash flow, or an outflow, because the firm will not receive the $400 from the sale of the lathe in 2022 if the new machine is purchased. Thus, the total terminal cash flow is $2,200 = $1,400 + $1,200 – $400.

Making the Decision. A summary of the data and the computation of the project's NPV are provided with the following cash flow timeline:

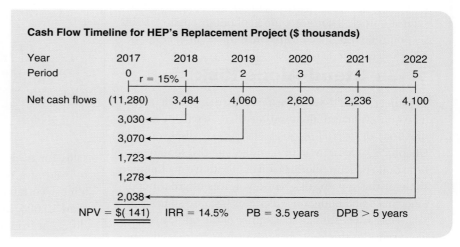

Cash Flow Timeline for HEP's Replacement Project ($ thousands)

According to the NPV and IRR methods, HEP should not replace the existing lathe with the new machine. Before we leave our discussion of replacement decisions, we should note that a replacement decision involves comparing two mutually exclusive projects: (1) retaining the old asset and (2) buying a new asset. To simplify matters, in our replacement example we assumed that the new machine had a life equal to the remaining life of the old machine. If, however, we were choosing between two mutually exclusive alternatives with significantly different lives, an adjustment would be necessary to make the results of the capital budgeting analysis for the two projects comparable. We mention the unequal-life problem here to make you aware that the evaluation of mutually exclusive projects with significantly different lives requires a slightly different analysis to ensure that a correct decision is made. Techniques that are used to adjust for unequal lives are included in more advanced finance textbooks.

10-3 Incorporating Risk in Capital Budgeting Analysis

To this point, we have assumed that the projects being examined have the same risk as the projects the firm currently possesses—that is, the investment risk associated with the projects is considered average, or normal—so that we could use the firm's *average* required rate of return to evaluate the acceptability of the investments. However, three types of risk, which we discuss in this section, must be examined to determine whether it is appropriate to use the firm's average required rate of return to evaluate a project. Although more difficult, evaluating the risk associated with a capital budgeting project is similar to evaluating the risk of a financial asset such as a stock. Therefore, much of our discussion in this section relies on the concepts introduced in Chapter 8.

10-3a Stand-Alone Risk

A project's **stand-alone risk** is the risk that it exhibits when evaluated alone rather than as part of a combination, or *portfolio*, of assets. As we discovered in Chapter 8, at least in theory stand-alone risk should be of little or no concern, because diversification can eliminate some of this type of risk. However, it is of great importance in capital budgeting decisions because stand-alone risk is easier to estimate than either of the other two risks we discuss in this section, and, in most cases, all three types of risk are highly correlated. As a result, management knows that it can get a good idea of a project's riskiness by determining its stand-alone risk.

The starting point for analyzing a project's stand-alone risk involves determining the uncertainty inherent in the project's cash flows. This analysis can be handled in a number of ways, ranging from informal judgments to complex economic and statistical analyses involving large-scale computer models. We will illustrate what is involved using Household Energy Products' appliance-control computer project, which we discussed earlier.

Many of the individual cash flows that were shown in Table 10.2 are subject to uncertainty. For example, although

Sergey Nivens/Shutterstock.com

sales for each year were projected at 15,000 units to be sold at a net price of $2,000 per unit, actual sales almost certainly would be somewhat higher or lower than 15,000, and the sales price might turn out to be different from the projected $2,000 per unit. In effect, estimates of the sales quantity and the sales price are expected values taken from probability distributions, as are many of the other values shown in Table 10.2. The distributions could be relatively "tight," reflecting small standard deviations and low risk, or they could be "wide," denoting a great deal of uncertainty about the final value of the variable in question and hence a high degree of stand-alone risk.

The nature of the individual cash flow distributions, and their correlations with one another, determine the nature of the NPV distribution and, thus, the project's stand-alone risk. Three techniques that are used for assessing a project's stand-alone risk include sensitivity analysis, scenario analysis, and Monte Carlo Simulation.

Sensitivity Analysis. Because the cash flows used to determine the acceptability of a project result from

stand-alone risk The risk an asset would have if it were a firm's only asset. It is measured by the variability of the asset's expected returns.

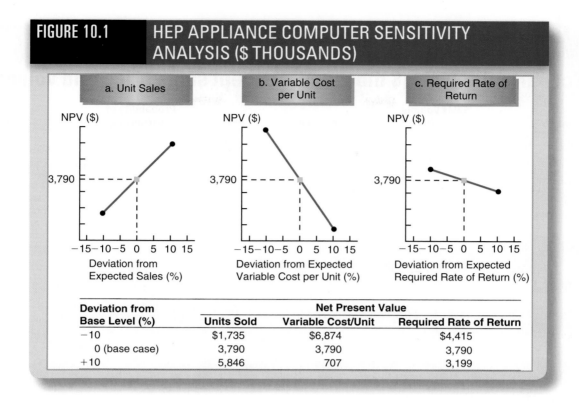

FIGURE 10.1 — HEP APPLIANCE COMPUTER SENSITIVITY ANALYSIS ($ THOUSANDS)

a. Unit Sales

b. Variable Cost per Unit

c. Required Rate of Return

Deviation from Base Level (%)	Net Present Value		
	Units Sold	Variable Cost/Unit	Required Rate of Return
−10	$1,735	$6,874	$4,415
0 (base case)	3,790	3,790	3,790
+10	5,846	707	3,199

forecasts of uncertain events, such as economic conditions in the future and expected demand for a product, we know the cash flow amounts used to determine the NPV of a project might be significantly different from what actually happens in the future. We also know that if a key input variable, such as units sold, changes, the project's NPV will also change. We can use a technique called **sensitivity analysis** to show exactly how much the NPV will change in response to a given change in an input variable, other things held constant. In a sensitivity analysis, we begin with the base-case situation that was developed using the expected values for each input; next, each variable is changed by specific percentage points above and below the expected value, holding other things constant; then a new NPV is calculated for each of these values; and, finally, the set of NPVs is plotted against the variable that was changed. Figure 10.1 shows sensitivity graphs for HEP's computer project for three of the key input variables. The table in the figure gives the NPVs that were used to construct the graphs. The slopes of the lines in the graphs show how sensitive NPV is to changes in each of the inputs; the steeper the slope, the more sensitive the NPV is to a change in the variable. In Figure 10.1, we see that the project's NPV is very sensitive to changes in variable costs, less sensitive to changes in unit sales, and fairly insensitive to changes in the required rate of return. So when estimating these variables' values, HEP should take extra care to ensure the accuracy of the forecast for variable costs per unit.

If we were comparing two projects, the one with the steeper sensitivity lines would be regarded as riskier, because, for that project, a relatively small error in estimating an extremely sensitive variable would produce a large error in the project's expected NPV. Thus, sensitivity analysis can provide useful insights into the riskiness of a project.

Scenario Analysis. In general, a project's stand-alone risk depends on both (1) the sensitivity of its NPV to changes in key variables and (2) the range of likely values of these variables, as reflected in their probability distributions. Sensitivity analysis considers only the first factor. **Scenario analysis** is a risk-analysis technique that considers both factors. In a scenario analysis, the financial analyst asks operating managers to pick a "bad" set of circumstances (low unit

sensitivity analysis A risk analysis technique in which key variables are changed and the resulting changes in the NPV and the IRR are observed.

scenario analysis A risk analysis technique in which "bad" and "good" sets of financial circumstances are compared with a most likely, or base case, situation.

Table 10.5

Scenario Analysis ($ thousands, except sales price and volume)

Scenario	Sales Volume (Units)	Sales Price	NPV	Probability of Outcome Pr_i	NPV × Pr_i
Best case	20,000	$2,500	$17,494	0.20	$3,499
Most likely case	15,000	2,000	3,790	0.60	2,274
Worst case	10,000	1,500	(6,487)	0.20	(1,297)
				1.00	Expected NPV = $4,475*
					σ_{NPV} = $7,630
					CV_{NPV} = 1.7

$$\text{Expected NPV} = \sum_{i=1}^{n} Pr_i(NPV_i) = 0.2(\$17,494) + 0.6(\$3,790) + 0.2(-6,487) = \$4,475$$

$$\sigma_{NPV} = \sqrt{\sum_{i=1}^{n} Pr_i(NPV_i - \text{Expected NPV})^2}$$

$$= \sqrt{0.2(\$17,494 - \$4,475)^2 + 0.6(\$3,790 - \$4,475)^2 + 0.2(-\$6,487 - \$4,475)^2} = \$7,630$$

$$CV_{NPV} = \frac{\sigma_{NPV}}{\text{Expected NPV}} = \frac{\$7,630}{4,475} = 1.7$$

*Rounding difference.

sales, low sales price, high variable cost per unit, high construction cost, and so on) and a "good" set of circumstances. The NPVs under the bad and good conditions are then calculated and compared to the expected, or *base case,* NPV.

As an example, let's return to the appliance-control computer project. Assume that HEP's managers are fairly confident of their estimates of all the project's cash flow variables except price and unit sales. Further, they regard a drop in sales below 10,000 units or a rise above 20,000 units as being extremely unlikely. Similarly, they expect the sales price as set in the marketplace to fall within the range of $1,500 to $2,500. Thus, 10,000 units at a price of $1,500 define the lower bound, or the **worst-case scenario**, whereas 20,000 units at a price of $2,500 define the upper bound, or the **best-case scenario**. Remember that the **base**, or **most likely, case** values are 15,000 units and a price of $2,000.

To carry out the scenario analysis, we use the worst-case variable values to obtain the worst-case NPV and the best-case variable values to obtain the best-case NPV.[5] We then use the results of the scenario analysis to determine the *expected* NPV, the standard deviation of NPV, and the coefficient of variation. To complete these computations, we need estimates of the probabilities of occurrence of the three scenarios, the Pr_i values. Suppose management estimates that there is a 20 percent probability of the worst-case scenario, a 60 percent probability of the base case, and a 20 percent probability of the best case. The scenario probabilities and NPVs constitute a probability distribution of returns just like those we dealt with in Chapter 8, except that the returns are measured in dollars instead of percentages, or rates of return.

We performed the scenario analysis using a spreadsheet model, and Table 10.5 summarizes the results of this analysis. We see that the base case (or most likely case) forecasts a positive NPV result; the worst case produces a negative NPV; and the best case results in a large positive

worst-case scenario An analysis in which all of the input variables are set at their worst reasonably forecasted values.

best-case scenario An analysis in which all of the input variables are set at their best reasonably forecasted values.

base (most likely) case An analysis in which all of the input variables are set at their most likely values.

[5]We could have included worst- and best-case values for fixed and variable costs, income tax rates, salvage values, and so on. For illustrative purposes, we limited the changes to only two variables. Also, note that we are treating sales price and quantity as independent variables; that is, a low sales price could occur when unit sales were low, and a high sales price could be coupled with high unit sales, or vice versa. As we discuss in the next section, it is relatively easy to vary these assumptions if the facts of the situation suggest a different set of conditions.

NPV. However, the expected NPV for the project is $4.475 million and the project's coefficient of variation is 1.7. Now we can compare the project's coefficient of variation with the coefficient of variation of HEP's average project to get an idea of the relative riskiness of the appliance-control computer project. For example, because HEP's existing projects, on average, have a coefficient of variation of about 1.0, on the basis of this stand-alone risk measure, HEP's managers would conclude that the appliance computer project is much riskier than the firm's "average" project.

Denis Vrublevski/Shutterstock.com

Monte Carlo Simulation. Scenario analysis is limited because it only considers a few discrete outcomes (NPVs) for the project, even though there really are many more possibilities. For this reason, firms often use **Monte Carlo simulation**, so named because this type of analysis grew out of work on the mathematics of casino gambling, to examine a wider range of possible outcomes. Simulation is more complicated than scenario analysis because the probability distribution of each uncertain cash flow variable must be specified. Once this has been done, a value from the probability distribution for each variable is randomly chosen to compute the project's cash flows; these values are then used to determine the project's NPV. Simulation is usually completed using a computer because the process just described is repeated again and again—say, 500 times—which results in 500 NPVs and a probability distribution for the project's NPV values. Thus, the output produced by simulation is a probability distribution that can be used to determine the most likely range of outcomes expected from a project. This provides the decision maker with a better idea of the various outcomes that are possible than is available from a single point estimate of the NPV.

10-3b Corporate (Within-Firm) Risk

Corporate, or **within-firm, risk** is the effect a project has on the total, or overall, riskiness of the company, without considering whether adding the project to existing assets affects the firm's systematic or unsystematic risk. To measure corporate, or within-firm, risk, we need to determine how the capital budgeting project is related to the firm's existing assets. Remember from our discussion in Chapter 8 that two assets can be combined to

reduce risk if their payoffs move in opposite directions, that is, when the payoffs from the assets are negatively related. In reality, it is not easy to find assets with payoffs that move opposite each other. However, we also discovered in Chapter 8 that as long as assets are *not* perfectly positively related (i.e., $\rho \neq +1.0$), some diversification, or risk reduction, can still be achieved. Many firms use this principle to reduce the risk associated with their operations by adding new projects that are not highly related to existing assets.

Corporate risk is important for three primary reasons:

1. Undiversified stockholders, including the owners of small businesses, are primarily concerned about the diversification that is associated with a particular firm (i.e., its corporate risk).

2. Empirical studies of the determinants of required rates of return generally find that investors, even those who are well diversified, give some consideration to corporate risk when they establish required returns.

3. The firm's stability is important to its managers, workers, customers, suppliers, and creditors, as well as to the community in which it operates. Firms that are in serious danger of bankruptcy, or even of suffering low profits and reduced output, have difficulty attracting and retaining good managers and workers. In addition, both suppliers and customers are

Monte Carlo simulation A risk analysis technique in which probable future events are simulated on a computer, generating a probability distribution that indicates the most likely outcomes.

corporate (within-firm) risk Risk that does not take into consideration the effects of stockholders' diversification; it is measured by a project's effect on the firm's earnings variability.

reluctant to depend on weak firms, and such firms have difficulty borrowing money at reasonable interest rates. These factors tend to reduce risky firms' profitability and hence the prices of their stocks; thus they also make corporate risk significant.

From this discussion, it is clear that corporate risk is important even if a firm's stockholders are well diversified.

10-3c Beta (Market) Risk

The types of risk analysis discussed to this point provide insights into a project's risk and thus help managers make better capital budgeting decisions. However, these risk measures do not take account of beta, or market, risk, which is project risk assessed from the standpoint of a stockholder who holds a well-diversified portfolio. Thus, in this section, we show how the capital asset pricing model (CAPM), which was introduced in Chapter 8, can be used to evaluate portfolio risk as well as to specify the rates of return that should be used to evaluate projects that have substantially different risks.

In Chapter 8, we developed the concept of beta, β, as a measure of the systematic risk for an individual stock. From our discussion, we concluded that systematic risk is the relevant risk of a stock because unsystematic, or firm-specific, risk can be reduced significantly, or eliminated, through diversification. This same concept can be applied to capital budgeting projects because the firm can be thought of as a composite of all the projects it has undertaken. Thus, the relevant risk of a project can be viewed as the impact it has on the firm's systematic risk (its portfolio of assets). This line of reasoning leads to the conclusion that if the beta coefficient for a project, β_{proj}, can be determined, then the **project required rate of return**, r_{proj}, can be found using the following form of the CAPM equation:

$$r_{proj} = r_{RF} + (r_M - r_{RF})\beta_{proj}$$

As an example, consider the case of Erie Steel Company, an integrated steel producer operating in the Great Lakes region. For simplicity, let's assume that Erie is financed with all equity (stock), so that the *average* required rate of return it needs to earn on capital budgeting projects is based solely on the average return demanded by stockholders; that is, there is no debt that might require a different return. Erie's existing beta = $\beta_{Existing}$ = 1.1; r_{RF} = 8%; and r_M = 12%. Thus, Erie's required rate of return is 12.4% = r_{Erie} = 8% + (12% − 8%)1.1, which suggests that investors should be willing to give Erie money to invest in average-risk projects if the company expects to earn 12.4 percent or more on this money.[6] Here again, by *average-risk projects* we mean projects with risk similar to the firm's existing assets.

Suppose, however, that taking on a particular project will cause a change in Erie's beta coefficient and hence change the company's required rate of return. For example, suppose Erie is considering the construction of a fleet of barges to haul iron ore, and barge operations have betas of 2.1 rather than 1.1. Because the firm itself can be regarded as a "portfolio of assets," Erie's beta, just like the beta of a portfolio of stocks, is a weighted average of the betas of its individual assets. Thus, taking on the barge project will cause the overall corporate beta to rise. If 80 percent of Erie's total funds end up in basic steel operations with a beta of 1.1 and 20 percent in the barge operations with a beta of 2.1, the new corporate beta will increase to 1.3 = 0.8(1.1) + 0.2(2.1). Thus, taking on the new project will cause the *overall* corporate required rate of return to rise from the original 12.4 percent to 13.2 percent; $r_{Erie,New}$ = 8% + (12% − 8%)1.3. This higher average rate can be earned only if the new project generates a return higher than the existing assets are providing. Because Erie's overall return is based on its portfolio of assets, the return required from the barge project must be sufficiently high so that, in combination with returns of the other assets, the firm's average return is 13.2 percent. Because its beta is higher, the barge project, with β_{Barge} = 2.1, should be evaluated at a 16.4 percent required rate of return—that is, r_{Barge} = 8% + (4%)2.1 = 16.4%. On the other hand, a low-risk project such as a new steel distribution center that has a beta of only 0.5 would have a required rate of return of 10 percent.

In Chapter 8, we discussed the estimation of betas for stocks, and we indicated that it is difficult to estimate *true* future betas. The estimation of project betas is even more difficult and more fraught with uncertainty. One way a firm can try to measure the systematic risk of a project is to find *single-product* companies in the same line of business as the project being evaluated and then use the betas of those companies to determine the

beta (market) risk That part of a project's risk that cannot be eliminated by diversification; it is measured by the project's beta coefficient.

project required rate of return, r_{proj} The risk-adjusted required rate of return for an individual project.

---

[6]To simplify things somewhat, we assume at this point that the firm uses only equity capital. If debt is used, the required rate of return used must be a weighted average of the costs of debt and equity. This point is discussed at length in Chapter 11.

required rate of return for the project being evaluated. This technique is termed the pure play method, and the single-product companies that are used for comparisons are called *pure play firms*. For example, if Erie could find some existing firms that only operate barges, it could use the average of the betas of those firms as a proxy for the barge project's beta.

10-3d Project Risk Conclusions

We have discussed the three types of risk normally considered in capital budgeting analysis—stand-alone risk, within-firm (or corporate) risk, and beta (or market) risk—and we have discussed ways of assessing each. However, two important questions remain: (1) Should a firm be concerned with stand-alone risk and corporate risk in its capital budgeting decisions? (2) What do we do when the stand-alone or within-firm risk assessments and the beta risk assessment lead to different conclusions?

These questions do not have easy answers. From a theoretical standpoint, well-diversified investors should be concerned only with beta risk, managers should be concerned only with stock price maximization, and these two factors should lead to the conclusion that beta risk should be given virtually all the weight in capital budgeting decisions. However, if investors are not well diversified, if the CAPM does not operate exactly as theory says it should, or if measurement problems keep managers from having confidence in the CAPM approach in capital budgeting, it might be appropriate to give stand-alone and corporate risk more weight than financial theorists suggest. Note also that the CAPM ignores bankruptcy costs, even though such costs can be substantial, and that the probability of bankruptcy depends on a firm's corporate risk, not on its beta risk. Therefore, one can easily conclude that even well-diversified investors should want a firm's management to give at least some consideration to a project's corporate risk instead of concentrating entirely on beta risk.

Although it would be desirable to reconcile these problems and to measure project risk on some absolute scale, the best we can do in practice is to determine project risk in a somewhat nebulous, relative sense. For example, we can generally say with a fair degree of confidence that a particular project has more or less stand-alone risk than the firm's average project. Then, assuming that stand-alone risk and corporate risk are highly correlated (which is typical), the project's stand-alone risk will be a good measure of its corporate risk. Finally, assuming that beta risk and corporate risk are highly correlated (as is true for most companies), a project with more corporate risk than average will also have more beta risk, and vice versa for projects with low corporate risk.

10-3e How Project Risk Is Considered in Capital Budgeting Decisions

From our discussion to this point, you should conclude that it is difficult to develop a really good measure of project risk. As a result, most firms incorporate project risk in capital budgeting decisions using the risk-adjusted discount rate approach. With this approach, the appropriate required rate of return at which the expected cash flows are discounted is adjusted if the project's risk is substantially different from the average risk associated with the firm's existing assets. Following this logic, average-risk projects would be discounted at the rate of return required of projects that are considered average, or normal, for the firm; above-average-risk projects would be discounted at a higher-than-average rate; and below-average-risk projects would be discounted at a rate below the firm's average rate of return. Unfortunately, because risk cannot be measured precisely, there is no accurate way of specifying exactly how much higher or lower these discount rates should be. Given the present state of the art, *risk adjustments are necessarily judgmental and somewhat arbitrary.*

Although the process is not exact, many companies use a two-step procedure to develop risk-adjusted discount rates for use in capital budgeting analysis. First, the overall required rate of return is established for the firm's existing assets. This process is completed on a division-by-division basis for very large firms, perhaps using the CAPM. Second, each project might be classified into one of three categories: high risk, average risk, and low risk.

pure play method An approach used for estimating the beta of a project in which a firm identifies companies whose only business is the product in question, determines the beta for each firm, and then averages the betas to find an approximation of its own project's beta.

risk-adjusted discount rate The discount rate (required rate of return) that applies to a particular risky stream of income; it is equal to the risk-free rate of interest plus a risk premium appropriate to the level of risk associated with a particular project's income stream.

Then, the firm or division uses the average required rate of return as the discount rate for average-risk projects, reduces the average rate by 1 to 3 percentage points when evaluating low-risk projects, and raises the average rate by several percentage points for high-risk projects. For example, if a firm's basic required rate of return is estimated to be 12 percent, an 18 percent discount rate might be used for a high-risk project and a 9 percent rate for a low-risk project. Average-risk projects, which constitute about 80 percent of most capital budgets, would be evaluated at the 12 percent rate of return. *If project risk is not considered in capital budgeting analysis, incorrect decisions are possible*: a high-risk project might be accepted when it actually should be rejected, or a low-risk project might be rejected when it should be accepted.

Although the risk-adjusted discount rate approach is far from precise, it does at least recognize that projects with different risks should be evaluated using different required rates of return.

10-4 Multinational Capital Budgeting

Although the basic principles of capital budgeting analysis are the same for both domestic and foreign operations, some key differences need to be mentioned. First, cash flow estimation generally is much more complex for overseas investments. Most multinational firms set up a separate subsidiary in each foreign country in which they operate, and the relevant cash flows for these subsidiaries are the earnings and dividends that can be *repatriated,* or returned, to the parent company (**repatriation of earnings**). Second, these cash flows must be converted into the currency of the parent company, and thus are subject to future exchange rate changes. Third, earnings and dividends normally are taxed by both foreign and home-country governments. Fourth, a foreign government might restrict the amount of cash that

repatriation of earnings The process of sending cash flows from a foreign subsidiary back to the parent company.

exchange rate risk The uncertainty associated with the price at which the currency from one country can be converted into the currency of another country.

political risk The risk of expropriation (seizure) of a foreign subsidiary's assets by the host country or of unanticipated restrictions on cash flows to the parent company.

can be repatriated to the parent company, perhaps to force multinational firms to reinvest earnings in the host country or to prevent large currency outflows that might affect the exchange rate. Whatever the host country's motivation, the result is that the parent corporation cannot use cash flows blocked in the foreign country to pay current dividends to its shareholders, nor does it have the flexibility to reinvest cash flows elsewhere in the world. Therefore, from the perspective of the parent organization, *the cash flows relevant to the analysis of a foreign investment are the cash flows that the subsidiary legally can send back to the parent.*

In addition to the complexities of the cash flow analysis, *the rate of return required for a foreign project might be different from that of an equivalent domestic project because foreign projects might be either riskier or less risky.* A higher risk could arise from two primary sources—exchange rate risk and political risk—while a lower risk could result from international diversification.

Exchange rate risk reflects the inherent uncertainty a company has about the value of cash flows that will be sent back to the parent at some date in the future, because the cash has to be converted from the foreign country's currency into the home country's currency. In other words, foreign projects have an added risk element that relates to what the basic cash flows will be worth in the parent company's home currency. The foreign currency cash flows that are to be turned over to the parent must be converted into U.S. dollars by translating them at *expected* future exchange rates. Actual exchange rates might differ substantially from expectations.

Political risk refers to any action (or the chance of such action) by a host government that reduces the value of a company's investment. It includes at one extreme the *expropriation* (seizure) without compensation of the subsidiary's assets. However, it also includes less drastic actions that reduce the value of the parent firm's investment in the foreign subsidiary, such as higher taxes, tighter repatriation or currency controls, and restrictions on prices charged. The risk of expropriation of U.S. assets abroad is low in traditionally friendly and stable countries such as the United Kingdom or Switzerland. However, in Latin America and the Middle East, for example, the risk might be substantial.

Generally, political risk premiums are not added to the required rate of return to adjust for this risk. If a company's management has a serious concern that a given country might expropriate foreign assets, it simply will not make significant investments in that country. Expropriation is viewed as a catastrophic or ruinous event, and managers have been shown to be extraordinarily risk averse when faced with ruinous loss possibilities. However, companies can take steps to reduce the potential loss from expropriation in three major ways: (1) by financing the subsidiary with capital raised in the country in which the asset is located, (2) by structuring operations so that the subsidiary has value only as a part of the integrated corporate system, and (3) by obtaining insurance against economic losses from expropriation from a source such as the Overseas Private Investment Corporation (OPIC). In the last case, insurance premiums would have to be added to the project's cost.

STUDY TOOLS

LOCATED AT BACK OF THE TEXTBOOK

- ☐ Problems are found at the end of this chapter.
- ☐ A tear-out Chapter Review card is located at the back of the textbook.

LOCATED AT WWW.CENGAGEBRAIN.COM

- ☐ Review Key Term flashcards and create your own cards.
- ☐ Track your knowledge and understanding of key concepts in corporate finance.
- ☐ Complete practice and graded quizzes to prepare for tests.
- ☐ Complete interactive content within CFIN5 Online.
- ☐ View the chapter highlight boxes for CFIN5 Online.

KEY CONCEPTS ABOUT PROJECT CASH FLOWS AND RISK

To conclude this chapter, we summarize some project cash flows and risk concepts (rules) that were discussed.

- In capital budgeting analysis, "relevant" cash flows include only those cash flows that are affected by the decision to purchase the project. If a cash flow does not change as a result of the purchase, it is not relevant.

- The relevant, or incremental, cash flows can be categorized as (1) the initial investment outlay, which includes cash flows that occur only at the beginning of the project's life; (2) supplemental operating cash flows, which include changes in the day-to-day operating cash flows during the life of the project; and

(3) the terminal cash flow, which includes cash flows that occur only at the end of the project's life.

- Identifying the relevant cash flows for a replacement project is somewhat more complicated than for an expansion project, because the cash flows that will be generated if the new project (the replacement asset) is purchased, as well as the cash flows that will be generated if the old project (the replaced asset) is retained, must be considered.

- If the risk associated with a capital budgeting project differs substantially from the average risk of the firm's existing assets, some adjustment should be made to the firm's required rate of return when evaluating the project. If the project has substantially higher risk, a higher-than-average required rate of return should be used in the capital budgeting evaluation. If the project's risk is lower than average, a lower required rate of return should be used.

- Although the same basic principles should be applied when conducting capital budgeting analysis for multinational operations, application of these principles often is more complicated when dealing with foreign subsidiaries.

PROBLEMS

For problems that refer to MACRS depreciation, see Table 10A.2 in Appendix 10A to determine the recovery allowance percentages.

10-1 Canadian Wilderness Company (CWC) just bought a machine that is expected to generate $25,000 in operating income before depreciation expenses each year. The machine, which has a depreciable basis equal to $60,000, falls into the MACRS 3-year class. What will be CWC's (a) after-tax operating income and (b) operating cash flow for both this year (Year 1) and three years from now (Year 3)? Assume that all sales and operating expenses, except depreciation, are cash. CWC's marginal tax rate is 40 percent.

10-2 Dave's Devilish Dogs (3D) expects to generate $92,000 in sales in the long term. 3D's operating costs, excluding depreciation, are 75 percent of sales. The company has only one asset, a machine that was just purchased for $150,000. The machine will be depreciated according to the MACRS 3-year class of assets. 3D's marginal tax rate is 35 percent, and it has no debt. Compute the company's (a) net income and (b) after-tax operating cash flow for the next four years.

10-3 Underwater Swimwear recently purchased a new machine for $350,000. It cost $20,000 to ship the machine to Underwater's facility, and it cost another $50,000 to get it installed. Purchase of the new machine will require Underwater to increase its working capital by $25,000. If the new machine falls into the MACRS 3-year class, what amount will the firm be able to depreciate during the next five years?

10-4 Xavier Corporation plans to purchase a new machine to replace an older machine on its assembly line. The new machine's purchase price is $500,000, and it will cost $75,000 to have the new machine shipped and installed. The old machine, which is fully depreciated, can be sold to another company for $45,000. The new machine falls into the MACRS 5-year class. Compute the depreciation expense associated with the new machine for the next five years?

10-5 Western Textiles is trying to determine whether to purchase a new weaving machine that costs $214,000. It would cost another $26,000 to install the machine. Western plans to use the machine for four years and then sell it for $80,000. The machine falls into the MACRS 5-year class. (a) What will be the depreciation associated with the machine each year Western uses it? (b) If its marginal tax rate is 40 percent, what after-tax net cash flow will Western receive when the machine is sold in four years?

10-6 Chiefland Campers is evaluating a project that will not affect revenues, but it will save the firm $110,000 per year in before-tax operating costs, excluding depreciation. The project's depreciable basis is $840,000, and it will be depreciated on a straight-line basis to a book value equal to zero ($0) over its 10-year life. If the firm's marginal tax rate is 34 percent, what are the annual supplemental operating cash flows?

10-7 Gator Bicycles just bought a new brake calibration machine that is expected to generate $30,000 in new revenues each of the next four years without increasing cash operating costs. The machine falls in the MACRS 3-year class, and its depreciable basis is $120,000. If Gator's marginal tax rate is 35 percent, what are the annual supplemental operating cash flows attributed to the machine?

10-8 Cool Cat Cabinets (CCC) is evaluating whether to replace an aging machine. The existing machine is being depreciated at $40,000 per year, whereas the depreciation for a new machine is expected to be $35,000 per year. CCC's operating income, excluding depreciation, is expected to be $90,000 no matter which machine is used. The firm's marginal tax rate is 40 percent. If the new machine is purchased, what effect will the change in depreciation have on the firm's (a) net income and (b) supplemental operating cash flows. CCC has no debt.

10-9 Towers Elevator Company plans to sell one of its machines to another company for $102,000. The book value of the machine is $90,000. Compute (a) the gain (loss) on the sale of the machine and (b) the net cash flow that will be generated from the sale of the machine. Towers' marginal tax rate is 40 percent.

10-10 Four years ago Progressive Products purchased a machine for $25,000. The machine's current book value is $6,000. Later today, Progressive plans to sell the machine for $4,000. The company's marginal tax rate is 35 percent. (a) Compute the tax effect of selling the machine and (b) the net cash flow that will be generated from selling the machine.

10-11 Rader Railway is determining whether to purchase a new rail setter, which has a base price of $432,000 and would cost another $52,000 to install. The setter falls into the MACRS 3-year class, and it would be sold after three years for $220,000. Using the setter requires a $22,000 increase in net working capital. Although it would have no effect on revenues, the setter should save the firm $185,000 per year in before-tax operating costs (excluding depreciation). Rader's marginal tax rate is 40 percent, and its required rate of return is 14 percent. Should the setter be purchased?

10-12 Artistic Adobes is considering growing its business by adding a paint machine that costs $90,000. The machine will generate an additional $29,800 in before-tax operating income (excluding depreciation) for the next five years. At the end of five years, the machine can be sold for $8,000. The machine falls into the MACRS 3-year class. Artistic's marginal tax rate is 34 percent, and its required rate of return is 15 percent. Should Artistic purchase the machine?

10-13 Emotion Cosmetics is considering whether to replace one of its manufacturing machines with a new one that will increase operating income (excluding depreciation) by $14,300 per year for the next three years. The new machine costs $37,500, and it falls in the MACRS 3-year class. If the new machine is purchased, the old machine, which has a current book value equal to $8,300, will be sold for $5,000. If the old machine is kept, it will continue to be depreciated on a straight-line basis at $2,300 per year, and then it will be sold in three years for $2,000. If the new machine is purchased, Emotion plans to sell it in three years for $6,000. The firm's marginal tax rate is 40 percent, and its required rate of return is 11 percent. Should the old machine be replaced?

10-14 Otter Outside Gear must decide whether to replace a 10 year-old packing machine with a new one that costs $153,800. Replacing the old machine will increase net operating income (excluding depreciation) from $70,000 to $110,000 and it will decrease net working capital by $18,000. The new machine falls in the MACRS 5-year class. If the new machine is purchased, it will be sold in six years for $25,000; whereas, if the old machine is kept, it will have no salvage value in six years. The old machine has a current market value of $10,860, and although its current book value is $8,000, in one year the old machine's book value will be zero ($0). The firm's marginal tax rate is 40 percent, and its required rate of return is 12 percent. Should the new packing machine be purchased?

10-15 Quiet Quilts is considering adding another division that requires a cash outlay of $29,500, and is expected to generate $6,250 in after-tax cash flows each year for seven years. The CFO has determined the new division's beta coefficient is 0.8. The market return is expected to be 11 percent and the risk-free rate of return is 4 percent. Should Quiet add the new division?

10-16 Logic Legal Leverage (LLL) is evaluating a project that has a beta coefficient equal to 1.3. The risk-free rate is 3 percent and the market *risk premium* is 6 percent. The project, which requires an investment of $405,000, will generate $165,000 in after-tax operating cash flows for the next three years. Should LLL purchase the project?

10-17 Qualil evaluated a project using scenario analysis. His results indicate that the project normally will generate a net present value (NPV) equal to $19,800, which will occur 70 percent of the time. But, he also discovered that 10 percent of the time the NPV will be −$20,100, and 20 percent of the time the NPV will be $31,500. The firm's policy is not to invest in projects that have coefficients of variation greater than 0.8. Should Qualil recommend that the project be purchased?

10-18 After completing a scenario analysis for a prospective investment, the CFO of a company reported to the CEO that there is a 60 percent chance the investment will provide the firm with a net present value (NPV) equal to $128,300, there is a 25 percent chance the investment's NPV will be $185,400, and there is a 15 percent chance the NPV will be −$77,600. The CEO will not purchase investments that have coefficients of variation greater than 0.7. Should the CEO purchase the investment?

10-19 Following are three *independent* projects Peanut/ Pecan Processing (PPP) is evaluating:

Project	IRR	Risk
P	10.0%	Low
Q	12.0	Average
R	14.5	High

PPP generally considers risk when examining projects by adjusting its average required rate of return, r, which equals 11 percent. A 4 percent adjustment is made for high-risk projects, and a 2 percent adjustment is made for low-risk projects. Which project(s) should PPP purchase?

10-20 The CFO of Bogey Golf has been given the following information about two *mutually exclusive* investments:

Project	IRR	Risk
X	14.0%	Average
Y	19.0	High

The CFO normally uses a risk-adjusted required rate of return to evaluate such investments. The firm's average required rate of return, which is 15 percent, is adjusted by 5 percent for high-risk projects, and it is adjusted by 3 percent for low-risk projects. Which project(s) should Bogey purchase?

APPENDIX 10A DEPRECIATION

Remember from your accounting course(s) that depreciation recognizes the annual effect of wear and tear, or reduction in value, for a long-term asset that is used to generate revenues over a number of years. The concept of depreciation is covered in detail in accounting courses, so in this appendix we simply summarize basic information that will help you conduct capital budgeting analysis.

1. Companies often calculate depreciation in one way when figuring taxes and in another way when reporting income to investors: many use the *straight-line* method for stockholder reporting (or book purposes), but they use the fastest rate permitted by law for tax purposes. Because we are concerned with the effect of depreciation on cash flows, not on net income, we use the same depreciation method that firms use when determining their taxes. This depreciation method is known as the Modified Accelerated Cost Recovery System (MACRS).

2. According to MACRS, each depreciable asset is classified into one of several "classes of life" according to its characteristics. The asset's depreciable basis can be written off according to the depreciation rates established by the Internal Revenue Service in each MACRS "life class." Table 10A.1 describes the types of property that fit into the different class-life categories and Table 10A.2 sets forth the MACRS recovery allowances

(depreciation rates) for selected classes of investment property. Property classified as having a life equal to or greater than 27.5 years (real estate) must be depreciated by the straight-line method, but assets classified in the other categories can be depreciated either by the accelerated method or by an alternate straight-line method. Most assets that qualify are depreciated using MACRS because depreciation expenses are higher in the early years of the assets' lives, and higher depreciation expenses result in lower taxes.

Table 10A.1 Major Classes and Asset Lives for MACRS

Class	Type of Property
3-year	Certain special manufacturing tools
5-year	Automobiles, light-duty trucks, computers, office machinery, and certain special manufacturing equipment
7-year	Most industrial equipment, office furniture and fixtures, and agricultural equipment
10-year	Certain longer-lived equipment and many water vessels
15-year	Certain land improvement, such as shrubbery, fences, and roads; service station buildings
20-year	Farm buildings
25-year	Property used in water treatment; municipal sewers
27½-year	Residential rental real property such as apartment buildings

Table 10A.2 Recovery Allowance Percentages for Personal Property

Ownership Year	Class of Investment			
	3-Year	5-Year	7-Year	10-Year
1	33%	20%	14%	10%
2	45	32	25	18
3	15	19	17	14
4	7	12	13	12
5		11	9	9
6		6	9	7
7			9	7
8			4	7
9				7
10				6
11				3
	100%	100%	100%	100%

Notes: These recovery allowance percentages were taken from the Internal Revenue Service website, http://www.irs.gov. The percentages are based on the 200 percent declining-balance method prescribed by MACRS, with a switch to straight-line depreciation at some point in the asset's life. For example, consider the 5-year recovery allowance percentages. The straight-line percentage would be 20 percent per year, so the 200 percent declining-balance multiplier is 2.0(20%) = 40% = 0.4. Because the half-year convention applies (see discussion), the MACRS percentage for Year 1 is 20 percent. For Year 2, 80 percent of the depreciable basis remains to be depreciated, so the recovery allowance percentage is 0.40(80%) = 32%. The same procedure is followed for subsequent years. Although the tax tables carry the allowance percentages to two decimal places, we have rounded the numbers for ease of illustration.

3. An asset's depreciable basis, which is the total amount that can be written off under MACRS, is equal to the purchase price of the asset plus any shipping and installation costs. The depreciable basis is not adjusted for salvage value when applying MACRS rates.

4. If a depreciable asset is sold, the sale price (salvage value) minus the then existing undepreciated book value is added to operating income and taxed at the firm's marginal tax rate. For example, suppose a firm buys a 5-year class life asset for $100,000 and sells it at the end of the fourth year for $25,000. The asset's book value is equal to $100,000(0.11 + 0.06) = $17,000. Therefore, $25,000 − $17,000 = $8,000 is added to the firm's operating income and is taxed. If this difference were negative, the firm would effectively receive a tax refund, which would be recognized as a cash inflow.

5. Under MACRS, in many cases it is assumed that property is placed in service in the middle of the first year. As a result for 3-year class life property, the recovery period begins in the middle of the year the asset is placed in service and ends three years later. The effect of the *half-year convention* is to extend the recovery period by one additional year, so 3-year class life property is depreciated over four calendar years, 5-year class property is depreciated over six calendar years, and so on. This convention is incorporated into the recovery allowance percentages given in Table 10A.2.

Depreciation Illustration. Suppose that Unilate Textiles buys a $150,000 machine that falls in the MACRS 5-year class life and places it into service on March 15, 2016. Unilate must pay an additional $30,000 for delivery and installation. Salvage value is not considered, so the machine's depreciable basis is $180,000 = $150,000 + $30,000. Each year's recovery allowance (tax depreciation expense) is determined by multiplying the depreciable basis by the applicable recovery allowance percentage. Thus, the depreciation expense for 2016 is 0.20($180,000) = $36,000, and for 2017 it is 0.32($180,000) = $57,600. Similarly, the depreciation expense is $34,200 for 2018, $21,600 for 2019, $19,800 for 2020, and $10,800 for 2021. The total depreciation expense over the six-year recovery period is $180,000, which is equal to the depreciable basis of the machine.

part **5**

After you finish this chapter go to **PAGE 222** for **STUDY TOOLS**

Sergey Nivens/Shutterstock.com

LEARNING OUTCOMES

After studying this chapter, you will be able to...

LO1 Compute the component cost of capital for (a) debt, (b) preferred stock, (c) retained earnings, and (d) new common equity.

LO2 Describe the weighted average cost of capital (WACC), and discuss the logic of using WACC to make informed financial decisions.

LO3 Describe how the marginal cost of capital (MCC) is used to make capital budgeting decisions.

LO4 Discuss the relationship between the firm's WACC and investors' required rates of return.

The Cost of Capital

11

Remember that investors provide the funds that firms use to purchase assets. As a result, the returns required (demanded) by investors determine the minimum rates that a firm must pay to attract the funds it uses. The average cost of these funds represents the firm's **required rate of return**, r, which is also called its **cost of capital**. It is vitally important that a firm knows its cost of capital, because this cost represents the minimum rate of return that must be earned from investments, such as capital budgeting projects, to ensure the value of the firm does not decrease.

In this chapter, we discuss the concept of cost of capital, how the average cost of capital is determined, and how the cost of capital is used in financial decision making. Because a firm's cost of funds is based on the return demanded by investors, most of the models and formulas used in this chapter are the same ones we developed in Chapters 6–8, where we described how stocks and bonds are valued by investors and how investors' required rates of return are determined. To attract their funds, a firm must offer (pay) the returns investors want (require), which means *the average rate of return that investors require on corporate securities represents a cost to the firm for using those funds*. Thus, it is the investors who determine a firm's cost of capital.

11-1 Component Costs of Capital

The items in the liability and equity sections of a firm's balance sheet—various types of debt, preferred stock, and common equity—are its **capital components**. *Capital* is a necessary factor of production, because any increase in total assets must be financed by an increase in one or more of the capital components. Like any other

factor of production, capital has a cost. The cost of each type of funds is called the *component cost* of that particular type of capital, and the *costs of capital* represent the rates of return that the firm pays to investors to attract various forms of capital funds. For example, if Unilate Textiles, the North Carolina textile company we introduced in earlier chapters, can borrow money at 10 percent, its component cost of debt is 10 percent because investors demand a 10 percent return to provide funds in the form of debt to the company. Throughout this chapter, we concentrate on debt, preferred stock, retained earnings, and new issues of common stock as the capital components for Unilate.

11-1a Cost of Debt, r_{dT}

In Chapter 6, we showed that yield to maturity (YTM) on a bond is the average rate of return that *investors require* to provide funds to the firm in the form of debt. This yield, which we designated r_d, is a cost to the firm for using investors' funds; thus we refer to the YTM, or r_d, on the firm's bonds as its *cost of debt*. However, because interest on debt is a tax-deductible expense to the firm, r_d does not represent the true cost of debt funds to the firm. To determine the actual cost of debt, we must adjust r_d to account for the tax savings associated with interest payments. Thus, the **after-tax cost of debt**, r_{dT}, which represents the actual cost to the firm, is the before-tax interest rate (yield) on debt, r_d, less the tax saving that

required rate of return The return that must be earned on invested funds to cover the cost of financing such investments; also called the *opportunity cost rate*.

cost of capital The firm's average cost of funds, which is the average return required by the firm's investors—what the firm must pay to attract funds.

capital components The particular types of capital used by the firm—that is, its debt, preferred stock, and common equity.

after-tax cost of debt, r_{dT} The relevant cost of new debt, taking into account the tax deductibility of interest.

results because interest is tax deductible. This relationship is shown in Equation 11.1:

11.1

$$\begin{pmatrix} \text{After-tax} \\ \text{component} \\ \text{cost of debt} \end{pmatrix} = r_{dT} = \begin{pmatrix} \text{Bondholders'} \\ \text{required} \\ \text{rate of return} \end{pmatrix} - \begin{pmatrix} \text{Tax} \\ \text{savings} \end{pmatrix}$$

$$= r_d - r_d \times T$$

$$= r_d(1 - T)$$

In effect, the government pays part of the cost of debt because interest is tax deductible. Therefore, if a firm can borrow at an interest rate of 8 percent, and if it has a marginal tax rate of 40 percent, its after-tax cost of debt is 4.8 percent:

$$r_{dT} = 8.0\%(1.0 - 0.4)$$
$$= 8.0\%(0.6) = 4.8\%$$

We use the after-tax cost of debt because the value of the firm's stock, which we want to maximize, depends on *after-tax* cash flows. It follows that because we are concerned with after-tax cash flows, the after-tax rates of return are appropriate for financial decision making.[1]

Note that the cost of debt is the interest rate on *new* debt, not on already outstanding debt. In other words, we are interested in the *marginal* cost of debt, which is the rate of return that the firm must pay to raise new funds by issuing debt. Our primary concern with the cost of capital is how it is used to make capital budgeting decisions involving investments that generate future cash flows. Thus, the rate at which the firm has borrowed in the past is a sunk cost, and it is irrelevant for cost of capital purposes.

In Chapter 6, we solved the following equation to find r_d, the rate of return, or yield to maturity (YTM), for a bond. Because YTM $= r_d =$ before-tax cost of debt, we can use Equation 11.2 to determine r_d when interest is paid annually.

11.2

$$V_d = \frac{INT}{(1 + YTM)^1} + \cdots + \frac{INT + M}{(1 + YTM)^N}$$

$$= \frac{INT}{(1 + r_d)^1} + \cdots + \frac{INT + M}{(1 + r_d)^N}$$

where INT is the dollar interest paid per period, M is the face value repaid at maturity, and N is the number of interest payments remaining until maturity.

Assume that Unilate issued a new bond five years ago. The bond has a face value of $1,000, 20 years remaining until maturity, and pays $90 interest annually. Unilate is going to issue new bonds in a couple of days that have the same general characteristics as this outstanding bond. If the current market price of the outstanding bond is $915, what should the r_d be for the new bond? We would expect that the return investors demand for the new bond should be about the same as that for the outstanding bond, because both bonds have the same characteristics. To determine the before-tax cost of debt, we can solve for r_d in the following equation:

$$\$915 = \frac{\$90}{(1 + r_d)^1} + \frac{\$90}{(1 + r_d)^2} + \cdots + \frac{\$90 + \$1,000}{(1 + r_d)^{20}}$$

Whether you use the trial-and-error method or the time value of money functions on your calculator, you should find $r_d = 10\%$, which is the before-tax cost of debt for this bond.[2] Unilate's marginal tax rate is 40 percent; so its after-tax cost of debt, r_{dT}, is $6.0\% = 10.0\%(1 - 0.40)$.

11-1b Cost of Preferred Stock, r_{ps}

In Chapter 7, we found that the dividend associated with preferred stock, which we designated D_{ps}, is constant, and that preferred stock has no stated maturity. We also discovered that we can determine the rate of return that investors require to provide funds to the firm in the form of preferred stock by solving for r_s in the model that was used to value stock with a constant growth rate equal to 0. (The annual dividend stays the same, which means it does not grow.) That is, we solved for r_s in the constant growth model, and the result was Equation 7.3. To determine the component

---

[1] If a company's tax rate is effectively zero, the cost of debt is not reduced; that is, in Equation 11.1 the tax rate equals zero, so the after-tax cost of debt is equal to the before-tax interest rate.

[2] It should also be noted that we have ignored flotation costs (the costs incurred for new issuances) on debt because nearly all debt issued by small and medium-sized firms, as well as that issued by many large firms, is privately placed, and hence has little or no flotation costs. However, if bonds are publicly placed and do involve flotation costs, the solution value of r_d in the following formula is used as the before-tax cost of debt:

$$V_d(1 - F) = \sum_{t=1}^{N} \frac{INT}{(1 + r_d)^t} + \frac{M}{(1 + r_d)^N}$$

Here F is the percentage amount (in decimal form) of the bond flotation, or issuing, cost; N is the number of periods to maturity; INT is the dollars of interest per period; M is the maturity value of the bond; and r_d is the cost of debt adjusted to reflect flotation costs. If we assume that the bond in the example calls for annual payments, that it has a 20-year maturity, and that F = 2%, then the flotation-adjusted, before-tax cost of debt is 10.23 percent (versus 10 percent before the flotation adjustment).

cost of preferred stock, which we designate r_{ps}, we apply Equation 7.3 for a stock with a growth rate equal to 0, but we adjust the current market price to reflect the fact that the firm incurs costs when it issues preferred stock to raise funds. These issuance costs, which are called *flotation costs*, reduce the amount of funds that the firm can use for financing capital budgeting projects, and thus effectively increase the rate that the firm must earn to pay the preferred dividend. In other words, flotation costs require the firm to invest funds provided by preferred stockholders at a higher rate than investors actually demand, because although the firm does not receive the entire amount that investors pay for the stock (due to flotation costs), it still must pay the same preferred dividend to all preferred stockholders. Thus, r_{ps} is computed using Equation 11.3:

11.3

$$\text{Component cost of preferred stock} = r_{ps} = \frac{D_{ps}}{P_0 - \text{Flotation costs}}$$
$$= \frac{D_{ps}}{P_0(1-F)} = \frac{D_{ps}}{NP_0}$$

Here F is the percentage cost (in decimal form) of issuing preferred stock and P_0 is the current market price of the stock.

To illustrate, although it has no preferred stock at present, Unilate plans to issue preferred stock that pays a $12.80 dividend per share and sells for $120 per share in the market. It will cost 3 percent, or $3.60 per share, to issue the new preferred stock, so Unilate will net $116.40 per share. Therefore, Unilate's cost of preferred stock is 11 percent:

$$r_{ps} = \frac{\$12.80}{\$120.00(1-0.03)} = \frac{\$12.80}{\$116.40}$$
$$= 0.11 = 11.0\%$$

No tax adjustments are made when calculating r_{ps} because preferred dividends, unlike interest expense

[3]The term *retained earnings* can be interpreted to mean either the balance sheet item "retained earnings," consisting of all the earnings retained in the business throughout its history, or the income statement item "additions to retained earnings." The income statement item is used in this chapter; for our purpose, *retained earnings* refers to that part of current earnings not paid out in dividends and hence available for reinvestment in the business this year.

[4]In reality, stockholders' preferences are also affected by the tax rates that are applied to dividends and to capital gains. If dividends are taxed at a much higher rate than capital gains, stockholders might prefer for the firm to retain earnings, even if it invests some of these funds at returns that are slightly lower than r_s. We do not consider the effects of investors' taxes on their preferences for dividends versus capital gains in this chapter. Even so, we know that investors prefer for the firm to reinvest any retained earnings at a rate that equals or exceeds r_s.

on debt, are not tax deductible, which means there is no tax savings associated with the use of preferred stock.

11-1c Cost of Retained Earnings (Internal Equity), r_s

The costs of debt and preferred stock are based on the returns investors require on these securities. Similarly, the **cost of retained earnings**, which we designate r_s, is the rate of return stockholders require on equity capital the firm "raises" by retaining earnings that otherwise could be distributed to common stockholders as dividends.[3]

The reason we must assign a cost to retained earnings involves the *opportunity cost principle.* Bondholders are compensated by interest payments and preferred stockholders are compensated by preferred dividends, so the earnings that remain after interest and preferred dividends are paid belong to the common stockholders, and these earnings help compensate these stockholders for the use of their capital. Management can either pay out the earnings in the form of dividends or retain earnings and reinvest them in the business. If management decides to retain earnings, there is an opportunity cost involved because common stockholders could have received the earnings as dividends and invested this money for themselves in other stocks, in bonds, in real estate, or in anything else. Thus, the firm should earn a return on earnings it retains that is at least as great as the return stockholders themselves could earn on alternative investments of comparable risk; otherwise, common stockholders will demand that all earnings be paid out as dividends.

What rate of return can stockholders expect to earn on equivalent-risk investments? First, recall from Chapter 8 that stocks normally are in equilibrium, with the expected rate of return, $\hat{r}_s$, equal to the required rate of return, r_s; that is, $\hat{r}_s = r_s$. Therefore, we can assume that Unilate's common stockholders expect to earn a return of r_s on their money. *If the firm cannot invest retained earnings and earn at least r_s, it should pay these funds to its common stockholders and let them invest directly in other assets (investments) that do provide this return.*[4]

Whereas debt and preferred stocks are fixed obligations that have easily determined costs, it is not as easy to measure r_s. However, we can employ the principles developed in Chapters 7 and 8 to produce reasonably good estimates of the cost of retained earnings. To begin, we know

cost of preferred stock, r_{ps} The rate of return investors require on the firm's preferred stock, r_{ps}.

cost of retained earnings, r_s The rate of return required by stockholders on a firm's existing common stock.

premium that is based on (1) the stock's relation to the market as measured by its beta coefficient, β_s, and (2) the magnitude of the market risk premium, RP_M, which is the difference between the market return, r_M, and the risk-free rate, r_{RF}.

To illustrate the CAPM approach, assume that $r_{RF} = 6\%$, $r_M = 10.5\%$, and $\beta_s = 1.6$ for Unilate's common stock. Using the CAPM approach, the return required by Unilate's common stockholders and thus its cost of retained earnings, r_s, is calculated as follows:

$$r_s = 6.0\% + (10.5\% - 6.0\%)(1.6)$$
$$= 6.0\% + 7.2\% = 13.2\%$$

that when a stock is in equilibrium (which is the typical situation), its required rate of return, r_s, is equal to its expected rate of return, $\hat{r}_s$. Further, its required return is equal to a risk-free rate, r_{RF}, plus a risk premium, RP, whereas the expected return on a constant growth stock is equal to the stock's dividend yield, $\hat{D}_1/P_0$, plus its expected growth rate, g. This relationship is shown in Equation 11.4:

11.4

Required rate of return = Expected rate of return

$$r_s = \hat{r}_s$$

$$r_{RF} + RP_s = \frac{\hat{D}_1}{P_0} + g$$

Because the two must be equal, we can estimate r_s using either the left side or the right side of Equation 11.4.

The CAPM Approach (Required Rate of Return, r_s). The capital asset pricing model (CAPM) we developed in Chapter 8 is stated as Equation 11.5:

11.5

$$r_s = r_{RF} + RP_s = r_{RF} + RP_M\beta_s = r_{RF} + (r_M - r_{RF})\beta_s$$

Equation 11.5 shows that the CAPM estimate of r_s begins with the risk-free rate, r_{RF}, to which is added a risk

Although the CAPM approach appears to yield an accurate, precise estimate of r_s, there actually are several problems with it. First, as we saw in Chapter 8, if a firm's stockholders are not well diversified, they might be concerned with total risk rather than with market risk only (measured by β). In this case, the firm's true investment risk will *not* be measured by its beta, and the CAPM procedure will understate the correct value of r_s. Further, even if the CAPM method is valid, it is difficult to obtain correct estimates of the inputs required to make it operational, because (1) there is controversy about which Treasury yields to use as a measure of r_{RF} and (2) both β_s and r_M should be estimated values, which often are difficult to obtain.

Discounted Cash Flow (DCF) Approach (Expected Rate of Return, $\hat{r}_s$). In Chapter 7, we learned that both the price and the expected rate of return on a share of common stock depend, ultimately, on the dividends the stock is expected to pay. We also discovered that, as long as the firm is growing at a constant rate, the expected rate of return of common stockholders can be determined by applying Equation 7.3. Restating Equation 7.3 in equilibrium form gives Equation 11.6, which we can use to estimate a firm's cost of retained earnings, r_s.

11.6

$$r_s = \hat{r}_s = \frac{\hat{D}_1}{P_0} + g$$

Here P_0 is the current price of the stock, $\hat{D}_1$ is the dividend that is *expected* to be paid at the end of the year (Year 1), g is the constant rate at which the firm will grow into perpetuity, and $\hat{r}_s$ is the expected rate of return.

Thus, investors expect to receive a dividend yield, $\hat{D}_1/P_0$, plus a capital gain, g, for a total expected return of $\hat{r}_s$. In equilibrium, this expected return is also equal to the required return, r_s. From this point on, we will assume that equilibrium exists, and we will use the terms r_s and $\hat{r}_s$ interchangeably, so we will drop the hat (^) above r_s.

It is relatively easy to determine the dividend yield, but it is difficult to establish the proper growth rate. If past growth rates in earnings and dividends have been relatively stable, and if investors appear to be projecting a continuation of past trends, then g can be based on the firm's historical growth rate. However, if the company's past growth has been abnormally high or low, either because of its own unique situation or because of general economic fluctuations, historical growth probably should not be used. Securities analysts regularly make earnings and dividend growth forecasts, looking at such factors as projected sales, profit margins, and competitive factors. For example, *Value Line,* which is available in most libraries, provides growth rate forecasts for approximately 1,700 companies, and Bank of America Merrill Lynch, Morgan Stanley Smith Barney, and other investment organizations make similar forecasts. Therefore, someone making a cost of capital estimate can obtain several analysts' forecasts, average them, and use the average as a proxy for the growth expectations, g.[5]

To illustrate the DCF approach, suppose Unilate's common stock currently sells for $22 per share; the common stock dividend expected to be paid in 2017 is $1.28 per share; and its expected long-term growth rate is 7.5 percent. Unilate's expected and required rate of return on retained earnings is 13.3 percent:

$$r_s = \hat{r}_s = \frac{\$1.28}{\$22.00} + 0.075$$
$$= 0.058 + 0.075 = 0.133 = 13.3\%$$

This 13.3 percent is the minimum rate of return that management must expect to earn to justify retaining earnings

[5]Analysts' growth rate forecasts are usually for five years into the future, and the rates provided represent the average growth rate over that five-year horizon. Studies have shown that analysts' forecasts represent the best source of growth rate data for DCF cost of capital estimates. See Robert Harris, "Using Analysts' Growth Rate Forecasts to Estimate Shareholder Required Rates of Return," *Financial Management,* Spring 1986, 58–67.

[6]People experienced in estimating equity capital costs recognize that both careful analysis and sound judgment are required. It would be nice to pretend that judgment is unnecessary and to specify an easy, precise way of determining the exact cost of equity capital. Unfortunately, this is not possible; finance is in large part a matter of judgment, and we simply must face that fact.

and plowing them back into the business rather than paying them out to stockholders as dividends.

Bond-Yield-Plus-Risk-Premium Approach. Empirical work suggests that the cost of retained earnings, r_s, can also be estimated by adding a risk premium of 3 to 5 percentage points to the before-tax interest rate on the firm's own long-term debt, r_d. The logic to applying this approach is that firms with risky, low-rated, and consequently high interest rate debt will also have risky, high-cost equity. Although this simplistic method is not likely to produce a precise cost of equity, it can get us into the right "ballpark." For example, Unilate's cost of equity might be estimated as follows:

$$r_s = \text{Bond YTM} + \text{Risk premium}$$
$$= 10.0\% + 4.0\% = 14.0\%$$

Because the 4 percent risk premium is a judgmental estimate, the estimated value of r_s is also judgmental.

We have described three methods to estimate the cost of retained earnings, which should be a single number. To summarize, we found the cost of common equity to be (1) 13.2 percent using the CAPM method, (2) 13.3 percent using the constant growth model (the DCF approach), and (3) 14.0 percent with the bond-yield-plus-risk-premium approach. It is not unusual to get different estimates, because each approach is based on different assumptions. The CAPM assumes investors are well diversified, the constant growth model assumes the firm's dividends and earnings will grow at a constant rate far into the future, and the bond-yield-plus-risk-premium approach assumes the cost of equity is closely related to the firm's cost of debt. Which estimate should be used? Probably all of them. Many analysts use multiple approaches to estimate a single value, then average the results. For Unilate, then, the average of the estimates is $r_s = 13.5\% = (13.2\% + 13.3\% + 14.0\%)/3$.[6]

11-1d Cost of Newly Issued Common Stock (External Equity), r_e

The cost of new common equity, or *external equity capital*, which we designate r_e, is similar to the cost of retained earnings, r_s, except it is higher because the firm incurs *flotation costs* when it issues new common stock. As mentioned earlier,

cost of new common equity, r_e The cost of external equity; based on the cost of retained earnings, but increased for flotation costs.

the **flotation costs**, which are the expenses associated with issuing new securities (equity or debt), reduce the amount of funds the firm receives, and hence the amount that can be used for investment. Only the amount of funds that is left after paying flotation costs—that is, the *net* amount received by the firm—is available for investment. As a result, *the cost of issuing new common stock (external equity), r_e, is greater than the cost of retained earnings, r_s,* because there are no flotation costs associated with retained earnings (internal equity) financing.

In general, the cost of issuing new equity, r_e, can be found by modifying the DCF formula used to compute the cost of retained earnings, r_s. Equation 11.7 shows the modified DCF formula:

11.7

$$r_e = \frac{\hat{D}_1}{NP_0} + g = \frac{\hat{D}_1}{P_0(1 - F)} + g$$

Here F is the percentage flotation cost (in decimal form) incurred in selling the new stock issue, so $P_0(1 - F)$ is the net price per share received by the company, NP_0.

If Unilate can issue new common stock at a flotation cost of 17 percent (remember from our discussion in Chapter 2 that the company's financial position is somewhat precarious), r_e is computed as follows:

$$r_e = \frac{\$1.28}{\$22.00(1 - 0.17)} + 0.075 = \frac{\$1.28}{\$18.26} + 0.075$$

$$= 0.70 + 0.075 = 0.145 = 14.5\%$$

Using the DCF approach to estimate the cost of retained earnings, we found that investors require a return of $r_s = 13.3\%$ on the stock. However, because of flotation costs, the company must earn more than 13.3 percent on funds obtained by selling stock if it is to provide stockholders a 13.3 percent return. Specifically, if the firm earns 14.5 percent on the net funds that are raised from issuing new stock, then earnings per share will not fall below previously expected earnings, the firm's expected dividend can be maintained, and, as a result, the price per share will not decline. If the firm earns less than 14.5 percent, then earnings, dividends, and growth will fall below expectations, causing the price of the stock to decline. If it earns more than 14.5 percent, the price of the stock will rise.

The reason for the flotation-cost adjustment can be made clear by a simple example. Suppose Weaver Realty Company has $100,000 of assets and no debt, it earns a 15 percent return (or $15,000) on

its assets, and it pays all earnings out as dividends, so its growth rate is zero. The company has 1,000 shares of stock outstanding, so earnings per share (EPS) and dividends per share (DPS) are the same—DPS = $15 = $15,000/1,000—and $P_0 = \$100 = \$100,000/1,000$. Weaver's cost of equity is thus $r_s = \$15/\$100 + 0 = 15.0\%$. Now suppose Weaver can get a return of 15 percent on new assets. Should it sell new stock to acquire new assets? If it sold 1,000 new shares of stock to the public for $100 per share, but it incurred a 10 percent flotation cost on the issue, it would net $100 - 0.10(\$100) = \$90$ per share, or $90,000 in total. It would then invest this $90,000 and earn 15 percent, or $13,500. Its new *total* earnings would be $28,500, which would consist of $15,000 generated from the old assets plus $13,500 from the new assets. However, the $28,500 would have to be distributed equally to the 2,000 shares of stock now outstanding. Therefore, Weaver's EPS and DPS would decline from $15 to $14.25 = $28,500/2,000. Because its EPS and DPS would fall, the price of the stock would also fall from $P_0 = \$100$ to $P_1 = \$14.25/0.15 = \$95.00$. This result occurs because investors have put up $100 per share, but the company received and invested only $90 per share. Thus, we see that the $90 must earn more than 15 percent (be put to work harder) to provide investors with a 15 percent return on the $100 they put up.

We can use Equation 11.7 to compute the return Weaver must earn on the $90,000 of new assets it purchases—that is, the amount it raises with the new issue:

$$r_e = \frac{\$15}{\$100(1 - 0.10)} + 0.0 = 0.1667 = 16.67\%$$

If Weaver invests the funds from the new common stock issue at 16.67 percent, here is what would happen:

$$\left(\begin{array}{c}\text{New } total \\ \text{earnings}\end{array}\right) = \left(\begin{array}{c}\text{Earnings from} \\ \textit{existing} \text{ assets}\end{array}\right) + \left(\begin{array}{c}\text{Earnings from} \\ \textit{new} \text{ assets}\end{array}\right)$$

$$= \quad \$15,000 \quad + \$90,000(0.16667)$$

$$= \quad \$30,000$$

$$\left(\begin{array}{c}\text{New EPS} \\ \text{and DPS}\end{array}\right) = \frac{\$30,000}{2,000} = \$15$$

$$\text{New price} = \frac{\$15}{0.15} = \$100$$

Thus, if the return on the new assets is equal to r_e as calculated by Equation 11.7, then EPS, DPS, and the stock price will all remain constant. If the return on the new assets exceeds r_e, then EPS, DPS, and P_0 will rise. Because of flotation costs, the cost of external equity exceeds the cost of equity raised internally from retained earnings—that is, $r_e > r_s$. If F = 0 (which is unlikely), however, then $r_e = r_s$.

11-2 Weighted Average Cost of Capital (WACC)

It is possible to finance a firm entirely with equity funds by issuing only common stock. In that case, the cost of capital used to analyze capital budgeting decisions should be the company's required return on common equity. However, most firms raise a substantial portion of their funds as long-term debt, and some also use preferred stock. For these firms, their cost of capital must reflect the average cost of the various sources of long-term funds used, not just the firms' costs of common equity.

Suppose that a firm has an 8 percent cost of debt and a 12 percent cost of equity. Further, assume that the company has decided to finance next year's projects by selling debt only. The argument is sometimes made that the cost of capital for these projects is 8 percent because only debt will be used to finance them. However, this position is incorrect. If the company finances a particular set of projects with debt only, the firm will be using up some of its potential for obtaining new debt in the future. As expansion occurs in subsequent years, the company will at some point find it necessary to raise additional equity to prevent the proportion of debt from becoming too large. For example, consider what would happen if the company borrows heavily at 8 percent during 2016, using up its debt capacity in the process, to finance projects yielding 10 percent. If it has new projects available in 2017 that yield 11.5 percent, which is above the return on 2016 projects, it cannot accept them because they would have to be financed with 12 percent equity funds. To avoid this problem, the company should be viewed as an ongoing operation, and *the cost of capital used in capital budgeting should be calculated as a weighted average, or combination, of the various types of funds generally used, regardless of the specific financing used to fund a particular project.*

11-2a Determining WACC

Each firm has an optimal capital structure—a mix of debt, preferred stock, and common equity that causes its stock price to be maximized. Therefore, a rational,

value-maximizing firm will establish a **target (optimal) capital structure** and then raise new capital in a manner that will keep the actual capital structure on target over time. In this chapter, we assume that the firm has identified its optimal capital structure, it uses this optimum as the target, and it raises funds so it constantly remains on target. How the target is established will be examined in Chapter 12.

The target proportions of debt, preferred stock, and common equity, along with the component costs of capital, are used to calculate the firm's **weighted average cost of capital (WACC)**. The WACC simply represents the average cost of each dollar of financing, no matter its source, that the firm uses to purchase assets. That is, *WACC represents the minimum rate of return the firm must earn on its investments (assets) to maintain its current level of wealth.*

To illustrate, suppose Unilate Textiles has determined that in the future it will raise new capital according to the following proportions: 45 percent debt, 5 percent preferred stock, and 50 percent common equity (retained earnings plus new common stock). In the preceding sections, we found that its before-tax cost of debt, r_d, is 10 percent, so its *after-tax* cost of debt, r_{dT}, is 6 percent; its cost of preferred stock, r_{ps}, is 11 percent; and its cost of common equity, r_s, is 13.5 percent if all of its common equity financing comes from retained earnings. Now we can calculate Unilate's weighted average cost of capital (WACC) using Equation 11.8:

11.8

$$\text{WACC} = w_d\,(r_{dT}) + w_{ps}\,(r_{ps}) + w_s\,(r_s)$$

Here w_d, w_{ps}, and w_s represent the proportions (weights) of debt, preferred stock, and common equity, respectively, that make up the firm's target capital structure; and, as previously

target (optimal) capital structure The combination (percentages) of debt, preferred stock, and common equity that will maximize the price of the firm's stock.

weighted average cost of capital (WACC) A weighted average of the component costs of debt, preferred stock, and common equity.

described, r_{dT} is the after-tax cost of debt, r_{ps} is the cost of preferred stock, and r_s is the cost of common equity (cost of retained earnings or cost of new equity).

Every dollar of new capital that Unilate obtains consists of $0.45 of debt with an after-tax cost of 6 percent, $0.05 of preferred stock with a cost of 11 percent, and $0.50 of common equity with a cost of 13.5 percent (if all of the common equity funds come from additions to retained earnings). The company's WACC is calculated as follows:

$$WACC = 0.45(6.0\%) + 0.05(11.0\%) + 0.50(13.5\%) = 10.0\%$$

The average cost of each whole dollar, WACC, is 10 percent as long as these conditions continue. If the component costs of capital change when new funds are raised in the future, then WACC changes. We discuss changes in the component costs of capital in the next section.

Determining a firm's WACC is more complicated than simply plugging numbers into Equation 11.8 and performing the math. Most large firms issue different types of debt as well as different classes of common stock that have different component costs, so that there is neither a single cost of debt nor a single cost of common equity. As a result, in practice, the cost of debt, r_d, that is used to compute the firm's WACC is a weighted average of the costs of the various types of debt the firm has issued. Similarly, when a firm raises capital by issuing new common stock, the total amount of equity capital often includes both the amount of earnings retained during the year and the amount raised with the new common stock issue, which means the cost of common equity should be a weighted average of r_s and r_e. To simplify our discussions and the subsequent computations, however, we assume that (1) the firm issues only one type of bond each time it raises new funds using debt and (2) when new common stock is issued, the average cost to the firm for *all* common equity used to finance new investments is the cost of the new common stock, r_e, even if retained earnings have provided some of the common equity capital.

11-2b The Marginal Cost of Capital (MCC)

The marginal cost of any item is the cost of adding another unit of that item. For example, the marginal cost of labor is the cost of adding one additional worker. The marginal cost of labor might be $25 per person if 10 workers are added, but $35 per person if the firm tries to hire 100 new workers because it will be harder to find that many people willing and able to do the work. The same concept applies to capital. As the firm tries to attract additional new dollars, at some point the cost of each dollar will increase. Thus, the marginal cost of capital (MCC) is defined as *the weighted average cost (WACC) of the last dollar of new capital that the firm raises,* and the marginal cost rises as more and more capital is raised during a given period.

In the preceding section, we computed Unilate's WACC to be 10 percent. As long as Unilate keeps its capital structure on target, and as long as its debt has an after-tax cost of 6 percent, its preferred stock has a cost of 11 percent, and its common equity in the form of retained earnings has a cost of 13.5 percent, its weighted average cost of capital will be 10 percent. Each dollar the firm raises will consist of some long-term debt, some preferred stock, and some common equity, and the cost of the whole dollar will be 10 percent; that is, its marginal cost of capital (MCC) will average 10 percent.

11-2c The MCC Schedule

A graph that shows how the WACC changes as more and more new capital is raised by the firm is called the MCC (marginal cost of capital) schedule. Figure 11.1 shows Unilate's MCC schedule if the cost of debt, cost of preferred stock, and cost of common equity *never change.* Here the dots represent dollars raised, and because each dollar of new capital will have an average cost equal to 10 percent, the marginal cost of capital (MCC) for Unilate is constant at 10 percent under the assumptions we have used to this point.

Do you think Unilate actually could raise an unlimited amount of new capital at the 10 percent cost? Probably not. As a practical matter, as a company raises larger and larger amounts of funds during a given time period, the costs of those funds begin to rise, and as this occurs, the WACC of each new dollar also rises. Thus, companies cannot raise unlimited amounts of capital at a constant cost. At some point, the cost of each new dollar will increase, no matter what its source—debt, preferred stock, or common equity.

How much can Unilate raise before the cost of its funds increases? As a first step in determining the point at which the MCC begins to rise, recognize that although the company's balance sheet

FIGURE 11.1

MARGINAL COST OF CAPITAL (MCC) SCHEDULE FOR UNILATE TEXTILES

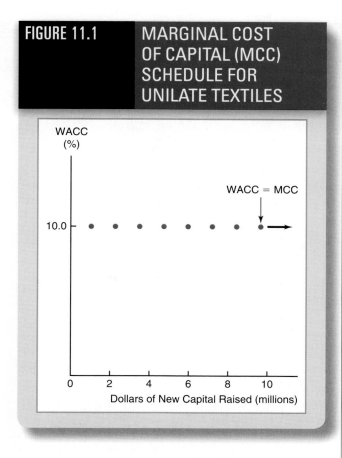

Earlier, we determined that the cost of issuing new common stock, r_e, will be 14.5 percent, because the flotation costs associated with the new issue will be 17 percent. Because the cost of common equity increases when common stock must be issued, the WACC also increases at that point.

How much new capital can Unilate raise before it exhausts its retained earnings and is forced to sell new common stock? In other words, where will an increase in the MCC schedule occur? Suppose that Unilate's 2017 net income will be $61 million and that $30.5 million will be paid out as dividends so that $30.5 million will be added to retained earnings (the payout ratio is 50 percent). In this case, Unilate can invest in capital projects to the point where the *common equity needs* equal $30.5 million before new common stock must be issued. Remember, though, that when Unilate needs new funds, the target capital structure indicates that only 50 percent of the total should be common equity; the remainder of the funds should come from issues of bonds (45 percent) and preferred stock (5 percent). Thus, we know that

Common equity = 0.50 × Total new capital raised

We can use this relationship to determine how much *total new capital*—that is, the combination of debt, preferred stock, and retained earnings—can be raised before the $30.5 million of retained earnings is exhausted and Unilate is forced to sell new common stock. Simply solve the following relationship:

$$\text{Retained earnings} = \$30.5 \text{ million}$$

$$= 0.50\left(\text{Total new capital raised}\right)$$

$$\left(\text{Total new capital raised}\right) = \frac{\$30.5 \text{ million}}{0.50} = \$61.0 \text{ million}$$

Thus, Unilate can raise a *total* of $61 million before it has to sell new common stock to finance new capital projects.

If Unilate needs exactly $61 million in new capital, the breakdown of the amount that would come from each source of capital would be as follows:

shows total long-term capital of $715 million at the end of 2016, all of this capital was raised in the past, and these funds have been invested in assets that are now being used in current operations. If Unilate raises new (marginal) capital based on its target capital structure—that is, 45 percent debt, 5 percent preferred stock, and 50 percent common equity—then to raise $1,000,000 in new capital, the company should issue $450,000 of new debt, $50,000 of new preferred stock, and $500,000 of additional common equity. The additional common equity could come from two sources: (1) retained earnings, defined as that part of the *current* year's profits that management decides to retain in the business rather than pay out as dividends (but not earnings retained in the past, because these amounts have already been invested in existing assets); or (2) proceeds from the sale of new common stock.

We know that Unilate's WACC will be 10 percent as long as the after-tax cost of debt is 6 percent, the cost of preferred stock is 11 percent, and the funds needed from common equity can be satisfied by retained earnings with a cost of 13.5 percent (r_s = 13.5%). But what happens if Unilate expands so rapidly that the retained earnings for the year are not sufficient to meet the common equity needs, forcing the firm to sell new common stock?

Capital Source	Weight, w	Amount ($ Millions)	Component Cost, r
Debt	0.45	$27.45	6.0%
Preferred stock	0.05	3.05	11.0
Common equity	0.50	30.50	13.5
	1.00	$61.00	

For this situation, the computation for the weighted average cost of capital (WACC) is:

$$\text{WACC} = 0.45(6.0\%) + 0.05(11.0\%) + 0.50(13.5\%)$$
$$= 10.0\%$$

Therefore, if Unilate needs *exactly* $61 million in new capital in 2017, retained earnings will be just enough to satisfy the common equity requirement, which means the firm will not need to sell new common stock and its weighted average cost of capital (WACC) will be 10 percent. But what will happen if Unilate needs more than $61 million in new capital? If Unilate needs $64 million, for example, the $30.5 million of retained earnings will not be sufficient to cover the $32 million common equity requirement (50 percent of the total *new* funds), so new common stock will have to be sold. The cost of issuing new common stock, r_e, is greater than the cost of retained earnings, r_s; hence, the WACC will be greater.

If Unilate raises $64 million in new capital, the breakdown of the amount that would come from each source of capital would be as follows:

Capital Source	Weight, w	Amount ($ Millions)	Component Cost, r
Debt	0.45	$28.80	6.0%
Preferred stock	0.05	3.20	11.0
Common equity	0.50	32.00	14.5
	1.00	$64.00	

For this situation, the computation for the weighted average cost of capital (WACC) is:

$$\text{WACC} = 0.45(6.0\%) + 0.05(11.0\%) + 0.50(14.5\%)$$
$$= 10.5\%$$

The WACC will be greater in this situation because Unilate will have to sell new common stock, which has a higher component cost than retained earnings (14.5 percent versus 13.5 percent). Consequently, if Unilate's capital budgeting needs are greater than $61 million, new common stock will need to be sold, and its WACC will increase. The $61 million in total new capital is defined

break point (BP) The dollar value of new capital that can be raised before an increase in the firm's weighted average cost of capital occurs.

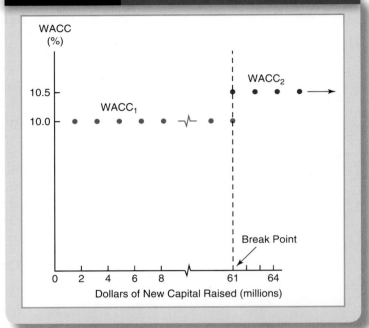

FIGURE 11.2 MARGINAL COST OF CAPITAL (MCC) SCHEDULE FOR UNILATE TEXTILES USING RETAINED EARNINGS AND NEW COMMON STOCK

as the *retained earnings break point,* because above this amount of total capital, a break, or jump, in Unilate's MCC schedule occurs. In general, a **break point (BP)** is defined as the last dollar of *new total capital* that can be raised *before* an increase in the firm's WACC occurs.

Figure 11.2 graphs Unilate's marginal cost of capital schedule with the retained earnings break point. Because the amount of retained earnings is sufficient to satisfy the common equity portion of total funds as long as financing needs range from $1 to $61 million, each dollar raised within this range has a weighted average cost of 10.0 percent. However, if Unilate raises one dollar over $61 million, each new dollar will contain $0.50 of equity *obtained by selling new common stock at a cost of 14.5 percent.* As a result, WACC jumps from 10.0 percent to 10.5 percent, as calculated previously and shown in Table 11.1.

At this point, we must note two important facts:

▶ Unilate's cost of equity will not actually jump from 13.5 percent to 14.5 percent when $0.50 of new equity is issued. In reality, the cost of common equity would only increase marginally. However, to simplify our discussion and computations, we assume that

Table 11.1
WACC and Break Points for Unilate's MCC Schedule

I. Break Points

1. $BP_{\text{retained earnings}} = \$30,500,000/0.50 = \$61,000,000$

2. $BP_{\text{debt}} = \$54,000,000/0.45 = \$120,000,000$

II. Weighted Average Cost of Capital (WACC)

1. If the firm's new capital needs range from $1 to $61,000,000

Capital Source	Breakdown of Funds if $61,000,000 Is Raised	Weight of Capital	×	After-Tax Component Cost	=	WACC
Debt, r_{dT1}	$27,450,000	0.45	×	6.0%	=	2.70%
Preferred stock, r_{ps}	3,050,000	0.05	×	11.0	=	0.55
Common equity, r_s	30,500,000	0.50	×	13.5	=	6.75
	$61,000,000	1.00				10.00% = WACC$_1$

2. If the firm's new capital needs range from $61,000,001 to $120,000,000

Capital Source	Breakdown of Funds if $120,000,000 Is Raised	Weight of Capital	×	After-Tax Component Cost	=	WACC
Debt, r_{dT1}	$ 54,000,000	0.45	×	6.0%	=	2.70%
Preferred stock, r_{ps}	6,000,000	0.05	×	11.0	=	0.55
Common equity, r_e	60,000,000	0.50	×	14.5	=	7.25
	$120,000,000	1.00				10.50% = WACC$_2$

3. If the firm's new capital needs are greater than $120,000,000

Capital Source	Breakdown of Funds if $130,000,000 Is Raised	Weight of Capital	×	After-Tax Component Cost	=	WACC
Debt, r_{dT2}	$ 58,500,000	0.45	×	7.1%	=	3.20%
Preferred stock, r_{ps}	6,500,000	0.05	×	11.0	=	0.55
Common equity, r_e	65,000,000	0.50	×	14.5	=	7.25
	$130,000,000	1.00				11.00% = WACC$_3$

NOTE: Each boxed number indicates which component cost differs from the WACC that is computed in the previous range. For example, if the amount of funds that Unilate needs to raise is from $61,000,001 to $120,000,000, new common equity must be issued, and thus equity will have a cost, r_e, equal to 14.5 percent, which is greater than the cost of equity if the firm needs funds equal to $61,000,000 or less ($r_s$ = 13.5%). Remember that the break point associated with retained earnings is $61,000,000; so at this point the amount of retained earnings is "used up."

once Unilate issues common stock, no matter the amount, the cost of equity increases so that the average cost of each dollar of equity is 14.5 percent even though the common equity financing also includes some retained earnings. For further simplification, we apply this same logic to all types of capital.

▶ Because we really don't think the MCC jumps by precisely 0.5 percent when we raise $1 over $61 million, Figure 11.2 should be regarded as an approximation rather than as a precise representation of reality. We will return to this point later in the chapter.

11-2d Other Breaks in the MCC Schedule

There is a jump, or break, in Unilate's MCC schedule at $61 million of new capital because new common stock must be sold. Could there be other breaks in the schedule? Yes, there could. For example, suppose Unilate can obtain only $54 million of debt at a before-tax cost of 10 percent, with any additional debt costing 11.85 percent (before taxes). This would result in a second break point in the MCC schedule, at the point where the $54 million of 10 percent debt is exhausted. At what amount of *total financing* would the 10 percent debt be used up? We know that this total financing will amount to $54 million of debt plus some amount of preferred stock and common equity. If we let BP_{Debt} represent the total financing at this break point for debt, then we know that 45 percent of BP_{Debt} will be debt, so

$$0.45\ (BP_{Debt}) = \$54\ \text{million}$$

Solving for BP_{Debt}, we have

$$BP_{debt} = \frac{\text{Maximum amount of 10\% debt}}{\text{Proportion of debt}}$$

$$= \frac{\$54\ \text{million}}{0.45} = \$120\ \text{million}$$

As you can see, in this case, there will be another break in the MCC schedule after Unilate has raised a total of $120 million, and this second break will result from an increase in the cost of debt. The higher after-tax cost of debt ($r_{dT2} = 11.85\%(1 - 0.4) = 7.1\%$ versus $r_{dT1} = 10\%(1 - 0.4) = 6.0\%$) will result in a higher WACC. For example, if Unilate raises $130 million to fund new capital budgeting projects, the amount of each source of capital that must be issued is:

Capital Source	Weight, w	Amount ($ millions)	Component Cost, r
Debt	0.45	$ 58.50	7.1%
Preferred stock	0.05	6.50	11.0
Common equity	0.50	65.00	14.5
	1.00	$130.00	

For this situation, the computation for the weighted average cost of capital (WACC) is:

WACC = 0.45(7.1%) + 0.05(11.0%) + 0.50(14.5%)
    = 11.0%

[7]The first break point is not necessarily the point at which retained earnings are used up; it is possible for low-cost debt to be exhausted *before* retained earnings have been used up. For example, if Unilate had available only $22.5 million of 10 percent debt, BP_{Debt} would occur at $50 million:

$$BP_{Debt} = \frac{\$22.5\ \text{million}}{0.45} = \$50\ \text{million}$$

Thus, the break point for debt would occur before the break point for retained earnings, which occurs at $61 million.

In other words, the next dollar beyond $120 million will consist of $0.45 of 11.85 percent debt (7.1 percent after taxes), $0.05 of 11 percent preferred stock, and $0.50 of new common stock at a cost of 14.5 percent (retained earnings were used up much earlier), and this marginal dollar will have a cost of $WACC_3 = 11\%$.

The effect of this second WACC increase is shown in Figure 11.3. Now there are two break points, one caused by using up all the retained earnings and the other caused by using up all the 6 percent debt (after-tax cost). With the two breaks, there are three different WACCs: $WACC_1 = 10.0\%$ for the first $61 million of new capital; $WACC_2 = 10.5\%$ in the interval between $61 million and $120 million; and $WACC_3 = 11.0\%$ for all new capital beyond $120 million.

There could, of course, still be more break points; they would occur if the cost of debt continued to increase with more debt, if the cost of preferred stock increased at some level(s), or if the cost of common equity rose as more new common stock was sold.[7] In general, a break point will occur whenever the cost of one (or more) of the capital components increases, and thus a break point can be determined by applying Equation 11.9:

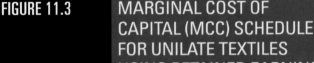

FIGURE 11.3 — MARGINAL COST OF CAPITAL (MCC) SCHEDULE FOR UNILATE TEXTILES USING RETAINED EARNINGS, NEW COMMON STOCK, AND HIGHER-COST DEBT

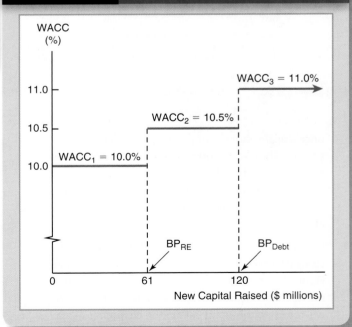

11.9

$$\text{Break point} = \frac{\left(\begin{array}{c}\text{Maximum amount of } lower \text{ cost} \\ \text{of capital of a given type}\end{array}\right)}{\left(\begin{array}{c}\text{Proportion of that type of capital} \\ \text{in the capital structure}\end{array}\right)}$$

As you can imagine, numerous break points are possible. At the extreme, an MCC schedule might have so many break points that it rises almost continuously beyond some given level of new financing.

The easiest sequence for calculating MCC schedules is as follows:

1. Use Equation 11.9 to determine each point at which a break occurs. A break will occur any time the cost of one of the capital components rises. (It is possible, however, that two capital components could increase at the same point.) After determining the exact break points, make a list of them.

2. Determine the cost of capital for each component in the intervals between breaks.

3. Calculate the weighted averages of these component costs to obtain the WACCs in each interval, as we did in Table 11.1. The WACC is constant within each interval, but it rises at each break point.

Notice that if there are n separate breaks, there will be n + 1 different WACCs. For example, in Figure 11.3 we see two breaks and three different WACCs. We should note again that a different MCC schedule will result if a different capital structure—that is, proportions of debt and equity—is used.

11-3 Combining the MCC and Investment Opportunity Schedules (IOS)

Now that we have calculated the MCC schedule, we can use it to develop a discount rate (required rate of return) for

use in the capital budgeting process—that is, *we can use the MCC schedule to find the appropriate cost of capital for determining projects' net present values (NPVs)* as discussed in Chapter 9.

To understand how the MCC schedule is used in capital budgeting, assume that Unilate Textiles has three financial executives: a financial vice president (VP), a treasurer, and a director of capital budgeting (DCB). The financial VP asks the treasurer to develop the firm's MCC schedule, and the treasurer produces the schedule shown in Figure 11.3. At the same time, the financial VP asks the DCB to draw up a list of all projects that are potentially acceptable. The list shows each project's cost, projected annual net cash inflows, life, and internal rate of return (IRR). These data are presented at the bottom of Figure 11.4. For example, Project A has a cost of $39 million, it is expected to produce inflows of $9 million per year for six years, and, therefore,

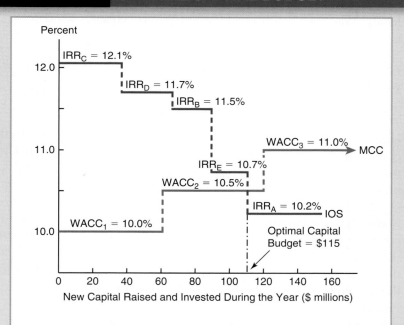

FIGURE 11.4 COMBINING THE MCC AND IOS SCHEDULES TO DETERMINE THE OPTIMAL CAPITAL BUDGET

Project	Initial Cost ($ millions)	Annual Net Cash Flows ($ millions)	Life (years)	IRR (%)
A	$39	$9	6	10.2%
B	25	6	6	11.5
C	36	10	5	12.1
D	29	7	6	11.7
E	25	8	4	10.7

it has an IRR of 10.2 percent. Similarly, Project C has a cost of $36 million, it is expected to produce inflows of $10 million per year for five years, and thus it has an IRR of 12.1 percent. (NPVs cannot be shown yet because we do not know the appropriate marginal cost of capital.) For simplicity, we assume now that all projects are independent as opposed to mutually exclusive, that they are equally risky, and that their risks are all equal to those of the firm's average existing assets.

The DCB then plots the IRR data shown at the bottom of Figure 11.4 as the **investment opportunity schedule (IOS)** shown in the graph. The IOS schedule shows, in rank order, how much money Unilate can invest at different rates of return (IRRs). Figure 11.4 also shows Unilate's MCC schedule as it was developed by the treasurer and plotted in Figure 11.3. Now consider Project C: Its IRR is 12.1 percent, and it can be financed with capital that costs only 10.0 percent. Consequently, it should be accepted. Recall from Chapter 9 that if a project's IRR exceeds the firm's cost of capital, its NPV will be positive; therefore, Project C must also be acceptable by the NPV criterion. Projects B, D, and E can be analyzed similarly. They are all acceptable because IRR > MCC = WACC, and hence NPV > 0. Project A, on the other hand, should be rejected because IRR_A < MCC; hence, NPV_A < 0.

People sometimes ask this question: "If we took Project A first, it would be acceptable because its 10.2 percent return would exceed the 10.0 percent cost of money used to finance it. Why couldn't we do this?" The answer is that we are seeking, in effect, to maximize the excess of *returns over costs*, or the area that is above the WACC but below the IOS. We accomplish this by graphing (and accepting) the most profitable projects first.

Another question that often arises is this: What would happen if the MCC cut through one of the projects? For example, suppose the second break point in the MCC schedule had occurred at $100 million rather than at $120 million, causing the MCC schedule to cut through Project E. Should we then accept Project E? If Project E could be accepted in part, we would purchase only the portion that caused the total capital budget to equal $100 million, which means we would purchase only $10 million of Project E.

investment opportunity schedule (IOS) A graph of the firm's investment opportunities ranked in order of the projects' internal rates of return.

The preceding analysis as summarized in Figure 11.4 reveals a very important point: *The cost of capital used in the capital budgeting process, as discussed in Chapters 9 and 10, actually is determined at the intersection of the IOS and MCC schedules. If the cost of capital at the intersection ($WACC_2$ = 10.5% in Figure 11.4) is used, then the firm will make correct accept/reject decisions, and its level of financing and investment will be optimal. If it uses any other rate, its capital budget will not be optimal.* This rationale follows the general economic principle that a firm should continue to manufacture and sell products to the point where marginal costs equal marginal revenues. Using this same logic, a firm should continue to invest in capital budgeting projects until its marginal cost of capital, MCC, equals the marginal return generated by the last project purchased, which is measured by the project's IRR.

The WACC intersection as determined in Figure 11.4 should be used to find the NPVs of new projects that are about as risky as the firm's existing assets, but this cost of capital should be adjusted up or down to find NPVs for projects with higher or lower risks than the average project. This point was discussed in Chapter 10 in connection with the Home Energy Products appliance-control computer example.

11-4 WACC versus Required Rate of Return of Investors

We introduced the concept of risk and rates of return in Chapter 8, where we discovered that investors demand higher rates of return to compensate them for taking higher levels of risk. In Chapters 6 and 7, we discovered that, everything else equal, an asset's value is inversely related to the rate of return investors require to invest in it. The following equation, with which you should be familiar by now, shows this relationship:

$$\text{Value} = \frac{\hat{CF}_1}{(1+r)^1} + \frac{\hat{CF}_2}{(1+r)^2} + \cdots + \frac{\hat{CF}_n}{(1+r)^n}$$

$$= \sum_{t=1}^{n} \frac{\hat{CF}_t}{(1+r)^t}$$

This equation shows that the value of any asset—real or financial—is based on (1) the cash flows that the asset is expected to generate during its life, $\hat{CF}_t$; and (2) the

Timurpix/Shutterstock.com

rate of return that investors require to "put up" their money to purchase the investment (asset), r. As a result, we know that investors purchase a firm's stocks and bonds—and thus provide funds to the firm—only if they expect to receive a return that sufficiently compensates them for the risk associated with those stocks and bonds. Consequently, *the investors who purchase a firm's stocks and bonds determine the rates of return, or costs, that the firm must pay to raise funds to invest in capital budgeting projects.*

In Chapters 6 and 7, we discussed valuation from the standpoint of investors. For example, we described r_s as the required rate of return of investors—that is, the rate of return investors demand to purchase the firm's common stock and thus provide funds to the firm. In this chapter, we described r_s as the cost of internal common equity, which represents the return that the firm must earn to satisfy investors' demands when it retains earnings for reinvestment in assets. Which description is correct? They both are. This point can be illustrated with a simple analogy. Assume

that Randy borrows money from his credit union to invest in common stocks. The loan agreement requires Randy to repay the amount borrowed plus 10 percent interest at the end of one year. The 10 percent interest rate represents both Randy's cost of borrowing—that is, cost of debt—and his required rate of return (assuming that this is his only debt). If he does not invest the borrowed funds in stocks that earn at least a 10 percent return—that is, have internal rates of return (IRRs) greater than 10 percent—then Randy will lose wealth because he has to pay the credit union 10 percent interest to use the money, regardless of what he does with the funds. The 10 percent interest rate also represents the return the credit union demands to lend money to Randy based on his credit risk; that is, 10 percent is the credit union's required rate of return. Although the situation is much more complex, this same relationship exists for firms that use funds provided by investors. Investors are similar to the credit union in the sense that they provide funds to the firms, whereas firms are similar to Randy in the sense that they use the funds provided by investors and must pay a return that is sufficient to raise (attract) such funds. Moreover, just as the credit union determines the interest rate that Randy must pay for his loan, investors determine the rates that firms must pay to use their funds.

As mentioned in Chapters 6–8, our discussions were presented primarily from the perspective of investors, whereas in this chapter we used the information introduced in these earlier chapters to explain the concept of cost of capital, which was discussed from the perspective of the firm. You should have noticed that the general concepts presented in this chapter are the same as the general concepts presented in Chapters 6–8; that is, determination of required rates of return and of their impact on value. In reality, all of these chapters present the same relationships from two perspectives: the investor's (Chapters 6–8) and the firm's (this chapter). In other words, the rates of return, or component costs of capital, discussed in this chapter are the same rates that were introduced in Chapters 6–8. For this reason, we thought it might be a good idea to summarize these rates here. Table 11.2 shows the rates of return discussed in Chapters 6–8 and compares them to the component costs of capital discussed in this chapter. Note that the equations shown in the column labeled "Return to Investors" are the same as those shown in the column labeled "Cost to Firms," except for adjustments for taxes and flotation costs.

Table 11.2

WACC versus Investors' Required Rates of Return

Investor's Required Rate of Return = Firm's Cost of Capital

$$\underset{\text{rate of return}}{\text{Investor's required}} = r = r_{RF} + \begin{bmatrix} \text{Risk} \\ \text{premium} \end{bmatrix} = r_d, r_{ps}, \text{ or } r_s = \underset{\text{cost of capital}}{\text{Firm's component}}$$

Financial Asset	Financial Asset's Market Value	Return to Investors	Cost to Firms
Debt, r_d	$P_0 = \dfrac{INT}{(1 + YTM)^1} + \cdots + \dfrac{INT + M}{(1 + YTM)^N}$	$YTM = r_d = $ Return investors require to purchase the firm's debt	$r_d = YTM = $ Before-tax cost of debt $r_{dT} = r_d(1-T) = $ After-tax cost of debt
Preferred stock, r_{ps}	$P_0 = \dfrac{D_{PS}}{r_{PS}}$	$r_{PS} = \dfrac{D_{PS}}{P_0} = $ Return investors require to purchase the firm's preferred stock	$r_{PS} = \dfrac{D_{PS}}{P_0(1 - F)} = $ Cost of preferred stock
Common equity, r_s (internal) or r_e (external)	$P_0 = \dfrac{\hat{D}_1}{r_s - g} = $; (constant growth firm)	$r_S = \dfrac{\hat{D}_1}{P_0} + g = $ Return investors require to purchase the firm's common stock	$r_S = \dfrac{\hat{D}_1}{P_0} + g = $ Cost of retained earnings (internal) $r_e = \dfrac{\hat{D}_1}{P_0(1 - F)} + g = $ Cost of new common equity (external)

Variable Definitions:

r_{RF} = nominal risk-free rate of return

P_0 = current market value of financial asset

INT = dollar interest payment

M = maturity (face) value of a bond

N = number of remaining interest payments

YTM = yield to maturity = r_d

g = constant growth rate of the firm

T = firm's marginal tax rate

D_{ps} = preferred stock dividend

$\hat{D}_1$ = next period's common stock dividend

F = cost of issuing new stock (in decimal form)

STUDY TOOLS

LOCATED AT BACK OF THE TEXTBOOK

☐ Problems are found at the end of this chapter.

☐ A tear-out Chapter Review card is located at the back of the textbook.

LOCATED AT WWW.CENGAGEBRAIN.COM

☐ Review Key Term flashcards and create your own cards.

☐ Track your knowledge and understanding of key concepts in corporate finance.

☐ Complete practice and graded quizzes to prepare for tests.

☐ Complete interactive content within CFIN5 Online.

☐ View the chapter highlight boxes for CFIN5 Online.

KEY COST OF CAPITAL CONCEPTS

To conclude this chapter, we summarize some cost of capital concepts (rules) that were discussed.

- To make appropriate capital budgeting decisions, the firm must know its required rate of return, which is defined as the average rate of return that the firm pays to attract investors' funds. Because the firm pays the average rate of return to investors who provide its long-term funds (capital), the firm's required rate of return is also referred to as its cost of capital.

- To determine its required rate of return, the firm must compute the cost of each source of funds or capital that investors provide; that is, the firm must compute the cost of debt, the cost of preferred stock, the cost of retained earnings, and the cost of new common equity. These costs are then combined by weighting each component by the proportion or weight that it contributes to the total capital of the firm. The result is the weighted average cost of capital, or WACC, which is the required rate of return that the firm should use when making capital budgeting decisions.

- Investors who participate in the financial markets determine firms' WACCs. Investors only provide funds to firms if they expect to earn sufficient returns on their investments; thus, firms must pay investors' demands (required returns) to attract funds.

- When investing in capital budgeting projects, a firm should follow the economics principle that asserts products should continue to be manufactured until marginal costs equal marginal revenues. That is, the firm should invest until the marginal cost of capital (marginal costs) equals the internal rate of return on the last project that is purchased (marginal revenues).

PROBLEMS

11–1 Global Products plans to issue long-term bonds to raise funds to finance its growth. The company has existing bonds outstanding that are similar to the new bonds it expects to issue. The existing bonds have a face value equal to $1,000, mature in 10 years, pay $60 interest annually, and are currently selling for $1,077 each. Global's marginal tax rate is 40 percent. (a) What should be the coupon rate on the new bond issue? (a) What is Global's after-tax cost of debt?

11–2 Notable Nothings plans to issue new bonds with the same yield as its existing bonds. The existing bonds have a coupon rate of interest equal to 5.6 percent (semiannual interest payments), 12 years remaining until maturity, and a $1,000 maturity value; they are currently selling for $918 each. (a) If Notable issues new bonds today, what will be its before-tax cost of debt? (b) What will be its before-tax cost of debt if the price of its existing bonds is $730 when Notable issues the new bonds?

11–3 Buoyant Cruises plans to issue preferred stock with a $120 par value and a 5 percent dividend. Even though the current market value of its preferred stock is $80 per share, Buoyant expects to net only $75 for each share issued. What is its cost of issuing preferred stock? The firm's marginal tax rate is 34 percent.

11–4 Jumbo Juice's preferred stock pays a constant dividend equal to $4.75 per share. The firm's marginal tax rate is 40 percent. Jumbo Juice incurs a 5 percent flotation cost each time it issues preferred stock. (a) If the firm issues 10,000 shares of preferred stock at $50 per share, how much of the total value of the issue will the firm be able to use (receive)? (b) What is Jumbo Juice's cost of preferred stock?

11–5 Suppose the current risk-free rate of return is 3.5 percent and the expected market return is 9 percent. Fashion Faux-Pas' common stock has a beta coefficient equal to 1.4. Using the CAPM approach, compute the firm's cost of retained earnings.

11–6 Suppose the current risk-free rate of return is 5 percent and the expected market *risk premium* is 7 percent. Using this information, estimate the cost of retained earnings for a company with a beta coefficient equal to 2.0?

11-7 Energetic Engines is trying to estimate its cost of retained earnings. The company has outstanding bonds that pay $20 interest every six months. The bonds, which have a $1,000 face value and mature in six years, are currently selling for $900. Estimate Energetic's cost of retained earnings using the bond-plus-risk-premium approach.

11-8 Tip Top Hats (TTH) is expected to grow at a 4 percent rate for as long as it is in business. Currently the company's common stock is selling for $34 per share. The most recent dividend paid by TTH was $4.25 per share. If new common stock is issued, TTH will incur flotation costs equal to 8.5 percent. (a) What is the company's cost of retained earnings? (b) What is its cost of new common equity?

11-9 Canyon Eatery's common stock, which is currently selling for $50 per share, has a beta coefficient equal to 0.75. Canyon has paid a dividend equal to $6 per share since it has been in business, and expectations are that the same dividend will be paid forever. Canyon's investment banker charges 7 percent when new common stock is issued. What is Canyon's (a) cost of retained earnings and (b) cost of new common equity?

11-10 Halo Hot Air Balloons is expected to grow at 5 percent forever. Its common stock is currently selling for $28 per share, and the most recent dividend paid to common stockholders was $2.40 per share. If Halo's cost of new common equity is 15 percent, what is the flotation cost charged by its investment banker?

11-11 Bonanza Gold's common stock currently sells for $32 per share. Bonanza's investment banker charges 6.5 percent flotation costs when new common stock is issued. The company expects to pay a $3.36 per share dividend at the *end of the year*. If Bonanza's cost of retained earnings is 15.5 percent, what is its cost of new common equity?

11-12 Tropical Tours is considering an expansion of its operations, which will require the company to issue new debt and equity. Tropical's investment banker provided the following information about the cost of issuing new debt:

Amount of Debt Issued	Yield to Maturity, r_d
$1 – $450,000	4.5%
450,001 – 750,000	5.8
Over 750,000	6.5

If Tropical's capital structure consists of 60 percent debt, what WACC break points are associated with issuing new debt?

11-13 Western Transportation's capital structure consists of 30 percent debt and 70 percent common equity. According to its investment banker, Western can issue up to $240,000 new debt at a 3.8 percent cost; for any amount of new debt greater than $240,000, the cost is 5.5 percent. Western expects to generate $560,000 in retained earnings this year. Compute the WACC break point(s) associated with raising new funds.

11-14 Divided Walls Construction (DWC) has determined that the yield to maturity (YTM) on new bonds is 5 percent, its cost of retained earnings is 8 percent, and its cost of new common stock is 11 percent. If DWC's capital structure consists of 40 percent debt and 60 percent common equity, what is its weighted average cost of capital (WACC) if it (a) does not have to issue new stock to raise additional funds and (b) must issue new stock to raise additional funds? DWC's marginal tax rate is 35 percent.

11-15 Killer Burgers' capital structure consists of 20 percent debt, 30 percent preferred stock, and 50 percent common stock. If Killer raises new capital, its *after-tax* cost of debt will be 3.5 percent, its cost of preferred stock will be 6 percent, its cost of retained earnings will be 10.2 percent, and its cost of new common equity will be 12.4 percent. If Killer needs to raise $220,000 and it expects to generate $100,000 in retained earnings this year, what is its marginal cost of capital to raise the needed funds?

11-16 Futuristic Coiffures (FC) needs to raise $85,000 to purchase a new machine. FC knows its component costs of capital are $r_d = 5\%$, $r_{ps} = 7\%$, $r_s = 11\%$, and $r_e = 13\%$. FC maintains a capital structure that consists of 60 percent debt, 10 percent preferred stock, and 30 percent common equity. The firm's marginal tax rate is 30 percent. If FC expects to generate $27,000 in retained earnings this year, what marginal cost of capital will it incur to raise the needed funds?

11-17 The CFO of Lazy Loungers is evaluating the following independent, indivisible projects:

Project	Cost	IRR
A	$10,000	21.0%
B	15,000	20.0
C	25,000	16.0

Lazy's weighted average cost of capital (WACC) is 14 percent if the firm does *not* have to issue new common equity; if new common equity is needed, its WACC is 17 percent. Lazy's capital structure consists of 40 percent debt. If Lazy has no preferred stock and expects to generate $24,000 in retained earnings this year, which project(s) should be purchased?

11-18 Over-the-Top Canopies (OTC) is evaluating two independent investments. Project S costs $150,000 and has an IRR equal to 12 percent, and Project L costs $140,000 and has an IRR equal to 10 percent. OTC's capital structure consists of 20 percent debt and 80 percent common equity, and its component costs of capital are $r_{dT} = 4\%$, $r_s = 10\%$, and $r_e = 12.5\%$. If OTC expects to generate $230,000 in retained earnings this year, which project(s) should be purchased?

11-19 Peter Piper's Pies (P^3) is evaluating four independent investments. The cost of each project is $214,000. The internal rates of return (IRRs) for the projects are $IRR_1 = 19\%$, $IRR_2 = 15\%$, $IRR_3 = 18\%$, and $IRR_4 = 14\%$. P^3's investment banker has provided the following WACC table:

Total Amount Raised	WACC
$1 – $520,000	11.0%
520,001 – 745,000	12.5
Over 745,000	15.2

Which project(s) should P^3 purchase?

11-20 Tri-Q Supply Company is considering an expansion project to increase sales. The project, which costs $2.6 million, has an IRR equal to 9.5 percent. Any portion of the project can be purchased. Tri-Q expects to retain $1.3 million of earnings this year. It can raise up to $420,000 in new debt with a before-tax cost equal to 5 percent; any additional debt will cost 7 percent before taxes. Tri-Q's cost of retained earnings is 12 percent, and its cost of new common equity is 14 percent. Its target capital structure consists of 35 percent debt and 65 percent common equity. If Tri-Q's marginal tax rate is 40 percent, what is the optimal capital budget?

After you finish this chapter go to **PAGE 244** for **STUDY TOOLS**

LEARNING OUTCOMES

After studying this chapter, you will be able to...

LO1 Describe how business risk and financial risk can affect a firm's capital structure.

LO2 Describe how businesses determine their optimal capital structures.

LO3 Describe how leverage can be used to make capital structure decisions, and discuss the effects (a) operating leverage, (b) financial leverage, and (c) total leverage have on risks associated with a firm.

LO4 Discuss how managers consider liquidity when determining the optimal capital structure for a firm.

LO5 Discuss the two general theories—(a) trade-off theory and (b) signaling theory—that have been developed to explain what firms' capital structures should be and why firms' capital structures differ.

LO6 Describe how and why capital structures vary among firms in the United States and around the world.

Capital Structure

12

In Chapter 11, when we calculated the weighted average cost of capital (WACC) for use in capital budgeting, we took the capital structure *weights*, or the mix of securities a firm uses to finance its assets, as a given. However, if the weights are changed, the calculated cost of capital, and thus the set of acceptable capital budgeting projects, will also change. Further, changing the capital structure will affect the riskiness inherent in the firm's common stock, and this will affect both the return demanded by stockholders, r_s, and the stock's price, P_0. Therefore, the choice of a capital structure is an important decision.

12-1 The Target Capital Structure

Firms can choose whatever mix of debt and equity they desire to finance their assets, subject to the willingness of investors to provide such funds. As we shall see, many different mixes of debt and equity, or **capital structures**, exist. In the next few sections, we will discuss factors that affect a firm's capital structure, and we will conclude that a firm should attempt to determine what its optimal, or best, mix of financing should be. It will become apparent that determining the exact optimal capital structure is not a science, so after analyzing a number of factors, a firm establishes a **target capital structure** that it believes is optimal and that it uses as guidance for raising funds in the future. This target might change over time as conditions vary, but at any given moment, the firm's management has a specific capital structure in mind, and individual financing decisions should be consistent with this target. If the actual proportion of debt is below the target level, new funds probably will be raised by issuing debt, whereas if the proportion of debt is above the target, stock probably will be sold to bring the firm back in line with the target ratio.

Capital structure policy involves a trade-off between risk and return. Using more debt raises the riskiness of the firm's earnings stream, but a higher proportion of debt generally leads to a higher expected rate of return. From the concepts we discussed in previous chapters, we know that the higher risk associated with greater debt tends to lower the firm's stock price. At the same time, however, the higher expected rate of return makes the stock more attractive to investors, which, in turn, ultimately increases the stock's price. Therefore, *the optimal capital structure is the one that strikes a balance between risk and return to achieve the ultimate goal of maximizing the price of the firm's stock.*

When we examined risk in Chapter 8, we distinguished between *market risk,* which is measured by the firm's beta coefficient, and *total risk,* which includes both beta risk and a type of risk that can be eliminated by diversification *(firm-specific risk).* In Chapter 10, we considered how capital budgeting decisions affect the riskiness of the firm. There we differentiated between *beta risk* (the effect of a project on the firm's beta) and *corporate risk* (the effect of the project on the firm's total risk). Now we introduce two new dimensions of risk: business risk and financial risk.

1. **Business risk** is defined as the uncertainty inherent in projections of future returns, either on assets (ROA) or on equity (ROE), if the firm uses no debt or debt-like financing (preferred stock);

capital structure The combination of debt and equity used to finance a firm.

target capital structure The mix of debt, preferred stock, and common equity with which the firm plans to finance its investments.

business risk The risk associated with the firm's operations, ignoring any financing effects.

that is, it is the risk associated with the firm's operations, ignoring any financing effects.

2. **Financial risk** is defined as the additional risk, over and above basic business risk, placed on common stockholders that results from using financing alternatives with fixed periodic payments, such as debt and preferred stock—that is, it is the risk associated with the types of funds the firm uses to finance its assets.

Conceptually, the firm has a certain amount of risk inherent in its production and sales operations; this is its business risk. When it uses debt, it partitions this risk and concentrates most of it on one class of investors: the common stockholders. This is its financial risk.[1] Both business risk and financial risk affect the capital structure of a firm.

12-1a Business Risk

Business risk is the single most important determinant of capital structure because it is based on the uncertainty that a company's future operations exhibit. Some companies have fairly stable, and thus somewhat predictable, production and sales patterns, whereas the operations of other companies are very unpredictable. It makes sense that firms with more stable operations generally can more easily take on, or handle, the fixed interest payments that are associated with debt, and therefore they use more debt in their capital structures than firms with less stable operations. In other words, everything else the same, firms with more stable operations have lower business risk than firms with less stable operations, and *firms with less business risk can take on more debt* (fixed financial payments) than firms that have greater business risk.

Business risk varies from one industry to another, and also among firms in a given industry. Further, business risk can change over time. Food processors and grocery retailers frequently are cited as examples of industries with low business risk, whereas cyclical manufacturing industries, such as steel and construction, are regarded as having especially high business risk. Smaller companies, especially single-product firms, also have relatively high degrees of business risk.[2]

financial risk The portion of stockholders' risk, over and above basic business risk, that results from the manner in which the firm is financed.

operating leverage The presence of fixed operating costs that do not change when the level of sales changes.

financial leverage The extent to which fixed-income securities (debt and preferred stock) are used in a firm's capital structure.

Business risk depends on a number of factors, the more important of which include the following:

1. ***Sales variability (volume and price)***—The more stable (certain) the unit sales (volume) and prices of a firm's products, the lower its business risk, other things constant.

2. ***Input price variability***—A firm with highly uncertain input prices—labor, product costs, and so forth—is exposed to a high degree of business risk.

3. ***Ability to adjust output prices for changes in input prices***—The greater the ability of the firm to adjust selling prices of its products when input costs change, the lower the degree of business risk. This factor is especially important during periods of high inflation.

4. ***The extent to which costs are fixed: operating leverage***—If a high percentage of a firm's operating costs are fixed and hence do not decline when demand falls off, this increases the company's business risk. This factor is called operating leverage; this topic will be discussed in detail later in the chapter.

Each of these factors is determined partly by the firm's industry characteristics, but each is also controllable to some extent by management. For example, most firms can, through their marketing policies, take actions to stabilize both unit sales and sales prices. However, this stabilization might require either large expenditures on advertising or price concessions to induce customers to commit to purchasing fixed quantities at fixed prices in the future. Similarly, some firms can reduce the volatility of future input costs by negotiating long-term labor and materials supply contracts. Of course, they might have to agree to pay prices somewhat above the current price to obtain these contracts.

12-1b Financial Risk

We define *financial risk* as the additional risk, over and above basic business risk, that is placed on common stockholders when the firm uses financing alternatives that require fixed periodic payments. Thus, financial risk results from using financial leverage, which exists when a firm uses fixed-income securities, such as debt and preferred stock, to raise capital. When financial leverage is created, a firm intensifies the business risk borne by the

---

[1]Using preferred stock also adds to financial risk. To simplify matters somewhat, in this chapter we shall consider only debt and common equity.

[2]We have avoided any discussion of market versus company-specific risk in this section. We note now that (1) any action that increases business risk will generally increase a firm's beta coefficient, but (2) a part of business risk as we define it will generally be company-specific and hence is subject to elimination through diversification by the firm's stockholders.

common stockholders. To illustrate, suppose 10 people decide to form a corporation to produce operating systems for personal computers. There is a certain amount of business risk in the operation. If the firm is capitalized only with common equity, and if each person buys 10 percent of the stock, then each investor will bear an equal share of the business risk. However, suppose the firm is capitalized with 50 percent debt and 50 percent equity, with five of the investors putting up their capital as debt and the other five putting up their money as equity. In this case, the cash flows received by the debtholders are based on a contractual agreement, so the investors who put up the equity will have to bear essentially all of the business risk, and their position will be twice as risky as it would have been had the firm been financed only with equity. Thus, *the use of debt intensifies the firm's business risk borne by the common stockholders.*

[3]In this chapter, we examine capital structures on a book value (or balance sheet) basis. An alternative approach is to calculate the market values of debt, preferred stock, and common equity, and then to reconstruct the balance sheet on a market value basis. Although the market value approach is more consistent with financial theory, bond rating agencies and most financial executives focus their attention on book values. Moreover, the conversion from book to market values is a complicated process, and because market value capital structures change with stock market fluctuations, they are thought by many to be too unstable to serve as operationally useful targets. Finally, exactly the same insights are gained from the book value and market value analyses. For all these reasons, a market value analysis of capital structure is better suited for advanced finance courses.

In the next section, we will explain how financial leverage affects a firm's expected earnings per share, the riskiness of those earnings, and, consequently, the price of the firm's stock. The objective of our analysis is to determine the capital structure at which *value is maximized;* this point is then used as the target capital structure.[3]

12-2 Determining the Optimal Capital Structure

We can illustrate the effects of financial leverage using the data shown in Table 12.1 for a fictional company, which we will call OptiCap. As shown in the top section of the table, the company currently has no debt. Should it continue the policy of using no debt, or should it start using financial leverage (debt)? If it does decide to substitute debt for equity, how far should it go? As in all such decisions, the correct answer is that the firm should *choose the combination of debt and equity, or capital structure, that will maximize the price of the firm's stock.*

To answer the questions posed here, we examine the effects of changing OptiCap's capital structure while

Table 12.1

Financial Information for OptiCap, 2016 ($ thousands, except per-share values)

I. Balance Sheet—12/31/16

Current assets	$100.0	Debt	$ 0.0
Net fixed assets	100.0	Common equity (10,000 shares)	200.0
Total assets	$200.0	Total liabilities and equity	$200.0

II. Income Statement for 2016

Sales	$200.0
Variable operating costs (60%)	(120.0)
Gross profit	80.0
Fixed operating costs	(48.0)
Earnings before interest and taxes (EBIT)	32.0
Interest expense	(0.0)
Earnings before taxes (EBT)	32.0
Taxes (40%)	(12.8)
Net income	$ 19.2
Common dividend	$ 19.2
Addition to retained earnings	$ 0.0

III. Per-Share Information

Earnings per share (EPS) = ($19,200/10,000 shares) =	$ 1.92
Dividends per share (DPS) = ($19,200/10,000 shares) =	$ 1.92
Market price per share (P_0)	$ 20.00

keeping all other factors, such as the level of operations, constant. To keep all other factors constant, we assume that OptiCap changes its capital structure by *substituting* debt for equity—that is, as new debt is issued, the proceeds are used to repurchase an equal amount of outstanding stock.

12-2a EPS Analysis of the Effects of Financial Leverage

If a firm changes the percentage of debt used to finance existing assets, we would expect the earnings per share (EPS) and, consequently, the stock price to change as well. To understand the relationship between financial leverage and EPS, we first examine how EPS is affected when our illustrative firm changes its capital structure to include greater relative amounts of debt.

First, to simplify our example, we assume that OptiCap's level of operations—that is, production and sales—will not change if its capital structure changes.[4] Table 12.1 shows that OptiCap's net operating income

(NOI), or earnings before interest and taxes (EBIT), was $32,000 in 2016. We expect that its EBIT will remain at this level when economic conditions are normal, but will rise to $84,000 when the economy is booming and will fall to −$6,000 when the economy is in a recession. The probabilities associated with each of these economic states are 0.5, 0.3, and 0.2, respectively. We give the different economic states so that we can see what happens to OptiCap's financial risk when its capital structure is changed.

[4]In the real world, capital structure does at times affect EBIT. First, if debt levels are excessive, the firm probably will not be able to finance at all if its earnings are low at a time when interest rates are high. This could lead to stop–start construction and research and development programs, as well as to the necessity of passing up good investment opportunities. Second, a weak financial condition (i.e. too much debt) could cause a firm to lose sales. For example, prior to the time that its huge debt forced Eastern Airlines into bankruptcy, many people refused to buy Eastern tickets because they were afraid the company would go bankrupt and leave them holding unusable tickets. Third, financially strong companies can bargain hard with unions as well as with their suppliers, whereas weaker ones might have to give in simply because they do not have the financial resources to carry on the fight. Finally, a company with so much debt that bankruptcy is a serious threat will have difficulty attracting and retaining managers and employees, or it will have to pay premium salaries. For all these reasons, it is not entirely correct to say that a firm's financial policy has no effect on its operating income.

Table 12.2

Cost of Debt, r_d, and Number of Common Shares Outstanding for OptiCap at Different Capital Structures ($ thousands)

Total Assets	Debt/Assets Ratio	Amount Borrowed[a]	Common Stock	Shares Outstanding[b]	Cost of Debt, r_d
$200	0%	$ 0	$200	10,000	—
200	10	20	180	9,000	8.0%
200	20	40	160	8,000	8.5
200	30	60	140	7,000	9.0
200	40	80	120	6,000	10.0
200	50	100	100	5,000	12.0
200	60	120	80	4,000	15.0

[a]We assume that the firm must borrow in increments of $20,000. We also assume that OptiCap cannot borrow more than $120,000, or 60 percent of assets because of restrictions in its corporate charter.

[b]We assume that OptiCap uses the amount of funds raised by borrowing (issuing debt) to repurchase existing common stock at the current market value, which is $20 per share; thus we assume that no commissions or other transaction costs are associated with repurchasing the stock. For example, if OptiCap's capital structure contains 40 percent debt, then $80,000 of the $200,000 total assets is financed with debt. We assume that if OptiCap borrows the $80,000, it will repurchase 4,000 shares = $80,000/$20 of its existing shares of common stock, so 6,000 shares (10,000 shares − 4,000 shares) remain.

OptiCap asked an investment banker to help determine what its before-tax cost of debt, r_d, will be at various levels of debt. The results are shown in Table 12.2. Naturally, we would expect that as a firm increases the percentage of debt it uses, lenders would perceive the debt to be riskier because the chance of financial distress is higher. As a result, lenders (bondholders) will charge higher interest rates to the firm as its percentage of debt increases, which is the pattern shown in the table.

We assume that OptiCap does not retain any earnings for reinvestment in the firm; that is, all earnings are paid to shareholders, which currently consist of stockholders only. As long as the firm pays all earnings to shareholders, and no additional funds are raised, growth will equal zero ($g = 0$), and future production and sales operations will continue as outlined previously; that is, the size of the firm will remain at its current level. Thus, any changes in EPS that we observe when the proportion of debt is changed will be a direct result of changing the firm's capital structure, not its level of operations.

Table 12.3 compares OptiCap's expected EPS at two levels of financial leverage: (1) zero debt, which is the existing capital structure, and (2) 50 percent debt. If OptiCap does not change its capital structure, all $200,000 of its assets will be financed with stock, so the interest expense will be zero because no debt exists. Section II of Table 12.3 shows that EPS is expected to be $2.40 with this capital structure. EPS will be as high as $5.04, and as low as −$0.36, but, on average, it will be $2.40. We also calculate the standard deviation of EPS (σ_{EPS}) and the coefficient of variation (CV_{EPS}) as indicators of the firm's risk with this capital structure: $\sigma_{EPS} = \$1.93$ and $CV_{EPS} = 0.80$.[5]

Section III of Table 12.3 shows the effect on EPS of shifting OptiCap's capital structure so that the mix of financing is 50 percent debt and 50 percent equity; that is, when the $200,000 in assets are financed with $100,000 debt and $100,000 equity. To accomplish this shift, OptiCap would issue $100,000 of debt and repurchase $100,000 of its existing equity. If we assume that stock can be repurchased at its current market price and transaction costs are negligible, then, using the information given in Table 12.1, we will find that OptiCap can repurchase 5,000 shares = $100,000/$20 per share.[6] Thus, the number of shares outstanding will decrease from 10,000 to 5,000. At the same time, because the firm now has debt, it will have to pay interest, which, according to the schedule given in Table 12.2, will equal $12,000 = $100,000 × 0.12 per year. The $12,000 interest expense is a fixed cost because it is the same regardless of OptiCap's level of sales.

[5]See Chapter 8 for a review of procedures for calculating standard deviations and coefficients of variation. Recall that the advantage of the coefficient of variation is that it permits better comparisons when the expected values of EPS vary, as they do here for the two capital structures.

[6]We assume in this example that the firm could change its capital structure by repurchasing common stock at the current market value, which is $20 per share. However, if the firm attempts to purchase a large block of its stock, demand pressures might cause the market price to increase, in which case OptiCap would not be able to purchase 5,000 shares with the $100,000 that was raised with its debt issue. In addition, we assume the flotation costs associated with the debt issue are negligible, so that OptiCap is able to use all $100,000 to repurchase stock. Clearly, the existence of flotation costs would mean OptiCap would have some amount less than $100,000 to repurchase stock. Neither of these assumptions affects the overall concept we are trying to provide through our illustration; only the numbers change.

Table 12.3

OptiCap: EPS at Different Capital Structures ($ thousands, except per-share values)

I. Economic States

	Recession	Normal	Boom
Type of economy			
Probability of occurrence	0.2	0.5	0.3
Sales	$ 105.0	$200.0	$330.0

II. Debt/Assets = 0% (current capital structure)

	Recession	Normal	Boom
EBIT	$ (6.0)	$ 32.0	$ 84.0
Interest expense	(0.0)	(0.0)	(0.0)
Earnings before taxes (EBT)	(6.0)	32.0	84.0
Taxes (40%)	2.4	(12.8)	(33.6)
Net income (NI)	$ (3.6)	$ 19.2	$ 50.4
Earnings per share (EPS) = NI/10,000 shares	$ (0.36)	$ 1.92	$ 5.04
Expected EPS		$ 2.40	
Standard deviation of EPS (σ_{EPS})		$ 1.93	
Coefficient of variation (CV$_{EPS}$)		0.80	

III. Debt/Assets = 50%

	Recession	Normal	Boom
EBIT	$ (6.0)	$ 32.0	$ 84.0
Interest expense = 0.12 × $100	(12.0)	(12.0)	(12.0)
Earnings before taxes (EBT)	(18.0)	20.0	72.0
Taxes (40%)	7.2	(8.0)	(28.8)
Net income (NI)	$ (10.8)	$ 12.0	$ 43.2
Earnings per share (EPS) = NI/5,000 shares	$ (2.16)	$ 2.40	$ 8.64
Expected EPS		$ 3.36	
Standard deviation of EPS (σ_{EPS})		$ 3.86	
Coefficient of variation (CV$_{EPS}$)		1.15	

With a debt/assets ratio of 50 percent, the expected EPS is $3.36, which is $0.96 higher than if the firm uses no debt. The EPS range is also greater; EPS can be as low as −$2.16 when the economy is poor or as high as $8.64 when the economy is booming. Thus, EPS has greater variability, which suggests that this capital structure is riskier than the capital structure of 100 percent equity financing. The standard deviation of EPS and the coefficient of variation computed for the capital structure with 50 percent debt are σ_{EPS} = $3.86 and CV$_{EPS}$ = 1.15. As you can see, these computations support our suspicion that this capital structure is riskier than the capital structure that consists of equity only.

Figure 12.1 shows the relationships among expected EPS, risk, and financial leverage for OptiCap for the all-equity capital structure and the various capital structures given in the lower section of the figure. The tabular data given in Figure 12.1 were calculated in the manner set forth in Table 12.3, and the graphs plot these data. In the left panel of Figure 12.1, we see that expected EPS rises until the firm is financed with 50 percent debt. Interest charges rise (Table 12.2), but this effect is more than offset by the decline in the number of shares outstanding as debt is substituted for equity. Beyond 50 percent debt, however, the interest rate rises so rapidly that EPS declines despite the smaller number of shares outstanding.

The right panel of Figure 12.1 shows that risk, as measured by the coefficient of variation of EPS, rises continuously and at an increasing rate as debt is

FIGURE 12.1

OPTICAP: RELATIONSHIPS AMONG EXPECTED EPS, RISK, AND FINANCIAL LEVERAGE

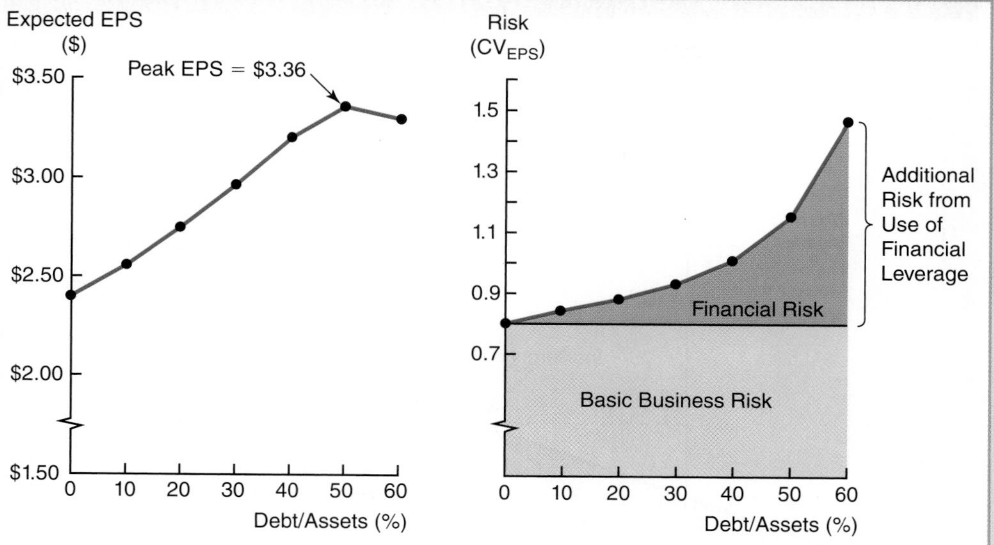

Debt Ratio = Debt/Assets	Expected EPS	Standard Deviation = σ_{EPS}	Coefficient of Variation = CV_{EPS}
0%	$2.40	$1.93	0.80
10	2.56	2.15	0.84
20	2.75	2.41	0.88
30	2.97	2.76	0.93
40	3.20	3.22	1.01
50	3.36	3.86	1.15
60	3.30	4.83	1.46

substituted for equity. We see, then, that using leverage has both good effects and bad effects. Higher leverage increases expected EPS (in this example, until the firm is financed with 50 percent debt), but it also increases the firm's risk. Clearly, for OptiCap, the debt/assets ratio should not exceed 50 percent. But where in the range of 0 to 50 percent is the best debt/assets ratio for OptiCap? This issue is discussed in the following sections.

12-2b EBIT/EPS Examination of Financial Leverage

In the previous section, we assumed that OptiCap's EBIT had to be one of three possible values: −$6,000, $32,000, or $84,000. Another way of evaluating alternative financing methods is to plot the EPS of each capital structure at many different levels of EBIT. Figure 12.2 shows such a graph for the two capital structures we considered for OptiCap in Table 12.3; that is, (1) 100 percent stock and (2) 50 percent stock and 50 percent debt. Notice that at low levels of EBIT,

and hence low levels of sales, EPS is higher if OptiCap's capital structure includes only stock. At high levels of EBIT, however, EPS is higher with the capital structure that includes debt. Notice also that the 50% Debt line has a steeper slope than the 100% Common Stock line, showing that earnings per share will increase more rapidly with increases in EBIT, and hence sales, if the firm uses debt. This relationship exists because the firm has a greater degree of financial leverage with the capital structure that includes 50 percent debt. In this case, the benefits of *additional sales need not be shared with debt holders because debt payments are fixed*; rather, any profits that remain after debt holders are paid "belong" to stockholders.

The point on the graph where the two lines intersect is called the **EPS indifference point**, and it is the level of EBIT (sales) where EPS is the same no matter which capital structure OptiCap uses. In Figure 12.2, the two lines cross where EBIT

EPS indifference point The level of sales at which EPS will be the same whether the firm uses debt or common stock financing.

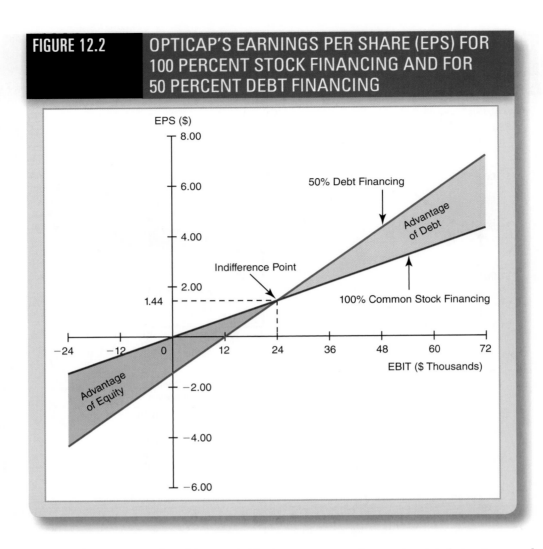

is equal to $24,000, which equates to sales of $180,000. If sales are below $180,000, EPS will be higher if the firm uses only common stock; above this level, the debt financing alternative will produce higher EPS. If we are certain that sales will never again fall below $180,000, some amount of bonds should be used to finance any increases in assets. We cannot know this for certain, however.

12-2c The Effect of Capital Structure on Stock Prices and the Cost of Capital

As we saw in Figure 12.1, OptiCap's expected EPS is maximized at a debt/assets ratio of 50 percent. Does this mean that OptiCap's optimal capital structure calls for 50 percent debt? The answer is a resounding no. *The optimal capital structure is the one that maximizes the price of the firm's stock, and this always calls for a debt/assets ratio that is lower than the one that maximizes expected EPS.* As we shall discover shortly, the primary reason this relationship exists is because P_0 reflects changes in risk that

accompany changes in capital structures and affect cash flows long into the future, whereas EPS generally measures only the expectations for the near term. That is, current EPS generally does not capture future risk, whereas P_0 is indicative of all future expectations. Our analysis to this point has, therefore, indicated that OptiCap's optimal capital structure should contain something less than 50 percent debt. The validity of this statement is demonstrated in Table 12.4, which develops OptiCap's estimated stock price and weighted average cost of capital (WACC) at different debt/assets ratios. The debt costs and EPS data in Columns 2 and 3 were taken from Table 12.2 and Figure 12.1. The beta coefficients shown in Column 4 were estimated. Recall from Chapter 8 that a stock's beta measures its relative volatility compared with the volatility of an average stock. It has been demonstrated both theoretically and empirically that a firm's beta increases with its degree of financial leverage. The exact nature of this relationship for a given firm is difficult to estimate, but the values given in Column 4 show the approximate nature of the relationship for OptiCap.

Table 12.4

Stock Price and Cost of Capital Estimates for OptiCap at Different Capital Structures

(1) Debt/ Assets	(2) After-Tax Cost of Debt, r_{dT}[a]	(3) Expected EPS (and DPS[b])	(4) Estimated Beta (β_s)	(5) Cost of Equity[c] $r_s = 4\% + 5\%(\beta_s)$	(6) Estimated Price[d]	(7) WACC[e]
0	—	$2.40	1.60	12.00%	$20.00	12.00%
10	4.8%	2.56	1.70	12.50	20.48	11.73
20	5.1	2.75	1.80	13.00	21.12	11.42
30	5.4	2.97	1.95	13.75	21.57	11.25
40	6.0	3.20	2.10	14.50	22.07	11.10
50	7.2	3.36	2.30	15.50	21.68	11.35
60	9.0	3.30	2.60	17.00	19.41	12.20

[a]The after-tax cost of debt, r_{dT}, is the before-tax cost of debt, r_d, given in Table 12.2 adjusted for the taxes: $r_{dT} = r_d(1 - T)$. For example, at a capital structure of 40 percent debt, $r_{dT} = 10.0\%(1 - 0.4) = 6.0\%$.

[b]OptiCap pays out all earnings as dividends, so DPS = EPS. Although the values in this column are rounded to the nearest penny, the values shown in Column 6 are computed based on DPS figures carried to four decimal places.

[c]We assume that $r_{RF} = 4\%$ and $r_M = 9\%$, so $r_{PM} = 9\% - 4\% = 5\%$, and, at debt/assets equal to 40 percent, $r_s = 4\% + (5\% \times 2.10) = 14.5\%$. Other values of r_s are calculated similarly.

[d]Because all earnings are paid out as dividends, no retained earnings are available to be reinvested in the firm, which means growth in EPS and DPS will be zero (g = 0). Therefore, we use the constant growth model, where g = 0, developed in Chapter 7 to compute the estimated stock price. To illustrate, at debt/assets equal to 40 percent, we have

$$\hat{P}_0 = \frac{\widehat{DPS}}{r_s} = \frac{\$3.20}{0.1450} = \$22.07$$

Other prices were computed similarly.

[e]The WACC, or weighted average cost of capital, is computed using Equation 11.8, which was developed in Chapter 11. At a capital structure that has 40 percent debt, the computation is

$$WACC = w_d[r_d(1 - T)] + w_s r_s = (0.40)\,6.00\% + (1 - 0.40)\,14.50\% = 11.10\%$$

The WACCs for the other capital structures were computed similarly.

If we assume that the risk-free rate of return, r_{RF}, is 4 percent and the required return on an average stock, r_M, is 9 percent, we can use the CAPM equation to develop estimates of the required rates of return on equity, r_s, for OptiCap as shown in Column 5. Here we see that $r_s = 12\% = 4\% + (9\% - 4\%)1.6$ if no financial leverage is used, but $r_s = 17\% = 4\% + (9\% - 4\%)2.6$ if the company finances with 60 percent debt, the maximum permitted by its corporate charter.

Figure 12.3 graphs OptiCap's required rate of return on equity at different debt levels. The figure also shows the composition of OptiCap's required return, including the risk-free rate of 4 percent and the premiums for both business and financial risk. As you can see from the graph, the business risk premium does not depend on the debt level. Instead, it remains constant at 8 percent at all debt levels, which is the difference between the 12 percent WACC when the firm is financed with 100 percent equity and the risk-free rate of 4 percent (i.e., $8\% = 12\% - 4\%$).

However, the financial risk premium varies depending on the debt level; the higher the debt level, the greater the premium for financial risk.

The zero growth stock valuation model (i.e., where g = 0) developed in Chapter 7 is used, along with the Column 3 values of dividends per share (DPS) and the Column 5 values of r_s, to develop the estimated stock prices shown in Column 6 in Table 12.4. Here we see that the expected stock price initially rises with additional financial leverage, hits a peak of $22.07 at a debt/assets ratio of 40 percent, and then begins to decline. Thus, OptiCap's optimal capital structure calls for 40 percent debt.

Finally, Column 7 shows OptiCap's weighted average cost of capital (WACC), calculated as described in Chapter 11, at the different capital structures. If the company uses zero debt, its capital is all equity, so WACC = r_s = 12%. As the firm begins to use lower-cost debt, its WACC declines. However, as the debt/assets ratio increases, the costs of both debt and equity rise,

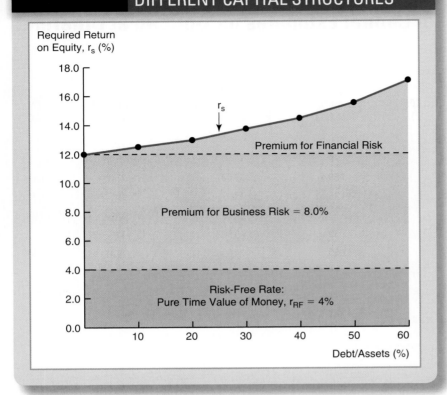

FIGURE 12.3	OPTICAP'S COST OF EQUITY, r_s, AT DIFFERENT CAPITAL STRUCTURES

and financial—are interrelated. If OptiCap can *reduce* its operating leverage, its optimal capital structure probably would call for *more* debt, and vice versa. In this section we show, through an analysis of the degree of leverage concept, how operating and financial leverage interact, which shows how business risk and financial risk affect a firm's projected income.

12-3a Degree of Operating Leverage (DOL)

The **degree of operating leverage (DOL)** is defined as the percentage change in net operating income (NOI)—that is, earnings before interest and taxes, or EBIT—associated with a given percentage change in sales. Thus, the degree of operating leverage is computed as in Equation 12.1:

and the increasing costs of the two components begin to offset the fact that larger amounts of the lower-cost debt are being used. At 40 percent debt, WACC hits a minimum at 11.10 percent, and then it begins rising as the debt/assets ratio is increased.

The cost of capital and stock price data shown in Table 12.4 are plotted in Figure 12.4 on the next page. As the graph shows, the expected stock price is maximized, and the cost of capital is minimized, at a 40 percent debt/assets ratio. Thus, *OptiCap's optimal capital structure calls for 40 percent debt and 60 percent equity. Management should set its target capital structure at these ratios, and if the existing ratios are off target, it should move toward the target when new securities offerings are made.*

12.1

Degree of operating leverage $= \text{DOL} = \dfrac{\%\Delta \text{ in NOI}}{\%\Delta \text{ in sales}} = \dfrac{\left(\dfrac{\Delta \text{EBIT}}{\text{EBIT}}\right)}{\left(\dfrac{\Delta \text{Sales}}{\text{Sales}}\right)}$

Here the Greek symbol Δ indicates change.

According to Equation 12.1, the DOL is an index that measures the effect of a change in sales on EBIT (operating income).

The DOL for a particular level of production and sales can be computed using Equation 12.2:

12.2

$\text{DOL} = \dfrac{Q(P-V)}{Q(P-V)-F} = \dfrac{S-VC}{S-VC-F}$

$= \dfrac{\text{Gross profit}}{\text{EBIT}}$

 ## 12-3 Degree of Leverage[7]

Leverage, whether operating or financial, is created when a firm has *fixed costs* associated either with its sales and production operations or with the types of financing it uses. These two types of leverage—operating

degree of operating leverage (DOL) The percentage change in operating income (EBIT) associated with a given percentage change in sales.

[7]A more detailed discussion of leverage is presented in Chapter 17, and the derivations of the equations contained in this section are included in the footnotes in that chapter.

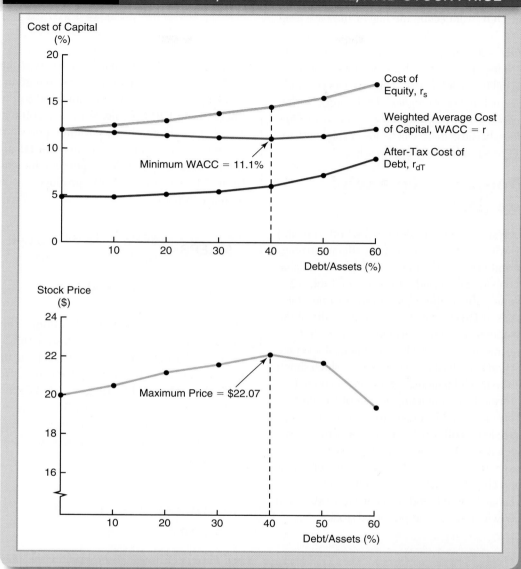

Here, Q is the intial units of output, P is the average sales price per unit of output, V is the variable cost per unit, F is fixed operating costs, S is initial sales in dollars, and VC is total variable costs in dollars.

Applying Equation 12.2 to data for OptiCap at a sales level of $200,000, as shown in Table 12.1, we find its degree of operating leverage to be 2.5:

$$\text{DOL}_{\$200,000} = \frac{\$200,000 - \$120,000}{\$200,000 - \$120,000 - \$48,000}$$

$$= \frac{\$80,000}{\$32,000} = 2.5\times$$

Thus, for every 1 percent change (increase; decrease) in sales there will be a 2.5 percent change (increase;

decrease) in EBIT. This situation is confirmed by examining Section II of Table 12.3, where we see that a 65 percent increase in sales, from $200,000 to $330,000, causes EBIT to increase by 162.5 percent (= 65% × 2.5), from $32,000 to $84,000. Note, however, that if sales decrease by 65 percent, then EBIT will decrease by 162.5 percent.

Also, note that the DOL is specific to a particular sales level; thus, if we evaluated OptiCap from a sales base of $330,000, DOL would be different:

$$\text{DOL}_{\$330,000} = \frac{\$330,000 - \$330,000(0.6)}{\$330,000 - \$330,000(0.6) - \$48,000}$$

$$= \frac{\$132,000}{\$84,000} = 1.57\times$$

Based on these examples, we conclude that when a firm's operations are closer to the breakeven level (at sales = $120,000, EBIT = $0), its degree of operating leverage will be higher, but DOL will decline the higher the base level of sales is above breakeven sales. (For example, at sales = $200,000, DOL = 2.5 times, whereas at sales = $330,000, DOL = 1.57 times.) Remember that in Chapter 8 we used the word "variability" to define risk. Thus, we can conclude that, all else equal, *a lower (higher) DOL suggests that lower (higher) risk is associated with the firm's normal operating activities*, because there will be lower (higher) variability in EBIT as a result of a change in sales.

12-3b Degree of Financial Leverage (DFL)

Operating leverage affects earnings *before* interest and taxes (EBIT), whereas financial leverage affects earnings *after* interest and taxes, or the earnings that are available to pay common stock dividends. In terms of Table 12.1, operating leverage affects the section of the income statement from sales to EBIT, which shows the results of the firm's normal operations and is termed the *operating section* of the income statement, whereas financial leverage affects the section from EBIT to net income, which shows the effects of the firm's financing arrangements on net income and is termed the *financing section* of the income statement. Thus, financial leverage takes over where operating leverage leaves off, further magnifying the effects on earnings per share (EPS) of changes in sales.

The degree of financial leverage (DFL) is defined as the percentage change in EPS that results from a given percentage change in EBIT, and is calculated as shown in Equation 12.3 (when there is no preferred stock):

12.3

$$\text{Degree of financial leverage} = DFL = \frac{\%\Delta \text{ in EPS}}{\%\Delta \text{ in EBIT}} = \frac{\left(\dfrac{\Delta \text{EPS}}{\text{EPS}}\right)}{\left(\dfrac{\Delta \text{EBIT}}{\text{EBIT}}\right)}$$

$$= \frac{\text{EBIT}}{\text{EBIT} - \text{I}}$$

Here, I is the firm's interest expense.

degree of financial leverage (DFL) The percentage change in earnings per share (EPS) associated with a given percentage change in earnings before interest and taxes (EBIT).

At sales of $200,000 and EBIT of $32,000, the degree of financial leverage when OptiCap has a 50 percent debt/assets ratio (Section III, Table 12.3) is[8]

$$DFL_{\$200,000, \text{Debt/TA} = 50\%} = \frac{\$32,000}{\$32,000 - \$12,000}$$

$$= \frac{\$32,000}{\$20,000} = 1.6\times$$

This index indicates that every 1 percent change in EBIT will result in a 1.6 percent change in net income and EPS. Therefore, the previous 162.5 percent change (increase) in EBIT would result in a 260% = 162.5% × 1.6 change (increase) in earnings per share. This can be confirmed by referring to Section III of Table 12.3, where we see that a 162.5 percent increase in EBIT, from $32,000 to $84,000, produces a 260 percent increase in EPS:

$$\%\Delta \text{EPS} = \frac{\Delta \text{EPS}}{\text{EPS}_0} = \frac{\$8.64 - \$2.40}{\$2.40} = \frac{\$6.24}{\$2.40}$$

$$= 2.60 = 260\%$$

If no debt were used, by definition, the degree of financial leverage would be 1.0, so a 162.5 percent increase in EBIT would produce exactly a 162.5 percent increase in EPS. This can be confirmed from the data in Section II of Table 12.3 (i.e., %ΔEPS = ($5.04 − $1.92)/$1.92 = 1.625 = 162.5%). We can conclude that, all else equal, *a lower (higher) DFL suggests that lower (higher) risk is associated with the firm's mix of debt and equity financing*.

12-3c Degree of Total Leverage (DTL)

We have seen that (1) the greater the degree of operating leverage (fixed operating costs), the more sensitive EBIT will be to a change in sales and (2) the greater the degree of financial leverage (fixed financial costs), the more sensitive EPS will be to a change in EBIT. Therefore, we can conclude that when a firm uses a considerable amount of both operating and financial leverage, even small changes in sales will lead to wide fluctuations in EPS.

Equation 12.2, which we use to compute DOL, can be combined with Equation 12.3, which we use to compute DFL, to produce an equation to compute

[8]We illustrate DFL at 50 percent debt rather than at OptiCap's optimal capital structure of 40 percent debt to save space. Because EPS figures are available in Table 12.3, they do not have to be computed for our illustration.

degree of total leverage (DTL), which shows how a given change in sales will affect earnings per share. Equation 12.4 gives equivalent equations for computing DTL (assuming no preferred stock exists):

12.4

$$\text{Degree of total leverage} = \text{DTL} = \frac{\%\Delta \text{ in EPS}}{\%\Delta \text{ in sales}}$$

$$= \text{DOL} \times \text{DFL}$$

$$= \frac{\text{Gross profit}}{\text{EBIT}} \times \frac{\text{EBIT}}{\text{EBIT} - \text{I}}$$

$$= \frac{\text{Gross profit}}{\text{EBIT} - \text{I}}$$

$$= \frac{Q(P - V)}{Q(P - V) - F - I}$$

$$= \frac{S - VC}{S - VC - F - I}$$

For OptiCap, at sales of $200,000 we can substitute data from Tables 12.1 and 12.3 into Equation 12.4 to find the degree of total leverage if the debt ratio is 50 percent:

$$\text{DFL}_{\$200,000,\text{Debt/TA} = 50\%} = \frac{\$200,000 - \$120,000}{\$200,000 - \$120,000 - \$48,000 - \$12,000}$$

$$= \frac{\$80,000}{\$20,000} = 4.0\times$$

$$= \text{DOL} \times \text{DFL} = 2.5 \times 1.6 = 4.0\times$$

We can use the degree of total leverage (DTL) to find the new earnings per share (EPS$_1$) for any given percentage change in sales, proceeding as shown in Equation 12.5:

⁹The degree of leverage concept is also useful for investors. If firms in an industry are classified as to their degrees of total leverage, an investor who is optimistic about prospects for the industry might favor those firms with high leverage, and vice versa if he or she expected industry sales to decline. However, it is very difficult to separate fixed from variable costs. Accounting statements generally do not contain this breakdown, so the analyst must make the separation in a judgmental manner. Note that costs really are fixed, variable, and semivariable, for if times get tough enough, firms will sell off depreciable assets and thus reduce depreciation charges (a fixed cost), lay off "permanent" employees, reduce salaries of the remaining personnel, and so on. For this reason, the degree of leverage concept generally is more useful in explaining the general nature of the relationship than in developing precise numbers, and any numbers developed should be thought of as approximations rather than as exact specifications.

12.5

$$\text{EPS}_1 = \text{EPS}_0 + \text{EPS}_0(\text{DTL} \times \%\Delta\text{Sales})$$

$$= \text{EPS}_0[1 + (\text{DTL} \times \%\Delta\text{Sales})]$$

For example, a 65 percent increase in sales, from $200,000 to $330,000, would cause EPS$_0$ ($2.40 as shown in Section III of Table 12.3) to increase to $8.64:

$$\text{EPS}_1 = \$2.40[1.0 + (4)(0.65)] = \$2.40(3.60)$$

$$= \$8.64.$$

This figure agrees with the one for EPS shown in Table 12.3. All else being equal, *a lower (higher) DTL suggests that lower (higher) risk is associated with both the firm's business risk and its financial risk,* which in combination represent total risk.

The degree of leverage concept is useful primarily for the insights it provides regarding the joint effects of operating and financial leverage on earnings per share. The concept can be used to show management the effect of financing the firm with debt versus common stock. For example, management might find that the current capital structure is such that a 10 percent decline in sales would produce a 50 percent decline in earnings, whereas with a different financing package, and thus a different degree of total leverage, a 10 percent sales decline might cause earnings to decline by only 20 percent. Having the alternatives stated in this manner gives decision makers a better idea of the ramifications of alternative financing plans, and hence of different capital structures.⁹

12-4 Liquidity and Capital Structure

Some practical difficulties are associated with the type of analysis described in the previous section, including the following:

1. It is difficult to determine exactly how either P/E ratios or equity capitalization rates (r_s values) are affected by different DFLs.

degree of total leverage (DTL)
The percentage change in EPS that results from a given percentage change in sales; DTL shows the effects of both operating leverage and financial leverage.

2. A firm's managers might be more or less conservative than the average stockholder, so management might set a somewhat different target capital structure than the one that would maximize the stock price. Managers of a publicly owned firm never would admit this, because they might be removed from office if they did.

3. Managers of large firms, especially those that provide vital services such as electricity or phones, have a responsibility to provide continuous service. Therefore, they must refrain from using leverage to the point where the firm's long-run survival is endangered. Long-run viability might conflict with short-run stock price maximization and capital cost minimization.[10]

For all these reasons, managers are concerned about the effects of financial leverage on the risk of bankruptcy, and an analysis of this factor is therefore an important input in all capital structure decisions. Accordingly, managers give considerable weight to financial strength indicators such as the **times-interest-earned (TIE) ratio**, which is computed by dividing EBIT by interest expense. The TIE ratio provides an indication of how well the firm can cover its interest payments with operating income (EBIT): the lower this ratio, the higher the probability that a firm will default on its debt and be forced into bankruptcy.

Following are expected TIE ratios that OptiCap would experience at the different debt/assets ratios we examined.

Debt/Assets Ratio	Expected TIE
10%	25.0×
20	11.8
30	7.4
40	5.0
50	3.3
60	2.2

As you can see, if the debt/assets ratio is only 10 percent, the expected TIE is very high at 25×, but the interest coverage ratio would decline rapidly if the debt/assets ratio is increased. Note, however, that these coverages are expected values at different debt/assets ratios; the actual TIE for any debt/assets ratio will be higher if sales exceed the expected level, but lower if sales fall

times-interest-earned (TIE) ratio A ratio that measures the firm's ability to meet its annual interest obligations; calculated by dividing earnings before interest and taxes (EBIT) by interest charges.

below this level. In general, we know that with less debt, there is a much lower probability of a TIE of less than 1.0, the level at which the firm is not earning enough to meet its required interest payments and thus is seriously exposed to the threat of bankruptcy.[11]

12-5 Capital Structure Theory

Over the years, researchers have proposed numerous theories to explain what firms' capital structures should be and why firms have different capital structures. The general theories of capital structure have been developed along two main lines: (1) tax benefit/bankruptcy cost trade-off theory and (2) signaling theory. These two theories are discussed in this section.

12-5a Trade-Off Theory

Modern capital structure theory began in 1958, when Professors Franco Modigliani and Merton Miller (hereafter MM) published what is considered by many to be the most influential finance article ever written.[12] MM proved—under a very restrictive set of assumptions, including that such financial costs as personal income taxes, brokerage costs, and bankruptcy do not exist—that due to the tax deductibility of interest on corporate debt, a firm's value rises continuously as more debt is used, and hence its value will be maximized by financing almost entirely with debt.

Because several of the assumptions outlined by MM obviously were, and still are, unrealistic, MM's position was only the beginning of capital structure research. Subsequent researchers, and MM themselves, extended the basic theory by relaxing the assumptions. Other researchers attempted to test the various theoretical models with actual data to see exactly how stock

---

[10]Recognizing this fact, most public service commissions that regulate utilities require them to obtain the commission's approval before issuing long-term securities, and Congress has empowered the SEC to supervise the capital structures of public utility holding companies. However, in addition to concern over the firms' safety, which suggests low debt ratios, both managers and regulators recognize a need to keep all costs as low as possible, including the cost of capital. Because a firm's capital structure affects its cost of capital, regulatory commissions and utility managers try to select capital structures that will minimize the cost of capital, subject to the constraint that the firm's financial flexibility not be endangered.

[11]Note that cash flows can be sufficient to cover required interest payments even though the TIE is less than 1.0. Thus, at least for a while, a firm might be able to avoid bankruptcy even though its operating income is less than its interest charges. However, most debt contracts stipulate that firms must maintain the TIE ratio above some minimum level, say, 2.0 or 2.5, or else they cannot borrow any additional funds, which can severely constrain operations. Such potential constraints, as much as the threat of actual bankruptcy, limit the use of debt.

[12]Franco Modigliani and Merton H. Miller, "The Cost of Capital, Corporation Finance, and the Theory of Investment," *American Economic Review*, June 1958, 261–297, and "Corporate Income Taxes and the Cost of Capital," *American Economic Review*, June 1963, 433–443. Modigliani and Miller both won Nobel Prizes for their work.

prices and capital costs are affected by capital structure. Both the theoretical and the empirical results have added to our understanding of capital structure, but none of these studies has produced results that can be used to precisely identify a firm's optimal capital structure. A summary of the theoretical and empirical research is expressed graphically in Figure 12.5.

Here are the key points in the figure:

1. The fact that interest is a tax-deductible expense makes corporate debt less expensive than common stock or preferred stock. In effect, the government pays, or subsidizes, part of the cost of debt capital; thus, using debt causes more of the firm's operating income (EBIT) to flow through to investors. Accordingly, the more debt a company uses, the higher its value.

2. A firm pays higher interest rates as it uses greater amounts of debt. In addition, expected tax rates fall at high debt levels, which further reduces the expected value of the debt tax shelter. Further, as the firm uses more debt, the probability of bankruptcy, which brings with it lawyers' fees and other costs, increases.

3. There is some threshold level of debt, labeled D/A_1 in Figure 12.5, below which the effects noted in point 2 are immaterial. Beyond D/A_1, however, the bankruptcy-related costs, especially higher interest rates on new debt, become increasingly important, and they reduce the tax benefits of debt at an increasing rate. In the range from D/A_1 to D/A_2, bankruptcy-related costs reduce but do not completely offset the tax benefits of debt, so the firm's stock price rises (but at a decreasing rate) as the debt/assets ratio increases. However, beyond D/A_2, bankruptcy-related costs exceed the tax benefits, so from this point on increasing the debt/assets ratio lowers the value of the stock. Therefore, D/A_2 is the optimal capital structure.

4. Although both theory and empirical evidence support the preceding discussion, researchers have not been able to identify points D/A_1 and D/A_2 precisely. As a result, the graphs shown in Figures 12.4 and 12.5 must be taken as approximations, not as precisely defined functions.

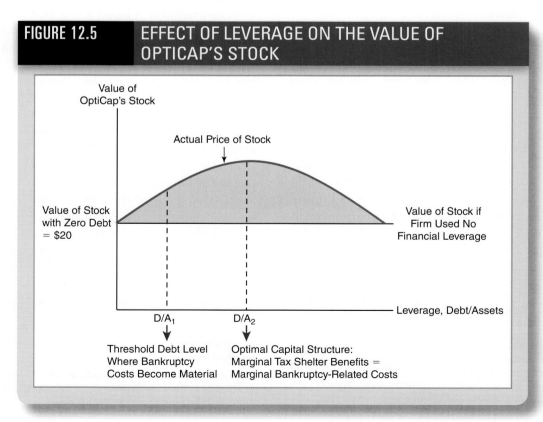

FIGURE 12.5 EFFECT OF LEVERAGE ON THE VALUE OF OPTICAP'S STOCK

Another disturbing aspect of capital structure theory as expressed in Figure 12.5 is the fact that many large, successful firms, such as Microsoft, use far less debt than the theory suggests. This point led to the development of signaling theory, which is discussed next.

12-5b Signaling Theory

MM assumed that investors have the same information about a firm's prospects as its managers. This is called **symmetric information**, because both those who are inside the firm (managers and employees) and those who are outside the firm (investors) have identical information. However, in reality, we know that managers have substantially more and better information about their firms than do outside investors. This is called **asymmetric information**, and it has an important effect on decisions to use either debt or equity to finance capital projects. To see why, consider two situations, one in which the company's managers know that its prospects are extremely favorable (Firm F) and one in which the managers know that the future looks very unfavorable (Firm U).

Suppose, for example, that Firm F's research and development labs have just discovered a cure for the common cold, but the product is not patentable. Firm F's managers want to keep the new product a secret for as long as possible to delay competitors' entry into the market. New plants and distribution facilities must be built to exploit the new product, so capital must be raised. How should Firm F's management raise the needed capital? If the firm sells stock, when profits from the new product start flowing in, the price of the stock will rise sharply and the purchasers of the new stock will have made a bonanza. The current stockholders (including the managers) also will do well, but not as well as they would have if the company had not sold stock before the price increased, because then they would not have had to share the benefits of the new product with the new stockholders. Therefore, *one would expect a firm with very favorable prospects to try to avoid selling stock* and, rather, to raise any required new capital by other means, including using debt beyond the normal target capital structure.[13]

Now let's consider Firm U. Suppose its managers have information that new orders are off sharply because a competitor has installed new technology that has improved its products' quality. Firm U must upgrade its own facilities at a high cost, just to maintain its existing sales level. As a result, its return on investment will fall (but not by as much as if it took no action, which would lead to a 100 percent loss through bankruptcy). How should Firm U raise the needed capital? Here the situation is just the reverse of that facing Firm F, which did not want to sell stock so as to avoid having to share the benefits of future developments. *A firm with unfavorable prospects would want to sell stock, which would mean bringing in new investors to share the losses!*[14]

The conclusion from all this is that firms with extremely bright prospects prefer not to finance through new stock offerings, whereas firms with poor prospects do like to finance with outside equity. How would you, as an investor, react to this conclusion? You ought to say, "If I see that a company plans to issue new stock, this should worry me because I know that management would not want to issue stock if future prospects looked good, but it *would* want to issue stock if things looked bad. Therefore, I should lower my estimate of the firm's value, other things constant, if I read an announcement of a new stock offering." Of course, the negative reaction would be stronger if the stock sale were by a large, established company such as General Electric or IBM, which surely would have many financing options, than if it were by a small company such as USR Industries. For USR, a stock sale might mean truly extraordinary investment opportunities that are so large they just could not be financed without a stock sale.

hxdbzxy/Shutterstock.com

symmetric information The situation in which investors and managers have identical information about the firm's prospects.

asymmetric information The situation in which managers have different (better) information about their firm's prospects than do outside investors.

[13]It would be illegal for Firm F's managers to purchase more shares on the basis of their inside knowledge of the new product. They could be sent to jail if they did.

[14]Of course, Firm U would have to make certain disclosures when it offered new shares to the public, but it might be able to meet the legal requirements without fully disclosing management's worst fears.

If you gave the preceding answer, your views are consistent with those of many sophisticated portfolio managers. Simply stated, the announcement of a stock offering by a mature firm that seems to have multiple financing alternatives is taken as a signal that the firm's prospects as seen by its management are not bright. This, in turn, suggests that when a mature firm announces a new stock offering, the price of its stock should decline. Empirical studies have shown that this situation does indeed exist.

What are the implications of all this for capital structure decisions? The answer is that firms should, in normal times, maintain a reserve borrowing capacity that can be used in the event that some especially good investment opportunities come along. This means that firms should generally use less debt than would be suggested by the tax benefit/bankruptcy cost trade-off expressed in Figure 12.5.

Signaling and asymmetric information concepts also have implications for the marginal cost of capital (MCC) curve discussed in Chapter 11. There we saw that the weighted average cost of capital (WACC) increased when retained earnings were exhausted and the firm was forced to sell new common stock to raise equity. The jump in the WACC, or the break in the MCC schedule, was attributed only to flotation costs. However, if the announcement of a stock sale causes a decline in the price of the stock, then r_e as measured by $r_e = \hat{D}_1/P_0(1 - F) + g$ will increase more because of the decline in P_0. This factor magnifies the effects of flotation costs, and perhaps it is an even more important explanation for the jump in the MCC schedule at the point at which new stock must be issued.

12-6 Variations in Capital Structures among Firms

As might be expected, wide variations in the use of financial leverage occur both across industries and among the individual firms in each industry. For example, drug and biotechnology companies generally do not use much debt (their common equity ratios are high), because the production of successful pharmaceuticals or biotech products is unpredictable. The uncertainties inherent in industries such as these as well as those that are cyclical, oriented toward research, or subject to huge product liability suits normally render the heavy use of debt unwise. On the other hand, utilities traditionally use large amounts of debt, particularly long-term debt. Their fixed

[15] The information provided in this section was obtained primarily from *OECD Financial Statistics, Part 3: Non-Financial Enterprises Financial Statement, 1996.*

assets make good security for mortgage bonds, and their relatively stable sales make it safe for them to carry more debt than would be true for firms with more business risk.

Wide variations in capital structures also exist among firms in particular industries. For example, although the average pharmaceutical firm had a capital structure consisting of approximately 30 percent debt at the end of 2014. Merck & Company had approximately 50 percent debt in its capital structure whereas GlaxoSmithKline had greater than 88 percent debt in its capital structure. Thus, we can conclude that factors unique to individual firms, including managerial attitudes, play an important role in setting target capital structures.

12-6a Capital Structures around the World[15]

As you might expect, when we examine the capital structures of companies around the world, we also find wide variations. Companies in Italy and Japan use greater proportions of debt (65 to 80 percent) than do companies in the United States and Canada (45 to 55 percent), and companies in the United Kingdom use the lowest proportion of debt of industrialized countries (30 to 35 percent). Of course, different countries use somewhat different accounting conventions, which make comparisons difficult. Still, even after adjusting for accounting differences, researchers find that Italian and Japanese firms use considerably more financial leverage than U.S. and Canadian companies.

It seems reasonable to attribute differences in firms' capital structures among countries to dissimilar tax structures. Although the interest on corporate debt is deductible in most countries, and individuals must pay taxes on interest received, both dividends and capital gains are taxed differently around the world. The tax codes in most developed countries encourage personal investing and savings more than the U.S. tax code does. For example, Germany, Italy, and many other European countries do not tax capital gains, and in most other developed countries, including Japan, France, and Canada, capital gains are not taxed unless they exceed some minimum amount. Further, in Germany and Italy, dividends are not taxed as income, and in most other countries, some amount of dividends is tax exempt. From these observations, we can make the following general conclusions: (1) From a tax standpoint, corporations should be equally inclined to use

signal An action taken by a firm's management that provides clues to investors about how management views the firm's prospects.

reserve borrowing capacity The ability to borrow money at a reasonable cost when good investment opportunities arise; firms often use less debt than specified by the optimal capital structure to ensure that they can obtain debt capital later if necessary.

debt in most developed countries. (2) In countries where capital gains are not taxed, investors should show a preference for stocks compared to investors in countries that have capital gains taxes. (3) Investor preferences should lead to relatively low equity capital costs in those countries that do not tax capital gains, and this, in turn, should cause firms in those countries to use significantly more equity capital than their U.S. counterparts. For the most part, however, this is exactly the opposite of the actual capital structures we observe, so differences in tax laws cannot explain the observed capital structure differences.

If tax rates cannot explain the different capital structures, perhaps risks, such as the risk of bankruptcy, can. Actual bankruptcy, and even the threat of potential bankruptcy, imposes a costly burden on firms with large amounts of debt. In the United States, *equity* monitoring costs are comparatively low because corporations produce quarterly reports and must comply with relatively stringent audit requirements, which are less prevalent in other countries. On the other hand, costs associated with monitoring debt probably are lower in such countries as Germany and Japan than in the United States, because most of the corporate debt in those countries consists of bank loans as opposed to publicly issued bonds. More importantly, though, the banks in many European and developed Asian countries are closely linked to the corporations that borrow from them, often holding major equity positions in, and having substantial influence over, the management of the debtor firms. Given these close relationships, the banks in Germany and Japan are much more directly involved than U.S. banks are with debtor firms' affairs, and as a result, they also are more accommodating than are U.S. bondholders in the event of financial distress. This, in turn, suggests that any given amount of debt gives rise to a lower threat of bankruptcy for a firm in Germany and Japan than for a U.S. firm with the same amount of business risk. Thus, an analysis of both bankruptcy costs and equity monitoring costs leads to the conclusion that U.S. firms should have more equity and less debt than do firms in countries such as Japan and Germany, which is what we typically observe.

We cannot state that one financial system is better than another one in the sense of making the firms in one country more efficient than those in another. However, as U.S. firms become increasingly involved in worldwide operations, they must become increasingly aware of worldwide conditions, and they must be prepared to adapt to conditions in the various countries in which they do business.

STUDY TOOLS

LOCATED AT BACK OF THE TEXTBOOK

- ☐ Problems are found at the end of this chapter.
- ☐ A tear-out Chapter Review card is located at the back of the textbook.

LOCATED AT WWW.CENGAGEBRAIN.COM

- ☐ Review Key Term flashcards and create your own cards.
- ☐ Track your knowledge and understanding of key concepts in corporate finance.
- ☐ Complete practice and graded quizzes to prepare for tests.
- ☐ Complete interactive content within CFIN5 Online.
- ☐ View the chapter highlight boxes for CFIN5 Online.

KEY CAPITAL STRUCTURE CONCEPTS

To conclude this chapter, we summarize some capital structure concepts that were discussed. Basic factors that influence capital structure decisions include the following:

- The greater the firm's *business risk*, or the riskiness that would be inherent in the firm's operations if it used no debt, the lower the amount of debt that is optimal.

- *Financial risk* is the risk common stockholders must take when the firm uses financing alternatives that require fixed periodic payments (e.g., debt and preferred stock).

- Firms that maintain *financial flexibility*, or the ability to raise capital on reasonable terms under adverse conditions, are less risky and find it easier to raise funds when money is tight than firms that don't have financial flexibility.

- Some managers are more aggressive than others when using debt; hence, managerial attitude (conservatism or aggressiveness) influences the amount of debt a firm takes on. This factor does not affect the optimal, or value-maximizing, capital structure.

- Leverage, which is the presence of fixed costs (both operating and financial), magnifies the effects of

changes in sales on operating income and net income. Everything else the same, more leverage generally indicates more risk. Thus, leverage should be considered when making capital structure decisions.

- Even though scientific models have not been developed to determine the optimal capital structure of a firm, it is important for a company to evaluate the effects of leverage on its value (as outlined in this chapter) to establish a target capital structure that can be followed when raising funds.

PROBLEMS

In all of the following problems, it is assumed that the firm's capital structure consists of debt and common equity only; preferred stock is not used to finance the firm.

12–1 Using the information provided in Tables 12.1 and 12.2, compute OptiCap's EPS when sales are $200,000 and the debt-to-total-assets ratio (D/TA) is 20 percent.

12–2 Loving Gardens (LG) has $6 million in assets, $700,000 EBIT, 80,000 shares of stock outstanding, and a marginal tax rate equal to 40 percent. If LG's debt-to-total-assets ratio (D/TA) is 70 percent, it pays 12 percent interest on debt, whereas if the D/TA ratio is 40 percent, interest is 9 percent. Calculate LG's EPS and ROE (ROE = Net income/Equity) for each capital structure. Which capital structure is better?

12–3 Firm AB and Firm YZ are identical except for their debt-to-total-assets ratios (D/TAs) and interest rates on debt. Each has $200,000 in assets, $40,000 EBIT, and a 40 percent marginal tax rate. Firm AB has a D/TA ratio of 40 percent and pays 7.5 percent interest on its debt, whereas YZ has a 60 percent D/TA ratio and pays 10 percent interest on debt. Each firm has 5,000 shares of common stock outstanding. Calculate each firm's EPS and ROE (ROE = Net income/Equity). Discuss your results.

12–4 Firm LM's debt-to-total-assets ratio (D/TA) is 25 percent, whereas Firm QR's D/TA ratio is 50 percent. LM has $800,000 in assets, $60,000 EBIT, and 15,000 shares of stock outstanding, and it pays 8 percent interest. QR has $400,000 in assets, $70,000 EBIT, and 25,000 shares of stock outstanding, and it pays 10 percent interest. The marginal tax rate for both firms is 40 percent. Calculate each firm's EPS and ROE (ROE = Net income/Equity). Discuss your results.

12–5 Senior management of Nancy's Nooks (NN) has determined that there is a 20 percent chance EPS will be $4.50 next year, there is a 60 percent chance EPS will be 1.50, and there is a 20 percent chance EPS will be –$1.80. Calculate the expected value, standard deviation, and coefficient of variation for NN's forecasted EPS.

12–6 Given the following information, calculate the expected value, standard deviation, and coefficient of variation of the EPS for both firms.

	Probability		
	0.3	**0.6**	**0.1**
Firm 1: EPS$_1$	$2.00	$1.30	($1.20)
Firm 2: EPS$_2$	$3.00	1.80	(2.20)

12–7 The CFO of Ink Imagination (II) wants to calculate next year's EPS using different leverage ratios. II's total assets are $5 million, and its marginal tax rate is 40 percent. The company has estimated next year's EBIT for three possible economic states: $1.2 million with a 0.2 probability, $800,000 with a 0.5 probability, and $500,000 with a 0.3 probability. Calculate II's expected EPS, standard deviation, and coefficient of variation for each of the following capital structures. Which capital structure do you recommend?

Leverage (Debt/Assets)	Interest Rate	Shares of Stock Outstanding
20%	6%	300,000
50	10	200,000

12–8 Absolute Corporation currently has $50 million in liabilities and common equity in combination. The firm has no preferred stock. After careful evaluation, the

CFO constructed the following table to show the CEO the effect of changing the firm's capital structure:

Amount of Debt in the Capital Structure	Earnings per Share (EPS)	Market Price per Share (P_0)
$10,000,000	$5.00	$125.50
20,000,000	5.50	130.75
30,000,000	5.70	130.00

According to this information, what is Absolute's optimal capital structure? Explain your answer.

12-9 Using the following information for Handy Hardware, determine the capital structure that results in the lowest weighted average cost of capital (WACC) for the firm. Explain your answer.

Proportion of Debt	Earnings per Share (EPS)	Stock Price, P_0
10%	$3.85	$95.40
30	3.98	97.25
50	4.10	96.80

12-10 Following is the latest income statement for Surfside Airlines:

Sales	$150,000
Variable operating costs	(105,000)
Gross profit	45,000
Fixed operating costs	(20,000)
Net operating income	25,000
Interest	(15,000)
Earnings before taxes	10,000
Taxes (40%)	(4,000)
Net income	$ 6,000

Compute Surfside's degree of operating leverage (DOL), degree of financial leverage (DFL), and degree of total leverage (DTL).

12-11 Data Recovery Systems (DRS) has a degree of operating leverage (DOL) equal to 3.2× and a degree of total leverage (DTL) equal to 8×. DRS forecasts that this year's sales will be $300,000 and that EBIT will be $180,000. If sales actually turn out to be $313,500, what will DRS's EBIT be?

12-12 The CFO of Jupiter Jibs (JJ) expects this year's sales to be $2.5 million. EBIT is expected to be $1 million. The CFO knows that if sales actually turn out to be $2.3 million, JJ's EBIT will be $880,000. What is JJ's degree of operating leverage (DOL)?

12-13 The CFO of The Chop Shop has determined that the company's degree of operating leverage (DOL) is

2.5× and that its degree of financial leverage (DFL) is 3.0×. According to this information, how will the firm's EPS be affected if its amount of EBIT turns out to be 5 percent higher than expected?

12-14 Enigma Energy has forecasted that its EPS will be $4 per share this year. If the firm's degree of operating leverage (DOL) is 3.0× and its degree of financial leverage (DFL) is 2.0×, what will its EPS be if sales turn out to be 10 percent lower than expected?

12-15 Muddy Murphy's degree of financial leverage (DFL) is 4×. The company knows that if sales are 6 percent higher than forecasted, its EPS will increase by 36 percent. What is Muddy's degree of operating leverage (DOL)?

12-16 Luxury Leisure's forecasted EBIT is $750,000. This year, Luxury will pay $250,000 interest on its debt and $320,000 dividends to its common stockholders. If its marginal tax rate is 40 percent, what is Luxury's degree of financial leverage (DFL)?

12-17 A firm has determined that its degree of operating leverage (DOL) is 5× and that its degree of financial leverage (DFL) is 2×. As a result, what will be the change in its expected EPS if sales are 7 percent lower than expected?

12-18 Smith Bottling Company (SBC) expects this year's sales to be $560,000. SBC's variable operating costs are 75 percent of sales and its fixed operating costs are $90,000. SBC pays interest on its debt equal to $30,000 per year and its marginal tax rate is 35 percent. (a) Compute SBC's DOL, DFL, and DTL. (b) If sales turn out to be $588,000 rather than $560,000, what will be SBC's EBIT and net income?

12-19 The CFO determined that the firm's degree of operating leverage (DOL) is 3× at sales equal to $900,000. She also determined that, if sales are actually $945,000, EPS will be $2.60 rather than the forecasted value of $2.00. What is the firm's degree of financial leverage (DFL)?

12-20 Expert Analysts Resources (EAR) has provided you with the following information about three companies you are currently evaluating:

Company	Degree of Operating Leverage (DOL)	Degree of Financial Leverage (DFL)
Acme	1.5×	6.0×
Apex	3.0×	4.0×
Alps	5.0×	2.0×

Which firm would be considered riskiest? Explain your answer.

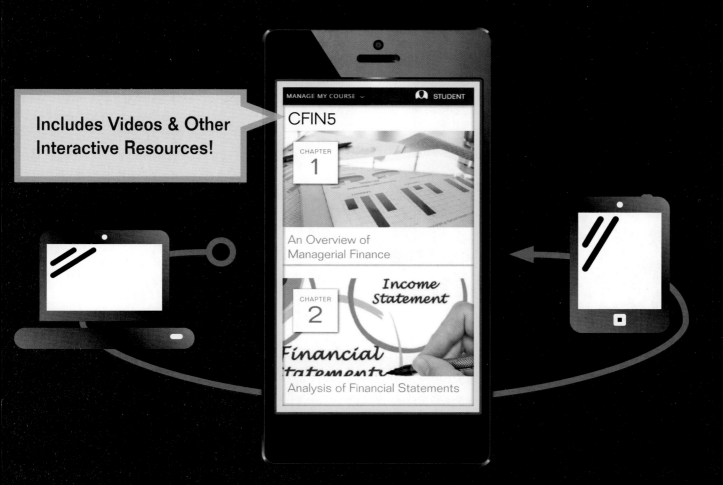

After you finish this chapter go to **PAGE 263** for **STUDY TOOLS**

LEARNING OUTCOMES

After studying this chapter, you will be able to…

LO1 Describe the views that have been proposed to explain why firms follow particular dividend policies and why investors react when firms change dividend policies.

LO2 Discuss (a) the types of dividend payments and (b) payment procedures that firms follow in practice.

LO3 Discuss factors that firms consider when making dividend policy decisions.

LO4 Describe stock dividends and stock splits, and discuss how stock prices are affected by these activities.

LO5 Describe stock repurchases and discuss reasons firms use repurchases.

LO6 Discuss differences in dividend polices around the world.

Distribution of Retained Earnings:
Dividends and Stock Repurchases

13

A firm's *dividend policy* involves the decision whether to pay out earnings or to retain them for reinvestment in the firm. Remember that, according to the constant dividend growth model introduced in Chapter 7, the value of common stock can be computed as $P_0 = \hat{D}_1/(r_s - g)$. This equation shows that if the firm adopts a policy of paying out more in cash dividends, $\hat{D}_1$ rises, which tends to increase the price of the stock. However, everything else equal, if cash dividends are increased, less money is available for reinvestment in the firm and the expected future growth rate, g, will be lowered, which will depress the price of the stock. Thus, changing the dividend has two opposing effects. *The **optimal dividend policy** for a firm strikes a balance between current dividends and future growth that maximizes the price of the stock.*

In Chapter 12, we discussed concepts related to determining a firm's optimal capital structure. In this chapter, we discuss activities that relate to capital structure because they affect the equity section of a firm's balance sheet: dividends and stock repurchases. An important decision that a firm faces each year is how to use the income that is earned. Thus, the basic question that management must answer is how much

of the earnings should be retained and reinvested in the firm, and how much should be distributed to stockholders.

13-1 Dividend Policy and Stock Value

How do dividend policy decisions affect a firm's stock price? Academic researchers have studied this question extensively for many years, and they have yet to reach definitive conclusions. On the one hand, there are those who suggest that dividend policy is *irrelevant* because they argue that a firm's value should be determined by the basic earning power and business risk of the firm, in which case value depends only on the income (cash) produced, not on how the income is split between dividends and retained earnings (and hence growth). Proponents of this line of reasoning, called the **dividend irrelevance theory**, would contend that investors care only about the *total returns* they receive, not whether they receive those returns in the form of dividends, capital gains, or both. Thus, *if the dividend irrelevance theory is correct, there exists no optimal dividend policy, because dividend policy does not affect the value of the firm.*[1]

optimal dividend policy The dividend policy that strikes a balance between current dividends and future growth, and maximizes the firm's stock price.

dividend irrelevance theory The theory that a firm's dividend policy has no effect on either its value or its cost of capital.

[1] The principal proponents of the *dividend irrelevance theory* are Miller and Modigliani (MM), who outlined their theory in "Dividend Policy, Growth, and the Valuation of Shares," *Journal of Business*, October 1961, 411–433. The assumptions MM made to develop their dividend irrelevance theory are similar to those they introduced in their capital structure theory mentioned in Chapter 12, which include no personal taxes, no brokerage costs, no bankruptcy, and so forth. Such assumptions are made to afford them the ability to develop a manageable theory.

On the other hand, it is quite possible that investors do prefer one dividend policy to another; if so, a firm's dividend policy is *relevant*. For example, it has been argued that investors prefer to receive dividends today because current dividend payments are more certain than the future capital gains that *might* result when a firm retains earnings to invest in growth opportunities. If this logic is correct, the required return on equity, r_s, should decrease as the dividend payout is increased, causing the firm's stock price to increase.[2]

Another factor that might cause investors to prefer a particular dividend policy is the tax effect of dividend receipts. Investors must pay taxes at the time dividends and capital gains are received. Thus, depending on his or her tax situation, an investor might prefer either a payout of current earnings as dividends, which would be taxed in the current period, or the capital gains associated with growth in stock value, which would be taxed when the stock is sold, perhaps many years in the future. Investors who prefer to delay the impact of taxes would be willing to pay more for companies with low dividend payouts than for otherwise similar high dividend-payout companies, and vice versa.

Those who believe that the firm's dividend policy is relevant are proponents of the **dividend relevance theory**, which asserts that dividend policy can affect the value of a firm through investors' preferences.

Although academic researchers have studied the dividend policy issue extensively, they cannot tell corporate decision makers exactly how dividend policy affects stock prices and capital costs. However, the research has provided some views concerning investors' reactions to dividend policy changes as well as why firms have particular dividend policies. Three of these views are discussed in this section.

13-1a Information Content, or Signaling

If investors expect a company's dividend to increase by 5 percent per year, and the dividend actually increases by 5 percent, the stock price generally will not change significantly on the day the dividend increase is announced. In Wall Street parlance, the announcement of such a dividend increase

would be *discounted*, or anticipated, by the market, so it would not be considered newsworthy. However, if investors expect a 5 percent increase but the company actually increases the dividend by 25 percent—say, from $2.00 to $2.50—this generally will be considered good, unanticipated news that should be accompanied by an increase in the price of the stock. Conversely, a lower-than-expected dividend increase, or an unexpected reduction, generally would result in a price decline.

It is a well-known fact that corporations are extremely reluctant to cut dividends, and therefore *managers do not raise dividends unless they anticipate higher, or at least stable, earnings in the future to sustain the higher dividends*. This means that a larger-than-expected dividend increase is taken by investors as a signal that the firm's management forecasts improved future earnings, whereas a dividend reduction signals a forecast of poor earnings. Thus, it can be argued that investors' reactions to changes in dividend payments do not show that investors prefer dividends to retained earnings; rather, stock price changes simply indicate that important information is contained in dividend announcements, because, in effect, such announcements provide investors with information previously known only to management. This theory is referred to as the **information content**, or **signaling**, **hypothesis**.

13-1b Clientele Effect

It also has been shown that it is possible for a firm to set a particular dividend payout policy, which then attracts a *clientele* consisting of those investors who like the firm's dividend policy. For example, some stockholders, such as retired individuals, prefer current income to future capital gains, so they invest in firms that pay out high percentages of their earnings as dividends. Other stockholders have no need for current investment income, so they favor low dividend-payout ratios. If investors could not invest in companies with different dividend policies, it might be very expensive for them to achieve their investment goals. For example, investors who prefer capital gains can reinvest any dividends they receive, but they first will have to pay taxes on the income. In essence, then, a **clientele effect** might exist if investors are attracted to certain companies because they have particular dividend policies. In reality, those investors who desire

dividend relevance theory The value of a firm is affected by its dividend policy— the optimal dividend policy is the one that maximizes the firm's value.

information content (signaling) hypothesis The theory that investors regard dividend changes as signals of management's earnings forecasts.

clientele effect The tendency of a firm to attract the type of investor who likes its dividend policy.

[2]Myron J. Gordon, "Optimal Investment and Financing Policy," *Journal of Finance*, May 1963, 264–272, and John Lintner, "Dividends, Earnings, Leverage, Stock Prices, and the Supply of Capital to Corporations," *Review of Economics and Statistics*, August 1962, 243–269.

current investment income can purchase shares in high dividend-payout firms, whereas those who do not need current income can invest in low-payout firms. Consequently, we would expect the stock price of a firm to change if the firm changes its dividend policy, because investors will adjust their portfolios to include firms with the desired dividend policy.

13-1c Free Cash Flow Hypothesis

If it is the intent of the financial manager to maximize the value of the firm, then investors should prefer that the firm pay dividends only if acceptable capital budgeting opportunities do not exist. We know that acceptable capital budgeting projects increase the value of the firm. We also know that, because flotation costs are incurred when new stock is issued, it costs a firm more to raise funds using new common equity than it does to use retained earnings. To maximize value, therefore, wherever possible a firm should use retained earnings rather than issue new common stock to finance capital budgeting projects. Proponents of this line of reasoning argue that dividends should be paid only when *free cash flows* in excess of capital budgeting needs exist; if management does otherwise, the firm's value will not be maximized. According to the **free cash flow hypothesis**, the firm should distribute any earnings that cannot be reinvested at a rate that is at least as great as the investors' required rate of return, which is the same as the cost of retained earnings, r_s, that was discussed in Chapter 11. In other words, free cash flows should be paid out as dividends. Everything else being equal, *firms that retain free cash flows have lower values than firms that distribute free cash flows*, because such firms decrease investors' wealth by investing in projects with IRRs less than r_s.

The free cash flow hypothesis might help to explain why investors react differently to identical dividend changes made by similar firms. For example, a firm's stock price should not change dramatically, and it might even increase, if dividends are reduced for the purposes of investing in capital budgeting projects with positive NPVs. On the other hand, a company that reduces its dividend simply to increase free cash flows should experience a significant decline in the market value of its stock, because the dividend reduction is not in the best interests of the stockholders. (In this case, an agency problem exists.) Thus, the free cash flow hypothesis suggests that a firm's dividend policy can provide information about management's behavior with respect to wealth maximization.

13-2 Dividend Payments in Practice

Although no one has been able to develop a formula that can be used to tell management specifically how a given dividend policy will affect a firm's stock price, management still must establish a dividend policy that specifies how much the annual dividend payment should be as well as when and how the payment should be made. In this section, we discuss dividend payout policies that are generally observed in practice.

13-2a Residual Dividend Policy

In practice, dividend policy is very much influenced by investment opportunities and by the availability of funds used to finance new investments. This fact has led to the development of a **residual dividend policy**, which states that a firm should follow these steps when deciding how much should be paid out as dividends each year: (1) Determine the optimal capital budget for the year. (2) To the extent possible, use retained earnings to provide the equity component of the total funds that are needed to finance the projects. (3) Pay dividends only if more earnings are generated than are needed to support the optimal capital budget. The word *residual* means "leftover," and the residual policy implies that dividends should be paid only out of *leftover earnings, which are the earnings that remain after capital budgeting funding requirements are satisfied.*

The basis of the residual policy is the fact that investors prefer to have the firm retain and reinvest earnings rather than pay them out in dividends *if the rate of return the firm can earn on reinvested earnings exceeds the rate investors, on average, can themselves earn on other investments of comparable risk.* For example, if the corporation can reinvest retained earnings at a 12 percent rate of return, whereas the best rate the average stockholder can obtain if the earnings are passed on in the form of dividends is 11 percent, stockholders should prefer to have the firm retain the profits.

To continue, we saw in Chapter 11 that the cost of retained

> **free cash flow hypothesis** All else equal, firms that pay dividends from cash flows that cannot be reinvested in positive net present value projects (*free cash flows*) have higher values than firms that retain free cash flows.

> **residual dividend policy** A policy in which the dividend paid is set to equal the actual earnings minus the amount of retained earnings necessary to finance the firm's optimal capital budget.

earnings is an *opportunity cost* that reflects rates of return available to equity investors. If a firm's stockholders can buy other stocks of equal risk and obtain an 11 percent return, then 11 percent is the firm's cost of retained earnings. The cost of new outside equity raised by selling common stock will be higher than 11 percent due to the costs associated with issuing the new stock (flotation costs).

From our discussion in Chapter 12, we know that most firms have target capital structures that call for at least some debt, so new financing is done partly with debt and partly with equity. As long as the firm finances with the optimal mix of debt and equity, and as long as it uses only internally generated equity (retained earnings), its marginal cost of each new dollar of capital will be less than if new equity financing is used. Internally generated equity is available for financing a certain amount of new investment, so beyond that amount the firm must turn to new common stock, which is more expensive. At the point where new stock must be sold, the cost of equity, and consequently the marginal cost of capital, rises.

These concepts are illustrated in Figure 13.1 with data from the Texas and Western (T&W) Transport Company. T&W has a marginal cost of capital (MCC) equal to 10 percent. However, this rate assumes that all additional equity comes from retained earnings. Therefore, MCC = 10% as long as retained earnings are available, but the MCC begins to rise at the point where new stock must be sold.

T&W has $60 million of net income and a 40 percent debt ratio at its optimal capital structure. If it does not pay cash dividends, T&W can make investments equal to $100 million, consisting of $60 million from retained earnings plus $40 million of new debt, at a 10 percent marginal cost of capital. Therefore, its MCC is constant at 10 percent up to $100 million of capital, beyond which the MCC rises as the firm begins to use more expensive new common stock.

Suppose T&W's director of capital budgeting has determined that the optimal capital budget requires a total investment equal to $70 million. The $70 million will be financed using $28 million debt (= $70 million × 0.40) and $42 million in common equity (= $70 million × 0.60). The $60 million retained earnings will be more than sufficient to cover the common equity financing requirement, so the *residual earnings* of $18 million (= $60 million − $42 million) can be paid out as dividends to stockholders.

Now suppose T&W's optimal capital budget is $150 million. Should dividends be paid? Not if T&W follows the residual dividend policy. Its $150 million capital budgeting needs will be financed with $60 million debt (= $150 million × 0.40) and $90 million common equity (= $150 million × 0.60). The common equity financing requirement of $90 million exceeds the $60 million of available retained earnings, so $30 million of new common equity will have to be issued. The new, or *external*, common equity will have a higher cost than retained earnings, so the marginal cost of capital

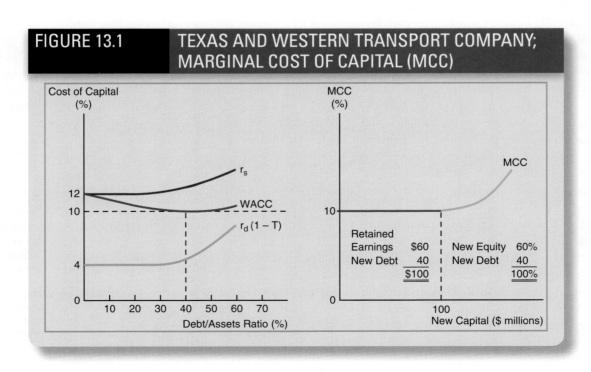

FIGURE 13.1   TEXAS AND WESTERN TRANSPORT COMPANY;
MARGINAL COST OF CAPITAL (MCC)

for T&W will be higher than 10 percent. Under these conditions, T&W should not pay dividends to its stockholders. If the company pays part of its earnings in dividends, the marginal cost of capital will be even higher because more common stock will have to be issued to account for the amount of retained earnings paid out as dividends. For example, if T&W pays stockholders $20 million in dividends, it still needs $90 million of common equity to satisfy the capital budgeting requirements. In this case, $50 million of external equity will be required [= $90 million − ($60 million − $20 million)], which means T&W's marginal cost of capital will increase sooner because new common equity will have to be issued when $40 million rather than $60 million of retained earnings are used. To maximize value, T&W should retain all of its earnings for capital budgeting needs in this case. Consequently, *according to the residual dividend policy, a firm that has to issue new common stock to finance capital budgeting projects does not have residual earnings, and thus should not pay dividends.*

Because both the earnings level and the capital budgeting needs of a firm generally vary from year to year, *strict adherence to the residual dividend policy would result in dividend variability*. One year the firm might declare zero dividends because investment opportunities are good, but the next year it might have a large dividend payout because investment opportunities are poor. Similarly, fluctuating earnings would also lead to variable dividends even if investment opportunities were stable over time. Thus, *following the residual dividend policy would be optimal only if investors were not bothered by fluctuating dividends*. If investors prefer stable, dependable dividends, r_s will be higher, and the stock price lower, if the firm follows the residual theory in a strict sense rather than attempting to stabilize its dividends over time.

13-2b Stable, Predictable Dividends

In the past, many firms set a specific annual dollar dividend per share and then maintained it, increasing the dividend only if it seemed clear that future earnings would be sufficient to maintain the new dividend. A corollary of this policy was the following rule: *Never reduce the annual dividend.*

Figure 13.2 illustrates a fairly typical dividend policy, that of United Parcel Service (UPS). As you can see, UPS's earnings per share (EPS) fluctuated fairly substantially from 1996 through 2015, but its dividends

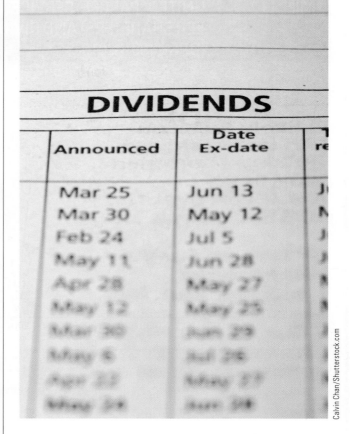

Calvin Chan/Shutterstock.com

steadily increased during this same period. UPS follows the **stable, predictable dividend policy**; its annual dividend has either stayed the same or increased each year since 1970.

There are two good reasons for paying stable, predictable dividends rather than following the residual dividend policy. First, given the existence of the information content (signaling) concept, a fluctuating payment policy would lead to greater uncertainty—and hence to a higher r_s and a lower stock price—than would exist under a stable policy. Second, many stockholders use dividends for current consumption, and they would be put to trouble and expense if they had to sell part of their shares to obtain cash if the company cut the dividend.

As a rule, everything else the same, *stable, predictable dividends imply more certainty than do variable dividends, and thus a lower r_s and a higher firm value*. Accordingly, most firms follow this dividend policy because they want investors to perceive stability (more certainty) in dividend payments.

> **stable, predictable dividend policy** Payment of a specific dollar dividend each year, or periodically increasing the dividend at a constant rate, so that the annual dollar dividend is relatively predictable by investors.

FIGURE 13.2

UNITED PARCEL SERVICE (UPS): EARNINGS PER SHARE (EPS) AND DIVIDENDS PER SHARE (DPS), 1991–2015

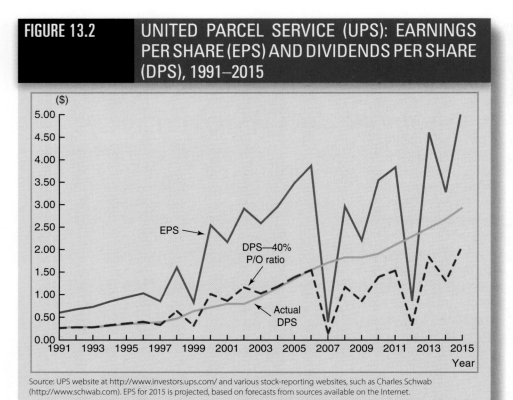

Source: UPS website at http://www.investors.ups.com/ and various stock-reporting websites, such as Charles Schwab (http://www.schwab.com). EPS for 2015 is projected, based on forecasts from sources available on the Internet.

13-2c Constant Payout Ratio

It would be possible for a firm to pay out a constant *percentage* of its earnings each year, but because earnings surely would fluctuate, this policy would mean that the dollar amount of dividends would also vary each year. For example, if UPS had followed the policy of paying a constant percentage of EPS, say 40 percent, the dividends per share paid since 1991 would have fluctuated exactly the same as the EPS, which means that the company would have had to cut its dividend in several years. The dashed line in Figure 13.2 represents the dividends per share that UPS would have paid had it followed a policy that specified dividends should equal 40 percent of earnings each year; as noted, the pattern for the DPS—40% P/O ratio plot (dashed line) mirrors the EPS pattern. Thus, we can conclude that *with the* **constant payout ratio** *dividend policy, if earnings fluctuate, investors have much greater uncertainty concerning the expected dividends each year, and chances are that r_s will also be*

constant payout ratio Payment of a constant *percentage* of earnings as dividends each year.

extra dividend A supplemental dividend paid in years when the firm does well and excess funds are available for distribution.

greater; hence, the firm's stock price will be lower.

13-2d Low Regular Dividend Plus Extras

A policy of paying a low regular dividend plus a year-end extra payment in good years represents a compromise between a stable, predictable dividend and a constant payout ratio. Such a policy gives the firm flexibility, yet investors can count on receiving at least a minimum dividend. Therefore, if a firm's earnings and cash flows are quite volatile, this policy might be a good choice. The board of directors can set a relatively *low regular dividend*—low enough so that it can be maintained even in low-profit years or in years when a considerable amount of retained earnings are needed to fund capital budgeting projects—and then supplement it with an **extra dividend** in years when excess funds are available.

13-2e Application of the Different Types of Dividend Payments: An Illustration

Table 13.1 illustrates the application of the four different types of dividend payments we described previously. Panel I in the table provides general information about each of the four dividend policies, Panel II gives financial information for a fictitious firm, and Panel III shows the dividends that this firm would pay over a four-year period if it followed each of the payout procedures. For reference, Panel IV shows how the dividend is determined in Year 1 for each of the policies for which a computation is required. Note that the annual dividend would vary under each type of payment except the stable, predictable dividend policy. This illustration shows that *firms with incomes and capital budgets that vary each year will pay fairly constant dividends only if they follow the stable, predictable dividend policy.* Therefore, as we mentioned

Table 13.1

Application of Different Types of Dividend Payments: Illustration

I. Dividend Policies

A. Residual dividend—pay dividends if earnings are "left over" after financing capital budgeting needs.

B. Stable, predictable dividend—pay $1 dividend each year.

C. Constant payout ratio—pay 60 percent of earnings each year.

D. Low regular dividend plus extras—pay a minimum dividend equal to $0.75, plus 40 percent of earnings greater than $400,000.

II. Financial Information

	Year 1	Year 2	Year 3	Year 4
Net income	$500,000	$300,000	$800,000	$150,000
Capital budget	$300,000	$350,000	$200,000	$140,000
Number of shares outstanding	250,000	250,000	250,000	250,000

III. Dividend Payments (Per Share)

	Year 1	Year 2	Year 3	Year 4
A. Residual dividend	$0.80	—	$2.40	$0.04
B. Stable, predictable dividend	$1.00	$1.00	$1.00	$1.00
C. Constant payout ratio (60%)	$1.20	$0.72	$1.92	$0.36
D. Low regular dividend plus extras	$0.91	$0.75	$1.39	$0.75

IV. Computations of Year 1 Dividend Payments for the Policies

A. Residual dividend

$$DPS_1 = \frac{\$500,000 - \$300,000}{250,000} = \frac{\$200,000}{250,000} = \$0.80$$

C. Constant payout ratio

$$DPS_1 = \frac{\$500,000(0.60)}{250,000} = \frac{\$300,000}{250,000} = \$1.20$$

D. Low regular (minimum) dividend

$$DPS_1 = \$0.75 + \frac{(\$500,000 - \$400,000)0.40}{250,000} = \$0.75 + \frac{\$40,000}{250,000} = \$0.91$$

earlier, because investors perceive more certainty with stable, predictable dividend payments, most firms try to follow this dividend policy in practice.

13-2f Payment Procedures

Dividends normally are paid semiannually or quarterly, and an announcement, or declaration, of the dividend is made prior to its payment. For example, on August 6, 2015, the board of directors of United Parcel Service (UPS) declared a $0.73 quarterly common stock dividend. Earlier in the year the board had indicated that it anticipated the annual dividend would be increased to $2.92 from its 2014 level of $2.68 per share. As a result, UPS's stockholders were not surprised when the $0.73 quarterly dividend was announced in August. In fact, this was the third time in 2015 that UPS had announced a $0.73 per share quarterly dividend; similar announcements were made in February and May. Stockholders would have been *shocked* if the dividend had been decreased, because UPS has not decreased its dividend payment in 45 years. (In most years, the dividend increased.)

When UPS declared the quarterly dividend on August 6, 2015, the following statement was issued:[3]

UPS BOARD ANNOUNCES QUARTERLY DIVIDEND

ATLANTA—(BUSINESS WIRE)—August 6, 2015 (GLOBE NEWSWIRE)—The UPS (NYSE: UPS) Board of Directors today declared a regular quarterly dividend of $0.73 per share on all outstanding Class A and Class B shares.

The dividend is payable September 1, 2015, to shareowners of record on August 17, 2015.

Earlier this year, the UPS Board increased the regular quarterly dividend by 9% to the current level of $0.73 per share. The company has paid either stock of cash dividends every year since 1955 and has more than quadrupled its dividend since it went public at the end of 1999.

The three dates mentioned in this announcement are important to current stockholders. These dates, as well as the ex-dividend date, are defined as follows:

1. *Declaration date.* On the **declaration date** (August 6, 2015, in the UPS case), the board of directors meets and declares the dividend. For accounting purposes, the declared dividend becomes an actual liability on the declaration date. On UPS's balance sheet, the amount equal to $0.73 \times$ (number of shares outstanding) would appear as a current liability, and retained earnings would be reduced by a like amount, because dividends are paid out of earnings that were retained in the current year and from previous years.

2. *Holder-of-record date.* At the close of business on the **holder-of-record date**, or **date of record**, the company closes its stock transfer books and produces a list of shareholders as of that date; these are the stockholders who will receive the next dividend payment. Thus, if UPS was notified of the sale and transfer of shares of stock before 5 p.m. on Monday, August 17, 2015, the new owner received the $0.73 dividend that the board declared on August 6. However, if notification was received after August 17, the previous owner of the stock received the dividend because his or her name appeared on the company's ownership records.

3. *Ex-dividend date.* The securities industry has established a convention of declaring that the right to the dividend remains with the stock until two *business days* prior to the holder-of-record date. This policy is meant to ensure the company is notified of an ownership transfer in time to record the new owner's information and thus pay the next dividend to him or her. The date when the right to receive the *next* dividend payment no longer goes with the stock—that is, when new purchasers will not receive the next dividend—is called the **ex-dividend date**. In the case of UPS, the ex-dividend date was Thursday, August 13, 2015, because the holder-of-record date was on Monday, August 17. As a result, any investor who purchased the stock on or after August 13 did not receive the $0.73 dividend payment on September 1, 2015. All else equal, we would expect the price of UPS's stock to drop on the ex-dividend date by approximately the amount of the next dividend.[4] Thus, assuming no other price fluctuations, the price at which UPS's stock opened on Thursday, August 13, 2015 should have been approximately $0.73 less than its price at the close of business on Wednesday, August 12.

4. *Payment date.* On Tuesday, September 1, 2015—the **payment date**—UPS paid dividends to the holders of record. Today most firms pay dividends electronically.

13-2g Dividend Reinvestment Plans (DRIPs)

Most large companies offer **dividend reinvestment plans (DRIPs)** whereby stockholders can automatically reinvest dividends they are "paid" in the stock of the paying corporation.[5] There are two basic types of DRIPs (referred to as "drips"): (1) plans that involve only already-outstanding ("old") stock that is traded in the financial markets and (2) plans that involve newly issued stock. In either case, the stockholder must pay income taxes on the amount of the dividends even though stock rather than cash is received.

declaration date The date on which the board of directors declares the amount and the specifics of the next dividend payment.

holder-of-record date (date of record) The date on which the company opens the ownership books to determine who will receive the next dividend; the stockholders of record on this date receive the dividend.

ex-dividend date The date on which the right to the next dividend no longer accompanies a stock; it usually is two working days prior to the holder-of-record date.

payment date The date on which a firm actually makes a dividend payment.

dividend reinvestment plans (DRIPs) Plans that enable stockholders to automatically reinvest dividends received in the stocks of the paying firms.

[3]UPS posted the announcement as shown here on its website at http://www.investors.ups.com/.

[4]Technically, the price should drop by the present value of the next dividend payment on the ex-dividend date.

[5]See Richard H. Pettway and R. Phil Malone, "Automatic Dividend Reinvestment Plans," *Financial Management*, Winter 1973, 11–18, for an excellent discussion of this topic.

Under the "old-stock" DRIP plan, a bank, acting as trustee, takes the total dividends available for reinvestment, purchases the corporation's stock on the open market, and allocates the shares purchased to the participating stockholders' accounts on a *pro rata* basis. Under this plan, because it merely acts as a buying agent for stockholders, the company does not generate any new funds. The transactions costs of buying shares (brokerage costs) are low because of volume purchases, so these plans benefit small stockholders who do not need cash dividends for current consumption.

The "new-stock" DRIP provides for dividends to be invested in newly issued stock; hence, these plans raise new capital for the firm. Companies sometimes use such plans to raise substantial amounts of new equity capital. No fees are charged to stockholders, and many companies offer stock at a discount of 3–5 percent below the actual market price. The companies absorb these costs as a trade-off against the flotation costs that would have been incurred had they sold stock through investment bankers rather than through the dividend reinvestment plans.[6]

13-3 Factors Influencing Dividend Policy

In addition to management's beliefs concerning which dividend theory is most correct, a number of other factors are considered when a particular dividend policy is chosen. The factors firms take into account can be grouped into these five broad categories:

1. **Constraints on dividend payments**—The amount of dividends a firm can pay might be limited due to (a) debt contract restrictions, which often stipulate that no dividends can be paid unless certain financial measures exceed stated minimums; (b) the fact that dividend payments cannot exceed the balance sheet item "Retained earnings" (this is known as the *impairment of capital rule*, which is designed to protect creditors by prohibiting the company from distributing assets to stockholders before debt holders are paid); (c) cash availability, because cash dividends can be paid only with cash; and (d) restrictions imposed by the Internal Revenue Service (IRS) on improperly accumulated retained earnings. If the IRS can demonstrate that a firm's dividend payout ratio is being held down deliberately to help its stockholders avoid personal taxes, the firm is subject to tax penalties. However, this factor generally is relevant only to privately owned firms.

2. **Investment opportunities**—Firms that have large numbers of acceptable capital budgeting projects generally have low dividend-payout ratios, and vice versa. However, if a firm can accelerate or postpone projects (i.e., has flexibility), then it can adhere more closely to a target dividend policy.

3. **Alternative sources of capital**—When a firm needs to finance a given level of investments and flotation costs are high, the cost of external equity, r_e, will be well above the cost of internal equity, r_s, making it better to set a low payout ratio and to finance by retaining earnings rather than through the sale of new common stock. In addition, if the firm can adjust its debt/assets ratio without raising capital costs sharply, it can maintain a stable dollar dividend, even if earnings fluctuate, by using a variable debt/assets ratio.

4. **Ownership dilution**—If management is concerned about maintaining control, it might be reluctant to sell new stock; hence, the company might retain more earnings than it otherwise would to finance capital budgeting projects.

5. **Effects of dividend policy on r_s**— The effects of dividend policy on the cost of common equity, r_s, might be considered in terms of four factors: (a) stockholders' desire for current versus future income; (b) the perceived riskiness of dividends versus capital gains; (c) any tax differences that apply to capital gains versus dividends; and (d) the information content of dividends (signaling). Because we discussed each of these factors earlier, we need only note here that the importance of each

[6]One interesting aspect of DRIPs is that they are forcing corporations to reexamine their basic dividend policies. A high participation rate in a DRIP suggests that stockholders might be better off if the firm simply reduced cash dividends, as this would save stockholders some personal income taxes. Quite a few firms survey their stockholders to learn more about their preferences and to find out how they would react to a change in dividend policy. A more rational approach to basic dividend policy decisions might emerge from this research. In addition, it should be noted that companies either use or stop using new-stock DRIPs depending on their need for equity capital.

factor in terms of its effect on r_s varies from firm to firm depending on the makeup of its current and possible future stockholders.

It should be apparent from our discussions that dividend policy decisions truly are exercises in informed judgment, not decisions that can be quantified precisely. Even so, to make rational dividend decisions, financial managers must consider all the points discussed in the preceding sections.

13-4 Stock Dividends and Stock Splits

Although little empirical evidence exists to support the contention, there is widespread belief that an *optimal, or psychological, price range* exists for stocks. *Optimal* means that if the price is within this range, the value of the firm will be maximized. A firm that follows this way of thinking might use a stock dividend or a stock split to adjust the per share market price of its stock when it moves outside the optimal price range.

The rationale for stock dividends and stock splits can best be explained through an example. We will use Porter Electronic Controls Inc., a $700 million electronic components manufacturer, for this purpose. Since its inception, Porter's markets have been expanding, and the company has enjoyed growth in sales and earnings. Some of its earnings have been paid out in dividends, but some have been retained each year, causing earnings per share and market price per share to grow. The company began its life with only a few thousand shares outstanding, and after some years of growth, Porter's stock had very high earnings per share (EPS) and dividends per share (DPS). When a normal price/earnings (P/E) ratio was applied, the derived market price was so high that Porter's management felt demand for the stock was restricted, which kept the total market value of the firm below what it

could have been if more shares, at a lower price, had been outstanding. To correct this situation, Porter might "split" its stock, as described next.

13-4a Stock Splits

If Porter believes that the best price range for its stock is from $40 to $80, then management probably will declare a 2-for-1 **stock split** when the price of the stock rises to greater than $80 per share. With a 2-for-1 split, each share of stock that currently exists is replaced with two *new* shares. In this way, the number of shares outstanding is doubled, and all per-share values—including EPS, DPS, and market value—are halved. All else equal, after a stock split each stockholder would have more shares, but each share would be worth less than the pre-split per-share value. For example, suppose that Porter declared a 2-for-1 split when the market value of its stock reached $90 per share. If the post-split price settles at $45 per share, stockholders will be *exactly as well off* after the split as they were before the split, because they will have twice as many shares at half the price as before the split. If the price of the stock stabilizes above $45, however, stockholders will be better off.

Stock splits can be of any size. For example, the stock could be split 2-for-1, 5-for-1, or in any other way. For example, on January 20, 2010, Berkshire Hathaway initiated a 50-for-1 split for its Class B common stock. The split was intended to lower the price of the stock, which was selling for $3,475 per share prior to the split, so that the stock would become more affordable to a greater number of investors. Reverse splits, which *reduce* the shares outstanding, can also be used. For instance, a company whose stock sells for $5 might employ a 1-for-5 reverse split, exchanging one new share for five old ones and raising the value of the shares to about $25, which might be considered to be within the stock's optimal range. For example, on June 16, 2003, Priceline.com initiated a 1-for-6 reverse split to avoid being delisted from NASDAQ. During the first six months of 2009, quite a few companies considered using reverse splits to increase the per-share values of their stocks, which were depressed as a result of a significant downturn in the financial markets.

stock split An action taken by a firm to decrease the per-share price of its stock.

wavebreakmedia/Shutterstock.com

13-4b Stock Dividends

Stock dividends are similar to stock splits in that they divide the pie into smaller slices without affecting the fundamental wealth position of the current stockholders. When a stock dividend is "paid," existing stockholders receive additional shares of stock rather than a cash payment. For example, on a 5 percent stock dividend, the holder of 100 shares would receive an additional 5 shares (without cost); on a 20 percent stock dividend, the same holder would receive 20 new shares; and so on. As in a stock split, the total number of shares is increased, so EPS, DPS, and price per share all decline proportionately. Because all stockholders receive the same proportion of additional shares, "payment" of a stock dividend neither affects the ownership structure of the firm nor the *total* value of the stock that is outstanding.

13-4c Price Effects of Stock Splits and Stock Dividends

If a firm wants to reduce the price of its stock, should it use a stock split or a stock dividend? Stock splits generally are used after a sharp price run-up to produce a large price reduction. Stock dividends typically are used on a regular annual basis to keep the stock price more or less constrained. For example, if a firm's earnings and dividends were growing at about 10 percent per year, its stock price would tend to go up at about that same rate, and it would soon be outside the desired trading range. A 10 percent annual stock dividend would maintain the stock price within the optimal trading range.

Stock splits and stock dividends have the same *economic* effect—none. In other words, these actions simply cut the pie into more slices in the sense that investors are neither better off nor worse off after a stock dividend is paid or a stock split is initiated. Investors own the same proportion of the company, just with more shares of stock than they owned before these actions were taken. To determine whether this reasoning is correct, several empirical studies have examined the effects of stock splits and stock dividends on stock prices. These studies suggest that investors see stock splits and stock dividends for what they are—*simply additional pieces of paper.* The studies show that investors bid up the price of the stock only if stock dividends and splits are accompanied by higher earnings and cash dividends. When stock dividends are not accompanied by increases in earnings and cash dividends, however, the dilution of earnings and dividends per share causes the price of the stock to drop by the same percentage as the stock dividend (or stock split). Because the fundamental determinants of price (value) are the underlying earnings and cash dividends

per share, stock splits and stock dividends merely cut the same pie into smaller slices.

13-4d Balance Sheet Effects of Stock Splits and Stock Dividends

Although the economic effects of stock splits and stock dividends are virtually identical, accountants treat them somewhat differently. On a 2-for-1 split, the shares outstanding are doubled and the stock's par value is halved in the equity section of the balance sheet. This treatment is shown for Porter Electronic Controls in Section II of Table 13.2 on the next page, using a pro forma 2017 balance sheet.

Section III of Table 13.2 shows the effect of a 20 percent stock dividend. With a stock dividend, the stock's par value is not changed, but an accounting entry is made to transfer funds from the Retained earnings account to the Common stock and Additional paid-in capital accounts. In essence, the payment of a stock dividend is treated as two simultaneous accounting events: the payment of a dividend and the sale of stock for an equal dollar amount. The transfer from retained earnings is calculated using Equation 13.1:

13.1

$$\text{Transfer from RE} = \left[(\text{shrs}) \times \left(\frac{\% \text{ stock}}{\text{divided}} \right) \right] P_0$$

Here "Transfer from RE" represents the dollar amount that must be taken out of Retained earnings and redistributed to the Common stock and Additional paid-in capital accounts, "Shrs" is the number of shares of common stock that is outstanding prior to the stock dividend, "% stock dividend" is the percentage of the stock dividend stated in decimal form, and P_0 is the current market price of the firm's common stock.

Porter has five million shares outstanding (Section I of Table 13.2), and each share currently sells for $90, so a 20 percent stock dividend would require the transfer of $90 million:

$$\text{Dollars transferred} = [(5,000,000)(0.2)][(\$90)]$$
$$= \$90,000,000$$

As shown in the table, $1 million (= $1 par value × 1 million shares) of this

stock dividends A dividend paid in the form of additional shares of stock rather than cash.

Table 13.2

Porter Electronic Controls, Inc.: Stockholders' Equity Accounts, Pro Forma, December 31, 2017 ($ millions, except per-share values)

I. Before a Stock Split or Stock Dividend

Common stock (5 million shares outstanding, $1 par value)	$ 5.0
Paid-in capital	10.0
Retained earnings	285.0
Total common stockholders' equity	$300.0
Book value per share = $300/5	$ 60.0

II. After a 2-for-1 Stock Split

Common stock (10 million shares outstanding, $0.50 par value)	$ 5.0
Paid-in capital	10.0
Retained earnings	285.0
Total common stockholders' equity	$300.0
Book value per share = $300/10	$ 30.0

III. After a 20 Percent Stock Dividend

Common stock (6 million shares outstanding, $1 par value)[a]	$ 6.0
Additional paid-in capital[b]	99.0
Retained earnings[b]	195.0
Total common stockholders' equity	$300.0
Book value per share = $300/6	$ 50.0

[a]Shares outstanding are increased by 20 percent, from 5 million to 6 million.

[b]A transfer equal to the market value of the new shares is made from the Retained earnings account to the Additional paid-in capital and Common stock accounts:

$$\text{Transfer} = [(5,000,000 \text{ shares})(.020)]\$90 = \$90,000,000$$

Of this $90 million, $1,000,000 = ($1 par)(1,000,000 shares) goes in the Common stock account and the remaining $89 million goes in the Additional paid-in capital account.

$90 million is added to the Common stock account and the remaining $89 million is added to the Additional paid-in capital account. The Retained earnings account is reduced from $285 million to $195 million ($195 million = $285 million − $90 million).[7]

 ## 13-5 Stock Repurchases

Rather than paying regular cash dividends, firms sometimes distribute earnings by repurchasing shares of their own stock in the financial markets. The primary reasons given for repurchasing stock are as follows:[8]

1. **To distribute excess funds to stockholders**—Firms

sometimes use stock repurchases to distribute funds that exceed capital budgeting needs in a particular year, especially when the price of the stock is considered low (undervalued). A firm might repurchase stock to distribute excess funds because, unlike regular dividend payments, a **stock repurchase** generally is not expected to continue in the future. Further, a repurchase has different tax implications than a cash dividend. With a repurchase, because investors sell their stock to the company, any gains they realize generally are taxed at

[7]Note that Porter could not pay a stock dividend that exceeded 71.25 percent of retained earnings; a stock dividend of that percentage would exhaust the retained earnings. Thus, a firm's ability to declare stock dividends is constrained by the amount of its retained earnings. Of course, if Porter had wanted to pay a 50 percent stock dividend, it could have just switched to a 1½-for-1 stock split and accomplished the same thing in terms of the number of shares owned by stockholders.

[8]See Amy K. Dittmar, "Why Do Firms Repurchase Stock?" *The Journal of Business*, Vol. 73, No. 3 (July 2000), 331–355, for an excellent discussion of this topic.

stock repurchase Distribution of earnings by a firm to stockholders by repurchasing shares of its stock in the financial markets.

the capital gains rate, which might be lower than the ordinary tax rate at which dividends are taxed.

2. **To adjust the firm's capital structure**—When a firm has more equity than its target capital structure suggests, it might issue debt and use the proceeds to repurchase shares of stock to bring the mix of debt and equity in line with the target.

3. **To acquire shares needed for employee options or compensation**—If a firm knows that many of the stock options that have been "paid" to employees as bonuses or incentives will be exercised soon, it might buy back shares in the financial markets to ensure sufficient shares are available when the options are exercised. Such repurchases also help support the price of the stock by reducing the dilution effect that occurs when employee stock options are exercised; that is, a repurchase reduces the impact on the market value of the stock that otherwise occurs if the number of shares of stock is increased by the number of exercised options.

4. **To protect against a takeover attempt**—A stock repurchase can be used to fend off a hostile takeover attempt because (a) repurchasing stock increases demand in the stock markets, which increases the value of the stock and thus increases the purchase price associated with the acquisition of the firm and (b) managers and other interested parties who hold their stock rather than selling back to the firm will have more concentrated ownership of the firm after the repurchase is complete, which might provide such groups with enough control to block the takeover.

Shares of stock that are repurchased are placed in the firm's treasury of stock, and thus are part of the *treasury stock* that can be reissued at some later date if funds are needed to support capital investments or for other purposes. Because a stock repurchase decreases the number of outstanding shares that are held by stockholders, as long as investors believe that the firm's basic earning power will not change or will improve following the repurchase, both earnings per share and the stock's market price per share should increase as a result of the repurchase.

13-5a Advantages and Disadvantages of Stock Repurchases

The principal advantages of repurchases include the following:

1. A company can use a stock repurchase to distribute excess cash (free cash flows) without increasing the amount of the dividends that might otherwise be paid during the year. As mentioned earlier, firms are extremely reluctant to decrease dividends even when there is good reason to do so because investors often interpret a dividend decrease as a bad signal with respect to the firm's future financial position. As a result, dividends generally are increased only when management believes that the higher dividend can be maintained in future years. A stock repurchase allows the firm to distribute earnings to stockholders without changing the amount of regular cash dividends.

2. A repurchase is an effective method to immediately change the firm's capital structure when the proportion of equity is substantially higher than the target capital structure prescribes. For example, if a firm issues debt and uses the proceeds to repurchase its stock, the capital structure will include a greater proportion of debt and a lower proportion of equity as soon as the process is completed.

3. When a firm expects managers and other employees to exercise stock options that have been paid to them as compensation in previous years, a repurchase can be used to minimize the dilution effect associated with exercising the options. That is, if the firm repurchases the number of shares needed to cover the stock options that it expects will be exercised, it will not have to issue new shares of stock, and the number of shares outstanding after the options are exercised will be the same as before the exercise. If a firm can predict the number of shares that will be needed to cover the exercise of the options and repurchase these shares in the stock markets, the effect of the exercise on the stock price and earnings per share should be minimal.

4. Stockholders do not have to sell their shares to the company during a repurchase period. Thus, those investors who need cash and don't mind paying the taxes associated with selling their stock will participate in the repurchase program; other stockholders will not. If the firm pays a cash dividend, all investors must pay taxes on the dividends they receive.

5. Many investors believe that a stock repurchase program is a signal from management that the firm's stock is undervalued in the financial markets, and thus it is a bargain to purchase. Empirical studies seem to support this belief. Hence, often when a firm initiates a stock repurchase, many investors who don't sell their shares to the company actually purchase additional shares in the stock markets.

The principal disadvantages of stock repurchases include the following:

1. The company might pay too much for stock that is repurchased. A firm that buys back substantial amounts of its stock will bid up the per-share price of the stock that remains outstanding, perhaps to an artificially high level. When this happens, the stock price will fall after the repurchase program ends, and this will harm new investors who purchased the company's stock during the repurchase period.

2. The interval between one stock repurchase and another one generally is irregular, which means that participating investors cannot rely on the cash that they receive from stock repurchases. As a result of the irregularity of stock repurchases, some investors might prefer to receive cash through regular dividend payments rather than through repurchases.

In recent years, the number of firms that have repurchased stock in the financial markets has increased dramatically; at the same time, the proportion of firms that pay regular dividends has decreased. In fact, currently more firms participate in stock repurchases than pay regular dividends to distribute earnings.[9]

13-6 Dividend Policies Around the World

The dividend policies of companies around the world vary considerably. Research indicates that the dividend payout ratios of companies range from 10.5 percent in the Philippines to nearly 70 percent in Taiwan.[10] The dividend payout ratios of companies in Canada, France, and the United States range from about 20 percent to 25 percent, in Spain and the United Kingdom the range is from 30 percent to 40 percent, in Germany and Mexico the rate is between 40 percent and 50 percent, and it is greater than 50 percent for companies in Japan and Southeast Asia. A study of firms in developing countries, such as Zimbabwe and Pakistan, shows that emerging market firms have average payout ratios that range from approximately 30 percent to 60 percent.[11]

Why do dividend payment policies differ so much around the world? As we mentioned in Chapter 12, it seems logical to attribute the differences to dissimilar tax structures, because both dividends and capital gains are taxed differently around the world. The tax codes in most developed countries encourage personal investing and savings more than the U.S. tax code does. For example, Germany, Italy, and many other European countries do not tax capital gains, and in most other developed countries, including Japan, France, and Canada, capital gains are not taxed unless they exceed some minimum amount. Furthermore, in Germany and Italy, dividends are not taxed as income, and in most other countries, some amount of dividends is tax exempt. The general conclusion we can draw, then, is that in countries where capital gains are not taxed, investors should show a preference for companies that retain earnings over those that pay dividends.

It has been found that differences in taxes do not fully explain the differences in dividend payout ratios among countries. A study by Rafael La Porta, Florencio Lopez-de-Silanes, Andrei Shleifer, and Robert W. Vishny offers some additional insight into the dividend policy differences that exist around the world.[12] They suggest that, all else equal, companies pay out greater amounts of earnings as dividends in countries that have measures that help protect the rights of minority stockholders. In such countries, however, firms with many growth opportunities tend to pay lower dividends, which is to be expected because the funds are needed to finance the growth, and shareholders are willing to forgo current income in hopes of greater future benefits. On the other hand, in countries where shareholders' rights are not well protected, investors are more likely to accept whatever dividends are offered, even if companies have numerous good investment opportunities, because great uncertainty exists about whether management will use earnings for self-gratification rather than to benefit

---

[9] See: Eugene F. Fama and Kenneth R. French, "Disappearing Dividends: Changing Firm Characteristics or Lower Propensity to Pay?," *Journal of Financial Economics*, Vol. 60, No. 1, (April 2001), 3–43; Malcolm Baker and Jeffrey Wurgler, "Appearing and Disappearing Dividends: The Link to Catering Incentives," *Journal of Financial Economics*, Vol. 73, No. 2, (August 2004), 271–288; Douglas J. Skinner, "The Evolving Relation between Earnings, Dividends, and Stock Repurchases," *Journal of Financial Economics*, Vol. 87, No. 3, (March 2008), 582–609; and Jim Hsieh and Qinghai Wang, "Stock Repurchases: Theory and Evidence," *Blackwell Companion to Dividends and Dividend Policy*, edited by H. Kent Baker (Blackwell Publishing: New York, 2009).

[10] Rafael La Porta, Florencio Lopez-de-Silanes, Andrei .Shleifer, and Robert W. Vishny, "Agency Problems and Dividend Policies Around the World," *Journal of Finance*, February 2000, 1–34.

[11] Varouj Aivazian, Laurence Booth, and Sean Cleary, "Do Emerging Market Firms Follow Different Dividend Policies from U.S. Firms?" *Journal of Financial Research*, Fall 2003, 371–387.

[12] Rafael La Porta, Florencio Lopez-de-Silanes, Andrei Shleifer, and Robert W. Vishny, "Agency Problems and Dividend Policies Around the World," *Journal of Finance*, February 2000, 1–34.

stockholders; investors prefer a "bird in hand." Some countries where minority shareholders have few, if any, protected rights, including Brazil, Chile, Colombia, and Venezuela, have regulations requiring firms to pay dividends.

Tateos/Shutterstock.com

In summary, it appears the most important factor that determines whether stockholders prefer earnings to be retained or paid out as dividends is the level of risk associated with future expected dividends, which is mitigated to some degree by regulations that protect minority shareholders' rights.

STUDY TOOLS

LOCATED AT BACK OF THE TEXTBOOK

- ☐ Problems are found at the end of this chapter.
- ☐ A tear-out Chapter Review card is located at the back of the textbook.

LOCATED AT WWW.CENGAGEBRAIN.COM

- ☐ Review Key Term flashcards and create your own cards.
- ☐ Track your knowledge and understanding of key concepts in corporate finance.
- ☐ Complete practice and graded quizzes to prepare for tests.
- ☐ Complete interactive content within CFIN5 Online.
- ☐ View the chapter highlight boxes for CFIN5 Online.

KEY DISTRIBUTION OF RETAINED EARNINGS CONCEPTS

To conclude this chapter, we summarize some of the concepts that were discussed.

- Because the firm's goal is to maximize shareholders' wealth, the optimal dividend policy is the one that maximizes the value of the firm. When a firm pays dividends, it decreases the amount of earnings that can be used to invest in acceptable capital budgeting projects. As a result, firms that have many acceptable capital budgeting projects generally pay few or no dividends because earnings are retained to reinvest in the firm. On the other hand, firms with few acceptable capital budgeting projects generally pay out most of their earnings as

dividends because not as much internal financing is needed.

- Of the different types of dividend payments discussed in the chapter, most firms follow the stable, predictable dividend policy. Everything else the same, it is believed that a stable, predictable pattern of dividend payments provides investors with a perception that there is less risk associated with the firm, and a perception of less risk often leads to a lower cost of capital. To maximize value, however, it might be better for a firm to follow the residual dividend policy so that cheaper funds (retained earnings rather than new equity) can be used to finance capital budgeting needs.

- Factors that influence a firm's dividend policy decisions include constraints on payments, investment opportunities, ownership dilution, and the effect on the firm's cost of capital. In some instances, these factors might prevent the firm from following either the optimal dividend policy or the policy it prefers.

- Both a stock split and a stock dividend increase the number of shares of outstanding stock. Neither action requires stockholders to invest any additional funds. Thus, although both actions reduce the per-share

value of the firm's stock, neither action *by itself* changes the *total* market value of the firm's stock.

- Firms use stock repurchases as an alternative to temporary changes in regular annual dividends when distributing earnings to stockholders. Recently, the use of repurchases has increased while the proportion of dividend-paying companies has decreased. In fact, currently a greater percentage of publicly traded firms engage in repurchase activities than pay regular dividends.

PROBLEMS

13–1 Desert A/C plans to invest $50 million to expand operations. The firm wants to maintain a 60 percent debt/assets ratio in its capital structure. If net income is expected to be $25 million this year and Desert follows the residual dividend policy, what amount of dividends will be paid this year?

13–2 Open Door Manufacturer earned $100,000 this year. The company follows the residual dividend policy when paying dividends. Open Door has determined that it needs a total of $120,000 for investment in capital budgeting projects this year. If the company's debt-to-asset ratio is 50 percent, what will its dividend payout ratio be this year?

13–3 The Hawaiian Corporation expects this year's net income to be $12 million. The firm's target debt/assets ratio is 30 percent. This year, Hawaiian has $20 million profitable investment opportunities. According to the residual dividend policy, what should be Hawaiian's dividend payout ratio this year?

13–4 In 2017, Seaworthy Dingy's earnings are expected to be $14.4 million, and the firm expects to have profitable investment opportunities of $8.4 million. Last year, the company paid dividends equal to $9 million. It is predicted that Seaworthy will grow at a constant rate of 5 percent in the future. What will be Seaworthy's total dividends for 2017 if it follows (a) a policy that requires dividends to grow at the long-run growth rate in earnings and (b) a pure residual dividend policy. Seaworthy's target debt/assets ratio is 40 percent.

13–5 Baker Island Tours (BIT) expects earnings to grow at a constant rate of 4 percent forever. Its target debt/assets ratio is 40 percent, and it expects to have profitable investments of $1.3 million this year. BIT plans to continue paying the same dividend that has been

paid the past 10 years, $2.25 per share, long into the future. The firm has 500,000 shares of stock outstanding. If net income is expected to be $2 million, what should be BIT's dividend payout ratio this year?

13–6 Darling's Dry Cleaning has been growing at a constant 6 percent rate for more than 20 years, and this growth is expected to continue forever. Last year, Darling's paid a dividend equal to $3.50 per share. If dividends grow at the same rate as the company's growth rate, what should be the per share dividend that Darling's pays this year?

13–7 Texas Tea's dividend policy calls for the dividend to be increased each year by the same rate. Last year, the company paid a dividend equal to $2.50 per share. This year, after the company initiates a 5-for-1 stock split, Texas Tea expects to pay a dividend equal to $0.54 per share. At what rate does Texas Tea increase its dividend each year?

13–8 Last year, Creative Artists retained $100,000 of the $250,000 net income it generated. This year, Creative generated net income equal to $275,000. If Creative follows the constant payout ratio dividend policy, how much should be paid in dividends this year?

13–9 Last year, Headline News Corporation paid $600,000 in dividends and retained $360,000 of the earnings it generated. The company follows a constant payout ratio dividend policy. If Headline generates $1.25 millon in income this year, how much will be paid in dividends?

13–10 Rapid Auto Transport (RAT) follows a constant payout ratio dividend policy, which requires the company to pay out 30 percent of income as dividends each year. If it wants to pay $840,000 in dividends next year, how much must RAT earn?

13–11 Ortinau's Office Products and Supplies (OOPS) follows the constant payout ratio dividend policy by paying out 40 percent of earnings each year. This year, OOPS expects the dividend payment to be 7 percent higher than last year's payment, which was $130,000. (a) What is the amount of net income that OOPS expects to generate this year? (b) If its target capital structure calls for 50 percent common equity, what will be the total funds the company can invest in capital budgeting projects this year before new common stock must be issued to raise new funds?

13–12 Universal Utilities (U2) applies the low regular dividend plus extras policy when determining how much of its income will be paid out as dividends each year. U2's policy states that the minimum dividend that will be paid each year is $0.50 per share. But, when net income is greater than $600,000, the total dividend will be increased by 25 percent of the amount that exceeds $600,000. The firm currently has 100,000 shares of stock outstanding. What will be the dividend per share if U2 earns (a) $760,000 and (b) $580,000?

13–13 Last year, Absolute Zero Freezers paid a dividend equal to $0.95 per share. Absolute follows the low regular dividend plus extras policy to determine its annual dividend. The policy requires the minimum dividend to be increased by 30 percent of the amount of earnings that exceeds $30,000. Last year's earnings were $50,000. If Absolute has 40,000 shares outstanding, how much is the minimum (low regular) dividend that the firm pays each year?

13–14 Dirty Dogs Grooming's optimal capital structure calls for 40 percent debt and 60 percent common equity. The company's weighted average cost of capital (WACC) is 10 percent if the amount of retained earnings generated during the year is sufficient to fund the equity portion of its capital budgeting requirements, whereas its WACC is 14 percent if new common stock must be issued. Dirty Dogs has the following independent investment opportunities:

> Project A: Cost = $684,000; IRR = 16%
>
> Project B: Cost = $640,000; IRR = 13%
>
> Project C: Cost = $660,000; IRR = 9%

If Dirty Dogs expects to generate net income of $720,000 and it pays dividends according to the residual policy, what will its dividend payout ratio be?

13–15 Aunt Bea's Barbeque (ABB) has two independent investment opportunities this year: Project S costs $45,000, and it has an IRR equal to 11 percent; Project T costs $52,000 and its IRR is 8 percent. The firm's weighted average cost of capital (WACC) is 9 percent as long as new common stock is not needed to finance capital budgeting projects, but its WACC is 12 percent if new common stock must be issued. ABB's target capital structure is 70 percent debt and 30 percent common equity. The firm expects to generate net income of $39,000 this year. ABB follows stable, predictable dividend policy by increasing its dividend payment by 5 percent each year. If ABB paid $20,000 in dividends last year, and it continues to follow the stable, predictable dividend policy, which capital budgeting project(s) should it purchase?

13–16 BKP plans to initiate a 10-for-1 stock split. BKP's stock currently sells for $225 per share. What will be the stock price immediately after the split takes place?

13–17 Coldwater Fishery is considering a 1-for-4 reverse stock split. Its stock is currently selling for $15 per share. Coldwater plans to pay a dividend equal to $0.48 per share after the split. But it would like to pay an equivalent dividend per share even if the split does not take place. (a) What will the price of the stock be immediately after the stock split? (b) What should the per share dividend be if Coldwater doesn't split the stock?

13–18 One week after Granddad's Kitchen split its stock 3-for-1, it paid a dividend of $0.55 per new share. The dividend payment was 10 percent greater than last year's pre-split dividend. What was last year's dividend per share?

13–19 Kitty Hawk Airlines recently declared a 10 percent stock dividend. Prior to the stock dividend, the equity section on Kitty Hawk's balance sheet was:

Common stock (12,000 shares outstanding, $2 par value)	$24,000
Additional paid-in capital	16,000
Retained earnings	10,000
Total common shareholders' equity	$50,000

Kitty Hawk's stock currently sells for $5 per share. Show what the equity section of the balance sheet will look like after the stock dividend is initiated.

13–20 Suppose that Kitty Hawk Airlines (see Problem 13–19) decided to initiate a 5-for-1 stock split rather than the stock dividend described in the problem. Show what the equity section of the balance sheet will look like after the stock split takes place.

part 6

After you finish this chapter go to **PAGE 281** for **STUDY TOOLS**

Jorg Greuel/Getty Images

LEARNING OUTCOMES

After studying this chapter, you will be able to…

LO1 Describe working capital management.

LO2 Describe the cash conversion cycle and how it can be used to better manage working capital activities.

LO3 Describe the policies that a firm might follow when financing current assets.

LO4 Describe the characteristics of different sources of short-term credit, including (a) accruals, (b) trade credit, (c) bank loans, (d) commercial paper, and (e) secured loans.

LO5 Discuss and compute the cost (both APR and EAR) of short-term credit.

LO6 Describe how working capital management differs in multinational firms compared to purely domestic firms.

Managing Short-Term Financing (Liabilities)

14

Generally, we divide financial management decisions into the management of assets (investments) and liabilities (sources of financing) in (1) the *long term* and (2) the *short term*. We discussed long-term decision-making techniques in previous chapters. In this and the next chapter, we discuss *short-term financial management*, also termed **working capital management**, which involves management of the current assets and the current liabilities of a firm. As you read these chapters, you will realize that a firm's value cannot be maximized in the long run unless it survives the short run. In fact, the principal reason firms fail is because they are unable to meet their working capital needs. Thus, *sound working capital management is a requisite for firm survival*.

14-1 Working Capital

It is useful to begin the discussion of working capital policy by reviewing some basic definitions and concepts.

1. The term **working capital**, sometimes called *gross working capital,* generally refers to current assets.

2. **Net working capital** is defined as current assets minus current liabilities. Thus, net working capital represents the amount of current assets that is financed with long-term funds.

3. **Working capital policy** refers to the firm's basic policies regarding (a) target levels for each category of current assets and (b) how current assets will be financed.

4. We must distinguish between those current liabilities that are specifically used to finance current assets and those current liabilities that result from long-term decisions. Such "long-term" current liabilities include (1) current maturities of long-term debt, (2) financing associated with a construction project that, after the project is completed, will be funded with the proceeds of a long-term security issue (perhaps a bond), and (3) the use of short-term debt to finance fixed (long-term) assets. All of these items are unaffected by changes in working capital policy because they resulted from long-term debt financing decisions. Thus, even though these items come due in the next accounting period and we classify them as current liabilities, they are not factors that should be considered when making current period working capital decisions. But, because such obligations

working capital management
The management of short-term assets (investments) and short-term liabilities (financing sources).

working capital A firm's investment in short-term assets—cash, marketable securities, inventory, and accounts receivable.

net working capital Current assets minus current liabilities—the amount of current assets financed by long-term liabilities.

working capital policy
Decisions regarding (1) the target levels for each current asset account and (2) how current assets will be financed.

are *due* in the current period, they must be taken into account when managers assess the firm's ability to pay off debt that is due in the current period using expected cash inflows.

We will use the financial statements of Unilate Textiles, the North Carolina textile manufacturer that was introduced in Chapter 2, to illustrate working capital analyses and decisions. First, we will examine balance sheets constructed for Unilate at three different dates, which are given in Table 14.1. According to the definitions given earlier, Unilate's December 31, 2016, working capital was $465 million, its net working capital was $335 million, and its current ratio was 3.6. Unilate's operations are seasonal, typically peaking in September and October. Thus, at the end of September, Unilate's inventories are significantly higher than they are at the end of the calendar year. As a result of this sales surge, Unilate's working capital is much higher at the end of September ($691.5 million) than it is at the end of December ($511.5 million). The working capital policy that Unilate follows determines the balances carried in current assets and how those balances are financed within the desired ranges at different times of the year.

Table 14.1
Unilate Textiles: Historical and Projected Financials ($ million)

	12/31/16 Historical	9/30/17 Projected	12/31/17 Projected
I. Balance Sheets			
Cash	$ 15.0	$ 30.0	$ 16.5
Accounts receivable	180.0	251.5	198.0
Inventories	270.0	410.0	297.0
Total current assets (CA)	$465.0	$ 691.5	$511.5
Net plant and equipment	380.0	408.5	418.0
Total Assets	$845.0	$ 1,100.0	$929.5
Accounts payable	$ 30.0	$ 90.0	$33.0
Accruals	60.0	100.0	66.0
Notes payable	40.0	129.0	46.8
Total current liabilities (CL)	$130.0	$ 319.0	$145.8
Long-term bonds	300.0	309.0	309.0
Total liabilities	$430.0	$ 628.0	$454.8
Common stock	130.0	159.3	159.3
Retained earnings	285.0	312.7	315.5
Total owners' equity	$415.0	$ 472.0	$474.8
Total Liabilities and Equity	$845.0	$ 1,100.0	$929.5[a]
Net working capital = CA − CL	$335.0	$ 372.5	$365.7
Current ratio = CA/CL	3.6×	2.2×	3.6×

	2016	2017
II. Partial Income Statements		
Sales	$1,500.0	$1,650.0
Cost of goods sold	(1,230.0)	(1,353.0)
Fixed costs	(140.0)	(154.0)
Earnings before interest and taxes	$ 130.0	$ 143.0

[a]Rounding difference.

14-2 The Cash Conversion Cycle

The following series of events, which make up a typical operating cycle, summarize the working capital management process that Unilate Textiles and other companies face:

1. Unilate orders and then receives the materials required to produce the textile products it sells. Unilate purchases from its suppliers on credit, so an account payable is created when the purchases are made. Credit purchases have no immediate effect on cash flows because payment is not made until some later date, perhaps 20 to 30 days after purchase.

2. Labor is used to convert the materials (cotton and wool) into finished goods (cloth products, thread, etc.). However, wages are not fully paid at the time the work is done, so accrued wages build up, maybe for a period of one or two weeks.

3. The finished products are sold, but on credit; so sales create receivables, not immediate cash inflows.

4. At some point during the cycle, Unilate must pay off its accounts payable and accrued wages. *If* these payments are made before Unilate collects cash from its receivables, a net cash outflow occurs that must be financed.

5. The cycle is completed when Unilate's receivables are collected, perhaps 30 to 40 days after the original sale. At that time, the company is in a position to pay off any credit that was used to finance the manufacture of the product. The cycle can then be repeated.

The preceding steps are formalized with the cash conversion cycle model, which focuses on the length of time between when the company makes cash payments to its suppliers, which is when it invests in the manufacture of inventory, and when it receives cash payment from the sale of the product, which is when it realizes a cash (inflow) return on its investment in the production process. The following terms are used in the model:

1. The **inventory conversion period (ICP)** is the average length of time required to convert materials into finished goods and then to sell those goods; it is the amount of time the product remains in inventory in various stages of completion. The inventory conversion period, which is equivalent to the average age of the firm's inventory, is calculated using Equation 14.1:

14.1

$$ICP = \frac{\text{Inventory}}{\text{Cost of goods sold per day}}$$

$$= \frac{\text{Inventory}}{\left(\dfrac{\text{Cost of goods sold}}{360}\right)}$$

$$= \frac{360}{\left(\dfrac{\text{Cost of goods sold}}{\text{Inventory}}\right)}$$

$$= \frac{360}{\text{Inventory turnover}}$$

In 2016, Unilate's cost of goods sold was $1,230 million; thus, its inventory conversion period was:

$$\text{Inventory conversion period(ICP)} = \frac{\$270 \text{ million}}{\left(\dfrac{\$1,230 \text{ million}}{360}\right)} = 79.0 \text{ days}$$

Thus, according to its 2016 operations, it takes Unilate 79 days to convert materials into finished goods and then to sell those goods.

Using the form of Equation 14.1 shown in the third line, we find that Unilate's inventory turnover is $4.6\times = (\$1,230$ million$)/(\$270$ million$)$. The inventory turnover indicates that Unilate sold, or *turned over*, its average amount in inventory 4.6 times during the year. As we discovered in Chapter 2, the industry average is $7.4\times$, which means that, compared to its peers, Unilate is not turning over (selling) its inventory quickly enough.

2. The **receivables collection period (DSO)** is the average length of time required to convert the firm's receivables into cash—that is, the time it takes to collect cash following a sale. The receivables collection period is also called the days sales outstanding (DSO), and it is calculated using Equation 14.2:

inventory conversion period (ICP) The amount of time a product remains in inventory in various stages of completion.

receivables collection period (DSO) The time it takes to collect cash following a sale; also known as days sales outstanding (DSO).

14.2

$$DSO = \frac{\text{Receivables}}{\text{Daily credit sales}}$$

$$= \frac{\text{Receivables}}{\left(\dfrac{\text{Annual credit sales}}{360}\right)}$$

$$= \frac{360}{\left(\dfrac{\text{Annual credit sales}}{\text{Receivables}}\right)}$$

$$= \frac{360}{\text{Receivables turnover}}$$

14.3

$$DPO = \frac{\text{Accounts payable}}{\text{Daily credit purchases}}$$

$$= \frac{\text{Payables}}{\left(\dfrac{\text{Cost of goods sold}}{360}\right)}$$

$$= \frac{360}{\left(\dfrac{\text{Cost of goods sold}}{\text{Payables}}\right)}$$

$$= \frac{360}{\text{Payables turnover}}$$

Because Unilate's sales in 2016 were $1,500 million, its DSO was:

$$DSO = \frac{\$180 \text{ million}}{\left(\dfrac{\$1,500 \text{ million}}{360}\right)} = 43.2 \text{ days}$$

A DSO equal to 43.2 indicates that Unilate does not collect cash payments associated with credit sales until an average of 43 days after the product is sold.

Using the form of Equation 14.2 shown in the third line, we find that Unilate's receivables turnover is 8.3× = ($1,500 million)/($180 million), which indicates that the company collected the average amount in receivables 8.3 times during the year. Because its days sales outstanding (DSO), which equals 43.2 days, is greater than the industry average (32.1 days), Unilate is not turning over its receivables accounts enough times during the year—that is, the company is not collecting its credit sales quickly enough.

Because Unilate's cost of goods sold was $1,230 million in 2016, its DPO was:

$$DPO = \frac{\$30 \text{ million}}{\left(\dfrac{\$1,230 \text{ million}}{360}\right)} = 8.8 \text{ days}$$

Therefore, on average, Unilate pays for raw materials about nine days after the materials are purchased from its suppliers.

Using the form of Equation 14.3 shown in the third line, we find that Unilate's payables turnover is 41.0× = ($1,230 million)/($30 million), which indicates that the company paid the average amount in payables 41 times during the year. Because the industry average DPO is 18 days, it appears that Unilate is paying its suppliers much too quickly.

4. The **cash conversion cycle** computation nets out the three periods just defined, resulting in a value that equals the length of time between when the firm pays cash for (invests in) productive resources (materials and labor) and it receives cash from the sale of products. In other words, the cash conversion cycle represents the length of time between paying for labor and materials and collecting on receivables. Thus, the cash conversion cycle equals the average length of time a dollar is tied up, or invested, in current assets. During this period, the firm must find ways to finance the operating cycle.

We can now use these definitions to analyze Unilate's cash conversion cycle. The concept, which is diagrammed in Figure 14.1, can be expressed by Equation 14.4:

payables deferral period (DPO) The average length of time between the purchase of raw materials and labor and the payment of cash for them; also known as days payables outstanding (DPO).

cash conversion cycle The length of time from the payment for the purchase of raw materials to manufacture a product until the collection of accounts receivable associated with the sale of the product.

3. The **payables deferral period (DPO)** is the average length of time between the purchase of raw materials and labor and the actual payment of cash for them. Also called days payables outstanding (DPO), the payables deferral period is computed using Equation 14.3:

FIGURE 14.1   THE CASH CONVERSION CYCLE FOR UNILATE TEXTILES

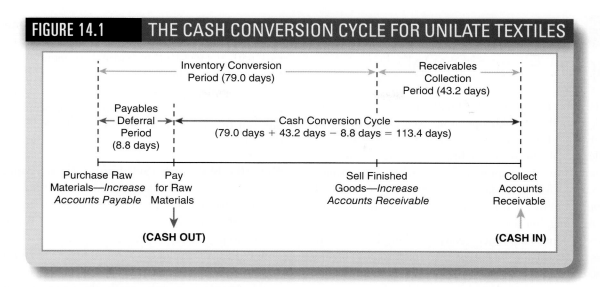

Inventory Conversion Period (79.0 days)

Receivables Collection Period (43.2 days)

Payables Deferral Period (8.8 days)

Cash Conversion Cycle (79.0 days + 43.2 days − 8.8 days = 113.4 days)

Purchase Raw Materials—*Increase Accounts Payable*

Pay for Raw Materials

Sell Finished Goods—*Increase Accounts Receivable*

Collect Accounts Receivable

(CASH OUT)

(CASH IN)

14.4

Cash conversion cycle = ICP + DSO − DPO

= 79.0 days + 43.2 days − 8.8 days

= 113.4 days

In Equation 14.4, ICP, DSO, and DPO represent the inventory conversion period, days sales outstanding, and days payables outstanding as defined in Equations 14.1, 14.2, and 14.3, respectively.

Based on our computations, we can conclude that Unilate's cash conversion cycle is about 113 days. As Figure 14.1 shows, the *receipt* of cash from manufacturing

and selling the products is delayed by approximately 122 days because (1) the product is tied up in inventory for 79 days and (2) the cash from the sale is not received until 43 days after the product is sold. However, the *disbursement* of cash for the raw materials purchased is delayed by nearly nine days. As a result, the net delay in cash receipts associated with the investment in inventory (cash disbursement) is approximately 113 days. What does this mean to Unilate?

Unilate's cash conversion cycle indicates that the manufacturing and other operating costs associated with the production and sale of products must be financed for a 113-day period. The firm's goal should be to shorten its cash conversion cycle as much as possible without harming operations. This effort would improve profits because the shorter the cash conversion cycle, the less the need for external, or nonspontaneous, financing (e.g., bank loans) that generally is more costly than internal financing (e.g., accruals). The firm can shorten its cash conversion cycle by (1) reducing the inventory conversion period by processing and selling goods more quickly (efficiently); (2) reducing the receivables collection period by speeding up collections; or (3) lengthening the payables deferral period by slowing down (delaying) payments to suppliers (and employees). To the extent that these actions can be taken *without harming the return* associated with the management of these accounts, they should be carried out. More specific actions that can be taken to reduce the length of the cash conversion cycle are discussed in the remainder of this chapter and the next chapter.

isak55/Shutterstock.com

14-3 Current Asset (Working Capital) Financing Policies

Most businesses experience fluctuations—seasonal, cyclical, or both—in their operating cycles. For example, construction firms have peaks in the spring and summer, retailers peak during the Christmas holidays, and the manufacturers that supply both construction companies and retailers follow similar patterns. Similarly, virtually all businesses must build up current assets when the economy is strong, but then they sell off inventories and have net reductions of accounts receivable when the economy slacks off. Even so, current assets rarely drop to $0, and this realization has led to the development of the idea that some current assets should be considered **permanent current assets** because their levels remain stable (at some minimum level) no matter the seasonal or economic conditions. Applying this idea to Unilate Textiles, Table 14.1 suggests that, at this stage in its life, total assets are growing at a 10 percent rate, from $845.0 million at the end of 2016 to a projected $929.5 million by the end of 2017, but seasonal fluctuations are expected to push total assets up to $1,100.0 million during the firm's peak season in 2017. Assuming Unilate's permanent assets grow continuously, and at the *same rate,* throughout the year, then 9/12ths (75 percent) of the 10 percent growth in assets will accrue by the end of September and permanent assets would equal $908.4 million ($845 million)[1 + 0.10(9/12)]. Because the actual level of assets is expected to be $1,100.0 million at the end of September, Unilate's total assets at that time consist of $908.4 million of permanent assets and $191.6 million = $1,100.0 million − $908.4 million of seasonal, or **temporary, current assets**. Unilate's *temporary* current assets fluctuate from zero during the slow season in December to nearly $192 million during

the peak season in September. Therefore, temporary current assets are those amounts of current assets that vary with respect to the seasonal or economic conditions of a firm. The manner in which the permanent and temporary current assets are financed is called the firm's *current asset financing policy,* which generally can be classified as one of the three approaches described next.

Maturity Matching (Self-Liquidating) Approach. The **maturity matching ("self-liquidating") approach** calls for matching the maturities of assets and liabilities. This strategy minimizes the risk that the firm will be unable to pay off its maturing obligations *if* the liquidations of the assets can be controlled to occur on or before the maturities of the obligations. At the limit, a firm could attempt to match exactly the maturity structure of all of its assets and liabilities. For example, inventory expected to be sold in 30 days could be financed with a 30-day bank loan, a 20-year building could be financed by a 20-year mortgage bond, and so forth. Clearly, two factors prevent this exact maturity matching: (1) there is uncertainty about the lives of assets; and (2) some common equity must be used, and common equity has no maturity. Still, if Unilate makes an attempt to match the maturities of its short-term assets and liabilities, we would define this as a *moderate current asset financing policy* with regard to risk and return.

Conservative Approach. With the **conservative approach**, permanent, or long-term, capital is used to finance all permanent asset requirements (both fixed assets and permanent current assets) and also to meet some or all of the seasonal, temporary demands. At the extreme, a firm could finance all of its seasonal needs with long-term financing alternatives, thereby eliminating the need to use short-term financing. However, this would be a difficult, if not impossible, task to accomplish. Most firms that follow this approach use some amounts of short-term credit to meet financing needs during peak-season periods. Even so, they will have "extra" permanent funds during off-peak periods, which allows them to "store liquidity" in the form of short-term investments, called marketable securities, during the off-season. As its name implies, this approach is a safe, conservative current asset financing policy, and it generally is not as profitable as the other two approaches discussed here.

Aggressive Approach. A firm that follows the **aggressive approach** finances all of its fixed assets (permanent long-term assets) and some of its permanent current assets with long-term capital; the remainder of the permanent current assets and all of the temporary

---

permanent current assets
Current assets' balances that remain stable no matter the seasonal or economic conditions.

temporary current assets
Current assets that fluctuate with seasonal or cyclical variations in a firm's business.

maturity matching ("self-liquidating") approach
A financing policy that matches asset and liability maturities; considered a moderate current asset financing policy.

conservative approach A policy under which all of the fixed assets, all of the permanent current assets, and some of the temporary current assets of a firm are financed with long-term capital.

aggressive approach A policy under which all of the fixed assets of a firm are financed with long-term capital, but *some* of the firm's permanent current assets are financed with short-term nonspontaneous sources of funds.

current assets are financed with such short-term financing as bank loans. Several different degrees of aggressiveness are possible. For example, one firm might finance nearly all of its permanent current assets with short-term credit, while another firm might finance relatively little of its current permanent assets with the same type of credit. The aggressive approach is riskier than either of the other two approaches because the short-term credit used to finance the permanent current assets must be renewed each time it comes due. As a consequence, the firm faces the threat of rising interest rates as well as loan renewal problems. Because short-term debt often is less expensive than long-term debt, however, some firms are willing to sacrifice safety for the chance of higher profits.

14-4 Sources of Short-Term Financing

The three different financing policies just described are distinguished by the relative amounts of short-term debt used under each alternative. The aggressive policy calls for the greatest use of short-term debt, the conservative policy requires the least, and maturity matching falls in between. It is clear that both risk and expected returns are influenced by which policy a firm elects to follow. While short-term debt generally is a riskier source of funds than long-term debt, it generally is also less expensive, and it can be obtained faster and under terms that are more flexible.

Statements about the flexibility, cost, and riskiness of short-term debt versus long-term debt depend to a large extent on the type of short-term credit that actually is used. Short-term credit generally is defined as any liability *originally* scheduled for payment within one year. In this section, we briefly describe five major types of short-term credit: (1) accruals, (2) accounts payable (trade credit), (3) bank loans, (4) commercial paper, and (5) secured loans.

14-4a Accruals

Firms generally pay employees on a weekly, biweekly, or monthly basis, so the balance sheet typically will show some accrued wages. Similarly, the firm's estimated income taxes, Social Security and income taxes

withheld from employee payrolls, and taxes collected on sales generally are paid on a weekly, monthly, or quarterly basis, so the balance sheet typically shows some taxes in accruals accounts as well. These accruals increase (decrease) automatically, or spontaneously, as a firm's operations expand (contract). This type of debt generally is considered "free" in the sense that no explicit interest is paid on funds raised through accruals. However, ordinarily, a firm cannot control its accruals: The timing of wage payments is set by economic forces and industry custom, while tax payment dates are established by law. Thus, firms use all the accruals they can, but they have little control over the levels of these accounts.

14-4b Accounts Payable (Trade Credit)

Most firms purchase from their suppliers on credit, recording these debts as *accounts payable*. This type of financing, which is called trade credit, typically is the largest single category of short-term debt. It is a *spontaneous* source of financing in the sense that it arises from ordinary business transactions. The amount of trade credit used by a firm depends on the terms of the credit purchase offered by suppliers and the size of the firm's operations. For example, lengthening the credit period, as well as expanding sales and purchases, generates additional trade credit.

14-4c Short-Term Bank Loans

Commercial banks, whose loans generally appear on firms' balance sheets as notes payable, are second in importance to trade credit as a source of short-term financing.[1] The influence of banks actually is greater than it appears from the dollar amounts they lend because banks provide *nonspontaneous* funds. That is, as a firm's financing needs increase, it specifically requests, or applies for, additional funds from its bank. If the request is denied, the firm might be forced to abandon attractive growth opportunities. Bank loans include the key features described next.

Maturity. Bank loans to businesses frequently are written as 90-day notes, so the loan must be repaid or renewed at the end of 90 days. Of

short-term credit Any liability originally scheduled for repayment within one year.

accruals Recurring short-term liabilities; liabilities such as wages and taxes that change spontaneously with operations.

trade credit The credit created when one firm buys on credit from another firm.

[1]Although commercial banks remain the primary source of short-term loans, other sources are available. For example, in 2015 GE Capital Corporation (GECC) had several billion dollars in commercial loans outstanding. Firms such as GECC, which was initially established to finance consumers' purchases of GE's durable goods, often find business loans to be more profitable than consumer loans.

course, if a borrower's financial position has deteriorated, the bank might refuse to renew the loan, which can mean serious trouble for the borrower.

Promissory Note. When a bank loan is approved, the agreement is executed by signing a **promissory note** that specifies (1) the amount borrowed, (2) the interest rate, (3) the repayment schedule, (4) whether collateral, or security, is required, and (5) any other terms and conditions to which the bank and the borrower have agreed.

Compensating Balances. Banks *often* require borrowers to maintain an average checking account balance, called a **compensating balance (CB)**, as a requirement of getting a loan. The funds used to maintain a compensating balance, which generally equals 10 to 20 percent of the loan amount, cannot be used by the firm to pay its bills or to invest. A compensating balance does not earn interest. Thus, a compensating balance essentially represents a charge by the bank for servicing the loan (bookkeeping, maintaining a line of credit, and so on).

Line of Credit. A **line of credit** is an agreement between a bank and a borrower indicating the maximum credit the bank will allow the borrower to have outstanding at any point in time. For example, a bank loan officer might indicate to a financial manager that the bank regards the firm as being "good" for a maximum of $200,000 during the forthcoming year. That is, the firm can have at most a $200,000 balance of loans outstanding from this source at any time during the year. When a line of credit arrangement is guaranteed, it is called a **revolving (guaranteed) credit agreement**. With a revolving credit agreement, the bank has a legal obligation to provide the funds requested by the borrower. The bank generally charges a **commitment fee** for guaranteeing the availability of the funds. This fee is usually charged on the unused balance of the credit line because, to guarantee that the funds will be available when requested, the funds must be accessed quickly, and as a consequence the bank must invest these funds in extremely liquid instruments that provide relatively low returns. Neither the legal obligation nor the fee exists under a "regular," or general, credit line because this type of credit provides funds to the firm only when they are available at the bank.

14-4d Commercial Paper

Commercial paper is a type of unsecured promissory note issued by large, financially strong firms. It is sold primarily to other businesses, insurance companies, pension funds, money market mutual funds, and banks. The use of commercial paper is restricted to a comparatively small number of firms that are *exceptionally* good credit risks. Maturities of commercial paper vary from one to nine months, with an average of about five months.[2] Using commercial paper permits a corporation to tap a wider range of credit sources, including financial institutions across the country, which can reduce interest costs. One potential problem with commercial paper is that a borrower (company) who is in temporary financial difficulty might receive little help from "lenders" because commercial paper dealings generally are less personal than are bank relationships.

14-4e Secured Loans

Most loans can be secured, or collateralized, if it is deemed necessary or desirable. Given a choice, it is usually better to borrow on an unsecured basis because the bookkeeping costs of **secured loans** often are high. Nevertheless, weak firms might find that they can borrow only if they put up an asset as security or if using security allows them to borrow at a lower rate.

Most secured, short-term business loans involve the use of short-term assets, such as accounts receivable and inventories, as collateral. Nearly every secured loan is established under the **Uniform Commercial Code**, which has standardized and simplified the procedures for establishing loan security. The heart of the Uniform

---

promissory note A document specifying the terms and conditions of a loan, including the amount, interest rate, and repayment schedule.

compensating balance (CB) A minimum checking account balance that a firm must maintain with a bank to borrow funds— generally 10 to 20 percent of the amount of loans outstanding.

line of credit An arrangement in which a bank agrees to lend up to a specified maximum amount of funds during a designated period.

revolving (guaranteed) credit agreement A formal, committed line of credit extended by a bank or other lending institution.

commitment fee A fee charged on the *unused* balance of a revolving credit agreement to compensate the bank for guaranteeing that the funds will be available when needed by the borrower; the fee normally is about 0.25 percent of the unused balance.

commercial paper Unsecured, short-term promissory notes issued by large, financially sound firms to raise funds.

secured loans Loans backed by collateral; for short-term loans, the collateral often is inventory, receivables, or both.

Uniform Commercial Code A system of standards that simplifies procedures for establishing loan security.

---

[2]The maximum maturity without SEC registration is 270 days. Also, commercial paper can only be sold to "sophisticated" investors; otherwise, SEC registration would be required even for maturities of 270 days or less.

Commercial Code is the *Security Agreement,* a standardized document on which the specific pledged assets are listed. The assets can be items of equipment, accounts receivable, or inventories.

Accounts Receivable Financing. When receivables are used as collateral for a loan, the firm is said to be **pledging** its **receivables.** With this arrangement, the lender has both a claim against the receivables if the borrowing firm defaults on the loan and **recourse** to the borrower. Recourse refers to the fact that the borrowing firm rather than the lender must take a loss when one of the borrowing firm's customers (a receivables account) does not pay. Therefore, the risk of default on the pledged accounts remains with the borrowing (pledging) firm. The customer of the pledging firm generally is not notified about the pledging of the receivables, and the financial institution that lends on the security of accounts receivable often is either a commercial bank or a large finance company.

Sometimes, receivables are actually sold to financial organizations. With this arrangement, the firm is said to be **factoring** its receivables, and the buyer is called a factor. The dollar amount the firm receives when receivables are sold is less than the full value of the receivables. The difference between the amount of the receivables and the selling price represents the potential gross profit to the factor (purchaser). With most factoring arrangements, because the factor buys the receivables, the factor must take the loss when a receivables account is not paid (i.e., there is no recourse). As a result, it is not uncommon for the factor to provide credit department personnel for the borrower (receivables seller) to carry out the credit investigation of its customers.

Inventory Financing. A substantial amount of credit is secured by business inventories. If a firm is a relatively good credit risk, the mere existence of the inventory might be a sufficient basis for receiving an unsecured loan. If the firm is a relatively poor risk, the lending institution might insist on security in the form of a lien against the inventory. The three major types of inventory liens include the following:

1. A *blanket lien* gives the lending institution a lien against all of the borrower's inventories without limiting the borrower's ability to sell the inventories. This type of lien generally is used when the inventory put up as collateral is relatively low priced, fast moving, and difficult to identify individually.

2. A *trust receipt* is an arrangement in which the goods are held in trust for the lender, perhaps stored in a public warehouse or held on the premises of the borrower. Such an arrangement generally is used for goods that are relatively high priced, slow moving, and easy to identify individually using serial numbers or other distinguishing characteristics. When the goods that are held in trust are sold, proceeds from the sale must be given to the lender.

3. *Warehouse receipt* financing refers to an arrangement in which inventory that is used as collateral is physically separated from the borrower's other inventory and then stored in a secured site located either on the premises of the borrower (field warehousing) or in an independent warehouse (terminal warehousing). To provide inventory supervision, the lending institution employs a third party in the arrangement—a warehousing company—that acts as its agent in the oversight and the sale of the inventory.

14-5 Computing the Cost of Short-Term Credit

In this section, we describe how the cost associated with using various sources of short-term financing is determined. To start, we compute the percentage cost of using the funds for a given period, r_{PER}, using Equation 14.5:

14.5

$$\text{Percentage cost per period} = r_{PER} = \frac{\left(\begin{array}{c} \$ \text{ cost of} \\ \text{borrowing} \end{array} \right)}{\left(\begin{array}{c} \$ \text{ amount of} \\ \text{usable funds} \end{array} \right)}$$

In this equation, the numerator represents the dollar amount that must be paid for using the borrowed funds, which includes the interest paid on the loan, application fees, charges for commitment fees, and so forth. The denominator represents the amount of the loan that actually can be used (spent) by the borrower. This amount is not necessarily the same as the principal amount of the loan because

pledging receivables Using accounts receivable as collateral for a loan.

recourse The lender can seek payment from the borrowing firm when receivables' accounts used to secure a loan are uncollectible.

factoring The outright sale of receivables.

discounts, compensating balances, or other costs might reduce the amount of the loan principal (amount borrowed) that the firm can actually use. We show that *when restrictions prevent the borrower from using the entire amount of the loan, the effective annual rate paid for the loan is higher than the stated interest rate.*

Using Equation 14.5 and the concepts described in Chapter 4, the effective annual rate (EAR) and the annual percentage rate (APR) for short-term financing can be computed as shown in Equations 14.6 and 14.7:

14.6

$$EAR = r_{EAR} = (1 + r_{PER})^m - 1.0$$

14.7

$$APR = r_{PER} \times m = r_{SIMPLE}$$

where m is the number of borrowing (interest) periods in one year—that is, if the length of the loan is one month, m = 12. Recall from our discussion in Chapter 4 that the EAR incorporates interest compounding in the computation, but the APR does not. Both computations adjust the percentage cost per period so that it is stated on an annual basis. We annualize the cost to make it easier to compare short-term credit instruments with different maturities.

Next we illustrate the application of these equations for computing the cost of three short-term financing alternatives: (1) trade credit, (2) bank loans, and (3) commercial paper.

14-5a Computing the Cost of Trade Credit (Accounts Payable)

Consider Microchip's credit terms of 2/10, net 30, which allows its customers, such as Personal Computer Company (PCC), to take a 2 percent discount from the purchase (invoice) price if payment is made on or before Day 10 of the billing cycle; otherwise, the entire bill is due by Day 30. If the invoice price is $100 and the firm does not take the discount, it effectively pays $2 to borrow $98 for a 20-day period, so the cost of using the funds for the 20-day period (i.e., the additional 20 days) is:

"free" trade credit Credit received during the discount period.

costly trade credit Credit taken in excess of "free" trade credit, whose cost is equal to the discount lost.

$$\text{Periodic rate} = r_{PER} = \frac{\$2}{\$98}$$
$$= 0.020408 \approx 2.0408\%$$

Because there are 18 = 360/20 20-day periods in a 360-day year, the APR, or simple interest rate, associated with trade credit with these terms is:

$$APR = 2.0408\% \times 18 = 36.73\%$$

The effective annual cost (rate), EAR, of using trade credit with these terms as a source of short-term financing is:

$$r_{EAR} = (1 + 0.020408)^{18} - 1.0 = 0.4386$$
$$= 43.86\%$$

According to this computation, if PCC chooses to pay its bill on Day 30, then it will "forgo" the 2 percent cash discount, which is equivalent to borrowing funds at a rate of nearly 44 percent per year.[3] PCC should forgo the cash discount to pay on Day 30 only if alternative financing, such as a bank loan, has a cost greater than 44 percent.

On the basis of the preceding discussion, trade credit can be divided into two components: (1) **"free" trade credit**, which involves credit received during the discount period; and (2) **costly trade credit**, which involves credit in excess of the free trade credit and whose cost is an implicit one based on the forgone discounts. *Financial managers always should use the free component, but they should use the costly component only after analyzing the cost of this source of financing to make sure that it is less than the cost of funds that could be obtained from other sources.*

14-5b Computing the Cost of Bank Loans

A bank loan can take the form of a *simple interest loan*, a *discount loan*, or an *installment loan*. The cost of bank loans varies for different types of loans and for different borrowers at any given point in time. Interest rates are higher for riskier borrowers, and rates also are higher on smaller loans because of the fixed costs involved in making and servicing such loans. Factors such as a compensating balance or application fees can affect the cost of borrowing for each of these types of loans. Here we give

[3]We assume that the firm pays its supplier on the last day possible. That is, if it takes the discount, payment is made on Day 10; if it doesn't take the discount, payment is made on Day 30. This is rational business behavior. If, however, the firm does not take the discount, but pays on Day 20 (or any other time before the final due date), then the cost associated with using this source of financing is higher than computed here. The funds cost more because the firm uses them for a shorter period.

Discount Interest Loan. With a **discount interest loan**, the interest due is deducted "up front" so that the borrower receives less than the principal amount, or face value, of the loan. Suppose Unilate Textiles receives a nine-month $10,000 discount interest loan with a 12 percent quoted (simple) interest rate. The interest payment on this loan is $900 = $10,000[0.12 × (9/12)]. Because the interest is paid in advance, Unilate is able to freely use only $9,100 = $10,000 − $900 of the $10,000 that it borrowed. Thus, the nine-month interest rate paid for the loan is:

some examples of how to compute the cost for each of these loans.

Simple Interest Loan. With a **simple interest loan**, the borrower receives the **face value** of the loan—that is, amount borrowed, or the principal—and repays both the principal and the interest at maturity. For example, with a simple interest loan of $10,000 at 12 percent interest for nine months, the borrower receives the $10,000 upon approval of the loan and pays back the $10,000 principal plus $900 = $10,000[0.12 × (9/12)] in interest at maturity. Note that interest is paid only for the portion of the year the loan is outstanding, which is nine months in this case. The 12 percent is the **quoted (simple) interest rate**.

The nine-month interest rate for this loan is:

$$r_{PER} = \frac{\text{9-month}}{\text{interest rate}} = \frac{\$10,000 \times \left[0.12 \times \left(\frac{9}{12}\right)\right]}{\$10,000}$$

$$= \frac{\$900}{\$10,000} = 0.09 = 9.00\%$$

The APR for this loan is:

$$APR = 9.0\% \times \left(\frac{12}{9}\right) = 12.00\%$$

The EAR is:

$$r_{EAR} = (1.09)^{(12/9)} - 1.0 = 0.1218 = 12.18\%$$

EAR > APR because this is a nine-month loan, which means interest compounding is assumed to occur every nine months.

$$r_{PER} = \frac{\text{9-month}}{\text{interest rate}}$$

$$= \frac{\$10,000 \times \left[0.12 \times \left(\frac{9}{12}\right)\right]}{\$10,000 - \left\{\$10,000\left[0.12 \times \left(\frac{9}{12}\right)\right]\right\}}$$

$$= \frac{\$900}{\$9,100} = 0.0989 = 9.89\%$$

The APR for this loan is:

$$APR = 9.89\% \times \left(\frac{12}{9}\right) = 13.19\%$$

The EAR is:

$$r_{EAR} = (1.0989)^{(12/9)} - 1.0 = 0.1340 = 13.40\%$$

What do you think the cost of the loan described here would be if Unilate's bank charged a $50 fee to cover the cost of processing the loan? To answer this question, first take a look at Equation 14.1 and determine whether the payment of the fee affects the numerator (that is, the dollar cost of borrowing), the denominator (that is, the amount of usable funds), or both the numerator and denominator. The general rule is that the numerator is affected by any expense associated

simple interest loan Both the amount borrowed and the interest charged on that amount are paid at the maturity of the loan.

face value The amount of the loan, or the amount borrowed; also called the *principal amount* of the loan.

quoted (simple) interest rate The annual percentage rate (APR) that is used to compute the interest rate per period (r_{PER}).

discount interest loan A loan in which the interest, which is calculated on the amount borrowed (principal), is paid at the beginning of the loan period; interest is paid in advance.

with the loan, and the denominator is affected if funds must be put aside (for example, to satisfy a compensating balance requirement) or costs are paid out of the loan proceeds at the beginning of the loan period. Thus, if Unilate uses the proceeds from the loan to pay the $50 fee, both the numerator and the denominator are affected, and the nine-month interest rate is:

$$r_{PER} = \frac{\text{9-month}}{\text{interest rate}} = \frac{\$900 + \$50}{\$9,100 - \$50} = \frac{\$950}{\$9,050}$$

$$= 0.1050 = 10.50\%$$

Check to see that the APR and the EAR are now 14.0 percent and 14.2 percent, respectively. (See the computation for the cost of commercial paper later in this section.)

Installment Loan: Add-On Interest. Lenders often charge **add-on interest** on various types of installment loans. The term *add-on* means that the interest is calculated and then added to the amount borrowed to determine the total dollar amount that will be paid back in equal installments. To illustrate, suppose Unilate borrows $10,000 on an add-on basis at a simple rate of 12 percent, with the loan to be repaid in nine monthly installments. At a 12 percent add-on rate, Unilate will pay a total interest charge of $900 as computed earlier, and a total of $10,900 in nine equal payments. The monthly payments would be $1,211.11 = $10,900/9. Therefore, each month Unilate would pay $100 interest (1/9 of the total $900 of interest) and $1,111.11 principal repayment (1/9 of the $10,000 borrowed). Because the loan is paid off in monthly installments, Unilate will be able to use the full amount of the loan—$10,000—only for the first month, and the outstanding balance declines by $1,111.11 each month such that the remaining principal due at the beginning of the last month of the loan is $1,111.11. As a result, the percent cost of the loan varies each month.

Unilate would pay $900 for the use of approximately 50 percent of the loan's face amount because the average outstanding balance of the loan is only about $5,000 = ($10,000 + $0)/2. (The $10,000 is paid down evenly over the life of the loan.) With this information we can *approximate* the rate for the nine-month period as follows:

$$\frac{\text{Approximate rate}}{\text{per period}} = \frac{\$900}{\$5,000} = 0.18 = 18.00\%$$

The *approximate* APR would be 24.0% = 18.0% × (12/9).

To determine the EAR, recognize that the $1,211.11 payment Unilate makes each month represents an annuity. The cash flow time line for this loan is:

Using a financial calculator, enter N = 9, PV = 10,000, PMT = −1,211.11, and then solve for r. The *monthly* rate equals 1.7591. In this case we assume monthly compounding, because the installment payments are made each month. When we annualize the monthly rate, the EAR is:

$$\text{EAR} = (1.017591)^{12} - 1.0 = 0.2328 = 23.28\%$$

14-5c Computing the Cost of Commercial Paper

Suppose Unilate issues 270-day commercial paper with a face value equal to $10,000. The simple annual interest rate on the commercial paper is 12 percent, and the total transactions fee, which includes the cost of a backup line of credit, is 0.5 percent of the amount of the issue. Because commercial paper is a discount instrument similar to a discount loan, Unilate will not be able to use the total $10,000 face value. Instead, investors will purchase the commercial paper issue for $9,100 = $10,000 − $10,000[0.10 × (9/12)], and then receive $10,000 at maturity. The transaction fee, which equals $50 = 0.005 × $10,000, is "taken off the top," so Unilate actually would receive only $9,050 = $9,100 − $50 to use from the commercial paper issue. The total dollar cost of borrowing using commercial paper would be $950, which includes interest equal to $900 and the $50 transaction fee. As a result, the nine-month cost of the commercial paper would be:

$$r_{PER} = \frac{\text{9-month}}{\text{interest rate}}$$

$$= \frac{\$900 + \$50}{\$10,000 - (\$900 + \$50)}$$

$$= \frac{\$950}{\$9,050} = 0.1050 = 10.50\%$$

The APR for this loan is:

$$\text{APR} = 10.50\% \times \left(\frac{12}{9}\right) = 14.00\%$$

The EAR is:

$$r_{EAR} = (1.1050)^{(12/9)} - 1.0 = 0.1424 = 14.24\%$$

14-5d Borrowed (Principal) Amount Versus Required (Needed) Amount

Compensating balances can raise the effective rate on a loan. To illustrate, suppose Unilate *needs* $10,000 to pay for some equipment it recently purchased. Atlantic/Pacific Bank offers to lend Unilate the money for nine months at a 12 percent simple rate, but the company must maintain a *compensating balance (CB)* equal to 20 percent of the loan amount (principal, or face value). First, note that Unilate must have $10,000 to pay for the equipment. If the firm's checking account balance is not sufficient to cover the compensating balance requirement, then the principal amount of the loan must be greater than $10,000 because some of the amount borrowed must be put aside to satisfy the compensating balance requirement. In this case, the question is, how much must be borrowed so the firm will have $10,000 available for use. To answer this question, first we must determine the *usable funds* from a loan using Equation 14.8:

14.8

$$\text{Usable funds} = \text{Principal} - \left(\begin{array}{c}\$ \text{ reductions from} \\ \text{principal amount}\end{array}\right)$$

Here "Principal" represents the face value of the loan, which is the amount that must be repaid at maturity, and "$ reductions from principal amount" includes anything that reduces the amount of money that the firm can actually use from the total amount that is borrowed.

If the dollar reductions from the face value of the loan are stated as percentages, Equation 14.8 can be written as Equation 14.8a:

14.8a

$$\text{Usable funds} = \text{Principal} \times \left[1 - \left(\begin{array}{c}\% \text{ reductions from} \\ \text{principal amount}\end{array}\right)\right]$$

Here "% reductions from principal amount" includes the items that reduce the amount that the firm can actually use from the borrowed amount stated in decimal form.

If we know how much of the amount borrowed actually is needed as usable funds, Equation 14.8a can be rearranged to solve for the amount that must be borrowed (principal amount) to provide these needed funds. The computation is shown in Equation 14.9.

14.9

$$\text{Principal amount} = \frac{\textit{Usable} \text{ funds}}{1 - \left(\begin{array}{c}\% \text{ reductions from} \\ \text{principal amount}\end{array}\right)}$$

Here "*Usable* funds" is the dollar amount that the firms must have (needs) to use as it wants.

If it does not have a checking account at Atlantic/Pacific Bank, then Unilate will have to borrow $12,500 to be able to satisfy the 20 percent compensating balance requirement and have $10,000 available to pay for the equipment. The computation follows:

$$\text{Required loan (principal) amount} = \frac{\$10,000}{1 - 0.20} = \$12,500$$

Let's check to ensure that this is the amount that the firm must borrow. If the firm borrows $12,500, but has nothing deposited in the bank, $2,500 = $12,500 × 0.2 must be taken out of the principal amount to satisfy the compensating balance requirement, which leaves the firm with $10,000 = $12,500 − $2,500 to use as it pleases (i.e., to pay for the equipment).

In this case, the nine-month rate for this loan would be:

$$r_{PER} = \frac{9\text{-month}}{\text{interest rate}} = \frac{\$12,500 \times \left[0.12 \times \left(\dfrac{9}{12}\right)\right]}{\$12,500 - \$12,500(0.20)}$$

$$= \frac{\$1,125}{\$10,000} = 0.1125 = 11.25\%$$

The APR and EAR are:

$$\text{APR} = 11.25\% \times \left(\frac{12}{9}\right) = 15.00\%$$

$$r_{EAR} = (1.1125)^{(12/9)} - 1.0 = 0.1527 = 15.27\%$$

If a firm normally keeps a positive checking account balance at the lending bank, it needs to borrow less to have a specific amount of funds available for use, which means the effective cost of the loan will be lower.

From the examples presented here, you should recognize that the percentage cost of short-term financing is higher when the dollar expenses, such as those associated with interest, clerical efforts, and loan processing, are higher, when the net proceeds from the loan are less than the principal amount, or when both these conditions exist. Thus, in most cases the effective interest rate (cost) of short-term financing is greater than its stated (quoted) interest rate. *The effective interest rate of a loan is equal to the quoted (simple) rate only if (1) the entire principal amount borrowed can be used by the borrower for the entire year and (2) the only dollar cost associated with the loan is interest charged on the outstanding balance.*

EDHAR/Shutterstock.com

14-6 Multinational Working Capital Management

For the most part, the techniques used to manage working capital accounts in multinational corporations are the same as those used in purely domestic corporations. But the task is far more complex for multinational corporations because they operate in many different languages, cultures, political environments, economic conditions, and so forth. Difficulties with these factors are more acute when managing working capital internationally because decisions made in the short run can have significant consequences on the long-run survival of the firm.

The results of one study provide some indication about the differences in the working capital policies of U.S. firms and European firms.[4] First, the average cash conversion cycle of European firms (about 263 days) was more than twice the average cash conversion cycle of U.S. firms (about 116 days). A possible explanation for this disparity is that European firms had much higher growth rates than their U.S. counterparts. Second, it appears that U.S. firms follow much more conservative working capital policies than European firms. The study reports that the average liquidity measure (e.g., current ratio) was significantly greater for U.S. firms than for European firms, which suggests that corporations in the United States use significantly greater proportions of long-term financing than European firms. One possible explanation for this observation could be the differences that exist in the banking systems in Europe and in the United States. As we mentioned in Chapter 3, U.S. financial institutions traditionally have been subject to more restrictions and regulations than banking organizations in other countries. For example, foreign banks often are permitted to own the firms to which they also lend funds. As a result, European banks often have very close relationships with the firms that borrow from them, which generally results in a greater willingness to provide more short-term, risky debt than we observe in U.S. banking organizations.

[4]Chun-Hao Chang, Krishnan Dandapani, and Arun J. Prakish, "Current Assets Policies of European Corporations: A Critical Examination," *Management International Review*, Special Issue 1995/2, 105–117.

STUDY TOOLS

LOCATED AT BACK OF THE TEXTBOOK

- ☐ Problems are found at the end of this chapter.
- ☐ A tear-out Chapter Review card is located at the back of the textbook.

LOCATED AT WWW.CENGAGEBRAIN.COM

- ☐ Review Key Term flashcards and create your own cards.
- ☐ Track your knowledge and understanding of key concepts in corporate finance.
- ☐ Complete practice and graded quizzes to prepare for tests.
- ☐ Complete interactive content within CFIN5 Online.
- ☐ View the chapter highlight boxes for CFIN5 Online.

KEY CONCEPTS FOR MANAGING SHORT-TERM FINANCING

To conclude this chapter, we summarize some concepts that were discussed.

- Working capital refers to the short-term, or current, assets of a firm. Liquidation of working capital accounts produces the cash that is needed to pay current bills. If a firm cannot pay its current bills, it will not survive to see the long term. As a result, poor working capital management generally results in financial distress and perhaps (often) bankruptcy.

- The cash conversion cycle represents the length of time funds are tied up, or invested, in current assets. Often a firm has to pay for the materials and labor that are needed to manufacture and sell its products before customers pay for their purchases. During the period from when the firm invests in the product—that is, pays for materials and labor—until it receives a cash payment from the sale of the product, external financing is needed to support operations. If a firm reduces its cash conversion cycle, it reduces its need for external financing to support day-to-day operations.

- A variety of sources of short-term credit exist, including accruals, which arise because firms do not pay salaries to employees daily; trade credit, which represents credit purchases from suppliers; short-term bank loans, which include lines of credit; commercial paper, which is unsecured debt issued by large, financially strong companies; and, secured loans, which are loans that often are secured by accounts receivable or inventories.

- The percentage cost of credit per period, r_{PER}, is based on both the dollar cost associated with the credit and the amount of the borrowed funds that the firm can use as it wants (available for use). Accruals and a portion of trade credit (the portion associated with cash discounts) are considered "free" in the sense that specific interest is not paid for using these types of credit. These sources of credit are also considered spontaneous in the sense that their balances automatically increase and decrease as a result of increases and decreases in normal business operations. Some form of cost (perhaps interest) is associated with other types of short-term credit.

- The effective interest rate on a loan is the same as its quoted rate only if all of the principal amount can be used for an entire year and the only cost associated with the loan is interest charged on the outstanding balance.

14–1 Balloon Payment Financial (BPF) has an inventory conversion period of 45 days, a receivables collection period of 30 days, and a payables deferral period of 20 days. (a) What is the length of the firm's cash conversion cycle? (b) If BPF's annual sales are $1.8 million and all sales are on credit, what is the average balance in accounts receivable? (c) How many times per year does BPF turn over its inventory? (d) What would happen to BPF's cash conversion cycle if, on average, inventories could be turned over 12 times a year?

14–2 The Flamingo Corporation is trying to determine the effect of its inventory turnover ratio and days sales outstanding (DSO) on its cash flow cycle. Last year, Flamingo's sales (all on credit) were $180,000 and its cost of goods sold were 85 percent of sales. Inventory was turned over eight times during the year and the accounts receivable turnover was 10. Flamingo's payables deferral period is 30 days. (a) Calculate Flamingo's cash conversion cycle. (b) Compute the average balances in accounts receivable, accounts payable, and inventory.

14–3 Stratosphere Wireless is examining its cash conversion cycle. The company expects its cost of goods sold, which equals 80 percent of sales, to be $480,000 this year. Stratosphere normally turns over inventory 24 times per year, accounts receivable are turned over 15 times per year, and the accounts payable turnover is 40. Calculate (a) the cash conversion cycle and (b) the average balances in accounts receivable, accounts payable, and inventory.

14–4 Look back in the chapter to Table 14.1, which showed the balance sheets for Unilate Textiles on three different dates. Assume all sales and all purchases are made on credit. Calculate the length of Unilate's cash conversion cycle on September 30, 2017 and December 31, 2017.

14–5 Swampy Ox Real Estate (SORE) has been growing at a constant 5 percent rate for many years, and it expects to continue this growth long into the future. On January 1 of this year, which is the slow part of its selling season, SORE's total assets were $420 million. At the height of its selling season, which is at the end of June, SORE expects total assets to be $480 million. How much of the $480 million in assets represents permanent assets, and how much represents temporary current assets?

14–6 If a firm buys on terms of 3/15, net 45, what is the APR of its non–free trade credit? What is the effective annual rate, r_{EAR}?

14–7 What is the APR and r_{EAR} on the non–free credit associated with credit terms of (a) 2/15, net 45 and (b) 3/5 net 45?

14–8 Calculate the APR and r_{EAR} of non–free trade credit associated with credit terms of 3/10, net 50, and 2.5/15, net 45, assuming that customers who do not take the discount (a) pay on the last due date and (b) delay payment until 10 days after the last due date.

14–9 Connecticut Advanced Technologies (CAT) is planning to get a 30-day $150,000 simple interest loan from its bank. The quoted interest rate on the loan is 10 percent. Calculate the APR and r_{EAR} assuming the loan (a) has no compensating balance requirement and (b) has a 20 percent compensating balance requirement, and CAT currently holds no funds at the lending bank.

14–10 Carefree Leisure has a 40-day discount interest loan outstanding. The principal amount of the loan is $60,000, its quoted interest rate is 12 percent, and there is no compensating balance requirement. Compute the loan's APR and r_{EAR}.

14–11 PanAir Reservations (PAR) borrowed $150,000 for 60 days from its bank. The simple interest rate on the loan is 12 percent. Calculate the APR and r_{EAR} assuming the loan is a simple interest loan with (a) no compensating balance requirement and (b) a 25 percent compensating balance requirement, and PAR currently holds no funds at the lending bank. (c) How much would PAR have to borrow if it needed $150,000 to pay bills and the loan required a 25 percent compensating balance?

14–12 Montana Allied Products (MAP) must borrow $1.7 million to finance its working capital requirements. The bank has offered a 45-day simple interest loan with a quoted interest rate of 8 percent. Calculate the loan's APR and r_{EAR} assuming there is (a) no compensating balance requirement and (b) a 15 percent compensating balance requirement, which MAP must satisfy from the loan proceeds. (c) How much does MAP have to borrow so that it has $5.1 million to pay its bills if the loan requires a 15 percent compensating balance?

14–13 Albatross Boats can borrow $450,000 from its bank using a 30-day discount interest loan. The loan has a quoted interest of 9 percent and no compensating balance requirement. (a) Compute the loan's APR and r_{EAR}. (b) Compute the amount Albatross must borrow so that it has $450,000 to use to pay bills. Compute the loan's APR and r_{EAR}.

14–14 United Sales Association (USA) recently borrowed $25,000 from its bank at a simple interest rate of 11 percent. The loan is for one year, and the loan agreement calls for the interest to be added to the amount borrowed and the total amount to be repaid in monthly installments. (a) What are the loan's monthly payments? (b) Compute the loan's APR and r_{EAR}.

14–15 Xenon Xrays (XX) recently issued 180-day commercial paper with a face value of $100,000 and a simple interest rate of 7 percent. XX paid a transaction fee equal to 0.3 percent of the issue, which was taken out of the issue amount before the company received any funds. Compute the commercial paper's APR and r_{EAR}.

14–16 Yunes' Yearlings (YY) is able to raise funds by issuing commercial paper with a face value of $100,000. If commercial paper is issued, the simple interest rate would be 5 percent, the time to maturity would be 90 days, and YY would have to pay a transaction fee equal to 0.25 percent of the issue, which would be taken out of the issue amount. Compute the commercial paper's APR and r_{EAR}.

14–17 Clicker Corporation must raise $50,000 to support operations for the next 12 months. Clicker buys from its suppliers on terms of 2.5/20, net 80, and it normally pays on Day 20 to take the cash discounts; but, it could forgo the discounts and pay on Day 90 to get the needed amount in the form of non–free trade credit. Alternatively, Clicker can borrow from its bank using a one-year discount interest loan that has a 12 percent quoted interest rate and requires a 15 percent compensating balance. Clicker normally maintains a negligible deposit at the bank. What is the EAR of the lower cost source? Assume the face value of the bank loan is $50,000.

14–18 PDQ Enterprise can borrow from its bank using a one-year (a) simple interest loan with a 12 percent quoted rate and no compensating balance or (b) a discount interest loan with a quoted rate equal to 10 percent that requires a 15 percent compensating balance. What is the EAR of the lower-cost loan? PDQ normally tries to keep its checking account balance close to $0.

14–19 Refer to the information provided in Problem 14-18. Suppose PDQ needs $90,000 today to pay past due bills. How much must PDQ borrow for each loan so that it has $90,000 available to pay the bills? Show how much of the total amount borrowed PDQ will actually be able to use.

14–20 BoGo Textbooks is evaluating two options for funding its working capital during the next year. Option 1 is borrowing from the bank using a 180-day discount interest loan, which has a quoted interest rate equal to 8 percent and requires a 20 percent compensating balance. BoGo normally maintains an average checking account balance of $10,000. Option 2 is to issue 180-day commercial paper, which has an annual interest equal to 9 percent and requires BoGo to pay a transaction fee equal to 0.3 percent. (a) If BoGo actually needs $200,000 to finance working capital during the next year, how much must BoGo borrow with each option so that $200,000 can be used to pay the bills? (b) Which option is better?

Michael R Ross/Shutterstock.com

After you finish this chapter go to **PAGE 302** for **STUDY TOOLS**

LEARNING OUTCOMES

After studying this chapter, you will be able to…

LO1 Describe the policies that a firm might follow when investing in current assets.

LO2 Discuss the goal of effective cash management and how (a) the cash budget, (b) techniques that exist to accelerate cash receipts, and (c) cash disbursement controls should be employed to develop an optimal cash management policy.

LO3 Explain the rationale for holding marketable securities, and describe the general characteristics of investments that should be included in portfolios of marketable securities.

LO4 Discuss accounts receivable (credit) management, and describe how a proposed credit policy change should be evaluated.

LO5 Explain the rationale for holding various forms of inventory, and describe how a firm can determine its optimal level of inventory.

LO6 Describe how management of current assets differs for multinational firms and for purely domestic firms.

Managing Short-Term Assets

15

In this chapter, we discuss working capital management policies with respect to the short-term assets of the firm. As you read the chapter, keep in mind that, although short-term assets generally are safer than long-term assets, they also earn lower rates of return. Thus, all else equal, firms that hold greater amounts of their total assets as short-term assets are considered less risky than firms that hold greater amounts of their total assets as long-term assets; at the same time, however, firms with more short-term assets earn lower returns than are earned by firms with more long-term assets. Consequently, financial managers are faced with a dilemma of whether to forgo higher returns to attain lower risk or to forgo lower risk to achieve higher returns.

15-1 Alternative Current Asset Investment Policies

A firm generally follows one of three alternative policies when determining the amount of current assets to carry relative to its total assets. These policies differ with respect to the amount of current assets that is carried to support a particular level of sales. The three policies are described as follows:

1. The **relaxed current asset investment** (or "fat cat") **policy** calls for relatively large amounts of current assets to be carried because sales are stimulated by the use of a credit policy that provides liberal financing to customers and a corresponding high level of receivables.

2. With the **restricted current asset investment** (or "lean-and-mean") **policy**, the amounts of current assets are minimized.

3. The **moderate current asset investment policy** lies between the relaxed current asset investment policy and the restricted current asset investment policy.

The more certain a firm is about its sales, costs, order lead times, payment periods, and so forth, the lower the level of current assets that is required to support operations and the closer the firm can follow the restricted current asset investment policy. If there is a great deal of uncertainty about operations, however, the firm requires some minimum amount of cash and inventories based on expected payments, expected sales, expected order lead times, and so on, plus additional amounts, or safety stocks, that enable it to deal with departures from the expected values. Similarly, accounts receivable levels are determined by credit terms; the tougher the credit terms, the lower the accounts receivable for any given level of sales. With a restricted current asset investment policy, the firm would hold minimal levels of safety stocks for cash and inventories, and it would have a tight credit policy even though such a policy would mean running the risk of losing sales.

A restricted, lean-and-mean current asset investment policy generally provides the highest expected return on investment, but it entails the greatest risk. The reverse is true under a relaxed policy, and the moderate policy falls in between the two extremes. In terms of the cash conversion cycle (discussed in Chapter 14),

relaxed current asset investment policy A policy under which relatively large amounts of cash and marketable securities and inventories are carried and under which sales are stimulated by a liberal credit policy that results in a high level of receivables.

restricted current asset investment policy A policy under which holdings of cash and marketable securities, inventories, and receivables are minimized.

moderate current asset investment policy A policy between the relaxed and restrictive current asset investment policies.

a restricted investment policy would tend to reduce the inventory conversion and accounts receivable collection periods, resulting in a relatively short cash conversion cycle. The opposite is true for the relaxed policy.

In the remainder of the chapter, we discuss factors firms consider when deciding which of the current asset investment policies to follow; that is, we discuss how firms determine the amount of current assets to carry as well as how these accounts are managed.

15-2 Cash Management

In earlier chapters, we discovered that managing cash flows is an extremely important task for a financial manager. Part of this task is determining how much cash a firm should have on hand at any time to ensure that normal business operations continue uninterrupted. For the purposes of our discussion, the term *cash* refers to the funds a firm holds that can be used for immediate disbursement. This includes the amount a firm holds in its checking account as well as the amount of actual coin and currency it holds. Cash is a *nonearning*, or *idle*, *asset* that is required to pay bills. When possible, cash should be "put to work" by investing it in assets that have positive expected returns. Thus, the goal of the cash manager is to minimize the amount of cash the firm must hold for use in conducting its normal business activities, yet, at the same time, to have sufficient cash to meet its cash needs (both expected and unexpected).

Firms generally hold cash for the following reasons:

1. Cash balances associated with routine business payments and collections are known as transactions balances.

2. A bank often requires a firm to maintain a compensating balance on deposit to help offset the costs of providing services such as check clearing and cash management advice.

3. Because cash inflows and cash outflows are somewhat unpredictable, firms generally hold some cash in reserve for random, unforeseen fluctuations in cash flows. These *safety* stocks are called precautionary balances. The less predictable the firm's cash flows, the larger such balances should be.

4. Sometimes cash balances are held to enable the firm to take advantage of bargain purchases that might arise. These funds are called speculative balances.

Although the cash accounts of most firms can be thought of as consisting of transactions, compensating, precautionary, and speculative balances, we cannot calculate the amount needed for each purpose, sum them, and produce a total desired cash balance, because the same money often serves more than one purpose. For instance, precautionary and speculative balances can also be used to satisfy compensating balance requirements. In addition, firms that have easy access to borrowed funds are likely to rely on their ability to borrow quickly rather than carrying cash balances. Firms do, however, consider all four factors when establishing their target cash positions.

In addition to these four motives, a firm maintains cash balances to preserve its credit rating by keeping its liquidity position in line with the average liquidity position of other firms in the industry. A strong credit rating enables the firm both to purchase goods from suppliers on favorable terms and to maintain ample short-term credit with its bank.

15-2a The Cash Budget

Perhaps the most critical ingredient of proper cash management is the ability to estimate the cash flows of the firm so that the firm can make plans to borrow when cash is deficient or to invest when cash is in excess of what is needed. Without a doubt, financial managers will agree that the most important tool for managing cash is the cash budget (forecast).

The firm estimates its general needs for cash as a part of its overall budgeting, or forecasting, process. First, the firm forecasts its operating activities, such as expenses and revenues, for the period in question. Then, the financing and investment activities necessary to attain that level of operations must be forecast. Such forecasts entail the construction of pro forma financial statements, which are discussed in Chapter 17. The information from these pro forma statements is combined with projections about the delay in collecting accounts receivable, the delay in paying suppliers and employees, tax payment dates, dividend and interest payment dates, and so on. All of this information is summarized in the cash budget, which shows the firm's projected cash inflows and cash outflows over some specified period.

---

transactions balance A cash balance necessary for day-to-day operations; the balance associated with routine payments and collections.

compensating balance A minimum checking account balance that a firm must maintain with a bank to help offset the costs of services such as check clearing and cash management advice.

precautionary balance A cash balance held in reserve for unforeseen fluctuations in cash flows.

speculative balance A cash balance held to enable the firm to take advantage of any bargain purchases that might arise.

cash budget A schedule showing cash receipts, cash disbursements, and cash balances for a firm over a specified time period.

The cash budget provides information concerning a firm's future cash flows that is much more detailed than the information provided in forecasted financial statements. For example, when we develop the forecasted financial statements for Unilate Textiles in Chapter 17, we project net sales in 2017 to be $1,650 million and net income to be $61 million. Based on the forecasted financial statements, we can determine that Unilate expects to generate a $50 million cash inflow through normal production and sales operations. Much of this $50 million will be used to satisfy the financing and investment activities of the firm. Even after these activities are considered, Unilate's cash account is projected to increase by $1.5 million in 2017. Does this mean that Unilate will not have to worry about cash shortages during 2017? To answer this question, we must construct Unilate's cash budget for 2017.

To simplify the construction of Unilate's cash budget, we will consider only the latter half of 2017 (July through December). Further, we will not list every cash flow that is expected to occur, but instead will focus on the operating cash flows. Remember that Unilate's sales peak in September and October. All sales are made on credit with terms that allow a 2 percent cash discount for payments made within 10 days of the billing period, and if the discount is not taken, the full amount is due in 30 days. However, like most companies, Unilate finds that some of its customers delay payment for more than 90 days. Experience has shown that payment on 20 percent of Unilate's *dollar* sales is made during the month in which the sales are made; these are the discount sales. On 70 percent of sales, payments are made during the month immediately following the month of sale, and payments are made on 10 percent of sales two months or more after the initial sale. To simplify the cash budget, however, we will assume the last 10 percent of sales is collected two months after the sales.

The costs to Unilate for cotton, wool, and other cloth-related materials average 60 percent of the sales prices of the finished products. These purchases generally are made one month before the firm expects to manufacture and sell the finished products. In 2017, Unilate's suppliers have agreed to allow payment for materials to be delayed for 30 days after the purchase. Accordingly, if July sales are forecast at $150 million, then purchases during June will amount to $90 million (= $150 million × 0.6), and this amount actually will be paid in July.

Other cash expenses, such as wages and rent, also are built into the cash budget, and Unilate must make estimated tax payments of $16 million on September 15 and $10 million on December 15; in addition, a $20 million payment for a new plant must be made in October. Assuming that Unilate's **target**, or **minimum**, cash balance is $5 million and that it projects $8 million to be on hand on July 1, 2017, what will the firm's monthly cash surpluses or shortfalls be for the period from July through December?

Unilate's 2017 cash budget for July through December is presented in Table 15.1. The approach used to construct this cash budget is termed the **disbursements and receipts method** (also referred to as **scheduling**) because the cash disbursements and cash receipts are estimated to determine the net cash flow that is expected to be generated each month. The format used in Table 15.1 is quite simple; it is much like balancing a checkbook. The cash receipts are lumped into one category and the cash disbursements are lumped into another category to determine the net effect monthly cash flows have on the cash position of the firm. Other formats also can be used, depending on how the firm prefers to present the cash budget information.

The first line of Table 15.1 gives the sales forecast for the period from May through December. These estimates are necessary to determine collections for July through December. Similarly, the second line of the table gives the credit purchases expected in each month based on the sales forecasts, so the monthly payments for credit purchases can be determined.

The Cash Receipts category shows cash collections based on credit sales originating in three different months—the current month and the previous two months. Take a look at the collections expected in July. Remember that Unilate expects 20 percent of the dollar sales to be collected in the month of the sales, and thus to be affected by the 2 percent cash discount that is offered, 70 percent of the sales will be collected one month after the sales occur, and the remaining 10 percent of the sales will be collected two months after the sales occur. (It is assumed that there are no bad debts.) So in July, $29.4 million = 0.20 × (1 − 0.02) × $150 million collections will result from sales in July; $87.5 million = 0.70 × $125 million will be collected from sales that occurred in June; and, $10.0 million = 0.10 × $100 million will be collected from sales that took place in May. Thus, the total collections expected in July equal $126.9 million (= $29.4 million + $87.5 million + $10.0 million).

The Cash Disbursements category shows payments for raw materials, wages, rent, and so forth. Raw materials are purchased on credit one month before the finished goods are expected to

target (minimum) cash balance The minimum cash balance a firm desires to maintain to conduct business.

disbursements and receipts method (scheduling) Method of determining net cash flow by estimating the cash disbursements and the cash receipts expected to be generated each period.

Table 15.1

Unilate Textiles: 2017 Cash Budget ($ millions)

	May	June	July	Aug	Sept	Oct	Nov	Dec
Credit sales	$100.0	$125.0	$150.0	$200.0	$250.0	$180.0	$130.0	$100.0
Credit purchases = 60 percent of next month's sales		90.0	120.0	150.0	108.0	78.0	60.0	

	May	June	July	Aug	Sept	Oct	Nov	Dec
Cash Receipts								
Collections of sales from:								
Current month = 0.2 × 0.98 × (current month's sales)			$ 29.4	$ 39.2	$ 49.0	$ 35.3	$ 25.5	$ 19.6
Previous month = 0.7 × (previous month's sales)			87.5	105.0	140.0	175.0	126.0	91.0
Two months previously = 0.1 × (sales two months ago)			10.0	12.5	15.0	20.0	25.0	18.0
Total cash receipts			$126.9	$156.7	$204.0	$230.3	$176.5	$128.6
Cash Disbursements								
Payments for credit purchases (one-month lag)			$ 90.0	$ 120.0	$ 150.0	$ 108.0	$ 78.0	$ 60.0
Wages and salaries (22 percent of monthly sales)			33.0	44.0	55.0	39.6	28.6	22.0
Rent			9.0	9.0	9.0	9.0	9.0	9.0
Other expenses			7.0	8.0	11.0	10.0	5.0	4.0
Taxes					16.0			10.0
Payment for plant construction						20.0		
Total cash disbursements			$139.0	$181.0	$241.0	$186.6	$120.6	$105.0
Net Cash Flow (Receipts − Disbursements)			($ 12.1)	($ 24.3)	($ 37.0)	$ 43.7	$ 55.9	$ 23.6
Beginning Cash Balance			8.0	(4.1)	(28.4)	(65.4)	(21.7)	34.2
Ending Cash Balance			(4.1)	(28.4)	(65.4)	(21.7)	34.2	57.8
Target (Minimum) Cash Balance			5.0	5.0	5.0	5.0	5.0	5.0
Surplus (Shortfall) Cash			($ 9.1)	($ 33.4)	($ 70.4)	($ 26.7)	$ 29.2	$ 52.8

be sold, but payments for the materials are not made until the month of the expected sales (that is, one month after the credit purchase). The cost of the raw materials is expected to be 60 percent of sales. July sales are forecast at $150 million, so Unilate will purchase $90 million of materials in June and pay for these purchases in July. Additional monthly cash disbursements include employees' salaries, which equal 22 percent of monthly sales; rent, which remains constant; and other operating expenses, which vary with respect to production levels. Cash disbursements that are not expected to occur monthly include taxes (September and December) and payment for the construction of additional facilities (October).

The line labeled Net Cash Flow shows whether Unilate's operations are expected to generate positive or negative net cash flows each month. However, this is only the beginning of the story. We need to examine the firm's cash position based on the cash balance that exists at the beginning of the month and based on the *target (minimum) cash balance* desired by Unilate. The bottom line provides information as to whether Unilate can expect a monthly cash surplus that can be invested temporarily in marketable securities or a monthly cash shortfall that must be financed with external, nonspontaneous sources of funds.

At the beginning of July, Unilate will have cash equal to $8 million on hand. During July, Unilate is expected to generate a negative $12.1 million net cash flow; thus, July cash disbursements are expected to exceed cash receipts by $12.1 million (deficit spending is expected). Because Unilate only has $8 million cash to begin July, the cash balance at the end of July is expected to be overdrawn by $4.1 million if the firm doesn't find additional funding. To make matters worse, Unilate has a target cash balance equal to $5 million. So, without any additional financing, its cash balance at the end of July is expected to be $9.1 million short of its target. As a result, Unilate must make arrangements to borrow $9.1 million in July to bring the cash balance up to the target balance of $5 million. Assuming that this amount is indeed borrowed, loans outstanding will total $9.1 million at the end of July. (We assume that Unilate does not have any bank loans outstanding on July 1 because its beginning cash balance exceeds the target balance.)

The cash surplus or required loan balance (shortfall) is given on the bottom line of the cash budget. A positive value indicates a cash surplus, whereas a negative value (in parentheses) indicates a loan requirement. Note that the *bottom line* surplus cash or loan requirement that is shown is a *cumulative amount*. Thus, Unilate must borrow $9.1 million in July. Because it has a cash shortfall of $24.3 million during August as reported on the Net Cash Flow line, Unilate's total loan requirement at the end of August is $33.4 million = $9.1 million + $24.3 million, as reported on the bottom line for August. Unilate's arrangement with the bank permits it to increase its outstanding loans on a daily basis, up to a prearranged maximum, just as you can increase the amount you are permitted to owe on a credit card. Unilate will use any surplus funds it generates to pay off its loans, and because the loans can be paid down at any time, on a daily basis the firm will never have both a cash surplus and an outstanding short-term loan balance. If Unilate actually does have a cash surplus and no short-term loans to repay, these funds will be invested in short-term, temporary investments.

This same procedure is used in the following months. Sales will peak in September, accompanied by increased payments for purchases, wages, and other items. Receipts from sales will also go up, but the firm will still be left with a $37 million net cash outflow during the month. The total short-term loan requirement at the end of September will hit a peak of $70.4 million, representing the cumulative cash deficits plus the target cash balance.[1]

---

[1]This figure is easily calculated as follows:

$$\text{Cash}_{\text{Sept}} = \begin{pmatrix} \text{Beginning cash} \\ \text{balance in July} \end{pmatrix} + \text{Net CF}_{\text{July}} + \text{Net CF}_{\text{Aug}} + \text{Net CF}_{\text{Sep}}$$

$$- \begin{pmatrix} \text{Target cash} \\ \text{balance} \end{pmatrix}$$

$$= \$8.0 + (-\$12.1) + (-\$24.3) + (-\$37.0) - \$5.0 = \$70.4$$

[2]The firm might even set the target cash balance at zero. This could be done if it carried a portfolio of marketable securities that could be sold to replenish the cash account, or if it had an arrangement with its bank that permitted it to borrow any funds needed on a daily basis. In that event, the target cash balance would simply be equal to zero. Note, though, that most firms would find it difficult to operate with a zero-balance bank account, just as you would. Therefore, most firms do set positive target cash balances.

Sales, purchases, and payments for past purchases will fall sharply in October, but collections will be the highest of any month because they will reflect the high September sales. As a result, Unilate will generate a healthy $43.7 million net cash inflow during October. This inflow can be used to pay off borrowings, so short-term loans outstanding will decline by $43.7 million to $26.7 million.

Unilate will generate an even larger cash surplus in November, which will permit the firm to pay off all of its short-term loans. In fact, the company is expected to have $29.2 million in surplus cash by the month's end, and another cash surplus in December will swell the excess cash to $52.8 million. With such a large amount of unneeded funds, Unilate's treasurer certainly will want to invest in interest-bearing securities or to put the funds to use in some other way.

Before concluding our discussion, we must make some additional points that should be considered and could easily be included in our simple cash budget.

1. For simplicity, our illustrative budget for Unilate omitted many important cash flows that are anticipated for 2017, such as dividends, proceeds from stock and bond sales, and investment in additional fixed assets.

2. Even though it could easily be included, our cash budget example does not reflect interest on the loans needed to finance cash deficits or income from investing surplus cash.

3. If cash inflows and outflows are not uniform during the month, we could seriously understate the firm's peak financing requirements. The data in Table 15.1 show the situation expected on the last day of each month, but on any given day during the month it could be quite different. For example, if all payments had to be made on the fifth of each month, but collections came in uniformly throughout the month, the firm would need to borrow much larger amounts than those shown in the table. In this case, we would have to prepare a cash budget identifying requirements on a daily basis.

4. Because the cash budget represents a forecast, all the values in the table are *expected* values. If the actual results differ from the forecasted levels, the projected cash deficits and surpluses will also differ.

5. Finally, we should note that the target cash balance will probably be adjusted over time, rising and falling with seasonal patterns and with long-term changes in the scale of the firm's operations. Thus, Unilate probably will plan to maintain larger cash balances during August and September than at other times, and as the company grows, so will its required cash balance.[2]

isak55/Shutterstock.com

15-2b Cash Management Techniques

Most cash management activities are performed jointly by the firm and its primary bank, but the financial manager ultimately is responsible for the effectiveness of the cash management program. Effective cash management encompasses proper management of both the cash inflows and the cash outflows of a firm, which entails consideration of the factors discussed next.

Cash Flow Synchronization. Companies try to arrange their finances so that cash inflows and cash outflows are matched as closely as possible. Having **synchronized cash flows** enables a firm to reduce its cash balances, decrease its bank loans, lower interest expenses, and boost profits. *The more predictable the timing of the cash flows, the greater the synchronization that can be attained.*

Check Clearing and the Use of Float. When a customer writes and mails a paper check, this does *not* mean that the funds are immediately available to the receiving firm. The check must be processed by the receiving firm, deposited at its bank, and cleared through the banking system before the funds are available for use. These activities result in a lag between the time when a firm deposits a check and records the amount on its books and when the funds are available for use. This lag results from factors associated with *float*.

Float is defined as the difference between the balance shown in a firm's (or individual's) checkbook and the balance on the bank's records. Suppose a firm writes, on average, checks for $5,000 each day, and it normally takes four days from the time a check is mailed until it is cleared and deducted from the firm's bank account. This will cause the firm's own checkbook to show a balance that is $20,000 = $5,000 × 4 days smaller than the balance on the bank's records; this difference is called **disbursement float**. Now suppose the firm also receives checks in the amount of $6,000 daily, but it loses two days while they are being processed, deposited, and cleared. This will result in $12,000 of **collections float**. In total, the firm's **net float**—the difference between the $20,000 positive disbursement float and the $12,000 negative collections float—will be $8,000, which means the balance the bank shows in the firm's checking account will be $8,000 greater than the balance the firm shows in its own checkbook.

Delays that create float arise because it takes time for checks (1) to travel through the mail (*mail delay*), (2) to be processed by the receiving firm (*processing delay*), and (3) to clear through the banking system (*clearing, or availability, delay*). Basically, the size of a firm's net float is a function of its ability to speed up collections on checks received and to slow down collections on checks written. Efficient firms go to great lengths to speed up the processing of incoming checks, thus putting the funds to work faster, and, at the same time, they try to delay their own payments for as long as possible.

15-2c Acceleration of Receipts

A firm cannot use customers' payments until they are received *and* converted into a spendable form. Thus, it would benefit the firm to accelerate the collection of customers' payments and conversion of those payments into cash. Although some of the delays that cause float cannot be controlled directly, the techniques described next can be used to manage collections.

Lockboxes. A **lockbox arrangement** requires customers to send their payments to a post office box located in the area near where they live rather than directly to the firm, which might be located a far distance from many customers. The firm arranges for a local bank to collect

synchronized cash flows A situation in which cash inflows coincide with cash outflows, thereby permitting a firm to hold low transactions balances.

float The difference between the balance shown in a firm's (or individual's) checkbook and the balance shown on the bank's records.

disbursement float The value of the checks that have been written and *disbursed* (paid) but have not yet fully cleared through the banking system, and thus have not been deducted from the account on which they were written.

collections float The amount of checks that have been received and deposited but have not yet been made available to the account in which they were deposited.

net float The difference between disbursement float and collections float; the difference between the balance shown in the company's checkbook and the balance shown on the bank's books.

lockbox arrangement A technique used to reduce float by having payments sent to post office boxes located near customers.

the checks from the post office box, perhaps several times a day, and to immediately deposit them into the company's checking account. By having lockboxes close to the customers, a firm can reduce float because, at the very least, (1) the mail delay is less than if the payment had to travel farther and (2) checks are cleared faster because the banks the checks are written on are in the same Federal Reserve district; thus, fewer parties are involved in the clearing process.

Preauthorized Debits. If a firm receives regular, repetitious payments from its customers, it might want to establish a **preauthorized debit system** (sometimes called *preauthorized payments*). With this arrangement, the collecting firm and its customer (paying firm) enter into an agreement whereby the paying firm's bank periodically transfers funds from the paying firm's account to the collecting firm's account, even if that account is located at another bank. Preauthorized debiting accelerates the transfer of funds because the collecting firm's mail and processing delays are completely eliminated, and availability delay is reduced substantially.

Concentration Banking. **Concentration banking** is a cash management arrangement used to mobilize funds from decentralized receiving locations, whether they are lockboxes or decentralized company locations, into one or more central cash pools. The cash manager then uses these pools for short-term investing or reallocation among the firm's various bank accounts. By pooling its cash, the firm is able to take maximum advantage of economies of scale in cash management and investment.

15-2d Disbursement Control

Accelerating collections represents one side of cash management, and controlling funds outflows, or disbursements,

represents the other side. Three methods commonly used to control disbursements include the following:

Payables Concentration. Centralizing the processing of payables permits the financial manager to evaluate the payments coming due for the entire firm and to schedule the availability of funds to meet these needs on a company-wide basis, and it also permits more efficient monitoring of payables and the effects of float. A disadvantage of a centralized disbursement system is that regional offices might not be able to make prompt payment for services received, which can create ill will and raise the company's operating costs.

Zero-Balance Accounts. A zero-balance account (ZBA) is a special disbursement account that has a balance equal to zero when there is no disbursement activity. Typically, a firm establishes several ZBAs in its concentration bank and funds them from a master account. As checks are presented to a ZBA for payment, funds are automatically transferred from the master account to ensure the checks are covered.

Controlled Disbursement Accounts. Whereas ZBAs typically are established at concentration banks, controlled disbursement accounts (CDA) can be set up at any bank. Such accounts are not funded until the day's checks are presented against the account. The firm relies on the bank that maintains the CDA to provide information in the morning (generally before 11 A.M. New York time) concerning the total amount of the checks that are expected to be presented for payment that day. This permits the financial manager (1) to transfer funds to the CDA to cover the checks presented for payment or (2) to invest excess cash at midday, when money market trading is at a peak.

Float, both collection and disbursement, has been reduced significantly with the increased use of electronic payment systems. As these systems become more sophisticated and widespread, float will continue to decrease, perhaps to the point where it is virtually nonexistent. Even so, as long as firms can use the postal service to submit payments, mail delay will

preauthorized debit system A system that allows a customer's bank to periodically transfer funds from its account to a selling firm's bank account for the payment of bills.

concentration banking A technique used to move funds from many bank accounts to a more central cash pool to more effectively manage cash.

zero-balance account (ZBA) A special checking account used for disbursements that has a balance equal to zero when there is no disbursement activity.

controlled disbursement accounts (CDA) Checking accounts in which funds are not deposited until checks are presented for payment, usually on a daily basis.

exist, which means that the effects of float must be considered when making cash management decisions (policy).

Marketable Securities

Realistically, the management of cash and the management of marketable securities cannot be separated. Management of one implies management of the other, because the amount of marketable securities held by a firm depends on its short-term cash needs.

Marketable securities, or *near-cash* assets, are extremely liquid short-term investments that permit the firm to earn positive returns on cash that is not needed to pay bills immediately but will be needed sometime in the near term, perhaps in a few days, weeks, or months. Although such investments typically provide much lower yields than other assets, nearly every large firm has them. The two basic reasons for owning marketable securities are:

1. Marketable securities serve as a *substitute for cash balances*. Firms often hold portfolios of marketable securities, liquidating part of the portfolio to increase the cash account when cash is needed, because the *marketable securities offer a place to temporarily put cash balances to work earning positive returns*. In such situations, the marketable securities could be used as a substitute for transactions balances, for precautionary balances, for speculative balances, or for all three.

2. Marketable securities are also used as a *temporary investment* (a) to finance seasonal or cyclical operations and (b) to amass funds to meet financial requirements in the near future. For example, if the firm has a conservative financing policy, as we discussed in Chapter 14, its long-term capital will exceed its permanent assets, and marketable securities will be held when inventories and receivables are low.

Because marketable securities are temporary investments, financial assets that are considered appropriate investments include those that are traded in the money markets. Examples of such short-term securities, which were described in Chapter 6, include Treasury bills, commercial paper, negotiable certificates of deposit, and Eurodollar time deposits. Depending on how long they will be held, the financial manager decides upon a suitable set of securities, and a suitable maturity pattern, to hold as *near-cash reserves* in the form of marketable securities. Long-term securities are not appropriate investments for marketable securities. As we have described in this section, safety, especially maintenance of principal, should be paramount when constructing a marketable securities portfolio.

15-4 Credit Management

Firms would prefer to sell products and services for cash only. So why do firms sell for credit? The primary reason many firms offer credit sales is that their competitors offer credit. Consider what you would do if you had the opportunity to purchase the same product for the same price from two different firms, but one firm required cash payment at the time of the purchase, whereas the other firm allowed you to pay for the product one month after the purchase without any additional cost. From which firm would you purchase? Like you, firms prefer to delay their payments, especially if there are no additional costs associated with the delay.

Effective credit management is extremely important, because too much credit is costly in terms of the investment in, and maintenance of, accounts receivable, whereas too little credit could result in the loss of profitable sales. Carrying receivables not only has both direct and indirect costs, but it also has an important benefit: granting credit should increase profits. Thus, to maximize shareholders' wealth, a financial manager needs to understand how to effectively manage the firm's credit activities.

15-4a Credit Policy

The major controllable variables that affect demand for a company's products are sales prices, product quality, advertising, and the firm's **credit policy**. The firm's credit policy, in turn, includes the factors we discuss next.

1. **Credit standards** refer to the strength and creditworthiness a customer must exhibit to qualify for credit. The firm's credit standards are applied to determine which customers qualify for its regular credit terms and how much credit each customer should receive. The major factors that are considered when setting credit standards relate to the likelihood that a given customer will pay slowly or perhaps even end up as a bad debt loss. Determining the credit

marketable securities
Securities that can be sold on short notice without loss of principal or original investment (liquid investments).

credit policy A set of decisions that includes a firm's credit standards, credit terms, methods used to collect credit accounts, and credit monitoring procedures.

credit standards Standards that indicate the minimum financial strength a customer must have to be granted credit.

quality, or creditworthiness, of a customer probably is the most difficult part of credit management. Nevertheless, good credit evaluation can provide reasonably accurate judgments of customers' default probabilities.

2. **Terms of credit** are the conditions of the credit sale, especially with regard to the payment arrangements. Firms need to determine when the **credit period** begins, how long the customer has to pay for credit purchases before the account is considered delinquent, and whether a cash discount for early payment should be offered. A variety of credit terms are offered by firms in the United States, ranging from cash before delivery (CBD) and cash on delivery (COD) to **cash discounts** for early payment. For example, a firm that offers terms of 2/10 net 30 gives its customers a 2 percent discount from the purchase price if the bill is paid on or before Day 10 of the billing cycle; otherwise the entire bill (the net amount) is due by Day 30.

3. **Collection policy** refers to the procedures the firm follows to collect its credit accounts. The firm needs to determine when and how notification of the outstanding bill is conveyed to the buyer. The more quickly a customer receives an invoice, the sooner the bill *can* be paid. In today's world, firms have increasingly turned to the use of electronics to send invoices to customers. Another important collection policy decision is how the past-due accounts should be handled—that is, when past-due notices should be sent, or when an account should be turned over to a collection agency.

15-4b Receivables Monitoring

Once a firm sets its credit policy, it wants to adhere to it. Thus, it is important that a firm periodically examine its receivables to determine whether customers' payment patterns have changed such that credit operations are outside the credit policy limits. **Receivables monitoring** refers to the process of evaluating the credit policy to determine whether a shift in customers' payment patterns has occurred. Traditionally, firms have monitored receivables by using methods that measure the amount of time credit remains outstanding. Two such methods are the *days sales outstanding (DSO)* and the *aging schedule*.

Days Sales Outstanding (DSO). The **days sales outstanding (DSO)**, which is sometimes called the *average collection period*, represents the average time it takes to collect credit accounts. DSO is computed by dividing *annual* credit sales by *daily* credit sales. For example, in the previous chapter (and in Chapter 2), we found the receivables collection period, or DSO, for Unilate Textiles was 43.2 days in 2016. The DSO of 43.2 days can be compared with the credit terms offered by Unilate. If Unilate's credit terms are 2/10 net 30, then we know there are quite a few customers who are delinquent when paying their accounts. One way to identify delinquent accounts is to use an aging schedule, as described next.

Aging Schedule. An **aging schedule** is a breakdown of a firm's receivables by age of account. Table 15.2 contains the December 31, 2016, aging schedule for Unilate Textiles. The standard format for aging schedules generally includes age categories broken down by month, because banks and financial analysts usually want companies to report their receivables' ages in this form. However, more precision, and thus better monitoring information, can be attained by using narrower age categories (for example, one or two weeks).

According to Unilate's aging schedule, only 40 percent of its

terms of credit The payment conditions offered to credit customers; these terms include the length of the credit period and any cash discounts offered.

credit period The length of time for which credit is granted; after that time, the credit account is considered delinquent.

cash discount A reduction in the invoice price of goods offered by the seller to encourage early payment.

collection policy The procedures followed by a firm to collect its accounts receivable.

receivables monitoring The process of evaluating the credit policy to determine whether a shift in the customers' payment patterns has occurred.

days sales outstanding (DSO) The average length of time required to collect accounts receivable; also called the *average collection period*.

aging schedule A report showing how long accounts receivable have been outstanding; the report divides receivables into specified periods, which provide information about the proportion of receivables that is current and the proportion that is past due for given lengths of time.

Table 15.2

Unilate Textiles: Receivables Aging Schedule for 2016

Age of Account (days)	Net Amount Outstanding ($ millions)	Percentage of Total Receivables	Average Days
0–30	$ 72.0	40%	18
31–60	90.0	50	55
61–90	10.8	6	77
Over 90	7.2	4	97
	$180.0	100%	

DSO = 0.40(18 days) + 0.50(55 days) + 0.06(77 days) + 0.04(97 days)
= 43.2 days

credit sales were collected within the credit period of 30 days; thus, 60 percent of the credit sales collections were delinquent. Some of the payments were delinquent by only a few days, while others were delinquent by three to four times the 30-day credit period.

Management should constantly monitor the DSO and the aging schedule to detect trends, to see how the firm's collection experience compares with its credit terms, and to see how effectively its credit department is operating in comparison with those of other firms in the industry. If the DSO starts to lengthen, or if the aging schedule begins to show an increasing percentage of past-due accounts, the firm's credit policy might need to be tightened.

We must be careful when interpreting changes in DSO or the aging schedule, however, because if a firm experiences sharp seasonal variations, or if it is growing rapidly, both measures could be distorted. For example, recall that Unilate's peak selling season is in the fall. Using the information provided in Chapter 14 (Table 14.1), we would determine that Unilate's DSO is expected to be 54.9 days on September 30, 2017 but 43.2 days on December 31, 2017. This decline in DSO would not indicate that Unilate had tightened its credit policy or more efficiently collected its receivables, but only that its sales and receivables had fallen due to seasonal factors. Similar problems arise with the aging

[3]See Eugene F. Brigham and Phillip R. Daves, *Intermediate Financial Management*, 12th ed. (Cincinnati, OH: Cengage Learning, 2016), Chapter 21, for a more complete discussion of the problems with the DSO and aging schedule and how to correct them.

schedule when sales fluctuate widely. If a firm generally experiences widely fluctuating sales patterns, some type of modified aging schedule should be used to correctly account for these fluctuations.[3] Still, days sales outstanding and the aging schedule are useful tools for evaluating customers' payment patterns.

15-4c Analyzing Proposed Changes in Credit Policy

The key question when deciding on a proposed credit policy change is this: How will the firm's value be affected? Unless the added benefits expected from a credit policy change exceed the added costs (on a present value basis), the policy change should *not* be made.

To illustrate how to determine whether a proposed change in a firm's credit policy is appropriate, let's examine what will happen if Unilate Textiles makes changes to reduce its average collection period. Suppose that Unilate's financial manager has proposed this task be accomplished in 2017 by (1) billing customers sooner and exerting more pressure on delinquent customers to pay their bills on time and (2) examining the accounts of existing credit customers and suspending the credit of customers who are considered habitually delinquent. These actions will result in a direct increase in the costs associated with Unilate's credit policy. At the same time, even though Unilate has an extremely loyal customer base, it is expected that some sales will be lost to competitors because some customers will have their credit decreased or even eliminated. However, because the credit policy changes do not affect the "good" credit customers, the financial manager does not expect there to be a change in the payments of those customers who currently take advantage of the cash discount. If the proposed credit policy changes are approved, the financial manager believes the average collection period, or DSO, for receivables can be reduced from 43.2 days to 34.8 days, which is more in line with the credit terms offered by Unilate (2/10 net 30) and is closer to the industry average of 32.1 days. In addition, if the average collection period is reduced, the amount carried in accounts receivable will be reduced, which means less funds will be tied up in receivables.

Table 15.3 provides information relating to Unilate's existing credit policy and the financial manager's proposed changes. According to this information, if the company changes its credit policy, its sales will drop by $2 million per year. Note that only the amount paid by customers who do not take the cash discount will be affected by this decrease. This group of customers

Table 15.3

Unilate Textiles: Existing and Proposed Credit Policies, 2017

	Existing Policy	Proposed Policy
I. General Credit Policy Information		
Credit terms	2/10 net 30	2/10 net 30
Days sales outstanding (DSO) for all customers[a]	43.2 days	34.8 days
DSO for customers who take the cash discount (20 percent)	10.0 days	10.0 days
DSO for customers who forgo the cash discount (80 percent)	51.5 days	41.0 days
II. Annual Credit Sales and Costs ($ millions)		
Net credit sales[b]	$1,650.0	$1,648.0
Amount paid by discount customers[c]	324.7	324.7
Amount paid by nondiscount customers[c]	1,325.3	1,323.3
Variable operating costs (82 percent of *net* sales)[d]	1,353.0	1,351.4
Bad debts	0.0	0.0
Credit evaluation and collection costs[d]	16.0	17.0
III. Daily Credit Sales and Costs ($ thousands)[e]		
Net sales	$4,583.3	$4,577.8
Amount paid by discount customers	901.9	901.9
Amount paid by nondiscount customers	3,681.4	3,675.8
Variable operating costs (82 percent of *net* sales)	3,758.3	3,753.9
Bad debts	0.0	0.0
Credit evaluation and collection costs	44.4	47.2

Notes:

[a]With the existing policy, 20 percent of the customers take the cash discount and pay on Day 10, and the remaining customers (80 percent) pay, on average, on Day 51.5; thus, the DSO for all customers is 43.2 days = 0.2(10 days) + 0.8(51.5 days).

[b]In Chapter 16, we determine that Unilate's 2017 *forecasted* sales are $1,650 million, which represent what the firm expects to collect from credit sales, net of cash discounts. The gross sales, which include cash discounts, can be computed as follows:

$$\text{Net sales} = 0.8(\text{Gross sales}) + 0.2(1 - 0.02)(\text{Gross sales}) = (\text{Gross sales})[0.8 + 0.2(0.98)] = (\text{Gross sales})(0.996)$$

$$= \$1{,}650 \text{ million}$$

$$\text{Gross sales} = \frac{\$1{,}650 \text{ million}}{0.996} = \$1{,}656.6 \text{ million}$$

[c]Currently, 20 percent of Unilate's customers pay on Day 10, taking advantage of the 2 percent cash discount. As a result, the amount expected to be paid by this group of customers is $324.7 million = 0.2 × (1.0 − 0.02) × $1,656.6 million. Customers who take the discount will not be affected by the credit policy changes that are intended to affect delinquent customers; thus the amount paid by customers who take the discount will be the same under either policy ($324.7 million). Consequently, the $2 million decrease in sales associated with the proposed credit policy will reduce the amount paid by customers who do not take the discount from $1,325.3 million (= 0.8 × $1,656.6 million) to $1,323.3 million (= $1,325.3 million − $2 million).

[d]The variable operating costs are paid at the time of the credit sale. Fixed operating costs are not included in the analysis because the amount does not change if the credit policy is changed. Expenses related to credit sales (evaluation and collection costs) are also paid at the time of the credit sale. These assumptions are made to simplify the analysis.

[e]Daily figures are required to evaluate whether the proposal should be adopted. See Figure 15.1 on the next page for the actual analysis. For consistency, we use a 360-day year to compute the daily figures.

includes the habitually delinquent payers, which is the category of customers the credit policy change is intended to affect. As a result, the amount paid by the *non-discount* customers will decrease if the proposed credit policy is adopted, but the amount paid by the discount customers will not change.

To determine whether Unilate should adopt the financial manager's proposal, we need to evaluate the effect the proposed changes will have on the value of the firm. Thus, we must compare the net present values (NPVs) of the two credit policies. To complete the analysis, we make two simplifying assumptions: (1) Sales occur evenly throughout the year. (2) Each production/selling cycle is constant; cash inflows and cash outflows occur at the same point in time relative to the credit sale, no matter what time of the year is examined. These assumptions allow us to evaluate the cash inflows and cash outflows associated with the credit sales for only one day to determine whether the proposed credit policy change should be made. Table 15.3 gives specific assumptions concerning the timing of the cash flows, and Figure 15.1 shows the results of the NPV analysis assuming Unilate's required rate of return is 10 percent annually. According to these results, the NPV for the existing credit policy is $725,800 per day, whereas the NPV for the proposed credit policy is $732,500 per day. If the company changes its credit policy, the change in the daily NPV shown in Section III of Figure 15.1 is $6,700. Given the assumptions we have stated here, as well as the assumptions given in Table 15.3, we would expect this change to have a permanent, or continuing, effect on the firm. Thus, the $6,700 change represents a daily perpetuity, which, according to Section III of Figure 15.1, will increase the value of the firm by $24.1 million. Clearly, then, the proposed changes should be made.

The analysis in Table 15.3 provides Unilate's managers with a vehicle for considering the impact of credit policy changes on the firm's value. A great deal of judgment must be applied to the decision, because customers' as well as competitors' responses to credit policy changes are difficult to estimate. Nevertheless, this type of analysis is essential.

(15-5) Inventory Management

If it could, a firm would prefer to have no inventory at all because while products are in inventory they do not generate returns and they must be financed. However, most firms find it necessary to maintain inventory in some form because (1) demand cannot be predicted with certainty and (2) it takes time to transform a product into a form that is ready for sale. Moreover, while excessive inventories are costly to the firm, so are insufficient

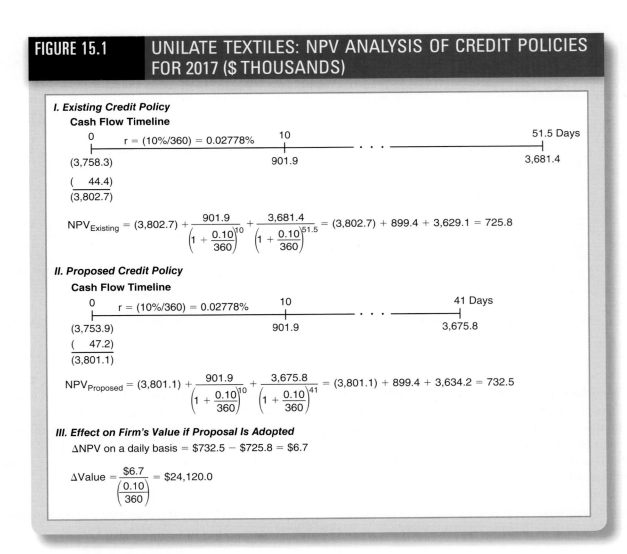

FIGURE 15.1 UNILATE TEXTILES: NPV ANALYSIS OF CREDIT POLICIES FOR 2017 ($ THOUSANDS)

I. Existing Credit Policy

Cash Flow Timeline

r = (10%/360) = 0.02778%

| 0 | 10 | 51.5 Days |
| (3,758.3) | 901.9 | 3,681.4 |

(44.4)
(3,802.7)

$$NPV_{Existing} = (3,802.7) + \frac{901.9}{\left(1 + \frac{0.10}{360}\right)^{10}} + \frac{3,681.4}{\left(1 + \frac{0.10}{360}\right)^{51.5}} = (3,802.7) + 899.4 + 3,629.1 = 725.8$$

II. Proposed Credit Policy

Cash Flow Timeline

r = (10%/360) = 0.02778%

| 0 | 10 | 41 Days |
| (3,753.9) | 901.9 | 3,675.8 |

(47.2)
(3,801.1)

$$NPV_{Proposed} = (3,801.1) + \frac{901.9}{\left(1 + \frac{0.10}{360}\right)^{10}} + \frac{3,675.8}{\left(1 + \frac{0.10}{360}\right)^{41}} = (3,801.1) + 899.4 + 3,634.2 = 732.5$$

III. Effect on Firm's Value if Proposal Is Adopted

ΔNPV on a daily basis = $732.5 − $725.8 = $6.7

$$\Delta Value = \frac{\$6.7}{\left(\frac{0.10}{360}\right)} = \$24,120.0$$

inventories, because customers might purchase from competitors if products are not available when demanded, which could result in lost future business.

Although inventory models are covered in depth in production management courses, it is important to understand the basics of inventory management, because proper management requires coordination among the sales, purchasing, production, and finance departments. Lack of coordination among these departments, poor sales forecasts, or both can lead to financial ruin.

15-5a Types of Inventory

An inventory item generally is classified into one of three groups:

1. **Raw materials** represent the new inventory items purchased from suppliers; they are the materials a firm purchases to transform into finished products for sale. As long as the firm has an inventory of raw materials, delays in ordering and delivery from suppliers do not affect the production process.

2. **Work-in-process** refers to inventory items that are at various stages in the production process. If a firm has work-in-process at every stage in the production process, it will not have to shut down production if a problem arises at one of the earlier stages.

3. **Finished goods** are the products that are ready for sale. Firms carry finished goods to ensure that orders can be filled when they are received. If there are no finished goods, demand might not be satisfied when it arrives. When a customer arrives and there is no

[4]In reality, both carrying and ordering costs can have variable and fixed cost elements, at least over certain ranges of average inventory. For example, utilities charges probably are fixed in the short run over a wide range of inventory levels. On the other hand, labor costs of receiving inventory could be tied to the quantity received, and hence could be variable. To simplify matters, we treat all carrying costs as variable and all ordering costs as fixed.

inventory to satisfy that demand, a **stockout** exists, and the firm might lose the demand to competitors, perhaps permanently.

15-5b Optimal Inventory Level

The goal of inventory management is to provide the inventories required to sustain operations at the lowest possible cost. Thus, the first step in determining the optimal inventory level is to identify the costs involved in purchasing and maintaining inventory; then, we need to determine at what point those costs are minimized.

Inventory Costs. We generally classify inventory costs into three categories: those associated with carrying inventory, those associated with ordering and receiving inventory, and those associated with running short of inventory (stockouts). First, let's look at the two costs that are most directly observable—carrying costs and ordering costs.

1. **Carrying costs** include any expenses associated with having products in inventory, such as rent paid for the warehouse where inventory is stored and insurance on the inventory. These costs generally increase in direct proportion to the average amount of inventory carried.

2. **Ordering costs** are those expenses associated with placing and receiving an order for new inventory, which include the costs of generating memos, fax transmissions, and so forth. For the most part, the total cost associated with each order is fixed regardless of the order size.[4]

If we assume that the firm knows how much total inventory it needs and that sales are distributed evenly during each period, we can use Equation 15.1 to combine the total carrying costs (TCC) and the total ordering costs (TOC) to determine total inventory costs (TIC).

raw materials The inventories purchased from suppliers that ultimately will be transformed into finished goods.

work-in-process Inventory in various stages of completion; some work-in-process is at the very beginning of the production process while some is at the end of the process.

finished goods Inventories that have completed the production process and are ready for sale.

stockout Occurs when a firm runs out of inventory *and* customers arrive to purchase the product.

carrying costs The costs associated with having inventory, which include storage costs, insurance, cost of tying up funds, and so on; these costs generally increase in proportion to the average amount of inventory held.

ordering costs The costs of placing an order; the cost of *each* order generally is fixed regardless of the average size of the inventory.

15.1

$$\text{Total inventory costs (TIC)} = \text{Total carrying costs} + \text{Total ordering costs}$$

$$= \left(\begin{array}{c}\text{Carrying cost}\\\text{per unit}\end{array}\right) \times \left(\begin{array}{c}\text{Average units}\\\text{in inventory}\end{array}\right) + \left(\begin{array}{c}\text{Cost per}\\\text{order}\end{array}\right) \times \left(\begin{array}{c}\text{Number of}\\\text{orders}\end{array}\right)$$

$$= (C \times PP) \times \left(\frac{Q}{2}\right) + O \times \left(\frac{T}{Q}\right)$$

The variables in the equation are defined as follows:

C = carrying costs as a percentage (stated as a decimal) of the purchase price of each inventory item.

PP = purchase price, or cost, per unit.

Q = number of units purchased with each order.

T = total demand, or number of units sold, per period.

O = fixed costs per order.

According to Equation 15.1, the average investment in inventory depends on how frequently orders are placed and the size of each order. If we order every day, the average inventory that is held will be much smaller than if we order once per year; inventory carrying costs will be lower, but the number of orders will be larger and inventory ordering costs will be higher. We can reduce ordering costs by ordering greater amounts less often, but then average inventory, and thus the total carrying cost, will be high. This trade-off between carrying costs and ordering costs is shown in Figure 15.2. Note from the figure that there is a point where the total inventory cost (TIC) is *minimized*; this is called the **economic (optimum) ordering quantity (EOQ)**.

The Economic Ordering Quantity (EOQ) Model. The EOQ is determined by using calculus to find the point where the slope of the TIC curve in Figure 15.2 is perfectly horizontal; thus, it equals zero. The result is Equation 15.2:

15.2

$$\text{Economic ordering quantity} = \text{EOQ} = \sqrt{\frac{2 \times O \times T}{C \times PP}}$$

economic (optimum) ordering quantity (EOQ) The optimal quantity that should be ordered; it is this quantity that will minimize the *total inventory costs*.

EOQ model A formula for determining the order quantity that will minimize total inventory costs.

The primary assumptions of the **EOQ model** given by Equation 15.2 are that (1) sales are evenly distributed throughout the period examined and can be forecast precisely,

(2) orders are received when expected, and (3) the purchase price (PP) of each item in inventory is the same regardless of the quantity ordered.[5]

To illustrate the EOQ model, consider the following data provided by Cotton Tops Inc., a distributor of custom-designed T-shirts that supplies concessionaires at Daisy World:

T = 78,000 shirts per year.

C = 25 percent of inventory value.

PP = $3.84 per shirt. (The shirts sell for $9, but this is irrelevant for our purposes here.)

O = $260 per order.

Substituting these data into Equation 15.2, we find an EOQ equal to 6,500 units:

$$\text{EOQ} = \sqrt{\frac{2 \times \$260 \times 78,000}{0.25 \times \$3.84}} = \sqrt{42,250,000}$$

$$= 6,500 \text{ units}$$

If Cotton Tops orders 6,500 shirts each time it needs inventory, it will place $78,000/6,500 = 12$ orders per year and carry an average inventory of $6,500/2 = 3,250$ shirts. Thus, at the EOQ quantity, Cotton Tops's total inventory costs would equal $6,240:

$$\text{TIC} = (C \times PP)\left(\frac{Q}{2}\right) + O\left(\frac{T}{Q}\right)$$

$$= [0.25 \times (\$3.84)]\left[\frac{6,500}{2}\right] + (\$260)\left[\frac{78,000}{6,500}\right]$$

$$= \$3,120 + \$3.120 = 46,240$$

Note these two points: (1) Because we assume the purchase price of each inventory item does not depend on the amount ordered, TIC does *not* include the $299,520 = 78,000($3.84)$ annual cost of purchasing the

[5]The EQQ model can also be written as follows:

$$\text{EOQ} = \sqrt{\frac{2 \times O \times T}{C^*}}$$

where C* is the annual carrying cost per unit expressed in dollars.

FIGURE 15.2 DETERMINATION OF THE ECONOMIC ORDERING QUANTITY

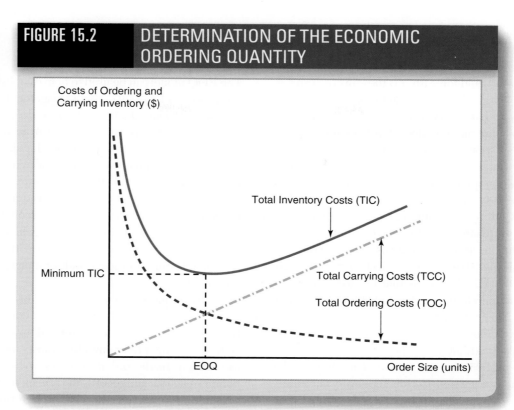

inventory itself. (2) As we see both in Figure 15.2 and in the numbers here, at the EOQ, total carrying cost (TCC) equals total ordering cost (TOC). This property is not unique to our Cotton Tops illustration; it always holds.

Table 15.4 contains the total inventory costs that Cotton Tops would incur at various order quantities, including the EOQ level. Note that (1) as the amount ordered increases, the total carrying costs increase but the total ordering costs decrease, and vice versa; (2) if less than the EOQ amount is ordered, then the higher ordering costs more than offset the lower carrying costs; and (3) if more than the EOQ amount is ordered, the higher carrying costs more than offset the lower ordering costs.

EOQ Model Extensions. It should be obvious that some of the assumptions necessary for the basic EOQ to hold are unrealistic. To make the model more useful, we can apply some simple extensions. First, if there is a delay between the time inventory is ordered and when it is received, the firm must reorder before it runs out of inventory. For example, if it normally takes two weeks to receive orders, then Cotton Tops should reorder when two weeks of inventory are left. Cotton Tops sells 78,000/52 = 1,500 shirts per week, so its **reorder point** is when inventory drops to 3,000 shirts. Even if Cotton Tops orders additional inventory at the appropriate reorder point, unexpected demand might

Table 15.4

Cotton Tops, Inc.: Total Inventory Costs for Various Order Quantities

	Quantity	Number of Orders	Total Ordering Costs	Total Carrying Costs	Total Inventory Costs
	3,000	26	$6,760	$1,440	$8,200
	5,200	15	3,900	2,496	6,396
	6,000	13	3,380	2,880	6,260
EOQ	**6,500**	**12**	**3,120**	**3,120**	**6,240**
	7,800	10	2,600	3,744	6,344
	9,750	8	2,080	4,680	6,760
	13,000	6	1,560	6,240	7,800
	78,000	1	260	37,440	37,700

T = annual sales = 78,000 shirts
C = carrying cost = 25 percent of inventory value
PP = purchase price = $3.84/shirt
O = ordering cost = $260/order

cause it to run out of inventory before the new inventory is delivered. To avoid this, the firm

reorder point The level of inventory at which an order should be placed.

could carry safety stock, which represents additional inventory that helps guard against stockouts. The amount of safety stock a firm holds generally *increases* with (1) the uncertainty of demand forecasts, (2) the costs (in terms of lost sales and lost goodwill) that result from stockouts, and (3) the chances that delays will occur in receiving shipments. The amount of safety stock *decreases* as the cost of carrying this additional inventory increases.

Another factor a firm might need to consider when determining appropriate inventory levels is whether its suppliers offer discounts to purchase large quantities. For example, if Cotton Tops's supplier offered a 1 percent discount for purchases equal to 13,000 units or more, the total reduction in the annual cost of purchasing inventory would be $[0.01(\$3.84)] \times 78,000 = \$2,995.20$. Looking at Table 15.4, we see that the total inventory cost (excluding purchase price) at 13,000 units is $7,800, which is $1,560 = \$7,800 - \$6,240$ greater than the cost at the EOQ level of 6,500 units. However, the net benefit of taking advantage of the quantity discount is $\$1,435.20 = \$2,995.20 - \$1,560.00$. Therefore, under these conditions, each time Cotton Tops orders inventory it will be more beneficial to order 13,000 units rather than the 6,500 units prescribed by the basic EOQ model.

In cases in which it is unrealistic to assume that the demand for the inventory is uniform throughout the year, the EOQ should not be applied on an annual basis. Rather, it would be more appropriate to divide the year into seasons within which sales are relatively constant, say, the summer, the spring and fall, and the winter; then the EOQ model can be applied separately to each period.

Although we did not explicitly incorporate the extensions we mentioned here into the basic EOQ, our discussion should give you an idea of how the EOQ amount should be adjusted to determine the optimal inventory level if any of these conditions exists.

safety stock Additional inventory carried to guard against unexpected changes in sales rates or production/shipping delays during the reorder period.

quantity discount A discount from the purchase price that is offered when inventory is ordered in large quantities.

redline method An inventory control procedure where a red line is drawn around the inside of an inventory-stocked bin to indicate the reorder point level.

computerized inventory control system A system of inventory control in which a computer is used to determine reorder points and to adjust inventory balances.

just-in-time system A system of inventory control in which a manufacturer coordinates production with suppliers so that raw materials of components arrive just as they are needed in the production process.

outsourcing The practice of purchasing components rather than making them in-house.

15-5c Inventory Control Systems

The EOQ model can be used to help establish the proper inventory level, but inventory management also involves the establishment of an *inventory control system*. Inventory control systems run the gamut from very simple to extremely complex, depending on the size of the firm and the nature of its inventories. For example, one simple control procedure is the redline method. Inventory items are stocked in a bin, a red line is drawn around the inside of the bin at the level of the reorder point, and the inventory clerk places an order when the red line shows. This procedure works well for parts such as bolts in a manufacturing process, and for many items in retail businesses.

Most firms employ some type of computerized inventory control systems. Large companies often have fully integrated computerized inventory control systems in which the computer adjusts inventory levels as sales are made, orders inventory when the reorder point is reached, and records the receipt of an order. The computer records are also used to determine whether the usage rates of inventory items change, so that adjustments to reorder amounts can be made. Another approach to inventory control that requires a coordinated effort between the supplier and the buyer is called the just-in-time system, which was refined by Japanese firms many years ago. With this system, materials are delivered to the company at about the same time they are needed, perhaps a few hours before they are used. Still another important development related to inventories is outsourcing, which is the practice of purchasing components rather than making them in house. Outsourcing often is combined with just-in-time systems to reduce inventory levels.

Inventory control systems require coordination of inventory policy with manufacturing and procurement policies. Companies try to minimize *total production and distribution costs*, and inventory costs are just one part of total costs. Still, they are an important cost, and financial managers should be aware of the determinants of inventory costs and how they can be minimized.

15-6 Multinational Working Capital Management

Although the methods used to manage short-term assets in multinational corporations are essentially the same as those used in purely domestic corporations, there are some differences in business, legal, and economic environments that make application of these methods somewhat more complex.

15-6a Cash Management

Like a purely domestic company, a multinational corporation wants to (1) speed up collections and to slow down disbursements where possible, (2) shift cash as rapidly as possible to those areas where it is needed, and (3) try to put temporary cash balances to work earning positive returns. Multinational companies use the same general procedures for achieving these goals as domestic firms use, but because of longer distances and more serious mail delays, lockbox systems and electronic funds transfers are even more important.

One potential problem a multinational company faces that a purely domestic company does not is the chance that a foreign government will restrict transfers of funds out of the country. Foreign governments often limit the amount of cash that can be taken out of their countries because they want to encourage domestic investment. Even if funds can be transferred without limitation, deteriorating exchange rates might make it unattractive for a multinational firm to move funds to its operations in other countries.

Once it has been determined what funds can be transferred out of the various nations in which a multinational corporation operates, it is important to get those funds to locations where they will earn the highest returns. Whereas domestic corporations tend to think in terms of domestic securities, multinationals are more likely to be aware of investment opportunities all around the world. To take advantage of the best rates available around the world, most multinational corporations use one or more global concentration banks, located in money centers such as London, New York, Tokyo, Zurich, or Singapore.

15-6b Credit Management

Credit policy generally is more important for a multinational corporation than for a purely domestic firm for two reasons. First, much U.S. trade is with poorer, less-developed nations, and in such situations, granting credit generally is a necessary condition for doing business. Second, and in large part as a result of the first point, developed nations whose economic health depends on exports often help their manufacturers compete internationally by granting credit to foreign countries that purchase from these firms.

When granting credit, the multinational firm faces a riskier situation than purely domestic firms because, in addition to the normal risks of default, (1) political and legal environments often make it more difficult to collect defaulted accounts and (2) multinational corporations must worry about exchange rate changes between the time a sale is made and the time a receivable is collected. We know that hedging can reduce this type of risk, but at a cost.

15-6c Inventory Management

Inventory management in a multinational setting is more complex than in a purely domestic setting because of logistical problems that arise with handling inventories. For example, should a firm concentrate its inventories in a few strategic centers located worldwide? While such a strategy might minimize the total amount of, and thus the investment in, inventories needed to operate the global business, it might also cause delays in getting goods from central storage locations to user locations around the world.

Exchange rates can significantly influence inventory policy. For example, if a local currency is expected to increase in value against the dollar, a U.S. company operating in that country will want to increase stocks of local products before the rise in the currency, and vice versa. Another factor that must be considered is the possibility of import or export quotas or tariffs. Quotas restrict the quantities of products firms can bring into a country, while tariffs, like taxes, increase the prices of products that are allowed to be imported. Both quotas and tariffs are designed to restrict the ability of foreign corporations to compete with domestic companies; at the extreme, foreign products are excluded altogether.

Another danger in certain countries is the threat of *expropriation*, or government takeover of the firm's local operations. If the threat of expropriation is large, inventory holdings will be minimized, and goods will be brought in only as needed. Similarly, if the operation involves extraction of raw material, processing plants might be moved offshore rather than located close to the production site.

Taxes also must be considered, because countries often impose property taxes on assets, including inventories. When this is done, the tax is based on holdings as of a specific date. Such rules make it advantageous for a multinational firm (1) to schedule production so that inventories are low on the assessment date and (2) if assessment dates vary among countries in a region, to hold safety stocks in different countries at different times during the year.

STUDY TOOLS

LOCATED AT BACK OF THE TEXTBOOK

☐ Problems are found at the end of this chapter.

☐ A tear-out Chapter Review card is located at the back of the textbook.

LOCATED AT WWW.CENGAGEBRAIN.COM

☐ Review Key Term flashcards and create your own cards.

☐ Track your knowledge and understanding of key concepts in corporate finance.

☐ Complete practice and graded quizzes to prepare for tests.

☐ Complete interactive content within CFIN5 Online.

☐ View the chapter highlight boxes for CFIN5 Online.

KEY CONCEPTS FOR MANAGING SHORT-TERM ASSETS

To conclude this chapter, we summarize some concepts that were discussed.

- Firms prefer not to hold cash, because cash is considered an idle asset that does not earn interest. However, firms find that they must hold some cash to ensure that day-to-day obligations can be paid.

  The firm should construct a cash budget to forecast its cash flows so that funds can be invested when there are cash surpluses, and arrangements can be made to borrow funds when there are cash deficiencies. To efficiently manage cash flows, the firm should try to collect funds it is owed as quickly as possible and try to delay payments of funds it owes for as long as possible. Of course, any actions taken should not be detrimental to the value of the firm.

- Marketable securities are short-term, highly liquid investments that have little risk. As a result, the returns on such investments are fairly low. Marketable securities provide the firm with safe instruments where *idle cash* that will be needed in the near term—perhaps in a few days or months—can be temporarily invested.

- Firms sell on credit because competitors sell on credit. A firm that sells on credit must have a credit policy

that specifies how customers qualify for credit, the maximum amount of credit that customers are allowed, the terms of credit sales to customers, and what actions will be taken if customers do not pay on time. To ensure that the credit policy is being followed and it is achieving the desired objective, a firm's credit policy should be monitored. Moreover, when customers' payment patterns change significantly, the firm should consider changing its credit policy. Proposed credit policy changes should be evaluated using net present value (NPV) to ensure the firm is maximizing its value.

- Firms carry inventory to ensure that demand is met when it arrives. If inventory is not available, then a sale cannot be made when a customer wants to purchase the firm's product, and arriving customers might take their business to competitors. Because carrying inventory is costly, firms do not want to have too much inventory on hand at any time. As a result, a firm determines how much inventory to hold by examining the demand for its product, the costs associated with not having enough inventory, and the costs of carrying sufficient inventory to satisfy demand. The EOQ, or economic ordering quantity, model is used to determine the optimal amount of inventory that a firm should carry.

PROBLEMS

15–1 Floribama Clothing has generated $130,000 in sales during the past few months, and it is expected that this level of sales will continue for the next year. Based on past experience, 40 percent of the sales will be collected in the month of the sale, and these customers will take the 3 percent cash discount that is offered for early payment. The remaining 60 percent of the sales will be collected one month after the sale. Floribama normally purchases and pays for raw materials, which cost 70 percent of the sales prices, in the same month the finished goods are sold. Employees' wages represent 15 percent of the sales price, and monthly rent is $15,000. The company currently has no cash, but its target cash balance is $6,000. Construct Floribama's cash budget for the next three months.

15–2 Vertical Ladder Company (VLC) forecasts that its sales for January through April will be $60,000, $70,000, $90,000, and $80,000, respectively. All sales are made on credit, and past experience indicates that 30 percent of the sales will be collected in the month of the sale and that the remaining 70 percent will be collected the following month. Customers who pay in the month of the sale will take the 2 percent cash discount offered by VLC for paying early. VLC normally purchases and pays for raw materials, which cost 55 percent of the sales prices, one month prior to selling the finished products. Employees' wages represent 25 percent of the sales price, and rent is $3,000 per month. At the beginning of February, VLC expects to have $4,000 in cash, which is $1,000 greater than its target cash balance. Using the information provided, construct a cash budget for February and March.

15–3 Smitty's Chop Shop normally writes checks in the amount of $15,000 each day. It takes five days for these checks to clear through the banking system. The firm also receives checks in the amount of $12,000 daily but loses four days while they are being deposited and cleared. What is the firm's disbursement float, collections float, and net float?

15–4 On average, Bowden Farms receives checks that amount to $420,000 each day, whereas the amount of checks the company writes each day averages $380,000. It normally takes three days for incoming checks to clear through the banking system, and outgoing checks generally clear in five days. What is the firm's disbursement float, collections float, and net float?

15–5 Currently, it takes six days for Apsoft Corporation to receive, process, and deposit its customers' payments. If it sets up a lockbox collection system, Apsoft estimates collection float would be reduced to two days. Apsoft receives an average of $125,000 in payments per day. If Apsoft has an opportunity cost of 12 percent, what is the maximum monthly charge it should pay for the lockbox system?

15–6 Currently, it takes five days from the time customers mail payments until Shark Bait Rafts (SBR) deposits them. SBR would like to set up a lockbox collection system that would reduce this collection float by three days. If SBR receives an average of $2,500 in payments per day and its opportunity cost is 18 percent, how much should SBR be willing to pay each month for the lockbox system?

15–7 Compute the DSO for Buckwell Corporation, which has the following aging schedule:

Account Age	Amount Outstanding	Average Days
0–30 days	$65,000	23
31–60 days	25,000	43
Over 60 days	10,000	63

15–8 Following is the aging schedule for QRM Corporation:

Account Age	Amount Outstanding	Average Days
0–30 days	$100,000	22
31–60 days	70,000	40
Over 60 days	30,000	?

If its DSO is 37 days, on average, on what day does QRM collect from customers who take longer than 60 days to pay for their purchases?

15–9 Finology Company's average collection period (DSO) is 37 days, which is only seven days longer than the net 30 terms the company offers credit customers. Fifty percent of Finology's customers pay on average on Day 20, and 30 percent pay on Day 40. On what day do the remaining credit customers pay? Assume Finology has no bad debts.

15–10 Great Munchies (GM) Corporation has a variable operating cost ratio of 60 percent, its cost of capital is 12 percent, and current sales are $100,000. All of its sales are on credit, and it currently sells on terms of net 30. Its accounts receivable balance is $20,000. GM is considering a new credit policy with terms of net 45. Under the new policy, sales will increase to $120,000, and accounts receivable will rise to $30,000. Compute the days sales outstanding (DSO) under the existing policy and the proposed policy.

15–11 Axis Wells and Excavation (AWE) currently generates $72,000 in annual credit sales. AWE sells on terms of net 50, and its accounts receivable balance averages $12,000. AWE is considering a new credit policy with terms of net 25. Under the new policy, sales will decrease to $68,000, and accounts receivable will average $13,600. Compute the days sales outstanding (DSO) under the existing policy and the proposed policy.

15–12 Lewis Lumber is considering changing its credit terms from net 55 to net 30 to bring its terms in line with other firms in the industry. Currently, annual sales are $360,000, and the average collection period (DSO) is 62 days. Lewis estimates that tightening the credit terms would reduce annual sales to $355,000, but accounts receivable would drop to 38 days of sales. Lewis' variable cost ratio is 65 percent and its average cost of funds is 12 percent. Should the change in credit terms be made? Assume all operating costs are paid when inventory is sold and that *all* sales are collected at the DSO.

15–13 The CFO of JJ's Jungle Equipment has decided that the company must sell its products on credit. As a result, she is evaluating two credit terms. (1) Net 45, which would generate $50,000 in annual sales and have an average collection period (DSO) equal to 55 days. (2) Net 30, which would generate $48,000 in sales and have an average collection period equal to 36 days. The firm's variable cost ratio is 70 percent, and its average cost of funds 14 percent. Which credit terms should the CFO recommend? Assume all operating costs are paid when inventory is sold and *all* sales are collected at the DSO.

15–14 Next Week's Technology (NWT) is evaluating whether to change its credit terms from 2/10, net 30 to 3/10, net 30. At present, 50 percent of NWT's sales are paid on Day 10, whereas, under the new terms, 60 percent of sales will be paid on Day 10. Regardless of the credit terms, half of the customers *who do not take the discount* are expected to pay on

Day 30, whereas the remainder will pay 15 days late (no bad debts exist). But, as a result of the higher cash discount offered with the new terms, sales are expected to increase from $360,000 to $396,000 per year. NWT's variable cost ratio is 80 percent and its cost of funds is 9 percent. All production costs are paid on the day of the sale. Should NWT change its credit terms?

15–15 Michael's Mechanical sells 6,000 jettison machines annually. Each machine costs Michael's $2,000 to purchase, inventory carrying costs are 45 percent of the purchase price, and the cost of placing an order with its supplier is $120. (a) What is the EOQ? (b) What is the total inventory cost at the EOQ level?

15–16 PC Calculators sells calculators that it purchases for $15 each. It costs PC $60 each time calculators are ordered, and carrying costs are 20 percent of the calculator's purchase price. Annual demand is 100,000 calculators. (a) Compute the EOQ. (b) Compute the inventory costs if PC orders (i) the EOQ amount, (ii) 1,000 calculators, and (iii) 2,500 calculators.

15–17 Media Moguls (M&M) normally sells 240,000 units per year. It costs M&M $52 to purchase each unit, the fixed cost of ordering is $260, and the carrying costs equal 15 percent of the unit's purchase price. (a) What is the EOQ? (b) How many orders should M&M place each year?

15–18 Refer to the information provided for M&M in Problem 15–17. Suppose that M&M must place orders in increments of 5,000 units and that it takes three days for each order to be delivered. (a) How many orders should M&M place each year? (b) At what inventory level should an order be placed?

15–19 Roybow Corporation sells lawn mowers that cost $160 each to purchase and prepare for sale. Annual sales are 5,000 mowers, carrying costs are 20 percent of inventory costs, and Roybow incurs a cost of $32 each time an order is placed. (a) What is the EOQ for the mowers? (b) What will be the total inventory costs if the EOQ amount is ordered?

15–20 Refer to the information provided for Roybow Corporation in Problem 15–19. Suppose that Roybow's supplier decides to offer a 2 percent cash discount if products are ordered in increments of 1.000. How many mowers should Roybow order each time an order is placed to minimize total inventory costs?

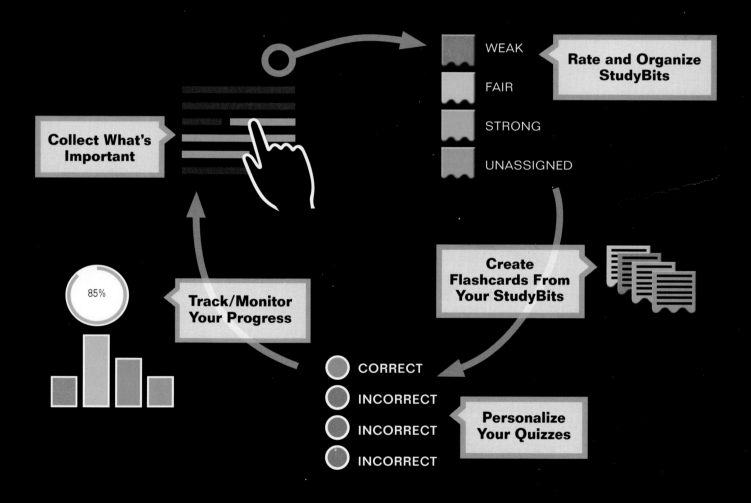

CFIN ONLINE

STUDY YOUR WAY WITH STUDYBITS!

WEAK

FAIR

STRONG

UNASSIGNED

Rate and Organize StudyBits

Collect What's Important

Create Flashcards From Your StudyBits

85%

Track/Monitor Your Progress

○ CORRECT

○ INCORRECT

○ INCORRECT

○ INCORRECT

Personalize Your Quizzes

4LTR PRESS

Access CFIN ONLINE at www.cengagebrain.com

part **7**

After you finish this chapter go to **PAGE 324** for **STUDY TOOLS**

Edhar/Shutterstock.com

LEARNING OUTCOMES
After studying this chapter, you will be able to…

LO1 Construct simple pro forma financial statements that can be used to forecast a firm's financing and investment needs.

LO2 Discuss some of the complications that management should consider when constructing pro forma financial statements.

LO3 Describe and compute (a) operating breakeven and operating leverage, (b) financial breakeven and financial leverage, and (c) total leverage.

LO4 Discuss how knowledge of leverage is used in the financial forecasting and control process and why financial planning is critical to firm survival.

Financial Planning and Control

16

The **financial planning** process begins with forecasts of financial statements to detemine the firm's future financing and investment needs. Once the base-case forecasted financial statements have been prepared, managers want to know (1) how realistic the results are, (2) how to attain the results, and (3) what impact changes in operations would have on the forecasts. At this stage, which is the **financial control** phase, the firm is concerned with implementing the financial plans and dealing with the feedback and adjustment processes that are necessary to ensure the goals of the firm are pursued appropriately. In this chapter, we show how the information obtained through financial statement analysis (discussed in Chapter 2) can be used for financial planning and control of future operations, which are vital to the future success of the firm.

16-1 Projected (Pro Forma) Financial Statements

Forecasting is an essential part of the planning process, and a **sales forecast** is the most important ingredient of financial forecasting. If the sales forecast is inaccurate, the consequences can be serious. First, if the market expands significantly more than the company has geared up for, demand likely will not be met, customers will buy competitors' products, and market share probably will be lost, perhaps for good. On the other hand, if the projections are overly optimistic, the company could end up with too much plant, equipment, and inventory. This would mean low turnover ratios, high costs for depreciation and storage, and the likelihood that obsolete and unusable inventory will have to be written off. All of this would result in a low rate of return on equity, which in turn would depress the company's stock price. Of course, if an unnecessary expansion is financed with debt, the firm's problems will be compounded. Thus, an accurate sales forecast is critical to the well-being of the firm.

The sales forecast generally starts with a review of sales during the past five to 10 years. For example, to form its sales forecasts, Unilate Textiles considers projections of economic activity, competitive conditions, and product development and distribution in the markets in which it currently operates, as well as in the markets the company plans to enter in the future. Based on its historical sales trend for the past five years, Unilate's planning committee has projected a 10 percent growth rate for sales during 2017.

Any forecast of financial requirements involves (1) determining how much money the firm will need during a given period; (2) determining how much money (funds) the firm will generate internally during the same period; and (3) subtracting the funds generated internally from the required funds to determine the *additional funds needed* (external financing) to support the level of forecasted operations. One method used to estimate external requirements is the *projected, or pro forma, balance sheet method*. The basic

financial planning The projection of sales, income, and assets, as well as the determination of the resources needed to achieve these projections.

financial control The phase in which financial plans are implemented; control deals with the feedback and adjustment process required to ensure adherence to plans and modification of plans because of unforeseen changes.

sales forecast A forecast of a firm's unit and dollar sales for some future period; generally based on recent sales trends plus forecasts of the economic prospects for the nation, region, industry, and so forth.

Table 16.1

Unilate Textiles: Actual 2016 and Projected 2017 Income Statements ($ millions, except per-share data)

	2016 Actual Results	Forecast Basis[a]	2017 Initial Forecast
Net sales	$ 1,500.0	× 1.10	$ 1,650.0
Cost of goods sold	(1,230.0)	× 1.10	(1,353.0)
Gross profit	$ 270.0		$ 297.0
Fixed operating costs except depreciation	(90.0)	× 1.10	(99.0)
Depreciation	(50.0)	× 1.10	(55.0)
Earnings before interest and taxes (EBIT)	$ 130.0		$ 143.0
Less: Interest	(40.0)	⟶	(40.0)[b]
Earnings before taxes (EBT)	$ 90.0		$ 103.0
Taxes (40%)	(36.0)		(41.2)
Net income	$ 54.0		$ 61.8
Common dividends	(29.0)	⟶	(29.0)[b]
Addition to retained earnings	$ 25.0		$ 32.8
Earnings per share	$ 2.16		$ 2.47
Dividends per share	$ 1.16		$ 1.16
Number of common shares (millions)	25.0		25.0

[a] × 1.10 indicates "times (1 + g)"; it is used for items that grow proportionally with sales.
[b] Indicates a figure carried over from 2016 for the preliminary forecast. See discussion for explanation.

steps that should be followed when constructing a pro forma balance sheet are explained in this section.

16-1a Step 1: Forecast the Income Statement

The **projected (pro forma) balance sheet method** begins with a forecast of sales. Next, the income statement for the coming year is forecast to obtain an initial estimate of the amount of retained earnings (internal equity financing) the company expects to generate during the year. This requires assumptions about the operating cost ratio, tax rate, interest charges, and dividends paid. In the simplest case, the assumption is made that costs will increase at the same rate as sales; in situations that are more complicated, each cost change is forecast separately. Still, the objective of this part of the analysis is to determine how much income the company will earn and then retain for reinvestment in the business during the forecast year.

projected (pro forma) balance sheet method A method of forecasting financial requirements based on forecasted financial statements.

Table 16.1 shows Unilate's actual 2016 income statement and the initial forecast of the 2017 income statement if the firm grows at 10 percent. To simplify our analysis, we assume that Unilate currently *operates at full capacity*, which means it will need to expand its plant capacity by 10 percent in 2017 to handle the increase in operations. As a result, in Table 16.1, *all* operating costs, including depreciation, are 10 percent greater than their 2016 levels. The result is that earnings before interest and taxes (EBIT) are forecast to be $143 million in 2017, which is 10 percent higher than in 2016 ($EBIT_{2016} = \$130$ million).

To complete the initial forecast of 2017 income, we assume no change in the external financing of the firm, because at this point it is not known whether additional financing is needed. Thus, *initially* we keep the 2017 interest expense and dividends the same as they were in 2016; that is, $40 million and $29 million, respectively. Of course, we know that both of these payments will increase if Unilate determines that it needs to raise additional funds by issuing new bonds and new shares of stock. At this stage of the forecasting process, however, we do not know whether such external financing is needed to support Unilate's projected growth in sales.

From the initial forecast, we see that $32.8 million dollars are *expected* to be added to retained earnings in 2017. This addition to retained earnings represents the amount Unilate is expected to invest in itself (i.e., internally generated funds) to support growth in operations in 2017, assuming that no additional (external) financing is used. To determine whether external financing is required, we must evaluate the impact this level of investment will have on Unilate's forecasted 2017 balance sheet.

16-1b Step 2: Forecast the Balance Sheet

If we assume the 2016 end-of-year asset levels were just sufficient to support 2016 operations (i.e., Unilate operated at full capacity), then if Unilate is to grow its sales in 2017, its assets must also grow. To simplify our analysis, we assume that each asset account, including plant and equipment, must grow at the same rate as sales (i.e., 10 percent).

Further, if Unilate's assets increase, its liabilities and equity must also increase, because the additional assets must be financed in some manner. Some liabilities will increase *spontaneously* due to normal business relationships. For example, as sales increase, so will Unilate's purchases of raw materials, and these larger purchases will spontaneously lead to higher levels of accounts payable. Similarly, a higher level of operations will require more labor, which will increase accruals. In general, current liabilities that change naturally (spontaneously) with changes in sales provide **spontaneously generated funds** that tend to change at the same rate as sales. On the other hand, notes payable, long-term bonds, and common stock will not change spontaneously with sales. Rather, the levels of these accounts depend on conscious financing decisions that are made once Unilate determines how much external financing it needs to support the projected operations. Therefore, until it is determined whether (and how much) external financing is needed, the account balances for notes payable, long-term debt, and common stock remain unchanged from their 2016 levels.

Table 16.2 contains Unilate's 2016 actual balance sheet and an initial forecast of its 2017 balance sheet. The mechanics of the balance sheet forecast are similar to those used to develop the forecasted income statement. First, those balance sheet accounts that are expected to increase directly with sales are multiplied by 1.10 to obtain the initial 2017 forecasts. Because we assume that all assets must grow at the same rate as sales, we multiply each asset account by 1.10. The result—$929.5 million—represents the total amount Unilate needs to invest in assets to support forecasted 2017 sales.

Next, the spontaneously increasing liabilities (accounts payable and accruals) are forecast by increasing each of these accounts by 10 percent. At this stage of the forecast, however, those liability and equity accounts whose values reflect conscious management decisions (notes payable, long-term bonds, and stock) *initially are not changed from* their 2016 levels. Thus, the amount of 2017 notes payable *initially* is set at its 2016 level of $40.0 million, the long-term bonds account is forecast at $300.0 million, and so forth. The forecasted 2017 level of retained earnings will be the 2016 level plus the forecasted addition to retained earnings, which was computed as $32.8 million in the projected income statement that we created in Step 1 (Table 16.1).

Because the forecast of total assets in Table 16.2 is $929.5 million, Unilate must add $84.5 million of new assets (compared to 2016 assets) to support the higher sales level expected in 2017. However, according to the initial forecast on the 2017 balance sheet, the total liabilities and equity sum to $886.8 million, which is an increase of only $41.8 million. Therefore, the forecasted amount of total assets exceeds the forecasted amount of liabilities and equity by $42.7 million = $929.5 million − $886.8 million. This indicates that $42.7 million of the forecasted increase in total assets will not be financed by liabilities that spontaneously increase with sales (accounts payable and accruals), or by an increase in retained earnings. Unilate can raise the additional $42.7 million, which we designate **additional funds needed (AFN)**, by borrowing from the bank (notes payable), by issuing long-term bonds, by selling new common stock, or by some combination of these actions.

The initial forecast of Unilate's financial statements shows that (1) higher sales must be supported by higher asset levels; (2) some of the asset increases can be financed by spontaneous increases in accounts payable and accruals as well as by an increased retained earnings; and (3) any shortfall must be financed from external sources, either by borrowing or by selling new stock.

spontaneously generated funds Funds that are obtained from routine business transactions.

additional funds needed (AFN) Funds that a firm must raise externally through new borrowing or by selling new stock.

Table 16.2

Unilate Textiles: Actual 2016 and Projected 2017 Balance Sheets ($ millions)

	2016 Actual Results	Forecast Basis[a]	2017 Initial Forecast	Change
Cash	$ 15.0	× 1.10	$ 16.5	$ 1.5
Accounts receivable	180.0	× 1.10	198.0	18.0
Inventory	270.0	× 1.10	297.0	27.0
Total current assets	$ 465.0		$ 511.5	
Net plant and equipment	380.0	× 1.10	418.0	38.0
Total assets	$ 845.0		$ 929.5	$84.5
Accounts payable	$ 30.0	× 1.10	$ 33.0	3.0
Accruals	60.0	× 1.10	66.0	6.0
Notes payable	40.0	⟶	40.0[b]	0.0
Total current liabilities	$ 130.0		$ 139.0	
Long-term bonds	300.0	⟶	300.0[b]	0.0
Total liabilities	$ 430.0		$ 439.0	
Common stock (25.0 million shares)	130.0	⟶	130.0[b]	0.0
Retained earnings	285.0	+$32.8[c]	317.8	32.8
Total owners' equity	$ 415.0		$ 447.8	
Total liabilities and equity	$ 845.0		$ 886.8	$41.8
Additional funds needed (AFN)			$ 42.7[d]	$42.7

[a] × 1.10 indicates "times (1 + g)"; it is used for items that grow proportionally with sales.
[b] Indicates a figure carried over from 2016 for the initial forecast.
[c] The $32.8 million represents the "addition to retained earnings" from the 2017 projected income statement given in Table 16.1.
[d] The additional funds needed (AFN) is computed by subtracting the forecasted amount of total liabilities and equity from the forecasted amount of total assets.

16-1c Step 3: Raising the Additional Funds Needed

Unilate's financial manager will base the decision of exactly how to raise the $42.7 million AFN on several factors, including its ability to handle additional debt, conditions in the financial markets, and restrictions imposed by existing debt agreements. Regardless of how Unilate raises the $42.7 million, the initial forecasts of both the income statement and the balance sheet will be affected. If Unilate takes on new debt, its interest expenses will increase; if additional shares of common stock are sold, *total* dividend payments will increase, assuming that the *same dividend per share* is paid to all common stockholders. Each of these changes, which we term *financing feedbacks*, will affect the amount of additional retained earnings that was originally forecast

financing feedbacks The effects on the income statement and balance sheet of actions taken to finance forecasted increases in assets.

in Step 1, which in turn will affect the amount of AFN that was computed in Step 2.

16-1d Step 4: Accounting for Financing Feedbacks

If Unilate raises the $42.7 million AFN by issuing new debt and new common stock, it will find that both the interest expense and the total dividend payments are higher than the amounts contained in the forecasted income statement shown in Table 16.1. Consequently, after adjusting for the higher interest and dividend payments, the forecasted addition to retained earnings will be lower than the initial forecast of $32.8 million. Because retained earnings will be lower than projected, a financing shortfall will exist even after the original AFN of $42.7 million is considered. Thus, Unilate must raise more than $42.7 million to account for the financing feedbacks that affect the amount of internal financing expected to be generated from the increase in operations. To determine the amount of external financing

Table 16.3

Unilate Textiles: 2017 Adjusted Forecast of Financial Statements ($ millions)

	Initial Forecast	Adjusted Forecast	Financing Adjustment
Income Statement[a]			
Earnings before interest and taxes (EBIT)	$143.0	$143.0	
Less: Interest	(40.0)	(41.4)	$ (1.4)
Earnings before taxes (EBT)	$103.0	101.6	(1.4)
Taxes (40%)	(41.2)	(40.6)	0.6
Net income	$ 61.8	$ 61.0	(0.8)
Common dividends	(29.0)	(30.5)	(1.5)
Addition to retained earnings	$ 32.8	$ 30.5	(2.3)[b]
Earnings per share	$ 2.47	$ 2.32	
Dividends per share	$ 1.16	$ 1.16	
Number of common shares (millions)	25.00	26.27	
Balance Sheet[a]			
Total assets	$929.5	$929.5	
Accounts payable	$ 33.0	$ 33.0	
Accruals	66.0	66.0	
Notes payable	40.0	46.8	$ 6.8
Total current liabilities	$139.0	$145.8	
Long-term bonds	300.0	309.0	9.0 ⎱ Total AFN = 45.0[c]
Total liabilities	$439.0	$454.8	
Common stock (26.27 million shares)	130.0	159.2	29.2
Retained earnings	317.8	315.5	(2.3)[b]
Total owners' equity	$447.8	$474.7	
Total liabilities and equity	$886.8	$929.5	
Initial amount of additional funds needed (AFN)			$ 42.7

[a]Because the operating section of the income statement and the asset section of the balance sheet are not affected by financing feedbacks, these sections are not shown in the table.

[b]The financing adjustment for the addition to retained earnings in the income statement is the same as the financing adjustment for retained earnings in the balance sheet.

[c]The total AFN (or external financing needs) equals the initial AFN of $42.7 million plus the $2.3 million decrease in retained earnings from the initial forecast. Thus the total external funds needed equal $45.0 million, of which $6.8 million will be from new bank notes, $9.0 million will come from issuing new bonds, and the remaining $29.2 million will be raised by issuing new common stock.

that is actually needed, we must adjust the initial forecasts of both the income statement (Step 1) and the balance sheet (Step 2) to reflect the impact of raising the additional external financing. This process must be repeated until AFN = 0 in Table 16.2, which means that Steps 1 and 2 might have to be repeated several times to fully account for the financing feedbacks.

Table 16.3 contains the adjusted 2017 preliminary forecasts for the income statement and the balance sheet of Unilate Textiles after all of the financing effects (feedbacks) are considered. To generate the adjusted forecasts, it is assumed that of the total external funds needed, 65 percent will be raised by selling new common stock at $23 per share, 15 percent will be borrowed from the bank at an interest rate of 7 percent, and 20 percent will be raised by selling long-term bonds with a coupon interest rate equal to 10 percent. Under these conditions, it can be seen from Table 16.3 that Unilate actually needs $45.0 million to support the forecasted increase in operations, not the $42.7 million contained in the initial forecast (Table 16.2). The additional $2.3 million is needed because the added amounts of debt and common stock will cause interest and dividend payments to increase, which in turn will decrease the contribution to retained earnings by $2.3 million compared to the initial forecast.

Equation 16.1 summarizes our discussion and provides a simple way to *estimate* the AFN for a firm that forecasts positive future growth and currently is operating at full capacity.

16.1

$$\text{Estimated AFN} = \begin{array}{c}\text{Forecasted} \\ \text{increase} \\ \text{in assets}\end{array} - \begin{array}{c}\text{Forecasted} \\ \text{increase} \\ \text{in liabilities}\end{array} - \begin{array}{c}\text{Forecasted} \\ \text{increase in} \\ \text{retained earnings}\end{array}$$

$$= [(TA_0 - SL_0) \times g] - [NI_0 (1 + g) - D]$$

Here TA_0 represents existing assets (in 2016), SL_0 represents existing spontaneous liabilities (which include accounts payable and accruals), g is the forecasted growth in sales in 2017, NI_0 represents existing net income, and D is the amount of dividends initially expected to be paid out of forecasted earnings. For firms that pay out a constant proportion of earnings as dividends each year, $D = [NI_0 (1 + g) \times (1 - P/O)]$, where P/O is the dividend payout ratio (P/O = Dividends/NI).

Using Equation 16.1 to estimate Unilate's AFN when sales are expected to grow by 10 percent and the firm expects to pay the same dividend in 2017 as it did in 2016, we find

$$\text{Estimated AFN} = [\$845 - (\$30 + \$60)](0.10)$$
$$- [\$54(1.10) - \$29]$$
$$= \$75.5 - \$30.4 = \$45.1 \text{ million}$$

The estimated AFN given here is higher than the *initial* forecast of $42.7 million shown in Table 16.2 primarily because the initial forecast of AFN assumes that the firm's interest expense does not change, whereas the result produced by Equation 16.1 assumes the interest expense changes proportionally with the change in sales and net income. Note, however, that estimated AFN computation is close to the *final* forecast of AFN given in Table 16.3 ($45 million).

16-1e Analysis of the Forecast

The 2017 forecast as developed here represents a preliminary forecast, because we have completed only the first stage of the entire forecasting process. Next, the projected statements must be analyzed to determine whether the forecast meets the firm's financial targets. If the statements do not meet the targets, then elements of the forecast must be changed.

Table 16.4 shows Unilate's 2016 ratios as they were reported back in Table 2.6 in Chapter 2, plus the projected 2017 ratios based on the preliminary forecast and the industry average ratios. As we noted in Chapter 2, the firm's financial condition at the close of 2016 was weak, with many ratios being well below the industry averages. The preliminary final forecast for 2017, which assumes that Unilate's past practices will continue into the future, shows an improved debt position. Nevertheless, the overall financial position still is somewhat weak, and this condition will persist unless management takes actions to improve things.

Unilate's management actually plans to take steps to improve its financial condition. The plans are to (1) close down certain operations, (2) modify the credit policy to reduce the collection period for receivables, and (3) better manage inventory so that products are turned over more often. These proposed operational changes will affect both the income statement and the balance sheet, so the preliminary forecast will have to be revised again to reflect the impact of such changes. When this process is complete, management will have its final forecast. To keep things simple, we do not show the final forecast here. Instead, for the remaining discussions we assume the preliminary forecast is not substantially different and use it as the final forecast for Unilate's 2017 operations.

Table 16.4

Unilate Textiles: Key Ratios

	2016	Adjusted Preliminary 2017	Industry Average
Current ratio	3.6×	3.5×	4.1×
Inventory turnover	4.6×	5.6×	7.4×
Days sales outstanding (DSO)	43.2 days	43.2 days	32.1 days
Total assets turnover	1.8×	1.8×	2.1×
Debt ratio	50.9%	48.9%	42.0%
Times interest earned (TIE)	3.3×	3.5×	6.5×
Profit margin	3.6%	3.7%	4.9%
Return on assets (ROA)	6.4%	6.6%	10.3%
Return on equity (ROE)	13.0%	12.8%	17.7%

16-2 Other Considerations in Forecasting

We have presented a simple method for constructing pro forma financial statements under rather restrictive conditions. In this section, we describe some other conditions that should be considered when creating forecasts.

16-2a Excess Capacity

The construction of the 2017 forecasts for Unilate was based on the assumption that the firm's 2016 operations were at full capacity, so any increase in sales would require additional assets, especially plant and equipment. If Unilate did *not* operate at full capacity in 2016, then plant and equipment would have to be increased only if the additional sales (operations) forecasted in 2017 exceeded the unused capacity of the existing assets. For example, if Unilate actually utilized only 80 percent of its fixed assets' capacity to produce 2016 sales of $1,500 million, then full-capacity sales would be computed as follows:

$$\$1,500 \text{ million} = 0.80 \times (\text{plant capacity})$$

$$\text{Plant capacity} = \frac{\$1,500 \text{ million}}{0.80} = \$1,875 \text{ million}$$

In this case, Unilate could increase sales to $1,875 million, or by 25 percent of 2016 sales, before full capacity—the point where plant and equipment would have to be increased to achieve additional growth—was reached. If Unilate did not have to increase plant and equipment, net fixed assets would remain at the 2016 level of $380 million, and depreciation and fixed operating costs would stay near $140 million. In this case, the AFN would actually be negative, which means that the amount of internally generated funds would be more than sufficient to support (finance) the forecasted 10 percent increase in sales in 2017. If this occurred, Unilate could increase the per-share dividend it pays to stockholders in 2017.

We can compute the sales capacity of the firm using Equation 16.2:

16.2

$$\text{Full capacity sales} = \frac{\text{Existing sales level}}{\left(\begin{array}{c}\text{Percent of capacity used} \\ \text{to generate existing sales level}\end{array}\right)}$$

In addition to the excess capacity of fixed assets, the firm could have excesses in other assets that can be used to support increases in operations. For instance, in Chapter 2, we concluded that Unilate's inventory level at the end of 2016 probably was greater than it should have been. If this is true, some increase in 2017 forecasted sales could be absorbed by the above-normal inventory, and production would not have to be increased until inventory levels were reduced to normal. This would require no additional financing.

In general, excess capacity means less external financing is required to support increases in operations than would be needed if the firm is currently operating at full capacity.

16-2b Economies of Scale

There are economies of scale in the use of many types of assets, and when such economies occur, a firm's variable cost of goods sold ratio is likely to change as the size of the firm changes (either increases or decreases) substantially. Currently, Unilate's variable cost ratio is 82 percent of sales; but the ratio might decrease to 80 percent of sales if operations increase significantly. If everything else is the same, changes in the variable cost ratio affect the addition to retained earnings, which in turn affects the amount of AFN.

16-2c Lumpy Assets

In many industries, technological considerations dictate that if a firm is to be competitive, it must add fixed assets in large, discrete units. Such assets often are referred to as **lumpy assets**. For example, in the paper industry, there are strong economies of scale in basic paper mill equipment, so when a paper company expands capacity, it must do so in large, lumpy increments. Lumpy assets primarily affect the turnover of fixed assets and, consequently, the financial requirements associated with expanding. For instance, if instead of $38 million, Unilate needed an additional $50 million in fixed assets to increase operations by 10 percent, the AFN would be much greater ($57.6 million rather than $45.0 million). With lumpy assets, it is possible that a small projected increase in sales would require a significant increase in plant and equipment, which would require a large financial commitment.

lumpy assets Assets that cannot be acquired in small increments, but instead must be obtained in large, discrete amounts.

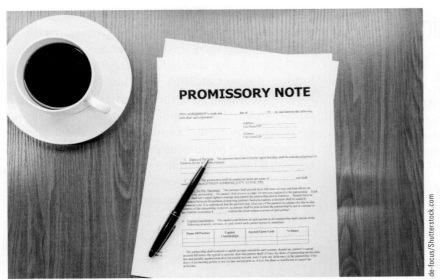

de-focus/Shutterstock.com

16-3 Financial Control—Budgeting and Leverage[1]

In the previous section, we focused on financial forecasting, emphasizing how growth in sales requires additional investment in assets, which in turn generally requires the firm to raise new funds externally. In the sections that follow, we consider the planning and control systems used by financial managers when implementing the forecasts. The planning process can be enhanced by examining the effects of changing operations on the firm's profitability, both from the standpoint of profits from operations and from the standpoint of profitability after financing effects are considered. In the next few sections, we will look at some of the areas financial managers evaluate to provide information about the effects of changing operations. To simplify our discussions, we assume that the firm has sufficient excess capacity to support any additional sales that are mentioned in the examples.

16-3a Operating Breakeven Analysis

The relationship between sales volume and *operating profitability* is explored in cost-volume-profit planning, or operating breakeven analysis. **Operating breakeven analysis** is a method of determining the point at which sales will just cover *operating costs*; that is, the point at

operating breakeven analysis
An analytical technique for studying the relationship between sales revenues, operating costs, and operating profits.

which the firm's operations will break even. It also shows the magnitude of the firm's operating profits or losses if sales exceed or fall below that point. Breakeven analysis is important in the planning and control process because the cost-volume-profit relationship can be influenced greatly by the proportion of the firm's investment in fixed assets. A sufficient volume of sales must be anticipated and achieved if both fixed and variable costs are to be covered; otherwise, the firm will incur losses from operations.[2]

Operating breakeven analysis deals only with the upper portion of the income statement—the portion from sales to net operating income (NOI).[3] This portion of the income statement generally is referred to as the *operating section*, because it contains only the revenues and expenses associated with the firm's *normal production and selling operations*. Table 16.5 gives the operating section of Unilate's forecasted 2017 income statement, which was shown in Table 16.1. For the discussion that

Table 16.5

Unilate Textiles: 2017 Forecasted Operating Income ($ million)

Sales (S)	$1,650.0
Variable cost of goods sold (VC)	(1,353.0)
Gross profit (GP)	$ 297.0
Fixed operating costs (F)	(154.0)
Net operating income (NOI = EBIT)	$ 143.0

Notes:

Selling price per unit = $15.00.

Sales in units = ($1,650.0 million)/$15 = 110 million units.

Variable costs per unit = ($1,353.0 million)/(110 million units) = $12.30 = 0.82($15.00).

Fixed operating costs = $154 million, which includes
$55 million depreciation and $99 million in other fixed costs, such as rent, insurance, and general office expenses. (See Table 16.1.)

[1]Because the numbers generated from the computations contained in the rest of the chapter are not rounded until final result is reported, you might find some slight rounding differences when performing the computations yourself.

[2]Costs that vary directly with the level of production generally include the labor and materials needed to produce and sell the product, whereas the fixed operating costs generally include costs such as depreciation, rent, and insurance expenses that are incurred regardless of the firm's production level.

[3]Net operating income (NOI) is the same as earnings before interest and taxes (EBIT); that is, NOI = EBIT.

FIGURE 16.1   UNILATE TEXTILES: OPERATING BREAKEVEN CHART

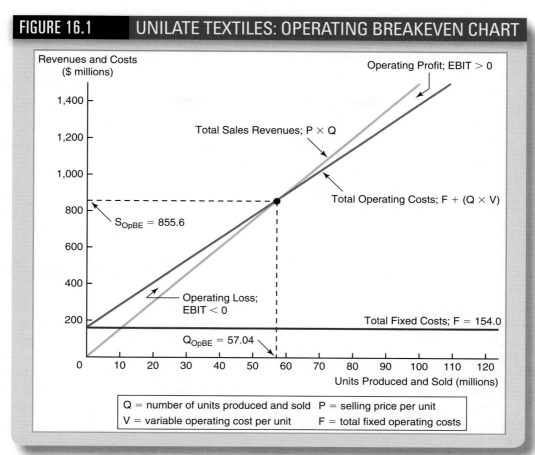

follows, we assume that all of Unilate's products sell for $15.00 each and that the variable cost of goods sold per unit is $12.30, which is 82 percent of the selling price.

Operating Breakeven Graph. Table 16.5 shows the net operating income for Unilate if 110 million products are produced and sold during the year. But, what if Unilate doesn't sell 110 million products? Certainly, the firm's net operating income will be something other than $143 million. Figure 16.1 shows the total revenues and total operating costs for Unilate at various levels of sales, beginning with zero. According to the information given in Table 16.5, Unilate has fixed costs, which include depreciation, rent, insurance, and so forth, equal to $154 million. This amount must be paid even if the firm produces and sells nothing, so the $154 million fixed cost is depicted by a horizontal line in Figure 16.1. If Unilate produces and sells nothing, its sales revenues will be zero; but *for each unit sold,* the firm's sales will increase by the selling price of $15. Therefore, the total revenue line starts at the origin of the X- and Y-axes, and it has a slope equal to $15 to account for the dollar increase

in sales for each additional unit sold. On the other hand, the line that represents the total operating costs intersects the Y-axis at $154 million, which represents the fixed costs incurred even when no products are sold, and it has a slope equal to the variable cost of goods sold per unit ($12.30). The point at which the total revenue line intersects the total operating cost line is the **operating breakeven point** (Q_{OpBE} on the X-axis and S_{OpBE} on the Y-axis), because this is where sales revenues just cover the *total operating costs* of the firm. Notice that prior to (to the left of) the breakeven point, the total cost line is above the total revenue line, which indicates that Unilate will suffer operating losses because the total costs cannot be covered by the sales revenues. Beyond (to the right of) the breakeven point, the total revenue line is above the total cost line because revenues are more than sufficient to cover total operating costs; thus, Unilate will realize operating profits in this region.[4]

Operating Breakeven Computation. Figure 16.1 shows that Unilate must sell 57.04 million units to be at its operating breakeven point. Remember, the operating breakeven point is where the revenues generated from sales just cover the total

operating breakeven point (Q_{OpBE} and S_{OpBE}) Represents the level of production and sales at which net operating income is zero; it is the point at which revenues from sales just equal total operating costs.

[4]In Figure 16.1, we assume the operating costs can be divided into two distinct groups: fixed costs and variable costs. It should be noted that some costs are considered semivariable (or semifixed). These costs are fixed for a certain range of operations, but change if operations are either higher or lower. For the analysis that follows, we have assumed there are no semivariable costs, so that the operating costs can be separated into either a fixed component or a variable component.

operating costs, which include both the costs directly attributable to producing each unit (variable costs) and the fixed operating costs that remain constant regardless of the production level. As long as the selling price of each unit (the slope of the total revenue line) is greater than the variable operating cost of each unit (the slope of the total operating cost line), each unit sold will generate revenues that contribute to covering the fixed operating costs. For Unilate, this contribution (termed the *contribution margin*) is $2.70, which is the difference between the $15.00 selling price and the $12.30 variable cost per unit. To compute the operating breakeven for Unilate, we have to determine how many units must be sold to cover the fixed operating cost of $154 million if each unit has a contribution margin equal to $2.70. Simply divide the $154 million fixed cost by the $2.70 contribution margin and you will discover that the breakeven point is 57.04 million units, which equates to $855.6 million in sales revenues.

More formally, the operating breakeven point can be found by setting the total revenues equal to the total operating costs so that net operating income (NOI) is zero. In equation form, NOI = 0 if

Sales revenues	=	Total operating costs	=	Total variable costs	+	Total fixed costs
$(P \times Q)$ =		TOC	=	$(V \times Q)$	+	F

Here P is the sales price per unit, Q is the number of units produced and sold, V is the variable operating cost per unit, and F is the total fixed operating costs. Solving for the quantity that must be sold, Q, produces Equation 16.3, which can be used to find the operating breakeven point:

16.3

$$Q_{OpBE} = \frac{F}{P - V} = \frac{F}{\text{Contribution margin}}$$

Thus, the operating breakeven point for Unilate is

$$Q_{OpBE} = \frac{\$154.0 \text{ million}}{\$15.00 - \$12.30} = \frac{\$154.0 \text{ million}}{\$2.70}$$

$$= 57.04 \text{ million units}$$

The operating breakeven point also can be stated in terms of the total sales. Simply restate the contribution margin as a percent of the sales price per unit (this is called the *gross profit margin*), and then apply Equation 16.4. That is,

16.4

$$S_{OpBE} = \frac{F}{1 - \left(\frac{V}{P}\right)} = \frac{F}{\text{Gross profit margin}}$$

Solving Equation 16.4 for Unilate, the operating breakeven stated in dollar sales is

$$S_{OpBE} = \frac{\$154.0 \text{ million}}{1 - \left(\frac{\$12.30}{\$15.00}\right)} = \frac{\$154.0 \text{ million}}{1 - 0.82}$$

$$= \frac{\$154.0 \text{ million}}{0.18} = \$855.6 \text{ million}$$

This computation shows that $0.18 of every $1.00 of sales goes to cover the fixed operating costs, which means nearly $856 million worth of the product must be sold for Unilate to break even. (In the remainder of the chapter, for simplicity we omit the word *million* in the computations and include it only in the final answer.)

From Equations 16.3 and 16.4, we can see that a firm's operating breakeven point is lower (higher) if its fixed costs are lower (higher), if the selling price of its product is higher (higher), if its variable operating cost per unit is lower (higher), or if some combination of these states exists.

Using Operating Breakeven Analysis. Operating breakeven analysis can shed light on three important types of business decisions: (1) When making new product decisions, breakeven analysis can help determine how large the sales of a new product must be for the firm to achieve profitability. (2) Breakeven analysis can be used to study the effects of a general expansion in the level of the firm's operations. An expansion would cause the levels of both fixed and variable costs to rise, but it would also increase expected sales. (3) When considering modernization projects where the fixed investment in equipment is increased in an effort to lower variable costs, particularly the cost of labor, breakeven analysis can help management analyze the consequences of purchasing these projects.

Care must be taken when using operating breakeven analysis. To apply breakeven analysis as we have discussed here requires that the sales price *per unit*, the variable cost *per unit*, and the *total* fixed operating costs do not change with the level of the firm's production and sales. Within a narrow range of production and sales, this assumption probably is not a major issue. However, if the firm expects either to produce a much greater (fewer)

Table 16.6

Unilate Textiles: Operating Income at Sales Levels of 110 Million Units and 121 Million Units ($ millions)

	2017 Forecasted Operations	Sales with 10% Increase	Unit Change	Percentage Change
Sales in units (millions) (Q)	110.0	121.0	11.0	+10.0%
Sales revenues (Q × $15.00)	$1,650.0	$1,815.0	$165.0	+10.0%
Variable cost of goods sold (Q × $12.30)	(1,353.0)	(1,488.3)	(135.3)	+10.0%
Gross profit	$ 297.0	$ 326.7	29.7	+10.0%
Fixed operating costs	(154.0)	(154.0)	(0.0)	0.0%
Net operating income (EBIT)	$ 143.0	$ 172.7	$ 29.7	+20.8%

number of products than normal or to expand (reduce) its plant and equipment significantly, these costs will change. Therefore, use of a single breakeven chart like the one presented in Figure 16.1 is impractical. Such a chart provides useful information, but the fact that it cannot deal with changes in the price of the product, changing variable cost rates, and changes in fixed cost levels suggests the need for a more flexible type of analysis. Firms generally perform breakeven analyses that are more complicated using computer simulation and other sophisticated models.

16-3b Operating Leverage

In Chapter 12 we defined operating leverage as the existence of fixed costs associated with normal operations. **Operating leverage** arises because the firm has *fixed operating costs* that must be covered no matter the level of production. The impact of this leverage, however, depends on the actual operating level of the firm. For example, Unilate has $154.0 million in fixed operating costs, which are covered rather easily because the firm projects sales of 110 million products, a quantity that is nearly double its operating breakeven point of 57.04 million units. But what would happen to its operating income if Unilate sold more or less than was forecast? To answer this question we need to determine the **degree of operating leverage (DOL)** associated with Unilate's forecasted 2017 operations.

Operating leverage can be defined more precisely in terms of the way a given change in sales volume affects operating income (NOI). To measure the effect of a change in sales volume on NOI, we calculate the

DOL, which is defined as the percentage change in NOI (or EBIT) that will result from a given percentage change in sales (Equation 16.5):

16.5

$$\text{Degree of operating leverage} = \text{DOL} = \frac{\% \Delta \text{ in NOI}}{\% \Delta \text{ in sales}} = \frac{\left(\dfrac{\Delta \text{NOI}}{\text{NOI}}\right)}{\left(\dfrac{\Delta \text{Sales}}{\text{Sales}}\right)}$$

$$= \frac{\left(\dfrac{\text{NOI}^* - \text{NOI}}{\text{NOI}}\right)}{\left(\dfrac{\text{Sales}^* - \text{Sales}}{\text{Sales}}\right)}$$

The symbol Δ—the Greek letter for "delta"—means *change*. The term with the asterisk (*) indicates the actual outcome, whereas the term without the asterisk is the forecasted result.

In effect, the DOL is an index that measures the effect a change in sales has on operating income or EBIT. Table 16.6 shows the EBIT for Unilate (1) if sales turn out to be 110 million units, which the firm has forecast and (2) if sales turn out to be 10 percent higher than expected (121 million units). The far right

operating leverage The existence of fixed operating costs such that a change in sales will produce a larger change in operating income (EBIT).

degree of operating leverage (DOL) The percentage change in NOI (or EBIT) associated with a given percentage change in sales.

column of the table shows that EBIT is magnified because fixed operating costs do not change when sales increase. As a result, a 10 percent increase in Unilate's forecasted 2017 sales will result in an *additional* 10.8 percent increase in operating income, so that the total increase is 20.8 percent.

Equation 16.5 can be simplified so that the degree of operating leverage at *a particular level of operations* can be calculated using one of the forms shown in Equation 16.6:[5]

16.6

$$DOL_Q = \frac{Q(P - V)}{Q(P - V) - F}$$

$$= \frac{S - VC}{S - VC - F}$$

$$= \frac{Gross\ profit}{EBIT}$$

To compute DOL using Equation 16.6, we only need information from Unilate's forecasted operations; we do not need information about the possible change in forecasted operations. Thus, Q represents the forecasted 2017 level of production and sales, and S and VC are the sales and variable operating costs, respectively, at that level of operations. For Unilate, the solution for DOL at sales equal to 110 million units is

$$DOL_{Q=110} = \frac{110(\$15.00 - \$12.30)}{110(\$15.00 - \$12.30) - \$154}$$

$$= \frac{\$1,650 - \$1,353}{\$1,650 - \$1,353 - \$154}$$

$$= \frac{\$297}{\$143} = 2.08\times$$

[5]Equation 16.6 can be derived by restating Equation 16.5 in terms of the variables we have defined previously, and then simplifying the result. Starting with Equation 16.5, we have

$$DOL = \frac{\%\Delta\ in\ NOI}{\%\Delta\ in\ sales} = \frac{\left(\dfrac{\Delta NOI}{NOI}\right)}{\left(\dfrac{\Delta Sales}{Sales}\right)}$$

NOI can be stated as the gross profit, Q(P − V), minus the fixed operating costs, F. So, if we use Q to indicate the level of operations forecasted for 2017 and Q* to indicate the level of operations that would exist if operations were different, the percent change in NOI is stated as

$$\%\Delta\ in\ NOI = \frac{[Q^*(P - V) - F] - [Q(P - V) - F]}{Q(P - V) - F} = \frac{(Q^* - Q)(P - V)}{Q(P - V) - F}$$

Substituting into Equation 16.5, restating the denominator, and solving, yields

$$DOL = \frac{\left[\dfrac{(Q^* - Q)(P - V)}{Q(P - V) - F}\right]}{\left[\dfrac{P(Q^* - Q)}{P(Q)}\right]} = \frac{(Q^* - Q)(P - V)}{Q(P - V) - F} \times \left(\frac{Q}{Q^* - Q}\right) = \frac{Q(P - V)}{Q(P - V) - F}$$

alejandro dans neergaard/Shutterstock.com

A DOL of 2.08× indicates that *each* 1 percent *change* in sales will result in a 2.08 percent *change* in operating income. What would happen if Unilate's sales turn out to be 10 percent lower than expected? According to the interpretation of the DOL figure, Unilate's operating income would be expected to decrease by 20.8 percent [= 2.02 × (−10%)]. If you compute Unilate's operating income at 99 million units, which is 10 percent less than the forecasted 110 million units, you will find that EBIT equals $113.3 million, which is 20.8 percent lower than the forecasted EBIT ($143 million). Therefore, *the DOL indicates the change (increase or decrease) in operating income that results from a change (increase or decrease) in the level of operations (sales).* It should be apparent that the greater the DOL, the greater the impact of a change in operations on operating income, whether the change is an increase or a decrease. And, as we discussed in Chapter 8, greater change (variability) suggests greater risk. Thus, we generally conclude that firms with higher DOLs have riskier business operations than firms with lower DOLs.

The DOL value found by using Equation 16.6 is the degree of operating leverage for a specific initial sales level. For Unilate, that sales level is 110 million units, or $1,650 million. The DOL value will differ if the initial (existing) level of operations differs. For example, if Unilate's operating cost structure is the same, but only 65 million units are expected to be produced and sold, the DOL would be

$$DOL_{Q=65} = \frac{65(\$15.00 - \$12.30)}{65(\$15.00 - \$12.30) - \$154}$$

$$= \frac{\$175.5}{\$21.5} = 8.16\times$$

The DOL at sales equal to 65 million units is nearly four times greater than the DOL at 110 million units. Thus, from a base sales of 65 million units, a 10 percent increase in sales (from 65 million units to 71.5 million units) would result in an 81.6% = 8.16 × 10% increase in operating income, from $21.5 million to $39.05 million. This shows that when Unilate's operations are closer to its operating breakeven point of 57.04 million units, its degree of operating leverage is higher.

Operating Leverage and Operating Breakeven.

In general, given the same operating cost structure, if a firm's level of operations is decreased, its DOL increases. Stated differently, the closer a firm is to its operating breakeven point, the greater is its degree of operating leverage. This occurs because, as Figure 16.1 indicates, the closer a firm is to its operating breakeven point, the more likely it is to incur an operating loss due to a decrease in sales. In other words, the closer its operations are to the operating breakeven point, the smaller the cushion, or buffer that exists for a firm to absorb a decrease in sales and still be able to cover the fixed operating costs. Similarly, at the same level of production and sales, a firm's DOL will be higher if the contribution margin for its products is lower. The lower the contribution margin, the less each product sold is able to help cover the fixed operating costs, and the closer the firm is to its operating breakeven point. Therefore, *it generally can be concluded that the higher the DOL for a particular firm, the closer the firm is to its operating breakeven point*, and the more sensitive its operating income is to a change in sales volume. Greater sensitivity generally implies greater risk; thus, it can be stated that *firms with higher DOLs generally are considered to have riskier operations than firms with lower DOLs.*

16-3c Financial Breakeven Analysis

Operating breakeven analysis deals with evaluation of production and sales to determine the level at which the firm's sales revenues will just cover its operating costs—the point where the operating income is zero.

Table 16.7

Unilate Textiles: 2017 Forecasted Earnings per Share ($ millions, except per-share data)

Sales in units (millions) (Q)	110.0
Earnings before interest and taxes (EBIT)	$ 143.0
Less: Interest	(41.4)
Earnings before taxes (EBT)	$ 101.6
Taxes (40%)	(40.6)
Net income (NI)	$ 61.0
Preferred dividends (D_{ps})	0.0
Earnings available to common stockholders (EAC)	$ 61.0
Earnings per share (EPS) = EAC/(26.27 million shares)	$ 2.32

Financial breakeven analysis is used to determine the operating income, or EBIT, the firm needs to generate to cover all of its *financing costs* and produce earnings per share equal to zero. Typically, the financing costs involved in financial breakeven analysis consist of the interest payments to bondholders and the dividend payments to preferred stockholders. Usually these financing costs are fixed, and, in every case, they must be paid before dividends can be paid to common stockholders.

Financial breakeven analysis deals with the lower section of the income statement—the portion from operating income (EBIT = NOI) to earnings per share (EPS). This portion of the income statement generally is referred to as the *financing section* because it contains the costs associated with the financing arrangements of the firm. The financing section of Unilate's forecasted 2017 income statement is shown in Table 16.7.

Financial Breakeven Graph. Figure 16.2 shows the earnings per share (EPS) for Unilate at various levels of EBIT. The point at which EPS equals zero is referred to as the **financial breakeven point (EBIT$_{FinBE}$)**. As the graph indicates, the financial breakeven point for Unilate is where EBIT equals $41.4 million. At this EBIT level, the income generated from operations is just sufficient to cover the financing costs and income taxes; thus, EPS equals zero at

financial breakeven analysis Determining the operating income (EBIT) the firm needs to just cover all of its financing costs and produce earnings per share equal to zero.

financial breakeven point (EBIT$_{FinBE}$) The level of EBIT at which EPS equals zero.

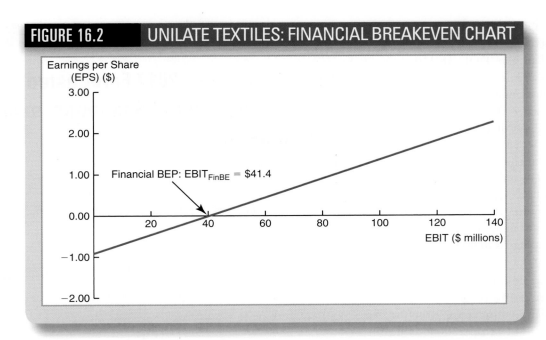

EBIT equal to $41.4 million. To see that this is the case, we can compute the EPS when EBIT is $41.4 million:

Earnings before interest and taxes (EBIT)	$41.4
Interest	(41.4)
Earnings before taxes (EBT)	0.0
Taxes (40%)	(0.0)
Net income	0.0
Preferred stock dividends	0.0
Earnings available to common stockholders (EAC)	$ 0.0
EPS = $0/26.27 =	$ 0.0

Financial Breakeven Computation. The results shown in Figure 16.2 can be translated algebraically to produce a relatively simple equation that can be used to compute the financial breakeven point of any firm. First, remember that the financial breakeven point is defined as the level of EBIT that generates EPS equal to zero. Equation 16.7, shows the definition of the financial breakeven point.

16.7

$$EPS = \frac{\left(\begin{array}{c} \text{Earnings available to} \\ \text{common stockholders} \end{array}\right)}{\left(\begin{array}{c} \text{Numbers of common} \\ \text{shares outstanding} \end{array}\right)} = 0$$

$$= \frac{(EBIT - I)(1 - T) - D_{ps}}{Shrs_C} = 0$$

Here EBIT is the earnings before interest and taxes, I represents the interest payments on debt, T is the marginal tax rate, D_{ps} is the amount of dividends paid to preferred stockholders, and $Shrs_C$ is the number of shares of common stock outstanding. Notice that EPS equals zero if the numerator in Equation 16.7, which is the earnings available to common stockholders, equals zero. Thus, the financial breakeven point also can be stated as follows:

$$(EBIT - I)(1 - T) - D_{ps} = 0$$

Rearranging this equation to solve for EBIT gives the level of EBIT that is needed to produce EPS equal to zero. Therefore, the computation for a firm's financial breakeven point is as shown in Equation 16.8:

16.8

$$EBIT_{FinBE} = I + \frac{D_{ps}}{(1 - T)}$$

Using Equation 16.8, the financial breakeven point for Unilate Textiles in 2017 is

$$EBIT_{FinBE} = \$41.4 + \frac{\$0.0}{(1 - 0.4)} = \$41.4$$

This is the same result shown in Figure 16.2.

According to Equation 16.8, the amount of preferred stock dividends must be stated on a before-tax basis to determine the financial breakeven point, because we want to determine the before-tax operating income (EBIT) that will result in EPS = 0. However, if it has no preferred stock, the firm only needs to cover its interest payments, so the financial breakeven point simply equals the interest expense. This is the case for Unilate, because it has no preferred stock. Because most corporations in the United States do not have preferred stock outstanding, we will not include preferred dividends in the discussions that follow.

Using Financial Breakeven Analysis. Financial breakeven analysis can be used to help determine the impact of the firm's financing mix on EPS.[6] When the financing mix includes financing alternatives that require fixed costs, such as interest, financial leverage exists. *Financial leverage affects the financing section* of the income statement like *operating leverage affects the operating section*. This point is discussed next.

16-3d Financial Leverage

While operating leverage considers how changing sales volume affects operating income, financial leverage considers how changing operating income (EBIT) affects EPS, or earnings available to common stockholders (EAC). Operating leverage affects the operating

section of the income statement, whereas financial leverage affects the financing section of the income statement. In other words, *financial leverage takes over where operating leverage leaves off, magnifying the effects on EPS of changes in operating income (EBIT).*

Like operating leverage, financial leverage arises because fixed costs exist. However, in this case, the fixed costs are associated with how the firm is financed. The **degree of financial leverage (DFL)** is defined as the percentage change in EPS that results from a given percentage change in EBIT. Thus, DFL is computed as shown in Equation 16.9:

16.9

$$\text{Degree of financial leverage} = \text{DFL} = \frac{\%\Delta \text{ in EPS}}{\%\Delta \text{ in EBIT}} = \frac{\left(\dfrac{\Delta\text{EPS}}{\text{EPS}}\right)}{\left(\dfrac{\Delta\text{EBIT}}{\text{EBIT}}\right)}$$

$$= \frac{\left(\dfrac{\text{EPS}^* - \text{EPS}}{\text{EPS}}\right)}{\left(\dfrac{\text{EBIT}^* - \text{EBIT}}{\text{EBIT}}\right)}$$

As in our previous discussions, the term with the asterisk (*) indicates the actual outcome, whereas the term without the asterisk is the forecasted result.

Table 16.8 shows the results of increasing Unilate's EBIT by 20.8 percent. The increase in EPS is 29.2 percent, which is 1.41 times the change in EBIT; thus, the DFL for Unilate equals 1.41.

The degree of financial leverage at a particular level of EBIT can be computed easily by using Equation 16.10:[7]

16.10

$$\text{DFL} = \frac{\text{EBIT}}{\text{EBIT} - \text{EBIT}_{\text{FinBE}}}$$

$$= \frac{\text{EBIT}}{\text{EBIT} - \text{I}} \quad \text{when } D_{\text{ps}} = 0$$

Using Equation 16.10, the DFL for Unilate Textiles at EBIT equal to $143.0 million (sales of 110 million units) is

$$\text{DFL}_{Q=110} = \frac{\$143.0}{\$143.0 - \$41.4}$$

$$= \frac{\$143.0}{\$101.6} = 1.41\times$$

financial leverage The existence of fixed financial costs such as interest and preferred dividends; occurs when a change in EBIT results in a larger change in EPS.

degree of financial leverage (DFL) The percentage change in EPS that results from a given percentage change in EBIT.

[6]The effect of financing the firm with various proportions of debt and equity is discussed in greater detail in Chapter 12.

[7]Equation 16.10 can be derived easily by expanding Equation 16.9, rearranging the terms, and then simplifying the results. If we use EPS and EBIT to indicate the forecasted 2017 EPS and EBIT, respectively, and EPS* and EBIT* to indicate the EPS and EBIT that would exist after a change in sales volume, then

$$\text{DFL} = \frac{\left(\dfrac{\Delta\text{EPS}}{\text{EPS}}\right)}{\left(\dfrac{\Delta\text{EBIT}}{\text{EBIT}}\right)} = \frac{\left(\dfrac{\text{EPS}^* - \text{EPS}}{\text{EPS}}\right)}{\left(\dfrac{\text{EBIT}^* - \text{EBIT}}{\text{EBIT}}\right)}$$

The computation for forecasted earnings per share is

$$\text{EPS} = \frac{(\text{EBIT} - \text{I})(1 - \text{T})}{\text{Shrs}_c}$$

where Shrs_c is the number of common shares outstanding. The percent change in EPS can be written and simplified as follows:

$$\Delta\text{EPS} = \frac{\left[\dfrac{(\text{EBIT}^* - \text{I})(1-\text{T})}{\text{Shrs}_c}\right] - \left[\dfrac{(\text{EBIT} - \text{I})(1-\text{T})}{\text{Shrs}_c}\right]}{\left[\dfrac{(\text{EBIT} - \text{I})(1-\text{T})}{\text{Shrs}_c}\right]}$$

$$= \frac{[(\text{EBIT}^* - \text{I})(1-\text{T})] - [(\text{EBIT} - \text{I})(1-\text{T})]}{(\text{EBIT} - \text{I})(1-\text{T})}$$

$$= \frac{\text{EBIT}^* - \text{EBIT}}{\text{EBIT} - \text{I}}$$

Substituting this relationship into the computation of DFL, we have

$$\text{DFL} = \frac{\left(\dfrac{\text{EBIT}^* - \text{EBIT}}{\text{EBIT} - \text{I}}\right)}{\left(\dfrac{\text{EBIT}^* - \text{EBIT}}{\text{EBIT}}\right)} = \frac{\text{EBIT}^* - \text{EBIT}}{\text{EBIT} - \text{I}} \times \frac{\text{EBIT}}{\text{EBIT}^* - \text{EBIT}}$$

$$= \frac{\text{EBIT}}{\text{EBIT} - \text{I}} = \frac{\text{EBIT}}{\text{EBIT} - \text{EBIT}_{\text{FinBE}}}$$

If a firm has preferred stock, the relationship given in Equation 16.8 should be substituted in this equation for the $\text{EBIT}_{\text{FinBE}}$.

Table 16.8

Unilate Textiles: Net Income and Earnings per Share at Sales Levels of 110 Million Units and 121 Million Units ($ million)[a]

	2017 Forecasted Operations	Sales with 10% Increase	Unit Change	Percentage Change
Sales in units (millions) (Q)	110.0	121.0	11.0	+10.0%
Earnings before interest and taxes (EBIT)	$143.0	$172.7	$29.7	+20.8%
Interest (I)	(41.4)	(41.4)	(0.0)	0.0%
Earnings before taxes (EBT)	$101.6	$131.3	$29.7	+29.2%
Taxes (40%)	(40.6)	(52.5)	(11.9)	+29.2%
Net income (NI)	$ 61.0	$ 78.8	$17.8	+29.2%
Earnings per share (26.3 million shares)	$ 2.32	$ 3.00	$ 0.68	+29.2%

[a]A spreadsheet was used to generate the results in this table. Only the final results are rounded. As a result, there might be rounding differences if you rely on some of the values in the table, which are rounded values, to compute the other values.

The interpretation of the DFL value is the same as for DOL, except that the starting point for evaluating financial leverage is EBIT and the ending point is EPS. Because the DFL for Unilate is 1.41×, the company can expect a 1.41 percent change in EPS for every 1 percent change in EBIT; a 20.8 percent increase in EBIT results in an approximately 29.2 percent (20.8 percent × 1.41) increase in EPS. Unfortunately, the opposite also is true—if Unilate's 2017 EBIT turns out to be 20.8 percent below expectations, its EPS will be 29.2 percent below the forecast of $2.32. To prove this result is correct, construct the financing section of Unilate's income statement when EBIT equals $113.3 million = $(1 − 0.208) × 143.0 million, and you will find EPS = $1.64, which is 29.2 percent lower than the forecasted amount of $2.32.

The DFL value found using Equation 16.10 pertains to one specific EBIT level. If the level of sales differs, and thus EBIT differs, so does the value computed for DFL. For example, at sales equal to 75 million units, Unilate's DFL would be

$$DFL_{Q=75} = \frac{75(\$15.00 - \$12.30) - \$154}{[75(\$15.00 - \$12.30) - \$154] - \$41.4}$$

$$= \frac{\$48.5}{\$7.1} = 6.83\times$$

Compared to sales equal to 110 million units, at sales equal to 75 million units Unilate would have greater difficulty covering the fixed financing costs, so its DFL is much greater. At EBIT equal to $48.5 million, Unilate is close to its financial breakeven point of $41.4 million,

so its degree of financial leverage is high. Consequently, the more difficulty a firm has covering its fixed financing costs with operating income, the greater its degree of financial leverage. In general then, *the higher the DFL for a particular firm, the closer the firm is to its financial breakeven point*, and the more sensitive its EPS is to a change in operating income. Greater sensitivity implies greater risk; thus, it can be stated that *firms with higher DFLs generally are considered to have greater financial risk than firms with lower DFLs*.

16-3e Combining Operating and Financial Leverage—Degree of Total Leverage (DTL)

Our analysis of operating leverage and financial leverage has shown that *(1) the greater the DOL, or fixed operating costs, for a particular level of operations, the more sensitive EBIT will be to changes in sales volume; and (2) the greater the DFL, or fixed financial costs, for a particular level of operations, the more sensitive EPS will be to changes in EBIT*. Therefore, if a firm has considerable amounts of both operating leverage and financial leverage, even small changes in sales will lead to wide fluctuations in EPS. Look at the impact leverage has on Unilate's forecasted 2017 operations. We found that if the sales volume increases by 10 percent, Unilate's EBIT will increase by 20.8 percent, and if EBIT increases by 20.8 percent, its EPS will increase by 29.2 percent. Thus, a 10 percent increase in sales volume would result in a 29.2 percent increase in EPS. This shows the impact of *total leverage*, which is the combination of both operating leverage and financial leverage, with respect to Unilate's current operations.

The **degree of total leverage (DTL)** is defined as the percentage change in EPS resulting from a 1 percent change in sales volume. This relationship, which represents the combination of DOL and DFL, can be written as Equation 16.11:

iStockphoto.com/E_Y_E

a 10 percent increase in sales will result in a 29.2 percent increase in EPS. This is exactly the impact expected.

The value of DTL can be used to compute the new earnings per share (EPS*) after a change in sales volume. We already know that Unilate's EPS will change by 2.92 percent for every 1 percent change in sales. Accordingly, the EPS* resulting from a 10 percent increase in sales can be computed as follows:

$$EPS^* = EPS[1 + (.10)(2.92)]$$
$$= \$2.32 \times (1 + 0.292) = \$3.00$$

This is the same result given in Table 16.8.

The degree of (total) leverage concept is useful primarily for the insights it provides regarding the joint effects of operating leverage and financial leverage on EPS. For example, the concept can be used to show management that a decision to finance new equipment with debt would result in a situation in which a 10 percent decline in sales would result in a nearly 30 percent decline in earnings, whereas with a different operating and financial package, a 10 percent sales decline would cause earnings to decline by only 15 percent. Having the alternatives stated in this manner gives decision makers a better idea of the ramifications of alternative actions with respect to the firm's level of operations and how those operations are financed.

16.11

Degree of total leverage $= DTL = DOL \times DFL$

$$= \frac{Gross\ profit}{EBIT} \times \frac{EBIT}{EBIT - EBIT_{FinBE}}$$

$$= \frac{Gross\ profit}{EBIT - EBIT_{FinBE}}$$

$$= \frac{S - VC}{EBIT - I} = \frac{Q(P - V)}{[Q(P - V) - F] - I} \Bigg\} \quad when \quad D_{ps} = 0$$

Using Equation 16.11, the degree of total leverage for Unilate would be

$$DTL_{Q=110} = 2.077 \times 1.407$$

$$= \frac{\$297.0}{\$143.0} \times \frac{\$143.0}{\$143.0 - \$41.4}$$

$$= \frac{\$1,650.0 - \$1,353.0}{\$143.0 - \$41.4}$$

$$= \frac{110(\$15.00 - \$12.30)}{[110(\$15.00 - \$12.30) - \$154.0] - \$41.4}$$

$$= \frac{\$297.0}{\$101.6} = 2.92 \times$$

This value indicates that for every 1 percent change in sales volume, Unilate's EPS will change by 2.92 percent; thus,

16-4 Using Leverage and Forecasting for Control

From the discussion in the previous sections, it should be clear what the impact on income would be if the 2017 sales forecast for Unilate Textiles is different from what is expected. If sales are greater than

degree of total leverage (DTL) The percentage change in EPS that results from a 1 percent change in sales.

expected, both operating and financial leverage will magnify the "bottom line" effect on EPS (DTL = 2.92). However, the opposite also holds. Consequently, if Unilate does not meet its forecasted sales level, leverage will result in a magnified loss in income compared to what is expected. This will occur because production facilities might be expanded too greatly, inventories might be built up too quickly, and so on, and the end result might be that the firm suffers a significant income loss. This loss will result in a lower than expected addition to retained earnings, which means that plans for additional external funds needed to support the firm's operations will be inadequate. Likewise, if the sales forecast is too low, then, if the firm is at full capacity, it will not be able to meet the additional demand, and sales opportunities will be lost—perhaps forever. In the previous sections, we showed only how changes in operations (2017 forecasts) affect the income generated by the firm; we did not continue the process to show the impact on the balance sheet and the financing needs of the firm. To determine the impact on the financial statements, the financial manager must repeat the steps discussed in the first part

of this chapter. At this stage, the financial manager needs to evaluate and act on the feedback received from the forecasting and budgeting processes. In effect, then, the forecasting (planning) and control of the firm is an ongoing activity, a vital function to the long-run survival of any firm.

The forecasting and control functions described in this chapter are important for several reasons. First, if the projected operating results are unsatisfactory, management can "go back to the drawing board," reformulate its plans, and develop targets that are more reasonable for the coming year. Second, it is possible that the funds required to meet the sales forecast simply cannot be obtained. If so, it obviously is better to know this in advance and to scale back the projected level of operations than to suddenly run out of cash and have operations grind to a halt. Third, even if the required funds can be raised, it is desirable to plan for their acquisition well in advance. Finally, any deviation from the projections must be dealt with to improve future forecasts and the predictability of the firm's operations, and therefore to ensure that the goals of the firm are being pursued appropriately.

STUDY TOOLS

LOCATED AT BACK OF THE TEXTBOOK

- ☐ Problems are found at the end of this chapter.
- ☐ A tear-out Chapter Review card is located at the back of the textbook.

LOCATED AT WWW.CENGAGEBRAIN.COM

- ☐ Review Key Term flashcards and create your own cards.

- ☐ Track your knowledge and understanding of key concepts in corporate finance.
- ☐ Complete practice and graded quizzes to prepare for tests.
- ☐ Complete interactive content within CFIN5 Online.
- ☐ View the chapter highlight boxes for CFIN5 Online.

KEY FINANCIAL PLANNING AND CONTROL CONCEPTS

To conclude this chapter, we summarize some concepts that were discussed.

- Financial planning requires the firm to forecast future operations. A firm forecasts its financial statements (called pro formas) so that arrangements can be made to accommodate expected changes in production, future financing needs, and so forth. A financial plan represents a "road map" for the firm to follow to attain future goals. The process doesn't stop when financial forecasts are completed, because the firm needs to monitor operations as the financial plan is implemented to determine whether modifications are needed.

- A firm evaluates its breakeven points and degrees of leverage to assess the risk associated with its forecasts. In general, a firm with a higher degree of leverage is considered riskier than a similar firm that has a lower degree of leverage. A firm uses the concept of leverage to estimate how fixed costs, both operating and financial, affect its "bottom line" (net) income. Everything else equal, a firm can decrease its risk by decreasing its relative fixed costs, by increasing sales, or by performing both actions. Remember from our discussions in previous chapters that, everything else equal, when a firm reduces its risk, its cost of capital decreases, and thus its value increases.

- Inadequate financial planning is the principal reason businesses fail. As a result, well-run companies generally base their operating plans on a set of well-designed forecasted financial statements. Simply stated, forecasting (planning) is an essential part of a successful business.

PROBLEMS

16–1 Midwest Mining (MWM) expects its sales to grow by 20 percent next year. Last year, when the firm was operating at *full capacity*, MWM generated sales equal to $250,000 with assets of $800,000. MWM's current balance sheet shows that accounts payable and accruals are $150,000, notes payable are $25,000, long-term debt is $100,000, common stock is $450,000, and retained earnings are $75,000. Next year, MWM's net profit margin is expected to be the same as this past year, 5 percent, and the company plans to continue to pay 60 percent of earnings as dividends. Estimate MWM's additional funds needed (AFN) for next year.

16–2 Esther's Egg Farm is constructing its pro forma financial statements for this year. At year end, assets were $400,000 and accounts payable (the only current liabilities account) were $125,000. Last year's sales were $500,000. Esther's expects to grow by 15 percent this year. Assets and accounts payable are expected to grow proportionally to sales. Common stock currently equals $140,000, and retained earnings are $98,000. Esther's plans to sell $15,000 of new common stock this year. The firm's profit margin on sales is 6 percent, and 40 percent of earnings will be paid out as dividends. How much *new* long-term debt financing will Esther's need this year to finance its expected growth? Esther's is currently operating at full capacity.

16–3 In its most recent fiscal year, SynoCorp generated $810,000 in sales. The firm was operating at 90 percent capacity. How much more sales can SynoCorp generate before it is at full capacity?

16–4 TransCan Industries has been operating at 60 percent capacity the past few years. In each of these years, TransCan generated sales of $5.4 million. By what percentage can TransCan increase its sales before full capacity is reached?

16–5 Prime Colors (PC) sells one-gallon cans of house paint for $25 each. The variable cost to produce each can is $17.50, and fixed operating costs are $1,500. PC normally sells 30,000 gallons of paint each year, has an interest expense equal to $300, and its marginal tax rate is 40 percent. Given this information, what is PC's operating breakeven point?

16–6 Maxine's Pumps (MP) sells bilge pumps for $250 each. Each pump costs $150 to produce, and MP's fixed operating costs equal $600,000. (a) What is MP's operating breakeven point? (b) What is MP's operating income (NOI) when 10,000 pumps are sold?

16–7 Flash Gordon Memory (FGM) sells memory cards for $45 each. Fixed costs are $900,000 for output up to 200,000 cards. Variable costs are $25 per card. (a) What is FGM's operating income at sales of 75,000 cards? (b) What is the operating breakeven point?

16–8 Last Chance Gaming manufactures slot machines that are sold to individuals for $575 each. Fixed operating costs are $690,000, and each machine's variable cost is 70 percent of its selling price. What is the firm's degree of operating leverage at sales equal to (a) 6,000 machines, (b) 9,000 machines, and (c) 12,000 machines?

16–9 Lost Time Watch (LTW) Company manufactures watches that are sold for $200 each. Fixed operating costs are $640,000 and variable costs are $120 per watch. (a) What is LTW's operating breakeven point? (b) What is LTW's degree of operating leverage (DOL) at sales of 10,000 units? (c) Everything else equal, what would happen to the operating breakeven point if the selling price is raised to $220?

16–10 Open Door Manufacturing (ODM) and Closed Window Industries (CWI) have identical operating cost structures. Both firms incur a fixed operating cost equal to $420,000, their variable cost ratio is 80 percent of the unit selling price, and they sell their products for $1,400 each. ODM normally sells 2,000 units per year, whereas CWI normally sells 2,500 units each year. (a) Compute the firms' operating breakeven point. (b) Compute the degree of operating leverage (DOL) for each firm at their normal sales levels, and show that ODM is operating closer to the operating breakeven point than CWI.

16–11 Mercury Air's debt consists of $50,000 in accounts payable, $100,000 in 10 percent notes payable, and $240,000 in 8 percent bonds. Mercury has no preferred stock. If its marginal tax rate is 35 percent, what is Mercury's financial breakeven point?

16–12 Juniper Jams' balance sheet shows that its outstanding debt consists of $15,000 in 9 percent notes payable and $48,000 in 6 percent bonds. In addition, Mercury has $60,000 preferred stock that pays a 5 percent dividend. If its marginal tax rate is 40 percent, what is Mercury's financial breakeven point?

16–13 Nuance Art has only one type of debt outstanding: a long-term bond with a face value of $300,000 and a coupon rate of interest equal to 11 percent. Nuance expects this year's EBIT to equal $99,000, and its marginal tax rate is 30 percent. (a) If Nuance has no preferred stock, what is its degree of financial leverage (DFL)? (b) If Nuance has preferred stock that pays an annual dividend equal to $18,480, what is its DFL?

16–14 Stumpy's Gator Farm forecasts that its net income will be $46,800 this year. The firm's marginal tax rate is 35 percent, and it must pay $36,000 interest on outstanding debt. Stumpy's has no preferred stock. What is the firm's degree of financial leverage (DFL)?

16–15 Debbie's Sod Farm (DSF) expects its EBIT to be $2,250 this year. DSF's marginal tax rate is 40 percent, it must pay $1,000 in interest this year, and it has 500 shares of common stock outstanding. (a) Compute the EPS that DSF expects to generate this year. (b) What is DSF's degree of financial leverage (DFL)? The firm has no preferred stock.

16–16 Beachcomber Treasures has determined that its degree of operating leverage (DOL) is 3.5 and its degree of financial leverage (DFL) is 2.0. (a) What is Beachcomber's degree of total leverage (DTL)? (b) What impact will a 5 percent decrease in sales have on Beachcomber's (i) EBIT and (ii) net income?

16–17 Ensured Insurance has a degree of financial leverage (DFL) equal to 4.0 and a degree of total leverage (DTL) equal to 10.0. Ensured expects sales to be $600,000 this year, and its net profit margin is 8 percent. (a) What is Ensured's degree of operating leverage (DOL)? (b) If Ensured's sales turn out to be 7 percent higher than expected, what will its net income be?

16–18 Analysts have evaluated the Wright Sign Company and discovered that when sales are $400,000, EBIT equals $125,000, the company's degree of operating leverage (DOL) is 2.0, its degree of financial leverage (DFL) is 4.0, and EPS equals $2.50. According to this information, what will Wright's EBIT be if sales actually equal $360,000 rather than $400,000? What will the EPS be?

16–19 Callie Corporation's products sell for $180 each. The variable cost of each product is $135, and fixed operating costs are $371,250. Callie pays $61,875 interest on its outstanding debt each year, and its marginal tax rate is 40 percent. If Callie expects to sell 11,000 units, what is its degree of operating leverage (DOL), its degree of financial leverage (DFL), and its degree of total leverage (DTL)? The firm has no preferred stock.

16–20 LPM Corporation sells its product for $10 each. Fixed operating costs equal $100,000, and variable operating costs are 75 percent of the selling price. The firm pays $37,500 in interest, and its marginal tax rate is 35 percent. (a) What are LPM's operating breakeven point and financial breakeven point? (b) If LPM expects to sell 65,000 units, what are its degree of operating leverage (DOL), degree of financial leverage (DFL), and degree of total leverage (DTL)? The firm has no preferred stock.

Appendix A
Using Spreadsheets to Solve Financial Problems

Like calculators, spreadsheets were developed to make mathematical computations easier to solve. In this appendix, we provide a brief tutorial on how to use spreadsheets to solve the problems discussed in Chapter 4. In the explanations that follow, we use Microsoft Excel 2013 to illustrate the spreadsheet applications.

A-1 Setting up Mathematical Relationships

It is easy to set up relationships to solve mathematical problems that require you to use such arithmetic operators as addition, subtraction, multiplication, division, and so on. Following are the common arithmetic operators used in Excel:

Operator	Description	Function
+	Plus sign	Addition
−	Minus sign	Subtraction
*	Asterisk (star)	Multiplication
/	Forward slash	Division
^	Caret	Exponentiation (raise to a power)

To solve a problem, put the cursor in the cell where you want the final answer to appear, type an equal sign (=), enter the relationship that you want to solve, and then press "Enter" to generate the result. For example, suppose that you want to compute how much $700 invested today will grow to in three years if it earns 10 percent interest compounded annually. This problem can be easily solved by entering into one of the cells of a spreadsheet the relationship shown in Equation 4.1 in Chapter 4. The solution shown in the chapter is:

$$FV_3 = \$700(1.10)^3 = \$931.70$$

Using a spreadsheet, this same solution can be determined as follows:

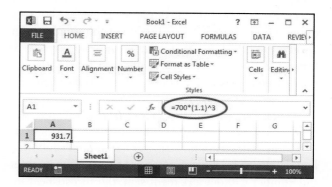

The equation entered into cell **A1** is shown in the circled area. As you can see, the relationship entered into the spreadsheet is FV = 700*(1.1)^3, which is the same as FV = 700(1.10)³. The result of the computation shown in cell **A1** is 931.7, or $931.70, which is the same result we reported earlier.[1]

Although it is easy to solve a problem by defining the relationship and entering numbers in one cell, it is better to create a table that contains the values needed to solve a particular equation and then set up a general relationship (equation) that refers to the locations of the specific cells where the needed values (numbers) are located. For example, for the current computation, the spreadsheet might be set up as follows:

---

[1]Neither the circles nor the ovals shown in the screenshots actually appear on the spreadsheets. We added these items for emphasis.

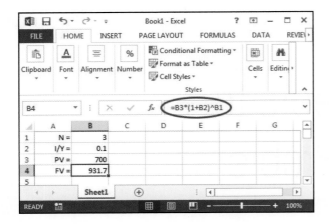

As you can see by the equation in the circled area, cell **B4** contains the relationship that computes the future value of the $700 investment. But the equation entered into cell **B4** contains no numbers; rather, the relationship refers to the cells where the numbers (values) required to solve the problem are located. By setting up the relationship (computation) in this manner, you can change any of the individual input values, and, using the new value(s), the new solution will be shown immediately in cell **B4.** Try setting up your spreadsheet as shown in the previous example. You should get the same answer we reported, 931.70. Now change the interest rate to 8 percent (0.08) in cell **B2.** When you input 0.08 and press "Enter," you will see the result in cell **B4** change to 881.7984, or $881.80.

Note that when you input a percentage into the spreadsheet, you must enter the number either in decimal form—for example, 0.10—or as a number followed by a percent (%) sign—for example, 10%.[2] If you enter the number without a percent sign, the spreadsheet interprets the number literally and solves the problem accordingly. For example, if you enter "10" rather than 0.10 or 10% in the original computation, the result shown in cell **B4** will be:

$$FV = 700(1 + 10)^3 = 100(11)^3 = 931,700$$

This clearly is an incorrect answer for the previous situation.

Although it is fairly easy to set up your own equations or relationships to solve most of the problems presented in the book, it is even easier to use the preprogrammed functions contained in the spreadsheet. In the remainder of this appendix, we show you how to use the time value of money functions that are preprogrammed into spreadsheets to solve the problems introduced in Chapter 4. The same functions can be used to solve time value of money problems given in other chapters.

A-2 Solving Time Value of Money (TVM) Problems Using Preprogrammed Spreadsheet Functions

The functions programmed into spreadsheets are the same as those programmed into financial calculators. In this section, we show how to use an Excel spreadsheet to solve some of the examples given in Chapter 4. Remember that in Chapter 4 we showed only the spreadsheet setup for computing the future value of a lump-sum amount. Here we show each step that should be followed when using the TVM functions discussed in Chapter 4. Note that we label the values entered into the cells of the spreadsheet (Column A) the same as the TVM keys on a Texas Instruments BAII PLUS financial calculator, which is the calculator used to solve the problems presented in the book.

Using Excel 2013, you can access the TVM functions from either the "HOME" menu or the "FORMULAS" menu. To access the functions from the "FORMULAS" menu, click the "Insert Function" icon that appears on the left side of the horizontal menu bar on the "FORMULAS" menu. The symbol "f_x" is also shown on "Insert Function" icon. To access the TVM functions from the "HOME" menu, either click the "f_x" icon on the left side of the formula bar, which is the blank space located above the letters that identify the columns, or click the *down arrow* to the right of the "Σ" sign in the "Editing" box on the right side of the horizontal menu bar on the "HOME" menu. The following screenshot shows the locations of the "f_x" icon (circled in green) and of the "Σ" sign (circled in red) on the "HOME" menu:

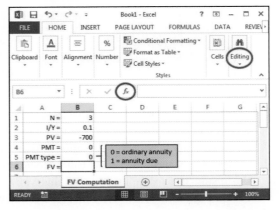

[2]If you input the number as 0.10, you can format the cell so that 10% is displayed with as many decimal places as you prefer by using the format function located on the "Home" menu, which allows you to format the contents of each cell. You can also use this function to format cells that contain such values as PV, PMT, and FV so that they are expressed in dollars and cents.

The following menu will appear after you click the "f_x" symbol on either the "HOME" menu or the "FORMULAS" menu:

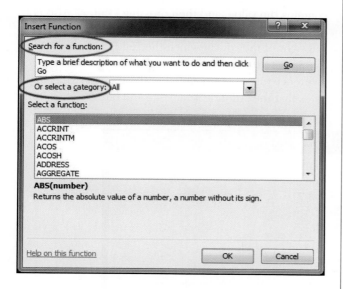

The "Search for a function:" option at the top of the menu (circled in red) allows you to search for a function that fits the type of computation you want to perform. You can also select a particular category of computations (functions) by using the drop-down menu labeled "Or select a category:" (circled in blue). Because we are going to use the financial functions, click the "Or select a category:" drop-down menu, and then click the category labeled "Financial" in the new menu that appears. The "Financial" category gives you access to the financial functions needed to solve time value of money problems. These financial functions are shown in the section labeled "Select a function:" in the new "Insert Function" menu that appears (shown in the next section).

A-2a Solving for Future Value (FV): Lump-Sum Amount and Annuity

The same spreadsheet function—"FV"—is used to solve for both the future value of a lump-sum amount and the future value of an annuity.

FV of a Lump-Sum Amount. If you want to find the FV in three years of $700 invested today at 10 percent

compounded annually, you might want to set up your spreadsheet as follows:

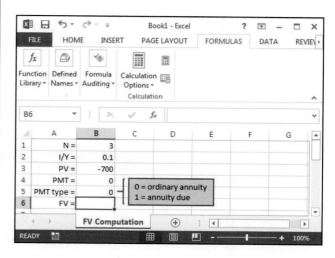

Note that the amount invested, $700, is entered as a negative number, just as it is when solving this problem using a financial calculator; that is, the $700 investment is a cash outflow.

To solve for the future value, place the cursor in cell **B6,** click the "Insert Function" (f_x) option on the "FORMULAS" menu, and scroll down the list of functions in the "Select a function:" menu until you reach "FV". You should see the following on your computer display:

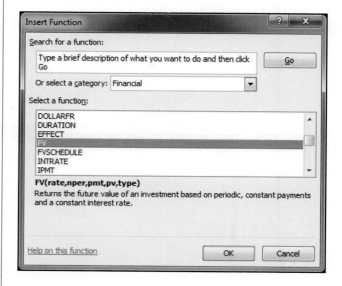

When you click "OK" or double-click "FV," the following dialog ("Function Arguments") box appears.

In this box, "Rate" represents the interest rate per period, "Nper" is the number of periods that interest is earned, "Pmt" is the periodic payment, or annuity amount (we will use this later), "Pv" is the present value of the amount, and "Type" refers to the type of annuity payment (0 = ordinary annuity; 1 = annuity due). You can read the definition for each variable by placing the cursor in the row in which the variable is located. For example, the definition for "Rate" is displayed in the dialog box shown here, because the cursor currently is located in the "Rate" box.

Note that you can also insert the appropriate location for each row in the dialog box by clicking the small box that contains a red arrow on the right side of the row (circled in green), placing the cursor in the cell that contains the value, and then pressing "Enter." Also note that the content of each cell to which you refer is given to the right of the row in which the cell is referenced. For example, to the far right of the row that contains the cell reference for "Rate" the number 0.1 appears, which indicates that the numerical value for the rate of return used

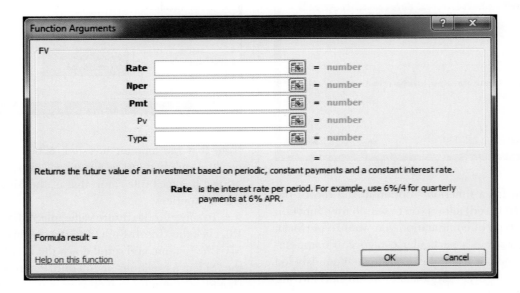

To solve our problem, refer to the appropriate cells in the spreadsheet that contain the requested values. You should insert **B2** in the first row of the dialog box (Rate), **B1** in the second row (Nper), **B4** in the third row (Pmt), **B3** in the fourth row (Pv), and **B5** in the last row so that the dialog box looks like the one below.

in the computation of the future value is 10 percent. When enough information is entered in the "Functions Arguments" box, the result of the computation appears at the bottom left portion of the box (circled in red).

Once the locations of all the appropriate values are entered in the dialog box, click "OK," and the result of

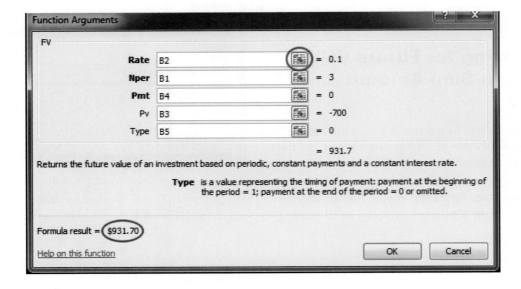

the computation will appear in cell **B6** in the spreadsheet. The spreadsheet now appears as follows:

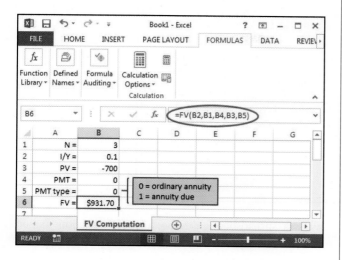

The future value amount computed here, $931.70, is the same result as found in the previous section. If you place the cursor in cell **B6** and press the F2 key, you will see the contents of the cell, which is "= FV(B2,B1,B4,B3,B5)." This relationship is also shown in the formula bar located above the letters that identify the columns (circled in red).

FV of an Annuity. To solve for the future value of an annuity, we use the same financial function discussed in the previous section—"FV". For example, in Chapter 4, we computed the future value of a three-year $400 annuity with an opportunity cost equal to 5 percent. Using the same spreadsheet setup shown earlier, change the values so that N = 3, I/Y = 0.05, PV = 0, and PMT = −400. You will see that the value for FV changes so that it is equal to $1,261.00, which is the same result as found in Chapter 4: that is, FVA = $1,261.00.

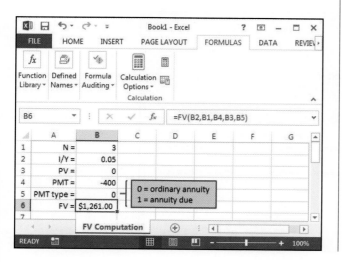

The result given here is the future value of an ordinary annuity. To find the future value of an annuity due, we must "flip a switch," just as we did on the financial calculator, to indicate that the computation should be for an annuity due rather than for an ordinary annuity. In our spreadsheet setup, we simply need to input a 1 rather than a 0 in cell **B5** when the situation calls for an annuity due. If you input a 1 in cell **B5** in the existing spreadsheet, you should see the answer in cell **B6** change to $1,324.05, which is the same answer shown in Chapter 4: that is, FVA(DUE) = $1,324.05.

A-2b Solving for Present Value (PV): Lump-Sum Amount and Annuity

To find the PV using a spreadsheet, follow the same steps as described to solve for FV, except use the "PV" financial function. The menus are the same as in the previous section, except the value for the future value (labeled "Fv" in the menu) is a required input rather than the present value (labeled "Pv" in the "FV" function). For example, if you want to determine the present value of $935 to be received in three years if your opportunity cost rate is 10 percent, the spreadsheet setup is as follows:

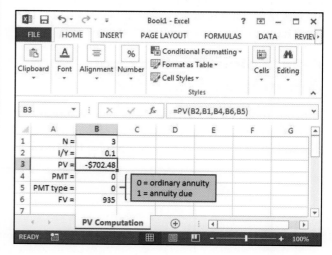

And, the PV "Function Arguments" window will be:

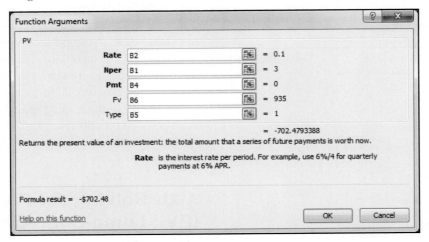

The result is the same as in Chapter 4: $702.48.

To compute the present value of an annuity using the "PV" function, simply enter the known values in the appropriate cells on the spreadsheet, and you will see the result appear in cell **B3**. For example, if you want to determine the present value of $400 to be received at the end of the next three years assuming an opportunity cost rate equal to 5 percent, you should input 3 in cell **B1**, 0.05 in cell **B2**, 400 in cell **B4**, 0 in cell **B5** (this is an ordinary annuity), and 0 in **B6**. The result of the computation, −$1,089.30, will appear in cell **B3**. If you input a 1 in cell **B5** to change the annuity from an ordinary annuity to an annuity due, you should see −$1,143.76 in **B3**. These are the same results as in Chapter 4.

A-2c Solving for r: Lump-Sum Amount and Annuity

Suppose you want to determine the rate of return that would be earned if you purchase an investment for $78.35 that will pay $100 after five years. To solve this problem using a spreadsheet, use the financial function named "RATE." The spreadsheet might be set up as follows:

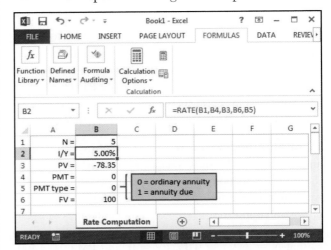

Once the appropriate cell locations are entered, the "Function Arguments" menu for the "RATE" function should be as follows:

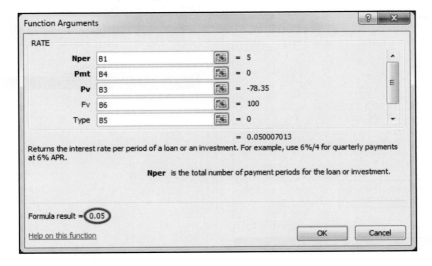

As you can see, the result of the computation is 5 percent (circled in red), which appears in cell **B2** when you press "OK." You would use the same financial function to find the interest rate, r, for an annuity.

A-2d Solving for n: Lump-Sum Amount and Annuity

Suppose you want to determine how many years it will take $68.30 invested today to grow to $100 if the interest rate is 10 percent. To solve this problem with a spreadsheet, use the financial function named "NPER." The spreadsheet might be set up as follows:

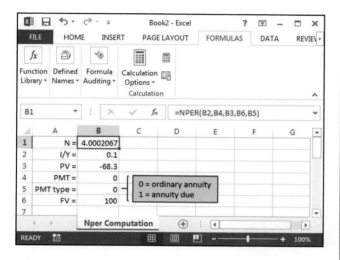

Once the appropriate cell locations are entered, the "Function Arguments" box for the "NPER" function is as follows:

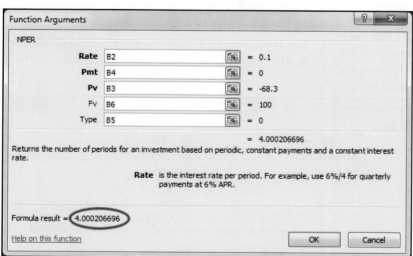

As you can see, the result of the computation is four years, which will appear in cell **B1** when you press "OK." You can use the same function to solve for n, the number of periods, for an annuity.

A-2e Solving for Present Value and Future Value: Uneven Cash Flows

To solve for the PV of an uneven cash flow stream, use the financial function named "NPV." Take care, however, to ensure that you understand what this spreadsheet function actually computes. The computation of NPV as presented in Chapter 9 represents the net present value of a series of cash flows that includes the *initial amount* invested in Period 0 *and* the *future cash flows* that the investment is expected to generate during its life. In the Excel spreadsheet, however, the financial function named "NPV" computes the present value of the *future cash flows only*. The current investment (in Period 0) should not be included when using the spreadsheet's "NPV" function, because this Excel function assumes that the cash flows in the computation are in sequential order beginning with the first *future* cash flow—that is, the order of the cash flows is CF_1, CF_2, ..., CF_n. If you want to compute the NPV as discussed in Chapter 9, use the Excel function named "NPV" to compute the present value of CF_1, CF_2, ..., CF_n and then simply add the negative initial investment outlay, CF_0, to the spreadsheet result.

Suppose that you are considering purchasing an investment that promises to pay $400, $300, and $250 at the end of the next three years, respectively. If your opportunity cost is 5 percent, how much should you pay for the investment? To answer this question, you need to determine the present value of the series of cash flows that the investment will generate in the future.

To compute the present value of a series of uneven cash flows using a spreadsheet, we must use the "NPV" function. For the current situation, we can set up the spreadsheet as follows:

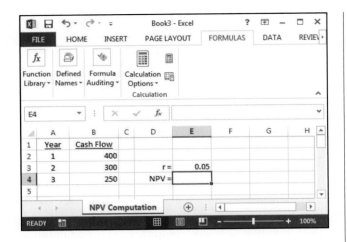

Place the cursor in cell **E4** as shown, select the "NPV" function in the financial category of the "Insert Function," and the following dialog box should appear:

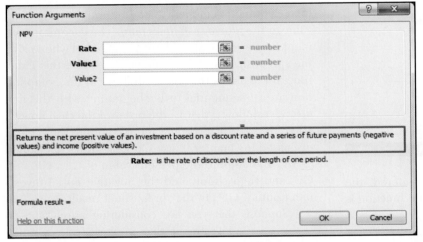

The description of this function, which we have highlighted in the red box, indicates that the result of the computation is the present value of all the *future* cash flows—both inflows and outflows—associated with the investment. Enter the appropriate cell locations that contain the cash flows for which you want to compute the present value. In the dialog box, Value1 refers to the series of cash flows. You can click the red arrow on the right side of the row labeled Value1 and use the cursor to highlight cells **B2** through **B4**. Then either enter **E3** in the box labeled "Rate" or click the red arrow on the right side of the row labeled "Rate," place the cursor in cell **E3**, and press return. Now the dialog box shows the cell locations of the needed values, and it should appear as follows:

The result of the computation, which is shown at the bottom of the dialog box, is 869.0206241 (circled in red). When you click the "OK" button, this result appears in cell **E4** of the spreadsheet. Thus, the present value of the series of cash flows in our example is $869.02, which is the same result we found in Chapter 4 using a financial calculator.

To compute the future value of the series of uneven cash flows, first compute its present value, and then compound this value to the future period at the appropriate opportunity cost. For our example, the future value is:

$$FV = \$869.02(1.05)^3 = \$1,006.00$$

This relationship can be entered into the spreadsheet so that it is automatically computed.

A-2f Setting Up an Amortization Schedule

To set up the amortization schedule using Excel, we use two financial functions—IPMT and PPMT. IPMT provides the interest payment for a particular period, given the amount borrowed and the interest rate. PPMT provides the principal repayment for a particular period, given the amount borrowed and the interest rate. The following spreadsheet shows the content required in each cell to construct an amortization schedule for a $15,000 loan that is repaid in three equal payments at the end of each of the next three years. The bank charges 8 percent interest, compounded annually. This is the amortized loan described in Chapter 4.

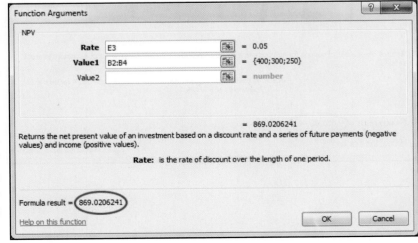

Note that the $ sign is used when referring to cells in the equations to fix the locations of common values that are required for each computation. Fixing the cell locations allows you to use the copy command to copy the relationships from row 9 to rows 10 and 11.

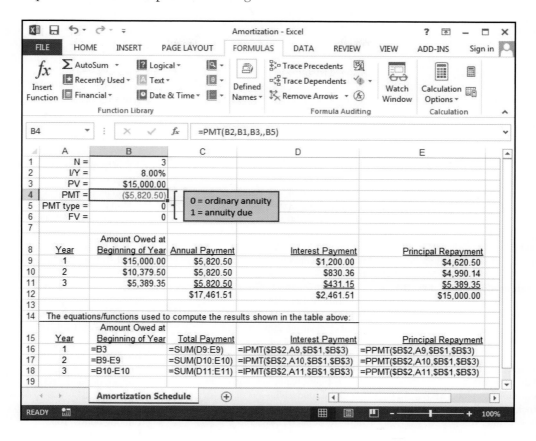

INDEX

A

Abnormal returns, defined, 45
Abnormal yield curve, 91
Acceleration of receipts, 290–291
Accounting
  balance sheet and, 24
  for financing feedbacks, 310–312
  importance of finance in, 5
  in international setting, 39
  ratio analysis and, 38
Accounting income, cash flow vs., 184–185
Accounting profits, 27
Accounts payable (trade credit), 273
  computing costs of, 276
Accruals, 273
Additional funds needed (AFN), 309, 310
Add-on interest, 278
After-tax cost of debt, 207–208
Agency problem, 12
Agency relationship, 11
Agent, 11
Aggressive approach, 272–273
Aging schedule, 293–294
American depository receipts (ADRs), 126
American Stock Exchange (AMEX), 50
Amortization schedule, 78
Amortized loans, 78–79
Annual compounding, 75
Annual percentage rate (APR), 75–78, 276
Annual report, 21
Annuity, 64. *See also* Ordinary annuity
Annuity due, 64
  future value of, 67–68
  present value of, 71
Archipelago Exchange (ArcaEX), 50
Asked price, 49
Asset account, 28
Asset management ratios, 32–33
Assets
  on balance sheet, 22
  cash and equivalents *vs.* other, 24
  claim against, 30
  current, 30, 272–273
  liquid, 30
  lumpy, 313
  priority to, 104
  replacement analysis, 190–194
  short-term (*See* Short-term assets, management of)
  stand-alone risk for, 194–197
  valuation of, 165–169
Asymmetric information, 242–243
Australian Securities Exchange, 48
Availability delay, 290
Average collection period (ACP), 33, 293

Average payoff, 142
Average-risk stock, 150
Average yield, 95
Aversion, risk, 144–145, 154–155

B

Balance sheet, 22–25
  defined, 22
  effects of stock splits and stock dividends, 259–260
  forecasting, 309–310
  projected (pro forma), 308–312
  sample format, 22
Banker's acceptance, 104
Bank loans
  computing cost of, 276–278
Bankruptcy, 124, 244
Banks/banking
  check clearing, 290
  commercial, 55
  concentration, 291
  credit union, 55
  investment banks, 44–45, 51–53
  mutual funds, 55
  thrift institutions, 55
Base (most likely) case, 196
Basel III Accord, 58
Beecham, 16
Benchmarking, 36
Best-case scenario, 196
Best-efforts arrangement, 51–52
Beta coefficient, 150–152, 155
Beta (market) risk, 198–199, 227
Bid price, 49
Blanket lien, 275
Bond indenture, 107
Bonds, 103–119
  Bulldog, 109
  contract features, 107–108
  convertible, 108
  corporate, 106
  defined, 105
  floating-rate, 107
  general obligation, 106
  government, 106
  income, 107
  indexed, 107
  interest rates and, 114–119
  international, 56
  junk, 107
  as long-term debt, 105–107
  long-term *vs.* short-term, 117
  mortgage, 106
  municipal, 106
  original issue discount, 107

  prices of, 118–119
  purchasing power, 107
  putable, 107
  ratings, 109–110
  revenue, 106
  Samurai, 109
  second-mortgage, 106
  time path of, 116
  treasury, 106
  valuation of, 111–114
  Yankee, 109
  yield to call, 113–114
  yield to maturity, 112–113
  zero coupon, 107
Bond-yield-plus-risk-premium approach, 211
Book values, *vs.* market values, 25
Borrowed (principal) amount, required amount *vs.*, 279–280
Boston Stock Exchange, 50
Brazil, 56
Break point (BP), 216
Brokers, 49
Budget, defined, 163
Budgeting, 314–323. *See also* Capital budgeting; Cash budgets
Bulldog bonds, 109
Business ethics, 12–13
Business goals, 9–13
Business organization, forms of, 5, 14–17
  corporation, 7
  limited liability company, 8
  limited liability partnership, 7–8
  partnership, 6–7
  proprietorship, 6
  S corporation, 8
Business risk, 227–228
Bylaws, corporate, 7

C

Callable bonds, 113
Call option, 46
Call premium, 108, 124
Call price, 113
Call protection, 108
Call provision, 107–108, 124
Canada, 15, 57, 243
Capital, 207
  alternative sources of, 257
  cost of (*See* Cost of capital)
  defined, 163
  raising, 51–53
Capital asset pricing model (CAPM), 152–155, 210, 211

To help you study, we have provided a review card for each chapter.

LEARNING OUTCOMES

LO.1

Explain what finance entails and why everyone should have an understanding of basic financial concepts.

- Finance is basically the study of money, both cash inflows and cash outflow[s] deal with ho[w] used by busi[ness] and individua[ls]

In this column, you'll find summary points often supported by key exhibits from the chapters.

- To make sound financial decisions you must understand three general, yet reasonable, concepts. Everything else equal, (1) more value is preferred to less; (2) the sooner cash is received, the more valuable it is; and (3) less-risky assets are more valuable than (preferred to) riskier assets.

- Everyone should have a basic understanding of finance because everyone is affected by finance both in their careers and their personal lives. Finance concepts are used

How to Use This Card:

How to use the card:

1. Look over the card to preview new concepts you will find in this chapter.

2. Read the chapter to fully understand the material.

3. Go to class (and pay attention)!

4. Review the card again to be sure you've registered the key concepts.

5. This card is only one of many CFIN learning tools available to help you succeed in the course. Check out CFIN online at cengagebrain.com for more tools.

[LO...]

Id[...] bu[...] w[...] di[...]

include: (1) easy to form, (2) subject to few government regulations, and (3) taxed like individuals. Dis-advantages include: (1) owners have unlimited personal liability for

the firm's debts, (2) the business has a limited life, (3) transferring ownership is similar to selling a house, and (4) raising large amounts of funds is difficult.

- Advantages to forming a business as a corporation include: (1) [o]wners have limited liability for [t]he firm's debts; (2) ownership is [e]asily transferred through stock [tr]ansactions; (3) the business has an unlimited life; and (4) raising large amounts of funds is easier than for partnerships, because corporations can issue stocks and bonds, whereas partnerships cannot. Disadvantages include: (1) setting up a corporation is more complex than setting up other forms of business, and (2) earnings paid to stockholders as dividends are taxed twice.

LO.3

Identify major goals that firms [pu]rsue and what a firm's [pri]mary goal should be.

- [F]irms pursue a variety of goals, [i]ncluding those that benefit [e]mployees, customers, and the [l]ocal community.

- [T]he primary goal of the firm should [b]e maximization of shareholders' [w]ealth, which is carrie[d] [out by] maximizing the value [of ...] that is, maximizing th[e] [f]irm's stock.

When it's time to prepare for an exam, use the card and the technique to the left to improve study sessions.

- Managers are encouraged to act in the best interests of shareholders through (1) compensation plans that reward them for pursuing the correct goal; (2) intervention by shareholders to correct conflicts of interest; and (3) threat of a

takeover, which probably would put top managers out of work.

LO.4

Explain the roles ethics and good governance play in successful businesses.

- Ethics refers to the standards of conduct that management follows when making business decisions. Firms that "behave" unethically have discovered they do not succeed in business, no matter how large they are.

- Corporate governance refers to the set of "rules" that a firm follows when conducting business. It is important for a firm to practice good corporate governance when dealing with its stakeholders because studies show that firms that practice good corporate governance generate higher returns for owners.

LO.5

Describe how foreign firms differ from U.S. firms and identify factors that affect financial decisions in multinational firms.

- Foreign firms are generally more [...]the U.S. firms of similar [...]ve fewer [... owne]rs, than U.S. [firms of the same size.]

- Some factors that affect multinational firms that typically do not affect purely domestic firms include differences in currencies, languages, cultures, government structures, and politics.

CHAPTER REVIEW 1

CHAPTER 1 KEY MANAGERIAL FINANCE CONCEPTS

- Financial decisions deal with cash flows, both inflows and outflows. To make sound financial decisions, students must understand three general, yet reasonable, concepts. Everything else equal, (1) more value is preferred to less; (2) the sooner cash is received, the more valuable it is; and (3) less risky assets are more valuable than (preferred to) riskier assets.

- The primary goal of the financial manager should be to maximize the value of the firm.

- The managers of a firm are the decision-making agents of its owners (stockholders in a corporation). When managers do not make decisions that are in the best interests of the owners, agency problems exist. Agency problems can be mitigated by rewarding managers for making decisions that help maximize the firm's value.

- Firms that are ethical and have good governance policies generally perform better than firms that are less ethical and have poor governance policies.

- Firms "go international" for a variety of reasons, including to operate in new markets, to search for raw materials, to attain production efficiency, and to avoid domestic regulations.

- Foreign firms generally are less open—that is, have fewer owners (stockholders)—than similar-sized U.S. firms.

KEY TERMS

> Here you'll find key terms from the chapter with page references for review.

proprietorship An unincorporated business owned by one individual. *p. 5*

partnership An unincorporated business owned by two or more persons. *p. 6*

corporation A legal entity created by a state, separate and distinct from its owners and managers, having unlimited life, easy transferability of ownership, and limited liability. *p. 6*

corporate charter A document filed with the secretary of the state in which a business is incorporated that provides information about the company, including its name, address, directors, and amount of capital stock. *p. 7*

bylaws A set of rules drawn up by the founders of the corporation that indicates how the company is to be governed; includes procedures for electing directors, rights of stockholders, and how to change the bylaws when necessary. *p. 7*

limited liability partnership (LLP) A partnership wherein at least one partner is designated as a *general partner* with unlimited personal financial liability, and the other partners are *limited partners* whose liability is limited to amounts they invest in the firm. *p. 7*

limited liability company (LLC) Offers the limited personal liability associated with a corporation; however, the company's income is taxed like that of a partnership. *p. 8*

S corporation A corporation with no more than 100 stockholders that elects to be taxed in the same manner as proprietorships and partnerships, so that business income is only taxed once. *p. 8*

stockholder wealth maximization The appropriate goal for management decisions; considers the risk and timing associated with expected cash flows to maximize the price of the firm's common stock. *p. 9*

value The present, or current, value of the cash flows that an asset is expected to generate in the future. *p. 10*

agency problem A potential conflict of interest between outside shareholders (owners) and managers who make decisions about how to operate the firm. *p. 11*

hostile takeover The acquisition of a company over the opposition of its management. *p. 12*

business ethics A company's attitude and conduct toward its stakeholders (employees, customers, stockholders, and community). Ethical behavior requires fair and honest treatment of all parties. *p. 13*

corporate governance Deals with the set of rules that a firm follows when conducting business; these rules identify who is accountable for major financial decisions. *p. 14*

stakeholders Those who are associated with a business, including managers, employees, customers, suppliers, creditors, stockholders, and other parties with an interest in the firm's well-being. *p. 14*

proxy votes Voting power that is assigned to another party, such as another stockholder or institution. *p. 14*

industrial groups Organizations of companies in different industries with common ownership interests, which include firms necessary to manufacture and sell products; networks of manufacturers, suppliers, marketing organizations, distributors, retailers, and creditors. *p. 15*

multinational companies Firms that operate in two or more countries. *p. 15*

exchange rates The prices at which the currency of one country can be converted into the currencies of other countries. *p. 16*

To access additional study tools, please visit CFIN Online at www.cengagebrain.com.

CHAPTER REVIEW 1

An Overview of Managerial Finance

LEARNING OUTCOMES

LO.1

Explain what finance entails and why everyone should have an understanding of basic financial concepts.

- Finance is basically the study of money, both cash inflows and cash outflows. Finance decisions deal with how money is raised and used by businesses, governments, and individuals.
- To make sound financial decisions you must understand three general, yet reasonable, concepts. Everything else equal, (1) more value is preferred to less; (2) the sooner cash is received, the more valuable it is; and (3) less-risky assets are more valuable than (preferred to) riskier assets.
- Everyone should have a basic understanding of finance because everyone is affected by finance both in their careers and their personal lives. Finance concepts are used when financing a car or a house, in retirement decisions, and so forth.

LO.2

Identify different forms of business organization as well as the advantages and disadvantages of each.

- The three basic forms of business are: proprietorship, partnership, and corporation.
- Advantages to forming a business as a proprietorship or a partnership include: (1) easy to form, (2) subject to few government regulations, and (3) taxed like individuals. Disadvantages include: (1) owners have unlimited personal liability for

the firm's debts, (2) the business has a limited life, (3) transferring ownership is similar to selling a house, and (4) raising large amounts of funds is difficult.
- Advantages to forming a business as a corporation include: (1) owners have limited liability for the firm's debts; (2) ownership is easily transferred through stock transactions; (3) the business has an unlimited life; and (4) raising large amounts of funds is easier than for partnerships, because corporations can issue stocks and bonds, whereas partnerships cannot. Disadvantages include: (1) setting up a corporation is more complex than setting up other forms of business, and (2) earnings paid to stockholders as dividends are taxed twice.

LO.3

Identify major goals that firms pursue and what a firm's primary goal should be.

- Firms pursue a variety of goals, including those that benefit employees, customers, and the local community.
- The primary goal of the firm should be maximization of shareholders' wealth, which is carried out by maximizing the value of the firm—that is, maximizing the value of the firm's stock.
- Managers are encouraged to act in the best interests of shareholders through (1) compensation plans that reward them for pursuing the correct goal; (2) intervention by shareholders to correct conflicts of interest; and (3) threat of a

takeover, which probably would put top managers out of work.

LO.4

Explain the roles ethics and good governance play in successful businesses.

- Ethics refers to the standards of conduct that management follows when making business decisions. Firms that "behave" unethically have discovered they do not succeed in business, no matter how large they are.
- Corporate governance refers to the set of "rules" that a firm follows when conducting business. It is important for a firm to practice good corporate governance when dealing with its stakeholders because studies show that firms that practice good corporate governance generate higher returns for owners.

LO.5

Describe how foreign firms differ from U.S. firms and identify factors that affect financial decisions in multinational firms.

- Foreign firms are generally more closed than U.S. firms of similar sizes—that is, they have fewer stockholders, or owners, than U.S. firms of the same size.
- Some factors that affect multinational firms that typically do not affect purely domestic firms include differences in currencies, languages, cultures, government structures, and politics.

CHAPTER REVIEW 1

CHAPTER 1 KEY MANAGERIAL FINANCE CONCEPTS

- Financial decisions deal with cash flows, both inflows and outflows. To make sound financial decisions, students must understand three general, yet reasonable, concepts. Everything else equal, (1) more value is preferred to less; (2) the sooner cash is received, the more valuable it is; and (3) less risky assets are more valuable than (preferred to) riskier assets.

- The primary goal of the financial manager should be to maximize the value of the firm.

- The managers of a firm are the decision-making agents of its owners (stockholders in a corporation). When managers do not make decisions that are in the best interests of the owners, agency problems exist. Agency problems can be mitigated by rewarding managers for making decisions that help maximize the firm's value.

- Firms that are ethical and have good governance policies generally perform better than firms that are less ethical and have poor governance policies.

- Firms "go international" for a variety of reasons, including to operate in new markets, to search for raw materials, to attain production efficiency, and to avoid domestic regulations.

- Foreign firms generally are less open—that is, have fewer owners (stockholders)—than similar-sized U.S. firms.

KEY TERMS

proprietorship An unincorporated business owned by one individual. *p. 6*

partnership An unincorporated business owned by two or more persons. *p. 6*

corporation A legal entity created by a state, separate and distinct from its owners and managers, having unlimited life, easy transferability of ownership, and limited liability. *p. 7*

corporate charter A document filed with the secretary of the state in which a business is incorporated that provides information about the company, including its name, address, directors, and amount of capital stock. *p. 7*

bylaws A set of rules drawn up by the founders of the corporation that indicates how the company is to be governed; includes procedures for electing directors, rights of stockholders, and how to change the bylaws when necessary. *p. 7*

limited liability partnership (LLP) A partnership wherein at least one partner is designated as a *general partner* with unlimited personal financial liability, and the other partners are *limited partners* whose liability is limited to amounts they invest in the firm. *p. 8*

limited liability company (LLC) Offers the limited personal liability associated with a corporation; however, the company's income is taxed like that of a partnership. *p. 8*

S corporation A corporation with no more than 100 stockholders that elects to be taxed in the same manner as proprietorships and partnerships, so that business income is only taxed once. *p. 8*

stockholder wealth maximization The appropriate goal for management decisions; considers the risk and timing associated with expected cash flows to maximize the price of the firm's common stock. *p. 9*

value The present, or current, value of the cash flows that an asset is expected to generate in the future. *p. 11*

agency problem A potential conflict of interest between outside shareholders (owners) and managers who make decisions about how to operate the firm. *p. 12*

hostile takeover The acquisition of a company over the opposition of its management. *p. 12*

business ethics A company's attitude and conduct toward its stakeholders (employees, customers, stockholders, and community). Ethical behavior requires fair and honest treatment of all parties. *p. 13*

corporate governance Deals with the set of rules that a firm follows when conducting business; these rules identify who is accountable for major financial decisions. *p. 14*

stakeholders Those who are associated with a business, including managers, employees, customers, suppliers, creditors, stockholders, and other parties with an interest in the firm's well-being. *p. 14*

proxy votes Voting power that is assigned to another party, such as another stockholder or institution. *p. 15*

industrial groups Organizations of companies in different industries with common ownership interests, which include firms necessary to manufacture and sell products; networks of manufacturers, suppliers, marketing organizations, distributors, retailers, and creditors. *p. 15*

multinational companies Firms that operate in two or more countries. *p. 16*

exchange rates The prices at which the currency of one country can be converted into the currencies of other countries. *p. 17*

To access additional study tools, please visit CFIN Online at www.cengagebrain.com.

CHAPTER REVIEW 2
Analysis of Financial Statements

LEARNING OUTCOMES

LO.1

Describe the basic financial information that is produced by corporations and explain how the firm's stakeholders use such information.

- A corporation must provide stockholders with a report on its operations each year. This annual report generally includes (1) a discussion of the operations and (2) basic financial statements. Stakeholders—stockholders, bondholders, and others—use information provided by the firm to form opinions and make decisions about the future success of its operations.

LO.2

Describe the financial statements that corporations publish and the information that each statement provides.

- The financial statements that are published by a firm include (1) the balance sheet, which gives a picture, as of a specific date, of the firm's assets and how the assets are financed (liabilities and equity); (2) the income statement, which shows the results of operations by summarizing the revenues that the firm generates and the expenses that it incurs over a particular time period; (3) the statement of cash flows, which shows the firm's financing activities (sources of funds) and investment activities (uses of funds) during a specified period; and (4) the statement of retained earnings, which provides information about the changes in the common equity accounts between balance sheet dates, including the effects of the firm's operations on retained earnings.

LO.3

Describe how ratio analysis should be conducted and why the results of such an analysis are important to both managers and investors.

- Financial statement analysis (ratio analysis) generally consists of an examination and interpretation of various ratios to forecast the *future* financial position of a firm. Ratios that should be evaluated can be classified in one of five categories: (1) liquidity ratios, which give an indication as to how well the firm can meet its current obligations; (2) asset management ratios, which show how efficiently the firm utilizes its assets (investments) to generate revenues; (3) debt management ratios, which give an indication of how well the firm is servicing its current debt and whether the firm can take on more debt; (4) profitability ratios, which show the combined effects of liquidity management, asset management, and debt management on operating results; and (5) market value ratios, which give an indication of what stockholders think of the firm's future prospects.
- Two general types of analyses should be completed when examining ratios: (1) comparative analysis, which is a comparison of how the firm's current financial position compares to that of its peers (or some benchmark); and (2) trend analysis, which is an examination of the firm's financial position during the most recent three to five years to determine whether its financial position is likely to improve or deteriorate in the future.

LO.4

Discuss potential problems (caveats) associated with financial statement analysis.

- Some potential problems that are associated with ratio analysis include: (1) many large firms operate a number of divisions in very different industries, which makes it difficult to develop a meaningful set of industry averages for comparative purposes; (2) most firms want to be better than average, so merely attaining average performance is not necessarily good; (3) because many values on a balance sheet are historical, inflation might distort the figures; (4) seasonal factors can distort a ratio analysis; (5) firms can employ "window dressing" to make their financial statements look stronger than they really are; (6) use of different accounting practices can distort comparisons among firms; (7) at times it is difficult to generalize about whether a particular ratio is "good" or "bad"; and (8) a firm might have some ratios that look "good" and others that look "bad," making it difficult to tell whether the company is, on balance, strong or weak.

CHAPTER REVIEW 2

CHAPTER 2 KEY FINANCIAL STATEMENT ANALYSIS CONCEPTS

- The information provided in financial reports is used by the firm's managers, its creditors and stockholders, potential creditors and stockholders, and other stakeholders and interested parties.
- If a financial analyst were permitted to use only one of the financial statements mentioned in this chapter, he or she probably would choose the statement of cash flows because it provides information about how a firm generated funds during the year and how those funds were used.
- Although ratio analysis is used to determine the current financial position of a firm, it is primarily used to indicate the direction the firm's operations are headed in the future.
- When evaluating the financial position of a firm, an analyst must be aware that different accounting techniques exist to measure the same event, that the firm might use techniques to "dress up" its financial statements, that the effects of inflation can distort values from different time periods, and so forth. Probably the most important ingredient in financial statement analysis is the judgment the analyst uses when interpreting the results.

KEY TERMS

annual report A report issued by a corporation to its stockholders that contains basic financial statements, as well as the opinions of management about the past year's operations and the firm's future prospects. *p. 21*

balance sheet A statement that shows the firm's financial position—assets and liabilities and equity—at a specific point in time. *p. 22*

stockholders' equity (net worth) The funds provided by common stockholders—common stock, paid-in capital, and retained earnings. *p. 23*

common size balance sheet Dollar amounts on the balance sheet are stated as a percent of total assets. *p. 24*

retained earnings The portion of the firm's earnings that have been reinvested in the firm rather than paid out as dividends. *p. 24*

book values Amounts reported in financial statements—accounting numbers. *p. 25*

market values Values of items—such as assets, liabilities, and equities—in the marketplace outside the firm. *p. 25*

income statement A statement summarizing the firm's revenues and expenses over an accounting period, generally a quarter or a year. *p. 25*

operating cash flows Those cash flows that arise from normal operations; the difference between cash collections and cash expenses associated with the manufacture and sale of inventory. *p. 27*

accounting profits A firm's net income as reported on its income statement. *p. 27*

statement of cash flows A statement that reports the effects of a firm's operating, investing, and financing activities on cash flows over an accounting period. *p. 27*

statement of retained earnings A statement reporting the change in the firm's retained earnings as a result of the income generated and retained during the year. The balance sheet figure for retained earnings is the sum of the earnings retained for each year that the firm has been in business. *p. 29*

liquid asset An asset that can be easily converted into cash without significant loss of the amount originally invested. *p. 30*

liquidity ratios Ratios that show the relationship of a firm's cash and other current assets to its current liabilities; they provide an indication of the firm's ability to meet its current obligations. *p. 32*

asset management ratios A set of ratios that measure how effectively a firm is managing its assets. *p. 32*

financial leverage The use of debt financing. *p. 34*

debt management ratios Ratios that provide an indication of how much debt the firm has and whether the firm can take on more debt. *p. 34*

profitability ratios A group of ratios showing the effect of liquidity, asset management, and debt management on operating results. *p. 35*

market value ratios A set of ratios that relate the firm's stock price to its earnings and book value per share. *p. 35*

comparative ratio analysis An analysis based on a comparison of a firm's ratios with those of other firms in the same industry at the same point in time. *p. 36*

trend analysis An evaluation of changes (trends) in a firm's financial position over a period of time, perhaps years. *p. 36*

window-dressing techniques Techniques employed by firms to make their financial statements look better than they actually are. *p. 38*

To access additional study tools, please visit CFIN Online at www.cengagebrain.com.

LEARNING OUTCOMES

LO.1

Describe the role that financial markets play in improving the standard of living in an economy.

- Financial markets facilitate the transfer of funds from savers (investors) to borrowers. Financial markets that provide an efficient flow of funds provide lower interest rates to borrowers than do inefficient financial markets. At the same time, efficient markets provide good returns (interest rates) to investors who supply the funds that borrowers use. The more efficient the process of the flow of funds, the more productive the economy is in terms of both manufacturing and financing. As a result, financial markets help improve the standard of living in an economy by providing opportunities to borrow and invest at good rates, which provides businesses with opportunities to be more productive than they could be without financial markets. Greater productivity provides more employment and higher salaries than would otherwise exist.

LO.2

Describe how various financial markets are differentiated.

- Some of the categories into which financial markets are classified include:
  - Money markets versus capital markets—short-term investments (initial maturities of one year or less) are traded in the money markets, whereas long-term investments are traded in the capital markets.
  - Debt markets versus equity markets—loans are traded in the debt markets and stocks are traded in the equity markets.
  - Primary versus secondary markets—firms issue new securities in the primary markets to raise funds, whereas already issued, outstanding securities are traded among investors in the secondary markets.
  - Derivatives markets—securities, such as options and futures, that "derive" their values from other assets are traded in the financial markets.

LO.3

Discuss the role that an investment banking house plays in the financial markets.

- Investment banking houses are companies that specialize in assisting corporations when they issue stocks and bonds to raise funds.

- Investment bankers help companies determine how and when to raise funds. The investment banking house generally buys the issue from the company and then resells the securities to investors in the financial markets.

LO.4

Describe the role that financial intermediaries play in the financial markets, and explain why there are so many different types of intermediaries.

- Financial intermediaries are organizations that facilitate the transfer of funds from savers to borrowers. Intermediaries "manufacture" financial products, such as savings accounts, money market funds, and pension funds to attract money that is then loaned to individuals and businesses in the form of debt instruments such as automobile loans, commercial loans, mortgages, and similar types of debt.

- There are many different types of intermediaries, including commercial banks, credit unions, mutual funds, and so forth; each was formed to meet a particular need of borrowers, investors, or both. For example, commercial banks generally provide services used by businesses.

LO.5

Describe how financial markets and financial intermediaries in the United States differ from those in other parts of the world.

- Financial markets and intermediaries have become much more globalized during the past few decades. Most U.S. financial markets and institutions are more heavily regulated than their foreign counterparts. As a result, the largest financial intermediaries in the world generally reside outside the United States.

CHAPTER REVIEW 3

CHAPTER 3 KEY FINANCIAL ENVIRONMENT CONCEPTS

- Financial markets represent the system, or mechanism, by which borrowers and lenders are brought together.

- Financial markets permit companies and individuals to "move" income from one time period to another—income is moved from future periods to the current period through borrowing, whereas income is moved from the present period to future periods through investing (saving).

- Corporations generally use the services of investment banking houses when raising funds through issues of stocks and bonds. Investment bankers provide advice and help firms issue securities to raise needed funds.

- Financial intermediaries, which include banks, credit unions, pension funds, and so forth, are important "players" in the financial markets. Such intermediaries generally take deposits and create loans (perhaps through investments) that are needed by individuals and businesses. If financial intermediaries did not exist, our standard of living would be much lower because bringing together borrowers and lenders would be more difficult and more costly than is possible when such markets exist.

- Even though foreign financial markets have increased their prominence during the past couple of decades, U.S. financial markets continue to dominate financial markets around the world.

KEY TERMS

financial markets A system consisting of individuals and institutions, instruments, and procedures that bring together borrowers and savers. *p. 43*

economic efficiency Funds are allocated to their optimal use at the lowest costs in the financial markets. *p. 45*

informational efficiency The degree to which prices of investments reflect existing information and how quickly they adjust when new information enters the markets. *p. 45*

abnormal return Return that exceeds what is justified by the risk associated with the investment. *p. 45*

money markets The segments of the financial markets where the instruments that are traded have original maturities equal to one year or less. *p. 46*

capital markets The segments of the financial markets where the instruments that are traded have maturities greater than one year. *p. 46*

debt markets Financial markets where loans are traded. *p. 46*

equity markets Financial markets where corporate stocks are traded. *p. 46*

primary markets Markets in which various organizations raise funds by issuing new securities. *p. 46*

secondary markets Markets where financial assets that have previously been issued by various organizations are traded among investors. *p. 46*

derivatives markets Financial markets where options and futures are traded. *p. 46*

initial public offering (IPO) market Market consisting of stocks of privately held companies that have recently gone public for the first time. *p. 47*

physical stock exchanges Formal organizations with physical locations that facilitate trading in designated ("listed") securities. The major U.S. stock exchange is the New York Stock Exchange (NYSE). *p. 47*

listing requirements Characteristics a firm must possess to be listed on a stock exchange. *p. 48*

over-the-counter (OTC) market A collection of brokers and dealers, connected electronically by telephones and computers, that provide for trading in securities not listed on the physical stock exchanges. *p. 49*

Securities and Exchange Commission (SEC) The U.S. government agency that regulates the issuance and trading of stocks and bonds. *p. 49*

dual listing When stocks are listed for trading in more than one stock market. *p. 50*

investment banker An organization that underwrites and distributes new issues of securities; it helps businesses and other entities obtain needed financing. *p. 51*

underwritten arrangement Agreement for the sale of securities in which the investment bank guarantees the sale by purchasing the securities from the issuer, thus agreeing to bear any risks involved in selling the securities in the financial markets. *p. 52*

best-efforts arrangement Agreement for the sale of securities in which the investment bank handling the transaction gives no guarantee that the securities will be sold. *p. 52*

flotation costs The costs associated with issuing new stocks or bonds. *p. 52*

registration statement A statement of facts filed with the SEC about a company that plans to issue securities. *p. 53*

prospectus A document describing a new security issue and the issuing company. *p. 53*

underwriting syndicate A group of investment banking firms formed to spread the risk associated with the purchase and distribution of a new issue of securities. *p. 53*

shelf registration Registration of securities with the SEC for sale at a later date. The securities are held "on the shelf" until the sale. *p. 53*

financial intermediaries Organizations that create various loans and investments from funds provided by depositors. *p. 54*

To access additional study tools, please visit CFIN Online at www.cengagebrain.com.

CHAPTER REVIEW **4**

Time Value of Money (TVM)

LEARNING OUTCOMES

LO.1

Identify various types of cash flow patterns (streams).

- Cash flows can take the form of (a) lump-sum, or single payment, amounts; (b) annuities, which represent equal payments over equal time periods; or (c) uneven cash flows, which represent different dollar amounts over multiple periods.

LO.2

Compute the future value of different cash flow streams. Explain the results.

- The future value (FV) and present value (PV) are computed to restate dollars from one time period into dollars at different time periods. FV is the amount to which a lump-sum investment (or a series of cash flows) will grow in the future, based on the return it earns over time. To compute the FV of a current amount, interest that can be earned during the life of the investment (or loan) is "added to" the current amount.

LO.3

Compute the present value of different cash flow streams. Explain the results.

- PV is the amount that must be invested today to accumulate a specific amount (or a series of cash flows) in the future based on the return that will be earned

during the investment period. To compute the PV of a future amount, interest that can be earned during the life of the investment (or loan) is "taken out" of the FV amount.

LO.4

Compute (a) the return (interest rate) on an investment (loan) and (b) how long it takes to reach a financial goal.

- TVM techniques can be used to determine the percentage return (r) an investment earns over time. The techniques can also be used to determine the length of time (n) it will take to reach a financial objective. Both of these pieces of information are important in financial decisions.

LO.5

Explain the difference between the annual percentage rate (APR) and the effective annual rate (EAR). Explain when it is appropriate to use each.

- APR represents an annual rate of return that does not consider the compounding of interest, whereas EAR is the return that recognizes interest compounding. Investors and borrowers should use the EAR to make financial decisions, because this figure

represents the "true" return on an investment (or loan). EAR > APR, except when interest is compounded annually.

LO.6

Describe an amortized loan. Compute (a) amortized loan payments and (b) the amount that must be paid on an amortized loan at a specific point during the life of the loan.

- An amortized loan is repaid in equal periodic payments. Each payment includes both repayment of a portion of the outstanding amount that is owed on the loan and payment of interest on the outstanding balance.

- To compute an amortized loan payment, you simply compute the annuity that you could pay yourself each period from the amount that is borrowed, assuming that you can invest the borrowed amount at the same rate as the interest charged on the loan.

- To compute the amount that is owed on an amortized loan before the last payment is made, you must "take out" any interest that is associated with the future loan payments (because you shouldn't have to pay this interest). That is, you find the present value of all remaining loan payments.

CHAPTER REVIEW 4

CHAPTER 4 KEY TVM CONCEPTS

- Before making financial decisions, dollars from different time periods must be stated in the same "time value," which means that all dollars must be valued at the same time period before they can be compared.

- An amount that is invested at a higher rate or for a longer time period will grow to a greater future amount (future value) because a greater amount of interest is earned.

- The further in the future an amount is received (paid) or the higher the opportunity cost rate, the lower the present value of the future amount—that is, the less money that must be invested today to accumulate the future amount. Based on this TVM rule, we know that, everything else equal, the current value of an investment is lower the higher the interest rate it earns in the future. This is an important financial concept that we will discuss throughout the book.

- Everything else equal, the greater the number of compounding periods per year, the greater the effective rate of return that is earned on an investment. In other words, the total dollar amount of interest that is earned on an investment is greater when interest is compounded more often during the year.

KEY TERMS

time value of money (TVM) The principles and computations used to revalue cash payoffs from different times so they are stated in dollars of the same time period. *p. 63*

opportunity cost rate The rate of return on the best available alternative investment of equal risk. *p. 64*

lump-sum amount A single payment (received or made) that occurs either today or at some date in the future. *p. 64*

annuity A series of payments of an equal amount at fixed, equal intervals for a specified number of periods. *p. 64*

ordinary annuity An annuity with payments that occur at the end of each period. *p. 64*

annuity due An annuity with payments that occur at the beginning of each period. *p. 64*

uneven cash flows Multiple payments of different amounts over a period of time. *p. 64*

future value (FV) The amount to which a cash flow or series of cash flows will grow over a given period of time when compounded at a given interest rate. *p. 64*

compounding The process of determining the value to which an amount or a series of cash flows will grow in the future when compound interest is applied. *p. 64*

payment (PMT) This term designates constant cash flows—that is, the amount of an annuity payment. *p. 68*

cash flow (CF) This term designates cash flows in general, including uneven cash flows. *p. 68*

terminal value The future value of a cash flow stream. *p. 68*

present value (PV) The value today—that is, the current value—of a future cash flow or series of cash flows. *p. 69*

discounting The process of determining the present value of a cash flow or a series of cash flows to be received (paid) in the future; the reverse of compounding. *p. 69*

perpetuities Streams of equal payments that are expected to continue forever. *p. 71*

annual compounding The process of determining the future (or present) value of a cash flow or series of cash flows when interest is paid once per year. *p. 75*

semiannual compounding The process of determining the future (or present) value of a cash flow or series of cash flows when interest is paid twice per year. *p. 75*

simple (quoted) interest rate (r_{SIMPLE}) The annual, non-compounded rate, quoted by borrowers and lenders; it is used to determine the rate earned per compounding period (periodic rate, r_{PER}). *p. 77*

annual percentage rate (APR) Another name for the simple interest rate, r_{SIMPLE}; does not consider the effect of interest compounding. *p. 77*

effective (equivalent) annual rate (r_{EAR}) The annual rate of interest actually being earned, as opposed to the quoted rate; considers the compounding of interest. *p. 77*

amortized loan A loan that requires equal payments over its life; the payments include both interest and repayment of the debt. *p. 78*

amortization schedule A schedule showing precisely how a loan will be repaid. It gives the payment required on each payment date and a breakdown of the payment, showing how much is interest and how much is repayment of principal. *p. 78*

To access additional study tools, please visit CFIN Online at www.cengagebrain.com.

CHAPTER REVIEW 5

The Cost of Money (Interest Rates)

LEARNING OUTCOMES

LO.1

Describe the cost of money and factors that affect the cost of money (interest rates).

- The cost of money, which refers to interest rates, is effectively the cost of "renting" (borrowing) funds from savers (investors). Factors that affect interest rates include production opportunities, time preference for consumption, risk, and inflation. All else equal, when there are more profitable production opportunities, greater time preference for funds, higher risk, and higher inflation expectations, interest rates are higher, and vice versa.

- Interest rates are determined by factors that affect the supply of and the demand for funds. Everything else equal, if demand increases or supply decreases, the general levels of interest rates increase.

LO.2

Describe how interest rates are determined.

- Interest rates represent the returns on investments. The return on any investment is equal to the nominal risk-free rate of return plus a premium for the risk that is associated with the investment. The nominal risk-free rate consists of the real risk-free return plus a return that compensates investors for the average rate of inflation they expect during the life of the investment. The risk premium includes an additional return that pays investors for taking the risks that are associated with the investment, which include default risk, maturity risk, and liquidity risk.

LO.3

Describe a yield curve and discuss how a yield curve might be used to forecast future interest rates.

- The yield curve shows the relationship between long-term and short-term interest rates at a particular point in time. Some experts believe that the shape of the yield curve indicates in which direction interest rates will move in the future. For instance, suppose that you think interest rates are going to increase. As an investor, should you invest your funds in long-term or short-term securities? Like other investors, you should invest short term, and wait until interest rates increase to lock up your money in long-term investments. Everything else equal, buying pressure on (demand for) short-term securities will increase prices, and thus decrease rates in the short-term markets. The opposite activity will occur in the long-term markets. As a result, when investors expect interest rates to increase, short-term interest rates should be lower than long-term rates, which will produce an upward-sloping yield curve. Such logic has been applied when using the yield curve to forecast future rates.

LO.4

Discuss how government actions and general business activity affect interest rates.

- The government affects interest rates through open market operations, its spending policies, and the balance of trade. Through open markets operations the Federal Reserve buys government securities when it wants to increase the money supply and thus decrease interest rates, and vice versa. When the government runs a deficit because it spends more money than it collects, it must borrow, which, everything else equal, increases demand for funds and thus increases interest rates. When imports are greater than exports, a trade deficit must be financed, which increases interest rates because the demand for funds in the financial markets is higher than it would be otherwise. In addition, as business activity increases in the economy, so do interest rates on loans that are used to finance those expanded activities.

LO.5

Describe how changes in interest rates (returns) affect the values of stocks and bonds.

- Higher interest rates indicate that investors demand higher returns. Everything else equal, the only way investors can earn higher returns is if they can purchase securities for lower prices. Thus, interest rates (returns) and prices are inversely related.

CHAPTER REVIEW 5

CHAPTER 5 KEY COST OF MONEY (INTEREST RATE) CONCEPTS

- The yield, or return, that is earned on an investment is comprised of two components: (1) income paid by the *issuer* of the financial asset and (2) the change in the market value of the financial asset over some time period (called capital gains).

- The cost of money (interest rates) is based on (1) the rate of return that borrowers expect to earn on their investments, (2) savers' preferences to spend income in the current period rather than delay consumption until some future period, (3) the risks associated with investments/loans, and (4) expected inflation.

- In general, the rate of return on an investment, or the interest rate on a loan, includes a minimum payment for delaying consumption until some future date, which is termed the risk-free rate of return, r_{RF}, and payment for the risk associated with the investment/loan, RP, which is termed a risk premium. Risks can include the risk that the borrower will default on the loan, the risk associated with the liquidity of the investment, and so forth.

- In most instances, long-term interest rates are greater than short-term interest rates—that is,

the yield curve is upward sloping. However, there are rare instances when the yield curve is inverted, or downward sloping, which occurs when long-term interest rates are lower than short-term interest rates. An inverted yield curve is likely to appear when the economy is in a recession.

- Everything else equal, when interest rates (returns) increase, the prices (values) of investments decrease. In other words, when investors want to receive higher returns, they lower the amount they are willing to pay for investments.

KEY TERMS

production opportunity The return available within an economy from investment in a productive (cash-generating) asset. *p. 84*

time preference for consumption The preference of a consumer for current consumption as opposed to saving for future consumption. *p. 84*

risk In a financial market context, the chance that a financial asset will not earn the return promised. *p. 84*

inflation The tendency of prices to increase over time. *p. 84*

nominal (quoted) risk-free rate, r_{RF} The rate of interest on a security that is free of all risk; r_{RF} is proxied by the T-bill rate and includes an inflation premium. *p. 87*

real risk-free rate of interest, r* The rate of interest that would exist on default-free U.S. Treasury securities if no inflation were expected. *p. 87*

inflation premium (IP) A premium investors add to the real risk-free rate of return to account for inflation that is

expected to exist during the life of an investment. *p. 88*

default risk premium (DRP) The difference between the interest rate on a U.S. Treasury bond and a corporate bond of equal maturity and marketability; compensation for the risk that a corporation will not meet its debt obligations. *p. 88*

liquidity premium (LP) A premium added to the rate on a security if the security cannot be converted to cash on short notice at a price that is close to the original cost. *p. 89*

maturity risk premium (MRP) A premium that reflects interest rate risk; bonds with longer maturities have greater interest rate risk. *p. 89*

term structure of interest rates The relationship between yields and maturities of securities. *p. 90*

yield curve A graph showing the relationship between yields and maturities of securities on a particular date. *p. 90*

normal yield curve An upward-sloping yield curve. *p. 90*

inverted (abnormal) yield curve A downward-sloping yield curve. *p. 91*

liquidity preference theory The theory that, all else being equal, lenders prefer to make short-term loans rather than long-term loans; hence, they will lend short-term funds at lower rates than they lend long-term funds. *p. 91*

expectations theory The theory that the shape of the yield curve depends on investors' expectations about future inflation rates. *p. 92*

market segmentation theory The theory that every borrower and every lender has a preferred maturity, and that the slope of the yield curve depends on the supply of and the demand for funds in the long-term market relative to the short-term market. *p. 93*

open market operations Operations in which the Federal Reserve buys or sells Treasury securities to expand or contract the U.S. money supply. *p. 95*

To access additional study tools, please visit CFIN Online at www.cengagebrain.com.

LEARNING OUTCOMES

LO.1
Describe the basic characteristics of debt and some of the different types of debt.

- Debt can have many different characteristics, which generally are outlined in the bond contract (called the indenture). Some of the characteristics include (1) the coupon rate, which specifies the annual interest that is paid; (2) the maturity date; and (3) whether the bond has a call provision, a sinking fund, or a conversion feature. In addition, there are various types of debt that are generally identified by the original term to maturity or by the issuer. Short-term debt instruments have original maturities equal to one year or less, and long-term debt instruments have original maturities greater than one year. Some of the different types of debt are government debt and corporate bonds. Different types of instruments with different characteristics exist in each of these categories.

LO.2
Discuss bond ratings and the information that they provide to investors.

- Bond ratings provide investors with an indication as to the risks that are associated with debt instruments. Risk is an important factor that investors consider when determining the rates of return that they require to purchase different debt instruments.

LO.3
Explain how bond prices are determined.

- Bond prices are based on two fundamental factors: (1) the future cash flows generated by the bonds and (2) the rates of return that investors require to purchase the bonds. The price of a bond is determined by computing the present value of the future cash flows that the bond is expected to generate during its life. A bond's cash flows include the annual interest that is paid and the repayment of the principal (maturity value).

LO.4
Explain how bond yields (market rates) are determined.

- The yield (return) on a bond is "set" by investors who participate in the financial markets. Investors determine the price at which the bond sells. The yield on the bond can be determined by computing the rate that equates the bond's current selling price with the present value of the cash flows it will generate during its life.

LO.5
Describe the relationship between bond prices and interest rates (yields), and explain why it is important for investors to understand this relationship.

- Interest rates and bond prices are inversely related. Because the cash flows that a bond generates are contractually fixed, the only way investors can earn higher returns is by paying a lower price for a bond.

- The inverse relationship between prices and rates of return exists for *all* investments. It is important that all investors understand this concept.

CHAPTER 6 KEY BONDS VALUATION CONCEPTS

- Other things held constant, the higher *the coupon rate, the higher the market price of a bond.*

- When interest rates change, the values of bonds change in an opposite direction—that is, when rates increase, bond prices decrease, and vice versa.

- Whenever the going market rate of interest, r_d, equals the coupon rate, a bond will sell at its par value; whenever r_d is greater than the coupon rate, a bond's price will fall below its par value (a discount bond); whenever r_d is less than the coupon rate, a bond's price will rise above its par value (a premium bond).

CHAPTER REVIEW 6

The market rate of interest, r_d, which represents the return that investors earn when buying and holding a bond to its maturity (called the yield to maturity, or YTM), is comprised of a return that is associated with (1) the annual interest payment, which is called the current yield, and (2) the annual change in the market value of the bond, which is called the capital gains yield.

• The market value of a bond will always approach its par value as its maturity date approaches, provided that the firm does not go bankrupt.

KEY TERMS

debt A loan to a firm, government, or individual. *p. 103*

discounted securities Securities selling for less than par value. *p. 103*

Treasury bills (T-bills) Discounted debt instruments issued by the U.S. government. *p. 104*

repurchase agreement An arrangement where one firm sells some of its financial assets to another firm with a promise to *repurchase* the securities at a later date. *p. 104*

federal funds Overnight loans from one bank to another bank. *p. 104*

banker's acceptance An instrument issued by a bank that obligates the bank to pay a specified amount at some future date. *p. 104*

commercial paper A discounted instrument that is a type of promissory note, or "legal" IOU, issued by large, financially sound firms. *p. 104*

certificate of deposit An interest-earning time deposit at a bank or other financial intermediary. *p. 105*

Eurodollar deposit A deposit in a foreign bank that is denominated in U.S. dollars. *p. 105*

money market mutual funds Pools of funds managed by investment companies that are primarily invested in short-term financial assets. *p. 105*

term loan A loan, generally obtained from a bank or insurance company, on which the borrower agrees to make a series of payments consisting of interest and principal. *p. 105*

bond A long-term debt instrument. *p. 105*

coupon rate Interest paid on a bond or other debt instrument stated as a percentage of its face (maturity) value. *p. 105*

government bonds Debt issued by a federal, state, or local government. *p. 106*

municipal bonds Bonds issued by a state or local government. *p. 106*

corporate bonds Long-term debt instruments issued by corporations. *p. 106*

mortgage bond A bond backed by tangible (real) assets. First-mortgage bonds are senior in priority to second-mortgage bonds. *p. 106*

debenture A long-term bond that is not secured by a mortgage on specific property. *p. 106*

subordinated debenture A bond which, in the event of liquidation, has a claim on assets only after the senior debt has been paid off. *p. 106*

income bond A bond that pays interest to the holder only if the interest is earned by the firm. *p. 107*

putable bond A bond that can be redeemed at the bondholder's option when certain circumstances exist. *p. 107*

indexed (purchasing-power) bond A bond that has interest payments based on an inflation index to protect the holder from loss of purchasing power. *p. 107*

floating-rate bond A bond whose interest rate fluctuates with shifts in the general level of interest rates. *p. 107*

zero coupon bond A bond that pays no annual interest but sells at a discount below par, thus providing compensation to investors in the form of capital appreciation. *p. 107*

junk bond A high-risk, high-yield bond; used to finance mergers, leveraged buyouts, and troubled companies. *p. 107*

indenture A formal agreement (contract) between the issuer of a bond and the bondholders. *p. 107*

call provision A provision in a bond contract that gives the issuer the right to redeem the bonds under specified terms prior to the normal maturity date. *p. 107*

sinking fund A required annual payment designed to amortize a bond issue. *p. 108*

conversion feature Permits bondholders to exchange their investments for a fixed number of shares of common stock. *p. 108*

foreign debt Debt sold by a foreign borrower but denominated in the currency of the country where it is sold. *p. 108*

Eurodebt Debt sold in a country other than the one in whose currency the debt is denominated. *p. 109*

LIBOR The London Interbank Offered Rate; the interest rate offered by the best London banks on deposits of other large, very creditworthy banks. *p. 109*

yield to maturity (YTM) The average rate of return earned on a bond if it is held to maturity. *p. 113*

yield to call (YTC) The average rate of return earned on a bond if it is held until the first call date, when it is called. *p. 113*

current (interest) yield The interest payment divided by the market price of the bond. *p. 115*

capital gains yield The percentage change in the market price of a bond over some period of time. *p. 115*

interest rate price risk The risk of changes in bond prices to which investors are exposed as the result of changing interest rates. *p. 116*

interest rate reinvestment risk The risk that income from a bond portfolio will vary because cash flows must be reinvested at current market rates. *p. 117*

To access additional study tools, please visit CFIN Online at www.cengagebrain.com.

LEARNING OUTCOMES

LO.1

Explain what equity is, and identify some of the features and characteristics of (a) preferred stock and (b) common stock.

- Equity in a corporation comes in two forms: (1) preferred stock and (2) common stock.

- Some of the characteristics that are associated with preferred stock include (1) fixed dividend payment, (2) no maturity, (3) cash dividends that are paid prior to distributions to common stockholders, and (4) no voting rights. Some preferred stock (1) is convertible into the firm's common stock; (2) is callable by the firm; or (3) has a sinking fund, which permits the firm to repurchase and retire a preferred issue.

- Some of the characteristics of common stock include (1) dividends that, if paid, are distributed to common stockholders after interest is paid to bondholders and preferred stock dividends are paid; (2) no maturity date; (3) voting rights, which allow common stockholders to elect the firm's board of directors; and (4) in some common stock issues, a preemptive right, which requires the firm to offer existing stockholders shares of a new stock issue before offering them to other investors.

LO.2

Describe how stock prices (values) are determined when (a) dividends grow at a constant rate and (b) dividend growth is nonconstant.

- The value of a common stock is determined by computing the present value of the cash distributions (dividends) that the firm is expected to pay during its life.

- When a firm is expected to grow at a constant rate long into the future, the value of its stock can be computed using the constant growth dividend discount model, $P_0 = [D_0(1 + g)]/(r_s - g)$.

- When a firm is expected to experience nonconstant growth in the future, to compute the value of its stock, (1) compute each dividend that grows at a nonconstant rate; (2) assume that the firm will begin to grow at a constant rate at some point in the future so that the constant growth model can be applied to determine the value of the stock at that time; (3) compute present values of the nonconstant dividends and the future stock price; and (4) sum the results.

LO.3

Describe some approaches (techniques) other than strict application of time value of money models that investors use to value stocks.

- Investors also evaluate stocks using P/E ratios and the economic value added (EVA) approach.

- The P/E ratio is an earnings multiplier that can be used to estimate a stock's current value by multiplying a benchmark, or "normal," P/E ratio by the firm's earnings per share (EPS).

- The EVA approach recognizes that to increase its value, the firm must produce earnings that are sufficient to cover the cost of the funds investors (bondholders and stockholders) provide.

LO.4

Identify factors that affect stock prices.

- Stock prices fluctuate continuously because conditions in the financial markets change. Investors react to changing market conditions by altering their expectations of (1) the risk associated with the investment, which affects the return that they require to purchase a stock, and (2) the cash distributions that the firm will make in the future, which are dependent on the firm's future growth rate(s). If investors require a return that exceeds the return they expect the firm to generate, they will not purchase the company's stock or they will sell the shares that they own. Such activity will tend to lower the price of the stock, and thus increase its expected return. The opposite reaction will occur if investors' expected return is greater than their required return.

CHAPTER 7 KEY STOCKS VALUATION CONCEPTS

- The current value of a stock is based on the stream of dividends investors expect the firm to pay during its life (generally considered to be infinite).

  - The current value of a stock is computed as the present value of the dividends the stock is expected to generate during the remainder of its life. If a company's dividends grow at a constant rate, its stock can be valued using a simple equation: $P_0 = [D_0(= + g)]/(r_s - g)$.

  - When a person sells stock that he or she owns, the investor who purchases the stock pays for the dividends that the stock is expected to generate in the future (during the remainder of the firm's life).

- Everything else equal, if the dividends that are expected to be paid in the future increase, the value of a stock also increases.

- Everything else equal, when investors demand higher rates of return—that is, when market rates increase—stock prices decrease. In other words, to earn higher rates of return, investors lower the prices they are willing to pay for their investments (stocks in this case).

- Investors often use P/E ratios to estimate the intrinsic values of stocks. The value of a stock can be estimated by multiplying a "normal" P/E ratio by the firm's existing earnings per share (EPS).

- The economic value added (EVA) approach can be used to determine whether the actions taken by a firm are sufficient to generate the funds that are needed to pay investors (stockholders and bondholders) who provide funds to the firm. If the firm generates more operating profits than are needed to pay taxes and cover its costs of funds, then its economic value increases.

KEY TERMS

cumulative dividends A protective feature on preferred stock that requires preferred dividends previously not paid to be disbursed before any common stock dividends can be paid. *p. 123*

call premium The amount in excess of par value that a company must pay when it calls a security. *p. 124*

income stocks Stocks of firms that traditionally pay large, relatively constant dividends each year. *p. 125*

growth stocks Stocks that generally pay little or no dividends so as to retain earnings to help fund growth opportunities. *p. 125*

proxy A document giving one person the authority to act for another; typically it gives them the power to vote shares of common stock. *p. 125*

preemptive right A provision that gives existing common stockholders the right to purchase new issues of common stock on a pro rata basis before any shares can be offered to other investors. *p. 126*

classified stock Common stock that is given a special designation, such as Class A, Class B, and so forth, to meet special needs of the company. *p. 126*

founders' shares Stock, owned by the firm's founders, that has sole voting rights but generally pays out only restricted dividends (if any) for a specified number of years. *p. 126*

American depository receipts (ADRs) "Certificates" created by organizations such as banks; represent ownership in stocks of foreign companies that are held in trust by banks located in the countries where the stocks are traded. *p. 126*

Euro stock Stock traded in countries other than the home country of the company, not including the United States. *p. 127*

Yankee stock Stock issued by foreign companies and traded in the United States. *p. 127*

market price (value), P_0 The price at which a stock currently sells in the market. *p. 127*

intrinsic (theoretical) value, $\hat{P}_0$ The value of an asset that, in the mind of a particular investor, is justified by the facts; $\hat{P}_0$ can be different from the asset's current market price, its book value, or both. *p. 127*

growth rate, g The expected rate of change in dividends per share. *p. 127*

required rate of return, r_s The minimum rate of return that stockholders consider acceptable on a common stock. *p. 127*

dividend yield The next expected dividend divided by the current price of a share of stock, $\hat{D}_1/P_0$. *p. 127*

capital gains yield The change in price (capital gain) during a given year divided by the price at the beginning of the year; $(\hat{P}_1 - P_0)/P_0$. *p. 127*

expected rate of return, $\hat{r}_s$ The rate of return that an individual stockholder expects to receive on a common stock. It is equal to the expected dividend yield plus the expected capital gains yield, $\hat{r}_s = \hat{D}_1/P_0 + (\hat{P}_1 - P_0)/P_0$. *p. 127*

constant growth model Also called the Gordon model, it is used to find the value of a stock that is expected to experience constant growth. *p. 129*

nonconstant growth The part of the life cycle of a firm in which its growth is either much faster or much slower than that of the economy as a whole. *p. 131*

P/E ratio The current market price of a stock divided by the earnings per share; P_0/EPS_0. *p. 134*

economic value added (EVA) An analytical method that seeks to evaluate the earnings generated by a firm to determine whether they are sufficient to compensate the suppliers of funds—both the bondholders and the stockholders. *p. 134*

To access additional study tools, please visit CFIN Online at www.cengagebrain.com.

LEARNING OUTCOMES

LO.1

Explain what it means to take risk when investing.

- Risk is defined as the possibility that you will not earn the return you expect when investing. Stated differently, risk exists when an investment has more than one possible outcome. Some risk can be considered "good" because greater returns than expected are possible, whereas some risk is "bad" because lower returns than expected are possible.

LO.2

Compute the risk and return of an investment, and explain how the risk and return of an investment are related.

- The risk associated with an investment is determined by measuring the variability of returns, or average deviation from the expected return. The standard deviation (σ) measures the scatter, or variability, of the possible outcomes for an investment; σ is a measure of the investment's total, or stand-alone, risk, which is the risk an investor takes when holding an investment by itself.

- The expected return on an investment is the weighted average return that investors will earn over a long period of time if the probability distribution that is associated with the investment is correctly specified.

- Generally, investments with greater risk earn higher rates of return

because their risk premiums are higher.

LO.3

Identify relevant and irrelevant risk, and explain how irrelevant risk can be reduced.

- The total risk of an investment consists of (1) firm-specific (unsystematic) risk, which is caused by events that are unique to a particular firm and can be reduced or eliminated through diversification, and (2) market (systematic) risk, which stems from factors that affect the general economy and thus cannot be reduced through diversification. Relevant risk refers to the risk that investors must take; thus, the relevant risk for an investment is its systematic, or market, risk because it cannot be eliminated.

LO.4

Describe how to determine the appropriate reward—that is, risk—that investors should earn for purchasing an investment.

- Investors should be rewarded for relevant risk only (the investment's systematic risk). Because the market as a whole is considered perfectly diversified, its variability (risk) is related to systematic risk only, and thus the market can be used as a benchmark for measuring the systematic risk of any investment. Thus, the systematic risk associated with

an individual investment can be determined by computing the relationship between the investment's variability and the variability of the market. This relationship, which is called the beta coefficient (β), indicates whether the investment's relevant risk is higher than ($\beta > 1.0$), lower than ($\beta < 1.0$), or equal to ($\beta = 1.0$) that of the market. Thus, the risk premium that investors should earn on an investment can be stated as a function of the market risk premium, RP_M. That is, the risk premium for an individual stock should be $RP_{Stock} = RP_M(\beta_{Stock})$, which means that (1) $RP_{Stock} > RP_M$ when $\beta_{Stock} > 1.0$, (2) $RP_{Stock} < RP_M$ when $\beta_{Stock} < 1.0$, and (3) $RP_{Stock} = RP_M$ when $\beta_{Stock} = 1.0$.

LO.5

Describe actions that investors take when the return they require to purchase an investment is different from the return they expect the investment to produce.

- If investors require a return that exceeds the return they expect an investment to generate, they will not purchase the investment, or they will sell the investment if they already own it. Such activity will tend to lower the price of the investment, and thus increase its expected return. Investors' reaction would be opposite if the expected return was greater than their required return.

CHAPTER REVIEW 8

Identify different types of risk, and classify each as relevant or irrelevant with respect to determining an investment's required rate of return.

- Risks that are unique to a particular firm are classified as firm-specific risks, which are considered irrelevant when determining an investment's required return. Risks that affect all firms, generally through the economy, are considered relevant because they cannot be eliminated through diversification. These systematic factors represent the risks for which investors should be rewarded.

CHAPTER 8 KEY RISK CONCEPTS

- In finance, we define risk as the chance that you will not receive the return that you expect, regardless of whether the actual outcome is better than expected or worse than expected.

- Riskier investments must have higher expected returns than less-risky investments; otherwise, people will not purchase investments with higher risks.

- The total risk of any investment can be divided into two components: diversifiable risk and nondiversifiable risk. Diversifiable risk is not important to informed investors, because they will eliminate its effects through diversification. Thus, the relevant risk is nondiversifiable risk, because it cannot be eliminated, even in a perfectly diversified portfolio.

- The effects of nondiversifiable risk, which is also called systematic risk or market risk, can be determined by computing the beta coefficient (β) of an investment. The beta coefficient measures the volatility of an investment relative to the volatility of the market, which is considered to be nearly perfectly diversified, and thus is affected only by systematic risk.

- According to the capital asset pricing model (CAPM), an investment's required rate of return can be computed as

$$r_i = r_{RF} + (r_{RF} - r_M)\beta_i = r_{RF} + (RP_M)\beta_i$$

KEY TERMS

risk The chance that an outcome other than the expected one will occur. *p. 141*

probability distribution A listing of all possible outcomes or events, with a probability (chance of occurrence) assigned to each outcome. *p. 141*

expected rate of return $\hat{r}$ The rate of return expected to be realized from an investment, which is the mean value of the probability distribution of possible results. *p. 142*

standard deviation, σ A measure of the tightness, or variability, of a set of outcomes. *p. 142*

coefficient of variation (CV) A standardized measure of the risk per unit of return. It is calculated by dividing the standard deviation by the expected return. *p. 144*

risk aversion Risk-averse investors require higher rates of return to invest in higher-risk securities. *p. 145*

risk premium (RP) The portion of the expected return that can be attributed to the additional risk of an investment. It is the difference between the expected rate of return on a given risky asset and the expected rate of return on a less risky asset. *p. 145*

expected return on a portfolio, $\hat{r}_p$ The weighted average of the expected returns on stocks held in a portfolio. *p. 146*

realized rate of return, $\bar{r}$ The return that is actually earned. The actual return ($\bar{r}$) usually differs from the expected return ($\hat{r}$). *p. 146*

diversification Reduction of stand-alone risk of an individual investment by combining it with other investments in a portfolio. *p. 147*

correlation coefficient, ρ A measure of the degree of relationship between two variables. *p. 147*

firm-specific (diversifiable) risk That part of a security's risk associated with random outcomes generated by events or behaviors, specific to the firm. It *can* be eliminated by proper diversification. *p. 149*

market (nondiversifiable) risk The part of a security's risk associated with economic, or market, factors that systematically affect all firms to some extent. It *cannot* be eliminated by diversification. *p. 149*

relevant risk The portion of a security's risk that cannot be diversified away; the security's market risk. It reflects the security's contribution to the risk of a portfolio. *p. 150*

beta coefficient, β A measure of the extent to which the returns on a given stock move with the stock market. *p. 150*

capital asset pricing model (CAPM) A model used to determine the required return on an asset, which is based on the proposition that an asset's return should be equal to the risk-free return plus a risk premium that reflects the asset's nondiversifiable (relevant) risk. *p. 152*

security market line (SML) The line that shows the relationship between risk as measured by beta and the required rate of return for individual securities. *p. 153*

market risk premium (RP$_M$) The additional return over the risk-free rate needed to compensate investors for assuming an average amount of risk. *p. 154*

equilibrium The condition under which the expected return on a security is just equal to its required return, $\hat{r} = r$, and the price is stable. *p. 156*

To access additional study tools, please visit CFIN Online at www.cengagebrain.com.

LEARNING OUTCOMES

LO.1 Describe the importance of capital budgeting decisions and the general process that is followed when making decisions about investing in fixed (capital) assets.

- Because capital budgeting decisions deal with funds that will be tied up for a long period of time, such decisions are among the most important ones that financial managers make.

- Making a capital budgeting decision is similar to making other financial decisions. Once the cash flows associated with a capital budgeting project are forecast, their present values must be computed. The sum of the present values, which represents the value of the project to the firm, is then compared to the cost (initial investment) of the project. If the project's cost is less than the present value of its expected future cash flows, the investment should be made.

LO.2 Describe how the net present value (NPV) technique and the internal rate of return (IRR) technique are used to make investment (capital budgeting) decisions.

- Net present value (NPV) is computed by subtracting the cost of a project from the present value of the cash flows the project is expected to generate during its useful life. NPV shows by how much the value of the firm will change if a project is purchased. Thus, if $NPV > 0$,

the project should be purchased; the project should be rejected if $NPV < 0$.

- Internal rate of return (IRR) represents the return any firm will earn if an asset is purchased and held for its useful life. A project is considered acceptable if its IRR is greater than the firm's required rate of return (r). When $IRR > r$, the firm will earn a higher return than it is paying for funds that are used to invest in assets, which means that the value of the firm will increase if the project is purchased.

LO.3 Compare the NPV technique with the IRR technique, and discuss why the two techniques might not always lead to the same investment decisions.

- NPV measures the dollar change in the value of the firm that would occur if a capital budgeting project is purchased; IRR measures the percentage return that the firm would earn if it purchased the same capital budgeting project. Thus, the NPV and IRR techniques provide the same accept/reject decisions when a capital budgeting project is evaluated. However, when evaluating two mutually exclusive projects, the NPV technique might suggest that one project is preferred, whereas the IRR technique might suggest that the other project is preferred. If the projects are independent, this conflict does not matter, because both projects should be purchased.

LO.4 Describe how conflicts that might arise when using the NPV and IRR techniques can be resolved using the modified internal rate of return (MIRR) technique.

- NPV assumes that cash flows produced by the project can be reinvested at the firm's required rate of return, whereas IRR assumes that the cash flows can be reinvested in projects with the same IRR. These differing assumptions can result in different rankings of mutually exclusive projects. MIRR helps resolve the ranking conflict by assuming that all cash flows can be invested at the firm's required rate of return. To compute a project's MIRR, compute the rate of return that equates the future value (FV) of the project's cash inflows to the present value (PV) of its cash outflows, where the FV and the PV are determined using the firm's required rate of return. If $MIRR > r$, the project is acceptable.

LO.5 Describe other capital budgeting techniques used by businesses to make investment decisions and which techniques are used most often in practice.

- Traditional payback (PB) period and discounted payback (DPB) period are two popular capital budgeting techniques that are used in addition to NPV and IRR. Both payback techniques determine the time it takes to recover the cost of a project from its expected future cash flows.

CHAPTER REVIEW 9

CHAPTER 9 KEY CAPITAL BUDGETING CONCEPTS

- Capital budgeting decisions are important because they involve long-term assets; thus, the firm loses some financial flexibility when such assets are purchased.

- The process of valuing a capital budgeting project (investment) to determine whether it should be purchased is the same process that is used to value financial assets, such as stocks and bonds: (1) compute the present value of the cash flows the asset is expected to generate during its useful life and (2) compare the present value of the asset to its purchase price (cost). If the present value of the project's cash flows is greater than its cost, the asset should be purchased.

- When making capital budgeting decisions, we generally compute an asset's net present value (NPV). NPV equals the present value of the cash flows the asset is expected to generate during its useful life minus the cost of the asset. Thus, the NPV indicates by how much the firm's value will change if the capital budgeting project is purchased. A project should be purchased if its NPV is positive.

- A project's internal rate of return (IRR) represents the average rate of return that a company will earn if the project is purchased and held until the end of its useful life. The IRR is the same for all companies that purchase a particular project. A project should be purchased if its IRR is greater than the firm's required rate of return (r).

- If a project has a positive NPV (i.e., NPV > 0), its IRR must be greater than the firm's required rate of return (i.e., IRR > r).

- A ranking conflict might occur when evaluating two or more mutually exclusive projects using the NPV technique and the IRR technique—that is, the NPV technique might favor one project whereas the IRR technique might favor the other project. This conflict, which results from the reinvestment assumptions associated with each of these capital budgeting techniques, generally can be resolved by using the modified internal rate of return (MIRR) technique rather than the traditional IRR technique.

- All capital budgeting techniques that consider the time value of money will provide the same accept–reject decisions—that is, for a particular project, if NPV > 0, then we know that IRR > r, MIRR > r, and DPB < Project's useful life, all of which indicate that the project is acceptable.

KEY TERMS

capital budgeting The process of planning and evaluating expenditures on assets whose cash flows are expected to extend beyond one year. *p. 163*

replacement decisions Decisions whether to purchase capital assets to take the place of existing assets to maintain or improve existing operations. *p. 164*

expansion decisions Decisions whether to purchase capital projects and add them to existing assets to increase existing operations. *p. 164*

independent projects Projects whose cash flows are not affected by decisions made about other projects. *p. 164*

mutually exclusive projects Projects in which the acceptance of one project means others cannot be accepted. *p. 164*

post-audit A comparison of actual and expected results for a capital project. *p. 165*

net present value (NPV) The present value of an asset's future cash flows minus its purchase price (initial investment). *p. 166*

internal rate of return (IRR) The discount rate that forces the PV of a project's expected cash flows to equal its initial cost; IRR is the same as the YTM on a bond. *p. 167*

required rate of return (hurdle rate) The discount rate (cost of funds) that the IRR must exceed for a project to be considered acceptable. *p. 168*

net present value (NPV) profile A graph that shows the NPVs for a project at various discount rates (required rates of return). *p. 169*

reinvestment rate assumption The assumption that cash flows from a project can be reinvested (1) at the firm's required rate of return, if using the NPV method or (2) at the internal rate of return, if using the IRR method. *p. 171*

multiple IRRs The situation in which a project has two or more IRRs. *p. 172*

modified IRR (MIRR) The discount rate at which the present value of a project's cash outflows is equal to the present value of its terminal value, where the terminal value is found as the sum of the future values of the cash inflows compounded at the firm's required rate of return and the present value of the cash outflows is found using the same required rate of return. *p. 172*

traditional payback period (PB) The length of time it takes to recover the original cost of an investment from its unadjusted (raw) expected cash flows. *p. 174*

discounted payback period (DPB) The length of time it takes for a project's discounted cash flows to repay the cost of the investment. *p. 175*

To access additional study tools, please visit CFIN Online at www.cengagebrain.com.

LEARNING OUTCOMES

LO.1

Describe the relevant cash flows that must be forecast to make informed capital budgeting decisions.

- When identifying relevant cash flows for capital budgeting decisions, two rules should be followed: (1) after-tax cash flows should be used and (2) only cash flows that are affected by the capital budgeting decision are relevant to the analysis.

- Relevant cash flows can be classified into one of three categories: (1) initial investment outlays, which occur only at the start of the project's life, (2) supplemental operating cash flows, which occur throughout the life of the project, and (3) terminal cash flows, which occur only at the end (termination) of the project's life.

LO.2

Identify the relevant cash flows and perform a capital budgeting analysis for (a) an expansion project and (b) a replacement project.

- Evaluation of an expansion project generally is easier than evaluation of a replacement project. The relevant cash flows that must be evaluated for an expansion project consist of any costs or savings the project will generate, whereas the relevant cash flows that must be evaluated for a replacement project consist of the *change* in cash flows that will occur as a result of replacing an existing asset with a new asset. Whether an expansion project or a replacement project, once the relevant cash flows are determined, capital budgeting techniques such as net present value (NPV) and internal rate of return (IRR) should be used to make a final decision as to whether to invest in the project.

LO.3

Describe how the riskiness of a capital budgeting project is evaluated and how the results are incorporated in capital budgeting decisions.

- The firm's required rate of return should be used when evaluating capital budgeting projects that have the same risk as the firm's existing assets (i.e., average risk). When evaluating either an above-average-risk project or a below-average-risk project, a risk-adjusted required rate of return should be used. A higher-than-average required rate of return should be used to evaluate an above-average-risk project, and vice versa.

LO.4

Describe how capital budgeting decisions differ for firms that have foreign operations and for firms that only have domestic operations.

- Factors that make capital budgeting decision making more complex in an international setting include: (1) the amount of cash that can be returned to the parent company (repatriation of earnings), (2) the risk that the foreign government will seize assets or impose tariffs or taxes (political risk), and (3) the risk that value will be lost due to currency fluctuations (exchange-rate risk).

CHAPTER 10 KEY CONCEPTS ABOUT CAPITAL BUDGETING CASH FLOWS AND RISK

- In capital budgeting analysis, "relevant" cash flows include only those cash flows that are affected by the decision to purchase the project. If a cash flow does not change, it is not relevant.

- The relevant, or incremental, cash flows can be categorized as (1) the initial investment outlay, which includes cash flows that occur only at the beginning of the project's life; (2) supplemental operating cash flows, which include changes in the day-to-day operating cash flows during the life of the project; and (3) the terminal cash flow, which includes cash flows that occur only at the end of the project's life.

- Identifying the relevant cash flows for a replacement project is somewhat more complicated than for an expansion project, because the cash flows that will be generated if the new project (the replacement asset) is purchased, as well as the cash flows that will be generated if the old project (the replaced asset) is retained, must be considered.

- If the risk associated with a capital budgeting project differs substantially from the "average" risk of the firm's existing assets, some adjustment should be made to the firm's required rate of return when evaluating the project.

If the project has substantially higher risk, a higher-than-average required rate of return should be used in the capital budgeting evaluation. If the project's risk is lower than average, a lower required rate of return should be used.

- Although the same basic principles should be applied when conducting capital budgeting analysis for multinational operations, application of these principles often is more complicated when dealing with foreign subsidiaries.

KEY TERMS

relevant cash flows The specific cash flows that should be considered in a capital budgeting decision. *p. 183*

incremental (marginal) cash flow The change in a firm's net cash flow attributable to an investment project. *p. 185*

sunk cost A cash outlay that has already been incurred and that cannot be recovered regardless of whether the project is accepted or rejected. *p. 185*

opportunity cost The return on the best alternative use of an asset; the highest return that will not be earned if funds are invested in a particular project. *p. 185*

externalities The effect accepting a project will have on the cash flows in other parts (areas) of the firm. *p. 185*

initial investment outlay The incremental cash flows associated with a project that will *occur only at the start of a project's life*. *p. 186*

supplemental operating cash flows The changes in day-to-day cash flows that result from the purchase of a capital project and continue until the firm disposes of the asset. *p. 187*

terminal cash flow The *net* cash flow that occurs at the end of the life of a project, including the cash flows associated with (1) the final disposal of the project and (2) returning the firm's operations to where they were before the project was accepted. *p. 187*

expansion project A project that is intended to increase sales. *p. 187*

replacement analysis An analysis involving the decision as to whether to replace an existing asset with a new asset. *p. 191*

stand-alone risk The risk an asset would have if it were a firm's only asset. It is measured by the variability of the asset's expected returns. *p. 194*

sensitivity analysis A risk analysis technique in which key variables are changed and the resulting changes in the NPV and the IRR are observed. *p. 195*

scenario analysis A risk analysis technique in which "bad" and "good" sets of financial circumstances are compared with a most likely, or base case, situation. *p. 195*

worst-case scenario An analysis in which all of the input variables are set at their worst reasonably forecasted values. *p. 196*

best-case scenario An analysis in which all of the input variables are set at their best reasonably forecasted values. *p. 196*

base (most likely) case An analysis in which all of the input variables are set at their most likely values. *p. 196*

Monte Carlo simulation A risk analysis technique in which probable future events are simulated on a computer, generating a probability distribution that indicates the most likely outcomes. *p. 197*

corporate (within-firm) risk Risk that does not take into consideration the effects of stockholders' diversification; it is measured by a project's effect on the firm's earnings variability. *p. 197*

beta (market) risk That part of a project's risk that cannot be eliminated by diversification; it is measured by the project's beta coefficient. *p. 198*

project required rate of return, r_{proj} The risk-adjusted required rate of return for an individual project. *p. 198*

pure play method An approach used for estimating the beta of a project in which a firm identifies companies whose only business is the product in question, determines the beta for each firm, and then averages the betas to find an approximation of its own project's beta. *p. 199*

risk-adjusted discount rate The discount rate (required rate of return) that is equal to the risk-free rate of interest plus a risk premium appropriate to the level of risk associated with a particular project's income stream. *p. 199*

repatriation of earnings The process of sending cash flows from a foreign subsidiary back to the parent company. *p. 200*

exchange rate risk The uncertainty associated with the price at which the currency from one country can be converted into the currency of another country. *p. 200*

political risk The risk of expropriation (seizure) of a foreign subsidiary's assets by the host country or of unanticipated restrictions on cash flows to the parent company. *p. 200*

To access additional study tools, please visit CFIN Online at www.cengagebrain.com.

LEARNING OUTCOMES

LO.1

Compute the component cost of capital for (a) debt, (b) preferred stock, (c) retained earnings, and (d) new common equity.

- The before-tax cost of debt, r_d, equals a bond's yield to maturity (YTM), which is determined by computing the rate of return that equates the present value of the bond's future cash flows with its current selling price. The after-tax cost of debt is $r_{dT} = r_d(1 - \text{Tax rate})$.

- The cost of preferred stock is computed as: $r_{ps} = D_{ps}/[P_0(1 - F)]$, where D_{ps} is the preferred dividend, P_0 is the current selling price of the preferred stock, and F is the percentage cost of issuing preferred stock stated as a decimal.

- The earnings retained by the firm have an opportunity cost to the firm, because common stockholders will demand that earnings be paid out as dividends if the firm cannot reinvest those earnings in assets that generate returns stockholders consider appropriate. The cost of retained earnings, r_s, can be computed using one of the following methods:

  - $r_s = \hat{D}_1/P_0 + g$, where $\hat{D}_1$ is the dividend that is expected to be paid at the end of the year, P_0 is the current selling price of the common stock, and g is the *constant* rate at which the firm will continue to grow long into the future.

  - $r_s = r_{RF} + (r_M - r_{RF})\beta_s$, where r_{RF} is the nominal risk-free rate of return, r_M is the return on the market, and β_s is the stock's beta coefficient.

  - $r_s = r_d + (\text{Risk premium})$, where r_d is the before-tax cost of debt and (Risk premium) is a 3 to 5 percent premium that is added for the additional risk that is associated with common stock compared to debt.

- The cost of new common equity is computed as: $r_e = \hat{D}_1/[P_0(1 - F)] + g$, where the variables are as defined earlier. The cost of new common equity is greater than the cost of retained earnings because the firm incurs flotation (issuing) costs when new equity is issued.

LO.2

Describe the weighted average cost of capital (WACC), and discuss the logic of using WACC to make informed financial decisions.

- The weighted average cost of capital (WACC) represents the average cost of each dollar of financing used by the firm, regardless of its source. The WACC is determined by first multiplying each component cost of capital by the proportion, or weight, that the source contributes to the firm's total capital, and then summing the results. The WACC is the firm's required rate of return, r.

LO.3

Describe how the marginal cost of capital (MCC) is used to make capital budgeting decisions.

- Because the MCC is the firm's required rate of return, it represents the minimum rate a capital budgeting project must generate to be considered an acceptable investment. In other words, a project is acceptable if (MCC = r) > IRR.

LO.4

Discuss the relationship between the firm's WACC and investors' required rates of return.

- Because investors provide the funds that finance a firm's investments (assets), its WACC is essentially determined by the required rates of return that investors demand to purchase the firm's securities (debt, preferred stock, and common equity). That is, WACC = investors' required rate of return = r.

CHAPTER 11 KEY COST OF CAPITAL CONCEPTS

- To make appropriate capital budgeting decisions, the firm must know its required rate of return, which is defined as the average rate of return that the firm pays to attract investors' funds. Because the firm pays this average rate of return to investors, the firm's required rate of return is also referred to as its cost of capital.

- To determine its required rate of return, the firm must compute the cost of each source of funds or capital that investors provide—that is, the firm must compute the cost of debt, the cost of preferred stock, the cost of retained earnings, and the cost of new common equity. These costs are then combined by weighting each component by the proportion or weight that it contributes to the total capital of the firm. The result is the weighted average cost of capital, or WACC, which is the required rate of return, r, that the firm should use when making capital budgeting decisions.

- Investors who participate in the financial markets determine firms' WACCs. Investors only provide funds to firms if they expect to earn sufficient returns on their investments; thus, firms must pay investors' demands to attract funds.

- When investing in capital budgeting projects, a firm should follow the economic principle that asserts products should continue to be manufactured until marginal costs equal marginal revenues. That is, the firm should invest until the marginal cost of capital (marginal costs) equals the internal rate of return on the last project that is purchased (marginal revenues).

KEY TERMS

required rate of return The return that must be earned on invested funds to cover the cost of financing such investments; also called the *opportunity cost rate*. p. 207

cost of capital The firm's average cost of funds, which is the average return required by the firm's investors—what the firm must pay to attract funds. p. 207

capital components The particular types of capital used by the firm—that is, its debt, preferred stock, and common equity. p. 207

after-tax cost of debt, r_{dT} The relevant cost of new debt, taking into account the tax deductibility of interest. p. 207

cost of preferred stock, r_{ps} The rate of return investors require on the firm's preferred stock, r_{ps}. p. 209

cost of retained earnings, r_s The rate of return required by stockholders on a firm's existing common stock. p. 209

cost of new common equity, r_e The cost of external equity; based on the cost of retained earnings, but increased for flotation costs. p. 211

flotation costs The expenses incurred when selling new issues of securities. p. 212

target (optimal) capital structure The combination (percentages) of debt, preferred stock, and common equity that will maximize the price of the firm's stock. p. 213

weighted average cost of capital (WACC) A weighted average of the component costs of debt, preferred stock, and common equity. p. 213

marginal cost of capital (MCC) The cost of obtaining another dollar of new capital; the weighted average cost of the last dollar of new capital raised. p. 214

MCC (marginal cost of capital) schedule A graph that relates the firm's weighted average cost of each dollar of capital to the total amount of new capital raised. p. 214

break point (BP) The dollar value of new capital that can be raised before an increase in the firm's weighted average cost of capital occurs. p. 216

investment opportunity schedule (IOS) A graph of the firm's investment opportunities ranked in order of the projects' internal rates of return. p. 220

To access additional study tools, please visit CFIN Online at www.cengagebrain.com.

LEARNING OUTCOMES

LO.1

Describe how business risk and financial risk affect a firm's capital structure.

- Business risk refers to the risk of a firm's normal operations, ignoring how it is financed. Financial risk refers to the risk that is associated with how the firm is financed. Firms that have greater business risk generally use less debt in their capital structures, because such firms normally generate cash flows that are less stable than firms that have less business risk. Firms that have greater financial risk generally either find it difficult to borrow additional funds or must borrow at higher rates than firms that have less financial risk.

LO.2

Describe how businesses determine their optimal capital structures.

- The primary objective of the firm is to maximize its value. As a result, when determining the optimal capital structure, a firm evaluates how changes in its capital structure will affect the value of its common stock. The optimal capital structure is the mixture of debt and equity that maximizes the value of the firm (minimizes its cost of capital).

LO.3

Describe how leverage can be used to make capital structure decisions, and discuss the effects (a) operating leverage, (b) financial leverage, and (c) total leverage have on risks associated with a firm.

- Leverage refers to fixed costs, whether those costs are associated with the firm's operations or its financing structure. Leverage magnifies the effects changes in sales and operating income have on the firm's net income; the possibility of greater changes implies greater risk.

- Operating leverage refers to fixed operating costs, which include expenses that do not change if there are changes in the level of production. The degree of operating leverage (DOL) indicates by what percentage operating income (EBIT) will change if sales turn out to be 1 percent different than expected.

- Financial leverage refers to fixed financing costs, which generally include interest payments and preferred stock dividends. The degree of financial leverage (DFL) indicates by what percentage EPS will change if EBIT turns out to be 1 percent different than expected.

- Total leverage is the combination of operating leverage and financial leverage. The degree of total leverage can be computed as: DTL = DOL × DFL. DTL indicates by what percentage EPS will change if sales turn out to be 1 percent different than expected.

LO.4

Discuss how managers consider liquidity when determining the optimal capital structure for a firm.

- Managers want to maintain a level of liquidity that will keep the firm operating. As a result, firms generally try to maintain a particular value for their times-interest-earned (TIE) ratios. In addition, debt covenants (restrictions) often require firms to maintain specific TIE values to ensure that interest payments can be covered with operating income.

LO.5

Discuss the two general theories—that is, (a) trade-off theory and (b) signaling theory—that have been developed to explain what firms' capital structures should be and why firms' capital structures differ.

- The trade-off theory suggests that a firm should issue debt as long as the tax deductibility of the interest payments is advantageous. Although interest is tax deductible, interest rates increase as more debt is used, because the chances that the firm will go bankrupt also increase (the trade-off).

- According to the signaling theory, firms might issue debt when funds are needed to invest in growth and value increasing projects so that existing stock-holders do not have to share the firm's future success with new stockholders. Stockholders don't mind sharing when prospects are poor, which suggests that stock would be issued in these instances.

LO.6

Describe how and why capital structures vary among firms in the United States and around the world.

- Firms that have more stable operations are able to take on more debt than firms with less stable operations. Internationally, whichever form of funding (debt or equity) is easier to monitor generally is more prevalent in firms' capital structures.

CHAPTER 12 KEY CAPITAL STRUCTURE CONCEPTS

- The greater the firm's *business risk*, or the riskiness that would be inherent in the firm's operations if it used no debt, the lower the amount of debt that is optimal.

- Because interest on debt is tax deductible, everything else equal, the effective after-tax cost of debt is lower for firms with high tax rates than for firms with low tax rates.

- Firms that maintain *financial flexibility*, or the ability to raise capital on reasonable terms under adverse conditions, are less risky and find it easier to raise funds when money is tight than firms that don't have financial flexibility.

- Some managers are more aggressive than others when using debt; managerial conservatism or aggressiveness influences the amount of debt a firm takes on. This factor does not affect the optimal, or value-maximizing, capital structure.

- Leverage, which is the presence of fixed costs (both operating and financial), magnifies the effects of changes in sales on operating income, net income, or both. More leverage generally indicates more risk. Thus, leverage should be considered when making capital structure decisions.

- Even though scientific models have not been developed to determine the optimal capital structure of a firm, it is important for a company to evaluate the effects of leverage on its value to establish a target capital structure that can be followed when raising funds.

KEY TERMS

capital structure The combination of debt and equity used to finance a firm. *p. 227*

target capital structure The mix of debt, preferred stock, and common equity with which the firm plans to finance its investments. *p. 227*

business risk The risk associated with the firm's operations, ignoring any financing effects. *p. 227*

financial risk The portion of stockholders' risk, over and above basic business risk, that results from the manner in which the firm is financed. *p. 228*

operating leverage The presence of fixed operating costs that do not change when the level of sales changes. *p. 228*

financial leverage The extent to which fixed-income securities (debt and preferred stock) are used in a firm's capital structure. *p. 228*

EPS indifference point The level of sales at which EPS will be the same whether the firm uses debt or common stock financing. *p. 233*

degree of operating leverage (DOL) The percentage change in operating income (EBIT) associated with a given percentage change in sales. *p. 236*

degree of financial leverage (DFL) The percentage change in earnings per share (EPS) associated with a given percentage change in earnings before interest and taxes (EBIT). *p. 238*

degree of total leverage (DTL) The percentage change in EPS that results from a given percentage change in sales; DTL shows the effects of both operating leverage and financial leverage. *p. 239*

times-interest-earned (TIE) ratio A ratio that measures the firm's ability to meet its annual interest obligations; calculated by dividing earnings before

interest and taxes (EBIT) by interest charges. *p. 240*

symmetric information The situation in which investors and managers have identical information about the firm's prospects. *p. 242*

asymmetric information The situation in which managers have different (better) information about their firm's prospects than do outside investors. *p. 242*

signal An action taken by a firm's management that provides clues to investors about how management views the firm's prospects. *p. 243*

reserve borrowing capacity The ability to borrow money at a reasonable cost when good investment opportunities arise; firms often use less debt than specified by the optimal capital structure to ensure that they can obtain debt capital later if necessary. *p. 243*

To access additional study tools, please visit CFIN Online at www.cengagebrain.com.

Distribution of Retained Earnings: Dividends and Stock Repurchases

LEARNING OUTCOMES

LO.1 Describe the views that have been proposed to explain why firms follow particular dividend policies and why investors react when firms change dividend policies.

- Firms follow particular dividend polices based on three primary factors: (1) information content, or signaling, which suggests that current dividends and any changes in future dividends signal information to investors; when investors interpret signals as good news, the price of the firm's stock increases, and vice versa; (2) clientele effect, which suggests that some investors purchase the stock of particular companies because of their dividend policies; and (3) the free cash-flow hypothesis, which suggests that firms should pay dividends only when earnings exceed the amounts needed to invest in value-increasing projects.

LO.2 Discuss (a) the types of dividend payments and (b) payment procedures that firms follow in practice.

- The primary types of dividend payments that firms follow include (1) residual dividend policy, which permits payment of dividends only after all capital budgeting needs have been supported by current earnings; (2) stable, predictable dividends, which require the firm to maintain a fairly predictable dollar dividend payment; (3) constant payout ratio, which requires the firm to apply the same dividend payout ratio (percentage of EPS paid out) when determining the annual dividend payment; and (4) low regular plus extras, which calls for a minimum dividend that is supplemented in the years when excess earnings are available.

- On the declaration date, the firm's board of directors announces the amount of dividends to be paid on the payment date. Stockholders who will receive the dividend payments are identified on the holder-of-record date. The ex-dividend date, which is two working days prior to the holder-of-record date, is important because those who purchase the stock on this day or later will not receive the next dividend payment. Thus, on the ex-dividend date, the market value of the stock should decrease by the present value of the next dividend payment.

LO.3 Discuss factors that firms consider when making dividend policy decisions.

- Factors that influence a firm's dividend policy include: (1) constraints placed on dividend payments by debt contracts or the firm's liquidity position, (2) whether the firm has investment opportunities that must be funded with earnings, (3) whether the firm can raise capital using sources other than earnings, (4) concern for dilution of ownership if additional shares of stock must be issued because dividends were paid, and (5) how dividend payments affect the cost of equity, r_s.

LO.4 Describe stock dividends and stock splits, and discuss how stock prices are affected by these activities.

- Stock dividends and stock splits are used to adjust the market value of a firm's stock. If the per-share stock price is considered too high, everything else equal, it can be reduced by increasing the number of shares outstanding through either a stock split or a stock dividend. Neither action by itself should affect the total value of the firm. After a stock split or stock dividend, there exist more shares at a lower per-share price, but the total value of all outstanding shares is the same.

LO.5 Describe stock repurchases and discuss reasons firms use repurchases.

- A firm might repurchase its stock to (1) distribute excess funds to stockholders, (2) adjust its capital structure, (3) acquire shares needed for employees' stock options or compensation plans, or (4) protect against a takeover attempt.

LO.6 Discuss differences in dividend policies around the world.

- Dividend policies differ substantially around the world. In countries where future payouts are extremely uncertain or little regulation exists, investors prefer companies that pay current dividends rather than those that retain earnings, and vice versa.

CHAPTER REVIEW 13

CHAPTER 13 KEY DISTRIBUTION OF RETAINED EARNINGS CONCEPTS

- Because the firm's goal is to maximize shareholders' wealth, the optimal dividend policy is the one that maximizes the value of the firm. When a firm pays dividends, it decreases the amount of earnings that can be used to invest in acceptable capital budgeting projects. Firms that have many acceptable capital budgeting projects generally pay few or no dividends because earnings are retained to reinvest in assets. Firms with few acceptable capital budgeting projects generally pay out most of their earnings as dividends because not as much internal financing is needed.

- Most firms follow the stable, predictable dividend policy.

- Everything else the same, it is believed that a stable, predictable pattern of dividend payments provides investors with a perception that there is less risk associated with the firm, and a perception of less risk often leads to a lower cost of capital. To maximize value, it might be better for a firm to follow the residual dividend policy so that cheaper funds (retained earnings rather than new equity) can be used to finance capital budgeting needs.

- Factors that influence a firm's dividend policy decisions include constraints on dividend payments, investment opportunities, ownership dilution, and the effect on the firm's cost of capital. In some instances, these factors might prevent the firm from following either the optimal dividend policy or the policy it prefers.

- Both a stock split and a stock dividend increase the number of shares of outstanding stock. Neither action requires stockholders to invest any additional funds. Thus, although both actions reduce the per share value of the firm's stock, neither action *by itself* changes the *total* market value of the firm's stock.

- Firms use stock repurchases as an alternative to temporary changes in annual dividends when distributing earnings to stockholders. Recently, the use of repurchases has increased while the proportion of dividend-paying companies has decreased.

KEY TERMS

optimal dividend policy The dividend policy that strikes a balance between current dividends and future growth, and maximizes the firm's stock price. *p. 249*

dividend irrelevance theory The theory that a firm's dividend policy has no effect on either its value or its cost of capital. *p. 249*

dividend relevance theory The value of a firm is affected by its dividend policy— the optimal dividend policy is the one that maximizes the firm's value. *p. 250*

information content (signaling) hypothesis The theory that investors regard dividend changes as signals of management's earnings forecasts. *p. 250*

clientele effect The tendency of a firm to attract the type of investor who likes its dividend policy. *p. 250*

free cash flow hypothesis All else equal, firms that pay dividends from cash flows that cannot be reinvested in positive net present value projects (*free cash flows*) have higher values than firms that retain free cash flows. *p. 251*

residual dividend policy A policy in which the dividend paid is set to equal the actual earnings minus the amount of retained earnings necessary to finance the firm's optimal capital budget. *p. 251*

stable, predictable dividend policy Payment of a specific dollar dividend each year, or periodically increasing the dividend at a constant rate, so that the annual dollar dividend is relatively predictable by investors. *p. 253*

constant payout ratio Payment of a constant *percentage* of earnings as dividends each year. *p. 254*

extra dividend A supplemental dividend paid in years when the firm does well, and excess funds are available for distribution. *p. 254*

declaration date The date on which the board of directors declares the amount and the specifics of the next dividend payment. *p. 256*

holder-of-record date (date of record) The date on which the company opens the ownership books to determine who will receive the next dividend; the stockholders of record on this date receive the dividend. *p. 256*

ex-dividend date The date on which the right to the next dividend no longer accompanies a stock; it usually is two working days prior to the holder-of-record date. *p. 256*

payment date The date on which a firm actually makes a dividend payment. *p. 256*

dividend reinvestment plans (DRIPs) Plans that enable stockholders to automatically reinvest dividends received in the stocks of the paying firms. *p. 256*

stock split An action taken by a firm to decrease the per-share price of its stock. *p. 258*

stock dividends A dividend paid in the form of additional shares of stock rather than cash. *p. 259*

stock repurchase Distribution of earnings by a firm to stockholders by repurchasing shares of its stock in the financial markets. *p. 260*

To access additional study tools, please visit CFIN Online at www.cengagebrain.com.

CHAPTER REVIEW 14
Managing Short-Term Financing (Liabilities)

LEARNING OUTCOMES

LO.1 Describe working capital management.

- A firm's working capital accounts include its current assets and the current liabilities that are used to finance current assets. Sound working capital management is a requisite for firm survival.

LO.2 Describe the cash conversion cycle and how it can be used to better manage working capital activities.

- The cash conversion cycle (CCC) represents the length of time from when the firm pays for inventory until it collects for the sale of that inventory; the CCC is the amount of time funds are tied up in inventory and receivables. A firm should strive to reduce its CCC so that funds can be freed up to invest in value-increasing projects. The CCC can be decreased by extending the time it takes to pay suppliers, reducing the amount of time it takes to sell inventory, or reducing the amount of time it takes to collect receivables.

LO.3 Describe the policies that a firm might follow when financing current assets.

- A firm generally follows one of three current asset financing approaches: (1) *maturity matching* (self-liquidating), which calls for matching the maturities of assets and liabilities; (2) *conservative*, which calls for use of permanent capital to finance all permanent asset

requirements (both fixed assets and permanent current assets) and also to meet some or all of the seasonal, temporary demands; and (3) *aggressive*, which calls for financing all fixed assets and some permanent current assets with long-term capital; the remainder of the permanent current assets and all temporary assets are financed with short-term funds.

LO.4 Describe the characteristics of different sources of short-term credit, including (a) accruals, (b) trade credit, (c) bank loans, (d) commercial paper, and (e) secured loans.

- Short-term credit includes debt instruments with original maturities equal to one year or less.

- Accruals (wages payable and taxes) increase spontaneously with the firm's operations, expanding during the height of the selling season and contracting when sales are slow.

- Trade credit (accounts payable) represents amounts that are owed to suppliers for credit purchases. Generally a portion of this type of credit is considered free because there is no explicit cost to using it.

- Bank loans (notes payable) can be in the form of (1) a specific amount that is borrowed and must be repaid on a particular date or (2) a line of credit, which represents an agreement with the bank that specifies the

maximum amount of credit that can be outstanding at any time.

- Commercial paper can best be described as an IOU that is issued by large firms with outstanding credit.

- Because they are expected to generate cash flows in the short term, both receivables and inventory make good collateral for short-term financing.

LO.5 Discuss and compute the cost (both APR and EAR) of short-term credit.

- The cost of any type of financing is based on the amount of funds that actually can be used by the firm and the total costs associated with such funds.

- To compute the cost of short-term credit, we must first determine the percentage cost that the firm pays each period, r_{PER}, and then annualize this rate by computing either the APR or the r_{EAR}. APR is the noncompounded cost of credit, whereas r_{EAR} is the effective, or compounded, cost.

LO.6 Describe how working capital management differs in multinational firms compared to purely domestic firms.

- Although the same general concepts apply, such factors as cultural differences and political risks make working capital management in multinational firms more complicated than in purely domestic firms.

CHAPTER 14 KEY CONCEPTS FOR MANAGING SHORT-TERM FINANCING (LIABILITIES)

- Working capital refers to the short-term, or current, assets of a firm. Liquidation of working capital accounts produces the cash that is needed to pay current bills. If a firm cannot pay its current bills, it will not survive to see the long term.

- The cash conversion cycle represents the length of time funds are "tied up," or invested, in current assets. Often a firm has to pay for the materials and labor that are needed to manufacture and sell its products before customers pay for their purchases. During the

period from when the firm invests in the product until it receives cash payment from the sale of the product, external financing is needed to support operations. If a firm reduces its cash conversion cycle, it reduces its need for external financing.

CHAPTER REVIEW 14

- Short-term financing generally is riskier but cheaper than long-term financing. Firms that are able to take on substantial amounts of financial risk are more likely to finance with more short-term debt (the aggressive approach) than firms that are not able to handle as much financial risk (the conservative approach). Most firms follow the maturity matching approach, a more moderate approach.

- A variety of sources of short-term credit exist, including accruals, which arise because firms do not pay salaries to employees daily; trade credit, which represents purchases from suppliers; short-term bank loans, which include lines of credit; commercial paper, which is unsecured debt issued by large, financially strong companies, and secured loans, which are generally secured by receivables and inventories.

- The percentage cost of credit per period, r_{PER}, is based on both the dollar cost associated with the credit and the amount of the borrowed funds that is available for use. Accruals and a portion of trade credit are considered "free" in the sense that specific interest is not paid for using these types of credit. Some form of interest is associated with other forms of short-term credit.

KEY TERMS

working capital management The management of short-term assets (investments) and short-term liabilities (financing sources). *p. 267*

working capital A firm's investment in short-term assets—cash, marketable securities, inventory, and accounts receivable. *p. 267*

net working capital Current assets minus current liabilities—the amount of current assets financed by long-term liabilities. *p. 267*

working capital policy Decisions regarding (1) the target levels for each current asset account and (2) how current assets will be financed. *p. 267*

inventory conversion period (ICP) The amount of time a product remains in inventory in various stages of completion. *p. 269*

receivables collection period (DSO) The time it takes to collect cash following a sale; also known as days sales outstanding (DSO). *p. 269*

payables deferral period (DPO) The average length of time between the purchase of raw materials and labor and the payment of cash for them; also known as days payables outstanding (DPO). *p. 270*

cash conversion cycle The length of time from the payment for the purchase of raw materials to manufacture a product until the collection of accounts receivable associated with the sale of the product. *p. 270*

permanent current assets Current assets' balances that remain stable no matter the seasonal or economic conditions. *p. 272*

temporary current assets Current assets that fluctuate with seasonal or cyclical variations in a firm's business. *p. 272*

maturity matching ("self-liquidating") approach A financing policy that matches asset and liability maturities; considered a moderate current asset financing policy. *p. 272*

conservative approach A policy under which all of the fixed assets, all of the permanent current assets, and some of the temporary current assets of a firm are financed with long-term capital. *p. 272*

aggressive approach A policy under which all of the fixed assets of a firm are financed with long-term capital, but *some* of the firm's permanent current assets are financed with short-term nonspontaneous sources of funds. *p. 272*

short-term credit Any liability originally scheduled for repayment within one year. *p. 273*

accruals Recurring short-term liabilities; liabilities such as wages and taxes that change spontaneously with operations. *p. 273*

trade credit The credit created when one firm buys on credit from another firm. *p. 273*

promissory note A document specifying the terms and conditions of a loan, including the amount, interest rate, and repayment schedule. *p. 274*

compensating balance (CB) A minimum checking account balance that a firm must maintain with a bank to borrow funds. *p. 274*

line of credit An arrangement in which a bank agrees to lend up to a specified maximum amount of funds during a designated period. *p. 274*

revolving (guaranteed) credit agreement A formal, committed line of credit extended by a bank or other lending institution. *p. 274*

commitment fee A fee charged on the *unused* balance of a revolving credit agreement to compensate the bank for guaranteeing that the funds will be available when needed by the borrower. *p. 274*

commercial paper Unsecured, short-term promissory notes issued by large, financially sound firms to raise funds. *p. 274*

secured loans Loans backed by collateral; for short-term loans, the collateral often is inventory, receivables, or both. *p. 274*

Uniform Commercial Code A system of standards that simplifies procedures for establishing loan security. *p. 274*

pledging receivables Using accounts receivable as collateral for a loan. *p. 275*

recourse The lender can seek payment from the borrowing firm when receivables' accounts used to secure a loan are uncollectible. *p. 275*

factoring The outright sale of receivables. *p. 275*

"free" trade credit Credit received during the discount period. *p. 276*

costly trade credit Credit taken in excess of "free" trade credit, whose cost is equal to the discount lost. *p. 276*

simple interest loan Both the amount borrowed and the interest charged on that amount are paid at the maturity of the loan. *p. 277*

face value The amount of the loan, or the amount borrowed; also called the *principal amount* of the loan. *p. 277*

quoted (simple) interest rate The annual percentage rate (APR) that is used to compute the interest rate per period (r_{PER}). *p. 277*

discount interest loan A loan in which the interest, which is calculated on the amount borrowed (principal), is paid at the beginning of the loan period; interest is paid in advance. *p. 277*

add-on interest Interest that is calculated and then added to the amount borrowed to obtain the total dollar amount to be paid back in equal installments. *p. 278*

To access additional study tools, please visit CFIN Online at www.cengagebrain.com.

LEARNING OUTCOMES

LO.1 Describe the policies that a firm might follow when investing in current assets.

- The three current asset investment policies firms follow are: (1) relaxed, which calls for large amounts of current assets to be carried; (2) restricted, which calls for minimal amounts of current assets to be held; and (3) moderate, which is between the first two policies.

LO.2 Discuss the goal of effective cash management and how (a) the cash budget, (b) techniques that exist to accelerate cash receipts, and (c) cash disbursement controls should be employed to develop an optimal cash management policy.

- Firms want to hold as little cash as possible, because cash is a non-earning asset. The cash budget helps the firm match its cash inflows and cash outflows, and thus minimize its cash holdings. A firm can use lockboxes, preauthorized debits, or concentration banking to speed up cash receipts; payables concentration,

zero-balance accounts, and controlled disbursement accounts can be used to control cash disbursements.

LO.3 Explain the rationale for holding marketable securities, and describe the general characteristics of investments that should be included in portfolios of marketable securities.

- Marketable securities provide a mechanism for a firm to temporarily "put cash to work." Such investments are short-term and extremely liquid, which means they have low risks and generate low returns.

LO.4 Discuss accounts receivable (credit) management, and describe how a proposed credit policy change should be evaluated.

- Although firms prefer to sell products for cash, competition often dictates that they sell on credit. A credit policy should be developed that maximizes the value of the firm. Receivables should be monitored to ensure that

the credit policy is followed. Any proposed policy changes should be evaluated using the NPV technique.

LO.5 Explain the rationale for holding various forms of inventory, and describe how a firm can determine its optimal level of inventory.

- Firms hold inventory because demand for their products cannot be predicted with certainty. Holding inventory in various forms helps a firm to continue its selling operations while inventory is converted into finished goods.

LO.6 Describe how management of current assets differs for multinational firms and for purely domestic firms.

- Some of the complications that arise in the management of current assets in multinational firms include: (1) difficulty moving cash to other countries, (2) higher risk associated with credit operations, and (3) import quotas, tariffs, and taxes that are imposed on inventory.

KEY TERMS

relaxed current asset investment policy A policy under which relatively large amounts of cash and marketable securities and inventories are carried and under which sales are stimulated by a liberal credit policy that results in a high level of receivables. *p. 285*

restricted current asset investment policy A policy under which holdings of cash and marketable securities, inventories, and receivables are minimized. *p. 285*

moderate current asset investment policy A policy between the relaxed and restrictive current asset investment policies. *p. 285*

transactions balance A cash balance necessary for day-to-day operations; the balance associated with routine payments and collections. *p. 286*

compensating balance A minimum checking account balance that a firm must maintain with a bank to help offset the costs of services such as check clearing and cash management advice. *p. 286*

precautionary balance A cash balance held in reserve for unforeseen fluctuations in cash flows. *p. 286*

speculative balance A cash balance held to enable the firm to take advantage of any bargain purchases that might arise. *p. 286*

cash budget A schedule showing cash receipts, cash disbursements, and cash balances for a firm over a specified time period. *p. 286*

target (minimum) cash balance The minimum cash balance a firm desires to maintain to conduct business. *p. 287*

disbursements and receipts method (scheduling) Method of determining net cash flow by estimating the cash disbursements and the cash receipts expected to be generated each period. *p. 287*

synchronized cash flows A situation in which cash inflows coincide with cash

CHAPTER REVIEW 15

outflows, thereby permitting a firm to hold low transactions balances. *p. 290*

float The difference between the balance shown in a firm's (or individual's) checkbook and the balance shown on the bank's records. *p. 290*

disbursement float The value of the checks that have been written and *disbursed* (paid) but have not yet fully cleared through the banking system, and thus have not been deducted from the account on which they were written. *p. 290*

collections float The amount of checks that have been received and deposited but have not yet been made available to the account in which they were deposited. *p. 290*

net float The difference between disbursement float and collections float; the difference between the balance shown in the checkbook and the balance shown on the bank's books. *p. 290*

lockbox arrangement A technique used to reduce float by having payments sent to post office boxes located near customers. *p. 290*

preauthorized debit system A system that allows a customer's bank to periodically transfer funds from its account to a selling firm's bank account for the payment of bills. *p. 291*

concentration banking A technique used to move funds from many bank accounts to a more central cash pool to more effectively manage cash. *p. 291*

zero-balance account (ZBA) A special checking account used for disbursements that has a balance equal to zero when there is no disbursement activity. *p. 291*

controlled disbursement accounts (CDA) Checking accounts in which funds are not deposited until checks are presented for payment, usually on a daily basis. *p. 291*

marketable securities Securities that can be sold on short notice without loss of principal or original investment (liquid investments). *p. 292*

credit policy A set of decisions that includes a firm's credit standards,

credit terms, methods used to collect credit accounts, and credit monitoring procedures. *p. 292*

credit standards Standards that indicate the minimum financial strength a customer must have to be granted credit. *p. 292*

terms of credit The payment conditions offered to credit customers; these terms include the length of the credit period and any cash discounts offered. *p. 293*

credit period The length of time for which credit is granted; after that time, the credit account is considered delinquent. *p. 293*

cash discount A reduction in the invoice price of goods offered by the seller to encourage early payment. *p. 293*

collection policy The procedures followed by a firm to collect its accounts receivable. *p. 293*

receivables monitoring The process of evaluating the credit policy to determine whether a shift in the customers' payment patterns has occurred. *p. 293*

days sales outstanding (DSO) The average length of time required to collect accounts receivable; also called the *average collection period*. *p. 293*

aging schedule A report showing how long accounts receivable have been outstanding; the report divides receivables into specified periods, which provide information about the proportion of receivables that is current and the proportion that is past due for given lengths of time. *p. 293*

raw materials The inventories purchased from suppliers that ultimately will be transformed into finished goods. *p. 297*

work-in-process Inventory in various stages of completion; some work-in-process is at the very beginning of the production process while some is at the end of the process. *p. 297*

finished goods Inventories that have completed the production process and are ready for sale. *p. 297*

stockout Occurs when a firm runs out of inventory *and* customers arrive to purchase the product. *p. 297*

carrying costs The costs associated with having inventory, which include storage costs, insurance, cost of tying up funds, and so on; these costs generally increase in proportion to the average amount of inventory held. *p. 297*

ordering costs The costs of placing an order; the cost of *each* order generally is fixed regardless of the average size of the inventory. *p. 297*

economic (optimum) ordering quantity (EOQ) The optimal quantity that should be ordered; it is this quantity that will minimize the *total inventory costs*. *p. 298*

EOQ model A formula for determining the order quantity that will minimize total inventory costs. *p. 298*

reorder point The level of inventory at which an order should be placed. *p. 299*

safety stock Additional inventory carried to guard against unexpected changes in sales rates or production/shipping delays during the reorder period. *p. 300*

quantity discount A discount from the purchase price that is offered when inventory is ordered in large quantities. *p. 300*

redline method An inventory control procedure where a red line is drawn around the inside of an inventory-stocked bin to indicate reorder point level. *p. 300*

computerized inventory control system A system of inventory control in which a computer is used to determine reorder points and to adjust inventory balances. *p. 300*

just-in-time system A system of inventory control in which a manufacturer coordinates production with suppliers so that raw materials of components arrive just as they are needed in the production process. *p. 300*

outsourcing The practice of purchasing components rather than making them in-house. *p. 300*

To access additional study tools, please visit CFIN Online at www.cengagebrain.com.

Financial Planning and Control

LEARNING OUTCOMES

LO.1 Construct simple pro forma financial statements that can be used to forecast a firm's financing and investment needs.

- Pro forma financial statements are forecasts that are used to help the firm plan for the future. The firm must (1) determine how much money is needed to achieve its goals, (2) determine how much money it expects to generate through normal operations, and (3) make arrangements to finance expected shortfalls and to invest expected surpluses. This process is accomplished in four repetitive steps: (1) Forecast the income statement for the next one or two years to determine the amount of funds that the firm expects to generate through normal operations. (2) Forecast the balance sheet for the next one or two years to determine (a) the amount that must be invested in assets to reach particular goals and (b) the amount of internally generated funds that basic operations are expected to provide during the forecast period. (3) If the amount that is needed for investment in assets exceeds the amount of funds that the firm expects to generate internally, then the firm must determine how the additional funds that are needed (AFN) will be raised externally. (4) Because raising new funds increases interest payments, dividends, or both, the firm must consider the effects of such "financing feedbacks" on the original forecasts. These steps should be continued until AFN = 0.

LO.2 Discuss some of the complications that management should consider when constructing pro forma financial statements.

- Some factors that firms must consider when constructing pro forma financial statements include (1) excess capacity, (2) economies of scale, and (3) lumpy assets.
- If a firm is not operating at full capacity (i.e., if excess capacity exists), existing assets can be used to satisfy some or all of an increase in production that is needed to attain growth goals.
- As a firm grows to particular levels of production, it attains economies of scale that decrease the per-unit cost of manufacturing products.
- Some assets can only be purchased in large, discrete amounts, which means that a firm might be required to invest a large percentage in assets to achieve a relatively small percentage increase in sales.

LO.3 Describe and compute (a) operating breakeven and operating leverage, (b) financial breakeven and financial leverage, and (c) total leverage.

- A firm's operating breakeven point is the level of sales that is just sufficient to cover all operating expenses, which include variable costs and fixed costs, so that EBIT = 0. Operating leverage refers to the firm's fixed operating costs. The degree of operating leverage (DOL) indicates by what percent operating income will change if sales change by 1 percent. Firms with higher DOLs experience greater changes in their operating incomes when their sales change, which suggests that such firms (1) have riskier operations and (2) are operating closer to their operating breakeven points than firms with lower DOLs.

- A firm's financial breakeven point is the level of EBIT (operating income) that is just sufficient to cover all financing expenses, which generally include interest payments and preferred dividends, so that EPS = 0. Financial leverage refers to the firm's fixed financing costs. The degree of financial leverage (DFL) indicates by what percent EPS will change if EBIT changes by 1 percent. Firms with higher DFLs experience greater changes in their net incomes when their EBITs change, which suggests that such firms (1) have riskier financing arrangements and (2) are operating closer to their financial breakeven points than firms with lower DFLs.

- Total leverage is a combination of operating leverage and financial leverage. The degree of total leverage (DTL) indicates by what percent EPS will change if sales change by 1 percent. Firms with higher DTLs experience greater changes in their net incomes when their sales change, which suggests that such firms are riskier, and thus have higher costs of capital, than firms with lower DTLs.

CHAPTER REVIEW 16

LO.4 Discuss how knowledge of leverage is used in the financial forecasting and control process and why financial planning is critical to firm survival.

- The forecasting and control process is continuous. A firm must forecast to plan for its future financing and investing activities. Forecasting is not an exact science, so managers must continuously evaluate and update forecasts to make them more accurate. It is important to learn from past mistakes and incorporate this learning in future forecasts.

CHAPTER 16 KEY FINANCIAL PLANNING AND CONTROL CONCEPTS

- Financial planning requires the firm to forecast future operations. A firm forecasts its financial statements (pro formas) so that expected changes in production and future financing needs may be accommodated. A financial plan represents a "road map" for the firm to follow to attain future goals. The process doesn't stop when financial forecasts are completed, because the firm needs to monitor operations as the financial plan is implemented to determine whether modifications are needed.

- A firm evaluates its breakeven points and degrees of leverage to assess the risk associated with its forecasts. A firm with a higher degree of leverage is considered riskier than a similar firm that has a lower degree of leverage. A firm uses the concept of leverage to estimate how fixed costs, both operating and financial, affect its "bottom line" (net) income. Everything else equal, a firm can decrease its risk by decreasing its relative fixed costs, by increasing sales, or by performing both actions. Remember from our discussions in previous chapters that, everything else equal, when a firm reduces its risk, its cost of capital decreases, and thus its value increases.

- Inadequate financial planning is the principal reason businesses fail. Well-run companies base their operating plans on a set of well-designed forecasted financial statements.

KEY TERMS

financial planning The projection of sales, income, and assets, as well as the determination of the resources needed to achieve these projections. *p. 307*

financial control The phase in which financial plans are implemented; control deals with the feedback and adjustment process required to ensure adherence to plans and modification of plans because of unforeseen changes. *p. 307*

sales forecast A forecast of a firm's unit and dollar sales for some future period; generally based on recent sales trends plus forecasts of the economic prospects for the nation, region, industry, and so forth. *p. 307*

projected (pro forma) balance sheet method A method of forecasting financial requirements based on forecasted financial statements. *p. 308*

spontaneously generated funds Funds that are obtained from routine business transactions. *p. 309*

additional funds needed (AFN) Funds that a firm must raise externally through new borrowing or by selling new stock. *p. 309*

financing feedbacks The effects on the income statement and balance sheet of actions taken to finance forecasted increases in assets. *p. 310*

lumpy assets Assets that cannot be acquired in small increments, but instead must be obtained in large, discrete amounts. *p. 313*

operating breakeven analysis An analytical technique for studying the relationship between sales revenues, operating costs, and operating profits. *p. 314*

operating breakeven point (Q_{OpBE} and S_{OpBE}) Represents the level of production and sales at which net operating income is zero; it is the point at which revenues from sales just equal total operating costs. *p. 315*

operating leverage The existence of fixed operating costs such that a change in sales will produce a larger change in operating income (EBIT). *p. 317*

degree of operating leverage (DOL) The percentage change in NOI (or EBIT) associated with a given percentage change in sales. *p. 317*

financial breakeven analysis Determining the operating income (EBIT) the firm needs to just cover all of its financing costs and produce earnings per share equal to zero. *p. 319*

financial breakeven point ($EBIT_{FinBE}$) The level of EBIT at which EPS equals zero. *p. 319*

financial leverage The existence of fixed financial costs such as interest and preferred dividends; occurs when a change in EBIT results in a larger change in EPS. *p. 321*

degree of financial leverage (DFL) The percentage change in EPS that results from a given percentage change in EBIT. *p. 321*

degree of total leverage (DTL) The percentage change in EPS that results from a 1 percent change in sales. *p. 323*

To access additional study tools, please visit CFIN Online at www.cengagebrain.com.

EQUATION CARD

Chapter 2
Analysis of Financial Statements

$$\text{Net cash flow} = \text{Net income} + \text{Depreciation and amortization} \qquad 2.1$$

$$\text{ROA} = \text{Net profit margin} \times \text{Total assets turnover}$$
$$= \frac{\text{Net income}}{\text{Sales}} \times \frac{\text{Sales}}{\text{Total assets}}$$
$$= \frac{\text{Net income}}{\text{Total assets}} \qquad 2.2$$

$$\text{ROE} = \text{ROA} \times \text{Equity multiplier}$$
$$= \frac{\text{Net income}}{\text{Total asssts}} \times \frac{\text{Total assets}}{\text{Common equity}} \qquad 2.3$$

$$\text{ROE} = \left[\left(\frac{\text{Profit}}{\text{margin}} \right) \times \left(\frac{\text{Total assets}}{\text{turnover}} \right) \right] \times \left(\frac{\text{Equity}}{\text{multiplier}} \right) \qquad 2.4$$
$$= \left[\frac{\text{Net income}}{\text{Sales}} \times \frac{\text{Sales}}{\text{Total assets}} \right] \times \frac{\text{Total assets}}{\text{Common equity}}$$

Chapter 3
The Financial Environment: Markets, Institutions, and Investment Banking

$$\text{Amount of issue} = \frac{NP + OC}{(1 - F)} \qquad 3.1$$

Chapter 4
Time Value of Money

$$FV_n = PV(1 + r)^n \qquad 4.1$$

$$FVA_n = PMT[(1 + r)^{n-1} + (1 + r)^{n-2} + \cdots + (1 + r)^0]$$
$$= PMT \sum_{t=0}^{n-1} (1 + r)^t = PMT \left[\frac{(1 + r)^n - 1}{r} \right] \qquad 4.2$$

$$FVA(DUE)_n = PMT \sum_{t=0}^{n-1} (1 + r)^t (1 + r)$$
$$= PMT \left\{ \left[\frac{(1 + r)^n - 1}{r} \right] \times (1 + r) \right\} \qquad 4.3$$

$$FVCF_n = CF_1(1 + r)^{n-1} + \cdots + CF_n(1 + r)^0$$
$$= \sum_{t=1}^{n} CF_t(1 + r)^{n-t} \qquad 4.4$$

$$PV = \frac{FV_n}{(1 + r)_n} = FV_n \left[\frac{1}{(1 + r)^n} \right] \qquad 4.5$$

$$PVA_n = PMT \left[\sum_{t=1}^{n} \frac{1}{(1 + r)^t} \right] = PMT \left[\frac{1 - \frac{1}{(1 + r)^n}}{r} \right] \qquad 4.6$$

$$PVA(DUE)_n = PMT \left\{ \sum_{t=1}^{n} \left[\frac{1}{(1 + r)^t} \right] (1 + r) \right\}$$
$$= PMT \left\{ \left[\frac{1 - \frac{1}{(1 + r)^n}}{r} \right] \times (1 + r) \right\} \qquad 4.7$$

$$PVP = PMT \left[\frac{1}{r} \right] = \frac{PMT}{r} \qquad 4.8$$

$$PVCF_n = CF_1 \left[\frac{1}{(1 + r)^1} \right] + \cdots + CF_n \left[\frac{1}{(1 + r)^n} \right]$$
$$= \sum_{t=1}^{n} CF_t \left[\frac{1}{(1 + r)^t} \right] \qquad 4.9$$

$$\text{Periodic rate} = r_{PER} = \frac{\left(\begin{array}{c} \text{Stated annual} \\ \text{interest rate} \end{array} \right)}{\left(\begin{array}{c} \text{Number of interest} \\ \text{payments per year} \end{array} \right)}$$
$$= \frac{r_{SIMPLE}}{m} \qquad 4.10$$

$$\text{Number of interest periods} = n_{PER} = \left(\begin{array}{c} \text{Number} \\ \text{of years} \end{array} \right) \times \left(\begin{array}{c} \text{Number of interest} \\ \text{payments per year} \end{array} \right)$$
$$= n_{YRS} \times m \qquad 4.11$$

$$\text{Effective annual rate (EAR)} = r_{EAR} = \left(1 + \frac{r_{SIMPLE}}{m} \right)^m - 1.0$$
$$= (1 + r_{PER})^m - 1.0 \qquad 4.12$$

Chapter 5
The Cost of Money (Interest Rates)

$$\text{Yield} = \frac{\text{Dollar return}}{\text{Beginning value}} = \frac{\text{Dollar income} + \text{Capital gains}}{\text{Beginning value}}$$
$$= \frac{\text{Dollar income} + (\text{Ending value} - \text{Beginning value})}{\text{Beginning value}} \qquad 5.1$$

$$\text{Rate of return} = r = \left(\begin{array}{c} \text{Risk-free} \\ \text{rate} \end{array} \right) + \left(\begin{array}{c} \text{Risk} \\ \text{premium} \end{array} \right) \qquad 5.2$$

$$r = r_{RF} + RP$$
$$= r_{RF} + [DRP + LP + MRP] \qquad 5.3$$

$$r_{Treasury} = r_{RF} + MRP = (r^* + IP) + MRP \qquad 5.4$$

$$\text{Yield (\%) on an n-year bond} = \frac{R_1 + R_2 + \cdots + R_n}{n} \qquad 5.5$$

Value of an asset $= \dfrac{\hat{CF}_1}{(1 + r)^1} + \dfrac{\hat{CF}_2}{(1 + r)^2} + \cdots + \dfrac{\hat{CF}_n}{(1 + r)^n}$

$$= \sum_{t=1}^{n} \dfrac{\hat{CF}_t}{(1 + r)^t} \qquad 5.6$$

Chapter 6
Bonds (Debt)—Characteristics and Valuation

Bond value $= V_d = INT \left[\dfrac{1 - \dfrac{1}{(1 + r_d)^N}}{r_d} \right] + M \left[\dfrac{1}{(1 + r_d)^N} \right]$ 6.1

$$V_d = \left(\dfrac{INT}{2} \right) \left[\dfrac{1 - \dfrac{1}{(1 + r_d/2)^{2 \times N}}}{(r_d/2)} \right] + \dfrac{M}{(1 + r_d/2)^{2 \times N}} \qquad 6.2$$

Bond yield = Current yield + Capital gains yield

$$= \dfrac{INT}{V_{d,\,Begin}} + \dfrac{V_{d,\,End} - V_{d,\,Begin}}{V_{d,\,Begin}} \qquad 6.3$$

Chapter 7
Stocks (Equity)—Characteristics and Valuation

Stock value $= V_s = \hat{P}_0 = \dfrac{\hat{D}_1}{(1 + r_s)^1} + \cdots + \dfrac{\hat{D}_\infty}{(1 + r_s)^\infty}$

$$= \sum_{t=1}^{\infty} \dfrac{\hat{D}_t}{(1 + r_s)^t} \qquad 7.1$$

$$\hat{P}_0 = \dfrac{D_0(1 + g)^1}{(1 + r_s)^1} + \dfrac{D_0(1 + g)^2}{(1 + r_s)^2} + \cdots + \dfrac{D_0(1 + g)^\infty}{(1 + r_s)^\infty}$$

$$= \dfrac{D_0(1 + g)}{r_s - g} = \dfrac{\hat{D}_1}{r_s - g}$$

= value of a constant growth stock   7.2

$$\begin{array}{ccc} \text{Expected} & \text{Expected} & \text{Expected growth} \\ \text{rate of} = & \text{dividend} + & \text{rate, or capital} \\ \text{return} & \text{yield} & \text{gains yield} \\ \hat{r}_s = & \dfrac{\hat{D}_1}{P_0} + & g \end{array} \qquad 7.3$$

$$\hat{P}_t = \dfrac{\left(\begin{array}{c} \text{First constant} \\ \text{growth dividend} \end{array} \right)}{r_s - g_{norm}} = \dfrac{\hat{D}_t(1 + g_{norm})}{r_s - g_{norm}} = \dfrac{\hat{D}_{t+1}}{r_s - g_{norm}} \qquad 7.4$$

$$\begin{array}{c} \text{Economic} \\ \text{value added} \end{array} = EVA$$

$$= EBIT(1 - T) - \left[\left(\begin{array}{c} \text{Average cost} \\ \text{of funds} \end{array} \right) \times \left(\begin{array}{c} \text{Invested} \\ \text{capital} \end{array} \right) \right] \qquad 7.5$$

Chapter 8
Risk and Rates of Return

Expected rate of return $= \hat{r} = Pr_1 r_1 + \cdots + Pr_n r_n$

$$= \sum_{i=1}^{n} Pr_i r_i \qquad 8.1$$

$$\begin{array}{c} \text{Standard} \\ \text{deviation} \end{array} = \sigma = \sqrt{(r_1 - \hat{r})^2 Pr_1 + \cdots + (r_n - \hat{r})^2 Pr_n}$$

$$= \sqrt{\sum_{i=1}^{n} (r_i - \hat{r})^2 Pr_i} \qquad 8.2$$

$$\text{Estimated } \sigma = s = \sqrt{\dfrac{\sum_{t=1}^{n} (\ddot{r}_t - \bar{r})^2}{n - 1}} \qquad 8.3$$

$$\bar{r} = \dfrac{\ddot{r}_1 + \ddot{r}_2 + \cdots + \ddot{r}_n}{n} = \dfrac{\sum_{t=1}^{n} \ddot{r}_t}{n} \qquad 8.4$$

$$\text{Coefficient of variation} = CV = \dfrac{\text{Risk}}{\text{Return}} = \dfrac{\sigma}{\hat{r}} \qquad 8.5$$

Portfolio return $= \hat{r}_p = w_1 \hat{r}_1 + w_2 \hat{r}_2 + \cdots + w_N \hat{r}_N$

$$= \sum_{j=1}^{N} w_j \hat{r}_j \qquad 8.6$$

Portfolio beta $= \beta_p = w_1 \beta_1 + \cdots + w_N \beta_N$

$$= \sum_{j=1}^{N} w_j \beta_j \qquad 8.7$$

Risk premium for Stock j $= RP_j = RP_M \times \beta_j$

$$= (r_M - r_{RF}) \beta_j \qquad 8.8$$

$$\begin{array}{c} \text{Required} \\ \text{return} \end{array} = \begin{array}{c} \text{Risk-free} \\ \text{return} \end{array} + \begin{array}{c} \text{Premium} \\ \text{for risk} \end{array}$$

$$r_j = r_{RF} + RP_j \qquad 8.9$$

$$r_j = r_{RF} + (RP_M)\beta_j$$

$$= r_{RF} + (r_M - r_{RF})\beta_j \qquad 8.10$$

Chapter 9
Capital Budgeting Techniques

$$NPV = \hat{CF}_0 + \dfrac{\hat{CF}_1}{(1 + r)^1} + \dfrac{\hat{CF}_2}{(1 + r)^2} + \cdots + \dfrac{\hat{CF}_n}{(1 + r)^n}$$

$$= \sum_{t=0}^{n} \dfrac{\hat{CF}_t}{(1 + r)^t} \qquad 9.1$$

$$NPV = \hat{CF}_0 + \dfrac{\hat{CF}_1}{(1 + IRR)^1} + \cdots + \dfrac{\hat{CF}_n}{(1 + IRR)^n} = 0$$

or

$$\hat{CF}_0 = \dfrac{\hat{CF}_1}{(1 + IRR)^1} + \cdots + \dfrac{\hat{CF}_n}{(1 + IRR)^n} \qquad 9.2$$

EQUATION CARD CONT.

PV of cash outflows $= \dfrac{TV}{(1 + MIRR)^n}$

$$\sum_{t=0}^{n} \frac{COF_t}{(1 + r)^t} = \frac{\sum_{t=0}^{n} CIF_t(1 + r)^{n-t}}{(1 + MIRR)^n} \qquad 9.3$$

$$\text{Payback period} = \begin{pmatrix} \text{The year just } prior \\ \text{to the year of full recovery} \\ \text{of initial investment} \end{pmatrix}$$

$$+ \begin{pmatrix} \dfrac{\begin{array}{c}\text{Amount of the intial}\\ \text{investment that is } unrecovered \\ \text{at the start of the recovery year}\end{array}}{\begin{array}{c}\text{Total cash flow generated} \\ \text{during the recovery year}\end{array}} \end{pmatrix} \qquad 9.4$$

Chapter 10
Project Cash Flows and Risk

$$\begin{aligned} \text{Supplemental operating } \hat{CF}_t &= \Delta\text{Cash revenues}_t - \Delta\text{Cash expenses}_t - \Delta\text{Taxes}_t \\ &= \Delta NOI_t \times (1 - T) + \Delta Depr_t \\ &= (\Delta NOI_t + \Delta Depr_t) \times (1-T) + T\Delta Depr_t \qquad 10.1 \end{aligned}$$

Chapter 11
The Cost of Capital

$$\begin{pmatrix} \text{After-tax} \\ \text{component} \\ \text{cost of debt} \end{pmatrix} = r_{dT} = \begin{pmatrix} \text{Bondholders'} \\ \text{required} \\ \text{rate of return} \end{pmatrix} - \begin{pmatrix} \text{Tax} \\ \text{savings} \end{pmatrix}$$

$$= r_d - r_d \times T$$

$$= r_d(1 - T) \qquad 11.1$$

$$\begin{aligned} V_d &= \frac{INT}{(1 + YTM)^1} + \cdots + \frac{INT + M}{(1 + YTM)^N} \\ &= \frac{INT}{(1 + r_d)^1} + \cdots + \frac{INT + M}{(1 + r_d)^N} \qquad 11.2 \end{aligned}$$

$$\begin{aligned} \text{Component cost of preferred stock} &= r_{ps} = \frac{D_{ps}}{P_0 - \text{Flotation costs}} \\ &= \frac{D_{ps}}{P_0(1 - F)} = \frac{D_{ps}}{NP_0} \qquad 11.3 \end{aligned}$$

Required rate of return $=$ Expected rate of return

$$r_s = \hat{r}_s$$

$$r_{RF} + RP_s = \frac{\hat{D}_1}{P_0} + g \qquad 11.4$$

$$r_s = r_{RF} + RP_s = r_{RF} + RP_M\beta_s = r_{RF} + (r_M - r_{RF})\beta_s \qquad 11.5$$

$$r_s = \hat{r}_s = \frac{\hat{D}_1}{P_0} + g \qquad 11.6$$

$$r_e = \frac{\hat{D}_1}{NP_0} + g = \frac{\hat{D}_1}{P_0(1 - F)} + g \qquad 11.7$$

$$WACC = w_d(r_{dT}) + w_{ps}(r_{ps}) + w_s(r_s \text{ or } r_e) \qquad 11.8$$

$$\text{Break point} = \begin{pmatrix} \dfrac{\begin{array}{c}\text{Maximum amount of } lower \text{ cost}\\ \text{of capital of a given type}\end{array}}{\begin{array}{c}\text{Proportion of that type of capital} \\ \text{in the capital structure}\end{array}} \end{pmatrix} \qquad 11.9$$

Chapter 12
Capital Structure

$$\text{Degree of operating leverage} = DOL = \frac{\% \, \Delta \text{ in NOI}}{\% \, \Delta \text{ in sales}} = \frac{\left(\dfrac{\Delta EBIT}{EBIT}\right)}{\left(\dfrac{\Delta Sales}{Sales}\right)} \qquad 12.1$$

$$\begin{aligned} DOL &= \frac{Q(P - V)}{Q(P - V) - F} = \frac{S - VC}{S - VC - F} \\ &= \frac{\text{Gross profit}}{EBIT} \qquad 12.2 \end{aligned}$$

$$\begin{aligned} \text{Degree of financial leverage (no preferred stock)} &= DFL = \frac{\% \, \Delta \text{ in EPS}}{\% \, \Delta \text{ in EBIT}} = \frac{\left(\dfrac{\Delta EPS}{EPS}\right)}{\left(\dfrac{\Delta EBIT}{EBIT}\right)} \\ &= \frac{EBIT}{EBIT - I} \qquad 12.3 \end{aligned}$$

$$\begin{aligned} \text{Degree of total leverage} = DTL &= \frac{\% \, \Delta \text{ in EPS}}{\% \, \Delta \text{ in sales}} \\ &= DOL \times DFL \\ &= \frac{\text{Gross profit}}{EBIT} \times \frac{EBIT}{EBIT - I} \\ &= \frac{\text{Gross profit}}{EBIT - I} \\ &= \frac{Q(P - V)}{Q(P - V) - F - I} \\ &= \frac{S - VC}{S - VC - F - I} \qquad 12.4 \end{aligned}$$

$$\begin{aligned} EPS_1 &= EPS_0 + EPS_0(DTL \times \%\Delta Sales) \\ &= EPS_0[1 + (DTL \times \%\Delta Sales)] \qquad 12.5 \end{aligned}$$

EQUATION CARD CONT.

Chapter 13
Distribution of Retained Earnings: Dividends and Stock Repurchases

$$\text{Transfer from RE} = \left[(\text{Shrs}) \times \binom{\% \text{ stock}}{\text{dividend}}\right]P_0 \qquad 13.1$$

Chapter 14
Managing Short-Term Liabilities (Financing)

$$\text{ICP} = \frac{\text{Inventory}}{\text{Cost of goods sold per day}}$$

$$= \frac{\text{Inventory}}{\left(\dfrac{\text{Cost of goods sold}}{360 \text{ day}}\right)}$$

$$= \frac{360 \text{ day}}{\left(\dfrac{\text{Cost of goods sold}}{\text{Inventory}}\right)}$$

$$= \frac{360 \text{ days}}{\text{Inventory turnover}} \qquad 14.1$$

$$\text{DSO} = \frac{\text{Receivables}}{\text{Daily credit sales}}$$

$$= \frac{\text{Receivables}}{\left(\dfrac{\text{Annual credit sales}}{360}\right)}$$

$$= \frac{360 \text{ days}}{\left(\dfrac{\text{Annual credit sales}}{\text{Receivables}}\right)}$$

$$= \frac{360 \text{ days}}{\text{Receivables turnover}} \qquad 14.2$$

$$\text{DPO} = \frac{\text{Accounts payable}}{\text{Credit purchases per day}}$$

$$= \frac{\text{Accounts payable}}{\left(\dfrac{\text{Cost of goods sold}}{360}\right)}$$

$$= \frac{360 \text{ days}}{\left(\dfrac{\text{Cost of goods sold}}{\text{Accounts payable}}\right)}$$

$$= \frac{360 \text{ days}}{\text{Payables turnover}} \qquad 14.3$$

$$\text{Cash conversion cycle} = \text{ICP} + \text{DSO} - \text{DPO} \qquad 14.4$$

$$\binom{\text{Percentage cost}}{\text{per period}} = r_{PER} = \frac{\binom{\$ \text{ cost of}}{\text{borrowing}}}{\binom{\$ \text{ amount of}}{\text{usable funds}}} \qquad 14.5$$

$$\text{EAR} = r_{EAR} = (1 + r_{PER})^m - 1.0 \qquad 14.6$$

$$\text{APR} = r_{PER} \times m = r_{SIMPLE} \qquad 14.7$$

$$\binom{\text{Usable}}{\text{funds}} = \text{Principal} - \binom{\$ \text{ reductions from}}{\text{principal amount}} \qquad 14.8$$

$$\binom{\text{Usable}}{\text{funds}} = \text{Principal} \times \left[1 - \binom{\% \text{ reductions from}}{\text{principal amount}}\right] \qquad 14.8a$$

$$\binom{\text{Principal}}{\text{amount}} = \frac{\textit{Usable} \text{ funds}}{1 - \binom{\% \text{ reductions from}}{\text{principal}}} \qquad 14.9$$

Chapter 15
Managing Short-Term Assets

$$\binom{\text{Total inventory}}{\text{costs (TIC)}} = \text{Total carrying costs} + \text{Total ordering costs}$$

$$= \binom{\text{Carrying cost}}{\text{per unit}} \times \binom{\text{Average units}}{\text{in inventory}} + \binom{\text{Cost per}}{\text{order}} \times \binom{\text{Number of}}{\text{orders}}$$

$$= (C \times PP) \times \left(\frac{Q}{2}\right) + O \times \left(\frac{T}{Q}\right) \qquad 15.1$$

$$\text{Economic ordering quantity} = \text{EOQ} = \sqrt{\frac{2 \times O \times T}{C \times PP}} \qquad 15.2$$

Chapter 16
Financial Planning and Control

$$\text{Estimated AFN} = \begin{pmatrix}\text{Forecasted}\\\text{increase}\\\text{in assets}\end{pmatrix} - \begin{pmatrix}\text{Forecasted}\\\text{increase}\\\text{in liabilities}\end{pmatrix} - \begin{pmatrix}\text{Forecasted}\\\text{increase in}\\\text{retained earnings}\end{pmatrix}$$

$$= [(TA_0 - SL_0) \times g] - [NI_0 (1 + g) - D] \qquad \text{16.1}$$

$$\text{Full capacity sales} = \frac{\text{Existing sales level}}{\begin{pmatrix}\text{Percent of capacity used}\\\text{to generate existing sales level}\end{pmatrix}} \qquad \text{16.2}$$

$$Q_{OpBE} = \frac{F}{P - V} = \frac{F}{\text{Contribution margin}} \qquad \text{16.3}$$

$$S_{OpBE} = \frac{F}{1 - \left(\dfrac{V}{P}\right)} = \frac{F}{\text{Gross profit margin}} \qquad \text{16.4}$$

$$\begin{aligned}\text{Degree of operating leverage} = DOL &= \frac{\%\,\Delta \text{ in NOI}}{\%\,\Delta \text{ in sales}} = \frac{\left(\dfrac{\Delta NOI}{NOI}\right)}{\left(\dfrac{\Delta Sales}{Sales}\right)}\\[2em] &= \frac{\left(\dfrac{NOI^* - NOI}{NOI}\right)}{\left(\dfrac{Sales^* - Sales}{Sales}\right)} \qquad \text{16.5}\end{aligned}$$

$$\begin{aligned}DOL_Q &= \frac{Q(P - V)}{Q(P - V) - F}\\[1em] &= \frac{S - VC}{S - VC - F}\\[1em] &= \frac{\text{Gross profit}}{EBIT} \qquad \text{16.6}\end{aligned}$$

$$\begin{aligned}EPS &= \frac{\begin{pmatrix}\text{Earnings available to}\\\text{common stockholders}\end{pmatrix}}{\begin{pmatrix}\text{Numbers of common}\\\text{shares outstanding}\end{pmatrix}} = 0\\[1em] &= \frac{(EBIT - I)(1 - T) - D_{ps}}{Shrs_C} = 0 \qquad \text{16.7}\end{aligned}$$

$$EBIT_{FinBE} = I + \frac{D_{ps}}{(1 - T)} \qquad \text{16.8}$$

$$\begin{aligned}\text{Degree of financial leverage} = DFL &= \frac{\%\Delta \text{ in EPS}}{\%\Delta \text{ in EBIT}} = \frac{\left(\dfrac{\Delta EPS}{EPS}\right)}{\left(\dfrac{\Delta EBIT}{EBIT}\right)}\\[2em] &= \frac{\left(\dfrac{EPS^* - EPS}{EPS}\right)}{\left(\dfrac{EBIT^* - EBIT}{EBIT}\right)} \qquad \text{16.9}\end{aligned}$$

$$\begin{aligned}DFL &= \frac{EBIT}{EBIT - EBIT_{FinBE}}\\[1em] &= \frac{EBIT}{EBIT - I} \qquad \text{when } D_{ps} = 0 \qquad \text{16.10}\end{aligned}$$

$$\begin{aligned}\text{Degree of total leverage} = DTL &= DOL \times DFL\\[1em] &= \frac{\text{Gross profit}}{EBIT} \times \frac{EBIT}{EBIT - EBIT_{FinBE}}\\[1em] &= \frac{\text{Gross profit}}{EBIT - EBIT_{FinBE}}\\[1em] &= \frac{S - VC}{EBIT - I} = \frac{Q(P - V)}{[Q(P - V) - F] - I} \left.\right\} \text{when } D_{ps} = 0 \qquad \text{16.11}\end{aligned}$$